CONCISE COLLEGE TEXTS

GENERAL PRINCIPLES
OF SCOTS LAW

ALSO IN THIS SERIES

Questions and Answers on the Law of Scotland, by Frank Bates and
James W. Coull (1970).

CONCISE COLLEGE TEXTS

GENERAL PRINCIPLES OF SCOTS LAW

BY

ENID A. MARSHALL, M.A., LL.B., Ph.D., Solicitor

Reader in Business Law at the University of Stirling,
Formerly Lecturer in Law at Dundee College of Technology

FOURTH EDITION

EDINBURGH

W. GREEN & SON LTD.

ST. GILES STREET

1982

First published in 1971
Second impression 1973
Second edition 1975
Second impression 1977
Third edition 1978
Second impression 1979
Fourth edition 1982
Second impression 1983
Third impression 1986
Fourth impression 1987
Fifth impression 1988

ISBN 0 414 00681 X

PRINTED IN GREAT BRITAIN BY
THE EASTERN PRESS LTD.
LONDON AND READING

To my mother

PREFACE TO FOURTH EDITION

THIS fourth edition's slight increase in length over the last edition is mainly accounted for by the inclusion, in response to requests, of outline treatment of diligence, legal aid, arbitration and termination of agency. On the other hand the repeal of the Scotland Act 1978 has saved some space.

A new section was called for on registration of title, that system having become operational from April 6, 1981, by virtue of the Land Registration (Scotland) Act 1979. The exceptionally variegated hue of the Law Reform (Miscellaneous Provisions) (Scotland) Act 1980 involved numerous amendments of the text. Other recent statutes which have received some notice include the Confirmation to Small Estates (Scotland) Act 1979, the Estate Agents Act 1979 and the Employment Act 1980. There has been an unusually large number of consolidating Acts which have entailed routine alterations—the Adoption (Scotland) Act 1978, the National Health Service (Scotland) Act 1978, the Interpretation Act 1978, the Employment Protection (Consolidation) Act 1978, the Wages Councils Act 1979, the Sale of Goods Act 1979, the Education (Scotland) Act 1980 and the Solicitors (Scotland) Act 1980.

Recent decisions now noted in the text are *Bluebell Apparel Ltd.* v. *Dickinson*, *Photo Production Ltd.* v. *Securicor Transport Ltd.* and *Varney (Scotland) Ltd.* v. *Burgh of Lanark.*

The law in this edition was at first intended to be stated as at October 1, 1980, but so far as the exigiencies of proofs have allowed I have attempted to add all relevant later material down to the date of this Preface.

I am again grateful to Philip Myers for his reading of Chapters 6 and 7; Professor J. Milnes Holden, Julian S. Danskin and Christine A. M. Davis have given their willing assistance to me on specific points; and I renew my thanks to Iris Stewart of Green's.

It is also fitting that I should acknowledge a further debt to the new (eighth) edition of *Gloag and Henderson* and to the new (fifth) edition of Professor Walker's *The Scottish Legal System.*

November 7, 1981   ENID A. MARSHALL

PREFACE TO FIRST EDITION

THIS book is intended for the use of students, mainly attending Scottish technical and commercial colleges, who take, along with a number of non-legal subjects, a subject which has some such title as "General Principles of Scots Law," "Building Law" or simply "Law."

The syllabuses for the various courses differ, and no claim is made that the material included in this book covers any one or more of them. In order to keep the book to a reasonable size and price, it has been necessary to treat certain subjects very sketchily, to omit topics, seemingly specialised but on which questions have been set for students on these courses, and to leave untouched considerable areas of particular syllabuses on the ground that inclusion of these areas would not have added proportionately to the general usefulness of the book. In spite of these limitations it is hoped that the book will provide suitable reading for a large proportion of the non-university students of Scots law, whose needs have hitherto been little catered for by publishers.

In the selection and presentation of material I have had in mind the needs of these students as I have been made aware of them in my work as a lecturer in law in the Department of Management and Social Studies of Dundee College of Technology over the past eleven years.

The student for whom this book is primarily intended is probably approaching the study of law for the first time. He may have no Latin, and his English vocabulary probably does not include either technical legal terms or those somewhat archaic, though non-technical, words (the "hereinafters," as one of my students habitually called them) which are intended by lawyers to clarify a meaning but which to a layman appear often to obscure it. The student probably hopes to complete his study of "General Principles of Scots Law" (or whatever other title the subject may be given in his particular curriculum) in no more than one session, although he may at a later stage take another law subject, such as mercantile law, company law, or law of contract. What such a student requires is an introductory book setting out in ordinary language those principles of Scots law of which he must have a reasonable grasp if he is to be allowed to pass to the next part of his course. *Gloag and Henderson*, despite its title, is not a suitable introduction to the law of Scotland for one who does not aim at a law degree, but it has frequently been recommended outside the universities as being the only available textbook covering in sufficient depth most, if not all, of the subjects in a given "General Principles of Scots Law" course.

In selecting the material to be included in this book I have unashamedly been influenced by the content of past examination papers. I have accordingly chosen to write at greater length on certain topics (*e.g.* contracts in restraint of trade, and the distinction between an employee and an independent contractor) than could have been justified had my aim been to give a comprehensive and concise statement of each of the selected branches of law. Omissions and unevenness of treatment have inevitably resulted. This is obvious, for instance, in the chapter on property: the student will find little in that chapter about moveable property or about incorporeal property beyond an explanation of their essential nature; but then a question on the ownership of land and buildings is much more likely to appear in his examination paper than a question on either moveable or incorporeal property. By thus treading in the paths already well trodden by examiners I hope that I have made the book more useful to students than it would otherwise have been.

In the presentation of material my first objective has been to state the law as clearly and simply as it can be stated without undue sacrifice of accuracy. Short paragraphs and the numbering of paragraphs have, as aids to the understanding, been preferred to the striving after elegance of style. Topics have been dealt with in the order in which they will probably be most easily understood by students, although this has in some instances produced an arrangement which to a lawyer would appear illogical or at least unorthodox. The attainment of simplicity of statement tends to involve some sacrifice of legal accuracy; where I have failed to see how to express a rule of law in straightforward language and also with complete accuracy, I have deliberately preferred simplification to accuracy; for this preference it may be deemed some apology that my intended readers have chosen not to make the law their career: for them "a little learning" is perhaps not such a dangerous thing as it would be for potential entrants to the legal profession.

My second main objective has been to foster the interest of students by the incorporation into the text of a manageable number of summaries of reported cases. Most of the students for whom this book has been written have neither the time nor the opportunity themselves to consult law reports; nor, indeed, have their lecturers in many cases. Hence footnotes containing bare references to law reports would be of little value in a book such as this. Yet knowledge of the facts of a reported case can often produce in students an interest in, and an understanding of, principle not readily attainable by any other means.

I am grateful to Philip Myers, my colleague at Dundee College of

Technology, for considerable assistance with Chapters 6 and 7, to John G. Downie of Culsalmond, Aberdeenshire, for his reading of my draft chapters and for his suggestions designed to improve their readability for the layman, and to Dr. G. R. Thomson of W. Green & Son Ltd. for his encouraging and patient guidance.

The law is intended to be stated as at 22nd March, 1971.

March, 1971.   ENID A. MARSHALL

ACKNOWLEDGMENTS

THE author of such a book as this necessarily owes much to standard works of greater learning. The sources from which most of the material for the book has been derived are mentioned in the "*Further Reading*" listed at the end of each chapter, and the author gratefully acknowledges the assistance obtained from all these sources.

In particular, the author's indebtedness to the following works on Scots law, which are referred to at the end of more than one chapter in the book, is both obvious and immense:

Gloag and Henderson, *Introduction to the Law of Scotland* (W. Green & Son Ltd.);

J. A. Lillie, *The Mercantile Law of Scotland* (W. Green & Son Ltd.);

J. D. B. Mitchell, *Constitutional Law* (The Scottish Universities Law Institute Series) (W. Green & Son Ltd.);

T. B. Smith, *A Short Commentary on the Law of Scotland* (W. Green & Son Ltd.);

David M. Walker, *Principles of Scottish Private Law* (Clarendon Press, Oxford); and

David M. Walker, *The Scottish Legal System* (W. Green & Son Ltd.).

E. A. M.

CONTENTS

TABLE OF CASES

TABLE OF STATUTES

PART I — INTRODUCTORY

CHAPTER 1

HISTORICAL BACKGROUND

SCOTS law is not in the form of a code created at some definite point of time and capable of being known apart from the country's history; it takes the form of a tradition, *i.e.* something handed down through generations, developed, and still developing, under the influence of historical factors.

HISTORY OF SCOTS LAW

The history of Scots law over the past 1,000 years falls broadly into four periods:

1. the feudal period;
2. the Dark Age;
3. the Roman period; and
4. the modern period.

1. The Feudal Period

This period extends from the establishment of the Kingdom of Scotland with its present boundaries by the Battle of Carham in 1018 to the Wars of Independence between Scotland and England at the end of the thirteenth century.

During this period English influence on Scottish institutions in general was strong, being fostered by the marriage of Malcolm Canmore to the English princess Margaret and by the Anglicisation of Scotland undertaken by the Scottish king, David I.

For Scots law the most important introduction from England during this period was the feudal system of landownership, by which grants of land were made by superiors to vassals in return for military service to be given by the vassals as and when required by their

1

superiors. The feudal system has continued as the basis for the Scots law of landownership up to the twentieth century.

The division of Scotland into sheriffdoms and the establishment of the office of sheriff date from this feudal period, and are usually attributed to David I. In each sheriff court the sheriff, as the king's officer, administered both civil and criminal justice in the king's name, and heard appeals against decisions of baron courts within his sheriffdom.

Another feature which has had a permanent influence on Scots law was the power enjoyed by the church courts which administered the canon law of the Roman church and from which an appeal might be made to Rome. This canon law has played an important part in Scots family law down to the present day, and was the medium through which Roman law itself first came to exert a significant influence on Scots law.

By the end of the thirteenth century Scots law had developed to a stage where considerable, but not slavish, borrowings from English law had been, along with a certain amount of canon and Roman law, superimposed upon the native customary law.

This early development of a system of Scots law different from, yet similar to, the English system came to an end with the Wars of Independence which brought with them a rejection of English influences for the next four centuries.

With these wars, and especially as from the death of Robert the Bruce in 1329, Scotland lost the strong government which had up to that time aided the development of her legal system, and Scots law entered its Dark Age.

2. The Dark Age

The Dark Age of Scottish legal history extends from the beginning of the fourteenth century to the establishment of the Court of Session in 1532.

The period was one of political strife, economic trouble, and mainly futile attempts to establish a government strong enough to maintain law and order. This was a climate unfavourable to the healthy development of Scots law. Yet the Dark Age did make significant contributions both to the whole future of the Scottish legal tradition and to particular aspects of the legal system:

(a) As regards the Scottish legal tradition as a whole, the rejection by Scotland at this time of English influence interrupted the early development in Scotland of a system of law which would have had much closer connections with the system which continued to evolve steadily in England. Under the "Auld Alliance" between Scotland

and France (an alliance which was particularly strong in the fourteenth and first half of the fifteenth centuries) the influence of France replaced that of England as the dominant influence on Scottish civilisation in general and on the Scottish legal system in particular. That influence operated both directly, through the adoption of French institutions, and indirectly, from the fact that many Scottish law students went to France for their education. The result has been to place Scots law outside the school of legal thought referred to as the "Anglo-American" school, which, from its beginnings in England, has over the centuries, partly owing to colonisation and partly by deliberate adoption, come to embrace the legal systems of a very considerable portion of the globe. The Scottish legal tradition has closer associations with the other great school of legal thought, referred to as the "Roman" or the "continental" or the "Franco-German" school, which, like the Anglo-American school, has spread its influence to large areas of the world far removed from its original home in Europe.

(b) As regards particular aspects of the Scottish legal system to which the Dark Age made significant contributions, the most noteworthy were:

(i) the growth of Parliament;

(ii) a number of remarkable statutes, e.g. an Act of 1424 dealing with free legal aid for the poor, and an Act of 1449 which still is today the corner-stone of the law of leases; and

(iii) the continuing power of the church courts administering canon law over a wide range of cases, such as those concerned with marriage, legitimacy, succession, and slander—cases which would today come before the ordinary courts.

The early years of the sixteenth century saw some improvement in the administration of justice, and the establishment of the Court of Session in 1532 is probably the most appropriate landmark for the end of the Dark Age of Scottish legal history and the transition to the period of Romanisation. Some authorities, however, regard the Dark Age as having lasted until about 1600.

3. The Roman Period

The period extending from the foundation of the Court of Session in 1532 to the Napoleonic wars at the beginning of the nineteenth century is the great formative period in the history of Scots law.

The establishment of the Court of Session provided Scotland with a permanent supreme court composed of professional judges adequately equipped to apply the law, and was a most important step forward in the proper administration of justice and in the development of the law.

The existence of this permanent court also resulted in the appearance in the sixteenth and seventeenth centuries of a type of legal writing known as "practicks." These were collections of notes on decided cases, originally made privately by judges for their own use and later handed on and taking the name of their compiler, *e.g.* Balfour's *Practicks*. Practicks were the forerunners of the two main sources of Scots law other than Acts of Parliament, namely law reports and the "institutional" writings of authorities on the law of Scotland such as Stair, Erskine, and Bell. The emergence of these literary sources of law greatly encouraged the development of a systematic body of legal principles.

The influence of Roman law on Scots law during this period sprang from that great revival of learning, known as the "Renaissance," which brought with it a renewed interest in Roman law as in other aspects of classical civilisation. From the fifteenth century onwards there was a great tide of "Reception" of Roman law in the continental countries of western Europe, and Scottish law students, who until about 1800 continued to flock in considerable numbers to famous continental universities, such as those of Paris and Orleans in France and of Leyden and Utrecht in the Low Countries, for their legal education, returned to Scotland inspired with the principles of the Roman school of legal thought. In their later professional work they naturally resorted to these Roman principles when they found no adequately established rule of law within their native system, and so there came to be incorporated into Scots law a great mass of Roman law as taught by the French and Dutch legal scholars of that time.

It is to this Roman period that most of the "institutional" writings belong. The term "institutional writings" is used to describe a limited number of books of recognised authority, all of considerable antiquity, and all dealing with either the whole or a large area of Scots law. The writings are called "institutional" because they followed the order and contents of Gaius' and Justinian's *Institutes* which were textbooks of Roman law.

The best-known of all the institutional writers was Viscount Stair, who may be regarded as the architect for the building of Scots law. In his work, *The Institutions of the Law of Scotland*, published in 1681, he virtually created modern Scots law by uniting elements of native customary law, of feudal law, and of Roman law into one system soundly based on principles and philosophy.

The most notable of the other institutional writings belonging to this period were Craig's *Jus Feudale* ("Feudal Law.") of 1603,

Bankton's *An Institute of the Laws of Scotland* of 1751–53, Erskine's *An Institute of the Law of Scotland* of 1773, and Hume's *Commentaries on the Law of Scotland respecting Crimes* of 1797.

Other important factors in the development of Scots law during this period were:

(a) the Reformation, with its culmination in 1560 when the power of the courts of the Roman Catholic Church over such matters as marriage, divorce, and legitimacy was brought to an end;

(b) the Union of the Crowns under James VI of Scotland and I of England in 1603, which altered the character of Scotland's government by removing the monarch from personal participation in it, and involved Scotland in that seventeenth century struggle between king and Parliament which laid the foundations of the British constitution;

(c) the setting up in 1617 of the General Register of Sasines, which has since then made available to the public a record of the ownership of, and burdens over, land and buildings, and which has been the mainstay of the whole Scots law of landownership up to the present day;

(d) the creation in 1672 of the High Court of Justiciary, which has since remained the highest criminal court in the Scottish judicial system;

(e) the Union of the Parliaments in 1707, which, in spite of the fact that by the Treaty of Union Scots law and the Scottish courts were to be preserved in all time coming, brought the law of Scotland into much closer contact with that of England, with the result that English law took the place of Roman law as the most powerful outside influence on the law of Scotland; and

(f) the second Jacobite rebellion of 1745, which resulted in the break-up of the clan system, the abolition of the holding of land in return for military service, and an increased power and prestige for the sheriff courts.

With the approach of the nineteenth century the influence of Roman law on Scots law gradually declined, and the year 1800 may be taken as the date for the end of the Roman period.

The following factors contributed to the decline of the Roman influence:

(a) The tradition of study on the continent was interrupted by the Napoleonic wars. France and the Netherlands codified their laws, *i.e.* put them into the form of a "code" (a comprehensive and systematic statement of rules of law). As a result Scottish students were less attracted, even after hostilities had ceased, to the universities of these countries, since the principal subject of study was thereafter a code which did not apply to their own country. Those

Scottish students who did go to the continent for their legal education after the Napoleonic wars mostly preferred German universities,
since German law was not then codified.

(b) Since the establishment of the Court of Session in 1532 Scots
law had gradually been attaining a maturity which made it less
receptive to foreign influences: a considerable body of Scottish case-
law had been built up over the years, and reference could be made
to the Scottish institutional writings instead of to the works of
continental commentators.

(c) The Union of the Parliaments in 1707 had brought Scots law
into close contact with a legal system which did not belong to the
Roman school of legal thought. Shortly after the Union it became
established that appeals could be made to the House of Lords from
the Court of Session, and the result was the introduction to Scots law
of doctrines which were alien to the Roman school of legal thought.
Particularly important was the doctrine of "judicial precedent," by
which an earlier decision on some point of law by a higher court
must be accepted by a lower court which is later called on to decide
the same point. Development of this doctrine mainly through the
influence of the House of Lords led Scots lawyers to attach more
importance to cases previously decided by the courts of their own
judicial system than to commentaries on Roman law.

4. The Modern Period

The two most outstanding features in the development of Scots
law since 1800 have been:

(a) the influence of English law; and
(b) the increase in statutory law.

The entry of the United Kingdom to the European Communities
has, since 1973, opened up the way for a further important feature:

(c) the impact of European Community law.

(a) The influence of English law

English law has been the principal foreign influence on Scots law
since 1800. That influence has been exerted mainly through two
channels:

(i) legislation; and
(ii) the House of Lords.

(i) Legislation

Parliament may, and sometimes does, pass Acts which apply
only to England or only to Scotland, but all too often shortage of
time has caused Parliament, instead of giving separate consideration
to Scottish needs, to extend to Scotland legislation designed primarily to meet English needs. With the ever-increasing number of
Acts of Parliament which have accumulated during the modern

period, the result has been to make Scots law much more similar to English law than it was at the beginning of the nineteenth century. This is particularly true of those branches of the law, such as commercial law and industrial law, which Parliament has been most active in controlling and reforming in the nineteenth and twentieth centuries.

(ii) *The House of Lords*

After the Union of the Parliaments in 1707 the House of Lords had become the final court of appeal for Scottish civil cases, and this fact led to the importation of much English law into Scotland, especially as the doctrine of judicial precedent came to be accepted as part of Scots law.

Considerable dissatisfaction has been expressed by Scottish lawyers with the power which the House of Lords, composed mainly, and sometimes entirely, of judges trained in the Anglo-American school of legal thought, has exerted over the development of Scots law. Judgments of the Court of Session have often been reversed by the House, there have been in many cases displays and confessions of ignorance of Scots law on the part of the English judges, and the principles and terms of English law have sometimes wrongly been assumed to be the exact equivalents of those of Scots law.

(b) **The increase in statutory law**

In the modern period there has been a great increase in the volume of statutory law, which includes, as well as Acts of Parliament, all those detailed rules and regulations made by government departments, local authorities, and other bodies in accordance with powers conferred on them by Parliament. The "common law," *i.e.* that part of the law which is not statutory and which consists of principles and rules developed over the years by decisions of the courts, is now a much smaller part of the whole of Scots law than it was in 1800.

This increase in the volume of statutory law has made many branches of the law much more complex than they were at the beginning of the nineteenth century, and has also led to the emergence of some new branches of law.

Obvious examples of branches of the law which have become much more complex are industrial law (also called "labour law") and mercantile law (also called "commercial law").

As regards industrial law, legislation on conditions of work in factories came in with the start of the nineteenth century, and from these beginnings there has accumulated a great mass of legislation governing very many aspects of the lives of workers of all categories. At the beginning of the nineteenth century there was little more to industrial law than study of the contract of employment made between an employer and his employees as individuals, whereas now that branch of the law includes numerous and detailed statutory provisions on conditions of work, social security, wages councils, trade unions, industrial disputes, redundancy, etc.

There has been a similar enlargement of mercantile law, which, owing to the economic developments of the nineteenth and twentieth centuries, is now a much more important subject of study than it was in 1800. Mercantile law today includes a considerable body of statutory law regulating the formation and trading of different types of business organisations, whereas at the beginning of the nineteenth century there was virtually no legislation applying to subjects such as partnerships, companies, sale of goods, hire-purchase, and monopolies and mergers.

Both in industrial law and in mercantile law there is now so much statutory material that in the study of these subjects the fundamental common law, which still exists as the base on which the statutory material has been built, is in danger of being lost sight of.

In some other branches of the law the submergence of the common law has been less complete, although the volume of statutory material superimposed on the common law has been considerable. These branches also are examples, though less obvious ones, of the growing complexity of the law. In the law of leases, for instance, a significant part of the law as it existed in 1800 has been carried forward unaltered, but in the modern period there has been added a great mass of statutory provisions dealing with various residential, business, and agricultural leases. The law of arbitration is in a similar position: little alteration has been made to its general principles since 1800, but there has been extensive legislation on particular types of arbitration.

Examples of new branches of law which have emerged in the modern period are the law of town and country planning and the law of taxation. The statutes which comprise the law of town and country planning enable the state to regulate the physical character of city, town, and rural areas, an activity which was not considered to be one of the state's functions in 1800, while the greatly increased revenue required by the state to finance all the functions which it now performs has made necessary the passing of the statutes which comprise the modern law of taxation.

The increase in the volume of statutory law is closely associated with the following further features of the modern period:

    (i) increased governmental participation;
    (ii) growth of administrative law;
    (iii) specialisation; and
    (iv) reform of the law.

(i) *Increased governmental participation*

The Government has come to take a much greater part in the regulation of the lives and conditions of the people than it did in earlier times. Its authority to do so has had to be conferred by Acts of Parliament.

(ii) *Growth of administrative law*

The increasing participation of the Government in the life of the community has led to the growth of administrative law, which was virtually unrecognised as a separate branch of law until the twentieth century. Administrative law consists of the rules of law relating to the administration of the country by the central government, by local authorities and by other official bodies, such as the public corporations (*e.g.* the National Coal Board and the Area Health Boards). The main problem with which administrative law has to deal is the conflict between the individual and the state as represented by an official of the Government or of some subordinate authority. Such conflicts could arise comparatively seldom under the system of law which existed before 1800.

(iii) *Specialisation*

Much of the statutory law of the modern period is so complex that its details are known only to specialists: for instance, factory law, company law, and the law of compulsory purchase and compensation, although only parts of industrial law, mercantile law, and the law of town and country planning, respectively, each requires for its full treatment a large work written by a lawyer who has for a considerable time, if not for his life-time, given undivided attention to the subject.

Even in the early years of the nineteenth century, when the latest of the institutional writings were published, there were signs of specialisation, and in the remainder of the nineteenth and in the twentieth centuries specialisation has intensified.

The most authoritative of the law books now being published are those which deal exhaustively with a small area or a single topic in which the author has specialised. These specialist writings, however, are not accepted by the courts as authoritative to the same extent as are the institutional writings.

(iv) *Reform of the law*

Reform of the law is made necessary by changes in society. Decisions of the courts reflect changes in society to a certain degree, and so can be regarded as altering the law to that limited degree;

but the only way in which radical and conscious reforms can be made is by Act of Parliament.

The modern period has seen a great volume of statutory law which has had as its aim radical and conscious reform of existing institutions, of established common law, and of earlier statutory law: institutions which have been reformed include Parliament, the Scottish Office, local authorities, and the courts; as regards the common law, there is now hardly any branch of it which has not been reformed to some extent by statute; and existing statutory law itself requires to be amended from time to time as its deficiencies come to light or as conditions change.

The most significant development of recent years in connection with law reform has been the setting up under the Law Commissions Act 1965 of the two Law Commissions—the Law Commission and the Scottish Law Commission—whose duty it is to promote the systematic development and reform of the law of England and the law of Scotland.

(c) The impact of European Community law

Since January 1, 1973, the United Kingdom has been a member of the European Communities (see p. 193, below). It is therefore bound to accept the laws properly made by the Council and the Commission of the European Communities, and to promote the objectives for which the Communities were formed.

The treaties by which the European Communities were established cannot be challenged in the United Kingdom courts. The Treaty of Accession of 1972, by which the United Kingdom became a member of the Communities, was made under the prerogative of the Queen, and the European Communities Act 1972 was passed in order to give the force of law in the United Kingdom to previous and subsequent Community law.

Where a question as to interpretation of a treaty arises in a case, the United Kingdom court may, and, if it is a court from which no appeal can be made in this country, must, refer the question to the European Court of Justice.

The treaties are referred to as "primary" legislation. In addition to the treaties, there is a great volume of "secondary" legislation consisting of regulations, directives, and decisions made by the Council and the Commission. Regulations are binding on the United Kingdom courts, and are said to be "directly applicable" because they do not require to be confirmed by any law-making body in this country: if our own law is inconsistent with the terms of a regulation it is the latter which must prevail. Directives are also binding, but only as to the results to be achieved: it is for the law-making body in this country to choose the form and method of implementing the directive. Decisions are binding on the state or individual to whom they are addressed.

The courts of this country must now take account of all such primary and secondary legislation and also of decisions and opinions of the European Court of Justice.

The impact of European Community law was picturesquely described by Lord Denning M.R. in the (English) Court of Appeal in *H. P. Bulmer Ltd.* v. *J. Bollinger S.A.* [1974] Ch. 401, a case which arose out of a contention by French producers of "Champagne" that the use of the terms "Champagne Cider" and "Champagne Perry" to describe beverages other than wine produced in the Champagne District of France was contrary to European Community law. Lord Denning, defining the word "treaty" as including regulations made under the EEC treaty as well as the treaty itself, said (at p. 418):

"When we come to matters with a European element, the treaty is like an incoming tide. It flows into the estuaries and up the rivers. It cannot be held back. Parliament has decreed that the treaty is henceforward to be part of our law. It is equal in force to any statute. . . . Any rights or obligations created by the treaty are to be given legal effect in England without more ado. Any remedies or procedures provided by the treaty are to be available here without being open to question. In future, in transactions which cross the frontiers, we must no longer speak in or think of English law as something on its own. We must speak and think of Community law, of Community rights and obliga- tions, and we must give effect to them. This means a great effort for the lawyers. We have to learn a new system. The treaty, with the regulations and directives, covers many volumes. The case law is contained in hundreds of reported cases both in the European Court of Justice and in the national courts of the nine. Many must be studied before the right result can be reached. We must get down to it."

SCOTTISH LEGAL TRADITION

The review of the history of Scots law given above indicates the principal factors which have led to the existence in twentieth-century Scotland of a distinct legal system. At the present day, with the ever-increasing similarities between Scots law and English law and with the strong emphasis on reform of the law, it is particularly important to appreciate the historical distinctiveness of the Scottish and English legal systems.

While, however, Scots law is a distinct legal system, it is far from being an original legal system in the sense of having developed independently of outside influences: there is little in Scots law which is purely native to the country; most of Scots law has been contributed to Scotland by other legal systems, and the distinctiveness of the Scottish legal system springs from the original way in which the law-makers of Scotland have over past centuries formed a coherent body of law out of these diverse contributions.

The most influential factors in the Scottish legal tradition have been:

1. feudal law;
2. canon law;
3. Roman law;
4. English law; and
5. statute law.

1. Feudal Law

The most notable contribution made by feudal law to Scots law was to provide the basis for the Scots law of landownership. This branch of Scots law has been little influenced by any other foreign legal system down to the present day, and provides a pre-eminent illustration of how Scots law, left to itself, has been capable of evolution to meet the needs of a changed society.

2. Canon Law

The canon law administered by the church courts of pre-Reformation Scotland made a lasting contribution to Scots family law, including the law of marriage, wills and succession, and also to the Scots law of contract.

3. Roman Law

While feudal law and canon law have long since ceased to be active forces in the development of Scots law, it is only in the modern period that the influence of Roman law on Scots law has markedly declined. It was at its strongest during the most formative period in the history of Scots law, and was exerted on all the then-existing branches of law.

The terminology, the principles, and the whole ethos of Scots law all still today bear witness to the importance of the Roman law influence.

As regards terminology, even the most elementary study of Scots law cannot avoid the use of Latin words and phrases: for instance, Scots law divides persons under the age of majority into "pupils" and "minors," terms directly derived from Latin, refers to contracts which require writing as a solemnity as "obligationes literis," and expresses many of its rules in the form of Latin maxims such as assignatus utitur jure auctoris ("an assignee enjoys only the right which his cedent had").

The use of such Latin words and phrases indicates the origin in Roman law of the principles with which they are associated, and whereas terminology may be superficial, principles are certainly not. Latin terminology is used in this book only where there is no well-recognised equivalent terminology in the English language; yet to a student who is new to Scots law the amount of Latin which he must still master is likely to appear considerable. A quick glance through Chapter 9 of the book ("Contract") will give the student a preliminary idea of how much of the Scots law of contract still uses the terminology, and is based on the principles, of Roman law.

The illustrations given above of the Roman influence have been drawn from the law of contract. Other branches of the law might have been chosen instead. With the exception of those branches of law which are wholly or mainly creations of the modern period, the terminology of Roman law employed throughout Scots law gives some indication of the extent to which Scots law is indebted to Roman law for its leading principles. Moreover, a more scientific study of Scots law than is attempted in this book would reveal a much greater debt owed by Scots law to Roman law, both in content and in terminology, than is made evident by the amount of Latin necessarily included in an elementary study.

Further, the influence of Roman law on Scots law has an importance which extends beyond mere terminology and even beyond principles to its whole ethos. Historically, Scots law as a system belongs to that school of legal thought founded on the law of Rome and now including the legal systems of many countries in continental Europe and throughout the world. The legal systems belonging to the Roman school of legal thought are predominantly systematic and deductive, i.e. they are composed of a body of principles from which the law to be applied in a particular case is deduced. In contrast, the legal systems of the Anglo-American school of legal thought are predominantly empirical and inductive, i.e. they are built up from experience derived from particular instances, the legal principle being the result, not the origin, of the law applied in particular cases. In so far, therefore, as Scots law has fallen under the influence of Roman law it is a systematic and deductive legal system, and essentially different from English law.

However, the decline of Roman influence on Scots law from the latter part of the eighteenth century and the closer association thereafter with English law have had the result that Scots law now stands in an intermediate position between the two opposing schools of legal thought: broad principles and a process of reasoning from principles to instances remain essential characteristics of Scots law; yet there has been no adoption of a code in Scotland, although that would have been the natural development in modern times for a system properly belonging to the Roman school, and there is a tendency, aided by the strong influence of English law, for Scots law to accept the empirical and inductive reasoning of the Anglo-American school.

4. English Law

English law did not come to exert a decisive and permanent influence on Scots law until the most formative stages in the creation of Scots law were already past. By about 1800 Scots law had matured as a systematic and deductive legal system, and this subsequent, very strong, influence of a member of the opposing school of legal thought has involved some distortion of the structure of Scots law. English doctrines have sometimes been wrongly imported into Scots law through a Parliament and a final court of appeal insensitive to the distinctiveness of Scots law, and the whole influence of English law on Scots law has not been without its critics in the legal profession in Scotland.

On the other hand, the advantages of the close association between English law and Scots law must not be overlooked: English law is a great legal system, with a distinct tradition of which English lawyers are justly proud, and in the nineteenth and twentieth centuries Scots law has been greatly enriched by the English influence.

While the merits and demerits of the influence of English law may be argued about, it is beyond doubt that that influence is the dominant foreign influence on the Scots law of the twentieth century. This is ensured by the facts that:

(a) England and Scotland are a political unit, sharing most of the increasing volume of statutory law;

(b) the House of Lords is the final court of appeal in civil cases for both countries;

(c) Scots law has accepted the doctrine of judicial precedent; and

(d) Scots lawyers resort frequently to the English law reports and to English legal literature for the law to be applied in the cases before them.

5. Statute Law

The system of Scots law at the beginning of the nineteenth century, when English influence was becoming really strong, was mainly a common law system, *i.e.* it consisted mainly of principles worked out in decided cases and laid down by the judges in their judgments. Since that time statute has progressively encroached on the common law until at the present day it is doubtful whether Scots law can any longer claim to be mainly a common law system. Yet, with the exception of certain Acts in the field of mercantile law—the Bills of Exchange Act 1882, the Partnership Act 1890, the Sale of Goods Act 1893,[1] and the Marine Insurance Act 1906—there has been no codification of the whole or of parts of Scots law. Statutory additions to the common law have been haphazard, and made to suit the needs of the community for the time being.

The encroachment of statute law on the common law seems almost as likely to be a permanent influence on the Scots law of the twentieth century as does the influence of English law. Codification of the *whole* of Scots law remains a very remote possibility, although the Law Commissions Act 1965 makes particular mention of possible codification, and substantial *parts* of Scots law may yet be codified within the present century. Should this happen, Scots law will once again have taken a leaf from the books of the Roman school of legal thought.

Concluding Note

An appreciation of what is involved in the Scottish legal tradition gives a warning against assumptions, made all too often today, that Scots law on certain matters does not differ, or does not much differ, from English law. Similarities between Scots law and English law are admittedly extensive and on the increase with every year that passes, but they are sometimes superficial; the differences may be less obvious, but they are usually deep-rooted.

It is important for the future of the Scottish legal tradition that those who, in Parliament and in the courts, are mainly responsible for the development of the law should give adequate consideration to the distinctiveness of Scots law, and that those who, as practising lawyers or as students, have the task of discovering what Scots law is should beware of relying on English law reports and English legal literature without making an independent search for the Scottish principles.

Further Reading
Lord Cooper, *The Scottish Legal Tradition* (The Saltire Society)
David M. Walker, *The Scottish Legal System*

[1] Repealed by the Sale of Goods Act 1979 which consolidated the provisions of the 1893 Act with other later statutory provisions concerned with the sale of goods.

CHAPTER 2

COURTS, LEGAL PROFESSION, DILIGENCE, LEGAL AID AND ARBITRATION

THIS chapter outlines the structure of the judicial system and indicates who are the personnel of the law (judges, juries, and members of the legal profession).

Brief accounts are also given of diligence, legal aid and arbitration.

COURTS

The judicial system consists of a hierarchy or range of courts of different types, with different powers and composed of different

16

judges and juries. The term "jurisdiction" denotes the extent of the power which a court may exercise.

Only the national courts of the Scottish judicial system are considered in this chapter. For the European Court of Justice, see p. 195, below.

A vital preliminary to the understanding of the structure of the judicial system is to appreciate the distinctions:

1. between civil and criminal jurisdiction; and
2. between fact and law.

1. *Civil and criminal jurisdiction*

The civil courts are machinery provided by the state for the settlement of disputes between citizens of the state. The word "civil" is derived from the Latin "civis" ("a citizen"). When a dispute arises between two citizens and it cannot be resolved by agreement or in any other way, then it will be for a civil court to decide which of the two parties is in the right. The civil courts do not of their own accord intervene in disputes between citizens: one of the parties to the dispute must invoke the aid of the court by bringing an "action" in court against the other party. This resort to the court for the settlement of the dispute is referred to as "litigation." The party who brings an action in court is called the "pursuer," and the party against whom an action is brought is called the "defender." (The corresponding terms of English law for "pursuer" and "defender" are "plaintiff" and "defendant," respectively.)

The criminal courts, on the other hand, are machinery provided by the state for the enforcement of law and order and for the suppression of conduct which is contrary to the standard of behaviour required by the state of its citizens. Proceedings in the criminal courts are referred to as "prosecutions," and they are brought not by private individuals or by the police but by officials who represent the state. The function of a criminal court is to decide whether there has been a breach of the criminal law in the case before it, and, if there has been, what penalty is to be imposed on the guilty party.

2. *Fact and law*

The situation with which a court has to deal may involve one or more questions of fact, questions of law, and mixed questions of fact and law.

A question of fact concerns the existence of something which can be appreciated by one of the senses; *e.g.* what a person did or said, and when and where, are questions of fact. Such questions are decided by the bringing forward of evidence to show what exactly happened.

A question of law, on the other hand, concerns some doctrine' or principle, or rule of law; *e.g.* what interpretation is to be given to an Act of Parliament or to any other document is a question of law. Questions of law are decided by legal argument, *i.e.* by the bringing forward of Acts of Parliament, reports of earlier cases, and other authoritative statements of the law, such as may persuade the judge to apply the law (which he is always presumed to know and which he does not require to have proved to him by evidence) in the particular way desired by the party concerned.

In very many questions fact and law are intermixed; *e.g.* in civil proceedings a question may arise of whether a partnership exists between two parties, and the court will have to decide (a) what the terms of the agreement between the parties were (a question of fact), and (b) whether, according to the law of partnership, that agreement does constitute partnership (a question of law); similarly, in criminal proceedings a question may arise of whether the accused is guilty of murder, and this will involve evidence of what the accused actually did (a question of fact) and may also involve consideration of whether what the accused is proved to have done amounts to the crime of murder (a question of law).

In a court which consists of a judge or judges without a jury, questions of all three types are decided by the judge or judges. In a court which has a jury, certain questions of fact are decided by the jury, and certain mixed questions of fact and law are decided by the jury with guidance as to the legal elements from the presiding judge, but other questions, including all questions of pure law, are decided by the judge or judges.

Classification of Courts

Courts may be divided into:
1. civil courts;
2. criminal courts; and
3. courts of special jurisdiction.

In addition to traditional courts there are now very many administrative tribunals (*e.g.* industrial tribunals, rent tribunals, and the Lands Tribunal for Scotland) set up to deal with matters which arise in the field of administrative law. Where a citizen is in dispute with the state, *e.g.* about whether he is entitled to some benefit, such as unemployment benefit, which he is claiming from the state, or about the amount of compensation to which he is entitled because the state proposes to deprive him of the full use of his own property, he is generally not entitled to resort to a court of law for the decision of the matter in dispute; his case can be dealt with normally only by the appropriate administrative tribunal. In this connection there is an interesting instance provided by the Licensing (Scotland) Act 1976 of the replacement of a system of licensing "courts" (and courts of appeal) by a system of licensing "boards" (with a right of appeal from a board's decision to the sheriff and, on a point of law, from the sheriff's decision to the Court of Session). The Clayson Committee, on whose recommendations the Act of 1976 was based, had concluded that, since liquor licensing involved the exercise of an administrative discretion in the interests of the community, it was not an appropriate function for a court of law, and that the function should be carried out instead by a tribunal composed of local authority district council members. On administrative tribunals, see p. 226, below.

1. *Civil Courts*

Civil courts are concerned with the rights and duties of citizens of the state towards each other.

The civil courts in the Scottish judicial system are:

  (a) the sheriff court;
  (b) the Outer House of the Court of Session;
  (c) the Inner House of the Court of Session; and
  (d) the House of Lords.

The J.P. small debt courts constituted under the Justices of the Peace Small Debt (Scotland) Act 1825 were abolished as from May 16, 1975 by the District Courts (Scotland) Act 1975.

(a) The sheriff court

The sheriff court is the most important of the civil courts in that it undertakes the greatest volume of business.

In 1967 a committee under the chairmanship of Lord Grant, after an exhaustive study of all aspects of the sheriff court, recommended various reforms (*The Sheriff Court* (1967: Cmnd. 3248)). The general aim underlying most of the recommendations was "to secure the more speedy, economical and satisfactory dispatch of civil and criminal business" (paragraphs 2 and 28). The Committee suggested that the required legislation might be undertaken in two stages. The Sheriff Courts (Scotland) Act 1971 represents the first stage.

Sheriffs-principal and sheriffs

The office of sheriff dates from Anglo-Saxon times, and was introduced to Scotland from England in the twelfth century. Originally the sheriff, as the local representative of the king, was responsible for the military organisation of the area and the collection of the royal revenues from it, as well as for the preservation of law and order in it. Later the office became in many cases a hereditary one, with a resulting loss of control for the king.

After the Jacobite rebellion of 1745 the hereditary office of sheriff was abolished, and the Crown appointed instead "sheriffs-depute" with legal qualifications. These sheriffs-depute had power to appoint substitutes, and since the sheriffs-depute generally lived in Edinburgh and not in their sheriffdoms, it was the substitutes who undertook most of the court work in the sheriffdoms. The right to appoint sheriffs-substitute was transferred from the sheriffs-depute to the Crown by the Sheriff Courts (Scotland) Act 1877.

The person holding the office of sheriff-depute came to be referred to properly as "the sheriff." Colloquially, however, he was often referred to as "the sheriff-principal," while the term "sheriff" was often used of a sheriff-substitute. The Sheriff Courts (Scotland) Act 1971 made these colloquial titles the official ones, and also provided that the qualification for either office is ten years' standing as an advocate or as a solicitor.

By the Sheriffs' Pensions (Scotland) Act 1961 sheriffs-principal and sheriffs must retire at the age of seventy-two.

Procedure for their removal from office on the grounds of inability, neglect of duty or misbehaviour is laid down in the Act of 1971; the Lord President of the Court of Session and the Lord Justice-Clerk must first make a joint investigation, and the Secretary of State for Scotland may then, if the sheriff-principal or sheriff is reported unfit, make an order which is subject to annulment by either House of Parliament.

Under the Sheriff Courts (Scotland) Act 1907 sheriffs-principal have power to appoint honorary sheriffs, who may or may not have legal qualifications. Honorary sheriffs who are not legally qualified are appointed mainly as an honour, and seldom sit in court. Those who are legally qualified are appointed partly as an honour and partly to assist with court business.

Organisation and administration of the sheriff court

The Sheriff Courts (Scotland) Act 1971 has made important changes in the organisation and administration of the sheriff court. In order that court business might be authoritatively directed both centrally and at local level the Act conferred new and extensive powers on the Secretary of State for Scotland and on sheriffs-principal. The Secretary of State's powers are exercised on his behalf by the Scottish Courts Administration, a body which was set up in 1971 for this purpose and which has now a variety of other functions in the field of law.

Up to the end of 1974 Scotland was divided into twelve sheriff-doms based on groupings of the counties, *e.g.* the sheriffdom of Fife and Kinross, and the sheriffdom of Perth and Angus. Each sheriffdom had one sheriff-principal, whose appointment was, except in the sheriffdoms of Lanarkshire and of the Lothians and Peebles, a part-time one. Each sheriffdom also had a number of sheriffs-substitute, residing in the sheriffdom and holding full-time appointments.

By the Act of 1971 it is the duty of the Secretary of State "to secure the efficient organisation and administration of the sheriff courts." For that purpose he has power to make orders altering the boundaries of sheriffdoms, forming new sheriffdoms or abolishing existing sheriffdoms. Any such order requires to be approved by a resolution of each House of Parliament.

By an order taking effect on January 1, 1975, the Secretary of State abolished the twelve former sheriffdoms and created six new sheriffdoms, namely:

Grampian, Highland and Islands;
Tayside, Central and Fife;
Lothian and Borders;
Glasgow and Strathkelvin;
North Strathclyde; and
South Strathclyde, Dumfries and Galloway.

All sheriffs-principal now hold full-time appointments and are required to reside in their respective sheriffdoms. In each sheriffdom there are about ten full-time resident sheriffs, except that in the sheriffdom of Glasgow and Strathkelvin the number is about fifteen.

As from May 16, 1975, the boundaries of the six sheriffdoms were altered so as to correspond with the then new local government areas. With the exception of Strathclyde, each local authority region and islands authority falls wholly within one sheriffdom.

Each sheriffdom is divided into sheriff court districts, each district being centred on a town in which the sheriff court is held. By the Act of 1971 the Secretary of State has power by order to alter the boundaries of sheriff court districts, form new districts, abolish existing districts and to provide that sheriff courts shall be held, or shall cease to be held, at any place. A sheriff's jurisdiction extends to all parts of the sheriffdom for which he is appointed and is not confined to any particular sheriff court district.

The Secretary of State has wide powers under the Act of 1971 to give directions of an administrative nature to any sheriff-principal, sheriff or person engaged in the administration of the sheriff courts,

for the purpose of securing the efficient organisation and administration of the courts and, in particular, the speedy and efficient
disposal of business. He has also power on the occurrence of vacancies, illness or other inability to arrange for a sheriff-principal or a
sheriff from another sheriffdom to perform additional duties, and in
similar circumstances he may appoint a temporary sheriff-principal
or a temporary sheriff. A few "floating" sheriffs have been appointed
to undertake duties in any sheriffdom in Scotland where assistance
is needed.

A sheriff-principal is by the Act of 1971 under a duty to secure
the speedy and efficient disposal of business within his own sheriffdom and for that purpose may give instructions of an administrative
nature to sheriffs and administrative staff in the sheriffdom. Subject
to any direction given by the Secretary of State, he has power to
provide for the distribution of the business amongst the sheriffs, and
he may make special temporary arrangements in the event of illness
or other circumstances which would cause delay.

Jurisdiction of the sheriff court

The civil jurisdiction of the sheriff court is very wide. It is
governed mainly by the Sheriff Courts (Scotland) Act 1907 as
amended by the Sheriff Courts (Scotland) Act 1913, and has two
aspects:

(i) jurisdiction over persons; and
(ii) subject-matter of the jurisdiction.

(i) *Jurisdiction over persons.* Before a court can hear a case, it
must have jurisdiction over the defender. The maxim expressing
this general principle is actor sequitur forum rei (literally, "the
pursuer follows the court of the defender"), which means that the
pursuer must bring his action in the court which has jurisdiction over
the defender.

Since the sheriff court is a local court, its jurisdiction is in general
limited to those within the locality of the sheriffdom. For the exact
grounds of jurisdiction reference must be made to the Acts of 1907
and 1913; *e.g.* a sheriff court has jurisdiction:

1. where the defender resides within the sheriffdom, *or*, having
resided there for at least forty days, has ceased to reside there for
less than forty days and has no known residence in Scotland;

2. where the defender carries on business and has a place of
business within the sheriffdom, *and* is cited (*i.e.* summoned to answer
the case in court) either personally or at his place of business;

3. where the defender is owner or tenant of heritable property

(*i.e.* land and buildings) within the sheriffdom, *and* the action is connected with that property; and

4. where the action is concerned with a contract performed in the sheriffdom, *and* the defender is personally cited there.

In actions founded on delict (*i.e.* a wrongful act) the sheriff court has jurisdiction where the delict was committed within the sheriffdom (Law Reform (Jurisdiction in Delict) (Scotland) Act 1971).

(ii) *Subject-matter of the jurisdiction.* The main limitations in this connection are:

1. Certain types of action can be brought only in other courts, *e.g.* actions involving a person's status (such as divorce, nullity of marriage, and legitimacy), actions of reduction (*i.e.* actions to set aside something), and actions for proving the "tenor" (*i.e.* the terms or meaning) of lost documents are reserved for the Court of Session, questions as to the right to bear arms are reserved for the Court of the Lord Lyon, and appeals against rateable valuations of property are reserved for the Lands Valuation Appeal Court.

2. In certain types of action either of the parties has the right to require the action to be remitted to (*i.e.* sent to) the Court of Session, *e.g.* certain actions concerned with heritable right and title.

Apart from such limitations, the jurisdiction of the sheriff court is unlimited as regards subject-matter. It extends to actions of debt and actions for damages however large the sum involved, and to many other types of action, *e.g.* actions concerned with leases and rents, actions of separation of husband and wife (not to be confused with divorce), custody of children, and succession to a deceased's estate.

Further, there are certain cases in which the jurisdiction of the sheriff court is exclusive or "privative," which means that these cases must be dealt with by the sheriff court and cannot be either brought originally in, or taken on appeal to, the Court of Session. The Sheriff Courts (Scotland) Act 1971 raised the upper limit of the privative jurisdiction of the sheriff court from £50 to £250, and also enabled the figure to be varied in future by Order in Council. By the Sheriff Courts (Scotland) Act 1971 (Privative Jurisdiction, etc.) Order 1976, the limit was raised to £500 as from September 1, 1976.

Procedure in the sheriff court

There is now no jury in civil proceedings in the sheriff court, and trial is by a sheriff alone. The only exceptions were actions of damages brought by employees against their employers for injuries caused by accidents arising out of and in the course of employment: in such actions there might be a jury of seven persons. The Law

Reform (Miscellaneous Provisions) (Scotland) Act 1980 included a provision abolishing civil jury trials in the sheriff court, and this came into force on December 22, 1980.

The degree of formality of procedure varies according to the importance of the case. Formerly civil actions were divided into:

    (i) small debt causes;

    (ii) summary causes; and

    (iii) ordinary causes.

By provisions of the Sheriff Courts (Scotland) Act 1971, which were brought into force on September 1, 1976, the division is now into:

    (i) summary causes; and

    (ii) ordinary causes.

(i) *Summary causes.* The "summary cause" is a form of process used for actions for payment of money, actions relating to heritable and moveable property, and several other types of action. The sum being sued for must not exceed £500.[1] The action is commenced by a summons in a form prescribed by Act of Sederunt made by the Court of Session in consultation with the Sheriff Court Rules Council which was set up by the Act of 1971. The evidence, if any, given in a summary cause is not recorded.

Provision is made for a summary cause to be treated, as from any stage, as an ordinary cause and then to proceed as an ordinary cause for all purposes (including appeal). There are three situations where this may occur:

1. On a *joint* motion of the parties to the summary cause, the sheriff *must* direct that the cause be then treated as an ordinary cause.

2. On a motion of *one* of the parties to the summary cause, the sheriff *may* give such a direction, if he is of the opinion that the importance or difficulty of the cause makes this appropriate.

3. In the case of an action for the recovery of possession of heritable or moveable property, the sheriff *may of his own accord* give such a direction.

(ii) *Ordinary causes.* Actions for more than £500 [1] and most of the actions which involve a decision other than an award of a sum of money come under this heading. The action begins with an "initial writ." The procedure is similar to that followed in the Court of Session, and there is a verbatim record of the evidence. There are full rights of appeal.

At any stage, on the joint motion of the parties to an ordinary cause, the sheriff must direct that the cause be treated as a summary cause.

A provision of the Law Reform (Miscellaneous Provisions)

---

[1] Raised to £1000 by Sheriff Courts (Scotland) Act 1971 (Summary Cause) Order 1981.

(Scotland) Act 1980 confers a discretion on the sheriff, on the motion of any of the parties to the cause, to remit the cause to the Court of Session if he is of the opinion that the importance or difficulty of the cause makes it appropriate to do so. By the same Act, the sheriff may, of his own accord, remit to the Court of Session an action relating to the custody or adoption of a child.

Appeals from the sheriff court

Rights of appeal depend on the procedure under which the case has been heard.

In a civil jury trial there was a right of appeal to the Inner House of the Court of Session on certain grounds, but the Court of Session was reluctant to disturb the findings of the jury on questions of fact and of damages.

In summary causes, the only appeals which may be made are:
1. from the sheriff to the sheriff principal on a point of law; and
2. from the sheriff principal to the Inner House of the Court of Session on a point of law if the sheriff principal certifies the cause as suitable for such an appeal.

In ordinary causes there is a right of appeal *either* to the sheriff-principal and then to the Inner House of the Court of Session, *or* directly to the Inner House of the Court of Session. The possibility of a double appeal has the advantage of allowing an appeal to be heard locally without so much expense, but the disadvantage of being capable of being misused merely to secure delay.

(b) The Outer House of the Court of Session

The Court of Session, which sits in Edinburgh, was established in 1532, but its present structure resulted from a reorganisation in the first quarter of the nineteenth century. It consists of a number of judges who together make up the Inner House, which is mainly a court of appeal, and the Outer House, which is a court "of first instance" (*i.e.* a court deciding cases brought before it originally, as distinct from appeals).

The number of judges authorised to be appointed to the Court of Session as a whole was for many years 15, but the number has been progressively increased, and by the Maximum Number of Judges Order 1977, made under the Administration of Justice Act 1968, is now 22. One is Chairman of the Scottish Law Commission, eight sit in the Inner House, and 13 in the Outer House.

By the Judicial Pensions Act 1959 the retiring age for Court of Session judges is seventy-five.

Composition of the Outer House

The Outer House consists of a number of courts, each presided over by a junior Lord of Session (*i.e.* judge of the Court of Session other than one of the eight who form the Inner House), known as a "Lord Ordinary."

In certain classes of cases (principally claims of damages arising out of industrial and street accidents) there is a jury of twelve persons.

Jurisdiction of the Outer House

The Outer House does not have an appellate jurisdiction, *i.e.* it is not a court of appeal.

Both as regards persons and as regards subject-matter the jurisdiction of the Outer House is more extensive than that of the sheriff court.

(i) *Jurisdiction over persons.* The jurisdiction is not restricted to one locality but extends to the whole of Scotland.

There are two general grounds of jurisdiction over a particular individual:

1. that he is resident in Scotland; and
2. that he is the owner or tenant of heritable property in Scotland (the action need not be connected with the property).

Other grounds of jurisdiction apply in special cases; *e.g.* the court has jurisdiction if:

1. in an action concerned with a contract to be performed in Scotland, the defender is cited personally in Scotland; or
2. the defender has no fixed place of residence and is cited personally in Scotland.

In an action founded on delict it is sufficient that the delict was committed in Scotland: the rule which formerly required personal citation of the defender in Scotland was abolished by the Law Reform (Jurisdiction in Delict) (Scotland) Act 1971.

Actions involving status are subject to special rules. Many of these actions are governed by the Domicile and Matrimonial Proceedings Act 1973 which provides that the Court of Session has jurisdiction in such actions as divorce, separation and declarator of nullity of marriage if (and only if) either of the parties to the marriage:

1. is *domiciled* (*i.e.* has the home which the law regards as his permanent home) in Scotland on the date when the action is begun; *or*

2. was habitually resident in Scotland throughout one year immediately before that date.

(ii) *Subject-matter of the jurisdiction.* The jurisdiction of the Outer House extends to all classes of civil claims except those for which the sheriff court has privative jurisdiction and those which are excluded by some other statutory provision: in particular, it includes actions involving status (of which divorce actions are by far the most numerous), actions of reduction, actions for proving the tenor of lost documents, and the other actions similarly reserved for the Court of Session.

It follows from (i) and (ii) above that, except for those cases in which either the Court of Session or the sheriff court has privative jurisdiction, the pursuer is normally free to choose between the sheriff court and the Outer House of the Court of Session. On the one hand, he may prefer the sheriff court because it is within easier reach of his own home, and because proceedings in that court will normally be less expensive since he will not require to pay the fees of an Edinburgh solicitor and of counsel as well as those of a local solicitor. On the other hand, if a large sum of money or some other important matter is at stake, he may consider it desirable to have a ruling which will carry more authority than that of a sheriff, and further, in the limited class of cases in which jury trial is available in the Outer House, he may feel that a jury, guided by a judge, will view his case more sympathetically than a judge sitting alone.

Procedure in the Outer House

Proceedings are usually started by a summons, which is a document setting out the pursuer's claim and summoning the defender to appear in court to answer that claim. The summons includes a "condescendence" (*i.e.* a statement of facts which the pursuer alleges to exist) and also "pleas-in-law" (statements of the legal principles on which the pursuer is basing his case).

If the defender ignores the summons, the case is an undefended one, and the pursuer is as a general rule entitled to obtain from the court a decree in absence giving him the remedy which he claims. Consistorial actions (actions between husband and wife involving their status as a married couple) are exceptions to the general rule: in such actions proof is always required; however, since 1978 in undefended actions of divorce and of judicial separation the proof may take the form of "affidavits" (written statements made on oath before a notary public or a J.P.) and there is then no need for witnesses to attend the court.

If the defender wishes to defend the action, he must lodge written defences answering, statement by statement, the pursuer's allegations in the condescendence and including pleas-in-law for the defender.

Out of the summons and the defences an "open record" [1a] is then drawn up, setting out in one document the points of fact and

[1a] "Record" is pronounced with the emphasis on its second syllable.

of law on which each party is basing his case. In the open record each paragraph of the pursuer's condescendence is followed by the corresponding paragraph of the defender's defences, and the pleas-in-law for each party appear at the end of the document.

There follows a period of adjustment of the record, during which each party may make alterations in his written pleadings, and at the end of this period a "closed record" [1] is drawn up. The closed record is the written statement of the case on which the court's decision is sought.

The next step after the closing of the record depends on whether the case involves a question of fact only or a question of law.

If the case involves only a question of fact, there will be a "proof" (*i.e.* a trial by a Lord Ordinary alone) or a "jury trial" (*i.e.* a trial by a Lord Ordinary with a jury of twelve).

If, however, the case involves a question of law, it is not suitable, or not yet suitable, for a proof or jury trial: there must first be a decision by the Lord Ordinary on the question of law. The case is, therefore, sent to the "procedure roll" for the pleas-in-law to be considered. At this stage it is assumed that any facts alleged can be proved, and the procedure takes the form of a legal debate, with one party challenging the legal basis of the other party's case; *e.g.* the defender may be claiming that the court has no jurisdiction to grant the remedy sought, or either party may be claiming that the "averments" (the statements in the case) of the other are not "relevant" (*i.e.* not sufficient *in law*, even if they are admitted or proved to be true, to justify the remedy sought).

After the debate the Lord Ordinary issues an "interlocutor," which "sustains" (*i.e.* upholds and gives effect to) one or more of the pleas-in-law of one party and "repels" (*i.e.* rejects) other pleas-in-law. The case may then be at an end, but, if a question of fact as well as a question of law is involved, a proof or a jury trial may then be necessary in order that the facts may be proved.

At a proof or jury trial the object is to ascertain the facts, and for this purpose evidence is led first for the pursuer and then for the defender, each witness in turn being sworn by the judge, examined by counsel on one side, cross-examined by counsel on the other side, and often then re-examined by counsel on the first side. The evidence is recorded verbatim by a shorthand writer.

In a proof the Lord Ordinary may either give his decision at once or "make avizandum" (*i.e.* consider the case privately for a few days). In a jury trial his function is to "charge" the jury (*i.e.* instruct the jury as to points which they must consider in reaching their verdict), and it is then for the jury to decide the question of fact either immediately or, more usually, after retiring to the jury room; the verdict may be either unanimous or by a majority. Both in a proof and in a jury trial the decision of the court on the question of fact takes the form of a "decree." This may grant to the pursuer the remedy which he seeks or it may "assoilzie"[2] the defender, *i.e.* declare that the defender is not liable.

Normally, as is indicated by the outline of procedure given above, a question of law in a case is decided before any question of fact. A slightly different procedure, however, referred to as "proof before answer," is followed where the Lord Ordinary considers that he cannot give a decision on the point of law without knowing the facts of the case more fully; the evidence is then heard before the point of law is decided.

The procedure described above applies where the proceedings have been started by a summons. In some cases the proper way of approaching the court is not by a summons, but by a petition, or by some other less usual form of application.

A petition is appropriate, for instance, where the court is being asked to appoint new trustees or to wind up a company. Very often there is no opposition to the granting of a petition, and the petitioner may immediately obtain from the court the appointment, remedy, or authority which he seeks, though in some cases the court will remit the petition to a person with suitable qualifications (usually a member of the Bar or an experienced solicitor) for an inquiry and a report before it disposes of the petition. If there is opposition to a petition, this takes the form of "answers," and the party lodging answers is called the "respondent"; the court may then hear the parties, have a proof, or remit to a reporter and hear the parties on his report, before it disposes of the petition.

Appeals from the Outer House

Appeals lie (*i.e.* can be brought) to the Inner House by means of a "reclaiming motion."

If the appeal is on a question of fact, the evidence is not reheard but the shorthand-writer's transcript of the evidence is considered by the Inner House. There is no power to order a fresh proof, but on certain limited grounds a fresh jury trial may be allowed.

If the appeal is on a question of law, the Inner House will be concerned only with legal argument, and its decision will normally take the form of "adhering" to the Lord Ordinary's interlocutor (*i.e.* refusing the appeal) or of "recalling" that interlocutor and substituting a different one for it (*i.e.* allowing the appeal).

---

[2] The "z" in this word is not pronounced.

(c) The Inner House of the Court of Session

Composition of the Inner House

The Inner House has two Divisions, equal to one another in authority.

The First Division consists of the Lord President and three other "Lords of Session" (judges of the Court of Session), and the Second Division consists of the Lord Justice-Clerk and three Lords of Session.

The quorum for each Division is normally three judges. Therefore, if pressure of business requires it, a judge from a Division may sit instead in the Outer House as an additional Lord Ordinary. Absence of a judge from a Division may also be necessary in connection with the circuit sittings of the High Court of Justiciary. On the other hand, it is sometimes necessary for a Division to call in a judge from the other Division or from the Outer House to make up the quorum.

The Lord President may, if the volume of Inner House business makes it desirable, set up an Extra Division, consisting of any three judges of the Court of Session. The most senior judge of the three presides over the Extra Division.

Decisions of a Division are given either unanimously or by a majority. The presiding judge has no casting vote, and if opinion is equally divided a rehearing is necessary.

In cases of importance or difficulty (including those which require to be reheard) a larger court is often convened by having the First and Second Divisions sitting together to make a court of seven judges or by including also judges from the Outer House to make an even fuller court, *e.g.* a court of fifteen judges.

Jurisdiction of the Inner House

The Divisions are of equal jurisdiction, and a party is no longer entitled to choose the Division which is to hear his case.

In a limited number of cases the Inner House is a court of first instance. These are:

(i) "special cases," *i.e.* cases in which the parties are agreed as to the facts and seek the opinion of the Inner House only on a question of law (*e.g.* where there is a dispute as to the interpretation of a will or other document);

(ii) revenue "stated cases," *i.e.* cases in which the opinion of the Inner House is sought on certain questions in the law of taxation;

(iii) certain petitions, *e.g.* petitions by limited companies for confirmation of reduction of capital; and

(iv) certain appeals against decisions of some administrative tribunals and other bodies similarly placed outside the judicial system proper.

In most cases, however, the Inner House is a court of appeal affirming or reversing judgments of sheriffs, sheriffs-principal or Lords Ordinary.

Procedure in the Inner House

Only in exceptional circumstances will evidence be heard in an Inner House case; where the hearing of evidence is necessary, it will be before only one judge of the Division.

Normally the Inner House will hear only legal argument on the transcript of evidence given in the lower court and on questions of law.

After this hearing the judges may give their decision at once, one of them explaining the reasons for the decision orally in an "opinion," and the others adding shorter opinions usually "concurring" with the leading opinion. If, however, the case is a difficult one, the judges will make avizandum, prepare written opinions, and read these in court on a later occasion. That later stage is termed "advising." A judge who does not agree with the decision of the majority gives a "dissenting" opinion.

An interlocutor, signed by the presiding judge, then gives effect to the decision. The interlocutor of the sheriff or of the Lord Ordinary is adhered to or recalled according to whether the appeal is refused or allowed respectively.

Appeals from the Inner House

An appeal can be made against a decision of the Inner House by means of a petition to the House of Lords "praying" that the interlocutor of the Inner House be altered.

The appeal may be either on a question of law or on a question of fact, except that if the case originated in the sheriff court, only an appeal on a question of law is allowed. The right of appeal may be excluded by Acts of Parliament in particular situations, but otherwise an appeal may be made against any final judgment of the Inner House and also against any other judgment of the Inner House if either the Court of Session gives leave to appeal or the judges were not unanimous.

Because of the great expense and delay of an appeal to the House of Lords, parties do not normally take their cases beyond the Inner House unless a large sum or some other important issue is at stake.

An appeal to the House of Lords on a question of fact is unlikely to succeed because of the great weight given by that House to the views of the judge who actually saw and heard the witnesses.

Only about a dozen cases are appealed from the Inner House in a year.

After the House of Lords has given judgment, the case returns to the Inner House for the Inner House to "apply the judgment."

(d) The House of Lords

Before the Union of the Parliaments in 1707 a right of appeal to the House of Lords from the English courts had become established, but the Treaty of Union left it doubtful whether there was to be a similar right of appeal from the Court of Session.

In *Greenshields* v. *Magistrates of Edinburgh*, (1710–11) Rob. 12, Colles p. 427, English Reports 1, p. 356, however, the House of Lords held that such an appeal could be made, and after that case the right of appeal to the House of Lords in Scottish civil cases came to be accepted.

Considerable dissatisfaction was felt with a system which enabled English judges who had no training in or experience of Scots law to reverse judgments of the most eminent of Scottish judges. From the beginning of the nineteenth century, in particular, there was mounting discontent at the continuing imposition of English law on Scotland resulting from the ignorance displayed, and sometimes openly admitted, by the House of Lords.

A partial remedy was provided when in 1866 Lord President McNeill became a peer and took his seat in the House of Lords as Lord Colonsay, and further improvement became possible under the Appellate Jurisdiction Act 1876, which authorised the appointment of legally qualified life peers known as "Lords of Appeal in Ordinary." Since 1876 there has always been at least one Scottish Law Lord in the House of Lords, and by convention (*i.e.* by established custom) there are now at least two.

Composition of the House of Lords

In theory the composition of the House of Lords as a court of appeal is the same as its composition as a law-making body, but in practice only the legally qualified members take part in the judicial business. These are the Lord Chancellor, the Lords of Appeal in Ordinary and peers who hold or have held high judicial office.

The Lords of Appeal in Ordinary, authorised to be appointed by the Appellate Jurisdiction Act 1876, must either have held high judicial office for two years or be barristers or advocates of fifteen years' standing. They are entitled to sit in the House of Lords for life (because they are barons for life), but they must retire from office at the age of seventy-five (Judicial Pensions Act 1959).

Their number has been gradually increased from the original two, and is now, under the Administration of Justice Act 1968, eleven.

Although by convention at least two of the Law Lords are of Scottish origin, there is no rule that they or even one of them must be present when a Scottish appeal is being heard. As a result, the final decision in a Scottish case may be given by an appeal court consisting wholly of English judges.

The quorum of the House as a court of appeal is three legally qualified members. Decision is by a majority. Often five members sit, but if the case is a particularly important one the number sitting may be seven or more.

Procedure in the House of Lords

The theory is that an appeal to the House of Lords is an appeal to Parliament; therefore the procedure is for a petition to be presented to the House "praying" that the interlocutor be altered, the judgments of the Law Lords are technically speeches in support of or against a motion put to the House by the presiding judge that the appeal be allowed or be dismissed, and the decision reached by the majority is not in the form of an operative decree but in the form of a judgment which takes effect only when it is applied by the Inner House of the Court of Session.

Formerly appeals were heard in the House of Lords debating chamber, but a change of practice took place during the last war, and the practice is now for appeals to be heard by an Appellate Committee consisting of Law Lords sitting in a committee room and then reporting to the House where the vote is taken on the motion to allow or dismiss the appeal.

2.   Criminal Courts

Criminal courts are concerned with the punishment of persons who have been guilty of conduct which the state considers should be repressed.

The criminal courts in the Scottish judicial system are considered below under these headings:

(a) the district court;
(b) the sheriff court;
(c) the High Court of Justiciary as a court of trial; and
(d) the High Court of Justiciary as a court of appeal.

The prosecution of crimes is under the control of the Lord Advocate who acts through the Crown Office in Edinburgh. Neither the police nor private individuals prosecute in Scotland. Crimes are reported by the police to the procurator-fiscal who is the local representative of the Lord Advocate, and it is then for him, after consulting the Crown Office if the crime is serious, to decide whether to prosecute, and if so in which court.

There are two types of criminal jurisdiction—summary and solemn. In the former there is no jury whereas in the latter there is a jury of fifteen. Summary procedure takes the form of trial "on complaint," and solemn procedure of trial "on indictment." [3]

Of the courts of trial listed in (a) to (c) above, the first exercises only summary criminal jurisdiction, the High Court of Justiciary exercises only solemn criminal jurisdiction, and in the sheriff court the procedure may be either summary or solemn.

The most serious crimes of all can be tried only in the High Court of Justiciary, while at the other end of the scale there are crimes created by statute for which the statute lays down that only summary procedure is to be followed. Apart from such restrictions the prosecutor has a discretion as to the mode of trial, and he will make his choice according to the gravity of the crime, since there are limits on the power of the lower courts to punish offenders.

Statutory provisions relating to criminal procedure were consolidated by the Criminal Procedure (Scotland) Act 1975, which has 464 sections and ten schedules. Some notable amendments have since been made by the Criminal Law Act 1977 and the Criminal Justice (Scotland) Act 1980.

(a) The district court

District courts were provided for by the District Courts (Scotland) Act 1975. They took the place of the J.P. courts and the burgh police courts which were abolished as from May 16, 1975, the date when local government reform took effect.

The provisions of the Act enabled a district court to be established for each "commission area," *i.e.* each district or islands area for the purposes of the Local Government (Scotland) Act 1973. The Secretary of State might, however, direct that a district court be not established in a particular area if there is likely to be a lack of business for such a court in that area; the sheriff court would then deal with such cases as occurred.

The judges in the J.P. and burgh police courts had been laymen except that "stipendiary magistrates" (full-time professional judges)

[3] Pronounced "inditement."

had been appointed in Glasgow. The Act of 1975 preserved this tradition. A district court consists of one or more justices of the peace or of a stipendiary magistrate. A person appointed to be a stipendiary magistrate must have been for at least five years either an advocate or a solicitor; the appointment is made by the local authority but requires the prior approval of the Secretary of State for Scotland.

When the court is composed of laymen, its jurisdiction extends to the less serious criminal cases, including those involving drunkenness, breaches of the peace, petty thefts and minor road traffic offences. The maximum sentence is a fine of £200 [4] and sixty days' imprisonment. When the court is constituted by a stipendiary magistrate, it has the same jurisdiction and powers as the sheriff has in summary proceedings.

Prosecutions are conducted by a procurator-fiscal appointed by the Lord Advocate.

The Act of 1975 enabled the Secretary of State to introduce courses of instruction for justices of the peace, made legal aid available to the accused and conferred on each district and islands council the right to nominate up to one quarter of their members to serve as "ex-officio justices," *i.e.* to hold office for only so long as they remain members of the council and retain its nomination.

(b) The sheriff court

In criminal proceedings there is no distinction between the powers of the sheriff-principal and those of the sheriff, and there is no appeal to the one from the other.

The sheriff court is the most important of the lower criminal courts. Its jurisdiction extends to all crimes and offences committed within the sheriffdom other than those serious crimes, such as treason, murder and rape, which are reserved for the High Court of Justiciary.

There are, however, limits on the sentencing powers of the sheriff, and this fact may lead the prosecutor to prefer to bring the case before the High Court.

In summary cases the sheriff's sentencing powers are normally limited to a fine of £1,000 [4] and imprisonment of three months. If the accused has a previous conviction for dishonesty or violence, the sheriff may impose a sentence of up to six months' imprisonment for an offence of a similar kind. Particular statutory provisions may enlarge or narrow these general limits.

In solemn proceedings the sheriff can impose an unlimited fine, but not a longer period of imprisonment than two years.

[4] Criminal Law Act 1977.

Prosecutions are conducted normally by the procurator-fiscal or one of his deputes, but sometimes in difficult cases by an advocate-depute.

(c) The High Court of Justiciary as a court of trial

The High Court of Justiciary was established in 1672.

It now consists of the Lord President of the Court of Session (who in this capacity takes the title of "Lord Justice-General"), the Lord Justice-Clerk, and all the other judges of the Court of Session (who take the title of "Lords Commissioners of Justiciary" when acting in this capacity).

The jurisdiction of the court extends to the whole of Scotland and to all crimes unless the jurisdiction has been excluded by statute (as is the case for certain minor offences). The most serious crimes of all, such as treason, murder and rape, cannot be tried in any lower court. Because of the limits on the sentencing powers of the sheriff all the most serious cases of crime are dealt with by the High Court, even although they might have been brought before the sheriff court instead.

When acting as a court of trial, the High Court usually consists of only one judge with a jury of fifteen, but in difficult or important cases there may be more than one judge; for such cases the usual number is three.

Sittings of the court take place both in Edinburgh and on circuit. For this purpose Scotland is divided into four circuits:

    (i) Home (*i.e.* Edinburgh);

    (ii) West (Glasgow, Stirling, and Oban);

    (iii) North (Inverness, Aberdeen, Dundee, and Perth); and

    (iv) South (Dumfries, Jedburgh, and Ayr).

Sittings may take place at other towns than those mentioned if some other town is convenient to or near the place where the crime was committed.

Normally sittings on circuit are held only once a quarter and are taken by only one judge, but in Glasgow the volume of business makes it necessary for sittings to be held there every month and for two judges to go on the West circuit. A sitting need not be held if there is no business.

Prosecutions are conducted sometimes by one of the Law Officers (*i.e.* the Lord Advocate and the Solicitor-General for Scotland) but normally by one of the advocates-depute.

(d) The High Court of Justiciary as a court of appeal

When sitting as a court of appeal the High Court consists of three or more Lords Commissioners of Justiciary, the number depending on the importance attached to the particular case, *e.g.* in a specially important case, *H.M. Advocate* v. *Kirkwood,* 1939 J.C. 36, the court consisted of thirteen judges.

The appeal may be from a court of summary criminal jurisdiction, the usual modes of appeal being the "stated case" (available both to the accused and to the prosecutor) and the "bill of suspension" (available only to the accused). Appeals in this category are referred to as the "justiciary roll."

If the appeal is from a court of solemn criminal jurisdiction, the High Court will be acting in its capacity as the Scottish court of criminal appeal, which was set up by the Criminal Appeal (Scotland) Act 1926 as a result of a miscarriage of justice in the case of Oscar Slater. Appeals in this category are referred to as the "criminal appeal roll."

Sittings are always in Edinburgh and are normally held every three or four weeks. Since the judges are the same persons as comprise the Court of Session, the usual practice is for either the First or the Second Division of the Inner House not to sit during the hearing of criminal appeals and for three of the judges who would otherwise have formed that Division to sit instead as the High Court; the fourth judge of the Division may meantime go on circuit or act as a Lord Ordinary in the Outer House.

The Secretary of State for Scotland has power to refer a case to the High Court for an opinion.

There is no right of appeal from the High Court to the House of Lords. This point was finally decided in *Mackintosh* v. *Lord Advocate* (1876) 3 R.(H.L.) 34.

3. *Courts of Special Jurisdiction*

These are courts which fall outside the major division of courts into civil courts and criminal courts, and include the following:

(a) The Court of the Lord Lyon

This court has jurisdiction, both civil and criminal, in matters of heraldry and of the right to bear arms. It may, for instance, interdict (*i.e.* forbid) the use of heraldic devices or clan badges by persons who are not entitled to them, and it has power to fine and imprison offenders as well as to seize goods on which arms have been wrongfully used.

The office of the Lord Lyon King of Arms who presides over the Lyon Court is of very ancient origin.

There is a right of appeal from the Lyon Court to the Inner House of the Court of Session and from there to the House of Lords.

(b) The Scottish Land Court

This court was originally concerned with small land-holdings, but with the increased statutory control of agriculture in modern times the scope of its work has been greatly extended.

The chairman must have legal qualifications and experience. The other four members of the court are practical agriculturists. One must speak Gaelic.

Either party to a dispute which has been decided by the court may require a case "to be stated" by the court on a point of law. That "stated case" is then decided by one of the Divisions of the Inner House of the Court of Session.

(c) The Lands Valuation Appeal Court

This consists of three judges of the Court of Session.

It deals with appeals against decisions of the local valuation appeal committees which themselves in the first instance hear appeals against valuations of property made by a regional assessor for the purpose of the raising of local rates. The actual rateable value is not normally challenged in the Lands Valuation Appeal Court; the question will often be one of statutory interpretation, e.g. whether particular premises are "agricultural buildings" or a "retail shop" for the purposes of the statutory provision.

An appeal comes before the court by way of a "stated case," which sets out the facts as established before the valuation appeal committee and the question of law which is to be decided by the Appeal Court.

There is no appeal from the decision of this court.

(d) The Restrictive Practices Court

This court was established by the Restrictive Trade Practices Act 1956 to examine agreements which restrict trading and to prohibit those which are contrary to the public interest. The Registrar of Restrictive Trading Agreements, with whom restrictive agreements had to be registered, might bring a registered agreement before this court for the purpose of having the court decide whether or not the restrictions were contrary to the public interest. The functions of the Registrar were, by the Fair Trading Act 1973, transferred to the Director General of Fair Trading.

The jurisdiction of the court was extended by the Resale Prices Act 1964, which abolished resale price maintenance, but which allowed exemption from this general ban to be claimed for particular goods. Successful claims for exemption were made in respect of books and medicines. The jurisdiction of the court under this

Act is now at an end, the last case (decided in June 1970) having been that on medicines (*Re Medicaments Reference* (*No.* 2) [1971] 1 All E.R. 12).

The power of the court was further extended—to restrictive agreements for the supply of services—by the Fair Trading Act 1973.

The legislation on all these matters was consolidated in three Acts of 1976—the Restrictive Practices Court Act, the Restrictive Trade Practices Act, and the Resale Prices Act.

A peculiarity of the court is that it is a United Kingdom court. It consists of five judges and not more than ten lay members. Of the five judges, three are judges of the High Court in England, one is a judge of the Court of Session, and the other is a judge of the Supreme Court of Northern Ireland. The court may sit anywhere in the United Kingdom.

The quorum of the court is three, and the court may sit either as a single court or in two or more divisions.

Appeals from the court on points of law are fitted into the judicial system of the country in which it is sitting. In Scotland appeal lies to the Court of Session.

(e) Children's hearings

These were introduced by the Social Work (Scotland) Act 1968 to deal with children under sixteen who are alleged to have committed offences.

A " children's panel " is formed for every local authority area, *i.e.* for every region and every islands area in the new local government structure. Persons are appointed to the panels by the Secretary of State on the advice of local committees.

Sittings of members of the children's panel are referred to as "children's hearings." Each children's hearing consists of a chairman and two other members, and must have both a man and a woman among its members. Cases are brought before a hearing by a local authority officer called "the reporter."

There is a right of appeal from a hearing's decision to the sheriff, and also a further right of appeal, only on a point of law or for an irregularity in the conduct of the case, to the Court of Session by way of "stated case."

If the offence is a serious one the child may be dealt with in the sheriff court or in the High Court of Justiciary instead of by a children's hearing.

(f) Church courts

These exercise jurisdiction only in matters of church discipline.

(g) Courts-martial

These deal with offences against the codes of discipline applicable to the forces.

An appeal may in certain circumstances be made to the Courts-Martial Appeal Court, consisting, so far as Scotland is concerned, of an uneven number of at least three Lords Commissioners of Justiciary, and from that court (but only if a point of law of general public importance is involved) to the House of Lords.

Technical Terms connected with Civil Jurisdiction

Res judicata

A court will normally refuse to consider the same case twice; otherwise there would be no end to litigation. This principle is given effect to in the doctrine of res judicata (literally, "matter decided"), which means that the question raised has already been decided by a competent court in an action between the same parties or between parties representing the same interest.

Res judicata is a "preliminary plea," *i.e.* a plea which is put forward at the beginning of an action, and which, if successful, will prevent the court from considering the "merits" (*i.e.* the substance) of the case at all.

For the plea to be successful, the question in the later case must be the same as that in the earlier, and the parties in the two actions, if they are not actually the same persons, must represent the same interest.

Examples of situations where parties represent the same interest are:

(a) In a dispute about the ownership of property, heirs to the property or purchasers of it represent the same interest as the original parties.

(b) Where one member of the public has unsuccessfully attempted in a court action to have a public right of way established, any other member of the public represents the same interest.

(c) In the law of trusts, if one beneficiary has unsuccessfully brought an action alleging that there has been a breach of trust by the trustees, any other beneficiary represents the same interest.

Res noviter

The full title of this plea is res noviter veniens ad notitiam (literally, "a matter newly coming to knowledge").

The plea means that new evidence has become available, of which the party was not aware at the time of the former trial and which he could not then, by the exercise of reasonable diligence, have discovered. For instance, some important document, supposed to have been lost, may have come to light.

The plea of res noviter can be used as a "replication" (*i.e.* an answer) to the plea of res judicata; in that case, while one party maintains that the question has already been decided, the other party contends that the question ought to be reconsidered because of the discovery of new evidence.

The plea may also be used as a ground for the reduction (*i.e.* the setting aside) of a decree.

Arrestment to found jurisdiction

Ownership of moveable property (*i.e.* of property other than land and buildings) within the area of a court's jurisdiction does not of itself give the court jurisdiction over the owner. However, by the process of arrestment to found jurisdiction, moveable property (such as a ship, or a sum of money) belonging to the defender and present within the area of the court's jurisdiction may be "arrested" under a warrant from the court for the purpose of giving the court jurisdiction over the defender in a particular action. This applies only to actions for payment of money or delivery of an article, and not, for example, to actions affecting a person's status such as divorce.

Arrestment to found jurisdiction is to be distinguished from arrestment as a form of diligence (see p. 52, below). The latter is resorted to by a creditor seeking payment of a debt out of a sum of money or other moveable property belonging to his debtor and for the time being in the hands of a third party. Arrestment to found jurisdiction creates no nexus ("bond") over the property and does not prevent the third party from handing it over to the debtor; its only effect is to give the court jurisdiction in the particular case.

Reconvention

The Court of Session may have jurisdiction conferred on it by reconvention, which means that where a party raises an action voluntarily in the Court of Session he thereby submits himself to its jurisdiction in any counter-action arising out of the same undertaking or belonging to the same class. In this way, for instance, if cross-actions arise out of a collision between two ships, the Court of Session may be entitled to exercise jurisdiction over a foreigner who would not have been subject to the jurisdiction of that court had he not himself raised one of the actions.

So far as the sheriff court is concerned, an extension of the principle of reconvention is provided for by the Sheriff Courts (Scotland) Act 1907: the defender is subject to the jurisdiction of a sheriff court if he is at the same time in another action within the sheriffdom himself suing the pursuer; the two actions need not be related.

Prorogation

Prorogation of jurisdiction means voluntary submission to a court's jurisdiction.

It applies where a person who would not otherwise be subject to the jurisdiction of the court agrees, expressly or impliedly, to submit himself to its jurisdiction. A defender will be considered to have agreed *impliedly* if he has lodged defences to an action without objecting to the jurisdiction.

Forum non conveniens

The court will refuse to exercise jurisdiction if the plea of forum non conveniens (literally, "court not appropriate") is successfully put forward by the defender.

The plea is used where there is some foreign element in a case. The defender admits that the Scottish court does have jurisdiction, but claims that there is in a civilised country some other court which also has jurisdiction and in which it would be more appropriate for the case to be heard.

When this plea is put forward, the court has a discretion whether to sustain (*i.e.* to accept or give effect to) it or not. The court considers the convenience of the parties involved, whether Scots law or foreign law is to be applied, and in general how the ends of justice can best be served.

The plea was sustained, for instance, in *Société du Gaz de Paris* v. *Armateurs français*, 1925 S.C. 332, affd. 1926 S.C.(H.L.) 13, a case in which, although the Dumbarton sheriff court had had jurisdiction conferred on it by the use of arrestments, the parties were both carrying on business in France, the witnesses all resided in France or in England, and the court would have had to consider a claim for damages for unseaworthiness of a French ship.

Declinature

Declinature of a judge means that the judge declines to exercise jurisdiction in a particular case on the ground that he is related to one of the parties or that he has some financial or other interest in the subject-matter of the action.

LEGAL PROFESSION

Legal practitioners, colloquially called "lawyers," are in Scotland either advocates or solicitors. There is a corresponding division of legal practitioners in England into barristers and solicitors. A lawyer, if suitably qualified, may change from one branch of the profession to the other, but no one can belong to both branches at the same time.

The two branches of the profession are distinct in tradition, organisation, qualifications for entry, and professional etiquette. The role of the advocate differs from that of the solicitor, appeals to a different type of person, and requires somewhat different talents and training.

There are about twenty times as many solicitors as advocates engaged in active practice.

Advocates work mainly at or in connection with the courts in Edinburgh, although at times they will be required to appear elsewhere, as when the High Court of Justiciary is on circuit, or when they are engaged for a sheriff court case or for an appeal to the House of Lords.

Solicitors, on the other hand, have their practices in towns and cities throughout Scotland. They may (but not all do) appear on behalf of clients in the sheriff courts, but they are not allowed to plead in higher courts. Usually quite a small proportion of the work of a solicitor's office relates to court proceedings. The solicitor's functions include giving advice to clients as to any legal matter on which he is consulted by them, carrying through commercial and personal negotiations on their behalf, and drawing up formal legal documents, such as wills and the deeds connected with the transfer of property. Much of the solicitor's work, therefore, is of a non-contentious character, *i.e.* it involves no dispute, and does not call for that fluency of debate which is essential for a successful advocate. The solicitor's time is usually devoted more to routine matters in his office and to personal contacts with clients and on their behalf than to court proceedings, and a successful solicitor must have the qualities appropriate for such work.

1. Advocates

Advocates are referred to collectively as "the Bar," a term derived from the fact that when pleading in the Court of Session advocates stand behind a wooden bar or barrier which runs across the court room. They are members of the Faculty of Advocates which had its origin in the group of pleaders who regularly appeared before the courts which existed prior to the foundation of the Court of Session in 1532. The head of the Faculty is the Dean.

Advocates are divided into senior and junior counsel, senior counsel being Q.C.s (Queen's Counsel), and junior counsel being advocates who have not attained that rank. When an advocate becomes a Q.C. he is said to "take silk," because a Q.C. wears a silk gown.

In all important cases it is usual for a Q.C. to be "instructed" (*i.e.* employed), but there is no objection to a person's instructing only junior counsel. A Q.C. need not be, but often will be, accompanied by junior counsel.

Counsel work together only for the duration of the case for which they have been instructed. They may very well find themselves opposing one another in a later case. It is an essential part of professional etiquette that opposition is confined to the court room and not carried over into personal relationships.

Every counsel, whether senior or junior, practises on his own account: no partnership or agreement for sharing of work or profits is allowed.

A client cannot instruct counsel directly, but may do so only through a solicitor. Whenever there is a consultation between the client and counsel, the solicitor must be present. The client is free to choose which counsel he is to instruct, but in practice he relies on the recommendations of his solicitor who is usually better able to make an informed choice.

Mutual confidence is essential between client and counsel. Therefore, an advocate is not bound to accept instructions and is even free to give up at any stage instructions which he has accepted; similarly, the client is free to cancel instructions.

During the conduct of a case the advocate has a discretion as to the course of action to be followed. He may even abandon or compromise (*i.e.* make some agreed settlement of) a claim unless he has been expressly forbidden to do so. However, he would in practice normally consult the client before taking any decisive step.

An advocate is not liable in damages for wrong advice in law, negligence, error of judgment, or mismanagement of a case, unless he has acted fraudulently or treacherously or there is an express agreement making him liable.

In court cases in which counsel have been instructed much of the preliminary work is done by the solicitor, but papers and pleadings are normally revised and signed by counsel, and all the actual pleading in court is undertaken by them.

Opinions of counsel

Counsel may be consulted on matters which do not, or have not yet, come to court. Where some legal difficulty arises or seems likely to arise in the interpretation of a document or in connection with some other matter, a solicitor may consider it advisable to obtain an "Opinion" of counsel.

The practice is for a "Memorial" to be prepared by the solicitor, setting out the problem on which an Opinion is desired. The Memorial is sent, along with the documents, to the chosen Q.C. or advocate, and the answers to the questions set out in the Memorial are given in the form of a written Opinion, which usually refers to statutes and decided cases in support of the answers.

This procedure is often adopted as a means of settling a dispute without litigation.

2. Solicitors

Solicitors were formerly called "writers" or "law agents," but since the Solicitors (Scotland) Act 1933 the term "solicitor" has been the proper one.

The Solicitors (Scotland) Acts 1933 to 1976 were consolidated by the Solicitors (Scotland) Act 1980. Some amendments to the consolidating Act are included in the Law Reform (Miscellaneous Provisions) (Scotland) Act 1980.

Not all solicitors are in practice: many are full-time employees of large business concerns and of local and other public authorities.

A solicitor who is in practice must take out a practising certificate every year. Solicitors may practise on their own account or in partnership with other solicitors, or they may be employed by another solicitor or firm of solicitors.

All practising solicitors must be members of the Law Society of Scotland, which was established in 1949. Amongst the functions of the Law Society are the following:

(a) control of the Legal Aid Scheme under which persons of modest means may obtain assistance in the payment of legal fees;

(b) supervision over the handling of clients' money by solicitors; and

(c) administration of a guarantee fund out of which payments are made to compensate persons who have suffered financial loss because of a solicitor's dishonesty.

In addition to the Law Society there are several other smaller professional societies, some of which are associated with a particular locality. The best-known are the Society of Writers to the Signet (W.S.), the Scottish Law Agents Society, the Society of Solicitors in the Supreme Courts (S.S.C.), the Royal Faculty of Procurators in Glasgow, and the Society of Advocates in Aberdeen.

Solicitors are in the position of agents for their clients, and are subject to the general principles of the law of agency.

The exact extent of a solicitor's authority depends on the class of business for which he has been engaged. In the conduct of a court case he is entitled to some discretion, but, unlike the advocate, he must not, without the client's authority, abandon a claim or take any extraordinary step in procedure. Transactions entered into by the solicitor on his client's behalf are binding on the client, provided the solicitor has not exceeded the authority usually conferred on a solicitor for the type of work in question.

The solicitor is under a duty to his client to exercise proper diligence and skill in the professional work for which he has been engaged, and if he fails in this duty he will be liable in damages for loss suffered by the client. A solicitor is not, however, liable for giving wrong advice if the law on the particular point is doubtful. To advise on doubtful points is a function of counsel, and a solicitor who has duly obtained and acted on an Opinion of counsel is not liable in damages even if counsel's Opinion ultimately proves incorrect. On the other hand, in certain circumstances it may amount to professional negligence for a solicitor to fail to obtain an Opinion of counsel, and for that breach of duty he could be made liable. By the Solicitors (Scotland) Act 1980 the Council of the Law Society has power to make rules requiring solicitors to insure against professional liability.

The Scottish Solicitors' Discipline Tribunal investigates complaints of professional misconduct made against solicitors, and may strike the name of a solicitor off the roll of solicitors. The Tribunal consists of solicitor members and lay members (persons who are neither solicitors nor advocates). There is a right of appeal against the Tribunal's decision to the Court of Session.

The Solicitors (Scotland) Act 1976 introduced the "lay observer," a person (other than a solicitor, advocate or member of the House of Commons) appointed by the Secretary of State for Scotland to examine allegations made by any member of the public who is dissatisfied with the way in which the Law Society has handled a complaint made by him against a solicitor.

Notaries public

Some solicitors are also notaries public (N.P.).

The office of notary public has a history dating back to Roman times, and is not confined to Scotland.

A notary public has certain functions which cannot be performed by an ordinary solicitor, *e.g.* formalities connected with bills of exchange and with maritime and foreign business.

Only solicitors are qualified to become notaries, and most of the functions which in earlier times required the services of a notary can now be performed by any solicitor.

Law Officers

The Law Officers are the Crown's official advisers. In Scotland these are the Lord Advocate and the Solicitor-General for Scotland, corresponding to the Attorney-General and the Solicitor-General in England.

Appointments are generally on a political basis and are made by the Prime Minister. One or both of the Law Officers may be in Parliament, and, if so, they are largely responsible for piloting Scottish legal measures through Parliament.

The Law Officers represent the Crown in both civil and criminal cases, and in important cases one or other of them will personally appear for the Crown.

The Lord Advocate, as head of the system of prosecution of crimes, has control over procurators-fiscal, and full discretion and ultimate responsibility in all prosecutions in the criminal courts in Scotland.

To assist in the work of prosecution the Lord Advocate appoints "advocates-depute," who may be either senior or junior counsel, except that the "Home Depute" (appointed for cases in Edinburgh) is always a Q.C. There are at present ten advocates-depute.

The Lord Advocate also has the assistance of the permanent staff of the Crown Office in Edinburgh. The head of the Crown Office is the Crown Agent, who is solicitor to the Lord Advocate in his official capacity.

Royal Commission on Legal Services

In 1976 a Royal Commission was established with the following terms of reference:

> "To inquire into the law and practice relating to the provision of legal services in Scotland and to consider whether any, and if so what, changes are desirable in the public interest in the structure, organisation, training, regulation of, and entry into, the legal profession, including the arrangements for determining its remuneration, whether from private sources or public funds, and in the rules which prevent persons who are neither advocates nor solicitors from undertaking conveyancing and other legal business on behalf of other persons."

The chairman of the Commission was Lord Hughes, and there were ten other members.

The Commission's *Report* was published in May 1980 (Cmnd. 7846 and 7846–1). The following are some of the recommendations made in the *Report*:

(a) The legal profession should no longer have a monopoly in conveyancing (the legal procedures followed to give effect to a purchase or sale of land and buildings); domestic conveyancing (*i.e.* the legal procedures for transferring people's homes, but not commercial property) could be undertaken by members of other professional bodies who satisfied prescribed standards of safety for clients' money, who had the education, training, and competence to do the work, and who had adequate indemnity insurance, proper rules of conduct and proper procedures for dealing with complaints.

(b) Sheriff courts should be granted jurisdiction in actions for divorce, and all divorce actions should be commenced in a sheriff court, though the sheriff should have power to remit the action to the Outer House of the Court of Session, if he thought fit.

(c) The two branches of the legal profession (advocates and solicitors) should not be fused, nor should the right to plead in the supreme courts (the Court of Session, the High Court of Justiciary and the House of Lords) be extended to solicitors.

(d) A new government department ("Department of Legal Affairs") should be set up whose sole function would be to take responsibility for all Scottish legal affairs other than the Lord Advocate's functions of providing legal advice to the Government and of prosecuting crime.

(e) A Legal Services Commission should be established whose guiding principle would be to secure in legal services the best possible value for money (*e.g.* it would be responsible for providing public information as to legal rights and services, for making grants to advice centres and Law Centres, and for publishing advice on how to leave one's affairs in good order).

DILIGENCE

Diligence is the procedure which enables a person who has been successful in a court action to compel the unsuccessful party to comply with the court's decree. It is possible that the unsuccessful party will comply voluntarily, and there will then be no need to resort to diligence.

Where an unsuccessful party fails to comply with a decree the reason usually is that he has insufficient funds to pay to the other party the amount for which the court has held him to be liable. As a result, diligence is often a stage on the road to bankruptcy. Once it is established that a person is bankrupt, he is liable to sequestration under the Bankruptcy (Scotland) Act 1913, *i.e.* to the formal legal process by which all his assets are gathered in by a trustee and sold and the proceeds are divided (as far as they will go) pari passu ("rateably") among the bankrupt's creditors. In the case of a bankrupt registered company the process corresponding to sequestration is liquidation, governed by the Companies Acts.

Since a major aim of sequestration and liquidation is to ensure equal treatment of all the creditors, there are statutory provisions which "cut down" diligence which has been "used" (*i.e.* resorted to) within a specified time (*e.g.* sixty days) before bankruptcy. This discourages the "race of diligence" which would otherwise occur as more and more of the creditors resorted to diligence for the purpose of obtaining, each for himself, full payment of his own debt out of the debtor's dwindling assets. Once a sequestration or liquidation has begun, the time for diligence is past.

In resorting to diligence a creditor is said to "attach" the person or property of his debtor.

The form of diligence by which the debtor's *person* is attached is civil imprisonment. This is to be distinguished from the imprisonment which may be the penalty imposed by a criminal court; diligence is concerned with civil law.

Civil imprisonment is now rare. The most important restriction of it was made by the Debtors (Scotland) Act 1880 which abolished (with some exceptions) imprisonment for debt. There still is a limited power to imprison for not more than six weeks a person who wilfully fails to pay a sum awarded as aliment; the claim must have been a direct one (as distinct from a claim for reimbursement to an authority which has been paying aliment) and must not have been for arrears after the right to aliment has ceased. Where the court decree is not for the payment of money but for the performance of some act (referred to as a "decree ad factum praestandum"), the court has power to imprison for not more than six months a person who wilfully fails to comply with the decree; as soon as he complies or if his failure to comply is no longer wilful failure, the court must liberate him.

The rest of this section is concerned only with the forms of diligence by which a debtor's *property* is attached. These fall into two groups, according to whether the property is heritable (*i.e.* land and buildings) or moveable (other than land and buildings).

Diligence is at present being comprehensively reviewed by the Scottish Law Commission.

(a) Diligence Applicable to Heritable Property

(i) Adjudication

This form of diligence is based on the Adjudications Act 1672, which abolished an earlier form known as "apprising."

Adjudication takes the form of an action. It must be raised in the

Court of Session, starting with a summons of adjudication and ending in a decree.

A notice of the summons is entered in the Register of Inhibitions and Adjudications, a public register kept in Edinburgh, and that has the effect of making the property "litigious," *i.e.* the debtor is no longer entitled to transfer the property voluntarily and any person to whom he transfers it takes it with the burden of the diligence attached to it.

The decree has the effect of conveying the property to the creditor, and he will then complete his title to the property by recording the decree in the General Register of Sasines, the public register of heritable property kept in Edinburgh.

There then follows a period of ten years (referred to as "the legal") during which the debtor may demand a reconveyance of the property on paying the debt.

On the expiry of "the legal" the creditor may raise an action known as "an action of declarator of expiry of the legal," and decree in this action will give him an irredeemable title to the property. If he does not take these proceedings, the debtor could still redeem the property even although the legal had expired.

Adjudication, as well as being available to a creditor who has obtained a decree against his debtor, may be used in security for a debt which is future (not yet due) or contingent (dependent on a condition being fulfilled), but only if the debtor is vergens ad inopiam ("on the verge of bankruptcy") or has had other adjudications used against him.

(ii) Inhibition

By this form of diligence a creditor can prevent his debtor from disposing of his heritable property or otherwise dealing with it in a way which will prejudice the creditor (*e.g.* granting security over it).

The procedure is either by "letters of inhibition" or by warrant (court authority) for inhibition. "Letters of Inhibition" are given under the Signet and follow a style which is set out in a schedule to the Titles to Land Consolidation (Scotland) Act 1868: the debtor is in the Queen's name to be inhibited (prevented) from "selling, disponing, conveying, burdening, or otherwise affecting his lands or heritages to the prejudice of the complainer." The other procedure (warrant for inhibition) is applicable where the creditor does not yet have a decree against the debtor but has raised an action in the Court of Session for payment of money alleged to be due and seeks an inhibition "on the dependence of" the action; a warrant for inhibition is then regarded as being implied in the summons of the action.

The letters or the summons must be served on the debtor, and a notice of the inhibition must be registered in the Register of Inhibitions and Adjudications.

Inhibition is only prohibitive or negative in its effect: it gives the creditor no positive right to become the owner of the debtor's property, but merely preserves the property as part of the debtor's assets.

When the debt for which the inhibition was used has been paid, the creditor must, at the debtor's expense, record a discharge in the Register; the effect is to "clear the record" thus enabling the debtor again to produce a good title to his property should he wish to sell it or grant security over it.

Where an inhibition has been used on the dependence of an action and the action is unsuccessful (with the result that the defender is assoilzied), the court grants an order on the Keeper of the Register to have the inhibition marked as recalled.

An inhibition prescribes in five years from the date of registration.

(b) Diligence Applicable to Moveable Property

(i) Poinding [5]

This form of diligence, sometimes referred to as "personal poinding" to distinguish it from poinding of the ground (see (iv), below), is the diligence by which moveable property in the possession of the debtor (or sometimes of the creditor) is attached and sold for the creditor's benefit.

The normal procedure, governed by the Debtors (Scotland) Act 1838 is in outline as follows: the creditor, having been successful in his action against his debtor, will have a decree in his favour registered in the court books; his first step is to obtain an "extract decree" (*i.e.* a copy of the decree extracted from the court books), which is handed over to an officer of court (a messenger-at-arms if the decree is a Court of Session one or a sheriff officer if the decree is a sheriff court one or if the sheriffdom has no messengers-at-arms); there must then be a "charge" (formal demand for payment); this is executed by the officer of court delivering to the debtor a "schedule of charge"; there then follow certain days of charge, known as "induciae," within which payment may be made, the number of days varying between six and fifteen according to the nature of the claim and the debtor's residence; on the expiry of the days of charge, if no payment has been made, the poinding may be executed by the officer; the articles poinded are left in the debtor's possession along with a schedule listing them and their value as assessed by two

[5] Pronounced "pinding."

valuators appointed by the officer for that purpose; the effect at this stage is that the debtor is prohibited from parting with the articles to the prejudice of his creditor; the poinding must be reported to the sheriff, who, if required, grants warrant (authority) for a sale by auction; if no offer is made, the articles or enough of them to satisfy the debt and expenses are delivered to the creditor; if the articles are sold, the result of the sale must be reported to the sheriff, and the creditor will, on the sheriff's order, be entitled to payment of his debt and expenses out of the proceeds.

The property which may be poinded is in general corporeal moveable property of commercial value and capable of being sold by auction. There are exemptions at common law for the debtor's wearing apparel and the working tools of his trade and by the Law Reform (Diligence) (Scotland) Act 1973 for beds or bedding material, chairs, tables, and facilities for cooking, eating or storing food and for heating, provided the articles are in a dwelling-house in which the debtor is residing and are reasonably necessary to enable him and others living in family with him to continue to reside there without undue hardship. Documents such as share certificates and cheques cannot be poinded except where the diligence is being used by the Crown.

(ii) Arrestment

This is the form of diligence which is appropriate where the moveable property to be attached is in the hands of a third party (*i.e.* someone other than the debtor or the creditor) who is under an obligation to account for it to the debtor. The effect of the arrestment is to prohibit the arrestee (the third party) from parting with the property.

Just as poinding is not complete until it is followed by a sale, so arrestment is not complete until it is followed by a decree of furthcoming; it is only when this latter stage is reached that the creditor is entitled to demand that the arrestee transfer the property to him instead of to the debtor.

Arrestment may be either in execution or in security.

Arrestment in execution is applicable where the creditor has been successful in an action, and so is in a position to obtain an extract decree which is of itself a sufficient warrant for arrestment.

Arrestment in security may be resorted to where the creditor does not yet have a decree in his favour. The debt may be a future one (*e.g.* a bill of exchange payable on a future date); it is then possible for the creditor to obtain a warrant for arrestment in security, but only if he alleges special circumstances (*e.g.* that the debtor is vergens ad inopiam ("on the verge of bankruptcy") or in meditatione fugae ("contemplating flight")). The usual form of arrestment in security is "arrestment on the dependence," applicable where the creditor is raising an action against his debtor and seeks to attach property which then belongs to the debtor but which could otherwise disappear before the action reached its conclusion. Earnings and pension cannot be arrested on the dependence (Law Reform (Miscellaneous Provisions) (Scotland) Act 1966).

In outline the procedure for either type of arrestment (governed by the Debtors (Scotland) Act 1838) is as follows: the officer of court (messenger-at-arms or sheriff officer) serves on the arrestee a schedule of arrestment specifying the debt or other property which is being arrested and also referring in general to all other goods, money, etc., held by the arrestee and belonging to the debtor; this has the effect of making the property "litigious," *i.e.* the arrestee must not part with it to the prejudice of the arrester; the arrester must then bring an action of furthcoming, the purpose of which is to find out precisely the nature and extent of the property which has been arrested and to settle the creditor's claim out of the property.

The property which may be arrested includes, in addition to corporeal moveables, such incorporeal moveables as funds held by a bank for the debtor, shares in a company, and an insurance policy (the arrestee being in these cases the bank, the company and the insurance company respectively). The item most commonly arrested is the amount of wages or salary due to the debtor but still in his employer's hands; such arrestment is, however, subject to a number of statutory provisions, the general effect of which is to ensure that the debtor is left with a reasonable amount for his own aliment. Some debts are by statute entirely excluded from arrestment (*e.g.* family allowances, social security benefits and certain pensions).

In certain circumstances an arrestment may be "recalled" or may be "loosed" by the court. The effect of a recall is to extinguish the diligence completely. The effect of a loosing is to entitle the arrestee to transfer the property to the debtor, but if he does not do so the arrestment is preserved. The circumstances in which there may be a recall or a loosing include payment of the debt by the debtor to the creditor, proof by the debtor that the arrestment is nimious (excessive) or oppressive, and a claim by the arrestee that the property in question is his own.

An arrestment in execution prescribes in three years from its date if it is not insisted on within that time. An arrestment in security for a future debt prescribes in three years from the time when the debt becomes due, and an arrestment on the dependence prescribes in three years from the date of the decree which constitutes the debt.

For "arrestment to found jurisdiction" see p. 41, above.

(iii) Landlord's sequestration for rent

This is the form of diligence by which a landlord may make effective the hypothec (security) which he has over his tenant's invecta et illata (literally, "things brought in and carried in"), a phrase which covers all the ordinary moveable property in the premises (*e.g.* the tenant's furniture and stock-in-trade). (See also p. 481, below.)

Sequestration for rent takes the form of a sheriff court action: a warrant to sequestrate is granted to the landlord by the sheriff, and the property is then inventoried (listed) and valued by a sheriff officer; the effect at this stage is that the property is regarded as in manibus curiae ("in the hands of the court") and must not be removed from the premises; a separate warrant from the sheriff may then be obtained authorising a sale by auction.

(iv) Poinding of the ground

This form of diligence attaches moveables on land (not the land itself) and is available only to a creditor who holds a debitum fundi ("heritably secured debt"), *i.e.* who has a heritable security over the land. The creditor may be the superior claiming feu-duty, a heritable creditor holding a standard security over the property, or any other creditor who has a right to a "real" (*i.e.* heritable) burden over the land. Poinding of the ground is therefore described as being a "real" diligence for attaching moveables.

The diligence takes the form of an action (brought either in the Court of Session or in the sheriff court) in which the creditor obtains a warrant to poind the moveables situated on the land and belonging to the owner of the land or his tenants (to the extent of the rents due from them).

The procedure resembles that for personal poinding (see (i), above), except that no charge for payment is required.

(v) Maills and duties

The term "maills" means money payment and the term "duties" denotes the personal services which a tenant formerly could be called on to perform for his landlord. The modern equivalent for the phrase "maills and duties" is therefore "rents."

The type of diligence referred to as an "action of maills and duties" enables a creditor in a heritable security to attach the rents due by the tenants of the land over which his security exists. The rents would otherwise be payable by the tenants to their landlord, the debtor who is the owner of the land.

The normal procedure is governed by the Heritable Securities (Scotland) Act 1894: the creditor raises an action in the Court of

Session or in the sheriff court against the owner, and notice of the raising of this action is given to the tenants by a registered or a recorded delivery letter in a statutory form warning them that if, after receiving the notice, they pay their rents to the owner, they do so at the risk of having to pay again to the creditor; the effect is that the owner is unable to obtain payment of the rents from his tenants; decree in the action gives the creditor the right to the rents and a further statutory form of notice is sent to the tenants informing them of this fact.

LEGAL AID

As early as 1424 an Act was passed to provide a system of free legal aid for the poor, and that Act remained on the statute-book until 1949.

The modern system of legal aid originated in the Legal Aid and Solicitors (Scotland) Act 1949, described as "truly a watershed in legal history" (C. N. Stoddart, *Legal Aid in Scotland*, p. 14). This Act, however, did not suitably provide for the extension of legal aid to criminal cases until it was amended by the Criminal Justice (Scotland) Act 1963, which was given effect to in 1964. The major legislation now applicable to legal aid in both civil and criminal court proceedings is the Legal Aid (Scotland) Act 1967.

Where legal aid is sought for matters other than court proceedings it is governed principally by the Legal Advice and Assistance Act 1972.

This brief section on legal aid is therefore divided into three parts:

    (a) legal aid in civil proceedings;
    (b) legal aid in criminal proceedings; and
    (c) legal advice and assistance.

The Acts themselves lay down only broad principles; details of the various Legal Aid Schemes are to be found in copious subordinate legislation. In this connection it is useful as a preliminary to look at the functions of:

    1. the Law Society of Scotland;
    2. the Secretary of State for Scotland; and
    3. the courts.

1. *Functions of the Law Society of Scotland*

The Law Society's functions fall broadly under two headings: it has functions concerned with the granting of legal aid to persons applying for it (see (i), below), and functions concerned with the financial aspects (see (ii), below).

(i) Administering legal aid and advice

The Society in exercising this function operates through its Council and a network of committees and sub-committees. The committees include:

(a) the Scheme-Making Committee, consisting of members of the Law Society and persons nominated by the Faculty of Advocates; it is not a standing committee but is set up as and when the need arises; every Scheme requires the approval of the Secretary of State and the concurrence of the Treasury, and may be varied or revoked by a later Scheme;

(b) the Central Committee, consisting of solicitors and advocates together with two laymen appointed by the Secretary of State; solicitors are in the majority and the chairman is a solicitor; members hold office for five years; the Committee's functions include supervision of the Supreme Court Committee and the Local Committees, submission of financial statements and an annual report to the Law Society, publication of information on legal aid to the legal profession and to applicants for legal aid, and decision of appeals from the Supreme Committee and the Local Committees;

(c) the Supreme Court Committee, consisting of an equal number of solicitors appointed by the Law Society and advocates appointed by the Faculty of Advocates; members hold office for three years, and the chairman is usually a Q.C.; the Committee's main function is to administer the Legal Aid Schemes affecting proceedings in the Court of Session, the High Court of Justiciary sitting as a court of appeal, the Lands Valuation Appeal Court and the Restrictive Practices Court; it must also supply financial and other information to the Central Committee;

(d) the sixteen Local Committees distributed throughout Scotland, each consisting of solicitors practising in the sheriff courts of the area concerned; members hold office for three years; the main function of each Local Committee is to decide applications for civil legal aid in the sheriff courts in its area; it also has functions in connection with legal aid in criminal cases and with the Legal Advice and Assistance Scheme;

(e) the Complaints Committee, a committee of the Law Society; it deals with complaints against solicitors referred to it by the Law Society after they have been considered by the Supreme Court Committee or by a Local Committee; (complaints against counsel are dealt with by the Faculty of Advocates).

(ii) Administering the Legal Aid (Scotland) Fund

The Law Society has the duty of administering the Legal Aid

(Scotland) Fund. All receipts and expenses of the Society relating to legal aid are paid into or out of this fund.

The Secretary of State makes payments into the Fund out of money granted by Parliament to the Scottish Home and Health Department. Other receipts include contributions from assisted persons. Where damages or other money has been recovered on behalf of assisted persons in a court case this must also be initially paid into the Fund so that a complete accounting may be made.

The expenses for which the Fund is liable are mainly fees due to solicitors and counsel and the costs of administration.

The Society must prepare annual accounts which are audited by qualified accountants appointed by the Secretary of State and eventually laid before Parliament.

2. Functions of the Secretary of State for Scotland

The Secretary of State makes regulations in the form of statutory instruments, dealing with such matters as the proceedings for which legal aid may be given, the financial limits which make a person entitled to legal aid, and the contributions which may be required from applicants.

Other functions include laying before Parliament an annual report from the Law Society on the Legal Aid Schemes, and approving any new Scheme.

3. Functions of the Courts

The Court of Session has power to regulate a number of matters concerning legal aid by Acts of Sederunt (see p. 88, below); e.g. it may regulate the procedure of any civil court in relation to legal aid and provide for the "taxation" (official assessment by an auditor of court) of accounts of expenses.

The High Court of Justiciary may exercise similar powers by Acts of Adjournal (see p. 88, below); e.g. solicitors' fees in all criminal legal aid cases are fixed by Acts of Adjournal.

(a) Legal Aid in Civil Proceedings

The history has been one of gradual extension since the Act of 1949. With minor exceptions (e.g. defamation and breach of promise of marriage) legal aid is now available for proceedings in the civil courts (House of Lords, Court of Session, and sheriff courts), for proceedings in some of the courts of special jurisdiction (the Scottish Land Court, the Lands Valuation Appeal Court, the Restrictive Practices Court and the Courts-Martial Appeal Court), and for proceedings in the Employment Appeal Tribunal and the Lands Tribunal for Scotland. Legal aid is not available for proceedings before some of the courts of special jurisdiction (*e.g.* the Court of the Lord Lyon, the Election Petition Court, the church courts and courts-martial), and has not yet been extended to proceedings before the great mass of tribunals although the Legal Aid Act 1979 enables the Legal Advice and Assistance Scheme to be extended to such proceedings. There is a special Scheme applicable to certain stages in children's hearings (*e.g.* on an appeal to the Court of Session from the decision of a sheriff).

Applications for legal aid are made to the Law Society acting through the Supreme Court Committee or the appropriate Local Committee, except that for an appeal to the House of Lords application is made to the Central Committee. The applicant must be an individual: a body of persons, such as a company or a partnership, is not eligible. The purpose of the application is to obtain a legal aid certificate.

Four questions arise before the Committee decides to grant or refuse the certificate:

(i) Has the applicant a probabilis causa litigandi?

"Probabilis causa litigandi" means a legal case capable of being proved. The criterion to be applied here is not whether the Committee feels that the proposed action will be successful, but whether, on an assessment of what the case looks like on paper, the applicant has shown that he has a case which *could* be proved; where there is a reasonable doubt, the Committee gives the applicant the benefit of the doubt. Legal aid is, therefore, often granted to both parties, particularly in consistorial causes (actions concerned with marriage).

(ii) Is it reasonable in the particular circumstances of the case that the applicant should receive legal aid?

The object here is to prevent abuse of the legal aid system as by the bringing of frivolous or worthless actions; *e.g.* where there already was before the court a divorce action which was undefended, it could be considered unreasonable that legal aid should be granted for a cross-action of divorce (*i.e.* an action by the defender in the undefended action). Few applications, however, are refused on the ground of unreasonableness.

(iii) Is the applicant financially eligible for legal aid?

The original statutory financial limits laid down in the Act of 1949 have been frequently raised. They are fixed by the Legal Aid (Scotland) (Assessment of Resources) Regulations 1960 as amended.

Calculation of the applicant's resources is made by an "assessment officer" authorised by the Secretary of State. This officer assesses the applicant's "disposable income" and "disposable capital" and on the basis of these figures computes the applicant's "maximum contribution," *i.e.* the maximum amount which the applicant can be called upon to pay towards his legal expenses. These assessments are based on the financial declarations made by the applicant in his application form. The assessment officer usually interviews the applicant and may call for further information.

(iv) What contribution should the applicant be called upon to pay towards the cost of the proceedings?

This refers to the *actual* contribution payable by the applicant. It is distinct from (but never greater than) the "maximum contribution" fixed by the assessment officer. The actual contribution is fixed by the Committee after it has estimated the probable cost of the proceedings. The amount is often made payable by instalments, and it may be increased or decreased on a change of circumstances.

After these four matters have been considered, the Committee either grants a legal aid certificate (in which case the applicant becomes an "assisted person") or refuses a certificate.

An applicant has a right of appeal to the Central Committee if he has been refused a legal aid certificate or if he is dissatisfied with the *actual* contribution fixed. He has no right of appeal against the assessments by the assessment officer of disposable income, disposable capital or maximum contribution, but he may ask the assessment officer to re-assess these amounts if his circumstances have altered. In the House of Lords Scheme (in which the application is made to the Central Committee) there is no right of appeal.

Where a legal aid certificate has been granted, it is still necessary to obtain special sanction for abnormal steps in the proceedings; *e.g.* for the employment of counsel in a sheriff court case the prior consent of the Local Committee is required.

(b) Legal Aid in Criminal Proceedings

When introduced in 1964 criminal legal aid was available only in the sheriff courts and in the High Court of Justiciary (both as a court of trial and as a court of appeal) and not in the inferior criminal courts (the pre-1975 J. P. and burgh police courts). In 1975, however, legal aid was extended to the then newly established district courts.

The most prominent features of the criminal legal aid Scheme may be considered under these headings:

    (i) the duty solicitor system;
    (ii) legal aid for a criminal trial; and
    (iii) legal aid for a criminal appeal.

If legal aid is granted, the accused pays no contribution towards the expenses of his defence.

(i) The duty solicitor system

Under this system any person appearing from custody at the start of criminal proceedings is entitled to free advice and representation from a "duty solicitor." At these early stages there is no formal application for legal aid, and no inquiry into the resources of the accused.

Every Local Committee must prepare annually a duty plan for each sheriff and district court, providing a rota of solicitors who will be available to operate the duty solicitor system throughout the year. Each solicitor is allotted a period of duty, often a week or a month at a time. The plan requires to be approved by the Central Committee.

At the end of his period of duty, a duty solicitor sends a report to the Central Committee. This gives details of the period of duty, the names of the accused persons represented and the fees claimed.

(ii) Legal aid for a criminal trial

An accused person wishing legal aid for criminal trial proceedings other than the proceedings covered by the duty solicitor system must make a formal application to the court for a legal aid certificate.

If the trial is to be in the sheriff court or the High Court of Justiciary the application is normally decided by the sheriff in whose court the accused makes his first appearance. If the trial is to be in the district court, the application is decided by a justice of the peace or stipendiary magistrate.

The questions which arise in the determination of a claim are:

1. *Can the expenses of the case be met without undue hardship to the accused or his dependants?* On the basis of the declaration of means made by the accused in his application form and any further particulars which he has been required by the Law Society or by the court to furnish, the court must decide whether the applicant's financial circumstances are such that, without legal aid, undue hardship would be caused to him or to his dependants.

If the court is satisfied that undue hardship would ensue, the accused has passed the financial test. If the court is not satisfied that undue hardship would ensue, the application for legal aid is refused.

2. *Are other rights or facilities available to the accused making it unnecessary for him to obtain legal aid?* If the court is satisfied that

an applicant has available rights or facilities making it unnecessary for him to obtain legal aid, or has a reasonable expectation of obtaining financial or other help from a body of which he is a member, it must refuse the application, except on cause shown.

Instances of "rights or facilities" which could disqualify an applicant occur where he is insured under an insurance policy which covers payment of legal expenses and where he is a member of a motoring organisation or trade union which runs such a scheme.

3. *Is it in the interests of justice that legal aid be granted?* This question arises only in summary cases. Before granting legal aid in such cases the court must be satisfied that it is in the interests of justice that legal aid be made available. (The assumption is that in solemn proceedings it is always in the interests of justice that legal aid be made available provided the other conditions are fulfilled.)

This somewhat vague test has been differently interpreted in different summary courts, and has attracted much criticism.

The accused is bound to attend the court when his application is being dealt with. If he fails to do so, the application is refused.

If the application is granted, the clerk of court sends a legal aid certificate to the Local Committee, and that Committee then formally nominates the solicitor who is to act—usually the solicitor chosen by the accused.

If the application is refused, there is no appeal, but a further application may be made on a material change in circumstances.

The legal aid granted covers only the normal services provided for an accused. What is "normal" depends on the whole circumstances and in particular on whether the proceedings are solemn or summary. Abnormal services require the prior sanction of the Local Committee (*e.g.* the employment of counsel in the sheriff court, whether under solemn or summary procedure).

(iii) Legal aid for a criminal appeal

An application for legal aid for a criminal appeal is decided by the Law Society and not by the court. The accused must obtain an appeal certificate from the Supreme Court Committee, and to qualify for this he must surmount a number of hurdles designed to prevent frivolous appeals being made at the public expense.

In certain circumstances (*e.g.* where the appeal is by "stated case" (see p. 37, above) or where the accused has only a provisional financial certificate (see below)) the accused must first obtain an interim appeal certificate before applying for the full appeal certificate.

The accused may or may not have been legally aided at the trial.

The following questions arise in connection with the grant of an appeal certificate:

1. *Is the accused financially eligible for legal aid?* If the accused received legal aid for the trial proceedings, the general rule is that he continues to be regarded as financially eligible for legal aid in the appeal proceedings.

If, however, the accused did not receive legal aid for the trial proceedings, his means must first be assessed. He will apply to the clerk of the court in which the proceedings started for a provisional financial certificate, and the tests applied are whether he is able, without undue hardship to himself or his dependants, to meet the expenses of the appeal proceedings and whether he has other rights or facilities. On the grant or refusal of a provisional financial certificate the clerk of the court makes a report to the court in order that the court may decide on financial eligibility. The court's decision is reported to the Local Committee.

2. *Has the accused substantial grounds for taking appeal proceedings?* and

3. *Is it reasonable in the particular circumstances of the case that the accused should receive legal aid?* In answering these two questions the Supreme Court Committee relies on its experience of appeal proceedings, taking into account the due preservation of public funds.

The Supreme Court Committee does not deal with the application until the question of financial eligibility has been finally settled by the lower court.

The Committee normally reaches its decision on the basis of the written papers but has power to make further inquiries (*e.g.* by requiring the accused and his legal advisers to attend before the Committee or by appointing some person to interview the accused and report to the Committee).

The Committee's decision is final.

Where an appeal certificate has been granted, the solicitor chosen by the accused and nominated by the Committee, has authority to provide and arrange all normal services, such as instructing one junior counsel to represent the accused, but for other services (*e.g.* for instructing senior counsel or additional counsel in non-murder appeals) the sanction of the Supreme Court Committee must first be obtained.

(c) Legal Advice and Assistance

Before 1973 there were some rather fragmentary and unsatisfactory facilities for legal advice and assistance on matters not involving court proceedings, but these were abandoned with the passing of the Legal Advice and Assistance Act 1972, most of which was brought into force in April 1973.

Unlike the Legal Aid (Scotland) Act 1967 which is the principal Act on legal aid for court proceedings in Scotland, the Act of 1972 applies to the whole of Great Britain. In Scotland the Act is to be read along with the Act of 1967. It was amended by the Legal Aid Act 1979, which likewise includes provisions applicable to England and Wales as well as provisions applicable to Scotland.

The collective title for the Acts on legal aid and legal advice and assistance applicable to Scotland is "the Legal Aid and Advice (Scotland) Acts 1967 to 1979."

The phrase "legal advice and assistance" denotes any oral or written advice:

(i) on the application of Scots law (where the advice is given in Scotland) to particular circumstances which have arisen and which involve the person seeking the advice; and

(ii) as to any steps which that person might appropriately take (*e.g.* settling a claim out of court, bringing or defending court proceedings, making an agreement or a will, or obtaining further advice or assistance).

The Legal Advice and Assistance Scheme is therefore a comprehensive one, extending to the whole field of legal practice. The Act of 1972, however, expressly excluded:

(i) advice and assistance given to a person in connection with any court or tribunal proceedings at a time when he is receiving legal aid under one of the other legal aid schemes; and

(ii) the taking on behalf of a person of any step in court or tribunal proceedings (as distinct from assisting the person to take such a step for himself).

The effect of (ii) was that as a general rule the Scheme was available for preparatory work concerned with court or tribunal proceedings but stopped at the stage when the case actually came before the court or tribunal. The Act of 1979 removed that restriction by adding to the Scheme a new category of assistance, namely "assistance by way of representation" meaning assistance given to a person by taking on his behalf a step in court or tribunal proceedings, *e.g.* appearing and speaking on his behalf before a court or tribunal. The Act does not itself specify the proceedings covered by this provision: this is left to be defined in regulations made under authority of the Act.

Two further important aspects of the Legal Advice and Assistance Scheme may be briefly noted:

(i) Financial eligibility

A distinctive feature of the Scheme is that the decision as to whether an applicant is financially eligible to receive legal advice and assistance is taken by the solicitor whom he approaches. It is for the solicitor to calculate, in accordance with regulations, the applicant's "disposable capital," "disposable income," and the amount of any contribution for which the applicant is liable. The solicitor is responsible for collecting the contribution and may arrange that it be paid by instalments. If he fails to collect the full amount of it, the loss falls on him.

(ii) Limit on expenditure

The Act of 1972 placed a limit of £25 on the expenditure which could be incurred without any special authorisation. This limit has been increased to £40 as from October 1, 1980 (Legal Advice and Assistance (Scotland) (Prospective Cost) Regualtions 1980).

Where it appears at any time to the solicitor from whom advice is sought that the cost of giving advice is likely to exceed the statutory limit (£40 from October 1, 1980), he must, before giving the advice, obtain from the Local Committee authority to exceed the limit. The Local Committee must consider:

1. whether it is reasonable for the advice or assistance to be given; and

2. whether the estimated amount of the cost is fair and reasonable.

The Local Committee, if it approves of the application, fixes whatever larger amount it thinks fit.

The client has a right of appeal to the Central Committee against a refusal by the Local Committee to increase the authorised expenditure.

ARBITRATION

Parties to a dispute are, as a general rule, entitled to have their dispute settled by litigation (*i.e.* by bringing or defending an action in the courts). In many situations, however, the parties will prefer arbitration to litigation. In an arbitration the dispute is referred by the parties to a person of their own choice (called an "arbiter") and the parties acquiesce in his decision (called the "decree-arbitral" or "award") instead of resorting to the courts. The effect of the arbitration is to "oust" (exclude) the jurisdiction of the courts.

Some arbitrations are "statutory"; *i.e.* an Act of Parliament compels the parties to settle a dispute connected with the provisions of the Act by arbitration. Statutory arbitrations became common from the middle of the nineteenth century for the settlement of disputed claims for compensation where land was required for large undertakings such as railways (*e.g.* the statutory arbitrations provided for by the Lands Clauses Consolidation (Scotland) Act 1845 and the Railways Clauses Consolidation (Scotland) Act 1845). Other instances of statutory arbitrations include those provided for by the Agricultural Holdings (Scotland) Act 1949 for the settlement of claims between landlord and tenant. The scope of and procedure for such arbitrations depend on the provisions of the particular Act in question (*e.g.* the Act may provide, as does the Agricultural Holdings (Scotland) Act 1949, that the arbiter may be required to "state a case" for the opinion of the court on any question of law arising in the course of the arbitration).

Other arbitrations arise out of the agreement of the parties. There are two principal ways in which this may happen:

(a) The parties may have made no prior arrangement for the settling of disputes, but once the dispute has arisen, they agree that it be settled by arbitration; they then at that stage enter into a "contract of submission," which will govern the scope of and procedure for the arbitration.

(b) The parties may already be parties to another contract (the "main contract") such as a contract of co-partnery or a contract for the sale of goods which includes as one of its clauses an arbitration clause providing that *if* a dispute arises it will be referred to arbitration. In the event of a dispute arising, the parties will then at that stage submit their dispute to their arbiter, and the scope of and procedure for the arbitration will be governed by the terms of the arbitration clause. Such arbitrations are referred to as "ancillary arbitrations."

It is sometimes difficult to decide, especially in ancillary arbitrations, whether a disputed matter is within the scope of the arbitration agreement. An arbitration clause may be interpreted as merely "executorial" of the main contract, *i.e.* as covering only disputes occurring during the execution of the main contract, or the clause may be of the "ample" variety, *i.e.* sufficiently broad to cover disputes occurring after the completion of the main contract (*e.g.* a claim for damages for unsatisfactory performance of the contract). Difficulties of interpretation may lead to a court action, since only the court can finally decide whether its own jurisdiction has been effectively ousted by the agreement of the parties.

Once it has been established that the parties have agreed to go to arbitration on a particular matter, the parties must abide by their agreement: the court would "sist" (stop) any court action so that the matter could be decided by the arbiter. The court would also, if necessary, enforce the award when issued by granting "decree conform to it" (*i.e.* a court order in conformity with the award).

Arbitration may be considered to have the following advantages over litigation:

(a) *Speed*: In an arbitration the timetable is arranged by the parties and the arbiter, whereas in litigation the case would have to await its turn in the court timetable. An arbiter's decision may therefore be more speedily obtained.

(b) *Informality*: In an arbitration the parties are free to decide on the degree of formality or may leave that matter to the arbiter's discretion. Strict adherence to court procedures is not required unless the parties so specify. The arbiter is, however, bound to do equal justice to both sides.

(c) *Cheapness*: Litigation is often costly, especially for the unsuccessful party. An arbitration is, however, not necessarily cheaper: litigants do not pay remuneration to the judge or the clerk of court or a hire charge for the court room, whereas in an arbitration the arbiter's fee may be substantial and there may also be a charge for a clerk's services and for suitable accommodation for the hearing.

(d) *Privacy*: Most court proceedings take place in public, and may be reported in the press. Parties may wish to keep their disputes from the public gaze: they may, for instance, have been on intimate terms as partners or they may be business organisations wishing to avoid disclosure of financial details.

(e) *Expertise*: The arbiter chosen may be an expert in a particular line of business, perhaps capable of giving a decision as to the quality of goods by a simple "sniff and look," or well acquainted with the circumstances and terminology of the branch of commerce concerned. The parties may feel more satisfied with such an expert's findings than with a judge's decision.

Two further points should be noted by way of introduction to the short account of the law of arbitration which follows:

First, there are some questions which, on grounds of public policy, cannot be decided by arbitration but only by courts of law, *e.g.* criminal matters and disputes as to a person's status (such as whether he is legitimate or married).

Secondly, the general Scots law of arbitration (in contrast to the English law on the subject) is almost wholly common law. Statutory arbitrations, each governed by the particular statute under which it operates, are not further considered here. In the general law of arbitration applicable to Scotland only four statutory provisions need be mentioned—the Articles of Regulation of 1695, the Arbitration (Scotland) Act 1894, section 3 of the Administration of Justice (Scotland) Act 1972, and section 17 of the Law Reform (Miscellaneous Provisions) (Scotland) Act 1980. The last-mentioned of these statutory provisions enables a Court of Session judge to accept appointment as arbiter or oversman in a commercial dispute provided the Lord President of the Court of Session informs him that, having regard to the state of business in that court, he could be made available to do so; the fees for the judge's services would be payable in the Court of Session and be of an amount prescribed by statutory instrument. [6] The limited effect of the other three statutory provisions is explained in the course of the following paragraphs.

The main principles of the law of arbitration may be considered under the following headings:

    (a) arbiters and oversmen;

    (b) conduct of the arbitration; and

    (c) challenge of the award.

There is also a short section on:

    (d) judicial references.

(a) Arbiters and Oversmen

The parties to a dispute may agree on the nomination of one particular individual as their arbiter. However, it is quite possible that the parties, being already in disagreement or at least having opposing interests, would fail to agree on the question of who should be their arbiter, and so it is common for a dispute to be referred to two arbiters, one nominated by each party. In such a case it is appropriate to have an "oversman," who will make the final decision if (and only if) the two arbiters disagree; the matter is then, at the stage of disagreement, said to "devolve upon" the oversman.

(i) Selection and qualifications

The parties may choose whomsoever they wish as arbiters and oversmen, but it is an implied condition of the contract of arbitration that the persons selected have no interest, however slight, in the result of the dispute. If they do have such an interest, the award can be set aside by an action of "reduction" (setting aside) brought in the Court of Session.

An illustration is *Sellar* v. *Highland Railway Co.*, 1919 S.C.(H.L.) 19:

In an arbitration between S., the owner of certain fishings, and a

6 The fees prescribed are £500 on appointment plus £500 for each additional day of the hearing.

railway company, the arbiters disagreed, and the reference devolved upon the oversman. After the oversman had issued proposed findings, S. discovered that the arbiter appointed by the railway company was a holder of a small quantity of ordinary stock in the company, a fact now known to the directors personally at the time of the appointment. S. notified the company that he would not regard himself as bound by the award. Later the oversman issued his final award, and S. brought a successful action for reduction of the oversman's award on the ground of the arbiter's disqualification.

However, an interest which is known may be waived by the parties, and will then be no disqualification. In practice, an arbiter often is an interested party; he may, for instance, be the architect or the engineer of one of the parties (e.g. "the engineer of the Forth Bridge Railway Company for the time being" in the well-known case *Tancred, Arrol & Co.* v. *The Steel Co. of Scotland Ltd.* (1890) 17 R. (H.L.) 31).

The common law relating to the appointment of arbiters and oversmen was partly altered by the Arbitration (Scotland) Act 1894.

It had been recognised at common law that the appointment of an arbiter involved delectus personae (literally, "choice of person"), and so the common law rule was that the parties had to make a deliberate selection of a named individual, not merely agree that the arbiter would be the holder of a particular office for the time being or would be named by another party. The courts would not, as a general rule, enforce an arbitration agreement in which the arbiter was not named. There were some exceptions to the general rule (e.g. the arbitration agreement would be enforceable if the arbitration was necessary for the purpose of giving effect to another contract), but on the whole the common law rule proved unsatisfactory since its effect was to bring before the courts matters which the parties had really intended should be settled by arbitration. The defect was particularly noticeable in connection with ancillary arbitrations, as was shown in *Tancred, Arrol & Co.* v. *The Steel Co. of Scotland Ltd.*: an arbitration clause included in a contract for the building of the Forth Railway Bridge stated that any dispute that might arise as to the meaning of the contract was to be referred to "the engineer of the Forth Bridge Railway Company for the time being"; the clause was held to be ineffectual because of the absence of delectus personae. Lord Watson said in that case (at p. 36):

> "It has been settled by a uniform course of judicial decisions, extending over nearly a century, that according to the law of Scotland an agreement to refer future disputes, if and when they shall arise, to the person who shall then be the holder of a certain office is not binding."

The main purpose of the Act of 1894 was to abolish this common law rule. The Act also included a few other provisions designed to facilitate arbitrations, *e.g.* by preventing such deadlock as could arise at common law where two arbiters with no express power to nominate an oversman disagreed as to their decision.

The provisions of the Arbitration (Scotland) Act 1894 are:

1. An agreement to refer to arbitration is no longer ineffectual merely because the reference is to a person not named or to a person to be named by another, or to a person described as the holder of an office for the time being.

2. Where parties have failed to agree on the nomination of a single arbiter, and there is no machinery under their contract to meet such a situation, then either party may apply to the court for an appointment to be made by the court.

3. If a reference is to be to two arbiters and one party refuses to make his nomination, the court may be applied to for it to make an appointment.

4. Where there is a reference to two arbiters, these two arbiters have, unless the contract stipulates otherwise, power to nominate an oversman. Further, if there are two arbiters and they fail to agree on an oversman, the court has power to appoint an oversman.

(ii) Remuneration

The original rule of the common law was that an arbiter or oversman had no legal claim to be remunerated unless he had stipulated for remuneration before he accepted appointment. The rule has been modified over the years, and it can no longer be assumed that an arbiter or oversman is acting gratuitously even where no remuneration has been mentioned. In particular, a professional man, such as a chartered surveyor employed as arbiter on a valuation question, will be entitled, where there is no express agreement as to his remuneration, to charge a reasonable customary fee, which will probably be based on a scale of charges fixed by the professional body of which he is a member (*Wilkie* v. *Scottish Aviation Ltd.*, 1956 S.C. 198).

(b) Conduct of the Arbitration

The parties may in their agreement to resort to arbitration lay down conditions as to the way in which the arbitration is to be conducted, and the arbiter, since his jurisdiction is derived solely from the agreement of the parties, will be bound to observe these conditions. More usually the parties will not expressly specify the procedure which is to be followed, and in that case the arbiter's powers and duties in the conduct of the proceedings will depend on what was implied in the arbitration agreement and in other respects on his own discretion. For instance, where the arbitration is started by a formal deed of submission in probative form, it is implied. that the award also will require to be in a similar form. Likewise, the arbiter has implied power to deal with the question of expenses, but he would not be entitled to find a party liable in damages unless there was an express power to do so in the arbitration agreement.

The degree of formality of the procedure varies greatly: at one extreme the procedure may be as formal as court procedure and counsel may be instructed to plead the case of the parties; at the other extreme the procedure may be very informal, particularly in agricultural and mercantile circles where the arbiter's function often is rather to fix the value of crops, stock or other goods than to decide a dispute. There is no distinct line in Scots law between what are sometimes called "arbitrations proper" on the one hand and "valuations" on the other hand (*Stewart* v. *Williamson*, 1910 S.C.(H.L.) 47).

It is usual for an arbiter to appoint a clerk to take charge of the documents in the case and to act as a channel of communication between the parties and the arbiter. If the arbiter is not himself a lawyer but a layman chosen for his technical knowledge and experience, the clerk is often a solicitor and in practice will take a key role in the proceedings since the arbiter will to a great extent rely on his guidance when a point of law arises in the course of the proceedings.

The procedure often followed is for one party to lodge written claims which will be followed by written answers from the other party. A "record" may then be made up and closed in much the same way as in a court case (see p. 27, above). The arbiter will then decide what "proof" (*i.e.* evidence) should be allowed. He may wrongly allow or disallow certain evidence, but such errors are part of the risk which the parties have taken in resorting to arbitration and will not be a ground on which the award could be challenged. Sometimes it will be necessary for the arbiter to inspect premises or other property in order to inform himself of the matters in dispute. The arbiter will almost always allow a hearing to both parties at the conclusion of the proof, and will often issue "proposed findings" so that the parties may have an opportunity to make final "representations" criticising the proposed findings. Another hearing may be allowed for these representations. Although the steps mentioned in this paragraph are commonly taken, there are many arbitrations where the procedure is much less formal; in particular, in agricultural and mercantile arbitrations where a practical question is to be decided by an arbiter chosen for his knowledge and experience of such practical questions, there may be no objection to the arbiter's dispensing with both a proof and a hearing and deciding the question on the basis of a personal inspection.

Although the arbiter usually has a wide discretion as to the procedure to be followed, he is in all circumstances subject to the overriding principle of impartiality: he must adhere to "equal and even-handed procedure towards both parties alike" (J. M. Bell, *Treatise on the Law of Arbitration in Scotland*, 2nd ed., p. 23). He must not allow to one party what he denies to the other. If, for instance, he allowed a hearing to one party and not to the other, his award would be open to challenge unless it was wholly in favour of the party not heard. Similarly, if he is to be accompanied at an inspection of property by one of the parties, he ought to give the other party the opportunity of being present as well. In *Black* v. *John Williams & Co. (Wishaw) Ltd.*, 1924 S.C.(H.L.) 22, an arbiter had excluded one of the parties during the hearing of evidence, and this would have invalidated the award had it not been that the arbiter decided that part of the case in favour of the party who had been excluded.

Circumstances may arise in which an arbiter will be justified in proceeding ex parte ("without a party"), *e.g.* where a party refuses to take any further part in the proceedings although given full opportunity by the arbiter to do so.

The deed of submission or other document by which the parties refer their dispute to the arbiter may impose a time-limit within which the arbiter is to give his decision (*e.g.* the period of a year and a day from the date of the deed of submission). If the time-limit is allowed to pass without an award being made, the submission will fall (*i.e.* will cease to have effect). It is possible that the parties, seeing that the duration of the submission is nearing its end, will agree to "prorogate" (extend) the submission. It is safer, however, that the power of prorogation should have been conferred on the arbiter, because one of the parties, suspecting that the arbiter's decision would be disadvantageous to himself, might decline to agree on a prorogation. An arbiter has no *implied* power to prorogate the submission; in this as in other matters his jurisdiction is confined strictly within the bounds set on it by the agreement of the parties.

It may be necessary for an arbiter during the course of the arbitration to state a case for the opinion of the court on a question of law which has arisen. As has been noted, this duty is sometimes imposed on an arbiter in a statutory arbitration. In non-statutory arbitrations the stated case was introduced by the Administration of Justice (Scotland) Act 1972, s. 3, which provides that unless there is an express provision to the contrary in the arbitration agreement, the arbiter or oversman *may*, on the application of a party to the arbitration, at any stage in the arbitration state a case for the opinion of the Court of Session on any question of law arising in the arbitration, and the arbiter or oversman *must* do so if the party applies to the Court of Session and that court directs a case to be stated. It is important to note that the right of a party to apply for a stated case can be excluded by an "express provision" in the arbitration agreement. The application to have a case stated must be made "at any stage in the arbitration"; an application made after the award has been issued is too late (*Fairlie Yacht Slip Ltd.* v. *Lumsden*, 1977 S.L.T.(Notes) 41).

The conduct of the arbitration comes to an end when the award is issued. The arbiter is then said to be "functus," an abbreviation of "functus officio" ("having performed his duty"). The effect is that he no longer has any jurisdiction in connection with the matter in question.

(c) Challenge of the Award

The parties to an arbitration have voluntarily agreed to take the arbiter's decision instead of a court's decision. In doing so they have taken the risk that the arbiter will err on questions of fact and on questions of law, and the parties have no right to appeal to the court on the "merits" (substance) of their case. The finality of the arbiter's decision is expressed in memorable, but perhaps unduly strong, terms by Lord Jeffrey in *Mitchell* v. *Cable* (1848) 10 D. 1297, a case in which the Court of Session set aside an arbiter's award because he had decided the case after considering proof from one party without allowing the other party a fair opportunity of bringing forward his counter-proof. Lord Jeffrey said (at p. 1309):

> "On every matter touching the merits of the case, the judgment of the arbiter is beyond our control; and beyond question or cavil. He may believe what nobody else believes, and he may disbelieve what all the world believes. He may overlook or flagrantly misapply the most ordinary principles of law; and there is no appeal for those who have chosen to subject themselves to his despotic power."

Lord Jeffrey then goes on to explain that a decree-arbitral can stand only when the arbiter has done his duty "fairly," *i.e.* has dealt equally with both parties.

The passage quoted may be criticised on the ground that it suggests that an arbiter could with impunity draw on his own imagination for the facts and deliberately ignore legal principles. The arbiter has a duty to be honest as well as fair; he must take the facts as he finds them and the law as it is, and if there has been a stated case in which the court has decided a question of law the arbiter is bound to apply the court's finding to the facts before him (however wrong he may consider the finding to be).

The limited grounds on which an arbiter's decree-arbitral or award may be "reduced" (set aside) by the Court of Session are considered below under these headings:

   (i) "corruption, bribery or falsehood";
  (ii) ultra fines compromissi ("beyond the bounds of the sub-mission");
 (iii) improper procedure; and
 (iv) defective award.

Partial reduction is possible where one part of the award is open to objection, another part is valid and the two parts are clearly severable.

(i) "Corruption, bribery or falsehood"

The phrase is quoted from the twenty-fifth Act of the Articles of Regulation of 1695. These Articles were made by Commissioners under authority of a statute of the Scottish Parliament of 1693, and the twenty-fifth of them dealt with the grounds on which an arbiter's award might be challenged. It was in these terms:

> "That, for the cutting off of groundless and expensive pleas and processes in time coming, the Lords of Session sustain no reduction of any decreet-arbitral that shall be pronounced hereafter upon a Subscribed Submission, at the instance of either of the parties-submitters, upon any cause or reason whatsoever, unless that of corruption, bribery or falsehood, to be alleged against the judges-arbitrators who pronounced the same."

The effect of this provision can be appreciated only if the provision is viewed in its historical context: before 1695 the courts of law had come to allow an award to be challenged in court on the grounds of "iniquity" committed by an arbiter or of "enorm lesion" suffered by a party, *i.e.* on the grounds that an arbiter had gone wrong or that a party had suffered undue hardship; the result was that in practically every case an award could be reviewed upon its merits at the discretion of the court—a situation which was contrary to the whole essence of arbitration, since by resorting to arbitration the parties wished to exclude the jurisdiction of the courts. The aim of the twenty-fifth Article was to end the practice of review by the courts: arbiters' awards were to be final and binding on the parties and were no longer to be open to challenge merely because the arbiter had made a mistake or one party had suffered undue hardship.

Corruption, bribery and falsehood on the part of the arbiter, however, were to remain grounds on which an award could be challenged in court.

If this statutory provision had been given a literal interpretation it would have prevented an award from being set aside on any ground other than corruption, bribery or falsehood. Decided cases, however, and particularly *Adams* v. *Great North of Scotland Railway Co.* (1890) 18 R.(H.L.) 1, have established that the object for which the provision was made must be looked to: the provision had never been intended to go beyond the point of putting an end to the practice of review upon the merits; other common law grounds of challenge (see (ii) to (iv), below) remained available.

In some cases there were attempts to extend the word "corruption" so as to include "legal corruption" or "constructive corruption," *i.e.* conduct on the part of the arbiter which was mistaken but not strictly corrupt. In *Adams* v. *Great North of Scotland Railway Co.* there were strong protests about this extended meaning of "corruption"; actual corruption was considered to be necessary if the award was to be set aside on the ground of the Articles of Regulation: if the arbiter's mistake was innocent, it could not be brought within the term "corruption," though it might lead to reduction of the award on one of the other grounds (ii) to (iv), below.

(ii) Ultra fines compromissi

An award which is ultra fines compromissi may be set aside. This follows from the very nature of arbitration, since the parties have agreed to implement the judgment of their private judge on certain questions only. Any question which is beyond the bounds of the submission continues to be within the court's jurisdiction, and any attempted decision of such a question by the arbiter has no authority behind it.

(iii) Improper procedure

The parties may specify the procedure which the arbiter is to follow. If he then fails to do so, his award may be open to challenge. More often the procedure is left to the arbiter's discretion, and if so, failure to observe strict court procedure will not be a ground for challenging the award. There are, however, in every submission to arbitration implied conditions of honesty and impartiality, breach of which is a ground of reduction.

The arbiter will satisfy the test of honesty if he conscientiously believes that what he is doing is right and just, however much he may err in judgment. To satisfy the test of impartiality there must be "equal and even-handed procedure towards both parties alike."

The parties themselves, as well as the arbiter, must refrain from fraudulent and unfair procedure; *e.g.* an award would be set aside if a deliberately false case had been presented to the arbiter.

(iv) Defective award

An award should be clear in its terms: if it is unintelligible, it will be set aside by the court; if it is merely ambiguous or obscure, the court (but not the arbiter) has the right to interpret it.

An award must also be in the proper form. What is the proper form depends on circumstances: if, for instance, the arbitration proceedings were started by a formal deed of submission in probative form, the award also would require to be in a similar form; on the other hand, an informal award would be quite sufficient where the reference to arbitration was itself informal.

An award must be exhaustive of the submission, *i.e.* it must give a complete decision: the parties have agreed that certain disputes be decided by arbitration, and it is not a proper fulfilment of their agreement if the arbiter decides one question but leaves another question undecided. An instance of reduction on the ground of failure to exhaust the submission is *Donald* v. *Shiell's Executrix*, 1937 S.C. 52:

In an arbitration between the outgoing and the incoming tenants of a farm the questions submitted for the arbiter's decision were (1) what sum should be paid by the incoming tenant to the outgoing tenant for corn crop and various other items, and (2) the sum, "if any," to be paid by the outgoing tenant to the incoming tenant in order to put the buildings on the farm into the condition provided for under the conditions of let in favour of the incoming tenant.

The decree-arbitral ordered the incoming tenant to pay certain sums under the first head, but made no mention of items under the second head.

The incoming tenant brought an action for reduction of the decree-arbitral, and was successful on the ground of the omission: it could not be assumed that the arbiter had considered items under the second head and had found nothing to be due for them.

(d) Judicial References

By a judicial reference is meant the procedure by which parties to a court action agree to withdraw the decision of the whole or part of the questions raised in the action from the decision of the court and, while still formally leaving the action in court, refer these questions to an arbiter.

A judicial reference is started by the lodging with the court of a "minute" stating the agreement of the parties, and the court then, if it thinks fit, "interpones authority to the minute," *i.e.* authorises the judicial reference to be proceeded with.

The selection of the judicial referee is a matter for the parties to decide. Like an ordinary arbiter, a judicial referee is not bound by strict court procedure.

The decision of a judicial referee is set out in a report to the court (not in an award). The report may be challenged on the same grounds as an award in an arbitration. The court will either approve of the report and grant "decree conform," *i.e.* make a court order in conformity with the terms of the report, or set the report aside; the court has no power to amend the report.

Further Reading

David M. Walker, *The Scottish Legal System*
Gloag and Henderson, *Introduction to the Law of Scotland*
T. B. Smith, *A Short Commentary on the Law of Scotland*
The Scottish Office, *The Legal System of Scotland* (H.M.S.O.)
C. N. Stoddart, *The Law and Practice of Legal Aid in Scotland* (W. Green & Son Ltd.).

CHAPTER 3

SOURCES OF LAW

THE phrase "sources of law" has at least three meanings:

1. *HISTORICAL SOURCES*

These are the incidents in legal history from which the principles and rules of law have arisen. They include the ancient native customs of the community, canon law, Roman law, and English law. The historical source of an Act of Parliament may be a decision of the courts; *e.g.* the Trade Disputes Act 1965 was passed as a result of the case of *Rookes* v. *Barnard* [1964] A.C. 1129.

Historical sources merely explain how the principles and rules came to be part of Scots law; they do not confer on the principles and rules any binding force.

2. *PHILOSOPHICAL SOURCES*

These are to be found in the various beliefs and theories which have prevailed from time to time in the community. The philosophical basis for a rule or principle of law may lie in some moral or religious belief or in some social, political or economic theory. For instance, the Equal Pay Act 1970, the effect of which was to eliminate by the end of 1975 discrimination between men and women in pay and in other terms and conditions of employment, was based on the theory of the equality of the sexes.

These philosophical bases explain the underlying reasons for particular rules and principles of law, but do not, any more than the historical sources, give the principles and rules binding force.

3. *FORMAL SOURCES*

These are the sources from which rules and principles of law derive their authority or binding force. They explain what the law is and why it has to be applied.

These formal or authoritative sources are considered below under the headings:

1. legislation;
2. judicial precedent;
3. authoritative writings;
4. custom;
5. equity; and
6. extraneous sources.

Definitions of law

Formal sources are the only sources which *must* be taken into consideration in any attempt to define "law," although historical and philosophical sources also may contribute to the definition.

Attempted definitions of law are part of the subject-matter of the branch of law known as "jurisprudence."

Any valid definition of "law" for the purposes of legal studies should not be so wide as to embrace the "laws" of the natural sciences (such as the "law" of gravity), or moral "laws" (which lay down ideal standards of what is right and with which persons ought to conform although they are not obliged to do so).

The many varied definitions of "law" which have been put forward emphasise different aspects of law: some emphasise its connections with the ideal standard of justice, others its associations with the customary rules and practices accepted in particular communities, others its enforceability as being the command of the sovereign or superior authority in a state, and others again its function in society (*e.g.* the function of settling disputes).

While no one definition, therefore, can be regarded as providing the final answer to the abstract question "What is law?" that given by Salmond, a New Zealand writer with an international reputation, in his book *Jurisprudence* (§ 15) may be quoted as a workable definition so far as Scots law is concerned:

"The law may be defined as the body of principles recognised

and applied by the State in the administration of justice. In
other words, the law consists of the rules recognised and acted
on by Courts of justice."

This definition has the merit of including an express reference to the
state and an implied reference (in the words "administration of
justice") to the courts (for it is clear from the second sentence
quoted that the phrase "administration of justice" stresses not so
much the ideal of justice as the administration, *i.e.* the application
in the courts, of what the state recognises as justice). These are the
very aspects of law which are of most importance in connection with
the formal or authoritative sources of law.

If one seeks a purely practical answer to the concrete question
"What is the law?" then one must look to the courts to find what
rules they, as part of the machinery of the state and with the authority
of the state, will apply in a given situation. So far as Scots law is
concerned, the purely practical answer to that question lies in the
formal sources dealt with below.

Writings on law

It must be emphasised that books and other writings on law are,
with a few exceptions, not formal sources of law at all. Of course,
students, practitioners, and even judges all consult legal writings, and
students and practitioners may be well advised to accept (not un-
questioningly, however) the views of legal scholars who have greater
knowledge and experience than they themselves. The courts, however, are in general not bound to apply in their judgments the views
of writers on law, however well-known the writers may be and however high may be the standard of scholarship in their works. If a
court chooses to accept the view of a writer, then that view is
authoritative because of the court's acceptance of it, and not because
of its appearance in the writing.

There are two exceptions to this general rule that writings on
law are not authoritative:

1. There is a very limited class of writings, referred to as
"institutional writings," which are authoritative sources of law.
The best-known are those of Stair, Erskine and Bell. Institutional
writings are sometimes described as "literary sources of law," while
other writings are described as "legal literature."

2. Some writings on law, other than the institutional writings,
are extraneous sources of law, *i.e.* are consulted by the court for
guidance where none of the other sources yields a decisive answer.
As a result some "legal literature" can properly be considered as a
secondary source of law, although only "literary sources of law" are
primary sources.

1. Legislation

Legislation is considered below under three headings:

(a) statutes (Acts of Parliament);

(b) delegated legislation, which is legislation made by some other body or by some person, to which or to whom Parliament has delegated its legislative (*i.e.* its law-making) power; and

(c) legislation of the European Communities.

In addition, there is a limited amount of prerogative legislation, which is legislation made by the Crown (*i.e.* the King or Queen for the time being) in the exercise of the royal prerogative. Prerogative legislation takes the form of Orders in Council, Letters Patent, or Proclamations. It relates mostly to some colonial and other overseas matters, and is little used for home affairs except in war-time.

(a) Statutes

A statute is a declaration as to the law made by the highest law-making power, namely, "the Queen in Parliament." In other words, before a Bill becomes an Act of Parliament, it must be passed by both Houses of Parliament and receive the royal assent.

While the noun "statute" denotes only an Act of Parliament and does not include delegated legislation, the adjectives "statute" and "statutory" have a wider meaning: they cover delegated legislation as well as Acts of Parliament, *e.g.* the distinction between "common law" and "statute law" (p. 126), and the phrase "statutory interpretation" used in the sense of interpretation of all legislation.

Statutes applicable to Scotland

The Acts of Parliament which apply to Scotland are either Acts passed by the Scottish Parliament before the Union of the Parliaments of Scotland and England in 1707 (referred to as "Scots Acts") or Acts of the Westminster Parliament since that date.

(i) *Scots Acts.* Scots Acts differ from Acts of the Westminster Parliament in two respects:

1. Scots Acts are subject to the doctrine of "desuetude" (obsolescence). This means that a Scots Act, although never expressly repealed, may have been repealed by implication through its having fallen out of use.

For the doctrine to operate it is not enough that the Act is a very ancient one or even that it has not been relied on in court in any recent case; there must in addition be proof either that there has been practice contrary to the Act for a substantial time, or that the Act is out of keeping with modern conditions. An example of a

Scots Act repealed by desuetude is the Act of James I of Scotland prohibiting the playing of football.

Many Scots Acts were, however, expressly repealed by the Statute Law Revision (Scotland) Acts of 1906 and 1964 and the Statute Law (Repeals) Act 1973, and it is presumed that remaining Scots Acts are not in desuetude.

The doctrine of desuetude does not apply to Acts of the Westminster Parliament: they cease to have force only if and when they are repealed.

2. Scots Acts are given a more liberal interpretation than modern Acts of the Westminster Parliament.

Many Scots Acts are very short in comparison with modern statutes, and it was left to the courts to draw the full meaning out of the words used.

When a court is now called on to interpret a Scots Act, it attaches great weight to the interpretation placed on the Act by the courts immediately after it was passed. This type of interpretation is referred to as contemporanea expositio ("contemporary interpretation").

(ii) *Acts of the Westminster Parliament.* The Acts of the Westminster Parliament which apply to Scotland may be either Acts of the Parliament of Great Britain from 1707 to 1800, or Acts of the Parliament of the United Kingdom since 1801.

Not all statutes passed by the Westminster Parliament since 1707 extend to Scotland, but the rule is that a statute passed by the United Kingdom Parliament prima facie applies to the whole of the United Kingdom, *i.e.* it is presumed to apply to the whole of the United Kingdom until there is proof that Parliament's intention was to the contrary.

An Act which is not intended to apply to Scotland usually contains an express provision near the end of the Act that it does not extend to Scotland.

Some Acts of the Westminster Parliament apply to Scotland only. These can be immediately recognised by the word "Scotland" in brackets, *e.g.* Sheriff Courts (Scotland) Act 1907, or Conveyancing and Feudal Reform (Scotland) Act 1970. These Acts must not be confused with Scots Acts.

There is no corresponding system applicable to Acts which extend to England only, *e.g.* it is not immediately obvious that the Bankruptcy Act 1914 does not extend to Scotland, which has its own Act on the subject, namely the Bankruptcy (Scotland) Act 1913.

The necessary Parliamentary time is often not available for the passing of a separate Act for Scotland, and the device has often been

resorted to (not without criticism from Scots lawyers) of extending
to Scotland statutes primarily intended to apply to England and
expressed in English legal terminology. The device takes the form
of an "application-to-Scotland" section which gives the Scottish
terms which are to be substituted for the English terms used throughout the Act. Difficulties, however, arise from the fact that the terms
of English and of Scots law are seldom exact equivalents.

Classification of statutes

The main classification is into general Acts, local Acts, and
personal Acts.

General Acts apply to the whole community, whereas local and
personal Acts are limited in respect of the area or the persons,
respectively, affected by them. Local and personal Acts may be
required, for instance, to confer special powers on a local authority
or to deal with private estates or other personal affairs of individuals.

General Acts result from public Bills, *i.e.* from Bills which seek
to alter the general law of the land. Public Bills are mostly Government Bills, introduced to Parliament by ministers on behalf of the
Government of the day, but some public Bills are private members'
Bills, introduced by individual M.P.s who may or may not belong
to the party which has formed the Government. Only very limited
time is allowed in Parliament for private members' Bills, and there
is little chance of a private member's Bill becoming an Act unless the
Government assists its passage through Parliament by adopting it.

Local and personal Acts result from private Bills, *i.e.* from Bills
intended to benefit the person or the body promoting them. The
procedure for the passing of private Bills includes a hearing, similar
to the hearing of a court case, at which evidence is brought forward
on behalf of both promoters and opponents. A private Bill is quite
distinct from a private member's Bill.

An alternative to the private Bill is "provisional order procedure,"
which is governed by the Private Legislation Procedure (Scotland)
Act 1936, and involves less expense than a private Bill. Under this
procedure the local authority or other body or the individual concerned obtains from the Secretary of State for Scotland (after an
inquiry if there is opposition) a provisional order granting the
powers sought, and this order is later confirmed by the passing of a
"provisional order confirmation Act" introduced to Parliament as
a public Bill by the Secretary of State for Scotland, *e.g.* Strathclyde
University and Mackintosh School of Architecture Order Confirmation Act 1976, Aberdeen Shoemakers Incorporation Order Confirmation Act 1977 and West Lothian District Council Order
Confirmation Act 1980.

Descriptive terms applied to statutes

A "codifying" Act is one passed to reduce to the form of a code all the existing law on a particular topic. The Bills of Exchange Act 1882, the Partnership Act 1890, the Sale of Goods Act 1893,[1] and the Marine Insurance Act 1906 are codifying Acts.

A "consolidating" Act is one which brings together into a single Act the provisions contained in several earlier Acts. Consolidating Acts may include minor improvements, but, in general, their function is to re-enact the existing statute law in a more convenient form, not to make any major change in its substance. Examples are the Companies Act 1948 and the Criminal Procedure (Scotland) Act 1975.

A "declaratory" Act is one passed to declare what the existing law is on some point. Such an Act may be aimed at the removal of doubts which have arisen or at the setting aside of some decision of the courts which is considered by Parliament to have been wrong. An example is the Truck Act 1940, passed as a result of *Pratt* v. *Cook, Son & Co. (St. Paul's) Ltd.* [1940] A.C. 437.

A "statute law revision" Act is an Act passed to repeal statutory provisions which are obsolete, *e.g.* the Statute Law Revision (Scotland) Act 1964. The work of statute law revision is now undertaken by the Law Commission and the Scottish Law Commission, and a "statute law (repeals)" Act is passed from time to time to give effect to their recommendations; *e.g.* the Statute Law (Repeals) Act 1973 repealed 118 whole Acts and parts of 140 other Acts in accordance with a draft statute law (repeals) Bill prepared by the Commissions in 1972 (*Statute Law Revision: Fourth Report*, Law Com. No. 49, Scot. Law. Com. No. 26 (1972: Cmnd. 5108)).

A "clauses" Act is an Act designed to reduce the length of private Bills, *e.g.* when in the nineteenth century many railway companies were being formed and promoters were, by the introduction of private Bills to Parliament, seeking powers such as powers of compulsory purchase of land for their undertakings, some general Acts were passed setting out standard clauses which could be incorporated in any private Bill relating to a proposed railway. Examples are the Railways Clauses Consolidation (Scotland) Act 1845, and the Lands Clauses Consolidation (Scotland) Act of the same year. Clauses Acts were appropriate for an era when large-scale undertakings such as those for railways, water, gas, and electricity were the concern of private enterprise, and they are of little significance in relation to the nationalised undertakings of the twentieth century.

A "law reform (miscellaneous provisions)" Act is an Act passed

---

[1] Repealed by the Sale of Goods Act 1979 (a consolidating Act—see footnote on p. 15, above).

to reform the law on several different subjects which may be quite unconnected with each other. Some of the changes made may be important and others minor. An example is the Law Reform (Miscellaneous Provisions) (Scotland) Act 1980.

Contents of statutes

Statutes are divided into sections, subsections, paragraphs, and sub-paragraphs, in that order; *e.g.* "Companies Act 1948, s. 5 (7) (*b*) (ii)" stands for sub-paragraph (ii) of paragraph (*b*) of subsection (7) of section 5 of the Companies Act 1948.

In a Bill the terms "clauses" and "subsections" are used for what become in the Act sections and subsections, respectively.

Statutes, other than very short ones, are usually also divided into Parts, each Part consisting of a group of sections on the same subject-matter. Division into Parts does not interrupt the numbering of the sections; *e.g.* the Sale of Goods Act 1979 has sixty-four sections and is divided into seven Parts, Part I dealing with "Contracts to which Act Applies" and consisting of section 1, Part II dealing with "Formation of the Contract" and consisting of sections 2 to 15, Part III dealing with "Effects of the Contract" and consisting of sections 16 to 26, and so on.

The "title" of an Act is strictly the formal long title which appears at the beginning of the Act, *e.g.* "Act of Parliament to consolidate the law relating to the sale of goods." The titles of some of the older Acts are very long indeed.

Modern Acts are provided also with a "short title," which is given in a section of the Act, usually near the end of the Act; *e.g.* the last section of the Act just mentioned provides: "This Act may be cited as the Sale of Goods Act 1979." The Short Titles Act 1896 gave short titles to many older Acts which did not then have them, and the Statute Law Revision (Scotland) Act 1964 gave short titles for all the remaining Scots Acts.

Groups of Acts are sometimes given a "collective" title, which includes the dates of the earliest and the latest only of the Acts in the group, *e.g.* "Weights and Measures Acts 1963 to 1979."

Some statutes have a "preamble" (a preface) explaining the need for the Act. In older statutes preambles are sometimes very long. Modern statutes often have no preamble, and if they do have one, it is usually brief.

Many statutes have "schedules" attached to them, containing lists, forms, and other matters of detail which cannot conveniently be included in the body of the Act. The schedules are referred to in sections of the Act, and they are themselves part of the Act and must be given effect to as such. Schedules are numbered (if there is more than one), and each schedule may, if necessary, be divided into paragraphs and sub-paragraphs.

Commencement of statutes

Prima facie (*i.e.* until the contrary is proved) an Act comes into operation when it is passed, and the date when it is passed is the date of the royal assent. This date appears at the beginning of the Act, immediately after the (long) title.

However, provision is often made for an Act to come into operation at some later date than the date of its passing. This later date may be fixed by the Act itself, or alternatively the Act may give a minister or some other person the power to fix the date of commencement of the Act.

Amendment of statutes

A later statute may "amend" (alter) an existing statute to any extent, and the amending statute may in turn be amended.

Amendment may be express or implied. Amendment is express if a later statute provides that a word, phrase or section in the earlier statute is to be extended or restricted or otherwise altered, or that some addition, deletion or substitution is to be made. Amendment is implied where a later statute contains some provision which is inconsistent with a provision in an earlier statute. The later provision must be given effect to in preference to the earlier one, since the later provision represents the later intention of Parliament.

Repeal of statutes

A statute other than a Scots Act remains on the statute book until it is repealed.

Repeal may be express or implied. Express repeal may be by a later statute on the same subject-matter or by a "statute law revision" or "statute law (repeals)" Act (p. 83 above). There is implied repeal when a later Act is so contradictory of an earlier one that the two cannot both be given effect to; however, the courts are reluctant to infer a repeal in this way, and if it is at all possible they read the two statutes together and give effect to both.

(b) Delegated legislation

Delegated legislation, also called "subordinate legislation," consists of regulations, rules, orders, by-laws, and the like, made by persons or bodies lower than Parliament.

Delegated legislation is possible only because Parliament, the supreme law-making authority, has chosen, by an Act, to delegate to a subordinate authority part of its own legislative power.

The delegated power is subject to the control of Parliament: the power may at any later time be restricted or taken away altogether by Parliament, and the most important principle applied by the courts in interpreting delegated legislation is that it must, to be valid, be intra vires ("within the powers") of the delegating Act (sometimes referred to as "the enabling Act"); delegated legislation which is ultra vires ("beyond the powers") is invalid and is not given effect to by the courts. Provided, however, delegated legislation has been made by the proper procedure and is intra vires, it is valid, and has the same force as if it were itself an Act of Parliament.

Forms of delegated legislation

The main forms of delegated legislation may be considered under four headings:

   (i)   statutory instruments;
  (ii)   by-laws;
 (iii)   Acts of Sederunt and Acts of Adjournal; and
 (iv)   sub-delegated legislation.

(i) *Statutory instruments.* The term " statutory instruments " was introduced by the Statutory Instruments Act 1946. It has a complicated definition, but, in general, it covers two types of delegated legislation:

1.   Orders in Council; and
2.   ministerial regulations, rules, orders, etc.

1.   *Orders in Council.* These are orders made by the "Queen in Council" (*i.e.* the Queen with the advice of the Privy Council). In practice the Queen follows the advice of her ministers, with the result that Orders in Council are just as much the product of the Government of the day as are other statutory instruments.

Some Orders in Council are not delegated legislation at all, but are an exercise of the royal prerogative; no authority from Parliament is necessary for the issue of Orders in Council in that category.

Other Orders in Council, however, are properly classed as delegated legislation, since power to issue them depends on Parliament's having in an Act conferred power on "Her Majesty in Council" to make Orders in Council for particular purposes.

This type of delegated legislation is usually reserved for matters of some national or constitutional importance; *e.g.* the Emergency Powers (Defence) Act 1939 authorised the making of Orders in Council to secure public safety and to maintain essential supplies on the outbreak of war, and the Southern Rhodesia Act 1965 authorised the making of Orders in Council in connection with unconstitutional action taken in Southern Rhodesia.

2. *Ministerial regulations, rules, orders, etc.* This is the commonest type of delegated legislation. Very often an Act of Parliament lays down a general principle only, and confers on an appropriate minister of the Crown power to make regulations, rules, orders, etc., which will have the effect of filling in details which could not conveniently have been included in the Act itself. It will then not be necessary to amend the Act itself on each occasion when a new or unforeseen point of detail arises.

Normally only specialists in the various branches of law are expected to know the contents of the great volume of statutory instruments which come under this heading.

Examples are:

Census (Scotland) Regulations 1980, made under the Census Act 1920; these provide for the detailed arrangements necessary for the census, and set out the forms which require to be completed by householders and others;

Scottish Local Elections Rules 1974, made under the Local Government (Scotland) Act 1973; these deal with the conduct of elections of councillors for regions, islands areas and districts; and

Valuation Roll (Scotland) Order 1977, made under the Local Government (Scotland) Act 1975; this prescribes the form of the valuation roll which came into force on April 1, 1978.

The first example shows that separate regulations may be made for Scotland under an Act which is not itself restricted to Scotland; the corresponding regulations for England are the Census Regulations 1980.

(ii) *By-laws.* These differ from statutory instruments in that they are made not by the Government but by some other public body, such as a local authority or a public corporation, and also in that they require to be confirmed by a minister of the Crown if they are to be effective.

Local authorities derive their power to make by-laws from general legislation, such as the Local Government (Scotland) Act 1973, and also from any special local Act obtained by the particular local authority. Different local authorities may, therefore, have different powers, and, even where their powers are the same, they may, in the exercise of these powers, make different by-laws. The by-laws can be enforced against any member of the public who is within the area of the local authority; they have no force outside that area.

Amongst the other bodies empowered to make by-laws are the public corporations set up to manage the nationalised industries, such as the British Railways Board. Some other special bodies, such as the National Trust, also have power to make by-laws. These by-laws will govern the rights and duties of the public in relation to the public corporation or other body, and can be enforced against any member of the public.

The fact that a by-law has been confirmed by the appropriate authority does not mean that its validity cannot be challenged. In fact, the validity of by-laws may be challenged, not only on the grounds that the correct procedure has not been followed in the making of them or that they are ultra vires, but also on the grounds that they are uncertain, or repugnant to some express general rule of law, or unreasonable (in the sense of oppressive).

By-laws must be distinguished from the rules made by numerous bodies such as trade unions, professional societies and clubs. The rules of such bodies are binding on *members*, because the members, by their contract of membership, have agreed to be bound by them, but, unlike by-laws, they do not affect the public. These rules are contractual rules, and not delegated legislation.

(iii) *Acts of Sederunt and Acts of Adjournal.* An Act of Sederunt is a rule made by the Court of Session to regulate procedure in the civil courts. There was a codifying Act of Sederunt in 1913. An instance of an Act of Sederunt is "Act of Sederunt (Appeals under the Licensing (Scotland) Act 1976) 1977," made under the Sheriff Courts (Scotland) Act 1971 and the Licensing (Scotland) Act 1976, to specify the procedure for appeals to the sheriff against decisions of a licensing board.

An Act of Adjournal is a rule made by the High Court of Justiciary to regulate procedure in the criminal courts. An instance of an Act of Adjournal is "Act of Adjournal (Circuits) 1977," made under the Criminal Procedure (Scotland) Act 1975 to provide for sittings of the High Court of Justiciary on circuit in 1978.

Certain Acts of Adjournal were included in the consolidating Criminal Procedure (Scotland) Act 1975, and now appear as sections in that Act. However, by express provisions of the Act of 1975, these sections are not given the full force of an Act of Parliament but are treated as still having the characteristics of delegated legislation in that they may be challenged on the ground that they are ultra vires (see p. 86, above) and in that they may be varied or repealed by later Acts of Adjournal.

Acts of Sederunt and Acts of Adjournal are now usually in the form of statutory instruments.

(iv) *Sub-delegated legislation.* Normally an Act of Parliament authorises only one stage of delegation. This is in accordance with a fundamental rule of the common law, applicable generally to any situation where one person has been appointed as the agent of another, namely the rule that the agent must not delegate to another the work which he personally has been appointed to do. The maxim in which this rule is expressed is delegatus non potest delegare ("a delegate cannot delegate"). There is, therefore, a presumption that Parliament did not intend to confer on the person or body authorised to make delegated legislation the right to delegate that legislative power to another.

In some cases, however, the terms of the enabling Act are very general, and give rise to general delegated legislation, which is followed by more specific sub-delegated legislation.

The example usually given of sub-delegated legislation involved four stages of delegation: the Emergency Powers (Defence) Act 1939 conferred wide powers on His Majesty (in practice on His Majesty's advisers, namely the Cabinet) to make by Order in Council any regulations which he thought necessary in view of the outbreak of war; the Defence Regulations made under that provision authorised ministers to make "orders," which in turn authorised ministers or other agencies to give "directions," which in turn authorised the issue of "licences" in particular cases.

Need for delegated legislation

The need for delegated legislation arises from the fact that in the last hundred years the state has increased its activities in very many fields, such as housing, employment, education, welfare, town and country planning, and the economy. It is no longer possible for all the necessary legislation to be enacted by Parliament itself. Delegated legislation is inevitable if the state is to fulfil the role expected of it in the twentieth century.

The reasons for and advantages of delegated legislation were summarised under six headings by the Donoughmore Committee on Ministers' Powers in its *Report* in 1932 (Cmd. 4060):

   (i)   pressure on Parliamentary time;
   (ii) technicality of subject-matter;
  (iii) unforeseen contingencies;
  (iv) flexibility;
   (v) opportunity for experiment; and
  (vi) emergency powers.

(i) *Pressure on Parliamentary time.* The bulk of legislation is so great that Parliament does not have the time to concern itself with all the details. It considers only the general policy and confers on some other person or body the power to fill in the details. For example, the Town and Country Planning (Scotland) Act 1972 and the Health and Safety at Work etc. Act 1974, although both fairly long Acts, merely lay down general principles, and for the detailed application of the Acts the numerous regulations passed under them must be consulted.

(ii) *Technicality of subject-matter.* Members of Parliament are in general not qualified to discuss, for instance, the pattern of miners' safety lamps, or whether a particular disease, or substance, or poison should come within the scope of some general statutory provision. It is appropriate for such matters to be left to experts, this being usually done by a power conferred on a minister to make delegated legislation; the technicalities are then dealt with by the experts in the government department concerned.

(iii) *Unforeseen contingencies.* At the time when an Act is being passed it is difficult to foresee, especially if some large and complex scheme of reform is being introduced, what difficulties may arise in the application of the Act: special categories of persons and special local conditions might call for exceptions and exemptions; scientific discoveries and other developments might make some additional provision advisable or essential; changes in social or economic conditions might necessitate some adjustment of standards or values which would hardly merit the attention of Parliament itself.

Delegated legislation enables a minister or other person or body to deal with these contingencies as they arise.

(iv) *Flexibility.* By means of delegated legislation statutory provisions may be more easily and quickly adapted to meet changed circumstances or special cases, to take account of experience gained in the application of some statutory scheme, and to enable improvements to be made after consultation with interested parties.

(v) *Opportunity for experiment.* Delegated legislation can be used to enable a scheme to be tried out for a limited time or in a limited area by way of experiment. The experience gained may lead to the scheme being abandoned or perfected and extended, without the need for further recourse to Parliament.

Road traffic law is a branch of law in which delegated legislation is often used for this purpose.

(vi) *Emergency powers.* Emergencies arise both in war-time and in peace-time which call for more speedy legislation than that of which Parliament itself is capable. For the use of delegated legislation in war-time, see on the Emergency Powers (Defence) Act 1939 (p. 89, above). In peace-time, emergency powers are usually less in evidence, but include numerous, though mostly less extensive, powers to take immediate action, *e.g.* to safeguard public health, to control an outbreak of foot-and-mouth disease, to regulate the economy of the country, etc.

Criticisms of delegated legislation

The main criticisms of delegated legislation may be summarised under four headings:

    (i) skeleton statutes;
    (ii) inadequate controls;
    (iii) inadequate publicity; and
    (iv) wide and uncertain powers.

(i) *Skeleton statutes.* The process of confining the statute itself to a skeleton form containing only the barest general principles and of leaving all the flesh-and-blood details to be filled in by a subordinate authority can be carried too far. Parliament may thus lose its real supremacy, and the citizen be denied his right of opposing proposed legislation through his elected representative in Parliament.

(ii) *Inadequate controls.* Some controls are exercised by Parliament ("Parliamentary" controls), and others by the courts ("judicial" controls).

Of the Parliamentary controls, the most notable, apart from the obvious one of deciding the contents of the "parent" Act, are:

1. the procedure of "laying" before Parliament, by which a particular statutory instrument must be laid on the table of either House of Parliament for a prescribed time;

2. the Joint Committee on Statutory Instruments, consisting of select committees of the two Houses of Parliament, which considers statutory instruments and draws attention to certain aspects of them; and

3. questions put in the House of Commons by M.P.s to ministers.

The judicial controls over delegated legislation are that the courts will declare void delegated legislation which has not been made by the proper procedure or which is beyond the powers delegated.

Parliamentary control is necessarily limited by the very nature, complexity and volume of delegated legislation. Neither the time nor the opportunity is available to make the control fully effective.

Judicial control is sometimes ineffective because the delegated powers have been so widely expressed as to give the minister or other authority virtually complete discretion. Moreover, judicial control is bound to be to some extent unsatisfactory, since it will be exercised only after the harm has been done, or at least attempted, and the court is asked to declare the invalidity of the legislation in some actual individual case. Further, the person affected may be unable or unwilling to face the expense or publicity of court proceedings, or may, through ignorance of or indifference to his rights, fail to challenge the validity of the legislation.

(iii) *Inadequate publicity.* Adequate publicity is not always given to delegated legislation, nor are all interested parties always consulted before it is made.

However, the Statutory Instruments Act 1946 provided for the printing, numbering, and publication for sale of statutory instruments, and it has become the practice for an enabling Act to require a minister to consult certain committees or other bodies before he makes the subordinate legislation.

(iv) *Wide and uncertain powers.* Criticism has been directed in particular against the "Henry VIII clause," which has sometimes been included in an enabling Act. That type of clause gives power to a minister to modify the provisions of the Act itself "so far as may appear to him to be necessary" for the purpose of bringing the Act into operation. The clause derived its nickname from the fact that Henry VIII was regarded as the typical absolute monarch.

While the Henry VIII clause seems now to have been abandoned, the criticism remains valid that delegated powers are in some instances so wide and uncertain that the citizen is virtually powerless in opposing their exercise.

(c) Legislation of the European Communities

The legislation of the European Communities which applies to the United Kingdom may be either primary or secondary.

Primary legislation consists of the treaties by which the European Communities were originally established and certain subsidiary treaties which have since been made. The treaties which originally established the Communities are the Treaty of Paris of 1951 which set up the European Coal and Steel Community, and two Treaties of Rome of 1957 which set up the European Economic Community and the European Atomic Energy Community. Amongst the later treaties are the Treaty of Brussels of 1965, which merged the main institutions of the Communities, and the Treaty of Accession of 1972 which prepared the way for the accession of the United Kingdom to the Communities as from January 1, 1973.

Secondary legislation consists of regulations, directives and decisions made by the Council and the Commission of the Communities in accordance with powers conferred on these bodies by the treaties.

Regulations have general application, do not require any Act of Parliament to be passed in this country to give them effect, and override any part of our national law which is contrary to them.

Directives indicate objectives to be achieved, and impose on the
United Kingdom, as a member state, an obligation to bring the
national law into line with the aim stated in the directive, leaving to
the national authorities the choice of form and methods. Decisions
are binding on the states or persons to whom they are addressed. They
are used to explain policies (which may be incorporated in subsequent regulations or directives), and also to provide for some action
to be taken, such as the setting up of a committee on a Community
question.

In general, secondary legislation is recommended by the Commission, and passed by the Council.

The legality of all secondary legislation is controlled by the
European Court of Justice, which has power to declare acts of the
Council or of the Commission to be void if they infringe the treaties.

Various arrangements have been made in Parliament to keep
members informed of Community developments and to enable
members to scrutinise and debate matters which are being considered by Community institutions. These arrangements include
the setting up of the Select Committee on European Secondary
Legislation to consider draft proposals for secondary legislation and
to report as to whether these proposals raise questions of legal or
political importance.

2. Judicial Precedent

The most authoritative source of law after legislation is judicial
precedent, also referred to as "the principle of stare decisis" ("standing by decisions").

According to this principle the court is bound to give effect to
the law laid down by a superior court in an earlier case.

The principle has always been more strictly applied in England
than in Scotland. It gradually came to be accepted in Scotland in
the nineteenth century, mainly through the influence of the House
of Lords and improved methods of law-reporting. In Scotland
before the nineteenth century the courts considered a *series* of
decided cases as authoritative, but did not recognise a single decision
as having binding force.

The word "precedent" simply means "previous case," and a
"judicial precedent" is a case previously decided by the courts.
The phrase "the doctrine of judicial precedent," therefore, is wide
enough to cover the former Scottish practice, but it is now generally
used, and will be used here, only of the more rigid (and originally
English) practice, properly referred to as "stare decisis," which gives
even a single decision binding force.

In the European Court of Justice there is no rigid doctrine of judicial precedent: that court is willing to depart from its own previous decisions.

It is essential for the operation of the doctrine of stare decisis that there should be in existence reliable reports of the decisions of the superior courts. There are several different series of law reports both in Scotland and in England, and the letters and numbers which appear in textbooks after the name of a case enable the account of the case to be traced in the appropriate series of reports.

At present the most important decisions of the Scottish courts are published in the series known as "*Session Cases.*" Each annual volume of *Session Cases* consists of three parts, the first devoted to Scottish cases decided by the House of Lords, the second to cases decided by the High Court of Justiciary and the third (by far the largest section of the volume) to cases decided by the Court of Session. Each of the three parts of the volume has its pages separately numbered, and so the case reference must indicate not only the year but also the court in which the case was decided. The first part of the volume is referred to by the letters "S.C.(H.L.)", the second part by the letters "J.C." (for "Justiciary Cases") and the third part by the letters "S.C." In each case the letters are preceded by the year and followed by the number of the page on which the report starts. Examples are:

(a) *Donoghue* v. *Stevenson*, 1932 S.C.(H.L.) 31;
(b) *H.M. Advocate* v. *Kirkwood*, 1939 J.C. 36; and
(c) *Smith* v. *Oliver*, 1911 S.C. 103.

Before 1906 there were five series of *Session Cases* which are referred to by the initial letter of the editor's surname:

First Series:
    Shaw . . . 16 volumes covering the period 1821–1838
Second Series:
    Dunlop . . 24 volumes covering the period 1838–1862
Third Series:
    Macpherson. . 11 volumes covering the period 1862–1873
Fourth Series:
    Rettie . . . 25 volumes covering the period 1873–1898
Fifth Series:
    Fraser . . . 8 volumes covering the period 1898–1906

Examples of references to these series are:
Countess of Dunmore v. *Alexander* (1830) 9 S. 190;
Wilson v. *Marquis of Breadalbane* (1859) 21 D. 957;
Goldston v. *Young* (1868) 7 M. 188;
Bruce v. *Smith* (1890) 17 R. 1000; and
Douglas & Co. v. *Stiven* (1900) 2 F. 575.

A reference to a House of Lords case is written thus:
Lord Elphinstone v. *Monkland Iron and Coal Co. Ltd.* (1886) 13 R. (H.L.) 98;

and a reference to a justiciary case thus:
Mortensen v. *Peters* (1906) 8 F.(J.) 93.

It will be observed that in references to these five series of *Session Cases* brackets appear round the dates of the cases; this is because the date is not an essential part of the reference.

Of earlier Scottish reports the best-known is Morison's *Dictionary of Decisions*, referred to by the letter "M." or by the abbreviation "Mor.," and consisting of twenty-two volumes, the pages of which are numbered continuously; references are to the page number only, *e.g.:*

Earl of Orkney v. *Vinfra* (1606) M. 16,481.

The *Dictionary* was compiled from decisions of the Court of Session in the period from 1540 to 1808.

Apart from the series of *Session Cases* there have been at various times other series of reports which include some Court of Session cases not included in the *Session Cases* and some of which include sheriff court cases. The only current series additional to the *Session Cases* is *The Scots Law Times*, which is issued as a weekly periodical and includes reports of cases in the House of Lords, the High Court of Justiciary, the Court of Session, the sheriff courts, the Scottish Land Court and the Lands Tribunal for Scotland. A reference to *Session Cases* is regarded in court as preferable to a reference to any other series of reports in which the case may also have been included. However, *The Scots Law Times* has advantages over the *Session Cases* in that it reports cases, including many Outer House cases, which do not appear in the *Session Cases,* and in that its reports are published at an earlier date than the *Session Cases. The Scots Law Times* dates from 1893. An example of a reference to a recent case is:

Alexander Stephen (Forth) Ltd. v. *J. J. Riley (U.K.) Ltd.,* 1976 S.L.T. 269 (O.H.).

References to English reports mentioned in this book include the following abbreviations:
A.C. for Appeal Cases;
Q.B. for Queen's Bench;
Ch. for Chancery;
W.L.R. for Weekly Law Reports;
All E.R. for All England Law Reports; and
T.L.R. for Times Law Reports.

The doctrine of judicial precedent does not mean that decisions of judges in earlier cases must always be followed, for:

(a) the precedent, if it is to be binding, must be a precedent "in point"; it must not be "distinguishable";

(b) unless it is the decision of a higher court, it is merely persuasive and not binding; and

(c) the only part of the precedent which is binding is the ratio decidendi ("reasoning of the decision").

It is for the court which is later called on to consider the precedent to decide whether the precedent is "in point" or "distinguishable" and whether binding or merely persuasive, and what the ratio decidendi of the precedent is.

(a) Precedents "in point"

A precedent is "in point" if there was decided in it the same question of law as arises in the case presently before the court. The phrase "on all fours with" is sometimes used instead of "in point."

The doctrine is concerned only with the question of law, not with questions of fact, although the facts of the two cases will be of the same general kind.

Much argument is sometimes devoted to the question of whether a precedent is in point or not. If the precedent is not exactly in point, the court will not be bound, although it may be persuaded, to apply it.

Where a court decides that a precedent is not in point, it is said to "distinguish" the precedent by pointing out the essential differences between the two cases.

(b) Binding and persuasive precedents

The authority of a precedent depends on the position occupied by the court which decided it.

On questions of Community law (e.g. interpretation of one of the treaties), the courts of the United Kingdom must follow any available precedents of the European Court of Justice.

On questions of Scots law, the precedents to be considered will very often include decisions of courts in other parts of the United Kingdom as well as decisions of courts in the Scottish judicial system. The general rule is that, provided the precedent is in point, it will be binding if it was decided by a superior court, but merely persuasive if it was decided by a court of equal or lower standing.

Precedents of the courts of England and of Northern Ireland are regarded by the Scottish courts as persuasive in varying degrees, according to the similarity between Scots and English or Irish law on the particular matter.

The doctrine of judicial precedent is stronger in the Scottish civil courts than in the other Scottish courts, probably because in the House of Lords, the final court of appeal for civil cases, judges of English training predominate.

Until 1966 it was generally accepted that, according to the decision in the English case of *London Street Tramways* v. *London County Council* [1898] A.C. 375, the House of Lords was bound by its own precedents pronounced in Scottish appeals, but in that year the Lord Chancellor stated that in future the House would depart from a previous decision if it considered that the right course ([1966] 3 All E.R. 77).

Decisions of the House of Lords in Scottish appeals are binding on all other civil courts in the Scottish judicial system.

In the Inner House of the Court of Session one Division normally regards itself as bound by a precedent either of itself or of the other Division. Where there are conflicts of precedents, as where one Division has not followed a precedent of itself or of the other Division, a "full bench" of the Court of Session or some other specially large court (*e.g.* a court of seven judges) is usually convened for the later case, and that larger court may quite freely overrule a precedent of either Division. A "full bench" is not bound by previous decisions of itself.

A Lord Ordinary in the Outer House of the Court of Session is bound to apply precedents of the Inner House, but not precedents of another Lord Ordinary (although he will treat them with respect).

A sheriff is bound by the same precedents as are binding on a Lord Ordinary, and he will treat with respect, but will not be bound to follow, decisions of Lords Ordinary and other sheriffs.

In the criminal courts the doctrine of judicial precedent is less rigid: the High Court of Justiciary when sitting as a court of appeal is not bound by its own previous decisions, although in practice a larger court would be convened for a case involving a doubtful precedent; a Lord of Justiciary sitting singly in the High Court when it is acting as a court of trial is not bound to follow an earlier decision of any other one Lord of Justiciary, although he will regard that decision as very persuasive; and similarly a sheriff is not bound by decisions of other trial judges (whether Lords of Justiciary or sheriffs), but normally follows these decisions.

The doctrine of judicial precedent has little place in the courts of special jurisdiction.

(c) Ratio decidendi

The ratio decidendi (often referred to simply as "the ratio") is the reason on which the earlier decision was based, the point of law which was necessary for the decision.

The ratio may be an instance of the application of a general principle of law to a particular set of facts, but it is not itself a general principle. The view of the deductive school of legal thought, to which Scots law historically belongs, is that the ratio for each individual case is deduced from an existing general principle, whereas the view of the inductive school, to which English law belongs, is that the ratio for each individual case contributes to the building up of a general principle out of numerous specific cases.

It is often a very difficult task to find the ratio of a case. This is especially so where a judge has followed two or more different trains of reasoning in reaching his decision, and where in an appeal court the opinions of the several judges (or of the majority of them if they are not unanimous) do not yield the same ratio. Some cases yield no useful or discoverable ratio at all.

A distinction must be drawn between ratio decidendi and obiter dicta. The phrases "obiter dictum" ("a thing said by the way") and "obiter dicta" ("things said by the way") are used of any statement or statements by the judges which go beyond the ratio. Obiter dicta are the remarks which are not essential for the disposal of the case.

An obiter dictum may be easily recognised if it is introduced by words such as, "The case would have been different if . . .", but sometimes it is difficult to distinguish with certainty between the ratio and obiter dicta, and this can lead to arguments in later cases.

The importance of the distinction lies in the fact that only the ratio is binding in later cases; obiter dicta are never more than persuasive, the degree of persuasiveness depending mainly on the standing and reputation of the judge who pronounced them.

Advantages and disadvantages of doctrine of judicial precedent

The main advantages of the doctrine of judicial precedent are:

(a) It helps to make the law certain. By consulting the law reports members of the public or their legal advisers can discover what the law is. Without this doctrine previous cases could not be relied on to the same extent.

(b) It helps to make the law consistent. There is less room than there would otherwise be for different decisions to be given in similar cases, and less likelihood of mistakes being made by the inferior courts. Equality of treatment is generally recognised as being an essential element of justice.

(c) It assists the orderly development of the law. Although in theory judges regard their function as being to declare, not to create, law, they do in fact make new law, often under camouflage of extending or limiting a principle established in a previous case. The existence of the doctrine of judicial precedent makes it easier for a legal adviser to predict how the law will be developed by the courts in subsequent cases.

On the other hand, the doctrine has these disadvantages:

(a) It tends to make the law rigid, so preventing it from keeping pace with changes in society. This may result in more legislation being required than would be necessary if case-law were more flexible.

(b) It leads to fine, and sometimes artificial, distinctions being drawn whenever a court feels compelled to avoid applying a binding precedent.

(c) There are practical difficulties in the operation of the doctrine; these include the difficulty of finding an apt precedent amongst the reported cases, and the difficulty of discovering the essential reasoning behind the decision in the precedent. It is unsatisfactory that the law should depend on the chance of a particular earlier case having been reported or on the chance of its essential reasoning having been made clear in the opinions delivered in it.

3. Authoritative Writings

The only authoritative writings are the institutional writings. Their authority is always less than that of legislation and case-law, and so the court must always apply the legislation or the binding precedent in the event of a conflict.

All the institutional writers belonged to earlier centuries, and all covered in their works either the whole of Scots law, or large areas of it.

With the great increase in the volume of legislation in modern times and with the development of the doctrine of judicial precedent since 1800, the scope of the authority attaching to institutional writings has considerably decreased. Where, however, there is nothing to the contrary in legislation or in decided cases, a statement in an institutional writing is still almost certain to be accepted as settling the law. Institutional writings are usually regarded as carrying an authority about equal to that of a Division of the Inner House of the Court of Session.

The importance of the institutional writers so far as Scots law of the present day is concerned is to be measured not so much by the actual references now made to their works as by the influence which their works have exerted in the past towards the development of the Scots law which exists today.

The most notable institutional writings are, in order of date, those of:

(a) Sir Thomas Craig;
(b) Sir George Mackenzie;
(c) Viscount Stair;
(d) Lord Bankton;
(e) Professor John Erskine;
(f) Baron David Hume; and
(g) Professor George Joseph Bell.

Although the number of institutional writers is very small, not all authorities agree as to the exact number; *e.g.* some authorities regard Henry Home, Lord Kames, whose best-known work was his *Principles of Equity* (1760), as institutional, and most authorities regard Archibald Alison, whose writings on criminal law were published in 1832 and 1833, as institutional, but these names are not always included in the list.

A writer may be an institutional writer without all his works being necessarily institutional writings: the writer's lesser works, or works not revised by him, or works published without his authority may not attain to institutional status: they are merely part of "legal literature," not "literary sources." Examples of non-institutional writings are Erskine's *Principles of the Law of Scotland* (published as a textbook for his students at Edinburgh University), Hume's *Lectures on Scots Law* (not finally revised or published by him), and possibly also Mackenzie's *The Institutions of the Law of Scotland*.

(a) Sir Thomas Craig

Sir Thomas Craig of Riccarton (1540–1607) was the author of the earliest institutional writing, *Jus Feudale* ("Feudal Law").

(b) Sir George Mackenzie

Sir George Mackenzie of Rosehaugh (1636–1691) distinguished himself at the Bar, in politics, and as a prose writer, and founded the Advocates' Library (now the National Library of Scotland). As criminal prosecutor in the days of the Covenanters he acquired the nickname "bluidy Mackenzie."

Of his many legal works, *The Laws and Customs of Scotland in Matters Criminal* (1678) is the one which is undoubtedly of institutional status.

(c) Viscount Stair

James Dalrymple, first Viscount Stair, (1619–1695) was prominent in politics and as a judge as well as being the most notable of all the institutional writers.

A native of Ayrshire, Stair devoted himself at first to the study and, after service in the army, to the teaching of philosophy at

Glasgow University, a fact which is of significance for the philosophical approach which he later adopted in his legal writings.

In 1647 he resigned from his post at Glasgow University and
went to Edinburgh, where he became an advocate in 1648, a judge
of the Court of Session under Cromwell's Protectorate in 1657, and
Lord President of the Court of Session in 1671.

Meantime, however, he took a leading part in the troubled
political and religious scene of his day, and it was in that connection
that he was ejected from his post as Lord President in 1681. He
withdrew to Leyden and devoted himself to writing.

While in Holland, he came to be much in favour with William
of Orange, and in 1688 he returned with that Prince. In the following year he was reappointed Lord President, and this time held the
office until his death in 1695.

The title of "Viscount Stair" was conferred on him in 1690.

Stair's institutional work, *The Institutions of the Law of Scotland*,
was published first in 1681 and in a revised and enlarged form in
1693. It is usually regarded as marking the creation of modern Scots
law. Stair drew on native customary law, feudal law, Roman law,
the law of nature, the Bible, and philosophy for his work, and used
the deductive approach, basing the rules of law on broad principles.
His originality and the emphasis which he laid on first principles
were of great value for the future systematic development of Scots
law.

While in retirement at Leyden, Stair sent to Edinburgh for
publication his *Decisions of the Court of Session from 1661 to 1681*,
which were the first series of law reports actually published in Scotland.

(d) Lord Bankton

The institutional writing of Andrew McDouall, Lord Bankton,
(1685–1760) was *An Institute of the Laws of Scotland*, published in
three volumes in 1751–53. It is notable for the comparisons which
it makes between Scots law and English law, and is a work of considerable value and authority. It was, however, soon overshadowed
by the slightly later work of Erskine.

(e) Professor John Erskine

John Erskine (1695–1768) was primarily an academic lawyer who
attained a place second only to that of Stair.

Born in the year of Stair's death, Erskine became an advocate
in 1719 and Professor of Scots law at Edinburgh University in 1737.

His institutional work, *An Institute of the Law of Scotland*, on
which he worked after his retirement from Edinburgh University,
was published posthumously in two volumes in 1773.

In contrast to Stair's *Institutions,* Erskine's *Institute* has the merits rather of lucidity than of originality, and of precise scholarship rather than of philosophic breadth. It is the final and most authoritative statement of the classical Scots law of Erskine's day, when the rules of the common law could still be deduced from first principles and were not yet overburdened with innumerable, and sometimes conflicting, precedents or with volumes of detailed legislation.

(f) Baron David Hume

Baron David Hume (1756–1838), a Baron of Exchequer, was, like Erskine, an academic lawyer. He was Professor of Scots law at Edinburgh University from 1786 to 1822.

Hume's standing as an institutional writer depends, like that of Mackenzie, on his writing on the criminal law: his *Commentaries on the Law of Scotland respecting Crimes* were published in two volumes in 1797.

(g) Professor George Joseph Bell

George Joseph Bell (1770–1843) became an advocate in 1791, and in 1822 succeeded Hume as Professor of Scots law at Edinburgh University, a post which he held until his death.

In addition to his writings he took a prominent part in the improving of Court of Session procedure.

Bell's two institutional works were his *Commentaries on the Law of Scotland and on the Principles of Mercantile Jurisprudence* and his *Principles of the Law of Scotland.*

The *Commentaries* were published in 1810, and were an enlarged version of a treatise on the law of bankruptcy in Scotland published by Bell some years earlier. The work met the need, becoming evident with the expansion of commerce at the time, for an authoritative and systematic treatment of mercantile (*i.e.* commercial) law. Bell's aim was to harmonise the principles of the "law merchant" (*i.e.* the body of law built up from customs generally and continuously recognised in trading) with the fundamental principles of Scots law.

Bell's other institutional work, his *Principles,* was originally published in 1829 as a textbook for students and was later revised and enlarged.

Bell also published other legal textbooks, including a case-book for students.

4. Custom

Custom as an authoritative source of new law must be distinguished from custom which forms part of the common law and also from custom which merely incorporates some term into a contract.

(a) Custom forming part of the common law

The historical, as distinct from the formal, source of the common law (*i.e.* the law other than statutory law) lies in the customs of the people which have been so generally and consistently recognised and given effect to over the centuries that they have acquired the force of law. Thus, the common law is described by Stair as "our ancient and immemorial customs."

There are examples of such customs in the legal rights of a widow and of children in a deceased person's estate, in the legal relationship between landlord and tenant, and in many other branches of the law.

Customs forming part of the common law do not require to be proved in court, since the courts are considered to know what the common law is. The customs are said to be "judicially noticed." When a court is called upon to apply some part of the common law which has not been applied in any previous case, the function of the court is, in theory at least, merely to *declare* what the existing common law on the matter is, not to create any new law: the common law is regarded as deriving its original binding force, not from any court decision, but from its recognition as law within the community.

It is now rare for a court to be called on to give effect to custom as a *formal* source of part of the common law, for most of the customs which are of legal force have already been given effect to in past decisions or are stated in the institutional writings, with the result that the doctrine of judicial precedent or the authority of the institutional writing is their formal source; further, many customs which would otherwise form part of the common law have been, expressly or by implication, recognised by Acts of Parliament and either reinforced or abolished or modified in some way by a statutory provision.

(b) Custom as an authoritative source of new law

This differs from the customs which have already been absorbed into the common law in that it requires to be proved before the courts will recognise it and give effect to it as law.

Certain conditions must be fulfilled: the custom must:

(i)   have been acquiesced in for so long as to justify the belief that it has been accepted as law; no precise time is laid down, and the length of time will vary according to circumstances;

(ii)   be definite and certain; if it is vague or if there are too few instances of its being applied, it will not have the force of law;

(iii)   be fair and reasonable; there is an instance of a custom which failed this test in *Bruce* v. *Smith* (1890) 17 R. 1000: landlords in Shetland claimed that by custom they were entitled to one-third of the proceeds of whales killed on the seashore; the court held that this custom was unreasonable since the landlords made no return for the exaction;

(iv)   be in some way an exception to, or a qualification of, the general law, without being inconsistent with any absolute statutory or common law rule; it may, for instance, be confined to a particular locality as is the special form of land tenure enjoyed by the "kindly tenants of Lochmabon."

It can be seen from these conditions that custom is a very limited source of new law.

(c)   Custom incorporating a term into a contract

It often happens in commercial contracts that the parties use words and expressions in a special sense recognised by usage of the particular trade, or do not express the terms of the contract in full, leaving unmentioned certain terms which are generally recognised by usage of that trade.

Custom may then be looked to by the courts either to assist in the interpretation of the contract, or to introduce an implied term into the contract.

This type of custom is not law at all, but merely part of the agreement between the parties; so far as the courts are concerned, it has no binding force, and so a court may hold that, in spite of some trade usage, the parties have chosen to use words and expressions in their ordinary sense or have chosen to negative a term which would normally be implied.

There is an instance of custom being looked to by the court to assist in the interpretation of a phrase of otherwise doubtful meaning in *Douglas & Co.* v. *Stiven* (1900) 2 F. 575: a contract for the sale of timber contained a provision that if a dispute arose it was to be settled by "arbitration in the customary manner of the timber trade"; it was proved that the most usual kind of arbitration in the timber trade was for each party to choose an arbiter and for the two arbiters to appoint an oversman who would decide the question if the two arbiters failed to agree; the court found that the parties had to be considered as having had that mode of arbitration in view when they made their contract.

The type of custom which merely incorporates a term into a contract differs from customs which are law in that the custom must be proved to have been within the knowledge of the contracting parties. So far as customs which are law are concerned, there is no need to prove to the court that the parties knew of the existence of the custom, since everyone is presumed to know the law; the maxim applicable is ignorantia juris neminem excusat ("ignorance of the law excuses no-one"), which means that no-one can ever put forward ignorance of the law as a valid defence.

5. Equity

In England there was, and to some extent still is, a distinction between law and equity: until 1875 England had a system of courts of equity distinct from its system of courts of common law.

In Scotland there has never been a corresponding separation between law and equity: the Scottish courts have always administered law and equity together.

The term "equity," therefore, does not have the same technical associations in Scots law as it does in English law. It is used in two senses in Scots law:

(a) In its broad sense "equity" means "fairness," "reasonableness," or "natural justice."

In this sense it has been in the past and is still a very important, although in many cases not a very obvious, source of law. It has been responsible for the granting by the courts of remedies for wrongs; *e.g.* the remedies of "specific implement" and of "interdict" are available where the court thinks that it is just and appropriate that a person who is in breach of contract should be required to perform his part of the contract instead of merely paying damages. Further, in connection with breach of contract, equity prevents a party from exacting exorbitant penalties from the other party even although that other party may have taken no objection to the penalties at the time when the contract was entered into; in such a situation equity is limiting the strict rule of law that the courts will give effect to the terms agreed on by the parties; application of the strict rule would in the circumstances be unjust.

These instances of the force of equity have for long been accepted as part of the common law. Equity is also still, however, an unexhausted source of new law: in many situations the common law requires a judge to exercise his discretion as to the way in which he applies the law, and in doing so he will have regard for equity; even in the interpretation and application of statutory provisions, although the court will be bound to give effect to a rule which is stated in absolute terms, however harsh, rigid, and inequitable it may be, there are numerous statutory provisions which expressly require the court to do what appears to it to be "just and equitable," or "reasonable," or to do what it "sees fit," and any such expressions give room for the operation of equity as a source of the law to be applied in the particular case.

(b) In a more specific sense "equity" refers to the nobile officium ("equitable power"), according to which the Court of Session and, to a less notable extent, the High Court of Justiciary may, as a last resort, provide a remedy where justice requires it and where none is otherwise available.

The nobile officium of the Court of Session is especially important in the law of trusts: for instance, under the nobile officium, that court may appoint new trustees whenever the administration of the trust makes that necessary, and in a charitable trust, if the truster's intention cannot be given effect to exactly as he directed, that court may arrange for the trust funds to be applied in a way which is as close as possible to the intention (a cy près ("similar") scheme).

Apart from trusts, however, situations in which the Court of Session will exercise its nobile officium are rare; there must generally be some precedent for its exercise in the particular situation. There are such precedents in cases where it is necessary to supply a casus omissus ("an omitted event") in a statute or document.

There is a casus omissus, also referred to as a casus improvisus ("an unforeseen event"), when circumstances arise which were not foreseen by the persons who drew up the statute or document in question, and for which there was, therefore, as a result of this accidental oversight, no provision made. The nobile officium enables the Court of Session to supply the type of provision which would have been expressly included in the statute or document if the eventuality had been foreseen; it does not entitle the court to make any substantial extension or other alteration of an express provision.

An example of a casus omissus being supplied in a statute is given in *Roberts, Petitioner* (1901) 3 F. 779: Roberts was a bankrupt who had done everything necessary for his discharge except that he had not made the formal statutory declaration about having fully and fairly disclosed his assets and about not having entered into any secret arrangements with his creditors; having become insane, he was unable to make that declaration; in these very special circumstances, which were not covered by the statute, the Court of Session, in the exercise of its nobile officium, dispensed with the declaration, with the result that Roberts obtained his discharge.

Similarly, in *The Law Society of Scotland, Petitioners*, 1974 S.L.T. (Notes) 66, where a notice in the *London Gazette*, required under the Bankruptcy (Scotland) Act 1913, had not been inserted timeously because of an industrial dispute in London, the nobile officium was successfully invoked to remedy the situation.

6. Extraneous Sources

These are all other sources to which a court may refer if it obtains no guidance from sources 1 to 5 above.

Extraneous sources are secondary, as distinct from primary, sources of law.

The main extraneous sources are:

(a) **Obiter dicta**

See p. 98, above.

(b) **Legal literature**

Legal literature, as distinct from literary sources of law (the institutional writings), consists of all the non-institutional works of the institutional writers and all other writings on law including text-books, reference books, periodicals and articles.

So far as the courts are concerned legal literature is composed merely of statements of what the various authors believe the law to be. In theory the courts are quite free to ignore any writing which is merely part of legal literature, and to decide a case in a way which proves to have been wrong any statement in legal literature, however highly regarded the author may have been.

In practice, however, the courts are influenced by legal literature, and often give their approval of views expressed by authors who are held in high regard.

The degree of influence exerted by a work within legal literature varies according to the reputation of the author, the nature of the work (*e.g.* whether it is comprehensive, scholarly, up to date, etc.), and the extent to which it has been relied on in practice.

There was formerly said to be a rule that a work could not be quoted in court unless its author either was dead, or had been appointed a judge, but this rule is not strictly observed today, and so works of high reputation by living authors, and, to an increasing extent, articles by academic lawyers in legal periodicals are in practice now referred to in court and may be accepted by the court as containing a true statement of the law.

(c) **Foreign law**

The foreign law which is most likely to be looked at first is English law, and there are many matters, especially in the fields of commercial and industrial law, on which assistance may legitimately enough be drawn from that source. However, there is an ever-present danger that English law will be allowed to exert an influence which is out of keeping with the Scottish legal tradition; this applies especially to those branches of the law which have their roots in the

Roman period of Scottish legal history and are of less recent growth than most of commercial and industrial law.

Traditionally, Roman law is the appropriate foreign law for the courts to look to for guidance on the long-established and non-statutory branches of the law.

Other foreign systems of law may occasionally give assistance. These may be either of the Anglo-American school (*e.g.* the law of the United States or of Commonwealth countries), or of the Roman school (*e.g.* the Roman-Dutch law of South Africa or the law of continental countries). The fact that the United Kingdom is now a member of the European Communities makes it especially appropriate to look to the law of other member states of the Communities for assistance on economic matters.

(d) The judge's conscience

Where no assistance is available from any other source at all, the judge will rely on his own conscience. The essence of the question before him will be "What does justice require in this situation?" and his answer will be based on the ideal of justice as he sees it.

Further Reading

David M. Walker, *The Scottish Legal System*

T. B. Smith, *A Short Commentary on the Law of Scotland*

Gloag and Henderson, *Introduction to the Law of Scotland*

The Stair Society, *An Introductory Survey of the Sources and Literature of Scots Law* (various authors)

Lawrence Collins, *European Community Law in the United Kingdom* (Butterworths).

CHAPTER 4

INTERPRETATION OF LEGISLATION

INTERPRETATION (or "construction") of legislation is the process by which the courts (or a legal adviser, if the matter has not reached the courts) ascertain whether a particular statutory provision applies to a given set of facts, and, if so, what effect it has.

Where a question as to the interpretation of legislation of the European Communities arises in a case before a national court, it *may* be referred to the European Court of Justice at Luxembourg, and *must* be so referred if the national court is one from which no further appeal can be made under the national law. In the European Court the approach to interpretation is predominantly "telelogical" or "purposive," *i.e.* the Court looks above all to the principles and objectives of the treaties governing the European Communities, and sees its role as the dynamic one of contributing to the development of the Communities.

This chapter is confined to the interpretation of United Kingdom legislation (whether Acts of Parliament or delegated legislation).

Interpretation of legislation is always a question of law, not a question of fact. It is, therefore, always to be decided by the judge, not by a jury, and to be decided after legal argument, not after the hearing of evidence.

In most cases (ideally in all cases) the meaning of the statutory provision will be clear. The draftsmen, who are responsible for the actual wording used in statutes and in subordinate legislation, are at great pains to ensure that the language is accurate and unambiguous, and that all possible situations are covered by it. However, language, from its very nature, does not have the precision of mathematics, and inevitably circumstances arise which were not foreseen by the law-making authority or by the draftsman. Difficulties can also arise from the complexity of modern legislation and the prolixity of its wording. In such cases it is for the court, when required to do so for the decision of a particular matter brought before it, to interpret, or construe (hence the word "construction") the statutory provision in accordance with the principles of statutory interpretation.

These principles of statutory interpretation have not been codified and, with the exception of the Interpretation Act 1978, are all part of the common law.

The Interpretation Act 1978 gives only very limited assistance in matters of interpretation. It was passed to consolidate the Interpretation Act 1889 (which it repealed) and a few other statutory provisions concerned with the interpretation and operation of Acts of Parliament; it also includes some minor but useful amendments suggested by the Law Commission and the Scottish Law Commission in June 1978 (*The Interpretation Bill*, Law Com. No. 90, Scot. Law Com. No. 53; Cmnd. 7235). It defines some expressions which are often used in legislation, *e.g.* "month," "Rules of Court," and "writing," and makes some provision for keeping the wording shorter than it would otherwise be, *e.g.* the provision that the masculine includes the feminine and the singular includes the plural (so that it is not necessary, for instance, to have "he or she or they," but only "he"), and the provision that the word "person" includes a body of persons, corporate or unincorporate (*e.g.* a company or a partnership). These definitions and provisions, however, apply only if there is no contrary indication in the particular piece of legislation which the court is interpreting.

In 1969 the Law Commission and the Scottish Law Commission published a major report on interpretation of legislation in which they made some proposals for reform of this branch of law (*The Interpretation of Statutes*, Law. Com. No. 21, Scot. Law Com. No. 11, 1968-69 H.C.P. 256). The Commissions did not recommend any comprehensive codification of the principles of interpretation, but suggested that legislation be introduced to clarify certain aspects of interpretation and to make some innovations which the Commissions considered desirable.

The main principles of the common law applied by the courts in the interpretation of legislation may be outlined under these headings:

1. general approaches to interpretation;
2. internal aids to interpretation;
3. external aids to interpretation; and
4. presumptions applicable in interpretation.

1.   *GENERAL APPROACHES TO INTERPRETATION*

It is the duty of the courts to give effect to the intention of Parliament as that intention is expressed in the statutory provision. Judges are not entitled to usurp the law-making function of Parliament (or of the subordinate authority to which Parliament has delegated some of its own power) either by extending a statutory provision to some situation which it clearly does not cover or by refusing to apply a statutory provision which has been enacted in unambiguous language. This applies not only where the judges disapprove of what has been, or not been, enacted but also where they believe that Parliament's *real* intention was different from Parliament's intention *as expressed in the statutory provision*; the judges must always give effect to the actual words of the enactment.

Where, however, Parliament's intention has not been made perfectly clear by the language used, there is room for some difference of approach in interpretation. The two extremes are the literal approach and the liberal approach. The approach adopted depends on the nature of the statutory provision and also on the inclination of the individual judge.

Where the literal approach is favoured, the language is strictly and narrowly construed, and in no way extended even although the result may be contrary to the common-sense idea of what Parliament's intention was. This literal approach may be supported by the argument that if Parliament intended to cover the particular situation, then it would have done so by using more ample language.

There is an instance of the literal approach in the interpretation given to the Married Women's Property (Scotland) Act 1881 in the case of *Eddington* v. *Robertson* (1895) 22 R. 430:

The common law of Scotland gave widowers and widows certain legal rights in the estates of their deceased spouses, and amongst these legal rights was jus relictae ("right of the widow"), which was the right of a widow to a certain share of the moveable estate (*i.e.* property other than land and buildings) of her deceased husband. At common law the widower had no legal right in his deceased wife's estate corresponding to the widow's jus relictae, but by the Married Women's Property (Scotland) Act 1881 he was given a corresponding right, known as "jus relicti" ("right of the widower").

At common law, however, legal rights arose not only on the death of a husband or wife but also on a divorce, the guilty spouse being treated as dead with the result that the innocent spouse had an immediate claim to a share of the guilty spouse's property. The Act of 1881 did not expressly provide for an innocent husband to have jus relicti in his divorced wife's estate, and in *Eddington* v. *Robertson* the court had to decide whether Colonel Eddington, who had obtained a decree of divorce on the ground of desertion, was entitled to jus relicti as a result of the divorce.

The words which the court had to interpret were (s. 6):

"The husband of any woman who may die domiciled in Scotland shall take by operation of law the same share and interest in her moveable estate which is taken by a widow in her deceased husband's moveable estate."

The argument for Colonel Eddington was that the word "die" had to be interpreted as including "be divorced" because at common law divorce was in this connection considered to be equivalent to natural death.

The court, however, giving a restrictive interpretation to the statutory words, held that jus relicti did not arise on divorce, but only on actual death.

Had a liberal approach been adopted, the court might have held that Parliament had intended to introduce for the widower a right which would, in every way, have corresponded to a widow's common law jus relictae.

Where a liberal approach is favoured, stress is laid on the general policy underlying the statutory provision rather than on the words actually used. This approach may result in a more sensible application of the statutory provision, but even where a judge adopts this general approach he must consider primarily the actual words used and he is not free to read into the provision words which are plainly not there.

Liberal interpretation is appropriate for Scots Acts, which are often restricted to the enactment, in no more than seven or eight lines, of some general principle. There is less scope for liberal interpretation in modern legislation, where the wording is full and detailed but instances do occur.

One of these instances is the interpretation of legislation applying to trade unions. The Trade Union Act 1871 did not expressly confer legal personality on trade unions, but after the passing of that Act the courts in a series of cases interpreted the Act as having conferred on trade unions sufficient legal personality for certain purposes, notably for the purpose of being made liable for wrongs done by them (*Taff Vale Ry. Co.* v. *Amalgamated Society of Ry. Servants* [1901] A.C. 426) and for the purpose of being sued for breach of contract (*Bonsor* v. *Musicians' Union* [1956] A.C. 104). (The position under the Trade Union and Labour Relations Act 1974 is similar: a trade union, though not a body corporate, has most of the attributes of such a body.)

Had a literal approach been adopted, the courts might have held that if Parliament had intended to confer that degree of personality on trade unions it would have expressly provided for it in the Act of 1871.

The difference in approach between the two extremes of literal on the one hand and liberal on the other hand is sometimes considered as being represented by three "rules" of interpretation. These "rules" are:

(a) the "literal" rule, which stresses the actual words used;

(b) the "mischief" rule, according to which the court takes account not only of the actual words used but also of the "mischief" (the evil or difficulty) which Parliament intended to remedy by the statutory provision; and

(c) the "golden" rule, which is a modified form of the "mischief" rule, and which seeks to give effect to the general intention of Parliament by assigning to the words used their ordinary and natural meanings except where this would lead to obvious absurdity or inconsistency, in which case the words are to be liberally interpreted so far as is necessary for the purpose of avoiding the absurdity or inconsistency.

The Law Commissions were critical of excessively literal interpretation and favoured the adoption by the courts of a more liberal approach than is now customary. They recommended that provision be made by statute to emphasise the importance of the general purpose underlying legislation, and proposed an extension of the range of materials to be consulted in order to ascertain that general purpose.

2. INTERNAL AIDS TO INTERPRETATION

The phrase "internal aids to interpretation" is used here to mean the assistance which may be derived in interpretation from within the limits of the statutory provision itself. Internal aids may be considered under three headings:

(a) interpretation sections;

(b) reference to context; and

(c) authoritative parts of statutes.

(a) Interpretation Sections

Many modern Acts include, usually near the end, an interpretation section, which gives a list of definitions of words used in the Act and provides that in the Act, unless the context otherwise requires, the words are to have the meanings assigned to them by the interpretation section.

The usual meanings of words may thus be extended or restricted by provisions in the interpretation section that certain words are to "include" or "exclude," respectively, particular cases.

If some special meaning assigned to a word by the interpretation section does not fit the context in which the word is used, then the word will be interpreted in that context according to its ordinary meaning.

(b) Reference to Context

When a word has not been defined in any interpretation section or when the definition of the word in the interpretation section does not fit the context, then the word must be interpreted according to its context.

If some unusual meaning had been intended, that would presumably have been covered by an interpretation section. Therefore, where the court is left without the assistance of an interpretation section, it will in the first place consider the possibility of giving the words the usual meaning which they had at the date of the Act. The words may be ordinary or technical, and they will, so far as the context permits, be given their usual ordinary or their usual technical meanings, respectively.

For instance, the word "shall" in a statutory provision normally has the meaning of "must," and so if a statute provides that a person "shall" do something he will be bound to do it; the word "shall" is "imperative" (*i.e.* it expresses a command). On the other hand, if the provision is that a person "may" do something or that "it shall be lawful" for him to do something, then he will normally be regarded as having a choice in the matter and not as being under any obligation to do the thing; the words are in that case merely "permissive" or "empowering" (*i.e.* they merely give him the necessary permission or power). The context, however, may indicate that a different meaning from the usual one was intended; *e.g.* where permissive or empowering words occur in a statute which is intended to confer some benefit on the general public, such as a statute dealing with the upkeep of highways, the permissive or empowering words may be interpreted as being imperative, with the result that the authority concerned will be held bound to exercise the powers conferred by the Act.

Reference to context involves both:

(i) consideration of the immediate context, *i.e.* the section, subsection, etc., in which the word being interpreted occurs; and

(ii) consideration of the whole Act, or at least of a Part of the whole Act.

(i) Reference to immediate context

Three "canons of construction" (rules of interpretation), all commonly expressed in the form of Latin maxims, apply in this connection. They are:

1. ejusdem generis ("of the same kind");
2. noscitur a sociis (literally, "it is known from its companions");
and
3. expressio unius est exclusio alterius ("expression of one is
exclusion of the other").

1. *Ejusdem generis*

Where a statute gives a list of items, all of the same kind, and
adds to the list general words such as "and other things," the general
words are interpreted as being limited to items of the same kind as
those specifically mentioned.

For instance, in *Henretty* v. *Hart* (1885) 13 R.(J.) 9, the court
had to construe a statutory provision which prohibited betting in any
"house, office, room, or other place." The question was whether
Henretty had been properly convicted under the provision for having
permitted betting at a race-course of which he was tenant. Applying ·
the ejusdem generis canon of construction, the court held that a race-
course was not covered by the statutory prohibition because it was
not a place of the same kind as house, office and room.

This canon of construction does not apply where the general
words are clearly intended to be absolutely general (*e.g.* "any other
place whatsoever"); nor does it apply where the particular items
listed do not all belong to one recognisable genus ("class") (*e.g.* in
Crichton Stuart v. *Ogilvie*, 1914 S.C. 888, the court, in interpreting the
phrase "building, feuing, planting or other purposes" as used in the
Agricultural Holdings (Scotland) Act 1908, held that, since building,
feuing and planting were not all of one genus, the words "other
purposes" in that context covered *any* other purpose).

2. *Noscitur a sociis*

According to this canon of construction where a word is vague
or ambiguous the accompanying words may fix the meaning to be
given to the word in the particular context. The canon has a limiting
effect similar to that of the ejusdem generis canon.

3. *Expressio unius est exclusio alterius*

The effect of this canon is that where express mention is made of
one item, and no mention is made of another similar or associated
item, the statutory provision is interpreted as not applying to the
item not mentioned, the presumption being that Parliament would
have expressly mentioned the second item also if it had intended the
statutory provision to apply to that item.

(ii) Reference to whole Act

Reference to the whole Act must be made to ensure that the

interpretation given to a word in its immediate context is not inconsistent with other provisions in the Act. For example, one section may provide for notice to be "given," without making it clear whether the notice is to be written, and another section of the same Act may refer to the notice being "left" at a particular place; the court would probably infer that the notice had to be in writing, because the word "left" would not be used of a notice given by word of mouth.

Moreover, apart from any possible inconsistency, consideration of the Act as a whole may reveal the general policy underlying it, and knowledge of that policy may assist in the interpretation of some particular word in its context.

In the case of Acts which are divided into Parts, it is particularly relevant to consider other provisions included in the same Part.

(c) Authoritative Parts of Statutes

The courts are entitled to look at the following parts of statutes for assistance in interpretation:

(a) the title (*i.e.* the formal long title), which may indicate the scope of the Act as a whole;

(b) the preamble (if there is one), which may state the reason for, and the general policy behind, the Act;

(c) headings, which are sometimes attached to Parts of, or to groups of sections in, an Act and which may give guidance in the interpretation of words within the Part or within the group of sections concerned; and

(d) schedules, although a mere form in a schedule will not be allowed to limit a provision in the body of the Act.

On the other hand, the courts are not entitled to look at the following for assistance in interpretation:

(a) the short title;

(b) punctuation, since punctuation is regarded as not being part of the Act at all; and

(c) marginal notes, which are printed in the margin at the beginning of each section and indicate very briefly the scope of the section.

However, the Law Commissions have recommended that the courts should be allowed to look for assistance in interpretation to the short title, punctuation and marginal notes, as well as to any other indications included in the officially printed copies of the Acts, and varying views have since been expressed in the House of Lords as to the guidance which may be obtained from headings, punctuation and marginal notes (*Reg.* v. *Schildkamp* [1971] A.C. 1).

3. EXTERNAL AIDS TO INTERPRETATION

The phrase "external aids to interpretation" is used here to mean the assistance which may be derived in interpretation from outside the statutory provision itself.

The courts are not entitled to look at what may be described as "the Parliamentary history" of the Act, such as reports of royal commissions and of committees appointed to examine the need for legislation on some particular subject, White Papers (which outline proposed legislation), *Hansard* (the full and official report of all debates and other proceedings in Parliament), and other papers circulated in Parliament at the time when the Act is being passed. None of these is considered an authoritative and reliable guide as to what Parliament finally intended to enact.

It is in this connection that the Law Commissions have made their most striking proposals for reform. While they considered that *Hansard* should still not be admitted as an external aid in interpretation, they recommended that the courts should take into account reports of royal commissions, of committees and of other bodies, Parliamentary documents concerned with the subject-matter of the legislation, and any other document which might be declared by the Act itself to be a relevant document for the purposes of interpretation. The Law Commissions seek to justify this extension of external aids by the argument that it is right for the courts to be able to consider any material which was in the contemplation of Parliament at the time when the statute was passed. The Commissions' recommendations have, however, been much criticised.

The present external aids may be considered under four headings:

    (a)   other statutes;

    (b)   the common law and decided cases;

    (c)   usage and contemporanea expositio ("contemporary interpretation"); and

    (d)   dictionaries and textbooks.

(a) Other Statutes

Other statutes in pari materia ("on the same subject-matter") may be looked to for assistance in interpretation. Statutes are considered to be in pari materia only if they are so closely related to one another that together they form one system of legislation. Statutes which are on merely similar subject-matter are of no assistance.

The statute being interpreted may have been passed in order to amend an earlier Act which was considered unsatisfactory, and the court may be aided in the interpretation of the amending Act by a knowledge of the provisions of the earlier Act.

Acts passed later than the one being interpreted may aid the court where a later Act has the express purpose of removing some doubt or ambiguity in the Act being interpreted or where a later Act impliedly removes the doubt or ambiguity by adding some new provision which is inconsistent with one of the alternative interpretations of the earlier Act.

(b) The Common Law and Decided Cases

Some defect in the common law, which may or may not have been brought to light by a court decision, may have led to the passing of the Act, and knowledge of the previously existing common law may, therefore, be of assistance to the court in interpretation of the statute which was intended to remedy the defect.

The court may also derive assistance from decided cases which were concerned with the interpretation of the same statutory provision, or with the interpretation of a corresponding provision in a statute in pari materia.

There is a presumption, which is not, however, a very strong one, that, if Parliament uses in an Act a word which has already been interpreted by the courts, that word has the same meaning in the new statutory provision. This presumption applies especially in connection with consolidating Acts: it may be that some provision in an earlier Act has been interpreted in a certain way by the court, and that Parliament, while repealing that earlier Act, substantially re-enacts its provisions in the consolidating Act; it will then be appropriate for the court, in interpretation of the consolidating Act, to have regard to the earlier decisions on the repealed, but re-enacted, provisions, since Parliament has by the re-enactment impliedly approved of the court's interpretation. For instance, it is appropriate for a court interpreting the Companies Act 1948 to be guided by decided cases in which the corresponding provisions of earlier, and now repealed, Companies Acts were interpreted.

In the case of statutes common to Scotland and England the court is entitled to look at English decided cases as well as at Scottish decided cases. This applies especially to matters such as taxation where uniform interpretation of the statutory provisions throughout the two countries is obviously desirable. Assistance may sometimes also be derived from English decided cases where Scotland and England are subject to distinct, but corresponding, statutes; for instance, English cases concerned with the interpretation of the Town and Country Planning Act 1971 may give guidance to the Scottish courts in the interpretation of the Town and Country Planning (Scotland) Act 1972.

(c) Usage and Contemporanea Expositio

If the meaning of a statute is clear, any usage to the contrary is of no avail, but if the meaning is doubtful then the court is entitled to interpret the statute in the way which is consistent with usage, *i.e.* with long-established practice generally believed to have been justified by the terms of the statute.

In contemporanea expositio (see p. 81, above) the court interprets a statute in the way in which it was interpreted by the courts immediately after it was passed.

Usage and contemporanea expositio are resorted to in the interpretation of Scots Acts and other old statutes, but are seldom of importance in the interpretation of modern statutes.

(d) Dictionaries and Textbooks

Dictionaries and textbooks are not authoritative, but the court may find them helpful. A standard dictionary may be consulted to discover the ordinary or technical meaning of a word, and a view expressed in a highly-regarded textbook as to the effect of a statutory provision may be adopted by the court, especially if the statute in question is an old one and the writer's view has long been accepted as correct.

4. *PRESUMPTIONS APPLICABLE IN INTERPRETATION*

Certain presumptions, some of greater weight than others, are applied by the courts in the interpretation of legislation. These presumptions can always be excluded by contrary provisions, express or implied, in the legislation itself.

The Law Commissions regarded presumptions as of doubtful value, although useful in a limited number of areas if their scope were precisely defined.

The main presumptions are:

(a) It is presumed that Parliament did not intend to infringe *international law*. Statutes are, therefore, if possible, interpreted in a way which is consistent with treaties made with foreign countries. The Law Commissions recommended that this presumption be given statutory force.

(b) It is presumed that *fundamental principles of constitutional law and of common law* will be altered only by express provisions in an Act, not by mere implication.

(c) It is presumed that the jurisdiction of the *ordinary courts* is not excluded, and that the citizen may bring an action in connection with the statute before these courts in the usual way. Therefore, if

Parliament intends the right of recourse to the ordinary courts to be limited in any way, or to be replaced by a right of appeal to an administrative tribunal or other administrative authority or to arbitration, that intention should be made express.

(d) It is presumed that a statutory provision, if properly interpreted, will be *workable*. Therefore, the courts will prefer an interpretation which fulfils some purpose to an interpretation which would result in the provision's having no effect.

(e) It is presumed that a statute does not have *retrospective* effect, *i.e.* that it affects only future cases and not past ones. Occasionally, Parliament considers that retrospective legislation is necessary or justified; *e.g.* the War Damage Act 1965 was passed to abolish retrospectively the common law right of a subject to compensation from the Crown for destruction of property by the Crown in connection with the outbreak of war; in particular, the Act had the effect of setting aside the right established by the House of Lords in *Burmah Oil Co. (Burma Trading) Ltd.* v. *Lord Advocate*, 1964 S.C. (H.L.) 117.

(f) It is presumed that a statute does not apply to the *Crown*, or to Crown officials, or Crown departments. If, therefore, Parliament intends that a statute is to be binding on the Crown, this will be expressly provided for in the statute. An example of an Act with such a provision is the Road Traffic Act 1972.

(g) In statutes which impose a *penalty* or create a *criminal offence* it is presumed that mens rea ("guilty intention") is necessary before a person will be liable to the penalty or guilty of the offence, mere ignorance or carelessness not being enough. However, in many modern statutes the words used rebut this presumption. The Law Commissions considered this an area in which a precisely-defined presumption would be useful.

(h) In statutes which *interfere with an individual's freedom or his property rights* it is presumed that Parliament did not intend the provisions to extend to any cases other than those expressly covered. A strict interpretation is therefore given to statutes which restrict a person's liberty, or which impose penalties or taxes, and if a statute authorises the taking away of an individual's property, as by compulsory purchase, there is a presumption that compensation is to be paid.

Further Reading

David M. Walker, *The Scottish Legal System*

Gloag and Henderson, *Introduction to the Law of Scotland*

CHAPTER 5

BRANCHES OF LAW

THE basic division of legal science is into six branches:

1. legal history;
2. jurisprudence;
3. comparative law;
4. public international law;
5. supranational law; and
6. state or municipal law.

It must, however, be noted:

(a) that law is a unity, and so no rigid division of it can ever be completely satisfactory; not all authorities agree as to how a particular legal subject is to be classified, and the greater the number of subdivisions made, the more overlapping there will be;

(b) that the practical problem with which a legal practitioner or a court has to deal will not necessarily fall neatly into one or other of the various divisions and sub-divisions, but may involve a consideration of several of them; however, a knowledge of the structure of the law will assist the practitioner or the court in tracing the law to be applied; and

(c) that the subjects studied by students are not all in their own right either divisions or sub-divisions of legal science; there is no more obvious illustration of that point than the subject "General Principles of Scots Law," which draws some of its topics from legal history and jurisprudence, and most of its topics from selected subdivisions of state or municipal law.

1. *LEGAL HISTORY*

The purpose of legal history is to explain how law and legal institutions, such as courts, have developed over the centuries.

So far as Scots law is concerned, the legal history which is most worthy of study is that of western Europe. In that legal history early Celtic law, Anglo-Saxon law, feudal law, the law merchant (*i.e.* the

121

law applied in trading transactions between merchants), and maritime law (of which the earliest traces are found in the Mediterranean
countries) are all of considerable importance, but the dominant
positions are held by:

    (a)   Roman law;

    (b)   canon law; and

    (c)   English law.

(a) Roman Law

Roman law (also called "Civil law") was the law first of the city
of Rome itself (the foundation of which is traditionally dated 753
B.C.), and then of the Roman empire, which fell in western Europe
in the fifth century A.D. but continued in the east until the capture
of Constantinople by the Turks in 1453.

Roman law is clearly a subject worthy of study in its own right
since it was applied and developed over such a long period and such
a wide area. It is, undoubtedly, one of the greatest legacies of the
ancient to the modern world.

Other reasons which make Roman law still an appropriate
subject of study at the present day are:

(i) Legal thinking and legal terminology throughout Europe are
based on Roman law.

(ii) Roman law is a key to the understanding of the many modern
systems of law which are derived from it. These include not only the
systems of law of continental countries, such as France and Germany,
but also those of overseas territories which were originally colonies
of, or were otherwise under the influence of, continental countries;
the French, for instance, took their law to Quebec, and the Dutch
theirs to South Africa. The common derivation of these many
modern systems from Roman law facilitates mutual understanding
among lawyers of the different countries, and gives to the various
systems a uniformity which they would not otherwise possess.

(iii) Public international law was founded on Roman law: the
rules which Grotius and his successors laid down as governing the
relationships of states to one another were, with some necessary
modifications, the rules of Roman law, and so, for instance, an
international dispute as to territory may at the present day be
settled by the application of a rule of the Roman law of property.

(b) Canon Law

"Canon law" means church law, and is used especially of the
law of the Roman Catholic church. Canon law in that latter sense
was based on Roman law and on the Bible, and had, like Roman
law itself, a powerful unifying influence over European legal systems
in the Middle Ages.

After the Reformation canon law came to have less importance in Protestant countries than in those which remained Catholic. Thus, canon law is no longer a subject for general legal study in Scotland, although it is still important because of the influence which it exerted in pre-Reformation times on the content and development of Scots law.

(c) English Law

English law has been, like Roman law, the founder-member of a great school of legal thought whose other members are located in widely-separated parts of the globe. For members of the Anglo-American school English law, with its characteristics of rigid adherence to precedents and of separation of law and equity, is of as much significance as is Roman law for members of the Franco-German school.

Because of the political and other close ties between England and Scotland, English law has also been in modern times of great significance in the development of Scots law, although Scots law traditionally belongs to the opposing school of legal thought.

2. *JURISPRUDENCE*

There have been many attempts to define "jurisprudence." For elementary purposes, jurisprudence may be described as the philosophy of the law.

It deals with such questions as the nature of law, the distinction between law and morality, the connection between law and justice, the way in which the state enforces law, and the meaning of the terms "right," "duty," "obligation," "ownership," "possession," "intention," etc., and in general it makes a critical examination of the philosophy which underlies the various actual rules of law.

An immense amount has been written on the subject, and in many different languages. Authorities differ from each other as to its scope and content, and as to their own approach to the subject. This has led to the division of jurists (legal scholars) into different schools.

The approach to jurisprudence which has been most favoured in English-speaking countries is that of analytical jurisprudence, whose founder was the London professor, John Austin (1790–1859). Analytical jurisprudence is concerned mainly with the analysis of law into fundamental concepts, such as "right," "duty," "obligation," "possession," etc., and with the examination and definition of these concepts.

Other approaches have been more favoured elsewhere: on the continent of Europe jurists have adopted the philosophical approach which emphasises the connections and distinctions between law and morality, and between law and justice, while in America sociological jurisprudence focuses attention on the way in which law works in society and gives effect to the various claims and duties of members of the society.

3. COMPARATIVE LAW

The function of comparative law is to compare different legal systems or particular branches of different systems.

Sometimes comparative law will suggest an answer to a question not hitherto decided by the native law, and sometimes it will give ideas for reform of the native law.

An appreciation of the distinctive features of the different schools of legal thought is basic to any study of comparative law.

Comparative law has been of considerable significance in the development of Scots law, the institutional writers Stair, Bankton, and Bell, having been especially notable for their comparative approach.

4. PUBLIC INTERNATIONAL LAW

Public international law consists of the rules which are recognised by civilised states as binding in their relationships with one another.

A greater need for this type of law arose with the breaking-up of the medieval European community which had owed allegiance to Pope and Emperor.

The foundation of modern public international law is usually dated from the publication in 1625 of *De Jure Belli ac Pacis* ("Concerning the Law of War and Peace") by the Dutch scholar, Hugo Grotius (1585–1645). As the title of that work indicates, there is both a public international law of war and a public international law of peace.

Public international law was based originally on Roman law, but notable contributions have also been made to it by custom, canon law, and theories of religion and of law, including the concept referred to as "the law of nature."

The academic question at the centre of public international law is "How far is public international law 'law' in the strict sense at all?"

On the one hand:

(a) There is no international legislative body with law-making powers comparable to those of, for instance, the British Parliament.

(b) There is no international legislation in the full sense of that term.

(c) Sanctions (*i.e.* the means by which law is enforced, such as punishment for disobedience) are in the international sphere of only very limited effectiveness.

(d) There is, in general, room for doubt about whether a body of rules of conduct, habitually observed but not legally enforceable, is properly termed "law."

On the other hand:

(a) The United Nations Organisation and the institutions and "organs" associated with it, such as the International Court of Justice, do to a certain extent undertake the functions of law-making and law-enforcing bodies.

(b) Treaties may be regarded as the international equivalent of legislation.

(c) Although sanctions may not always be effective, with the result that breaches of rules go unpunished, it is nevertheless true that countries for the most part regard the rules as binding on them and do almost always obey the rules, breaches of the rules being in practice as exceptional as they are notorious.

(d) If a state is accused of having violated some rule, that state does not attempt to justify its action by claiming that there is no such thing as public international "law" at all: it will rather attempt to show that the particular rule does not exist or that there has in fact been no violation of the rule. This general recognition of the existence of a body of international rules with binding force favours the view that public international law is properly termed "law."

The conclusion which may be drawn is that public international law *is* "law," but is as yet far from being as fully developed as the municipal law applicable within individual modern civilised states.

5. SUPRANATIONAL LAW

It is only in recent years that it has become necessary to recognise a division of law intermediate between public international law and state or municipal law. While public international law applies to states in their relations inter se ("between or among themselves"), and state or municipal law applies to the national and domestic affairs of individual states, "supranational law," as this intermediate division is being called, arises when several states in a group surrender some of their national sovereign power to some regional organisation, such as NATO, EFTA, or EEC.

Supranational law is distinct from public international law on the one hand in that it regulates the transactions of individual subjects of the member states, and distinct from municipal law on the other hand in that it overrides, and is of wider application than, the municipal law of any one member state.

Supranational law is likely to have a unifying influence on the different systems of municipal law in the various member states.

6. *STATE OR MUNICIPAL LAW*

State or municipal law is the law of a particular community, *e.g.* Scots law, English law, French law, etc.

A single state may have more than one system of municipal law applicable to different parts of the state; the United Kingdom is an example of such a state.

State or municipal law is binding on the individual subjects of the state, and is enforced by the courts, by administrative tribunals, by officials, or by some other agency of the state. It regulates the rights and duties of subjects inter se and also in relation to the state.

The subject-matter of this division of law may be classified in several different ways. Not every classification, however, is applicable to all the various national legal systems, *e.g.*:

(a) the distinction between law and equity, which is part of the English legal tradition, does not apply to any of the legal systems based on Roman law; and

(b) the distinction commonly found in legal systems of the Roman school between civil law (*i.e.* the law applicable to ordinary persons) on the one hand and commercial law (*i.e.* the law applicable to persons in business) on the other hand has led to the creation of separate civil and commercial codes in some states (*e.g.* France and Germany), whereas other states, such as the United Kingdom, do not recognise any such distinction.

For the purposes of Scots law the most important classifications of municipal law are:

(a) common law and statute law;
(b) civil law and criminal law;
(c) substantive law and adjective law; and
(d) public law and private law.

(a) Common Law and Statute Law

This distinction refers to the formal sources of the law.

Common law was originally the law "common to" the whole country, based on the customs of the community and declared and applied, as need arose, by the courts in individual cases. As opposed to statute law, common law is essentially the judge-made law, laid down in decisions of the courts, and found in the law reports.

Statute law is enacted law, created by the legislative organ of the state (*i.e.*, in the United Kingdom, by Parliament). Statute law usually alters the existing common law in some respect (although it may, in some cases, merely declare the common law on some point, *e.g.* where there is doubt as to what the common law is). Statute law includes delegated legislation.

(b) Civil Law and Criminal Law

This distinction refers to the courts and to the procedure by which law is enforced.

Civil law is the law applied in the civil courts by civil procedure, and criminal law is the law applied in the criminal courts by criminal procedure.

A fact not well appreciated by many laymen is that by far the greater volume of law is civil law. It is civil law which regulates all the rights, duties, and obligations arising from transactions between individuals within the state.

Criminal law is concerned only with conduct which the state has decided ought to be repressed and punished by fine or imprisonment. Normally, therefore, an individual can derive no direct benefit from any provision of the criminal law; it exists, not for his personal purposes, but for the protection of the community in general; he must seek his remedy in the civil courts. If, for instance, an individual finds that the person with whom he has made a contract breaks that contract and that he suffers loss as a result, he will have no right to fine or imprison the party in breach, but he may be able to recover his loss by making a claim for damages in the civil courts.

Some conduct gives rise both to civil and to criminal actions. This is especially so in connection with wrongs done to someone's person (*e.g.* assault, and injury caused by negligent driving), or to his property (*e.g.* theft and destruction of property): under civil law such wrongs are "delicts," for which reparation (*i.e.* compensation) can be claimed in the civil courts; under criminal law they are "crimes" or "offences," for which a penalty may be imposed in the criminal courts.

A different standard of proof applies in criminal courts from that which applies in civil courts. Before a conviction is made in a criminal case, the judge or jury must be satisfied "beyond reasonable doubt" that the accused is guilty, whereas in a civil case the court need be satisfied only "on the balance of probabilities" that the pursuer is entitled to the remedy which he seeks. It is, therefore, quite possible for a wrongdoer who has escaped conviction in a criminal court to be held liable in a civil court to make good, so far as money can do so, the damage which he has caused.

The separation of law into civil law and criminal law is a clear-cut division, based on court procedure.

It is not, however, a particularly useful division of the legal system as a whole, since it merely separates a small portion of the law,

criminal law, from the great mass of law. It is, moreover, open to
criticism in that it takes no account, in its simple form, of administrative law, or of matters dealt with by courts of special jurisdiction.
A three-fold division into civil, criminal, and administrative, or
alternatively a distinction between civil and administrative on the
one hand and criminal on the other hand would meet this criticism,
but would still leave this classification of law as fundamentally one
of procedure only and as not having much significance so far as the
substance of the law is concerned.

(c) Substantive Law and Adjective Law

Substantive law defines the rights, duties, obligations, and liabilities
of persons inter se, while adjective law is concerned with the enforcement of these rights, duties, obligations, and liabilities. Adjective
law includes, but is wider than, the law of procedure; it covers also
the constitution and jurisdiction of the various courts and administrative tribunals, the remedies which emerge when rights are
violated, matters of evidence, and questions of diligence (by means
of which decrees of courts are put into effect).

This division is less clear-cut than those into common law and
statute law and into civil law and criminal law. It has, however, a
vital importance in some of the questions which arise in private
international law (p. 139, below), e.g. when a court has to decide
the two quite distinct points of which country's courts have jurisdiction to deal with the case and which country's (substantive) law
is to be applied to the matter before the court.

There is considerable interaction between substantive law and
adjective law. For instance, a right recognised by substantive law
may be of little practical value if the rules of adjective law, such as
the rules of evidence, prevent that right from being enforced, and
substantive law in general is dependent for its value on the existence
of an efficient system of adjective law through which the substantive
law may be put into operation without undue expense and without
undue delay.

(d) Public Law and Private Law

Public law consists of the rules of law which specially relate to the
state, while private law is all the rest of the municipal law.

This division is not a clear-cut one: authorities differ about the
definition of it, and about the topics to be classified under the two
headings, and some authorities even deny the existence of the
division, on the ground that there is no essential difference in nature
(e.g. as to sources or procedure) between public law and private law.

The division is, however, the one which has been most generally accepted and used since Greek and Roman times.

(i) Public law

The branches of law included under this heading have greatly increased in scope and importance in modern times, especially in the twentieth century, as the state has come to exercise much more control over the activities of industrial, commercial, and private life. The branches usually classified as public law are:

1. constitutional law;
2. administrative law; and
3. criminal law.

1. *Constitutional law*

Constitutional law consists of the rules which regulate the organs of government in a state. The constitution of a state is the legal framework of it.

Much of the subject-matter of this branch of law relates to institutions which are common to England and Scotland, such as the monarchy, Parliament, the Government, and the Cabinet, and, since Scotland has had since 1603 the same monarch and since 1707 the same Parliament, and consequently the same Government and Cabinet, as England, it is usually assumed that on these topics at least the constitutional law of Scotland does not differ from that of England. Whether that assumption is justified or not is a question about which legal scholars may argue, but it is certainly true that the basic rules applying to these institutions do not now differ to any significant extent in the two countries. Further, a study of the historical background to and the development of these present-day institutions reveals that the basic rules are of English, rather than of Scottish, origin. For much of constitutional law, therefore, the student of Scots law may resort to English textbooks.

On the other hand, there are some aspects of constitutional law on which it may be obviously useless or latently dangerous to rely on English textbooks. For instance, a textbook which restricts itself to a description of the English courts is obviously of no direct use to a student of the Scottish judicial system, while in connection with proceedings against the Crown and Crown officials, and in connection with some of the individual's fundamental freedoms the student must beware of some less obvious differences between the laws of the two countries.

Constitutional law in any country, but especially in countries with "unwritten" constitutions (*e.g.* the British constitution which has never been embodied in a formal legal document), should be studied in close conjunction with the country's history. The position of the monarch, for instance, in the British constitution cannot be properly understood without some knowledge of the struggles between king and Parliament in the seventeenth century. The historical background to the constitution is sometimes made a separate subject of study under the title of "constitutional history."

A question arises in British constitutional law similar to that arising in public international law (p. 124, above), namely, "How far is British constitutional law 'law' in the strict sense at all?"

On the one hand, some of its sources have the full authority of law (*i.e.* statutes such as the Parliament Act 1911 and decided cases), and to that extent constitutional law is properly termed "law."

On the other hand, much of constitutional law is made up of mere usages, understandings, and practices, which are not of such a nature that a court would give effect to them; these are referred to as "conventions of the constitution." Without conventions, the British constitution would not have developed to what it is today, nor would it be workable in its present form. Although conventions are regarded as binding while they last, they may, without any legal consequences, be discarded when their usefulness is ended, and in this respect constitutional law differs from "law" in the strict sense.

2. *Administrative law*

Administrative law is the part of public law which has grown to the greatest extent as a result of the increased participation of the Government in the day-to-day life of the community. Until about 1930 this branch of law was not thought of as a separate branch at all, but merely as a chapter in constitutional law.

The subject-matter of administrative law is not usually considered as including the various statutory provisions which enable the Government to regulate housing, public health, town and country planning, conditions of work, industry, trade, agriculture, etc. Administrative law is usually restricted to the broad issues raised by the Government's powers of regulation, *e.g.* the structure of "the executive" (*i.e.* the governing power in the state), the general nature of delegated legislation, and the main characteristics of administrative tribunals.

The central point of administrative law is the conflict, or the possibility of conflict, between the executive and the individual: the greater the part played by the executive in the regulation of the life of the community, the greater is the risk that the individual will lose his fundamental freedoms.

Much of administrative law, therefore, relates to the safeguards which are available for these fundamental freedoms, *e.g.* the control of delegated legislation by Parliament and by the courts, the challenge of some administrative action in the courts, the review by the courts of decisions of administrative tribunals, the supervision of public corporations and other statutory bodies, such as the National Coal Board, the Health Boards, and the British Broadcasting Corporation, and the remedies open to the individual where a government official is in breach of contract or has done some wrong to the individual.

Administrative law is one of the liveliest legal subjects at the present day: it has given rise to problems, the solutions to which are still only in their experimental stages.

3. *Criminal law*

Criminal law consists of the rules relating to crimes and offences, *i.e.* relating to acts and omissions which the state wishes to suppress and which it has therefore declared wrong and punishable. The act or omission may or may not be also immoral; it will be criminal only if the state has declared it to be criminal, either in some statutory provision, or through the operation of the common law.

The subject-matter of criminal law includes not only the essential elements in various specific crimes, such as treason, murder, assault, theft and arson, but also the problems of criminal liability, such as the extent to which mens rea ("guilty intention") is required to be proved, and the extent to which liability may be "diminished" because of some mental abnormality.

Associated with, or part of, criminal law is criminal procedure, which is concerned with the structure of and proceedings in the criminal courts, including special rules of evidence, rights of appeal, and the sentences which may be imposed.

(ii) **Private law**

In spite of the great growth in public law in modern times, private law still is the more important part of the law in the sense that the ordinary citizen comes into contact with private law in almost everything he does or does not do in his day-to-day life, whereas he is comparatively seldom directly affected by public law.

The best-known division of private law is that of the Roman lawyers:

1. law of persons;
2. law of things; and
3. law of actions.

This division has been used as the basis for the arrangement of

European codes, and of legal writings including those of the institutional writers Stair, Bankton and Erskine.

1. *Law of persons*

The law of persons deals with legal personality.

The law attributes legal personality not only to human beings, but also to some groups of human beings and to some institutions. On the other hand, the law in some circumstances refuses to recognise full legal personality in a human being or holds that groups of human beings or institutions have only a limited personality.

Legal persons are, therefore, divisible into two groups:

(a) "natural" persons, namely, human beings; and

(b) "artificial" or "juristic" persons, namely, those groups of human beings and those institutions treated by the law as having a certain amount of personality distinct from that of the actual human beings of whom they consist.

(a) *Natural persons.* The law of persons has three main branches:

(i) *The status of natural persons in general.* A person's status is his standing in the eyes of the law; a person is not permitted of his own accord or by agreement with another person freely to alter his status. Nationality, age, legitimacy, sanity, bankruptcy, and imprisonment are some of the various factors which decide a person's status.

(ii) *Family law, or the law of domestic relations.* Under this heading are studied the rules of law which apply to a human being because of his membership of a family group. There are three main topics:

1. the law of husband and wife, which includes the constitution and legal consequences of marriage, and the reasons for and legal effects of divorce;

2. the law of parent and child, which includes legitimacy, aliment, custody, and adoption; and

3. the law of guardianship, or of guardian and ward, which is concerned with the rules which apply where a person (the "ward"), owing to his youth or his mental incapacity, requires to have a guardian, such as a "tutor" or a "curator," to act on his behalf.

(iii) *Status in extra-domestic relations.* A person's status may affect the transactions into which he enters with persons outside his family circle; *e.g.* in certain circumstances the law places restrictions on the capacity of aliens, young persons, and bankrupts. This third branch of the law of natural persons deals with the rules which arise out of some speciality in a person's status.

The first of these three branches is of a general and introductory nature in relation to the second and third branches.

(b) *Artificial persons.* Artificial persons may be "corporations" or "unincorporated associations."

(i) *Corporations.* Corporations (also referred to as "corporate bodies") are the artificial persons with the fullest personality. They are bodies created by ("incorporated by") the state for many different purposes: examples are the regional, islands and district councils in local government, registered companies, building societies, industrial and provident societies, the public corporations set up to manage public utilities and social services (such as the National Coal Board and the Health Boards), universities, and the various chartered institutions which exist for academic, professional, charitable, and other purposes.

The authority of the state which is necessary for the creation of a corporation may come from a royal charter or, directly or indirectly, from an Act of Parliament; *e.g.* a professional body, if it is a corporation, will normally have become one through its having obtained a royal charter; a public corporation set up for some national purpose will normally depend for its existence directly on a particular Act of Parliament (*e.g.* Post Office Act 1969); and an ordinary commercial concern, if it has corporate status, will normally have obtained that by registration under one of the Companies Acts (the present principal Companies Act being the Companies Act 1948).

(ii) *Unincorporated associations.* These are considered by the law to have a more limited personality than corporations, or no personality at all.

Some are recognised as "legal entities" distinct from the natural persons of whom they consist, and these come fairly close to having a legal personality as full as that of corporations. They are sometimes called "quasi-corporations." The main instances are partnerships and trade unions.

Examples of unincorporated associations regarded as having no personality at all and as being for legal purposes simply numbers of individuals are voluntary associations (such as clubs and societies) formed under the common law, and friendly societies, which provide relief for members and their relatives in sickness, old age, and other circumstances, and which may be registered under the Friendly Societies Act 1974.

The law of artificial persons covers such topics as the creation, capacity, rights, duties and liabilities of corporations and unincorporated associations, the relationships between the body and its

members and between the body and non-members, the position of
its representatives or officials, and the ways in which the body may
cease to exist.

2. *Law of things*

The law of things has two main branches:

(a) law of obligations; and

(b) law of property.

Whereas the former is concerned with "personal" rights (rights
which can be asserted against particular persons only), the latter is
concerned with "real" rights (rights which can be asserted against
any other person).

A simple example of a personal right is the right of a person to
claim damages for breach of contract; that is a right which can be
asserted only against the other party to the contract, since only that
other party is under an "obligation" in respect of the contract.

On the other hand, an example of a real right is the ownership
of a house, a watch, or any other type of property; the owner can
assert his right to the property against any other person who has
interfered, or threatens to interfere, with the property, for every
other person is under a "duty" not to interfere with the owner's right.

A personal right is referred to as a jus in personam ("right against
a person"), and a real right as a jus in re ("right in a thing"). See
also p. 242, below.

(a) *Law of obligations.* The law of obligations covers all the
circumstances in which the law places between parties a legal bond
or tie which gives rise to rights, duties, and liabilities between them.
It regulates very many of the relationships which arise daily in
ordinary private, commercial, and industrial life, and is therefore of
great practical importance. It has the following branches:

(i) law of contract;

(ii) law of quasi-contract; and

(iii) law of delict.

(i) *Law of contract.* This deals with the rules applied when
persons "contract" with one another (*i.e.* enter into legally binding
agreements with one another).

A contract should not be thought of as being always a formal
legal document: most contracts are never committed to writing;
they occur at every minute of the day, *e.g.* in shopping, travelling
by train, bus, or taxi, having a meal in an hotel or restaurant, instructing repairs to property, and countless other very ordinary transactions.

The law of contract is concerned with the general legal principles
which apply to all contracts. It examines the ways in which contracts
are formed, the factors which may make a contract invalid, the

circumstances which bring it to an end, the remedies available where there is breach of contract, and all the other legal aspects of contracts.

The law of contract also includes the special rules which apply to the different categories of contracts, *e.g.* contracts of employment agency, partnership, and carriage. In some cases the special rules are part of the common law (as are most of the rules of agency), and in other cases they are partly or mainly statutory (as in employment and carriage), while in a few cases they are embodied in a code (such as the Partnership Act 1890).

(ii) *Law of quasi-contract.* The rules of quasi-contract apply to situations where there is in fact no contract but where the parties stand in much the same relationship with one another as they would have been in had there been a contract; the law then imposes on them obligations (referred to as "quasi-contractual obligations") *as if* (which is the meaning of the Latin word "quasi") there had been a contract.

This branch of law covers only a limited number of rather special situations; in particular, it does *not* cover "implied" contracts (contracts formed without any written or spoken words); these come under the law of contract.

Examples of situations which do come under the law of quasi-contract are where a person finds goods which do not belong to him, and where money which is not due has been paid by mistake; the finder of the goods and the person who has received the money are under quasi-contractual obligations to restore the goods to their owner and to repay the money, respectively.

(iii) *Law of delict.* A " delict " is a legal wrong, an infringement of some legal right belonging to another party.

The law imposes on the party who has done the wrong an obligation to make "reparation" (compensation) for the wrong, and the law of delict is therefore often referred to as "the law of reparation."

An obvious example of a delict is assault, which is an infringement of a person's legal right not to be physically injured by another; the person assaulted is entitled to reparation for the assault, and this reparation takes the form of damages, a sum of money aimed at compensating the assaulted party.

The law of delict is concerned with the general legal principles which apply to all delicts. It examines the general nature of delict, the circumstances in which liability arises, vicarious liability (*i.e.* where one person is liable for wrongs done by another, as an employer may be for those of his employee), the defences to actions for reparation, and all the other legal aspects of delicts.

The law of delict also includes the special rules which apply to the different categories of delicts, *e.g.* physical wrongs (such as injury caused by negligent driving), wrongs to a person's reputation (such as slander), and wrongs to a person's property (such as trespass, and infringement of copyright). As in the case of specific categories of contracts, some of the special rules are part of the common law, while others are statutory.

The law of delict is of almost as widespread practical importance as the law of contract, for, although delicts do not occur as often as contracts, the whole pattern of behaviour of individuals is regulated by the law of delict: it is this branch of the law which protects the individual in the enjoyment of his normal legal rights such as freedom from physical injury, from having his character falsely brought into disrepute and from wrongful interference with his property.

Obligations, as well as being divided into contractual, quasi-contractual, and delictual, may be divided into obligations undertaken voluntarily or by agreement on the one hand and those imposed by the law on the other hand. The obligations in the first of these two groups are said to arise "ex voluntate vel ex conventione" (literally, "out of will or out of agreement"), *i.e.* by a voluntary undertaking by one party or by a contract between two parties. Those in the second group are said to arise "ex lege" (literally, "out of law"), *i.e.* by operation of law. The obligations with which the law of contract is concerned belong to the first group, while those resulting from quasi-contract and from delict belong to the second group.

(b) *Law of property.* The law of property covers all the legal aspects of ownership, possession, use, transfer, and disposal of things of all kinds, and is, like the law of obligations, a wide and important branch of private law.

The rules of the law of property vary substantially according to the nature of the property, and an examination of the different classifications of property is normally the first topic in this branch of law. These classifications result in a fourfold division of the law of property.

Cutting across this fourfold division, however, are branches of the law of property relating to special circumstances in which all four types of property may be involved. The most notable of these branches are the law of trusts, the law of bankruptcy, and the law of succession.

Another important subject concerned with property of all types is conveyancing.

Some further explanation of these aspects of the law of property is given below:

(i) *The four divisions of the law of property.* Property may be classified as either heritable or moveable: heritable property consists of land and of things built on or attached to land; all other property, *e.g.* cars, furniture, clothes, and money, is moveable.

Property may also be classified as either corporeal or incorporeal: corporeal property consists of objects which can be seen and touched, *e.g.* a house, food, cash; all other property is incorporeal; shares in a company, for instance, are not objects which can be seen and touched (although they are *represented by* a share certificate), and similarly any other right (*e.g.* a debt which is owing to a person, or the right of a tenant under a lease, or a registered trade mark) is incorporeal.

The four divisions of the law of property, therefore, are:

1. law of corporeal heritable property (*e.g.* buildings and crops);

2. law of incorporeal heritable property (*e.g.* a servitude, such as a right of way, over land (see p. 462, below) and a "bond" (security) over a house);

3. law of corporeal moveable property (*e.g.* books and stock-in-trade); and

4. law of incorporeal moveable property (*e.g.* a right to damages, and a patent).

(ii) *Law of trusts.* Property may be held on trust. In a trust there are three parties, namely, the truster, who formerly owned the property and who set up the trust, the trustee, to whom the property has been transferred and who holds and administers it, and the beneficiary, who is entitled to the benefit of the property. It is common for there to be several trustees and several beneficiaries in the one trust.

It is an important principle of the law of trusts that the trustees must not allow a conflict to arise between their own personal interests and the interests of the trust.

Trusts are often set up by a person's will, and come into operation only on the truster's death; these are referred to as "mortis causa" (literally, "for the sake of death") or "testamentary" trusts. Other trusts may be set up and come into operation during the lifetime of the truster; these are referred to as "inter vivos" (literally, "among the living") trusts.

The main classification of trusts is that into private trusts and public trusts: in a private trust the beneficiaries are private individuals, whereas in a public trust the trust property is held for some religious, educational, charitable, or other public purpose.

The law of trusts, as well as dealing with the powers and duties of trustees and the other legal relationships in ordinary private and public trusts, also covers the extensions of the trust concept found, for instance, in trustee savings banks, unit trusts, trust-deeds for creditors (used in bankruptcy), and in the law relating to judicial factors (appointed to manage and administer property where that is necessary to prevent loss of the property or to put an end to a deadlock in the administration of it).

(iii) *Law of bankruptcy.* A person who is bankrupt is subject to some restrictions in disposing of his property, and may even have his property compulsorily taken from him and divided amongst his creditors.

The term "bankruptcy," although used in the title of the statute which lays down most of the law on this subject, namely, the Bankruptcy (Scotland) Act 1913, is not itself a precise legal term: it may mean insolvency (*i.e.* inability to pay one's debts), or notour bankruptcy (which has a technical meaning, but which originally, and still basically, denotes insolvency which has become notorious or publicly known), or sequestration (the formal court process by which the bankrupt's property is taken from him, placed in the hands of a trustee, and distributed to creditors).

The law of bankruptcy covers the nature and effects of insolvency, notour bankruptcy, and sequestration, the procedure in sequestration, and the alternatives to sequestration (such as the voluntary trust-deed for creditors).

(iv) *Law of succession.* This consists of the rules which lay down who is to succeed to the property of a deceased person.

There are three main branches in the law of succession:

1. There are certain prior rights and legal rights which must be satisfied before any right of succession in the strict sense can arise; examples of legal rights are the widow's jus relictae ("right of the widow"), and a child's "legitim."

2. Where the deceased has left a will, the rules of "testate" succession apply; much of the subject-matter of this branch relates to the validity and interpretation of wills.

3. Where the deceased has left property which he has not disposed of by a valid will, the rules of "intestate" succession apply.

(v) *Conveyancing.* Conveyancing is concerned with the documents by which the various rights over property are created, transferred, or extinguished. It covers, for instance, examination of the title-deeds of heritable property, and the drawing up of leases, securities, wills, and many other types of "deeds" (formal legal documents).

Many solicitors and their assistants devote a considerable portion of their working hours to conveyancing. The subject is regarded as an art rather than as a sub-division of legal science, and calls for skill and experience in the use of legal forms and terminology, and for familiarity with the practices of the legal profession, as well as for a sound knowledge of the principles of law applicable to the various types of property.

3. *Law of actions*

The law of actions deals with the means by which the rules of the substantive law may be given effect to by the civil courts. Its topics include:

(a) the jurisdiction of the courts in various types of cases;

(b) procedure, including the system of appeals;

(c) the art of pleading, *i.e.* the drawing up of the written statements necessary for a court action;

(d) the law of evidence, which covers the admissibility of the various types of oral and written evidence, the onus (or burden) of proof, oaths and affirmations of witnesses, and the weight to be attached to evidence;

(e) diligence, which is concerned with the ways in which a court decree is enforced;

(f) legal aid, *i.e.* the system by which a person may obtain assistance from public funds in the payment of the expenses of an action;

(g) expenses (dealing with the question of which party must bear the cost of an action); and

(h) the law of arbitration, which regulates the extent to which the jurisdiction of the courts may be excluded by agreement of the parties or by some statutory provision, with the result that the parties must accept settlement of their dispute by some person or body other than the courts.

Private international law

A branch of private law which does not fall into one of the three traditional divisions ("persons," "things," and "actions") is private international law (also referred to as "conflict of laws").

The principles of this branch of law require to be applied when there is some foreign element in a case.

The main questions within the scope of private international law are which country's courts have jurisdiction to decide a dispute, which body of law is to be applied, and what effect is to be given to foreign judgments.

Private international law is quite distinct from public international law, since:

(a) whereas public international law regulates the relationships of states to one another, private international law relates to the rights, duties and obligations of individuals (often, but not always, nationals of different states);

(b) the institutions which make and enforce (so far as this is possible) the rules of public international law are international institutions, whereas the institutions which make and enforce private international law are the legislatures and the courts of individual states; and

(c) public international law is a separate division of legal science, whereas private international law is part of municipal law, from which fact it follows that private international law is undoubtedly "law" in the strict sense and that its rules vary from state to state.

The importance of private international law has increased in proportion to the extension of commerce, emigration, foreign travel, and the other conditions of modern life which have brought more frequent and closer contact between the nationals of different states.

In the United Kingdom private international law has a special significance owing to the existence of distinct systems of law within that one state. The close political, social, economic, and other ties between England and Scotland often result in there being in a case coming before the Scottish courts some English, *i.e.* some foreign, element, which requires to be dealt with according to the rules of the private international law of Scotland.

Concluding note

The place in the structure of Scots law as a whole occupied by the subjects dealt with in the following pages may be seen at a glance in this table, in which they are indicated by **:

(i) public law
   1. ** constitutional law
   2. ** administrative law
   3.   criminal law

(ii) private law
   1. law of persons
     (a) natural persons
       (i) status of natural persons in general
       (ii) family law
         1. ** law of husband and wife
         2. ** law of parent and child
         3.   law of guardianship
       (iii) status in extra-domestic relations

(b) artificial persons
   (i) corporations
   (ii) unincorporated associations

2. law of things
  (a) ** law of obligations in general
    (i) ** law of contract in general and law of particular contracts, *e.g.*—
      1. ** employment
      2. ** agency
      3.   partnership
      4.   carriage
    (ii) ** law of quasi-contract
    (iii) ** law of delict
  (b) law of property
    (i) ** the four divisions of the law of property
    (ii) ** law of trusts
    (iii)   law of bankruptcy
    (iv) ** law of succession
    (v)   conveyancing
3. law of actions
(also) private international law

The order in which the subjects marked ** are dealt with in the following pages is not the order in which they appear in the table but the order in which they can probably be most easily understood by a beginner in Scots law.

Further Reading
David M. Walker, *The Scottish Legal System*

PART II — PUBLIC LAW

CHAPTER 6

GENERAL PRINCIPLES OF CONSTITUTIONAL LAW

THE general characteristics and doctrines of the British constitution may be considered under the following headings:

1. general nature of the British constitution;
2. conventions of the constitution;
3. Parliament;
4. supremacy of Parliament;
5. the rule of law;
6. separation of powers; and
7. the European Communities.

At the end of the chapter a note is added on:

8. proposals for reform.

1. *GENERAL NATURE OF THE BRITISH CONSTITUTION*

The word "constitution" may denote the formal legal document which sets out the framework for the government of a state. Britain has no "constitution" in this sense.

In the phrase "the British constitution" the word "constitution" means the main structure of government.

The rules relating to the British constitution are to be found partly in the ordinary formal sources, especially Acts of Parliament, decided cases, custom, and textbooks. The Acts of Parliament affecting constitutional law have no special legal sanctity about them: they are merely ordinary, individual Acts of Parliament. Decided cases are, in constitutional law, a less important source than in many other branches of law, since questions of constitutional law seldom come before the courts. On the other hand, custom and textbooks are allowed wider scope than in most other branches.

However, many of the rules of British constitutional law are not to be found in any of the ordinary formal sources, but are merely "conventional" rules (rules binding by agreement only and not by force of law).

Two basic characteristics of the British constitution which result from the absence of any formal legal document which is "the constitution" are that the British constitution is:

(a) an unwritten constitution; and

(b) a flexible constitution.

(a) An Unwritten Constitution

The British constitution is "unwritten" in the sense that there is no single formal legal document setting out the framework for the government of the country.

The British constitution is in this respect commonly contrasted in particular with the constitution of the United States of America, which is a written constitution consisting of a document originally drawn up in 1787 and later (but only on a limited number of occasions) amended to meet changed circumstances.

When there is any change in the nature of the governing power in any country, *e.g.* after civil war, or as a result of a war of liberation, or on the attainment of self-government by a colony, the new constitution is usually embodied in a formal legal document.

Most civilised states, including almost all members of the Commonwealth, now have written constitutions.

The distinction between written and unwritten constitutions, however, is not, in itself, of any great practical importance, for:

(i) a written constitution does not usually contain more than the bare framework for the government of the country, with the result that much of constitutional law has to be sought in the ordinary sources of law; and

(ii) even in an unwritten constitution there are some fundamental principles which, whether they are embodied in particular legislation or not, are regarded as having just as much legal sanctity as the formally expressed provisions of a written constitution.

(b) A Flexible Constitution

A "flexible" constitution is one which may be changed by the same procedure as that used for the changing of any other part of the law, whereas a "rigid" constitution is protected from change by the fact that some special procedure must be followed if a change is to be made; *e.g.* a special majority of two-thirds or three-quarters of the legislative (law-making) body may be required, or the intervention of some other body may be necessary.

The constitution of the United States is again the example usually given of a rigid constitution, but the constitutions of almost all European states are also rigid.

The special procedure varies from one country to another: in some cases changes may be made relatively easily, while in other cases nothing short of revolution could achieve that end.

The British constitution is flexible since any part of it can in theory be changed by an ordinary Act of Parliament: however much Parliament might override fundamental principles, the courts, if called on, would be bound to give effect to the will of Parliament, and could never declare its legislation invalid on the ground that it was "unconstitutional."

A flexible constitution has the advantage that it may be comparatively easily adapted to suit changed conditions, and so it is less likely to fall out of date than is a rigid constitution. It can also be temporarily set aside without any special formality when an outbreak of war or some other emergency makes that desirable.

On the other hand, a flexible constitution has obvious dangers, and the legislative body has a special responsibility not to exercise its power to alter constitutional law except where this is really justified.

2. *CONVENTIONS OF THE CONSTITUTION*

It is in the British constitution and in constitutions derived from it (such as those of Commonwealth countries) that conventions are most widespread and have the greatest importance.

The significance of conventions in the British constitution was first emphasised by the best-known of all modern writers on this branch of the law, A. V. Dicey (1835–1922), whose most famous work, *The Law of the Constitution*, was first published in 1885. Earlier writers had, however, noted the existence of conventions, and the development of the constitution had been greatly influenced by conventions long before Dicey wrote.

Dicey stressed the distinction between those constitutional rules which were laws in the strictest sense and another set of constitutional rules consisting of "conventions, understandings, habits, or practices" which, though they might regulate the functioning of the organs of government, were not really laws at all since they were not enforced by the courts. This other set of rules he called "conventions of the constitution."

Later writers have suggested various definitions and descriptions of "conventions of the constitution." For example, the term has been stated to mean "certain rules of constitutional behaviour which are considered to be binding by and upon those who operate the Constitution, but which are not enforced by the law courts (although the courts may recognize their existence), nor by the presiding officers in the Houses of Parliament" (Marshall and Moodie, *Some Problems of the Constitution*, p. 29). This definition excludes from the category of conventions "the law and custom of Parliament" which define much of Parliamentary procedure and which are applied by, for instance, the Speaker of the House of Commons. Other writers prefer to include these in their definition of conventions.

While there are different views about the exact nature of conventions of the constitution, there is general agreement that they:

(a) regulate the operation of the organs of government;
(b) are not formal law; and
(c) are regarded as binding.

Conventions have historically been the means by which the modern "limited" or "constitutional" monarchy, the Cabinet system, and ministerial responsibility (*i.e.* the responsibility of ministers to Parliament) have become established. These are the conventions with which Dicey was most concerned.

Conventions also operate in other branches of constitutional law some of which were not as important branches in 1885 as they are today; for instance, there are conventions which regulate the relationship between the House of Lords and the House of Commons, between the Government and the Opposition, and between the United Kingdom and the other members of the Commonwealth.

Are Conventions "Law"?

The main question discussed in connection with conventions is whether they are properly classed as "law."

On the one hand, they are distinct from "law" in the strict sense of that term in that they are not enforced by the courts.

On the other hand, they come at least very close to being law in some respects:

(a) They are regarded as *binding*, and are distinct from mere practices; *e.g.* there is a convention that a minister is a member of either the House of Commons or the House of Lords, but it is a mere practice that on "budget" day the Chancellor of the Exchequer carries from Downing Street to the House of Commons the much-photographed dispatch case containing the budget.

(b)   They may be *impliedly recognised* by Acts of Parliament or in court decisions, both of which are "law" in the strictest sense; *e.g.* the offices of Prime Minister and of Leader of the Opposition, both of which rest on conventions, were impliedly recognised by the Ministers of the Crown Act 1937, which laid down salaries for the holders of these offices, and the case of *Liversidge* v. *Anderson* [1942] A.C. 206, which arose out of the detention of Liversidge in Brixton prison during the Second World War on the ground that he was a person of hostile associations, impliedly recognised the convention of ministerial responsibility (in this case the responsibility of the Home Secretary who had made the detention order) to Parliament.

(c)   Although conventions do not have legal "sanctions" attached to them, such as would result in some penalty being immediately imposed for the breach of them, breach of a convention would in many cases *ultimately lead to a breach of the law; e.g.* if Parliament were not summoned for a year, with the result that the annual Finance Act expired, collection of most of the national revenue would become illegal.

Advantages of Conventions

Most conventions have their origins in practices, and it is usually impossible to fix precisely the point of time at which a practice develops into a convention.

Moreover, conventions may, with the passage of time and with changes in circumstances cease to operate as such and either become totally obsolete or revert to being mere practices.

It is, therefore, impossible to state with complete certainty what the conventions of the constitution are for any given stage in history.

Although uncertainty in law is a disadvantage, it is the very flexibility of conventions which gives them their greatest value: they enable rules of constitutional law to be formed, adapted, and discarded imperceptibly, without formality, and at the precise time required for the smooth development of the constitution.

Examples of Conventions

(a)   **The monarch**

The Queen must appoint as her Prime Minister the leader of the party which commands a majority in the House of Commons, and must appoint as her other ministers those members of the House of Commons or of the House of Lords whom the Prime Minister advises her to appoint.

The Queen must not refuse to give the royal assent which finally converts a Bill into an Act of Parliament—a convention of particularly long standing, for no monarch since the time of Queen Anne has withheld the royal assent.

The Queen must act on the advice of her ministers; *e.g.* she must dissolve Parliament when asked to do so by the Prime Minister.

(b) The Cabinet system

An inner ring of the Queen's ministers forms the "Cabinet," the existence and functioning of which depend on conventions.

The Prime Minister is entitled to decide which ministers are to be included in the Cabinet, and no minister can insist on being included, but there is a convention that certain offices (*e.g.* that of Chancellor of the Exchequer) carry with them seats in the Cabinet.

Especially important for the working of the Cabinet system is the doctrine of "collective responsibility," by which all members of the Cabinet are collectively responsible to Parliament for the general conduct of affairs. Whatever dissenting views may have been expressed in the Cabinet by individual ministers, a decision once taken is treated as unanimous so far as responsibility to Parliament is concerned; a Cabinet minister must, therefore, vote with the Government in Parliament, defend its policy, and never express outside the Cabinet disagreement with the Cabinet's decision; his only alternative is to resign his office. This explains why it is necessary to keep secret all the proceedings in the Cabinet.

The importance of this convention of collective responsibility was emphasised by events in 1932, when the unanimity rule was departed from by an announcement that on a particular issue the members of the Cabinet had agreed to differ; only a few months later, however, the dissenting ministers resigned office over a related issue, and so the convention temporarily disregarded became even more firmly established. In 1975 the convention was deliberately departed from in connection with the referendum on membership of the EEC: while the Government supported continued membership, individual members of the Cabinet were free to express a contrary view. The occasion is regarded as a unique one and not as weakening the convention.

(c) Ministerial responsibility

A minister is also individually responsible to Parliament for what is done by the government department of which he has charge.

He must be prepared to answer questions in Parliament on the administrative action taken by officials of that department, and he can never shield himself by blaming a civil servant.

It is often said that where there has been a sufficiently serious error of administration, the minister himself must, by convention.

resign. This is not, however, a clear-cut convention, for a minister " may choose, and has not infrequently chosen in recent years, to brazen out appalling indiscretions, gross errors and omissions, plans gone awry and revelations of disastrous mismanagement within his Department " (S. A. de Smith, *Constitutional and Administrative Law*).

(d) The civil service

The civil service is governed by a mass of regulations, most of which would not be enforced in the courts but can properly be classed as conventions because within the service they are regarded as binding and are enforced by heads of departments.

Although normally conventions must not contradict the rules of strict law, there is, in connection with the civil service, an example of such a contradiction: the rule of strict law is that all servants of the Crown, whether they be ministers or civil servants, can be dismissed at the pleasure of the Crown; conventions, however, give civil servants greater security of tenure of office than is enjoyed by many other employees; it is a convention that civil servants are *not* dismissed purely at the pleasure of the Crown; serious misconduct would be necessary to justify instant dismissal.

(e) Parliament

Some parts of the law relating to Parliament have originated in statutes; *e.g.* the composition of the House of Commons is regulated by the Representation of the People Act 1949, which consolidated the law on "Parliamentary franchise" (*i.e.* the right to vote at a general election) and on certain other aspects of Parliamentary elections; matters such as the franchise have never depended on conventions.

There are other statutes which have merely reinforced previously existing conventions; *e.g.* it was formerly a convention that in case of conflict the House of Lords had to yield ultimately to the House of Commons, and this convention was given specific form by the Parliament Acts of 1911 and 1949; these Acts laid down a maximum period during which the House of Lords might delay a Bill which had passed the House of Commons.

Again, there are statutes which give implied recognition to conventions; *e.g.* in the Parliament Act 1911 there is implied recognition of the convention that money Bills are introduced only in the House of Commons.

Much of the procedure in the two Houses of Parliament depends on the Standing Orders of each House, which deal with such matters as the passage of legislation and the rules of debate. These Standing

Orders are similar to a code of law, but by some writers are classed as conventions since they are not enforced in the courts. An example of a convention of this type is the provision of Standing Order No. 89 of the House of Commons that a financial resolution is proposed only by a minister of the Crown.

Other aspects of the law relating to Parliament are embodied neither in statutes nor in Standing Orders but are purely conventional; *e.g.* the Speaker in the House of Commons must allow adequate expression of minority views, and the business of the House of Commons is arranged informally ("behind the Speaker's chair," as it is said) between the Government and the Opposition.

(However, not all the rules applying to Parliament have *constitutional* significance, and to qualify as a convention of the constitution a rule must have some purpose connected with the functioning of government and must not be merely a matter of administrative convenience; *e.g.* the rule that certain days are allocated for Parliamentary questions addressed to different ministers exists for administrative convenience and has no constitutional purpose, and is, therefore, not a convention of the constitution; similarly, the rule that peers who are not Law Lords do not sit in the House of Lords when it is acting as a court of appeal is sometimes regarded as not being a convention of the constitution, because it is a matter of Parliamentary and court practice rather than a part of constitutional law.)

(f) The Commonwealth

Conventions are of great importance in the relationships between members of the Commonwealth, *e.g.*:

(i) in appointing a Governor-General of an independent Commonwealth country the Queen must act on the advice of the Prime Minister of that country;

(ii) a Governor-General, as the representative of the Queen, must act on the advice of ministers of the Commonwealth country concerned; and

(iii) the Governments of the Commonwealth countries must keep one another informed of the negotiation of treaties and the conduct of foreign affairs.

Many of the conventions which have developed in this field have been made the subject of express agreement at Imperial Conferences or at meetings of Commonwealth ministers. These remain conventions, since such agreements have no legal sanction behind them.

Other conventions have received recognition in the Statute of Westminster 1931; *e.g.* the convention that the United Kingdom Parliament must not legislate for another independent member of the Commonwealth except at the request and with the consent of that other member, and the convention that an alteration in the succession to the throne requires the assent of the Parliaments of Canada, Australia, and New Zealand are both mentioned in the preamble to that Act, and the former convention is enacted in section 4 of the Act.

Why are Conventions Observed?

Dicey concluded that the reason why conventions are observed was that a breach of a convention would usually ultimately result in a breach of the "law" in the strict sense; if, for instance a Government which has ceased to command a majority in the House of Commons were to refuse to resign, that breach of convention would ultimately lead to illegal administrative action, because Parliament would not have authorised the necessary raising of revenue and expenditure of public funds. According to this view, conventions have an ultimate, although not an immediate, "legal sanction."

Dicey's conclusion has been criticised by other writers on constitutional law, notably Sir Ivor Jennings in his book *The Law and the Constitution*:

(a) Dicey was concerned mainly with conventions regulating the relationship between the Government and Parliament; in particular, he did not deal with conventions regulating the proceedings in Parliament or regulating Commonwealth relations—areas in which a breach of a convention could seldom lead, even ultimately, to a breach of the "law" in the strict sense; *e.g.* the courts would not be concerned with the results of the Speaker's failure to allow minority views to be expressed in the House of Commons or of a Government's failure to inform other Commonwealth countries of its conduct of foreign affairs. Dicey's argument, therefore, does not apply to all the conventions now recognised.

(b) Dicey's argument does not apply even to all the conventions of the class with which he deals; *e.g.* a Government which has committed a breach of some convention might, through its majority in the House of Commons, secure the passing of an Act which would legalise all the consequences of that breach, and so no breach of the "law" in the strict sense would, even ultimately, result.

A more satisfactory explanation of why conventions are observed is that they carry a "political sanction": in the internal affairs of the United Kingdom breach of conventions would result in a Government's losing the support of the House of Commons and falling into disfavour with the electorate, while in Commonwealth affairs breach of conventions would prejudice the unity of the Commonwealth and might lead to withdrawal from it.

It may, however, not be necessary to find any sanction, either legal or political, enforcing obedience to conventions. Sir Ivor Jennings, for instance, suggested that conventions were observed because they were *accepted as binding* and *fulfilled some constitutional purpose*. This view is in keeping with the characteristic of conventions that they can cease to operate when their usefulness is over. Those who must give their acceptance are mainly the persons who hold the reins of government for the time being and who have, therefore, the greatest interest in making the government work at least as efficiently as it has done in the past; they are consequently reluctant to abandon without good reason rules which have been shown by past experience to have some constitutional value.

The answer to the question of why conventions are observed may, therefore, lie in an attitude of mind, rather than in any legal or political sanctions: in internal affairs, those in power wish their power to continue, and accept conventions as being their greatest safeguard for a continuance of their power (*e.g.* the Queen may be regarded as accepting the conventions which have made the monarchy into a "limited" monarchy, because that is the surest means of retaining for the monarchy its present position and powers, and a Government may be regarded as accepting the conventions which make it "responsible" to the House of Commons, because that is the surest means of retaining the favour of the electorate and so being returned to power at the next general election); in Commonwealth affairs, members of the Commonwealth realise that smooth relationships bring greater mutual advantages, and they accept conventions as being the greatest safeguard for a continuance of smooth relationships (*e.g.* breach of the convention that the succession to the throne must not be altered except with the assent of the Parliaments of Canada, Australia, and New Zealand would not be in the best interests of a good relationship between the United Kingdom and these other members).

3. *PARLIAMENT*

The two principal functions of Parliament are:
(a) legislation; and
(b) control of the executive.

The word "Parliament" does not have the same meaning in connection with these two functions.

When "Parliament" denotes the British "legislature" (law-making body), it is short for "the Queen in Parliament"; the British legislature is composed of three parts, namely, the Queen and the two Houses of Parliament.

In relation to its function of controlling the executive, "Parliament" denotes the two Houses of Parliament only, and sometimes even the House of Commons only; *e.g.* debates on Government policy take place in both Houses of Parliament, while only the House of Commons, as representing the electorate, determines the composition of the Government.

Composition of Parliament

The Queen

The role of the Queen as part of Parliament has long been a merely formal one.

In earlier times the monarch was actually present in Parliament, but the practice now is for the monarch not to appear in person in Parliament except to read "the speech from the Throne" at the opening of a new session. This speech, also referred to as "the Queen's speech," outlines the Government's policy with regard to foreign affairs and proposed legislation in the new session; it is the work of the Cabinet, not of the Queen in person, and, if the Queen is not present, is read by the Lord Chancellor.

The Queen also has the formal function of dissolving Parliament. By convention, she exercises this function only at the time when she is asked to do so by the Prime Minister.

The royal assent which converts a Bill into an Act of Parliament is also a mere formality, since, by convention, the Queen never refuses it.

The formula used for the royal assent is in old French, and varies according to the type of Act. For a public Bill, other than one dealing with finance, the formula is "La Reine le veult" ("The Queen wishes it"); if the Bill is a financial one, the royal assent includes an expression of thanks from the Queen to her "good subjects" and of acceptance of their "kindness."

The tactful formula formerly used if a monarch refused the royal assent was "Le Roy s'avisera" ("The King will think about it"), or "La Reine s'avisera" ("The Queen will think about it").

The two Houses of Parliament

The British legislature is "bicameral," *i.e.* has two chambers—the House of Lords and the House of Commons.

Although the House of Lords is a peculiarly British institution and has taken its present shape as a result of a centuries-old tradition, Britain is by no means unique in having a bicameral legislature. In constitutions of more recent creation the second or "upper" chamber is usually formed on representative lines, which may be, but need not be, similar to the representative lines on which the "lower" chamber is formed. An example of a deliberately created bicameral legislature is the United States' Congress, which consists of the Senate and the House of Representatives, the former being the upper chamber.

(a) The House of Lords

The House of Lords has a membership of about 1,170, but of these about 80 do not apply for the "writ of summons" which must be issued to each peer before he is entitled to take his seat. Further, by a Standing Order (No. 20) of the House, adopted in 1958, members may be granted leave of absence for the duration of a particular Parliament or for a single session, and they are then expected not to attend unless they terminate their leave of absence by giving notice to that effect; this scheme for leave of absence reduces the potential attendance by about 175. The average daily attendance is about 300. Many attend only when a matter in which they are specially interested is being discussed.

Membership carries no salary, but resolutions of the House provide for recovery by members of expenses incurred by them on the days when they attend. The House consists of:

(i) lords temporal; and
(ii) lords spiritual.

The House is presided over by the Lord Chancellor, a Cabinet minister, who is the Speaker of that House. He sits on "the wool-sack" (a symbol of England's prosperity in medieval times), which is regarded as being technically outside the House. Unlike the Speaker of the House of Commons, he may take part in debates, and when he does so he moves away from the woolsack so that he may be technically within the House. In presiding over the House he has less extensive powers than those of the Speaker in the House of Commons since the House of Lords is master of its own procedure and itself decides matters of order.

When the House is in committee, the chair is taken by the Chairman of Committees.

(i) *Lords temporal.* The lords temporal are:
1. hereditary peers;
2. Lords of Appeal in Ordinary; and
3. life peers.

1. *Hereditary peers.* These account for the bulk of the membership of the House.

The peerages may be peerages of England or of Scotland created before the Union of the Parliaments of those two countries in 1707, or they may be peerages of Great Britain created between 1707 and 1800, or they may be peerages of the United Kingdom created since the union with Ireland in 1801.

Hereditary peerages are created by the Queen in virtue of the royal prerogative, which is now, by convention, exercised by the Queen only on the advice of her ministers. In the past this aspect of the royal prerogative featured in the struggle of the House of Commons for ascendancy over the House of Lords; *e.g.* in 1832, in the conflict between the Lords and the Commons over the passing of the Reform Bill to extend the franchise, there was a threat to create a sufficient number of peers to ensure the passage of the Bill by the House of Lords, and there was an even more notable instance of a similar threat in connection with the passing of the Parliament Act of 1911 which severely curtailed the legislative power of the House of Lords. No hereditary peerage has been created since 1965.

Formerly, a hereditary peerage could not be surrendered, and a person who succeeded to a hereditary peerage was, therefore, barred from a career in the House of Commons. This disability came into the limelight in the case of Mr. Anthony Wedgwood Benn, a Labour member of the House of Commons who wished to remain a member of that House after the death of his father, on which event he became Lord Stansgate (*Re Parliamentary Election for Bristol South East* [1964] 2 Q.B. 257). As a result of that case the Peerage Act 1963 allowed hereditary peers to disclaim their peerages. The number of peerages disclaimed under that Act is fifteen (August 1980).

It is because of the hereditary principle that the composition of the House of Lords has been so much criticised and that so many proposals for its abolition or reform have been made, especially in the twentieth century. Obviously many hereditary peers are unsuited, unable, or unwilling to form part of the British legislature, and the House of Lords is a workable institution only because so many hereditary peers choose to absent themselves from the House.

It is, however, generally agreed that a bicameral legislature is preferable to a unicameral (or single-chamber) one, and proposals for abolition of the House of Lords have, therefore, usually been linked with consideration of alternative methods of constituting a second or upper chamber. There have been numerous suggestions, but so far no final and decisive agreement.

2. *Lords of Appeal in Ordinary.* The appointment of these "Law Lords" was first authorised by the Appellate Jurisdiction Act 1876. See p. 32, above.

3. *Life peers.* Life peers are entitled to sit in the House of Lords under the provisions of the Life Peerages Act 1958.

Before the passing of that Act, although the Queen might create life peerages, such a peerage did not carry with it the right to a seat in the House of Lords; that had been decided in the *Wensleydale Peerage Case* (1856) 5 H.L.Cas. 958.

Although the number of life peerages (321 in 1980) is small in comparison with the number of hereditary peerages, life peers (who are, unlike hereditary peers, under a moral obligation to take part in the work of the House) form the most significant group of members in the "working" House.

A hereditary peer who has disclaimed his peerage under the Act of 1963 may later be created a life peer (*e.g.* Lord Hailsham and Lord Hume).

The effect of the Act of 1958 has been to increase regularity of attendance in the House and to give the House a political atmosphere similar to that of the House of Commons.

(ii) *Lords spiritual.* Only the Church of England is represented: the Church of Ireland and the Church in Wales are excluded because they are not "established" churches, and, although the Church of Scotland is an established church, and did make a claim in 1953 for representation in the House to correspond to that of the Church of England (Royal Commission on Scottish Affairs (Cmd. 9212)), it is not in fact as yet officially represented in the House. The twenty-six lords spiritual are:

1. the Archbishops of Canterbury and York;
2. the Bishops of London, Durham, and Winchester; and
3. twenty-one other diocesan bishops of the Church of England in order of seniority of appointment; when one of these twenty-one bishops dies or resigns his see, his place in the House of Lords is taken, not by his successor in the see, but by the bishop next in order of seniority of appointment.

(b) *The House of Commons*

The historical background to the present composition of the House of Commons is one of gradual approximation during the period from 1832 to 1948 to the principle "one man (or woman), one vote."

The Representation of the People Act 1832, often referred to as "the Reform Act," effected the first major extension of the franchise. It was specially important for its abolition of "rotten boroughs" (small communities with only a few voters which were represented in the House out of all proportion to their own population). As a result of that Act and of the Scottish "Reform Act" of the same year, the House of Commons became the dominant House of Parliament, and development of the principle that the making and unmaking of Governments depend on the will of "the people" was made possible.

The Acts of 1832, however, did not come near to establishing the democratic principle of "one man, one vote": a series of Acts in the nineteenth and twentieth centuries was required for that.

The final stage was reached with the Representation of the People Act 1948, which, unlike most of the earlier Acts in the series, did not extend the franchise, but abolished the last-surviving instances of "plural voting," namely, the additional votes allowed to occupiers of business premises and to university graduates.

Constituencies. Constituencies are regulated by the House of Commons (Redistribution of Seats) Acts 1949 to 1979.

By the provisions of these Acts there are four Boundary Commissions (one for each of England, Scotland, Wales, and Northern Ireland) whose duty it is to keep under review the representation in the House of Commons of that part of the United Kingdom with which each is concerned. The general aim is to prevent too great differences arising in the number of electors included in the different constituencies, and for this purpose reference is made to the "electoral quota", which is the number obtained by division of the total electorate for the part of the United Kingdom concerned by the number of constituencies in it. Rigid mathematical equality, however, is not insisted on.

The total number of constituencies in Great Britain must not be substantially greater or less than 613, and of these no fewer than seventy-one must be in Scotland and no fewer than thirty-five must be in Wales. The number of constituencies in Northern Ireland, formerly fixed at twelve, was altered by the Act of 1979 to between sixteen and eighteen.

For the election of May 1979, the total number of constituencies was 635, including seventy-one in Scotland, thirty-six in Wales, and the twelve in Northern Ireland.

Each constituency has the right to return only one member to the House of Commons: there is in the British constitution no "proportional representation," such as would enable candidates who poll a certain proportion (though a minority) of the votes cast to be returned to the House as representatives of the minorities concerned. It follows that a member of Parliament officially represents *all* the electors in his constituency, including those who did not vote for him.

The absence of proportional representation is criticised in particular by the Liberal party, since its candidates poll a considerable proportion of the votes of the electorate, yet seldom top the poll in any constituency, with the result that the number of Liberal members of Parliament is significantly out of proportion to the number of Liberal voters in the country.

Proportional representation would, however, be likely to undermine the two-party system of government, which is generally accepted as making a major contribution to the stability of British government.

The franchise. The law on the franchise was consolidated by the Representation of the People Act 1949. By that Act, as amended by the Representation of the People Act 1969, an elector in any constituency must be:

(i) at least eighteen years of age;

(ii) a British subject or a citizen of the Republic of Ireland;

(iii) not subject to any legal incapacity (as being an alien, a peer, an offender in prison or a person considered by the presiding officer at the poll to be mentally disordered, or as having been within the previous five years convicted of certain corrupt or illegal practices); and

(iv) resident in the constituency on the qualifying date (at present October 10).

Elections. The law relating to the conduct of elections is governed by the Representation of the People Act 1949, as amended by later Acts including the Representation of the People Acts 1969 and 1974.

A person is not entitled to vote in any constituency unless his name appears on the register of electors for that constituency. The compilation of this register is the responsibility of the "registration officer," who organises a door-to-door canvass for the purpose. The same official also deals with claims to vote by post and by proxy.

The conduct of the actual election is the responsibility of the "returning officer", who, by the Returning Officers (Scotland) Act 1977, is that officer of the regional or islands authority who has been appointed by the authority to be the returning officer for elections of regional or islands councillors; if the constituency is situated in more than one region or islands area, the Secretary of State for Scotland directs which of the two (or more) returning officers is to be the returning officer for the constituency.

A candidate must have a proposer and seconder, be supported by eight other electors, deposit £150 which will be forfeited if he fails to poll one-eighth of the votes cast, and make a declaration of his belief that he is not disqualified.

Much of the legislation on the conduct of election campaigns, now consolidated in the Representation of the People Act 1949, is aimed at preventing corrupt and illegal practices, and at keeping the campaign calm and fair.

Candidates' election expenses (now regulated by the Act of 1974) are strictly limited and must be declared and published.

The result of an election may be challenged by an election petition presented to the Election Petition Court, which consists, in Scotland, of two judges of the Court of Session, and whose decision is final.

An example of a petition to this court is the case of *Grieve* v. *Douglas-Home*, 1965 S.C. 315:

At the general election of October 1964 Sir Alec Douglas-Home, who was then Leader of the Conservative party and Prime Minister, was elected M.P. for the constituency of Kinross and West Perthshire. During the election campaign he had made television appearances in which he had urged the cause of the Conservative party. The expenses incurred in connection with these appearances were not authorised in writing by his election agent nor were they included in any statutory return of election expenses.

C. M. Grieve, a member of the Communist party, and one of the unsuccessful candidates in the constituency, presented a petition to have Sir Alec's election declared void on the ground that Sir Alec had failed to comply with the section of the Representation of the People Act 1949 which required expenses incurred with a view to procuring the election of a candidate to be authorised in writing by the candidate's election agent and which further required a return to be made of such expenses.

The court dismissed the petition, holding that the expenses incurred in connection with the television appearances had been incurred not with a view to procuring the election of Sir Alec as M.P. for the constituency but with a view to informing the public about matters of national political concern.

The Speaker. The chairman of the House of Commons derives his title of "the Speaker" from the fact that he is the channel of communication between that House and the Queen and between that House and the House of Lords.

The Speaker is appointed by the members of the House of Commons from among their own number at the beginning of each Parliament. Usually the Speaker of the previous Parliament is re-elected, if he is still a member and is willing to serve.

He does not take part in debates, and does not vote unless there is a tie. This impartial position of the Speaker means that his constituency is not politically represented in the House.

Amongst the functions of the Speaker are preserving order in the House, giving rulings on procedure and practice, and certifying "money Bills" for the purposes of the Parliament Acts 1911 and 1949.

At the beginning of each Parliament, the Speaker, in accordance with a tradition dating from the sixteenth century, makes a formal claim for certain "ancient and undoubted" privileges of the House of Commons; these are:

(i)   freedom from arrest;
(ii) freedom of speech in debates;

(iii) access to the Sovereign (a right which can only be exercised by members collectively through the Speaker); and

(iv) the right to have the most favourable interpretation placed by the Sovereign on the proceedings of the Commons.

The Speaker does not preside over committees of the House: when the House is in committee the chair is taken by the "Chairman of Ways and Means" or a "Deputy Chairman of Ways and Means" or by one of a Chairmen's panel consisting of members nominated by the Speaker. Either the Chairman or a Deputy Chairman of Ways and Means normally presides over the House itself in the absence of the Speaker.

Functions of Parliament

(a) Legislation

The primary function of Parliament is to legislate, *i.e.* to make law.

In modern Britain it is essential for Parliament to delegate much of its legislative power (see p. 85, above); hence, in practice, the legislative function of Parliament is restricted to consideration of such matters of general principle as can be appropriately embodied in Acts of Parliament and to control and supervision of the exercise by other authorities of the powers which it has delegated to them.

Further, many modern Acts are themselves so long and detailed that it is impossible for Parliament to give full consideration to all their provisions, and rules for the curtailment of debate sometimes result in substantial parts of a Bill passing into law without their having been debated and amended as fully as would have been desirable, or even at all.

Another important practical restriction on Parliament's legislative power arises from the dominant position of the Government party in the House of Commons. The great majority of Acts are passed because the Government requires or at least wishes them to be passed; individual members of Parliament have in practice little chance of initiating legislation.

Against these restrictions on Parliament's legislative power, however, must be set not only the doctrine of the supremacy of Parliament (see 4, below), but also the desire of the Government to retain the support of the electorate and its consequent willingness to conform to the wishes of the majority of the members of the House of Commons.

Thus, before important legislation is introduced, the Government often publishes first a "Green Paper" to promote discussion of tentative policy proposals and then a "White Paper" outlining the proposed legislation; the Parliamentary debate on the White

Paper may have a considerable influence on the Government's intentions; further, having been made aware, through Parliament, of criticisms of and hostility to certain provisions included in a Bill, the Government may choose to amend the Bill to meet criticism which it admits as justifiable or to avoid hostility which might cause it to lose favour with the electorate.

The most important aspects of the legislative function of Parliament may be considered under these headings:

    (i)   different types of legislation;

   (ii)   financial legislation;

  (iii)   Parliament Acts 1911 and 1949; and

  (iv)   procedure for passing public Bills.

(i) *Different types of legislation*

Bills are divided into:

1.   public Bills;

2.   private Bills; and

3.   hybrid Bills.

1. *Public Bills.* A public Bill is one which seeks to alter the general law of the land.

It may be either a Government Bill or a private member's Bill.

A Government Bill is one introduced by a minister on behalf of the Government; it is assured of the general support of the members of the Government party in the Houses of Parliament, and it is almost certain to pass duly through all its stages and become an Act.

A private member's Bill is one introduced by an individual member, who may or may not belong to the Government party, and who is acting on his own initiative without official backing from the Government. The Bill may deal with any subject except that its main object must not be the creation of a charge.

Very limited time is allowed for private members' Bills, and members must first be successful in the ballot for the time available for such Bills. Even then a private member's Bill is unlikely to reach the statute book unless the Government chooses to allot Government time to it.

A private member who has been unsuccessful in the ballot may be able to draw the attention of Parliament to the need for legislation on a subject by means of the "ten-minute rule": by a Standing Order of the House of Commons any member may get up in his place at the beginning of public business on Tuesdays or Wednesdays and ask leave of the House to introduce a Bill; the Speaker may allow him a few minutes to explain the purpose of the Bill and allow another member a similar time to speak against it; the House then "divides" (*i.e.* votes) on the question whether to give leave. A Bill introduced under this procedure is even less likely to reach the statute book than one which has been successful in the ballot.

For the distinction to be drawn between public bills which are financial and other public Bills, see (ii), below.

The procedure for passing public Bills is outlined in (iv), below.

2. *Private Bills.* A private Bill is one affecting a particular locality or a particular person or body of persons (such as a local authority).

Private Bills are introduced, not by members of Parliament, but by "promoters" (persons or bodies outside Parliament who petition Parliament to pass the Bill).

The procedure is governed by Standing Orders which provide for full notice being given so that persons affected may oppose the Bill. There are the same stages as for public Bills, namely first reading, second reading, committee stage, report stage, third reading, and royal assent, but in details the procedure differs from that for public Bills; in particular, the proceedings at the committee stage are of a judicial nature, with counsel presenting arguments and examining witnesses in much the same way as is done in a court case.

Private Bills are now comparatively rare. This is especially so in relation to Scotland, since the Private Legislation Procedure (Scotland) Act 1936 provides that, with the exception of estate Bills, all matters which would otherwise be dealt with by private Bills, must, so far as Scotland is concerned, be dealt with by "provisional order" procedure.

Provisional order procedure is in some ways similar to that for private Bills. A draft provisional order is prepared, and a petition is presented to the Secretary of State for Scotland requesting him to make a provisional order in the terms of that draft. Advertisement and notice are required. The petition is considered by the Chairman of Ways and Means and the Chairman of Committees of the House of Lords, and they make a report to the Secretary of State. If there is opposition to the order, the Secretary of State directs an inquiry to be held before four Commissioners (who are usually members of one or other House of Parliament). The inquiry is often held in Edinburgh or Glasgow, but it may be held in any other suitable place.

If the report of the Commissioners is against the making of the order, it is final, and the Secretary of State has then no power to make the order. If, however, the report is in favour of the making of the order, the Secretary of State is not bound by the report: he may or may not issue the order asked for, or he may choose to modify the draft order in some respects.

Thereafter the order goes before Parliament in the form of a confirmation Bill. There is another opportunity for opposition to the measure, and the possibility of a second inquiry, but normally the weight attached by Parliament to the Commissioners' report is sufficient to ensure that the confirmation Bill becomes a confirmation Act without difficulty.

Another alternative to the private Bill is a "special procedure order," made under the Statutory Orders (Special Procedure) Acts 1945 and 1965. This alternative is the one now generally resorted to in England. It is applicable where an Act (the "enabling" Act) provides that orders made under it are to be "subject to special Parliamentary procedure."

"Special procedure" resembles provisional order procedure in that it includes provision for notice, objection, inquiry, and Parliamentary control. The underlying principle is that matters of general policy are decided by Parliament itself, but that a procedure similar to private Bill procedure is applied in connection with the private rights affected. Under " special procedure " it is the objectors who petition, and not the promoters.

The order is first made by the minister concerned and is laid before Parliament. Either House of Parliament may annul it by resolution.

Any petition submitted for amendment of the order is referred to a Joint Committee of both Houses. If the order is approved by the Joint Committee, it comes into operation. If, however, the Joint Committee reports with amendments, the minister is not bound by the Joint Committee's report: he may accept the order as modified or withdraw it, or he may submit it to Parliament in a confirmation Bill.

Both the provisional order and the special procedure order have the advantage of saving much of the expense and delay involved in the promotion of a private Bill.

3. *Hybrid Bills.* A hybrid Bill is one which is introduced as a public Bill, but which affects private interests in such a way that, if it had been a private Bill, notice would have had to be given to the persons affected.

The procedure for the passing of hybrid Bills is designed to ensure that the private individuals concerned are given the opportunity of having their objections considered: after its second reading, a hybrid Bill is governed by a procedure similar to that for private Bills; persons whose interests are affected may lodge petitions against it (compare "special procedure order," above).

(ii) *Financial legislation*

Financial legislation includes all legislation which authorises expenditure or imposes taxation; it is not restricted to "money Bills" as defined in the Parliament Act 1911 (see p. 165, below).

Financial legislation is subject to special procedures which are based on the following general principles:

1. It is from the Crown that a demand for money must come; this means that a Bill which affects public finance must be introduced by a minister on behalf of the Government.

2. It is from the Commons that a grant of money must come; this means that a Bill which affects public finance must be introduced in the House of Commons, whereas other Bills may be introduced in either House; the function of the Lords is merely to assent to the grant made by the Commons.

3. An Act of Parliament is, by the Bill of Rights of 1688, required for the raising or spending of public money.

4. It is a convention of the constitution that the Lords must not amend a financial Bill.

Financial legislation must be passed every year, because both public revenue and public expenditure depend partly on annual Acts which remain in force for one year only.

Public revenue is derived partly from permanent sources, such as Crown lands and taxes imposed by Acts which remain in force until they are amended or repealed, and partly from income tax which is imposed by an annual Act.

Public expenditure also is partly permanent and partly annual. Examples of permanent expenditure are the interest on the "national debt" (loans made to the Government), the "Queen's Civil List" (a fixed annual sum paid by Parliament to the Queen),[1] and the salaries of judges, of the Speaker of the House of Commons, of the Leader of the Opposition, and of certain other office-holders. Such payments, authorised by permanent statutes, are made out of the "Consolidated Fund" or the "National Loan Fund," and are not open to annual debate. This has the effect of removing them from the realms of political controversy.

Examples of expenditure requiring annual authorisation are the costs of the army, navy, air force, civil service, and other public services. Such expenditure is said to be for "Supply services," and to be made "out of moneys provided by Parliament". It requires to be authorised every year and is open to annual debate.

The two Acts which round off the financial business of the year are the Finance Act and the Appropriation Act.

The Finance Act results from the budget. The proposals of the

---

[1] By the Civil List Act 1975, however, the Treasury may supplement this sum "out of moneys provided by Parliament."

Chancellor of the Exchequer for the levy of taxation take the from of budget resolutions of the House of Commons. These are not statutes, but, by the Provisional Collection of Taxes Act 1968 (which re-enacts an Act of 1913), they have statutory force for a limited period. The finding of money by the imposition of taxation is referred to as the business of "Ways and Means."

The Appropriation Act, on the other hand, is based on the estimates, which are introduced into the House of Commons normally in February and in any case before the beginning of the Government's financial year on April 1. It is the culmination of the business of "Supply" which commences with the demand in the speech from the Throne for a supply of money to maintain the public services. Until supply is fully granted the work of government is carried on by means of a "vote on account." The estimates are debated on a fixed number of "Supply days," allotted for that purpose. Scottish estimates, as well as being debated in the full House, are considered by the Scottish Grand Committee, which consists of all the members for the Scottish constituencies plus ten to fifteen other members. On the allotted Supply days the business of Supply takes precedence over all other business. According to custom the Opposition is allowed to choose which matters are to be discussed, and debates usually take the form of criticism and defence of the Government's general policy, not of detailed consideration of particular estimates.

The procedure relating to the estimates and the annual Appropriation Act is a traditional one which has lost much of its significance not only because so much Government expenditure on the public services is now fixed by other legislation (*e.g.* Social Security Acts), but also because major expenditure commitments are made for varying periods of years ahead.

In general, the role of Parliament in relation to financial legislation is not so much a legislative role as an administrative one, since it involves the principle of accountability of the Government to Parliament and affords an opportunity for criticism of Government policy as a whole. Financial legislation might, therefore, be considered as falling within Parliament's second function (control of the executive) instead of under its primary function (legislation).

(iii) *Parliament Acts* 1911 *and* 1949

These Acts may be regarded as the concluding chapters in the long history of conflict between the House of Lords and the House of Commons. The various earlier instances of conflict had, however, been resolved without resort to legislation.

The Parliament Act 1911 resulted from the conflict which emerged in 1905–6 when the Liberals obtained a huge majority in the House of Commons: the Liberals found that their policies were thwarted by continual rejection or amendment of their Bills by the House of Lords. A climax was reached in 1909 when that House rejected the annual Finance Bill. The controversy which followed involved two general elections and a threat by the King (on the advice of his ministers) to create enough new peers (about 400) to have the Parliament Bill passed without amendment by the Lords.

Although the passing of the Parliament Act 1911 aroused so much controversy, the Act probably did little more than declare what was the normal practice by that time.

The Act divided Bills into "money Bills" and other Bills.

The term "money Bill" is fairly narrowly defined in the Act: it means a public Bill which, in the opinion of the Speaker of the House of Commons, contains *only* provisions dealing with certain specified financial topics, including imposition or alteration of taxation, imposition of charges on the Consolidated Fund or on money provided by Parliament, supply, appropriation, and the raising, guaranteeing or repaying of loans by the Government; Bills relating to rates or loans raised by local authorities are not "money Bills."

When a money Bill is sent up to the House of Lords, it must have endorsed on it a certificate signed by the Speaker and stating that it is a money Bill. The Speaker's certificate is conclusive for all purposes.

The provision made by the Act for the passing of money Bills still applies today: if a money Bill has been passed by the Commons and has been sent to the Lords at least one month before the end of the session, and is not passed by the Lords without amendment within one month after it has been sent up, then that Bill, unless the Commons direct to the contrary, must be presented to the monarch for the royal assent, and once the royal assent has been given the Bill becomes an Act even although the Lords did not consent to the Bill. The effect of that provision was to abolish the House of Lords' power to delay or reject money Bills.

In relation to all other public Bills (with one important exception) the Act provided that if the Bill was passed by the Commons in three successive sessions, was sent to the Lords at least one month before the end of each of these sessions, and was rejected each time by the Lords, then the Bill, unless the Commons directed to the contrary, was to be presented to the monarch for the royal assent, and would become an Act; since a session of Parliament has no definite duration, the proviso was added that at least two years had to elapse between the date of the second reading in the Commons in the first session and the date of the third reading in the Commons in the third session.

The one important exception referred to was a Bill to extend the duration of Parliament, which was, in view of the increased power given to the House of Commons, reduced by the Act itself from seven to five years.

The power of the House of Lords to delay Bills other than money Bills was still further curtailed by the Parliament Act 1949, which was associated with the House of Lords' opposition to the Labour Government's Iron and Steel Bill.

The effect of the Act of 1949 was to substitute two successive sessions for the three successive sessions referred to in the Act of 1911, and to reduce the maximum period of delay from two years to one year.

These Acts ensure that ultimately the wishes of the House of Commons prevail over those of the House of Lords, although the delaying power still vested in the latter may sometimes, when combined with the statutory limit on Parliament's duration to five years, make it necessary for the wishes of the lower House to be endorsed by the electorate in a general election before they become law.

Granted that it would not be in keeping with a democratic constitution that an upper chamber formed mainly on the hereditary principle should have any real power to thwart the wishes of a lower chamber elected by the votes of the people, the curtailment of the powers of the House of Lords does bring Britain very near to having a unicameral legislature in effect at least, if not in theory.

That the House of Lords has a useful role, supplementary to that of the House of Commons, is seldom denied: proposed legislation which has been passed too hurriedly through the House of Commons is often improved by amendments introduced on behalf of the Government in the House of Lords; Bills of a non-controversial and non-political character may be introduced in the first instance in that House instead of in the House of Commons; and the proceedings of the House include valuable debates, some of which are on subjects which members of the lower House would, with their dependence on the electorate in mind, feel less free to discuss.

The limited powers now left to the House of Lords might in very special circumstances be of constitutional significance; *e.g.* if the House of Commons appeared to be acting contrary to the wishes of the electorate on some major matter, the House of Lords might be under a duty to exercise its remaining powers in the interests of the electorate. Apart from such exceptional circumstances, however, the House of Lords no longer has the power to act as an effective second chamber which would control and check the action of a determined House of Commons.

The question of the extent of the powers which the House of

Lords ought to have is inextricably linked to the question of reform of the composition of the House. This was expressly recognised by the statement in the Parliament Act 1911 that it was eventually intended to substitute for the House of Lords a second chamber constituted on a popular instead of an hereditary basis. Although the Life Peerages Act 1958 (see p. 154, above) was an important reform, comprehensive reshaping of the House has not yet been attempted.

A reformed House of Lords might appropriately have conferred on it greater powers than those which now remain to the House, and the reformed House would in that respect be a more effective second chamber. However, while it is generally agreed that the composition of the House of Lords requires to be reformed, there is no general agreement as to the powers which the reformed House should have. An increase in power would bring with it the risk of a fresh outbreak of conflict between that House and the Commons.

(iv) Procedure for passing public Bills

Most Bills are drafted by Parliamentary counsel to the Treasury, a group of lawyers in the civil service. Scottish Bills are drafted by the Lord Advocate's legal secretaries and Parliamentary draftsmen, who have their office in London.

Certain classes of Bills must originate in the House of Commons (e.g. Bills dealing with finance or with the franchise). Other Bills may originate in either House, but in practice only Bills which are not the subject of political controversy originate in the House of Lords.

Apart from the special procedure enacted by the Parliament Acts of 1911 and 1949, a Bill must pass through five stages in both Houses before it is sent for the royal assent.

A Bill which has passed through all stages in one House may pass through all stages in the other House without any further amendment; it then requires only the royal assent. If, however, it is amended by the other House, the Bill comes back to the House which first dealt with it, for the amendments to be either agreed to or dissented from. If the two Houses cannot reach agreement, the Bill lapses, unless the House of Commons decides to resort to the procedure of the Acts of 1911 and 1949.

The five stages are:

1. *First reading.* This is a mere formality, and consists only of the reading of the title of the Bill.

2. *Second reading.* This consists of a discussion of the main principles of the Bill.

In the Commons, if the Bill is non-controversial the second reading stage may be taken before the Second Reading Committee (a standing committee of sixteen to fifty members nominated for each Bill referred to it), while if the Bill relates only to Scotland the second reading stage may be taken before the Scottish Grand Committee (see p. 164, above).

A Bill which authorises expenditure (as most modern Bills do) requires, after its second reading, a recommendation from the Crown (which is a guarantee that the Government accepts responsibility for the charge on the public revenue), and also a financial resolution of the House of Commons.

3. *Committee stage.* After its second reading the Bill is referred to a committee.

The committee may be a "committee of the whole House." The composition of such a committee does not differ from that of the House itself, but there is a difference in procedure, and the chair is taken, not by the Speaker, but by the Chairman of Committees (in the House of Lords) or by the Chairman or a Deputy Chairman of Ways and Means or a member of the Chairmen's panel (in the House of Commons).

In the House of Lords the normal procedure is for a Bill to be referred to a committee of the whole House.

In the House of Commons a Bill is normally referred to one of the standing committees unless the House resolves that it be referred to a committee of the whole House (because, for instance, it is a Bill of major constitutional importance); one part of a Bill may be referred to a standing committee and another part to a committee of the whole House (*e.g.* the annual Finance Bill). Occasionally a Bill is referred to a select committee (*e.g.* the Abortion (Amendment) Bill in February 1975).

Standing committees are constituted as business requires. Each consists of a chairman and sixteen to fifty members nominated for each Bill by the Committee of Selection in such a way that the balance of political parties in the standing committee is approximately the same as that in the House itself.

Bills which relate to Scotland only are referred to one of the two Scottish standing committees. These are distinct from the Scottish Grand Committee. Each of the standing committees consists of sixteen to fifty members of whom not less than sixteen must represent Scottish constituencies.

It is at the committee stage that the details of a Bill are discussed and amendments are proposed. Procedure is less formal than in the House itself.

All amendments are discussed in detail except that the chairman may, in order to save time, select certain amendments only for discussion, the others being voted on without discussion; this device for curtailing discussion is referred to as "the kangaroo," because it involves "leaping" over amendments other than the selected ones.

4. *Report stage.* After the completion of the committee stage, the Bill is "reported" to the House, and at this "report stage" amendments similar to those which might have been made in committee may, with certain restrictions, be moved by the House.

The Speaker has power, under the kangaroo procedure, to select the amendments to be discussed, and his reason for excluding a particular amendment from discussion often is that the amendment has already been fully discussed in committee.

Bills which have been considered at the second reading stage by a Second Reading Committee or by the Scottish Grand Committee may have their report stage taken before a similarly constituted committee.

5. *Third reading.* Unless the Bill is recommitted to committee in order that further substantial amendments may be considered, the Bill is put down for its third reading.

At this stage debate is allowed only on a motion signed by at least six members. If there is a debate, it is confined to general principles, and only minor verbal amendments can be made.

Once the motion that the Bill "be read a third time" has been carried, the Bill is deemed to have passed that House, and will be sent to the other House (which will usually be the House of Lords) where it will pass through similar stages.

The " guillotine." This is a drastic form of closure sometimes adopted in the House of Commons to ensure that proceedings on a Bill are completed by a certain date. An allocation of time is made for each stage or for the different Parts of the Bill, and debate is automatically "cut off" when the time allocation has been used up. The guillotine is generally resorted to only where the Government and the Opposition have failed to agree on a voluntary timetable.

(b) Control of the executive

It is not the function of Parliament to govern the country; that is the function of the executive. Parliament does, however, have the important function of controlling the executive. As in the case of legislation, the dominant House in this connection is the House of Commons, with the result that ultimate control of the executive lies with the electorate.

The most general aspects of Parliamentary control over the executive are:

(i) Parliament makes and unmakes the executive: the Government consists of members of that political party which has a majority in the House of Commons.

Thus, at a general election, electors regard themselves not so much as choosing individual members to represent the various constituencies as deciding whether or not the existing Government is to continue in office. By convention, a Prime Minister belonging to the political party which loses a general election must tender his resignation and that of all his colleagues to the Queen, and make way for a ministry drawn from the political party to which the electorate has given the majority of seats in the House of Commons.

(ii) The executive cannot govern without the continuing support of Parliament: in order to carry out its policies, the Government must maintain the support of Parliament, or at least of the House of Commons, for its legislative programme, since only Parliament can legislate; it also relies on the House of Commons for the financial resources required. If Parliament does not continue to give its support to the Government (*e.g.* if it rejects some major Bill introduced on behalf of the Government or refuses to grant Supply), a general election must, by convention, normally be held, in order that the electorate may decide whether it wishes a change of Government. (This convention was modified during the period when the Labour Government of 1974 to 1979 was in a minority. The situation was that Parliament allowed the Government to remain in office but not to carry out its policy; the Government was frequently defeated in the House of Commons but chose to ignore such defeats although occasionally insisting on "votes of confidence" on issues which it considered fundamental.)

It must, however, be admitted that in practice this aspect of Parliamentary control is not of great significance as long as the political party to which members of the Government belong retains a clear majority in the House of Commons: members are reluctant to vote against the policies of a political party to which they owe their own membership of that House. The Government, therefore, can normally be confident that Parliament will comply with its wishes in respect both of legislation and of Supply. In relation to major issues at least, the control of the executive over Parliament is of greater practical importance than the control of Parliament over the executive.

(iii) The doctrine of ministerial responsibility has the effect of giving Parliament a significant degree of control over the administration: civil servants generally avoid taking administrative action which would be likely to embarrass the minister who is responsible to Parliament for their action.

Especially important in connection with ministerial responsibility is the Parliamentary question. A daily allocation of time is made for questions addressed by members to ministers, the purpose and effect of the questions being to focus public attention on matters of current concern or to secure the redress of particular grievances. There are rules which restrict the subject-matter of questions, and a minister can never be compelled to answer a question. The system does, however, enable Parliament to exert substantial influence over administrative action.

Amongst other Parliamentary procedures giving effect to the doctrine of ministerial responsibility are "debates upon the adjournment" (by which half-an-hour is allotted at the end of each day for the raising by private members of any matter involving ministerial responsibility) and "emergency motions" (by which a member may, in certain circumstances, interrupt the arranged business by moving the adjournment of the House in order that a "specific and important matter that should have urgent consideration" (House of Commons' Standing Order No. 9) be discussed).

(iv) Several committees have been established which enable Parliament to exercise a more detailed control over specific areas of executive action, e.g. select committees such as the Committee of Public Accounts, the Joint Committee on Statutory Instruments and the Committee on European Secondary Legislation; there are also fourteen departmentally related select committees appointed to examine the expenditure, administration and policy of the principal government departments and associated public bodies (such as nationalised industries); they include select committees on employment, energy, foreign affairs, industry and trade, Scottish affairs and Welsh affairs; most consist of a maximum of not more than eleven M.P.s, but the maximum for the Select Committee on Scottish Affairs is thirteen; meetings of that committee may be held in Scotland and be open to the public.

4. SUPREMACY OF PARLIAMENT

The doctrine of the supremacy, or "sovereignty" as Dicey called it, of Parliament is the most important of the general doctrines discussed in relation to the British constitution.

The phrase "supremacy of Parliament" may refer either to the legislative (or law-making) power of Parliament, or to its political power.

The legislative supremacy of Parliament means that Parliament, and no other body or person (unless Parliament grants permission), has the power to alter the law; in particular, the monarch has no power to do so. Parliament had a long struggle, culminating in the seventeenth century, to attain this legislative supremacy, which was finally established by the Bill of Rights of 1688.

The political supremacy of Parliament means that Parliament controls the executive. The attainment by Parliament of its political supremacy is closely associated with the extension of the franchise, and especially with the Reform Acts of 1832.

When the legislative supremacy of Parliament is referred to, "Parliament" denotes the House of Commons, the House of Lords, and the monarch, since a Bill becomes an Act by being passed by the two Houses of Parliament and then receiving the royal assent.

When the political supremacy of Parliament is referred to, "Parliament" denotes the Houses of Parliament only, and in particular the House of Commons, since it is the composition of the House of Commons which decides which political party is to form the Government, and it is in the two Houses of Parliament that ministers of the Crown must answer for their conduct of affairs.

The "doctrine of the supremacy of Parliament" refers to the legislative supremacy of Parliament.

Importance of the Doctrine of the Supremacy of Parliament

The supremacy of Parliament has two general aspects, one positive and the other negative.

The positive aspect is that Parliament can pass any legislation it pleases, and the negative aspect is that no court or other body can review and declare invalid the law made by Parliament. These two aspects were referred to by Dicey when he stated that Parliament had "the right to make or unmake any law whatever" and that no person or body was recognised by law as having "a right to override or set aside the legislation of Parliament" (*The Law of the Constitution*, 10th ed. (1959), p. 40).

In both its positive and negative aspects the doctrine is of great significance in British constitutional law.

In its positive aspect, it guarantees the flexibility of the British constitution because the most fundamental parts of the constitution, whether they have been embodied in statutes or depend on conventions, can be completely altered by Act of Parliament.

In its negative aspect, it ensures that there is not in Britain any power of "judicial review" of Acts of Parliament (*i.e.* any power in the courts to pronounce on the validity of Acts of Parliament), corresponding to the power which enables the courts of some countries with written constitutions to declare legislation invalid on the ground that it is "unconstitutional."

Illustrations of the Supremacy of Parliament

It must be noted that the doctrine applies only to Acts of Parliament, and not to mere resolutions of either House of Parliament; two well-known cases in constitutional law, *Stockdale* v. *Hansard* (1839) 9 A. & E. 1, and *Bowles* v. *Bank of England* [1913] 1 Ch. 57, involved this point.

The case of *Stockdale* v. *Hansard* was concerned with the House of Commons' privilege of freedom of speech. Stockdale sued the publisher of Parliamentary papers on the ground that a report published by order of the House of Commons and available for sale to the public contained defamatory matter. The House of Commons instructed the publisher to put forward the defence that the House of Commons had declared that the case was one of privilege and that a resolution of the House declaring its privileges could not be questioned in any court of law.

The court, however, rejected this defence, and held that only an Act of Parliament could alter the law, which at that time did not recognise the privilege which the House of Commons was claiming.

(As a result of the court's decision, the Parliamentary Papers Act 1840 was passed to alter the law on the matter.)

The case of *Bowles* v. *Bank of England* related to the budget resolutions passed by the House of Commons agreeing to the Chancellor's proposals for rates of income tax and for new customs and excise duties. These resolutions are ultimately incorporated in the annual Finance Act, which may make the new taxation provisions retrospective to the date of the budget.

Before 1913 it had been a well-established practice for the Government to collect taxation under authority of these budget resolutions, but the practice was successfully challenged in that year by Bowles, who sued the Bank of England on the ground that the Bank was not entitled to deduct income tax from dividends until the tax had been imposed by Act of Parliament.

(The case resulted in the passing of the Provisional Collection of Taxes Act 1913 which gave budget resolutions statutory force for a limited period each year.)

The extent of the supremacy of Parliament may be illustrated as follows:

(a) Parliament may alter the *succession to the throne*; thus, His Majesty's Declaration of Abdication Act 1936 varied the succession which had been laid down by the Act of Settlement of 1700.

(b) Parliament may alter its *own composition*; e.g. the composition of the House of Commons has been affected by various Acts which have redistributed seats and extended the franchise, while the composition of the House of Lords has been affected by statutory provisions on life peerages and Lords of Appeal in Ordinary.

An Act of Parliament could even abolish a part of Parliament itself: by convention, the monarch would be bound to give the royal assent to an Act abolishing the monarchy, while the House of Lords might be abolished even without its own consent by an Act passed under the Parliament Acts of 1911 and 1949.

(c) Parliament is *not bound by an Act of its predecessors* or of itself, nor can it bind itself or its successors; if it were otherwise, the present Parliament would not be supreme; thus, successive Acts, each repealing its predecessor, have fixed the maximum duration of Parliament as three years (the Triennial Act 1694), as seven years (the Septennial Act 1715), and as five years (the Parliament Act 1911), and indeed the very Parliament which enacted the Parliament Act 1911 itself renewed its own existence (because of the First World War) well beyond the five-year limit, while there were similar prolongations of Parliament's life during the Second World War; further, any words such as "for ever" contained in a statutory provision can be made of no effect by a later Act of Parliament.

(d) Parliament has the power to *legalise a past illegality*; exercise of this power may take the form of an "indemnity" Act (freeing a person from liability for some past illegal action) or of other retrospective legislation (*e.g.* the War Damage Act 1965 passed to set aside the decision of the House of Lords in *Burmah Oil Co. (Burma Trading) Ltd.* v. *Lord Advocate*, 1964 S.C.(H.L.) 117, in which the company had been held entitled to compensation from the Crown for destruction of property by the Crown in connection with the outbreak of war).

(e) Parliament's supremacy is, in theory, not subject to any *territorial limitations:* the British courts would be bound to give effect to any Act of Parliament, whatever the territory to which it applied; an Act might, for instance, be passed to deal with activities of foreigners on foreign territory, and, although section 4 of the Statute of Westminster 1931 enacted that the United Kingdom Parliament was not to have the right to legislate on its own initiative for independent Commonwealth states, there would, in theory, be nothing to prevent Parliament from acting in breach of that provision, or indeed repealing it.

(f) Parliament's supremacy is, in theory, not restricted by any rules of *international law:* the British courts would be bound to give effect to an Act of Parliament which was, by the rules of international law, a clear usurpation of the jurisdiction of a foreign state; in fixing territorial waters or fishery limits, for instance, Parliament might completely disregard the generally accepted rules of international law on the subject.

This aspect of the supremacy of Parliament can give rise to a situation such as that in *Mortensen* v. *Peters* (1906) 8 F.(J.) 93:

Mortensen, a Danish citizen and captain of a Norwegian ship, had been convicted in Dornoch Sheriff Court of an offence under the Herring Fishery (Scotland) Act 1889, which prohibited trawling in the Moray Firth. The offence had taken place outside the three-mile limit then generally recognised by the rules of international law. In an appeal to a " full bench " of the High Court of Justiciary, Mortensen's conviction and sentence were held to have been legal and competent.

Lord Justice-General (Dunedin) said (at p. 100):

"In this Court we have nothing to do with the question of whether the Legislature has or has not done what foreign powers may consider a usurpation in a question with them. Neither are we a tribunal sitting to decide whether an Act of the Legislature is ultra vires as in contravention of generally acknowledged principles of international law. For us an Act of Parliament duly passed by Lords and Commons and assented to by the King is supreme, and we are bound to give effect to its terms."

Diplomatic representations were made to the British Government against the conviction, and as a result the fine was remitted.

(By the Trawling in Prohibited Areas Prevention Act 1909 Parliament confirmed the correctness of the court's decision but removed the possibility of a similar diplomatically awkward situation arising in future by providing that where fish had been forfeited proceedings were not to be taken for a penalty under the Act of 1889.)

(g) The existence of *delegated legislation* does not detract from the supremacy of Parliament, for Parliament may take away the power which it has delegated and the courts will declare invalid any delegated legislation which is ultra vires ("beyond the powers").

Limitations on the Supremacy of Parliament

The most important limitations on the supremacy of Parliament are the practical limitations, but it is possible that the supremacy is not, even in theory, as absolute as it has traditionally been considered to be.

(a) Possible theoretical limitations

The possibility of there being theoretical limitations on Parliament's supremacy raises some complex questions, of which only a brief indication can be given here:

(i) Is the supremacy of the United Kingdom Parliament limited by the *Articles of Union*, which led to the Union of the Parliaments of Scotland and England in 1707?

The orthodox view has been that in 1707 the English and Scottish Parliaments extinguished themselves and transferred their powers to a new Parliament endowed with the characteristics of the former English Parliament (which characteristics included that of sovereignty).

However, in the case of *MacCormick* v. *Lord Advocate*, 1953 S.C. 396, which arose out of the official use in Scotland of the numeral "II" in the royal title "Elizabeth II," there were obiter dicta (observations with no binding force) which contradicted the orthodox view; these were to the effect that the United Kingdom Parliament has not necessarily inherited all the characteristics of the former English Parliament and none of the characteristics of the former Scottish Parliament, and that the United Kingdom Parliament *is* bound by the Articles of Union.

(ii) Problems relating to the supremacy of Parliament can arise in *supranational law*, *e.g.* the European Communities Act 1972, which was passed to give effect to rights and obligations arising from Britain's entry to the "Common Market," made existing and future Community law directly enforceable in this country, and the question has been asked whether by passing that Act Parliament was surrendering its sovereignty to the Community institutions, and, since there was no time limit for membership, binding itself and its successors for ever; however, the generally accepted view now is that Parliament did not surrender its sovereignty and that the Act of 1972 could be repealed as much as any ordinary Act of Parliament.

(iii) The United Kingdom has accepted as compulsory the jurisdiction of the *European Court of Human Rights*, and recognised the right of individuals to petition the European Commission of Human Rights. This has opened up the possibility of judicial review of Acts of the United Kingdom Parliament.

In recent years there has been much discussion as to whether the United Kingdom should have a "Bill of Rights," the primary purpose cf which would be to protect the individual citizen from unjustified interference by the State or its agents, and which could be expected to set out the various rights and freedoms protected by the European Convention on Human Rights and Fundamental Freedoms, such as the right to life, freedom from torture, inhuman treatment and slavery, rights to liberty and a fair trial, and freedom of thought, religion and expression.

On the one hand it has been maintained (Leslie Scarman, *English Law—The New Dimension* (Hamlyn Lectures, 1974), p. 69):

"A legal system at the mercy of a legislature, which is itself, save in a minority situation, at the mercy of the executive, is no sure guarantee of human rights. . . . Without a Bill of Rights protected from repeal, amendment, or suspension by the ordinary processes of a bare Parliamentary majority controlled by the governemnt of the day, human rights will be at risk."

Attempted legislation has been opposed on the grounds that:

1. if the courts were given power to set aside statutory provisions which they found to be in conflict with the Bill of Rights, this would undermine our doctrine of the supremacy of Parliament; and

2. appointments of judges, who would have the novel role of deciding conflicts between national interests and the rights of individuals, would come to be political appointments, with the result that the reputation of our judiciary would suffer.

(b) Practical limitations

The practical limitations on Parliament's supremacy may be illustrated as follows:

(i) There are *political* limitations: Parliament refrains, as far as possible, from antagonising the electorate, and normally does not make fundamental changes in the law unless it is satisfied that the majority of the electorate desires them; thus, Parliament does not normally alter the succession to the throne or its own composition, or prolong its own life, and does not normally pass retrospective legislation; further, there is a rather vague political doctrine, referred to as "the doctrine of the mandate," according to which Parliament is expected to give effect to the general policy of the political party which won the last general election as that general policy was expressed by that party at the time of the election; a referendum (a vote of the electorate on some individual issue) can operate as a more definite political limitation, confined, however, to the individual issue in question: the holding of a referendum in connection with major constitutional issues appears now to be establishing itself as a feature of the British constitution: a referendum was held in 1975 regarding continued membership of the European Communities, and another was held in Scotland on the question of devolution under the now repealed Scotland Act 1978.

(ii) There are *territorial* limitations: it is obviously pointless for Parliament to pass legislation concerning areas or persons completely beyond the jurisdiction of the United Kingdom courts, and violation of the provisions of the Statute of Westminster would similarly be of no effect so far as the courts of other Commonwealth countries were concerned.

(iii) Parliament generally adheres to the rules of *international law:* it normally refrains from usurping the jurisdiction of a foreign state; thus, it accepts for general purposes a three-mile limit on British territorial waters, and extends its legislation beyond these areas of the sea only where there is some possible justification in international law for that extension (*e.g.* the Continental Shelf Act 1964 which gave effect to some provisions of a Geneva Convention on the High Seas, and the Fishery Limits Act 1976 which extended British *fishery* limits to two hundred miles).

(iv) The practice of *consultation* has the effect of limiting Parliament's supremacy: it is now usual for the organisations and other bodies whose interests would be most affected by proposed legislation to be consulted in advance, the aim being to produce a system of legislation which not only gives effect to a general policy approved of by Parliament but also is workable and acceptable in its detailed application; the practice of consultation has naturally extended as the state has come to regulate more and more of the day-to-day life of the community; thus, organisations of employers and employed are consulted before legislation is introduced to regulate industrial relations, and professional bodies are consulted before legislation is introduced dealing with their professional work (*e.g.* consultation with the medical profession before the passing of the National Health Service Act 1946); Parliament is not, of course, bound to accept any advice which it receives.

The general purpose underlying all these practical limitations is the enforceability of legislation: normally Parliament will not pass legislation which is too absurd ever to command obedience, or which deals with territories and persons not subject to the jurisdiction of the United Kingdom courts, or which would threaten the stability of the British constitution or lead to strife with a foreign state, or which would be unacceptable to the classes most affected by it.

Many of the practical limitations on Parliamentary supremacy have become presumptions which are applied by the courts in the interpretation of legislation (see p. 119, above), *e.g.* the presumptions that:

(i) Parliament did not intend to infringe international law; statutes are, if possible, interpreted in a way which is consistent with treaties made with foreign countries;

(ii) fundamental principles of constitutional law and of common law will be altered only by express provisions in an Act, not by mere implication;

(iii) a statutory provision is workable; the courts will prefer an interpretation which fulfils some purpose to an interpretation which would result in the provision having no effect;

(iv) an Act does not have retrospective effect, *i.e.* it affects only future cases and not past ones.

5. *THE RULE OF LAW*

The phrase "the rule of law" has several different meanings.

In its most elementary sense it means that affairs are regulated by the appropriate organs of the constitution, such as Parliament, the courts, and administrative tribunals, and not by brute force. In this sense the rule of law operates in all civilised states.

Writers on constitutional and administrative law have given more sophisticated meanings to the phrase: most of these meanings have attributed to the rule of law the negative aim of protecting the individual from abuse of power on the part of his rulers.

A more positive aspect of the rule of law appears in the formulation of that rule contained in the Declaration of Delhi 1959. This Declaration was the work of the International Commission of Jurists (a voluntary body of lawyers from over fifty countries), and it resulted from a congress held at New Delhi in 1959. Emphasis was laid in this formulation of the rule of law on the need for the legislature and the executive to provide adequate social and economic conditions for the individual, and not merely on the need for an independent judiciary to provide protection from arbitrary rule.

For the purposes of an elementary study of British constitutional law, however, the most important formulation of the rule of law is still that of Dicey. Writing in 1885, Dicey gave three meanings to "the rule of law" as he saw it operating in the British constitution of his day, and the main question now asked is how far these meanings apply in the British constitution today.

(a) Dicey's Three Meanings of "The Rule of Law"

(i) **The first meaning—absence of arbitrary power**

"No man is punishable or can be lawfully made to suffer in body or goods except for a distinct breach of law established in the ordinary legal manner before the ordinary courts of the land. In this sense the rule of law is contrasted with every system of government based on the exercise by persons in authority of wide, arbitrary, or discretionary powers of constraint . . .

"It means, in the first place, the absolute supremacy or predominance of regular law as opposed to the influence of arbitrary power, and excludes the existence of arbitrariness, of prerogative, or even of wide discretionary authority on the part of the government" (*The Law of the Constitution*, 10th ed. (1959), pp. 188 and 202).

(ii) **The second meaning—"equality before the law"**

By "equality before the law" Dicey meant "the equal subjection of all classes to the ordinary law of the land administered by the ordinary law courts" (*ibid.*, pp. 202–203).

The second meaning of "the rule of law" he stated as being:
"not only that with us no man is above the law, but (what is a different thing) that here every man, whatever be his rank or condition, is subject to the ordinary law of the realm and amenable to the jurisdiction of the ordinary tribunals" (*ibid.*, p. 193).

Dicey contrasted this state of affairs with the droit administratif ("administrative law") of France: in that country, government officials were subject to a body of law distinct from that applicable as between private citizens, and disputes between government officials and citizens were dealt with by a special system of administrative courts.

(iii) The third meaning—constitution the result of the ordinary law of the land

Dicey's third meaning is that:
"with us the law of the constitution, the rules which in foreign countries naturally form part of a constitutional code, are not the source but the consequence of the rights of individuals, as defined and enforced by the courts; that, in short, the principles of private law have with us been by the action of the courts and Parliament so extended as to determine the position of the Crown and of its servants; thus the constitution is the result of the ordinary law of the land" (*ibid.*, p. 203).

By this, Dicey meant that the rights of the individual, such as his right to personal liberty and his freedom of speech, were the result either of decisions of the courts in particular cases or of individual Acts of Parliament, and were not set out in any formal code or constitution as they were in many foreign countries.

(b) How far does Dicey's "Rule of Law" Apply Today?

Dicey's explanation of the rule of law has been much criticised, *e.g.* on the ground that he overlooked the powers of the public authorities in his day and the considerable advantages enjoyed by the Crown over private individuals in litigation, and on the ground that he misunderstood the droit administratif.

Criticism of Dicey's explanation can be properly made only by a legal historian who has studied the British constitution as it existed in 1885.

The question with which the student of the present-day British constitution is concerned is whether "the rule of law" as explained by Dicey applies today, and a negative answer to that question is not in itself a valid criticism of Dicey's view.

In considering this question, the three meanings must be taken separately:

(i) The first meaning—absence of arbitrary power

So far as criminal law is concerned, Dicey's first meaning applies today: it is still a feature of the British constitution that a citizen will not be punished except for a breach of the ordinary law and that he will be tried in the ordinary courts and not, for instance, in a special tribunal set up to deal with crimes against the state.

In theory, the citizen knows, or has the means of knowing, all the crimes and offences for which he may be punished, and, except so far as a discretion is, in the interests of justice, left with the courts, he knows, or has the means of knowing, the exact penalties which he may incur.

In practice, however, the citizen is now less likely than he was in Dicey's day actually to know the criminal law which might affect him, for there has been a great increase in the number of statutory offences, many of them created by delegated legislation, many requiring no mens rea ("guilty intention") for their commission, and not all ascertainable with reasonable certainty.

There is, therefore, a practical, although not a theoretical, difference between the application of this first meaning to the criminal law of Dicey's day and its application to present-day criminal law.

Dicey's first meaning is not confined to the criminal law, but extends to arbitrariness, prerogative, and wide discretionary authority on the part of the Government in any branch of law. The Government now takes a much greater part in the regulation of the detailed conditions of life in the community than it did in Dicey's day, and this has made it necessary for government officials to have very wide powers conferred on them by statute or by delegated legislation. As a result it is now impossible for the citizen to foresee how he will be affected by the exercise of governmental powers.

The law of town and country planning is an obvious example of a branch of law in which the citizen cannot foresee how he may be restricted in the use of, or even deprived of, his property, but any "planning," in the general sense of control of private enterprise and private life by the state, involves some curtailment, often of an unforeseeable extent, of the individual's freedom of action.

Dicey's statement that "no man . . . can be lawfully made to suffer in . . . goods except for a distinct breach of law" must, therefore, now be interpreted in a different sense from that which Dicey intended, for an individual can now lawfully be deprived of rights in property in many circumstances which do not foreseeably involve a breach of law. However, it is still true that an individual cannot be deprived of property rights except by statutory authority, and that the courts protect him from any *unlawful* deprivation of these rights; Dicey's words are still applicable to that theoretical extent.

Dicey's contrast between the supremacy of "regular law" and the influence of arbitrary power still applies, provided "regular law" is interpreted as including all the mass of delegated legislation, and "arbitrary power" is taken to mean power which may be exercised without any lawful authority. However, Dicey does not distinguish in his application of the rule of law between arbitrary power on the one hand and wide discretionary power on the other hand, and this is a distinction which it is essential to make if the rule is to apply to the British constitution today: the Government acting through its officials still has no arbitrary powers, but it certainly has very wide discretionary powers.

A further qualification to the practical application of "the rule of law" in Dicey's first sense arises from the growth of "group law" since Dicey's day. An individual may, by his membership of a particular profession or his practice of a particular trade, become subject to special "group law" enforced by special tribunals, *e.g.* members of the medical profession may be tried by a committee of the General Medical Council on charges of serious professional misconduct and have their names erased from the Medical Register.

In theory, an individual can avoid subjection to group law by not joining the group to which it applies, but professions and trades are now so fully organised through trade unions and otherwise, and group law is consequently so widespread that in practice an individual would in many cases be deprived of a livelihood if he were to refuse to subject himself to any form of group law.

Through subjection, theoretically voluntary, to group law the individual may find that he "is punishable or can be lawfully made to suffer" for conduct which is not "a distinct breach of law established in the ordinary legal manner before the ordinary courts of the land."

(ii) The second meaning—"equality before the law"

There are two important respects in which Dicey's second meaning must be qualified if it is to be applied to the British constitution today:

1. *Special privileges*

Special privileges are given to different classes of persons for a variety of reasons; it cannot, therefore, be truly said that "every man, whatever be his rank or condition, is subject to the ordinary law of the realm."

Amongst those who enjoy special privileges are diplomatic agents (who are immune in some respects from proceedings in the British courts), and trade unions (which have a statutory privilege of not being sued for wrongs done by them), but the most important class of persons enjoying special privileges is that of government and other public officials.

In Dicey's time, when the state's function in home affairs did not greatly extend beyond the preservation of law and order, there was little need for special privileges for state officials other than police officers. At the present day, on the other hand, when the state takes such an active part in the whole life of the community it is essential that state officials of many different classes should enjoy the privileges necessary to enable them to carry out their several duties.

However, although there are now many more instances of special privileges for officials than there were in Dicey's day, the Crown Proceedings Act 1947, by restricting the immunity from legal proceedings enjoyed by the Crown and its officials, actually brought the British constitution closer to this second meaning of "the rule of law" than it was in 1885. This restriction of Crown immunity was itself a consequence of the greatly extended activities of officials in the modern state.

In theory, therefore, state officials are in a less privileged position than they were in Dicey's time, but in practice the desire of the individual citizen to make them liable arises much more often.

2. Administrative tribunals

There are in Britain today numerous special or administrative tribunals (e.g. national insurance local tribunals, rent tribunals, and industrial tribunals); it certainly cannot now be truly said that a man is amenable only "to the jurisdiction of the ordinary tribunals."

The modern administrative tribunals are, like the special privileges of officials, mainly the result of the extension of the Government's participation in the lives of individuals. They perform functions which could not all have appropriately been entrusted to the ordinary courts, and it is generally acknowledged that they are an essential feature of the modern state. The question now most debated concerning these tribunals is not whether they should exist at all, but how best they may be made to conform to the standards of the rule of law.

In connection with Dicey's second meaning, it is still relevant to contrast the situation in Britain and the droit administratif of France. Britain still has no distinct body of "administrative law" as such; the administrative law of Britain has merely grown out of "the ordinary law" since Dicey's time. Further, because of the haphazard way in which the British administrative tribunals have been created, from time to time as the need arose, they are lacking in uniformity, and cannot be said to comprise a system or hierarchy as do the administrative courts of France.

However, those who now contrast British and French administrative law do not all agree with Dicey in concluding that the situation in Britain is necessarily in all respects superior to, or better protects the individual against the state than, the droit administratif.

(iii) The third meaning—constitution the result of the ordinary law of the land

The third meaning does not now apply as fully as it did in 1885.

It is true that there is still no constitutional code guaranteeing the individual's fundamental rights. Freedom of speech, for instance, is a right which entitles a person to say what he wishes provided he does not infringe the criminal law or make himself liable to a civil action for defamation. Other fundamental rights such as freedom of person, freedom of meeting, and the right of enjoyment of property are similarly restricted and defined by the various provisions of criminal and civil law. To this extent rules which in foreign countries form part of the constitutional code are still in Britain "the result of the ordinary law of the land."

However, Dicey placed more emphasis than would now be justified on the decisions of the courts as being the source of the individual's fundamental rights: he described the constitution as being a "judge-made" constitution (*The Law of the Constitution*, p. 196). Statute law has, especially since the 1930s, progressively encroached on the common law in this area, with the result that a dispute about the exercise of a fundamental right now usually turns on the application of some statutory provision; *e.g.* freedom of meeting has had its scope defined by Acts such as the Public Order Act 1936 and Acts dealing with highways, and the right of enjoyment of property has been limited by Town and Country Planning Acts.

Further, the citizen now has many more rights than the fundamental rights which Dicey had in mind. These newer rights, which relate to such matters as education, pensions, unemployment benefit, sickness benefit, and redundancy payments, can usually be asserted only through administrative tribunals, and so, although they are the result of ordinary statutes, they are not the result of "the ordinary law of the land" in the sense that they are secured to the individual by the ordinary courts. These rights are not, of course, fundamental rights such as would be appropriately included in a constitutional code, but to the individual layman they may well appear of greater value than his fundamental rights.

6. SEPARATION OF POWERS

The phrase "separation of powers" has had different meanings in different writings.

The version of the doctrine of separation of powers which has been most discussed in relation to the British constitution is that associated with the French jurist Montesquieu (1689–1755), whose monumental work, *L'Esprit des Lois* ("The Spirit of the Laws"), was published in thirty-one books in 1748.

Montesquieu is often considered to have been the first to formulate the doctrine and to have regarded the British constitution of his day as conforming to the doctrine; neither of these commonly held views is fully justified, however. Further, the version of the doctrine now popularly associated with Montesquieu's name does not in fact exactly correspond to that actually given in *L'Esprit des Lois*. What follows here is restricted to the popularised version of the doctrine.

(a) Meaning of the Doctrine of Separation of Powers

The functions of government may be divided into three classes— legislative, executive (including administrative), and judicial. The organs of the state which perform these functions are, respectively, the legislature, the executive, and the judiciary.

(i) The legislature

The primary function of the legislature is to make law.

In the United Kingdom the legislature consists of "the Queen in Parliament."

(ii) The executive

The primary function of the executive is to carry out the law. This involves the direction of general policy, the maintenance of law and order, the promotion of social and economic welfare, and other aspects of the administration of the state.

A distinction is sometimes drawn between the executive function and the administrative function, the former being regarded as confined to the formulation of policy, and the latter as concerned with the implementation of policy by administrative action. It is, however, impossible to make any distinct separation between these two aspects of the executive function, because administrative action necessarily raises questions of policy, and policy which is not implemented by administrative action is of no effect.

In the United Kingdom the head of the executive is nominally the Queen, who is advised by her ministers. By convention the Queen always accepts the advice of her ministers, and so the Prime Minister is, along with the other ministers who form his Cabinet, the actual head of the executive. The lower ranks of the executive include all ministers not of Cabinet rank, and all government departments. While the Cabinet decides major questions of policy, the lower ranks of the executive deal with more specialised matters and with all the details of administration which are necessary to give effect to Cabinet policy.

(iii) The judiciary

The primary function of the judiciary is to declare, interpret, and apply the law; if the law applicable is common law, the function of the judiciary is to "declare" the law, whereas if the law applicable is statute law, the function of the judiciary is to "interpret" the law.

In the United Kingdom the judiciary is traditionally regarded as consisting of the various civil and criminal courts.

According to the doctrine of separation of powers, the three functions of government must be kept separate and never be exercised by the same organs; only in that way, it is maintained, can political liberty be safeguarded: if the same organ of government were to have both legislative and executive powers, that organ could enact tyrannical laws and proceed to carry them out in a tyrannical manner, and if the same organ were to have both executive and judicial powers, that organ could administer in an irresponsible and arbitrary manner; union of all three powers in one organ would amount to complete tyranny.

This doctrine has been very influential with those who have framed constitutions since Montesquieu's time. The standard example of the most rigid application of the doctrine is the constitution of the United States of America, drawn up in 1787. The framers of that constitution intended that there should be between the separate organs of government such a system of checks and balances that no one organ could ever become supreme: only Congress can legislate, only the President has supreme executive power and he cannot be removed from office by an adverse vote of either or both Houses of Congress, while the Supreme Court and the lower courts have a monopoly of judicial power.

In its practical application the doctrine of separation of powers can give rise to difficulties:

(i) It is not always possible to classify a power dogmatically under one or other of the three heads.

(ii) There are some organs of government which do not fit neatly into the traditional division, *e.g.* British administrative tribunals.

(iii) Rigid separation tends either to produce deadlock or to break down in the interests of workability, and greater political liberty is not necessarily actually enjoyed in countries which have given effect to the doctrine in their constitutions than in other countries in which the powers are inextricably intermingled.

There are three aspects of the doctrine of separation of powers; these relate to:

(i) *Persons*: the same persons should not form part of more than one of the three organs of government; in the British constitution this would mean, for instance, that ministers of the Crown, being part of the executive organ, could not sit in the House of Commons which is part of the legislative organ;

(ii) *Control*: one organ of government should not control, or interfere with, another organ; in the British constitution this would mean, for instance, that ministers would not be controlled by, or even be responsible to, Parliament;

(iii) *Functions*: one organ of government should not exercise the functions of another organ; in the British constitution this would mean, for instance, that ministers would not have power to make delegated legislation.

(b) How far is there Separation of Powers in the British Constitution Today?

There was no strict separation of powers in the British constitution of Montesquieu's day, and that fact has led to Montesquieu's being criticised for having misinterpreted the British constitution.

Whether or not that criticism is justified is a question for the legal historian, and the question with which the student of the present-day British constitution is primarily concerned is the extent to which the doctrine now applies to that constitution.

It is obvious from the examples given at the end of section (a), above, that the doctrine does not apply in any rigid or theoretical way to the British constitution today. This does not mean that political liberty is absent; indeed, some of the departures from the doctrine achieve the same end as the doctrine itself is supposed to achieve; *e.g.* the responsibility of ministers to the House of Commons ensures that the will of the electorate ultimately prevails.

On the other hand, there are instances of substantial adherence to the principle of separation, if not to the doctrine itself, where that is necessary for the maintenance of political liberty (*e.g.* the independence of the judiciary).

These conclusions can be justified by a consideration of the three aspects of the doctrine (persons, control, and functions) in relation to each pair of organs, namely:

    (i)   legislature and executive;
   (ii) legislature and judiciary; and
  (iii) executive and judiciary.

(i) Legislature and executive

1. *Do the same persons form part of both the legislature and the executive?*

The answer to this question is undoubtedly "Yes": the Queen is part of the legislature and is the nominal head of the executive, and, what is more important, the ministers of the Crown must, by convention, be members of one or other House of Parliament. This latter departure from separation of powers is vital to the working of the British system of Parliamentary government.

2. *Does the legislature control the executive or the executive control the legislature?*

Paradoxically, the answer to both of these questions is "Yes."

On the one hand, the House of Commons, the most important part of the legislature, controls the executive, since ministers of the Crown are chosen from the party which has a majority in that House, are responsible collectively and individually to Parliament for the performance of their executive functions, depend on the House of Commons for finance, and go out of office when they fail to command the support of a majority in that House.

On the other hand, so long as ministers are in power, and especially if their political party has a large majority in the House of Commons, they control the legislature, since they initiate most of the legislation, secure its passage through both Houses of Parliament by virtue of their party's majority in the House of Commons, advise the Queen to give the royal assent (advice which, by convention, she is bound to accept), and limit the time available in Parliament for business other than Government business (*e.g.* for private members' Bills).

In this respect, therefore, there is no separation of powers. On the contrary, there must be co-operation between the legislature and the executive if the Parliamentary government of modern Britain is to work at all. The detailed legislation, characteristic of the modern state, makes it essential for Parliament to rely on the executive to give practical effect to such legislation. Further, according to the rather vague doctrine of "the mandate," a Government, especially if there has been a recent general election, is regarded as being entitled to have the legislative changes which were proposed in the party's electoral programme given effect to by Parliament, so that in practice Parliament will usually do what the Government tells it to do; thus, the executive uses Parliament to obtain the necessary statutory authority for the carrying out of policy.

However, the system of co-operation also makes it essential for the Government so to govern that it retains the support of a majority in the House of Commons; otherwise it is bound either to resign, or to cause a general election to be held. Thus, the executive, in using Parliament, must constantly remember its own dependence on the electorate as represented in the House of Commons.

3. *Do the legislature and the executive exercise one another's functions?*

The most important inroad in this respect on separation of powers is the executive's extensive powers to make delegated legislation.

Provided Parliament has effective control over the delegated legislation made by the executive, this departure from separation of powers does not substantially threaten political liberty, and must be accepted as inevitable if the executive is to perform the functions required of it in the modern state.

However, Parliamentary supervision of delegated legislation is not always effective: sometimes unduly wide powers are conferred on the executive, and the mass of delegated legislation is so great that Parliamentary time is just not available for the adequate scrutiny of all of it.

On the other hand, Parliament sometimes exercises a function of the executive, since in dealing with private Bills it is performing an administrative action, although it uses the legislative form in doing so.

(ii) Legislature and judiciary

1. *Do the same persons form part of both the legislature and the judiciary?*

The theoretical answer to this question is "Yes, to a certain extent"; yet there is in fact no departure in this respect from the principle underlying the doctrine of separation of powers.

The House of Lords is both part of the legislature and the final court of appeal for civil cases from Scotland and for civil and criminal cases from other parts of the United Kingdom. The Lords of Appeal in Ordinary, specially appointed under the Appellate Jurisdiction Act 1876 to deal with the judicial business of the House, are full members of the House for life and are quite entitled to, and sometimes do, take part in the legislative business of the House. There is, in theory, nothing to prevent all the lay members of the

House from sitting in the House when it is acting as a court
of appeal.

On the other hand, there is in reality virtually no identity between
the persons who form the legislature and those who form the judiciary: under the House of Commons Disqualification Act 1975, all
salaried judges, including those of the Court of Session, sheriffs-
principal and sheriffs (other than honorary sheriffs), as well as
members of some administrative tribunals, are excluded from
membership of the House of Commons; the House of Lords in its
judicial capacity is in substance a court of law, composed of the
Law Lords only and sitting in circumstances different from those in
which the House sits in its legislative capacity.

2. *Does the legislature control the judiciary or the judiciary control
the legislature?*

Apart from formal Parliamentary procedure, virtually never
resorted to, for removal of certain judges in very exceptional circumstances, there is no control of the judiciary by the legislature other
than that which results from the doctrine of the supremacy of
Parliament and which enables Parliament to lay down the law which
must be applied by the courts in future cases, and even, by retrospective legislation, to set aside some past decision of the
courts.

The salaries of judges are charged on the Consolidated Fund,
and are therefore not subject to annual review by Parliament (see
p. 163, above).

The judiciary does not control the legislature except in so far as
there is necessarily an element of control in the performance by the
judiciary of its own primary function of applying and interpreting
statute law.

3. *Do the legislature and the judiciary exercise one another's
functions?*

Here again there is no substantial departure from separation of
powers.

The legislature does exercise some judicial functions: the House
of Lords is the final court of appeal for civil cases; each House of
Parliament has power to enforce its own privileges (such as freedom
of speech and the right to regulate its own proceedings) and to
punish persons, whether members or "strangers," who infringe
them; the power to punish members or others extends to any
"contempt" of the House, even although no breach of privilege is
involved; for instance, some disrespectful statement about a member
as such or disobedience to an order of the House may amount to

"contempt"; while the courts have refused to recognise the right of the House of Commons to decide what its privileges are (*Stockdale* v. *Hansard* (1839) 9 A. & E. 1, p. 173, above), each House has the right to decide in its own discretion whether some statement or action amounts to a "contempt."

It is also true that the judiciary exercises some legislative functions, since the Court of Session and the High Court of Justiciary have power to regulate procedure in the courts by Acts of Sederunt and Acts of Adjournal, respectively (p. 88, above).

These exceptions, however, are of a limited and specialised nature. Further, the rules on Parliamentary privilege and contempt are more likely to safeguard political liberty than to undermine it.

(iii) Executive and judiciary

1. *Do the same persons form part of both the executive and the judiciary?*

There are partial departures from separation of powers in this connection in relation to the Lord Chancellor and to the Judicial Committee of the Privy Council.

The Lord Chancellor is a Cabinet minister, and therefore part of the executive. He is also, as head of the English judicial system, an important part of the judiciary.

The Judicial Committee of the Privy Council has a distinguished membership including the Lord Chancellor and Lords of Appeal in Ordinary. In the judicial systems of the United Kingdom its jurisdiction is limited and specialised, *e.g.* an appeal may be made to it against a decision of the Professional Conduct Committee of the General Medical Council to strike a practitioner's name off the register. The Judicial Committee's most notable function is to hear appeals from the courts of British colonies and courts of some overseas Commonwealth countries; its decisions in such cases, although not binding on the Scottish courts, are treated as highly persuasive by them.

The Privy Council, out of which the Cabinet itself developed, was originally a select body of advisers to the monarch. Members were, in Henry VIII's reign, given the name of "privy councillors" to distinguish them from the larger number of the monarch's "ordinary councillors." The Judicial Committee of the Privy Council is, therefore, nominally a part of the executive, although in reality it is a court of law.

Apart from these exceptions, the same persons do not form part of both the executive and the judiciary.

2. *Does the executive control the judiciary or the judiciary control the executive?*

Although judges are the Queen's judges, and as such are appointed and paid by the executive, the judiciary is not, in the actual performance of its judicial functions, in any way controlled by the executive. Any interference by the executive with the work of the courts is quite alien to British standards of justice.

If the executive considers that a decision of the courts is unacceptable, it may initiate legislation to set the decision aside, and use its control over the legislature to have the legislation passed with retrospective effect (*e.g.* the War Damage Act 1965 passed to set aside the decision in *Burmah Oil Co. (Burma Trading) Ltd.* v. *Lord Advocate*, 1964 S.C.(H.L.) 117 (see p. 174, above)), but it is in Britain unthinkable that the executive could at its discretion overthrow the decisions of the courts.

On the other hand, it is a safeguard for political liberty that the judiciary should control the executive, so far as that is necessary to prevent the executive from exceeding its powers and from refusing to give to private citizens the rights and benefits to which they are entitled.

The control exercised by the judiciary over the executive for these purposes is one of the salient topics of administrative law. It is referred to as "judicial review of administrative action," and particularly important aspects of it are the ultra vires ("beyond the powers") doctrine, according to which the executive must not, either in procedure or in substance, exceed its powers, and the rules of "natural justice," according to which both sides must be heard ("audi alteram partem"—"hear both sides") and the person making the decision must be free from bias ("nemo judex in causa sua potest"—"no one can be judge in his own cause").

The judiciary is, however, sometimes barred from exercising this control over the executive because of total or partial exclusion of judicial review or because of the very wide discretion conferred by the particular statute on the executive authority. For instance, a statute may provide that certain administrative action is "not to be questioned in any legal proceedings whatsoever," or a time-limit of, say, six weeks, may be imposed on the right of judicial review, or a statute may confer on a minister power to do what "he may consider necessary" or to impose such conditions as "he sees fit." Such curtailment of judicial review is a potential threat to political liberty.

3. *Do the executive and the judiciary exercise one another's functions?*

The sheriff courts and the Court of Session exercise certain administrative functions, *e.g.* in connection with the winding-up of companies, the estates of deceased persons, and trusts, but these departures from strict separation of powers do not raise any question of principle.

On the other hand, a question of principle is raised by the tendency of modern legislation to entrust judicial functions to the executive or at least to take them away from the courts. In this connection, there is considerable room for debate, and the topic is one of the main ones in administrative law.

For instance, it is in practice difficult to draw a precise line between executive functions and judicial functions, although primarily an executive function involves the exercise of a discretion in the application of policy, while a judicial function involves the application of settled law to particular facts; further, the great variety of administrative tribunals makes it impossible to classify them all either under the executive or under the judiciary, and even where a judicial function is entrusted to the executive (as where the final decision is to be made by "the minister"), this does not necessarily mean that judicial forms and procedure are altogether abandoned.

The general conclusion on this point is that there are numerous executive functions which have some judicial content, and that a watch should be kept to ensure that in so far as these functions are judicial adequate standards of "openness, fairness and impartiality" (advocated in the Franks' *Report on Administrative Tribunals and Enquiries*, (1957) Cmnd. 218) are adhered to.

7. *THE EUROPEAN COMMUNITIES*

Because of the United Kingdom's membership of the European Communities, which dates from January 1, 1973, no account of our constitution can be complete without some reference to its European context (see also pp. 10, 92 and 176, above).

(a) **Historical Background**

The United Kingdom was not one of the original members of the European Communities.

In 1951, France, Germany, Italy, Belgium, the Netherlands and Luxembourg, by a Treaty of Paris, established the European Coal and Steel Community (ECSC), so that there was a single market without frontier barriers for these countries in iron, steel and coal.

This was followed in 1957 by two Treaties of Rome by which the same six countries established the European Economic Community (EEC, or, colloquially, "the Common Market") with the aim of removing all trade barriers between member states and formulating common economic policies, and the European Atomic Energy

Community (EURATOM) to develop and control nuclear industries in the member states.

In 1961, the United Kingdom applied for membership of EEC, and, in 1962, of ECSC and EURATOM also, but her accession was vetoed by France. A further application in 1967 was similarly rejected.

In 1971 the House of Commons voted in favour of the United Kingdom's entry, and in 1972 an Accession Treaty was signed at Brussels, admitting the United Kingdom, Ireland and Denmark to membership of the three European Communities as from January 1, 1973.

Certain changes in the law of the United Kingdom were required to enable her to comply with the obligations, and exercise the rights, of membership, and the European Communities Act 1972 was passed for that purpose.

After a change of government in 1974, the terms of the United Kingdom's entry to the Communities were renegotiated, and in a referendum (the first to be conducted in Britain) the electorate by a majority of approximately two to one voted in favour of continued membership on the renegotiated terms.

In 1975 Greece, and in 1977 Portugal and Spain, applied for membership of the Communities. Greece became a member on January 1, 1981.

(b) Institutions

As a result of a merger which took effect in 1967, the three Communities (ECSC, EEC and EURATOM) have had common, instead of separate, institutions. There are four permanent Community institutions, namely:

(i) the Council of Ministers;
(ii) the Commission;
(iii) the Court of Justice; and
(iv) the European Parliament.

In addition, there are several associated bodies (*e.g.* the European Investment Bank, whose function is to contribute, on a non-profit-making basis, to the balanced development of the Common Market, and the Economic and Social Committee (ESC), an advisory body consulted by the Council of Ministers and by the Commission on various categories of economic and social activity). There are also numerous sections and sub-divisions, based on subject-matter, within the institutions and other bodies. (*e.g.* the Commission has several specialised services (Legal Service, Environment and Consumer Protection Service, etc.) and nineteen directorates, and the Economic and Social Committee has nine sections).

(i) The Council of Ministers

The Council of Ministers has ten-members, one representing each of the ten national governments.

The Council is the executive body of the Communities, deciding final policy for the Communities and co-ordinating national policies with those of the Communities.

Many of the Council's decisions can be taken by "weighted" majority voting. For this purpose the votes of France, Germany, Italy and the United Kingdom count as ten each, those of Belgium, Greece and the Netherlands as five each, those of Denmark and Ireland as three each, and the vote of Luxembourg counts as two.

The matter before the Council may have been proposed by the Commission. If so, the majority required for a decision in favour of the proposal is 45 votes. If the Council is acting without a proposal from the Commission, the decision may be reached by the same number of votes, but the votes must have been cast by at least six members.

Where the matter before the Council is regarded by a member state as of vital interest to herself, unanimity is in practice required.

The office of President of the Council is held for six months at a time by the minister representing each member state in turn.

(ii) The Commission

The Commission has fourteen members, not more than two being from any one member state. Appointments are made by agreement among the member states, last for four years and may be renewed. The members are under a duty to act independently of their national governments and of other sectional interests. Each member is responsible for one or more of the main fields of activity of the Communities, but overall authority rests with the Commission as a whole. Meetings are held in Brussels at least once a week.

The role of the Commission is to be guardian of the treaties, to initiate and execute Community policies, and to act as mediator between the governments of member states. It reports to, and is responsible to, the European Parliament.

The President and Vice-Presidents are appointed from among the members for two years at a time, with the possibility of renewal.

(iii) The Court of Justice

The Court of Justice consists of eleven judges appointed for six years at a time (with the possibility of renewal) by agreement among the member states. The accepted practice is for each member state to provide at least one judge. The Court sits at Luxembourg.

Amendments to rules of procedure in 1979 enabled the Court to sit in three chambers, each consisting of a President and three other judges.

The function of the Court is to interpret, and ensure the observance of, the treaties of the Communities. The court deals with complaints that a member state is failing to fulfil treaty obligations, and it has power to declare an act of the Council or of the Commission to be void. It has also jurisdiction in relation to some cases before national courts: if a case before a national court necessarily involves a decision on a point of Community law (*e.g.* interpretation of the treaties or a question as to the validity of an act of one of the Community institutions), then the national court *may* request the European Court to give a preliminary ruling on the point, and if the national court is one from which in the country concerned no further appeal can be made (*e.g.* the House of Lords in the United Kingdom), the national court *must* make such a request. Judgments of the Court must be complied with by the Community institutions, and are enforceable by the courts of the member states.

The President of the Court is elected by the judges from among their own number, and holds office for three years, with the possibility of renewal.

The Court is assisted in its work by four Advocates-General who must have qualifications equal to those of the judges themselves. The Advocate-General in a case acts impartially and independently, making a statement to the Court after the representations of the parties have been presented and before the Court gives its judgment.

(iv) The European Parliament

The European Parliament at first consisted of members nominated by the Parliaments of the member states, but since 1979 members have been directly elected by the electorates of the member states.

The total membership is 434. France, Germany, Italy and the United Kingdom have eighty-one representatives each, the Netherlands twenty-five, Belgium and Greece twenty-four, Denmark sixteen, Ireland fifteen and Luxembourg six. Members are elected for a five-year term. The Parliament meets at Strasbourg.

In the United Kingdom elections are governed by the European Assembly Elections Act 1978, which provides for there being seventy-nine constituencies—sixty-six in England, eight in Scotland, four in Wales and one in Northern Ireland. Each of the constituencies in Great Britain elects one representative by the simple majority system, while the constituency of Northern Ireland elects three representatives by the single transferable vote system (a form of proportional representation which has been used in the past in Northern Ireland for other purposes).

The Parliament is consulted by the Council of Ministers and the Commission on policies and proposals. The Communities' annual budgets are subject to review by the Parliament. The Commission reports annually to the Parliament and may be dismissed on a two-thirds majority vote of its members.

The Parliament has a system of specialist committees, which, unlike the committees of the United Kingdom Parliament, consider draft legislation before it reaches the Parliament itself.

8. *PROPOSALS FOR REFORM*

Proposals for reform of the British constitution have in recent years centred mainly on the question of devolution.

In 1969 the Government set up a Royal Commission under the chairmanship of Lord Crowther "to examine the present functions of the central legislature and government in relation to the several countries, nations and regions of the United Kingdom," and to consider whether any changes were desirable in those functions or otherwise in present constitutional and economic relationships (including relationships between the United Kingdom and the Channel Islands and the Isle of Man). In March 1972 Lord Kilbrandon was appointed chairman of the Commission, following the death of Lord Crowther. The Commission's *Report* ("the Kilbrandon Report") was published in October 1973 (Cmnd. 5460).

Various proposals for devolution to Scotland and Wales were considered in the next five years until finally two major constitutional measures—the Scotland Act 1978 and the Wales Act 1978—reached the statute book. The Scotland Act provided for the setting up of a Scottish Assembly and a Scottish Executive, *i.e.* for both legislative and executive devolution; the Wales Act, in contrast, conferred no legislative powers on the Welsh Assembly.

Each scheme of devolution, however, was made conditional on the holding of a referendum in Scotland and Wales respectively, and it was provided that if *either* a majority of those voting were against devolution *or* the majority in favour of devolution was less than 40 per cent of the electorate, the Act was to be repealed by an Order in Council.

In the referenda, held on March 1, 1979, both schemes of devolution were rejected: in Scotland 32·8 per cent of the electorate voted "yes" and 30·8 per cent voted "no"; the corresponding figures for Wales were 11·9 per cent "yes" and 46·9 per cent "no". The two Acts were repealed in 1979.

It may be noted in this connection that the Select Committees on

Scottish Affairs and on Welsh Affairs, set up in the Parliamentary session 1979–80, hold a considerable number of their meetings in Scotland and Wales, respectively.

Further Reading

J. D. B. Mitchell, *Constitutional Law*

Central Office of Information, *The British Parliament* (Reference Pamphlets Series) (H.M.S.O.)

Wade and Phillips, *Constitutional and Administrative Law*, 9th edition by A. W. Bradley (Longman Group)

O. Hood Phillips, *Constitutional and Administrative Law* (Sweet & Maxwell)

Marshall and Moodie, *Some Problems of the Constitution* (Hutchinson of London)

S. A. de Smith, *Constitutional and Administrative Law* (Foundations of Law Series) (Penguin)

H. W. R. Wade, *Constitutional Fundamentals* (Hamlyn Lectures, 1980) (Stevens)

P. S. R. F. Mathijsen, *A Guide to European Community Law* (Sweet & Maxwell)

John P. Grant (editor), *Independence and Devolution: The Legal Implications for Scotland* (various authors) (W. Green & Son Ltd.)

Royal Commission on the Constitution 1969–1973 (Chairman: Lord Kilbrandon), *Report* (1973: Cmnd. 5460) and *Memorandum of Dissent* by Lord Crowther-Hunt and Professor A. T. Peacock (1973: Cmnd. 5460–1) (H.M.S.O.)

CENTRAL AND LOCAL GOVERNMENT

CENTRAL government is that part of the government which operates in the name of the Crown; it extends in general to the whole of the country, although some departments of it (*e.g.* the Scottish Office) are limited in their area of operation.

Local government is that part of the government which is the responsibility of local authorities; it is restricted to the particular locality in which the local authority operates.

CENTRAL GOVERNMENT

An outline of the structure and functioning of the central government is given in the following pages under these headings:

1. the monarch;
2. the royal prerogative;
3. the Privy Council;
4. ministers of the Crown;
5. the central government departments.

In addition mention must be made of the following, which are closely associated with the central government:

6. public corporations and other public bodies;
7. administrative tribunals.

The term "the Crown" sometimes means "the sovereign for the time being"; it is then synonymous with "the monarch." In other contexts it covers any organ of state which forms part of the executive; it is then synonymous with "the central government."

1. The Monarch

Succession to the throne is governed by the Act of Settlement 1700 as amended by His Majesty's Declaration of Abdication Act 1936.

By the Act of 1700 the right to succeed to the throne was conferred on Princess Sophia, Electress of Hanover, who was a granddaughter of James I of England (and VI of Scotland); on her death the right was to descend to the "heirs of her body," a phrase which brings into operation the feudal rules (similar to those formerly applicable to succession to heritable property) of:

(a) preference for males; e.g. a son of the monarch is entitled to succeed in preference to any daughter of the monarch;

(b) "primogeniture" (preference for the eldest); e.g. the monarch's eldest son is entitled to succeed in preference to younger sons; and

(c) representation, by which a child or a remoter descendant succeeds as representing his deceased parent or other ancestor who would, if he had survived, have succeeded; e.g. a granddaughter, the only child of a deceased eldest son, is entitled to succeed in preference to surviving younger sons.

The order of succession was altered in 1936 to give effect to the abdication of Edward VIII. His Majesty's Declaration of Abdication Act 1936 provided that the then Duke of York, later King George VI, was to succeed to the throne and that Edward VIII and his descendants were thereafter to have no right to the succession.

By the Bill of Rights of 1688 a person who becomes a Roman Catholic or marries a Roman Catholic forfeits all right to the throne.

Other statutory provisions are that the person succeeding to the throne must take the coronation oath, declare himself a faithful Protestant, swear to maintain the Church of Scotland and the Church of England and join in communion with the Church of England.

The term "heir apparent" is used of the eldest son of a reigning monarch, while the term "heir presumptive" is used of any other person who is at any given time the next in the order of succession but whose right may be nullified by a subsequent birth (e.g. the eldest daughter of a reigning monarch to whom no son has yet been born). The title of Prince of Wales is conferred on the heir apparent.

When a monarch dies his successor accedes to the throne automatically and immediately; hence the maxim "The king never dies." Two ceremonies, however, usually mark the accession of a new monarch: the first is the proclamation, which is authorised by an "Accession Council" (a special assembly of leading citizens including Privy Councillors and representatives of various Commonwealth countries), and the second is the coronation, which customarily takes place in Westminster Abbey some months later.

Although a person is never too young to accede to the throne, a monarch must, by the Regency Act 1937, have attained the age of eighteen before he is entitled to perform the royal functions. Statutory provisions relating to the exercise of royal functions when the monarch is under eighteen, is ill, or is absent from the United Kingdom are contained in that Act as amended by the Regency Acts of 1943 and 1953.

The royal functions are by the Act of 1937, to be exercised by a regent if:

(a) the monarch is under eighteen years of age; or

(b) a formal declaration is made by certain persons (*e.g.* the monarch's wife or husband, the Lord Chancellor, and the Speaker) that they are satisfied that the monarch either is incapable (physically or mentally) of performing the royal functions or is for some definite reason not available for their performance (*e.g.* by having been made a prisoner of war).

As a general rule the regent is the person next in the line of succession who is a British subject over eighteen years of age, domiciled in the United Kingdom and not disqualified on religious grounds, but the Act of 1953 provides for the Duke of Edinburgh's becoming regent in certain circumstances.

The regent may exercise all the royal powers except that he must not assent to a Bill altering the order of succession to the throne or altering or repealing the Scots Act which secured the Scottish church at the time of the Union of the Parliaments, namely the Protestant Religion and Presbyterian Church Act 1706.

The Act of 1937 further provided for the royal functions to be performed by "Counsellors of State" if the monarch:

(a) is to be absent from the United Kingdom; or

(b) is suffering from physical or mental infirmity which does not amount to incapacity such as would justify a regency.

The persons to be appointed Counsellors of State are the monarch's spouse and the four persons next in the line of succession who would not be disqualified from acting as regent. The Act of 1943 provided that a Counsellor of State who is to be absent from the

United Kingdom may be excepted during his absence, and the Act of 1953 added Queen Elizabeth the Queen Mother to the number of Counsellors of State.

The appointment is made by the monarch by letters patent which specify the functions which are being delegated to the Counsellors. Power to dissolve Parliament, however, must not be exercised except on the express instructions of the monarch, and the monarch's power to confer honours must not be delegated at all.

2. The Royal Prerogative

The royal prerogative is the residue of the power which at common law belonged to the monarch as such and which could be exercised at his discretion without the authority of Parliament. It is a "residue" because Parliament has taken away part of it (and may take away any remaining part); much of the seventeenth-century struggle between king and Parliament related to prerogative power, and the Bill of Rights of 1688 which marked the end of that struggle expressly limited that power in certain respects. Since the royal prerogative is a power to be exercised "at the discretion" of the monarch, the courts have no jurisdiction to question the exercise of the prerogative in any particular situation, although they may decide on whether the prerogative extends to that situation.

Although the royal prerogative is a "residue" of power, this does not mean that it is insignificant; in fact, it remains both important and extensive. Its existence in our present-day "limited" or "constitutional" monarchy is acceptable only because of the conventions which govern its exercise, in particular the convention that the monarch acts on the advice of his ministers; only to a limited extent does the prerogative now belong to the monarch in person; its importance now lies mainly in the scope which it gives to ministers acting in the name of the Crown to exercise, without the authority of Parliament and without being liable to be held responsible in the courts, those common law powers (so far as not taken away by Parliament) which formerly belonged personally to the monarch as such. Prerogative powers are, therefore, now divisible into:

    (a) personal prerogatives; and

    (b) governmental or political prerogatives.

(a) Personal prerogatives

So far as the governing of the country is concerned, the personal prerogative of the monarch is as a general rule limited to the right to be consulted, the right to encourage and the right to warn, all of which rights must be exercised in a spirit of political impartiality. Possible exceptions to this general rule are:

(i) the conferring of certain honours, such as the Order of the Thistle and the Royal Victorian Order;

(ii) the choice of a Prime Minister where the advice of the outgoing Prime Minister is not available and provided the choice has not been determined by any political machinery; the personal prerogative has been exercised in this connection several times in the present century, *e.g.* by the selection of Mr. Harold Macmillan in 1957 and of Sir Alec Douglas-Home in 1963, but since both the Labour party and, from 1965, the Conservative party have electoral systems for choosing their leaders, there is virtually no scope now for the exercise by the monarch of any personal choice; and

(iii) the right to refuse to dissolve Parliament when dissolution is requested by the Prime Minister and the right to dismiss a ministry; there are, however, no modern instances of the exercise of these rights; exercise of them would involve the monarch in political controversy and would not be justified except in extreme circumstances, *e.g.* where necessary for the preservation of the constitution.

Certain immunities and property rights of the monarch may also be classed as personal prerogatives. These include:

(i) the immunity expressed in the maxim "The king never dies," the effect of which is that there is never any "interregnum" (gap between one reign and the next);

(ii) the immunity expressed in the maxim "The king can do no wrong," the effect of which is that the monarch cannot be made liable in court for damages for delict; this immunity, which formerly extended to delicts of Crown servants, was reduced to an immunity personal to the monarch by the Crown Proceedings Act 1947 (see p. 437, below); and

(iii) the property rights, known as "regalia" ("royal rights"); these are divided into regalia majora (literally, "the greater royal rights"), which, being held in trust for the public, cannot be alienated by the Crown, and regalia minora (literally, "the lesser royal rights"), which are rights initially belonging to the Crown but capable of being alienated by it (see p. 467, below).

(b) Governmental or political prerogatives

The prerogatives in this group are often classified as legislative, executive and judicial according to the governmental function to which they relate.

(i) *Legislative prerogatives*

Prerogatives connected with legislation include the power to summon, prorogue and dissolve Parliament, the power to give the royal assent to Bills, and the immunity resulting from the presumption that a statute is not binding on the Crown unless it is expressly declared to be so.

(ii) *Executive prerogatives*

Possibly the most important executive prerogatives are those connected with foreign affairs; they cover such matters as declaration of war, making of peace, entering into treaties, and recognition of and relations with foreign states.

The existence of a state of war or other emergency in the country enlarges the scope of the prerogative to include power to requisition ships and other property, to enter on private land and to govern by martial law. The common law on this matter, however, is rather obscure, since on the occurrence of a particular emergency statutory provision is usually made for the Government to have extensive powers (*e.g.* the Emergency Powers (Defence) Act 1939 passed at the beginning of World War II), and, as was decided in *Att.-Gen.* v. *De Keyser's Royal Hotel Ltd.* [1920] A.C. 508, a statutory power takes the place of a prerogative power relating to the same subject-matter.

Amongst the other executive prerogatives are the powers to appoint and dismiss ministers, civil servants and members of the armed forces, to create peers and confer honours, and to constitute corporations by royal charter.

(iii) *Judicial prerogatives*

Although the Crown Proceedings Act 1947 had the general effect of abolishing the Crown's immunity from being sued in connection with acts done by its servants on its behalf, certain privileges were expressly preserved by the Act, *e.g.* in connection with defence, with liability for injuries to members of the armed forces, and with procedural matters such as disclosure of documents and enforcement of judgments.

The judges are "Her Majesty's Judges." Criminal proceedings are initiated and conducted on behalf of the Crown, and may be abandoned at the Crown's discretion.

The "prerogative of mercy" empowers the Crown to reprieve or pardon convicted persons.

3. The Privy Council

The origin of the Privy Council may be traced to the reign of Henry VIII when the distinction was first drawn between the monarch's "ordinary councillors," a fairly large body of lawyers and administrators, and his "privy councillors," a select group of nobles who were his actual advisers.

In course of time the Privy Council itself increased in size and became too unwieldy to be a practical instrument of government. Its function as an advisory body of the Crown was taken over in the course of the eighteenth century by the Cabinet, a select group of Privy Councillors.

The Privy Council, however, still exists as part of the formal structure of government. Its members (373 in number in August 1980) are appointed by letters patent issued by the monarch mainly on the advice of the Government of the day; they are entitled to the style "Right Honourable" and must on appointment take an oath which binds them to secrecy on Privy Council matters. The Council includes the following persons:

(a) the Lord President of the Council, who is a member of the Government; he usually presides at the Council's meetings;

(b) all present and past Cabinet ministers (but not other ministers of the Crown);

(c) the Speaker of the House of Commons;

(d) the Lords of Appeal in Ordinary and the holders of certain other high judicial offices;

(e) the Archbishops of Canterbury and of York; and

(f) leading statesmen from other Commonwealth countries.

Appointment is for life, and so Cabinet ministers who lose their seats in the Cabinet, through a change in the Government or otherwise, remain Privy Councillors.

The whole Privy Council is now called together only on the death of the monarch or when the monarch announces his intention to marry. The quorum of the Council is three, and when a meeting is required normally only four members, selected according to the business to be dealt with, are summoned to attend. A larger attendance is considered appropriate for matters of great importance to the state; *e.g.* on the occasion of George VI's assent to Princess Elizabeth's marriage twelve Privy Councillors were in attendance.

The function of the Council is now mainly to give formal effect to certain acts of the Crown done under the authority of the royal prerogative or of statute; the act is then said to have been done by "Her Majesty by and with the advice of her Privy Council." The form used may be a proclamation or an Order in Council; proclamations are customary for summoning, proroguing and dissolving Parliament, for declaring war or making peace, and for other solemn purposes requiring wide publicity; Orders in Council are employed for many varied purposes which may be legislative (*e.g.* when delegated legislation is made under prerogative or statutory power), executive (*e.g.* when a state of emergency is declared), or judicial (*i.e.* when effect is given to a decision of the Judicial Committee of the Council).

The Privy Council also serves as a source of political patronage.

Committees of the Privy Council are set up for various purposes, *e.g.* to advise on the grant of royal charters. Particularly important is the Judicial Committee; it consists of Privy Councillors who hold or have held high judicial office and it hears appeals from certain English courts and from courts in British colonies and in some other Commonwealth countries (see p. 191, above).

4. Ministers of the Crown

Because of the convention that the Queen acts on the advice of her ministers, it is the ministers of the Crown who now have the actual supreme executive power. They are appointed to office by the Queen on the advice of the Prime Minister and are referred to collectively as "the Government."

The rules which regulate the choice of ministers and the relationship between ministers and Parliament are almost entirely conventional. In essence their effect is to ensure:

(a) that the Government consists of members of either House of Parliament who belong to the political party which secured the majority of seats in the House of Commons at the last general election; and

(b) that the Government governs in such a way as to retain the approval of the majority of members of the House of Commons.

The system of government is described as "responsible government" because ministers of the Crown are responsible to the House of Commons, and through it ultimately to the electorate, for what they do in the Queen's name.

This responsibility is both collective and individual.

The collective responsibility of ministers means that the Government must present a united front to Parliament; a minister of the Crown, although he may not himself have been consulted on a policy beforehand and although he may not himself approve of it, must by vote and by speech support his ministerial colleagues; if, on a major issue, he openly disagrees with his ministerial colleagues, he must, by convention, resign office (see p. 147, above).

The individual responsibility of a minister means that he must account to Parliament for executive action which is within the sphere of his ministry. He may or may not in fact have obtained prior approval from his ministerial colleagues for the action taken. If, on an issue of sufficient importance, a minister fails to win the support of a majority of the House of Commons, he must, by convention, resign office. The issue may be a matter of policy, decided by the minister either on his own initiative or after consultation with other ministers or it may be administrative action taken by a civil servant within the minister's department. Where a minister resigns on a matter of policy, then, unless the Government as a body resigns or a general election is held, the minister is in effect being disowned by his ministerial colleagues: by sacrificing the minister with whom an unpopular policy is mainly associated the Government may renew its support in the House of Commons and so be able to continue in office. Where a minister resigns on an administrative matter, he is thereby accepting responsibility for the action of a civil servant who by the rules of Parliamentary government must remain anonymous and politically neutral, cannot be heard in his own defence and must be protected by his minister from attack and blame. However, resignations of ministers in accordance with this convention of individual responsibility are rare: usually a minister is shielded by the collective responsibility of the Government as a whole.

The Cabinet

While all ministers of the Crown form part of the Government, not all ministers are in the Cabinet, which is the inner ring of ministers who are most concerned with the general policy of the Government.

The functions of the Cabinet as defined in 1918 by the Haldane Committee set up to review the machinery of government in Britain are (*Report of the Machinery of Government Committee*, (1918) Cd. 9230, at para. 6):

(a) the final determination of the policy to be submitted to Parliament;

(b) the supreme control of the national executive in accordance with the policy prescribed by Parliament; and

(c) the continuous co-ordination and delimitation of the activities of the several Departments of State.

There are no fixed rules as to the number of ministers to be included in the Cabinet; the number must be small enough to make the Cabinet an effective machine for the taking of unanimous (or apparently unanimous) decisions on matters of general policy; apart from that consideration the Prime Minister has a discretion as to how many ministers are to be in his Cabinet. The holders of certain key ministries always have a seat in the Cabinet (*e.g.* the Chancellor of the Exchequer and the Secretary of State for Scotland), but the holders of other ministries may be included by some Prime Ministers only or on some occasions only.

Mrs. Thatcher's Cabinet during the Parliamentary session 1979–80 consisted of twenty-two ministers:

1. Prime Minister, First Lord of the Treasury and Minister for the Civil Service;
2. Secretary of State for the Home Department;
3. Lord Chancellor;
4. Secretary of State for Foreign and Commonwealth Affairs and Minister of Overseas Development;
5. Chancellor of the Exchequer;
6. Secretary of State for Industry;
7. Secretary of State for Defence;
8. Lord President of the Council and Leader of the House of Lords;
9. Secretary of State for Employment;
10. Lord Privy Seal;
11. Minister of Agriculture, Fisheries and Food;
12. Secretary of State for the Environment;
13. Secretary of State for Scotland;
14. Secretary of State for Wales;
15. Secretary of State for Northern Ireland;
16. Secretary of State for Social Services;
17. Chancellor of the Duchy of Lancaster and Leader of the House of Commons;
18. Secretary of State for Trade;
19. Secretary of State for Energy;
20. Secretary of State for Education and Science;
21. Chief Secretary to the Treasury;
22. Paymaster General.

Amongst the ministers not included in the Cabinet were the Parliamentary Secretary to the Treasury, the Minister of Transport, the Lord Advocate and various "Ministers of State" (ministers attached to departments headed by Secretaries of State who would otherwise be likely to be overburdened, *e.g.* Minister of State, Department of Energy, and Minister of State, Department of Employment).

Ministers of Cabinet rank become Privy Councillors and as such are bound to secrecy on Cabinet proceedings. Ministers not in the Cabinet are not necessarily Privy Councillors.

The British system of government is described as "Cabinet government" because it is in the nucleus of ministers who form the Cabinet that the vital decisions for the government of the country are taken. Ministers not in the Cabinet must accept and support Cabinet decisions, and, although the Government's policy may be criticised in Parliament, the House of Commons is almost certain to give a majority vote in favour of that policy since it is from the political party which occupies the majority of seats in that House that members of the Government have been chosen. While it is true that the Government is responsible to the House of Commons and cannot continue in office without the support of the majority in that House, it is also true that the Government, especially the core of it which forms the Cabinet, dominates the House of Commons because the members who comprise the majority in that House seldom take the extreme step of voting against their own party leaders in any matter of major importance. It follows that a Cabinet can normally secure for itself any Parliamentary approval, any finance and any legislation which is necessary for the implementation of its policies.

Cabinet committees

It is impracticable for all matters even of general policy to be adequately considered at meetings of the full Cabinet, and the practice has developed in the twentieth century of committees of the Cabinet being set up either as "standing" (*i.e.* continuing, but not necessarily permanent) committees or as "ad hoc" (literally, "for this purpose") committees, the latter being appropriate where a particular problem calls for consideration at Cabinet level. Ministers who are not normally in the Cabinet may sit as members of Cabinet committees where the matter in hand is relevant to their departments.

In practice the natural consequence of a system of Cabinet committees would be that the real decisions would be taken in the committees and the full Cabinet would normally accept the committees' reports. However, it is not usual for the setting up, the membership or the terms of reference of Cabinet committees to be made public during the lifetime of the particular Government, and so any possibility of apparent delegation which would infringe the principle of the unity and collective responsibility of the Cabinet is avoided.

The Prime Minister

The key position in the Cabinet is held by the Prime Minister, who is now always also appointed to the office of First Lord of the Treasury.

The office of Prime Minister is usually considered to have originated in the ministries of Walpole in the earlier half of the eighteenth century. The prestige of the office was enhanced in the course of the nineteenth century, especially by the outstanding personalities of Disraeli and Gladstone. The constitutional and political climate of the twentieth century has strengthened the position of the Prime Minister to such an extent that it is now said that Cabinet government is being replaced by "Prime Ministerial" government: the Prime Minister is no longer merely the minister who, as primus inter pares ("first among equals"), presides at meetings of the Cabinet; he is the personality who, as leader of a political party, appeals to the electorate at a general election, wins for himself as a political leader the support of a majority in the House of Commons, chooses his Cabinet colleagues and throughout his ministry plays the dominant role in the Cabinet and in the House.

The Prime Minister is chosen by the monarch, but conventions of the constitution leave little opportunity for the exercise of any personal choice by the monarch in this connection. The Queen is, by convention, bound to appoint the leader of the political party (or, if there are more than two political parties, the leader of the group of political parties) which has the support of a majority of the members of the House of Commons. When a Government is "defeated" in a general election, *i.e.* when as a result of changes made by the electorate in the membership of the House of Commons the Government no longer has the support of a majority of the members of that House, then, by convention, the Prime Minister in offering his own resignation and that of all his ministerial colleagues advises the monarch to send for the Leader of the Opposition. Only rarely and in exceptional circumstances has the monarch any real discretion as to who is to be appointed Prime Minister; the successor is usually marked out by political machinery.

It is now a convention that the Prime Minister must either be a member of the House of Commons at the time of his appointment or become a member within as short a time as is practicable after his appointment. The last Prime Minister to sit in the House of Lords was Lord Salisbury (1895–1902). In the earlier half of the twentieth century the convention was established that the Prime Minister had to be a member of the House of Commons, and the Peerage Act 1963 (which enables a peer to renounce his peerage), while it required a modification in the statement of the convention, was in effect a recognition of the substance of it. Accordingly, when in 1963 the Earl of Home, a member of the House of Lords, was appointed Prime Minister, he renounced his peerage four days after his appointment, and became a member of the House of Commons some two weeks later, having won a seat in that House at a by-election.

The first task of a Prime Minister is to choose his ministerial colleagues from among those members of the two Houses of Parliament who support his ministry; in the two-party system which normally operates at the present day these members will belong to the same political party as the Prime Minister himself. It is for the

Prime Minister to decide which ministries are to entitle their holders to seats in the Cabinet. Most of the ministers will be members of the House of Commons, but, by convention, it is necessary for the Government to be represented in the House of Lords. In earlier times statutory limits were imposed on the maximum number of ministers who might sit in the House of Commons, with the object of preventing that House from becoming filled with persons who were paid by, and so under the influence of, the monarch; by the House of Commons Disqualification Act 1975 the maximum number of ministers who may sit in the House of Commons is now ninety-five; in so far, therefore, as a Government consists of more than ninety-five ministers (and this is quite usual at the present day) statute requires that appointments be made of persons who are not members of the House of Commons.[1] By convention, ministers who are not in the House of Commons must normally be members of the House of Lords. If a Prime Minister wishes to appoint as one of his ministers a person from outside Parliament, he may recommend that that person be created a peer or he may "promote" to the House of Lords the holder of a "safe" seat in the House of Commons thereby enabling the person intended for office to stand for that House at the resulting by-election. The Chancellor of the Exchequer must, by the nature of his office, be a member of the House of Commons, since the House of Lords has no control over matters of finance. The holders of all the more important ministerial offices also are customarily members of the House of Commons (*e.g.* holders of the offices of Secretary of State).

The Prime Minister's functions during his term of office include the following:

(a) presiding at Cabinet meetings;

(b) acting as the main channel of communication between the Cabinet and the monarch;

(c) assuming personal control of such branches of government as he sees fit;

(d) determining the scope of the various ministries in his Government and reorganising them from time to time to such extent as he considers expedient;

(e) advising and consulting with ministerial colleagues on matters which have not yet come before the Cabinet;

(f) controlling the Cabinet Secretariat in the execution of its functions such as preparation of the agenda for Cabinet meetings;

(g) co-ordinating and guiding Government policy through the Cabinet and otherwise;

(h) being the chief spokesman for the Government in the House

---

[1] The number may be varied by Order in Council.

of Commons by answering questions and taking part in debates on matters of general policy;

(i) organising the business of the House of Commons (either personally or by delegating the task to the Leader of the House);

(j) communicating with other Commonwealth Prime Ministers;

(k) advising the monarch as to the persons to be appointed to various official positions in the state and as to the persons on whom honours are to be conferred; and

(l) deciding the time, within the five-year period laid down by the Parliament Act 1911, for the dissolution of Parliament, the holding of a general election and, if the result of the election justifies it, the tendering to the monarch of his own resignation and of that of all his colleagues.

5. The Central Government Departments

Each central government department, with the exception of departments which are non-political (*e.g.* that concerned with inland revenue), is headed by a member of the Government. He may have the title of "Secretary of State" (*e.g.* "Secretary of State for the Environment", "Secretary of State for Employment" and "Secretary of State for Scotland"); this title is reserved for the holders of the most important offices and all Secretaries of State are in the Cabinet. The heads of other departments may have the title of "Minister" (*e.g.* "Minister of Agriculture, Fisheries and Food") or may have some special title (*e.g.* "Lord Privy Seal"); these ministers may or may not be in the Cabinet (*e.g.* both the Minister of Agriculture, Fisheries and Food and the Lord Privy Seal were in Mrs. Thatcher's Cabinet during the Parliamentary session 1979–80).

In recent years the tendency has been to group functions together into departments with a wide span. It is now usual for one department to include several ministers, the head of the department being a Secretary of State and additional ministers (who are normally not in the Cabinet) having the titles of "Minister," "Minister of State," "Parliamentary Under-Secretary of State," and "Parliamentary Secretary." according to circumstances.

A "Minister" is appointed where a particular part of the work of a department is sufficiently important to justify the full attention of a minister with a status equivalent to that of a minister who is in charge of a distinct department. For instance, the Department of the Environment is headed by the Secretary of State for the Environment, a Cabinet minister who has responsibility for the department as a whole and is concerned primarily with strategic issues of policy; in the same department there is the Minister for Housing and Construction, who does not have a seat in the Cabinet.

A "Minister of State" is appointed where it is desirable that a particular part of the work of a department should receive the separate attention of a minister who enjoys greater political prestige than a Parliamentary Under-Secretary of State or a Parliamentary Secretary. The office of Minister of State may be used as a device to avoid the necessity for the creation of additional separate departments when an existing department becomes overburdened. For instance, there are Ministers of State in the Departments of Defence, of Employment and of Foreign and Commonwealth Affairs, and in the Treasury.

"Parliamentary Under-Secretaries of State" and "Parliamentary Secretaries" are titles given to junior ministers. The former title is used where the head of the department is a Secretary of State, and the latter is used in other cases. For instance, the Secretary of State for Education and Science has the assistance of two "Parliamentary Under-Secretaries of State." and the Secretary of State for Scotland of three "Parliamentary Under-Secretaries of State," whereas the junior minister assisting the Minister of Agriculture, Fisheries and Food is a "Parliamentary Secretary."

The Treasury

A particularly important central government department is the Treasury. It includes the following ministers:

(a) First Lord of the Treasury, who is now always the Prime Minister;

(b) Chancellor of the Exchequer, the effective head of the Treasury;

(c) Chief Secretary to the Treasury, who is a colleague of the Chancellor and has a seat in the Cabinet;

(d) Financial Secretary to the Treasury;

(e) two Ministers of State;

(f) Parliamentary Secretary to the Treasury, who is Government Chief Whip;

(g) five Lords Commissioners who act as Government Whips; and

(h) five Assistant Whips.

The Treasury is regarded as the senior department of the Government. It has control of national finance and has the responsibility for allocation of money and economic resources among the various departments. The main function of the Whips is to guard the Government's political majority in the House of Commons; a member of the House of Commons who fails to vote as he is directed to do by the Whips may be threatened with "withdrawal of the Whip," which means that he would be excluded from the political party to which he usually in practice owes his seat in the House and on which his future success in politics almost certainly depends.

The Scottish Office

A central government department which has special importance for Scotland is that known as "the Scottish Office." Its ministers are the Secretary of State for Scotland, a Minister of State and three Parliamentary Under-Secretaries of State.

The Scottish Office had its origin in the Secretary for Scotland Act 1885 but since that time it has been reorganised and expanded. It is centred in Edinburgh but has a liaison office in London. Although the Scottish Secretary is the Scottish counterpart of the (English) Home Secretary, his functions have a wider range than those of the Home Secretary and indeed of any other minister; thus, many of the functions assigned to the Department of the Environment, e.g. town and country planning and housing, are so far as Scotland is concerned the responsibility of the Scottish Office.

The general purpose of the existence of the Scottish Office is to give a measure of separate (rather than self-) government to Scotland in matters for which this is desirable in view of Scotland's distinctive history, law, church and society.

The Scottish Office comprises five departments:

(a) the Scottish Home and Health Department, which deals with public order and safety, the police and fire services, prisons and the health service;

(b) the Department of Agriculture and Fisheries for Scotland, which supervises the agriculture and fishing industries;

(c) the Scottish Education Department, which has responsibilities for schools and colleges and for social work;

(d) the Scottish Development Department, which controls town and country planning, housing, roads, water, local government and local transport; and

(e) the Scottish Economic Planning Department, which advises the Secretary of State on matters concerned with industrial and economic development in Scotland (including the development of North Sea oil) and is responsible for Scottish aspects of regional policies of the United Kingdom Government and the EEC.

The civil service

So far only the political aspects of the central government departments have been considered. When there is a change in the political allegiance of the House of Commons followed by the resignation of the Government, it is only the politicians in the departments who resign; all other servants of the Crown in the various government departments continue in their offices, unaffected by the resignation of the Government except that they are thereafter required to give effect to the policies of a different Government and a different minister. These "permanent" servants of the Crown comprise the civil service.

The head of the civil service in a central government department is referred to as "the Permanent Secretary." He has under him a hierarchy of civil servants of different grades and with experience and qualifications related to the departmental work which they are engaged to perform; some are experts in particular fields and some have professional or technical qualifications. The ministerial head of a department, on the other hand, is not an expert on the matters dealt with by the civil servants in his department; he may, indeed, if the Prime Minister "reshuffles" the Government find himself at short notice in control of a quite unrelated department; for matters requiring expert knowledge as for all routine administration he relies on civil servants.

It is obviously essential for the orderly government of the country that there should be continuity amongst the civil servants in a department. Further, in most of the day-to-day work of the department it makes little difference which political party is "in power" or who the individual politician may be who is the head of the department for the time being; the civil servant's function is in very many situations merely to give effect to law and procedures which are unlikely to be radically altered whichever political party forms the Government and whoever the minister appointed as head of the department may be.

On the other hand, a change of Government sometimes does mean that a civil servant, especially if he holds one of the higher posts, must act in accordance with principles quite different from those favoured by the former Government. The civil servant must be loyal to the Government of the day and prepared to abandon courses of action which are not in line with a new Government's policies. It follows that a civil servant must not, by active participation in politics, place himself in a position in which a conflict might arise between his own political career and his loyalty to the Government; a civil servant may exercise voting rights at elections but any more active participation in national and local politics is restricted to an extent which varies according to his grade: the higher the grade, the greater the restriction.

In theory, civil servants, being servants of the Crown, may be dismissed without notice at the pleasure of the Crown. In fact, they enjoy a high degree of security in their employment, but that is based on conditions of appointment which, unlike those applying to ordinary employees, are not legally binding in so far as they are inconsistent with the Crown's right of instant dismissal; civil servants have, however, the statutory right of appealing to an industrial tribunal on account of unfair dismissal (see p. 381, below). In practice no civil servant is dismissed without notice except for really serious misconduct. Conditions of appointment are regulated by the Civil Service Department the head of which is the Prime Minister.

For acts done by civil servants within the scope of their employment the Government has both a legal and a political responsibility.

Legal responsibility is now defined mainly by the Crown Proceedings Act 1947 which, with certain limitations, makes the Crown liable to be sued in respect of contracts and delicts of civil servants provided the circumstances are such that an ordinary employer would have been liable to be sued.

Political responsibility means that the Government, and in particular the political head of the department concerned, must answer in Parliament for what is done in the name of the Crown by civil servants in the government departments; a sufficiently serious fault in administration may involve the minister's resignation.

Accordingly, it is the duty of civil servants to act, if this is possible, in such a way that neither is any liability for improper action on their part incurred by the Government nor is a minister politically embarrassed as a result of the measures taken by his department.

6. Public Corporations and Other Public Bodies

Outside the ordinary framework of both central and local government but associated more closely with the former than with the latter is a host of public bodies which, from time to time, and increasingly since the late 1940s, have been established for purposes related to the administration of the country.

The variety of these bodies is more striking than their common features. It has been said of them: "Like flowers in spring, they have grown as variously and profusely and with as little regard for conventional patterns. They are even less susceptible of orderly classification: with quasi-government bodies, a new species often suggests a new genus" (Sir Arthur Street, "Quasi-Government Bodies since 1918" in *British Government since 1918* by Sir G. Campion and others, at p. 160).

This great variety may be seen from the following points:

(a) There is no uniformity in the names which have been given to individual bodies: they may be styled "boards" (*e.g.* "British Railways Board"), "corporations" (*e.g.* "New Town Development Corporations"), "authorities" (*e.g.* "Atomic Energy Authority"), "commissions" (*e.g.* "Forestry Commission"), "councils" (*e.g.* "Research Councils"), "committees" (*e.g.* "University Grants Committee"), etc., or they may have no such general word in their titles (*e.g.* "Post Office").

(b) There is no uniformity in the constitutions of the bodies: some are "bodies corporate," *i.e.* they have full legal personality because they have been incorporated by an Act of Parliament passed specially for the purpose of establishing the body (*e.g.* the Scottish Development Agency constituted by the Scottish Development Agency Act 1975), or by a royal charter (*e.g.* the British Broadcasting Corporation, and the Scottish Sports Council), or by registration as a limited company under the Companies Acts (*e.g.* the Scottish Business Education Council ("Scotbec") and the Scottish Technical Education Council ("Scotec")); others, though owing their existence directly or indirectly to an Act of Parliament, are not incorporated (*e.g.* the Council on Tribunals, the Criminal Injuries Compensation Board, and numerous advisory bodies set up to give specialist information to a minister or to a government department (*e.g.* the Advisory Committee on Scotland's Travelling People, the Ancient Monuments Board for Scotland, and the Parole Board for Scotland)). In addition to individual bodies, there are networks of bodies, such as industrial training boards, wages councils, and the networks of industrial, rent and other tribunals.

(c) There is no uniformity in the purposes for which the bodies have been established. A *Report on Non-Departmental Public Bodies* of January 1980 (Cmnd. 7797) (which expressly excluded the nationalised industries, the National Health Service bodies and the broadcasting authorities from its review) divided the bodies which it covered into three categories, according to purpose, as follows:

(i) executive, etc., bodies, *i.e.* bodies with executive, administrative and regulatory functions, which carry out a wide range of operational or regulatory functions, various scientific and cultural activities, and some commercial or semi-commercial activities (commonly described as "fringe" bodies to indicate that they function on the fringes of central government);

(ii) advisory bodies, *i.e.* bodies whose principal function is to advise ministers and central government departments; and

(iii) tribunals, etc., *i.e.* bodies with functions of a judicial kind, including tribunals whose jurisdiction extends to some specialised field of law (*e.g.* industrial tribunals and rent tribunals), licensing bodies, and appeal bodies.

In the Scottish Office, for instance, the review covered 244 bodies (84 executive, etc., 154 advisory, and 6 tribunal systems, etc.), employing in all a staff of 17,690 in 1978–79. Some bodies are set up for a purpose which is expected to be brought to an end in a number of years (*e.g.* New Town Development Corporations and Royal Commissions), others for a purpose which is likely to be continuing; in neither case is it usual for any express limit to be placed on a body's duration.

All these various public bodies have a few features in common:

(a) They are all recognisably part of the administration of the country (and so are properly part of the subject-matter of administrative law).

(b) They are part of the movement which has established itself in the twentieth century, and especially since the 1940s, for increased participation of the Government in the affairs of individual citizens.

(c) They are not themselves government departments or parts of government departments (and so do not come under the day-to-day direction of ministers or civil servants in government departments); nor are they part of local authority departments.

(d) They have been set up, each at the time when the need seemed to be apparent, to enable some central government function to be carried out "at arm's length" from the Government itself or to be "hived off" from the Government. Thus, it was considered right on the ground of public policy that nationalised industries should be free to operate as industrial or commercial enterprises without close supervision from the Government, and the Fulton Committee's *Report on the Civil Service* in 1968 (Cmnd. 3638) encouraged further "hiving off" to non-departmental bodies (such as the subsequent hiving off of a large part of the functions of the Department of Employment to the Manpower Services Commission ("MSC"), the Health and Safety Commission and the Advisory, Conciliation and Arbitration Service ("ACAS")).

In recent years there has been growing concern over the increasing number of public bodies, over the widening range of their functions and over the public expenditure involved. The *Report on Non-Departmental Public Bodies* of January 1980, already mentioned, was the result of a critical review aimed at eliminating any non-departmental bodies which had outlived their usefulness or which could not be justified in the light of the Conservative Government's objectives of reducing public expenditure and the size of the public sector. The *Report* (which contains much useful information about the individual executive, etc., advisory and judicial bodies connected with those government departments which were within the review) marks out thirty bodies in the executive, etc., group for winding up or rationalisation (*e.g.* amalgamation of nine wages councils in the retail trade to form two), 211 advisory bodies for similar treatment, and five tribunals, etc., for winding up.

Because of the variety of public bodies, it is impossible to find a collective word or phrase which will aptly cover them all. Popularly the bodies have in recent years come to be referred to as "quangos," an abbreviation of "quasi-autonomous non-governmental organisations." The principal objection to this term is that the great majority of the bodies are in fact governmental, rather than "non-governmental." Hence it has been suggested that the word "quango" should be taken as an abbreviation for "quasi-autonomous national government organisations," but "national government" is not an accepted term in the United Kingdom for "central government." The phrase "non-departmental public bodies" is open to the objection that the great majority of the bodies are in fact associated with a government department, as the Report of January 1980 clearly shows since the review was conducted department by department. Other terms which have been used include "quasi-government bodies" (whicn suggests closer associations with the Government than exist in some cases), "independent statutory authorities" (but not all the bodies are statutory, nor are they all independent), and "public boards" (a comprehensive but vague term, requiring further explanation).

The term "public corporations," used in the heading for this section is not a comprehensive term: it excludes the great many bodies which are not incorporated. It is, however, applicable to a considerable number of the most important of the public bodies, and the remainder of this section is therefore devoted to further consideration of this category.

General features of public corporations

The essential characteristics of a public corporation are as follows:

(a) It is a body corporate created by statute (or, rarely, by royal charter or registration under the Companies Acts).

(b) Its functions, defined by the statute (or other document by which it was constituted), are of a governmental character.

(c) It is to some extent independent of the central government. (The degree of independence, however, varies greatly, and some public corporations are so closely controlled by the central government that they merely serve the purpose of avoiding the creation of additional central government departments; *e.g.* the Forestry Commission is virtually part of the central government, for the Commissioners must comply with directions given to them by the Minister of Agriculture, Fisheries and Food and the Secretary of State for Scotland, and the doctrine of ministerial responsibility applies fully to it.)

(d) It has a governing body consisting of a chairman and a defined number of members, appointed in accordance with the statute (or other document by which it was constituted).

Other general, but non-essential, features are as follows:

(a) *Appointment of members*

Very often the power to appoint the chairman and the members is conferred on the minister whose department is most closely associated with the corporation's role. He may have complete discretion as to whom he is to appoint or he may be required to consult with other bodies or to limit his choice to certain categories of persons. The minister is responsible to Parliament in respect of the appointments which he makes.

Usually the chairman and the members are, by the statute, entitled to a salary, but there is a general rule in the House of Commons Disqualification Act 1975 that paid members of public corporations (with certain exceptions) are disqualified from membership of the House of Commons; therefore a member of that House who accepts appointment as a salaried member of a public corporation must generally resign his seat in the Commons.

(b) *Accounts and reports*

Public corporations are generally required to publish annually accounts audited by qualified auditors and a general report on the activities of the corporation. In many cases the accounts and the report must be presented to Parliament.

(c) *Status*

An important question in connection with the status of a public corporation is whether the corporation is a servant or agent of the Crown or not, since, apart from specific provisions in the statute or other constitutional document, the answer to that question decides the extent to which and the manner in which the corporation may be sued. It is now usual for a corporation's status to be expressly defined in the statute; *e.g.* there is in the Sex Discrimination Act 1975 which set up the Equal Opportunities Commission, an express provision that the Commission is not to act or be treated as the servant or agent of the Crown and is therefore not entitled to any immunity or privilege enjoyed by the Crown.

Where there is no specific provision applicable, the general principle is that a corporation which is required to act for and on behalf of the Crown is in the same legal position as an agent or servant of the Crown and so entitled to any immunity or privilege which could be claimed by the Crown in litigation; *e.g.* the former Central Land Board was required by statute to exercise its functions "on behalf of the Crown," and in *Glasgow Corporation* v.

Central Land Board, 1956 S.C.(H.L.) 1, the House of Lords held that the Secretary of State for Scotland was entitled on behalf of the Central Land Board to object to the production of certain documents by the Board, a Crown privilege available to the Board as representing the Crown. On the other hand, a corporation which is virtually its own master is regarded as legally independent and so enjoys none of the Crown immunities and privileges; public corporations managing the nationalised industries, for instance, are regarded as legally independent for this purpose.

Classification of public corporations

A neat and logical classification of public corporations is made impossible by the variety of their constitutions and functions, but for descriptive purposes they may be regarded as falling into four groups:

    (a)   those which manage industrial or commercial undertakings;
    (b)   those which manage social services;
    (c)   those which regulate private enterprise; and
    (d)   advisory and conciliatory agencies.

(a)   *Managerial bodies for industrial or commercial undertakings*

This group includes the corporations managing the nationalised industries. Examples are the National Coal Board, the British Gas Corporation, the Electricity Council and Boards, the British Steel Corporation, the British Broadcasting Corporation, the Independent Broadcasting Authority and the Atomic Energy Authority.

The functions of the corporations in this group are similar to those of large industrial or commercial companies, and the governing bodies of the corporations resemble the boards of directors of such companies. Usually these corporations are expected to be self-supporting; if, however, they are unable to meet their debts, the Government may provide the resources to enable them to continue operations. Most of the corporations enjoy a monopoly which they are expected to use for the benefit of the public and not purely for profit.

The corporations have a considerable measure of freedom from Parliamentary and Treasury control; this allows those in charge of the undertakings a scope for their enterprise similar to that available to the managers of large companies.

(b)   *Managerial bodies for social services*

This group comprises corporations set up to manage institutions which are not of an industrial or commercial nature but exist for certain specialised social purposes. Examples are the Health Boards, the New Town Development Corporations, the Housing Corporation, the Health and Safety Commission and the Health and Safety Executive, and the Tourist Boards, such as the Scottish Tourist Board.

Corporations in this group are not expected to be self-supporting: they are mainly or entirely dependent on grants from the Government.

They are subject to detailed control by the Government.

(c) *Regulatory bodies*

Corporations in this group are generally closer to the Government than those in either of groups (a) and (b). They are bodies set up to further certain social or economic policies (*e.g.* the Scottish Development Agency formed to promote commercial and industrial development in Scotland). Other examples are the Monopolies and Mergers Commission, the Medicines Commission, the Countryside Commission for Scotland, and the Crofters Commission.

The corporations in this group are often subject to detailed directions from a minister of the Crown.

(d) *Advisory and conciliatory agencies*

An example of an advisory corporation is the Local Government Boundary Commission for Scotland (see p. 234, below). However, most advisory bodies are not incorporated and so are not public corporations (*e.g.* the Council on Tribunals).

Examples of corporations whose primary function is the conciliation of differences are the Equal Opportunities Commission and the Advisory, Conciliation and Arbitration Service ("ACAS").

Control of public corporations

Public corporations are subject in varying degrees to control by:
- (a) ministers of the Crown;
- (b) the courts;
- (c) Parliament; and
- (d) the public.

(a) *Ministerial control*

A corporation is under the control of a minister of the Crown in so far as the minister has the right to appoint and often also to remove the members of its governing body and in so far as he is empowered by statute to give directions to the corporation, to make regulations applicable to its activities or to influence the corporation in other ways.

A right to remove members of the governing body is rarely exercised; for removal, as for appointment, of members the minister would be answerable in Parliament.

A power to give directions, although it entitles the minister to the right of ultimate control of the corporation in the interests of the public, is not in practice exercised to any considerable extent in the case of corporations (such as those managing the nationalised industries) which are considered to be likely to operate more efficiently if the managers are allowed discretionary powers; directions are a more appropriate form of control for corporations, such as the Countryside Commission, which depend on the central government for finance.

The regulations which a minister may have power to make may relate to the appointment of members of the governing body, to the way in which the corporation is to conduct its business or to any other matter as provided for by the statute; they may extend to technical matters, e.g. regulations made under the Gas Act 1972 as to standards of gas pressure and gas purity.

The influence actually exerted by a minister over a public corporation within his sphere of responsibility is usually greater than the formal statutory controls, such as directions and regulations, would suggest: the members of the governing body are in personal contact with the minister and with the senior civil servants of his department, and from their close working relationship there arises an indefinable, but considerable, amount of influence which makes resort to the formal controls comparatively seldom necessary.

(b) *Judicial control*

Most public corporations depend for their legal personality and their corporate powers on a statute and they are therefore subject to the ultra vires ("beyond the powers") doctrine, according to which any attempt by the corporation to extend its personality or exceed its powers is void. However, the ultra vires doctrine, although important, is in many situations of little practical value or hindrance since the statutory powers conferred on the corporation are wide enough to authorise it to undertake virtually any activity which it is ever likely to desire to undertake. The result is that there are few occasions when the control exercised by the courts over public corporations takes the form of a court declaration that a particular attempted act of a public corporation is void as being ultra vires.

A public corporation, being a legal person, may in general sue and be sued in the courts in the same way as any other artificial legal person, except that if it is a servant or agent of the Crown it may be entitled to claim the immunities and privileges of the Crown so far as these have been left standing by the Crown Proceedings Act 1947. This general rule is subject to any special provisions contained in the particular statute.

(c) *Parliamentary control*

The very reason for the creation of a public corporation often is to remove from the detailed scrutiny of Parliament some undertaking in which the Government participates. Since, however, public corporations are expected to exercise their functions in the public interest, it is appropriate that Parliament should have some measure of control over them. Parliamentary control may operate through:

    (i)   legislation;
    (ii) debates;
    (iii) questions to the minister; and
    (iv) the select committees.

(i) *Legislation.* Most public corporations are created by statute, and so it is for Parliament to confer on a public corporation only those powers and that measure of independence which it sees fit. Parliament may also amend the status of an existing public corporation and may even abolish it.

Legislation is, however, not a suitable form of control for the current and continuing operations of a public corporation once established.

(ii) *Debates.* Opportunities for debate on a public corporation may arise on several occasions, *e.g.* when the corporation is seeking financial assistance for its operations, when the annual accounts and reports are placed before Parliament and when a minister exercises a power to make regulations applicable to the corporation.

The debates, however, tend to be too restricted in scope to be a really effective check on the corporation's activities.

(iii) *Questions to the minister.* The doctrine of ministerial responsibility applies only in so far as a minister has statutory rights of appointment, dismissal and control; a minister is not, for instance, answerable to Parliament for an act done by a public corporation in the ordinary course of its administration of a nationalised industry.

However, in practice, a minister often accepts a question which is not strictly within the field of his responsibility. If, for instance, the question calls for information, the minister may state that he has been informed by the board of the corporation concerned that the position is as he proceeds to state, and if the question calls for remedial or other action by the corporation, the minister may state that he will bring the matter to the attention of the board.

This voluntary acceptance of questions, supplemented by the ingenuity of members in bringing the alleged grievance within the scope of one of the minister's statutory rights in respect of the corporation, makes this form of control a fairly effective one. The control is, however, not comprehensive but usually covers only some particular aspect of the corporation's activities or even only an isolated grievance.

(iv) *The select committees*. The fourteen departmentally related select committees set up in the Parliamentary session 1979–80 (see p. 171, above) have the function of examining the expenditure, administration and policy not only of the government departments themselves but also of "associated public bodies," an expression clearly intended to cover the public corporations within the particular government department's responsibility.

Complementary to this form of control is the scrutiny carried out by the Public Accounts Committee of those bodies whose accounts are audited by the Comptroller and Auditor General, or the Comptroller's audits of departmental expenditure.

(d) *Control by the public*

Control of public corporations by the public is especially desirable in the case of those corporations which enjoy a monopoly or a near-monopoly in an industry or trade. Thus, the corporations with monopolies in coal, gas, electricity and rail-transport are not expected to seek their own profit to the total exclusion of the public interest, and in some circumstances it is their duty to provide a service to the public or to certain sections of it although to do so is commercially unprofitable (*e.g.* where the National Coal Board has a duty to produce smokeless fuel on uneconomic terms in order to lessen air-pollution, where an Electricity Board has a duty to supply electricity to rural areas on uneconomic terms for the benefit of agriculture and where British Railways Board has a duty to run trains on uneconomic terms as a service to certain sections of the public).

Bodies have therefore been set up for the purpose of representing the public interest on the matters which come within the various monopolies of the public corporations. These bodies have names such as "consumers' council" (*e.g.* the "National Gas Consumers' Council" and the "Regional Gas Consumers' Councils"), "consultative council" (*e.g.* the "Consultative Councils" attached to each Area Electricity Board), "users' council" (*e.g.* the "Users' Councils" attached to the Post Office) and "advisory council" (*e.g.* the "Herring Industry Advisory Council" attached to the Herring Industry Board).

Members of these bodies are appointed by the minister but he is usually required by the statute to appoint persons of certain defined categories (*e.g.* persons nominated by local authorities or persons who hold certain qualifications related to the particular undertaking).

Consumer bodies are generally regarded as not having fully served the purpose for which they are intended. Members of the public are not well-informed about the existence of the bodies or about their functions and tend to regard them with suspicion as being rather the public-relations departments of the public corporations concerned than representatives of the public interest.

Another method of providing public control is for there to be a statutory requirement that some of the members of the corporation be nominated by, or appointed only after consultation with, local authorities or other bodies interested in the corporation's functions (*e.g.* under the National Health Service (Scotland) Act 1978 appointments to a health board are to be made after consultation with local authorities, universities, organisations representing medical, dental, etc., professions and other organisations which appear to be concerned).

A measure of public control was introduced to the public corporations in the health service by the provision in the National Health Service (Scotland) Act 1972[2] for the appointment of a Health Service Commissioner for Scotland. Corresponding legislation established the offices of Health Service Commissioner for England and Health Service Commissioner for Wales. Complaints may be made to a Health Service Commissioner directly by a member of the public.

(It should be noted that almost all public corporations are outside the jurisdiction of the Parliamentary Commissioner appointed under the Parliamentary Commissioner Act 1967 to investigate complaints of maladministration made to him, through M.P.s, against specified government departments and other specified bodies.)

7. Administrative Tribunals

The increased participation of the state in the private lives of its individual citizens has produced many situations in which conflict may arise between the interests of the state and those of individual citizens. The ordinary courts of law could obviously not deal with so great an addition to their traditional business unless there was to be a radical reorganisation of them including the appointment of many more judges. Further, many of the disputes arising between the state and its subjects are of such a nature that judges of the ordinary courts are not necessarily the persons best qualified to decide the questions raised; *e.g.* claims for state benefits are often too trivial in amount to justify the incurring of court expenses, decisions may require the application of specialised knowledge, and

---

[2] Now re-enacted in the consolidating National Health Service (Scotland) Act 1978.

court proceedings allow insufficient scope for policy (as distinct from law) and for the public interest (as opposed to the rights of an individual).

Accordingly, the various statutes conferring rights to benefits (*e.g.* unemployment benefit, pensions and child benefits), imposing restrictions and controls (*e.g.* the requirement of a licence for a public service vehicle or of planning permission for development of land) and levying charges (*e.g.* income tax and national insurance contributions) have also set up special statutory machinery for the resolution of the disputes relating to these rights, restrictions, controls and charges.

The machinery is not all of the same pattern. In some cases the decision of a dispute is, by the statute, left to "the minister"; in practice, the decision is that of a civil servant in the minister's department, and the effect of such a provision is to make the matter a purely administrative one; there may or may not be a right of appeal from the "minister's" decision to a court of law or to a tribunal. In other cases the decision of a dispute is to be made by the "minister" after the holding of an inquiry; the effect of such a provision is to make the decision ultimately an administrative one, although the inquiry itself is of a judicial nature. A third possibility is that the decision of a dispute is to be made by a tribunal the composition and jurisdiction of which is provided for by the relevant statute; the decision is then of a judicial nature, although the procedure is usually more speedy, more informal and cheaper than court procedure.

These statutory tribunals are commonly referred to as "administrative tribunals," a term which is justified in that the tribunals are associated with the administration. The function of the tribunals, however, is not administrative but judicial: they are machinery (distinct from the ordinary courts) set up by Parliament for the adjudication of disputes to which the state is specially a party; rules of procedure vary from one tribunal to the next according to the statutory provisions and the circumstances in which the tribunal performs its task, but it is an essential feature of a tribunal that although its members may in some cases be in the service of the Government it was intended by Parliament to be capable of giving a decision independently of a government department and by the application of rules of a judicial nature to the evidence before it.

Administrative tribunals are normally distinguishable from statutory inquiries in the following respects:

(a) Tribunals are set up on a permanent basis to deal with any disputes which may arise out of the application of the particular statutory provisions, whereas statutory inquiries are set up ad hoc (literally, "for this purpose"), *i.e.* to deal with a specific dispute which has arisen. For instance, a hierarchy of tribunals exists to decide such disputed claims for social security benefits as arise from time to time, whereas statutory inquiries are held where there are objections to a specific compulsory purchase order or to refusal of planning permission for a specific proposed development.

(b) Tribunals make decisions independently of the minister, whereas statutory inquiries make recommendations on which the minister's decision may be based. However, there is in some cases a right of appeal from the decision of a tribunal to the minister.

(c) Tribunals, although they are distinct from the traditional courts, can claim to be part of the "judicial" system in the wider sense of that term, whereas statutory inquiries are part of the administrative machinery of the state.

However the great variety in the structure, functions, powers, and procedure of tribunals makes the dividing line between tribunals and statutory inquiries rather blurred, as is that between tribunals and ordinary courts of law.

In 1955 a committee was appointed under the chairmanship of Sir Oliver Franks to consider and make recommendations on certain matters relating to tribunals and inquiries and many of the recommendations made in their report ("the Franks Report"), which was published in 1957 (Cmnd. 218), became law by the Tribunals and Inquiries Act 1958. The Report stressed the desirability of "openness, fairness and impartiality" in the working of both tribunals and inquiries (paras. 23 and 24):

> "There are certain general and closely linked characteristics which should mark these special procedures. We call these characteristics openness, fairness and impartiality.
>
> "Here we need only give brief examples of their application. Take openness. If these procedures were wholly secret, the basis of confidence and acceptability would be lacking. Next take fairness. If the objector were not allowed to state his case, there would be nothing to stop oppression. Thirdly, there is impartiality. How can the citizen be satisfied unless he feels that those who decide his case come to their decision with open minds?"

The general underlying aim of the Committee's recommendations was to bring tribunals and inquiries nearer to the attainment of these three ideal characteristics.

The Act of 1958 was amended by the Tribunals and Inquiries Act 1966, and these two Acts were consolidated in the Tribunals and Inquiries Act 1971.

Classification of administrative tribunals

Tribunals are sometimes classified according to their subject-matter, *e.g.*:

(a) those relating to personal welfare (including national insurance, industrial injuries insurance, child benefits and the national health service);

(b) those relating to land and buildings (including valuation, agriculture and rents);

(c) those relating to transport (including licensing and fares);

(d) those relating to employment; and

(e) those relating to immigration.

Such a classification is merely descriptive: it has no particular legal significance. Further, it is likely to be incomplete since new tribunals continue to be set up for new purposes.

The endless variety of purposes for which tribunals are created makes any neat and logical classification of the thousands of them now in existence impossible. The Tribunals and Inquiries Act 1958, however, although it did not attempt any formal classification of tribunals, introduced a distinction which has some legal significance: the distinction is between (a) tribunals listed in the First Schedule to the Act and those since added to that list either by statutory instruments made under authority of the Act or by other later legislation (all of which tribunals are referred to as "First Schedule tribunals") and (b) other tribunals. The main provisions of the Act of 1971 apply only to First Schedule tribunals.

To a limited extent there is uniformity in the general law relating to First Schedule tribunals; *e.g.* the constitution and working of these tribunals must be kept under review by the Council on Tribunals set up by the Act of 1958, and a minister who has power to make procedural rules for a First Schedule tribunal must not exercise the power without first consulting the Council. There are, however, other provisions of the Act of 1971 which apply to some only of the First Schedule tribunals; *e.g.* the provision allowing an appeal to the law courts on a point of law decided by a tribunal.

The Council on Tribunals

The setting up of this Council on the recommendation of the Franks Committee was the most important innovation made by the Tribunals and Inquiries Act 1958.

The Council has a maximum membership of sixteen persons including the Parliamentary Commissioner for Administration (popularly referred to as "the Ombudsman") who is an ex officio ("by virtue of his office") member. The Council has a Scottish committee, some of whose members are not members of the Council itself; the Parliamentary Commissioner is a member of the Scottish committee. Work of the Council is on a part-time basis and its meetings are held monthly. In addition, members of the Council visit sittings of tribunals from time to time and there is also much informal consultation with government departments. The Council is assisted by a small staff of lawyers and clerks.

The Council is an advisory body; it does not have executive functions or any power to consider appeals from tribunals. The main duties of the Council in relation to tribunals are:

(a) to keep under review the constitution and working of First Schedule tribunals and to make annual reports on these matters, the reports being laid before Parliament; and

(b) to consider and report on such particular matters as are referred to it concerning any tribunal, whether or not it is a First Schedule tribunal.

The Council has also a duty to consider and report on matters connected with the holding of statutory inquiries.

Membership of tribunals

The appointment of members to a particular tribunal is regulated by the statute which sets up the tribunal. Often the power of appointment is conferred on a minister of the Crown, but the minister may be required to select the persons whom he appoints from a panel nominated by various persons or organisations.

Members are not necessarily lawyers; they may be laymen or they may be experts in some technical field. The qualifications required will have been indicated in the relevant statute.

In the case of certain specified tribunals the chairman must be selected from a panel of persons appointed by the Lord Chancellor or by the Lord President of the Court of Session.

The Franks Committee recommended that members of tribunals be appointed by the Council on Tribunals, but this recommendation was not accepted. However, the Act of 1971 provides that the Council may make to the appropriate minister recommendations as to appointments to First Schedule tribunals. It appears that such recommendations are not often made.

A minister of the Crown who has power to terminate a person's membership of a First Schedule tribunal must obtain the consent of the Lord Chancellor or of the Lord President for the exercise of the power.

Procedure at tribunals

Many tribunals sit in divisions in local centres or have sittings in different places to suit the parties and the business which is in question. Public notice is given of the time and place of the sitting in order that interested parties may have the opportunity of attending. The accommodation used is often in the offices of the local council.

Procedure at the hearing itself is less formal than court procedure, but the circumstances of tribunals differ so widely that no standardisation of procedure is practicable. The principles of "natural justice" must always be followed: this means in particular that both sides must be heard and that the tribunal must be free from bias; if these principles are disregarded a court of law may review the tribunal's decision and set it aside. Some tribunals are subject to detailed statutory codes of procedure.

In almost every case a citizen appearing before a tribunal is entitled to engage the services of a legal representative. An exception is a tribunal investigating a complaint against a National Health Service practitioner, the justification being that if legal representation were allowed practitioners would avail themselves of the right and complainants might thus be discouraged from coming forward.

Legal aid was formerly not available for *representation* at a hearing, but the legal advice and assistance scheme, introduced by the Legal Advice and Assistance Act 1972, enabled a person to obtain some preliminary advice from a solicitor as to the law applicable and as to steps which might appropriately be taken. The Legal Aid Act 1979 extended this scheme by adding to it the new category of "assistance by way of representation" (see p. 63, above). The proceedings for which such assistance is to be available require to be specified in regulations, and no regulations have so far been made.

Appeals from decisions of tribunals

A distinction must be drawn between judicial review and an appeal.

Judicial review refers to the power which the courts have to set aside the decision of a tribunal on certain strictly limited grounds. The main grounds are that the tribunal has exceeded its jurisdiction and that the principles of natural justice have been violated. Normally the courts refuse to exercise their power in this connection unless the person aggrieved has exhausted all other possible remedies (*e.g.* by having availed himself of any right of appeal to a higher administrative tribunal).

The grounds on which an appeal, as distinct from a judicial review, may be made may be much more extensive; they vary according to the statutory provisions applicable to the particular tribunal and to the circumstances of the case. The appeal may be to a higher administrative tribunal, to the minister, or to a court of law.

The Franks Committee recommended that there should be a right of appeal on fact, law and merits from a tribunal of first instance to an appellate tribunal, unless the tribunal of first instance was so exceptionally strong and well qualified that an appellate tribunal would be no better qualified. That recommendation of the Committee has not been expressly enacted, but such a right of appeal exists in very many cases.

The Committee recommended that as a matter of principle there should be no right of appeal from the decision of a tribunal to the minister. This recommendation has not been accepted.

The Committee further recommended that there should generally be a right of appeal on a point of law from a tribunal's decision to a court of law. Effect was given to this recommendation in the Tribunals and Inquiries Act 1958.

LOCAL GOVERNMENT

The structure of local government in Scotland is quite distinct from that in England. In both countries major changes were recently made—by the Local Government Act 1972 in England and the Local Government (Scotland) Act 1973 in Scotland. The new Scottish structure came into operation on May 16, 1975.

The new Scottish structure had its origins in the recommendations of the Royal Commission on Local Government in Scotland, which was appointed under the chairmanship of Lord Wheatley in June 1966 and made its report in September 1969 (Cmnd. 4150). The Government subsequently, in February 1971, issued a White Paper, *Reform of Local Government in Scotland* (Cmnd. 4583), outlining the proposed legislation. With some modifications, these proposals were enacted by the Local Government (Scotland) Act 1973.

The Royal Commission saw reorganisation of the structure of local government as having four basic objectives (paragraph 128 of the Wheatley Report):

"*Power.* Local government should be enabled to play a more important, responsible and positive part in the running of the country—to bring the reality of government nearer to the people.

Effectiveness. Local government should be equipped to provide services in the most satisfactory manner, particularly from the point of view of the people receiving the services.

Local democracy. Local government should constitute a system in which power is exercised through the elected representatives of the people, and in which those representatives are locally accountable for its exercise.

Local involvement. Local government should bring the people into the process of reaching decisions as much as possible, and enable those decisions to be made intelligible to the people."

The White Paper stated that these objectives were believed by the Government to be "the corner stones on which the new structure must be founded" (paragraph 10).

Local Government Areas

The present local government areas are as set out in Schedule 1 to the Act of 1973. Scotland is divided into:
1. regions; and
2. islands areas.

1. Regions

Scotland (other than Orkney, Shetland and the Western Isles) is divided into nine regions—Highland, Grampian, Tayside, Fife, Lothian, Borders, Central, Strathclyde and Dumfries and Galloway —each with a regional council.

Each region is divided into a number of districts bearing names with local geographical associations, *e.g.* the Fife region is divided into the Kirkcaldy, North East Fife and Dunfermline districts. Most regions have three or four districts each, but the Grampian region has five, the Highland region eight and the Strathclyde region nineteen. The total number of districts is 53. Each district has a district council.

2. Islands areas

The three islands areas are Orkney, Shetland and Western Isles (consisting of the Outer Hebrides). Each islands area has an islands council.

Local Government Elections

The first elections of councillors for regional, islands and district councils took place in 1974. These were the councils which took over responsibilities from the former local government authorities in May 1975.

The scheme is that councils are elected every four years, with a gap of two years between elections of regional or islands councils and elections of district councils. According to this pattern the second elections of regional and islands councils took place in 1978. Until 1980 there were transitional arrangements for elections of district councils: the second election was in 1977 and the third was in 1980.

For the purpose of electing councillors each region and each islands area is divided into wards. There is a separate election for each electoral division or ward, and each division or ward returns one councillor.

The day of election is the first Thursday in May (Local Government (Scotland) Act 1978).

The Local Government Boundary Commission

With a view to preventing existing boundaries and electoral arrangements from becoming out of date, the Act of 1973 established a Local Government Boundary Commission, consisting of a chairman, a deputy chairman and up to four other members, appointed by the Secretary of State for Scotland.

The Boundary Commission is an advisory body whose functions are to review local government areas and electoral arrangements and to make reports to the Secretary of State. In conducting any review the Boundary Commission must consult the councils affected and any other interested bodies or persons and give adequate publicity to its reports; it may also cause a local inquiry to be held. Provision is made by the Act for an initial review, and thereafter for reviews at intervals of ten to fifteen years. The Commission may also, at the request of a local authority or otherwise, conduct interim reviews.

The Secretary of State, as well as having power to give directions to the Boundary Commission in relation to reviews, has a discretion as to whether to give effect to any proposals submitted to him by the Commission. If he sees fit to give effect to proposals, with or without modifications, he does so by an order, which, if it abolishes or alters the boundaries of any local government area, must be laid before Parliament and is subject to annulment by a resolution of either House of Parliament.

Local authorities no longer have power to promote private legislation for altering their areas or their electoral arrangements.

A regional, islands or district council may change its name by a procedure laid down in the Act. Consent of the Secretary of State is required.

Councillors

To be nominated as a candidate for election, a person must:

(i) have attained the age of twenty-one years;

(ii) be a British subject or a citizen of the Irish Republic;

(iii) not be subject to any legal incapacity; and

(iv) be a local government elector for the area, or for the preceding year have occupied as owner or tenant any land or other premises in the area, or for the preceding year have had his principal place of work in the area, or for the preceding year have resided in the area.

Disqualifications include:

(a) holding any paid office or employment with the local authority;

(b) being an undischarged bankrupt; and

(c) having, within the preceding five years, been convicted of an offence and sentenced to at least three months' imprisonment without the option of a fine.

A member of a local authority may at any time resign his membership by giving three weeks' notice of resignation. A member who fails to attend all meetings of the authority for six months ceases to be a member unless his failure was due to some reason approved by the authority.

When a casual vacancy occurs through the death or resignation of a member or otherwise, an election to fill the vacancy must normally be held within the next three months, but if the vacancy occurs within six months before the date of the next ordinary election, there is no election to fill the casual vacancy unless the total number of unfilled vacancies on the council exceeds one-third of the whole number of members. A person elected to fill a casual vacancy holds office until the next ordinary election.

A member who has any pecuniary interest, direct or indirect, in a contract or other matter being considered at a council meeting must disclose the fact that he has an interest, must not take part in the discussion and must not vote on the matter; failure to comply with these restrictions makes the member liable on summary conviction to a fine of up to £200 unless he proves that he did not know that the matter in which he had an interest was being considered at the meeting. A local authority may by standing orders provide for the exclusion of a member from a meeting during the consideration of the contract or other matter in which the member has an interest. Disclosures of interest must be recorded in a book kept by the authority for that purpose, and the book is open at all reasonable hours to inspection by electors for the area. The Secretary of State may remove these disabilities in any case in which the number of members having an interest is so great a proportion of the whole council as to impede the transaction of business or in any other case in which he considers that it would be in the interests of the inhabitants of the area that the disability be removed.

The Wheatley Commission recommended that salaries be paid to councillors, but this recommendation has not been adopted. The Act of 1973, however, provides that a councillor is entitled to an "attendance allowance" for performance of any approved duty, the amount of the allowance being a reasonable amount fixed by the local authority within limits prescribed by the Secretary of State. A councillor not entitled to an attendance allowance is entitled to a "financial loss allowance," *i.e.* a payment, within prescribed limits, for loss of earnings necessarily suffered or for necessary additional expenditure other than travelling and subsistence expenditure. The amounts paid for travelling (whether inside or outside the United Kingdom) and for subsistence are fixed by the local authority, subject to a maximum rate for travel within the United Kingdom specified by the Secretary of State.

Admission of Public and Press to Meetings

The right of the public and the press to attend local authority meetings is governed by the Public Bodies (Admission to Meetings) Act 1960, as extended by the Local Government (Scotland) Act 1973. Meetings to which the public and the press were entitled to be admitted under the Act of 1960 were full council meetings, meetings of a committee consisting of all members of the council and education committee meetings. By the Act of 1973 the right of admission is extended to all committee meetings. The council or committee may, however, by resolution exclude the public and the press whenever, for stated reasons, publicity would be prejudicial to the public interest.

Community Councils

Every islands council and every district council was required to submit to the Secretary of State a scheme for the establishment of community councils for the area.

The community councils are not part of the structure of local government, but are an important adjunct to that structure. The new local authorities, being fewer in number than their predecessors and responsible for wider areas, are necessarily more remote from the electors. The community councils represent an attempt to attain the fourth objective of the Wheatley Commission—local involvement—within the new structure.

The general purpose of a community council as defined in the Act of 1973 is:

> "to ascertain, co-ordinate and express to the local authorities for its area, and to public authorities, the views of the community which it represents, in relation to matters for which those authorities are responsible, and to take such action in the interests of that community as appears to it to be expedient and practicable."

Before submitting their schemes for community councils to the Secretary of State, the islands and district councils were required to invite suggestions from the public and give public notice of their draft schemes.

Regional, islands and district councils may make such contributions as they think fit towards the expenses of community councils within their area, may make loans to them and may, at the request of the community councils and on agreed terms, provide them with staff, services, accommodation, furniture, vehicles and equipment.

Community councils have met with little enthusiasm from the electorate. Their inherent defects are the lack of statutory powers and the absence of an independent source of income.

Internal Organisation

By the Act of 1973 local authorities were allowed greater flexibility in discharging their functions. With some exceptions, a local authority may arrange for the discharge of any of its functions by a committee of the authority, a sub-committee, an officer of the authority or by any other local authority in Scotland, and a committee, unless directed not to do so, may in turn delegate its functions to a sub-committee or officer. Two or more local authorities may appoint a joint committee of themselves. A committee or sub-committee, other than one controlling finance, may include persons who are not themselves councillors, but at least two-thirds of a committee (but not of a sub-committee) must consist of councillors.

The Act of 1973 also gave wider discretion to local authorities in the appointment of their staff. The general provision of the Act is that an authority must appoint such officers as it thinks necessary for the proper discharge of its functions. There are some exceptions to this general provision: appointment is still required of certain specified officers, e.g. chief officers of and members of fire brigades, directors of education, weights and measures inspectors, directors of social work and agricultural analysts.

A councillor must not be appointed to the staff of the authority. The disqualification lasts for twelve months after he has ceased to be a member of the authority.

An officer who knows that he has a pecuniary interest, direct or indirect, in a contract being entered into by the authority must give notice to the authority of the fact that he has an interest. He is also under a duty not to accept any fee or reward whatsoever other than his proper remuneration. Contravention of either of these provisions makes the officer liable on summary conviction to a fine of up to £200.

The details of the internal organisation of the new authorities were the subject of a study undertaken by a working group appointed by the Scottish local authority associations. The group's comments and proposals are set out in *The New Scottish Local Authorities: Organisation and Management Structures* (the "Paterson Report"), published for the Scottish Development Department by H.M.S.O. in 1973.

Functions

The functions of regional councils include:

   (i) education and youth employment;

   (ii) social work;

   (iii) major public services (roads, public transport, aerodromes, ferries, piers and harbours, flood prevention, coast protection, water (with special arrangements for central Scotland), sewerage and diseases of animals and plant health);

   (iv) consumer protection, including weights and measures and food standards and labelling;

   (v) registration of births, deaths and marriages; and

   (vi) valuation.

Police and fire services are also the responsibility of the regional councils, with the modification that for these functions there are two "combined areas":

   South-eastern, consisting of the Borders and Lothian areas; and Northern, consisting of the Highland and the Islands areas.

The functions of district councils include:

   (i) housing;

   *(ii) building control;

   (iii) public health (including cleansing, refuse collection, deposit of poisonous waste, clean air, noise abatement, burial grounds and cremation, food hygiene, civic restaurants, allotments and inspection of offices, shops and factories);

   *(iv) public libraries; and

   (v) licensing (including betting, gaming and lotteries, cinemas, theatres, house-to-house collections and animal boarding establishments).

In the Highland, Borders and Dumfries and Galloway regions the functions marked * are the responsibility of the regional and not the district councils.

Some functions are exercised concurrently by regional and district councils. These include industrial development, tourism, parks, recreation, museums and art galleries and community centres.

Islands councils undertake all the functions of both regional and district councils, subject to the exception stated above in relation to the police and fire services.

Special provisions have been made in the Act of 1973 for the town and country planning functions. Some amendment of the Town and Country Planning (Scotland) Act 1972 is involved.

Planning functions are divided into regional functions and

district functions, and the authorities which undertake these functions are regional planning authorities, general planning authorities and district planning authorities.

The general planning authorities are the regional councils for the Highland, Borders and Dumfries and Galloway regions and the islands councils. The regional planning authorities are the regional councils of the six other regions, and the district planning authorities are the district councils in these six regions.

The main regional planning functions are the drawing up of a regional report and the preparation of a structure plan. These functions are to be undertaken by regional planning authorities and general planning authorities.

District planning functions include the preparation of local plans, planning permission, enforcement of planning control, compensation, designation of conservation areas and ancient monuments. These functions are to be undertaken by general planning authorities and district planning authorities.

The effect of these provisions as to planning is that the regional councils for the regions which are predominantly rural have more detailed planning powers than the regional councils for the predominantly urban regions.

Finance

The revenue of local authorities comes mainly from two sources— local authority rates and government grants.

Rates fixed by regional and district councils are referred to as "regional" and "district" rates respectively. Rates fixed by islands councils are referred to as "general" rates.

The rating authorities are the regional and the islands councils. District councils must intimate to the regional councils the district rates which they have fixed, the regional councils prepare the demand notes and then make payments to the district councils on account of the district rates.

Rates are levied according to the rateable value of properties as appearing in the valuation roll. Each regional and each islands council is a valuation authority and must appoint an assessor to undertake this valuation function. The Secretary of State may, if he considers that it would be of public or local advantage, make an order combining the Highland regional council and the three islands councils or any two or more of them for valuation purposes.

The Secretary of State has power to prescribe by regulations a scheme for the grant by rating authorities of rebates from rates (the "standard "rate rebate scheme), and a rating authority may, with the consent of the Secretary of State, vary the standard scheme for its own area. A grant of nine-tenths of the rate rebates is payable by the Secretary of State to the local authority.

The accounts of every local authority must be audited by a professional accountant who is either an officer of the Commission for Local Authority Accounts or is an approved auditor appointed by the Commission. This Commission was established by the Act of 1973 and consists of nine to twelve members appointed by the Secretary of State. It must, subject to the approval of the Secretary of State, appoint a Controller of Audit, and it may also appoint such other officers, and such agents, as it may decide.

The Secretary of State may by regulations make provision as to the form of local authority accounts and related matters, and in auditing the accounts of any local authority an auditor must satisfy himself that the accounts comply with any such regulations and also that proper accounting practices have been observed in the preparation of the accounts.

The Controller of Audit may make a report to the Commission on any matters concerning a local authority's accounts. A copy of any report must be sent to the local authority. The Commission must consider any such report, may hold a hearing into any matter raised by the report and may then make recommendations to the Secretary of State, who has a discretion as to whether he will or will not make an order giving effect to the recommendations, with or without modifications.

The Local Government (Scotland) Act 1975, Part I,[3] amended the system of local government finance: in particular, it made changes in valuation and rating procedures and in the arrangements for grants to local authorities, consolidated, with amendments, legislation on borrowing and lending by local authorities and altered the local authority financial year so that it now ends on March 31 each year instead of on May 15.

Commissioner for Local Administration in Scotland

The Local Government (Scotland) Act 1975, Part II,[3] created the office of "the Commissioner for Local Administration in Scotland."

The Commissioner is appointed by the Queen on the recommendation of the Secretary of State for Scotland and must submit a general report on his work for each year to a body designated for that purpose by the Secretary State. That body arranges for the publication of the report.

The Commissioner has power to investigate complaints from

[3] Amended by the Local Government (Scotland) Act 1978 and by the Local Government (Miscellaneous Provisions) (Scotland) Act 1981.

members of the public who allege that they have sustained injustice as a result of maladministration in connection with action taken by a local authority in the exercise of its administrative functions. The power is a discretionary one: the Commissioner may, or may not, investigate a complaint, as he sees fit.

The Act further provides that normally the Commissioner *must not* investigate a complaint unless it is referred to him by a member of a local authority and unless the person aggrieved has exhausted all other possible remedies.

Many matters are, by the Act and a schedule to it, expressly made "not subject to investigation," *e.g.* the commencement or conduct of civil or criminal proceedings before any court of law, action taken concerning "personal matters," and the internal organisation of any educational establishment managed by the authority.

The full discretion conferred by the Act on the Commissioner as to whether he is to exercise his powers of investigation or not, coupled with the wide-ranging and vaguely-expressed catalogue of matters which are in any case "not subject to investigation," must leave many an aggrieved person with the impression that this institution is of little practical value.

Proposals for Reform

The Queen's speech at the opening of Parliament on November 4, 1981, promised legislation to implement the relatively uncontroversial recommendations of a committee of inquiry led by Lord Stodart into the functions of district and regional councils and also to confer additional powers on the Secretary of State enabling him to compel local authorities to repay to their ratepayers income which would otherwise have contributed to a level of expenditure regarded by the Secretary of State as excessive and unreasonable; legislation in the latter category is the Government's attempt to solve the major current problem in local government, namely the extent to which the central government is entitled to exercise control over local government expenditure.

Further Reading

J. D. B. Mitchell, *Constitutional Law*

Central Office of Information, *The Central Government of Britain* (Reference Pamphlets Series) (H.M.S.O.)

O. Hood Phillips, *Constitutional and Administrative Law* (Sweet & Maxwell)

J. F. Garner, *Administrative Law* (Butterworths)

James G. Kellas, *The Scottish Political System* (Cambridge University Press)

PART III — PRIVATE LAW

CHAPTER 8

OBLIGATIONS IN GENERAL

SOME study of the general law of obligations is a desirable preliminary to study of the three branches of the law of obligations—contract, quasi-contract and delict.

In law, obligations go hand in hand with rights: if one party is under an obligation, then some other party has a corresponding right.

RIGHTS

Detailed consideration of the nature of a right is the province of jurisprudence, and is beyond the scope of this book. However, the distinction must be made between real rights and personal rights, and for that purpose Stair's definition of a right is useful.

Stair defined a right as "a power, given by the law, of disposing of things, or exacting from persons that which they are due" (*The Institutions of the Law of Scotland*, I, 1, 22). The power of "disposing of things" is a real right, and the power of "exacting from persons that which they are due" is a personal right.

A real right is enforceable against all persons; a personal right is enforceable against a particular person only.

A real right is referred to as a jus in re ("right in a thing"), and a personal right is referred to as a jus in personam ("right against a person"). A personal right is also sometimes termed a jus ad rem ("right with regard to a thing").

The distinction between real and personal rights is expressed by Erskine thus: "A real right, or jus in re, whether of property or of an inferior kind—as servitude—entitles the person vested with it to possess the subject as his own; or, if it be possessed by another, to demand it from the possessor, in consequence of the right which he hath in the subject itself; whereas the creditor in a personal right or obligation has only a jus ad rem, or a right of action against the debtor or his representatives, by which they may be compelled to

242

fulfil that obligation, but without any right in the subject which the debtor is obliged to transfer to him" (*An Institute of the Law of Scotland*, III, 1, 2).

The typical example of a real right is the right of ownership: the owner of a thing can prevent anyone else from unlawfully interfering with his right of ownership. An example of a personal right is a right arising out of a contract; *e.g.* if A has agreed to transfer some property to B, but has not yet done so, B has a personal right against A, *i.e.* he can enforce his right against A, but not against anyone else; after the property has been transferred to B, B will have a real right in it.

OBLIGATIONS

The word "obligation" is used in two main senses:

1. It is used loosely for any legal tie, including the general duty to respect another person's right to liberty, reputation and property.

2. It is properly used only of that type of legal tie which can be enforced by a specific person only. It may be defined as a legal bond or juris vinculum (literally, "bond of law") between two persons, by which one person is bound to pay something to the other or is bound to perform something for the benefit of the other. When used in this strict sense, the term "obligation" does not include those general duties which are owed to all other persons, such as the duty to refrain from injuring or defaming them. Where, however, there has been a breach of one of these general duties, the person who is in breach of the duty comes under an obligation to the person whom he has wronged.

The distinction between "duty" and "obligation" as used in their strict senses in Scots law corresponds to that between a real right and a personal right. When one person has a real right, then all others are under a duty to respect that real right; *e.g.* real rights such as those to liberty, to reputation and to property can be asserted against the public generally and they correspond to general duties which members of the public have to respect these rights in others. In contrast, a personal right in one person corresponds to an obligation in one other person; *e.g.* if, as a result of a contract between A and B, B has a personal right against A, then B can enforce his right against A, and against A alone, and A, and only A, is under an obligation to satisfy B's right.

PERSONAL BAR

Sometimes a person is prevented by the doctrine of personal bar from exercising a real or a personal right. This doctrine corresponds to "estoppel" in English law.

The general effect of the doctrine is to prevent a person from asserting his right when assertion of that right would conflict with justice; *e.g.* if A has induced B to enter into a contract by fraudulently telling him that something is true which he (A) knows to be false, A has a right against B, but the law will not allow A to enforce that right, because it would not be just that A should be in a position to profit from his fraud; A is said to be "barred" from asserting his right.

Many of the applications of the doctrine of personal bar have in Scots law acquired special names according to the circumstances in which they appear; these include:

1. personal bar by representation;
2. personal bar by notice;
3. rei interventus;
4. homologation;
5. adoption;
6. acquiescence;
7. mora and taciturnity;
8. waiver; and
9. holding out.

1. Personal Bar by Representation

This was explained by Lord Chancellor Birkenhead in *Gatty* v. *Maclaine*, 1921 S.C.(H.L.) 1, at p. 7, as follows:

"Where A has by his words or conduct justified B in believing that a certain state of facts exists, and B has acted upon such belief to his prejudice, A is not permitted to affirm against B that a different state of facts existed at the same time."

For the principle to operate, A and B must have had relations with each other: if, for instance, A leaves his transistor radio on the beach, and it is stolen and sold by a thief to B, A's conduct may be said to have "justified B in believing" that the thief was the owner of the radio, but, since A had no relations with B, A is not barred from asserting the different, and true, state of facts, namely, that he (A) is the owner of the radio; he can recover it from B.

There is an example of the operation of the principle in *London Joint Stock Bank Ltd.* v. *Macmillan and Arthur* [1918] A.C. 777, which concerned a customer of a bank and the bank, parties standing in a relationship to each other:

On the morning of February 9, 1915, Mr. Arthur, one of the partners of the firm of Macmillan and Arthur, was going out to lunch about mid-day. He had his hat on, and was leaving the office when a clerk came up to him and said that he wanted £2 for petty cash, and produced a cheque for signature.

The clerk had repeatedly presented cheques for signature for petty cash, but usually for £3, and Mr. Arthur asked him why it was not £3 on this occasion. The clerk replied that £2 would be sufficient.

Mr. Arthur signed the cheque, which was then in the following condition: the space for words was entirely blank; in the space for figures, there appeared the figures " 2 0 0", but there were vacant spaces before and after the figure "2".

After Mr. Arthur had signed the cheque, the clerk wrote the words "One hundred and twenty pounds" in the space for words, and filled up the spaces on either side of the figure "2" by adding "1" on the left and "0" on the right.

He presented the cheque to the bank, received payment of £120, and absconded.

Macmillan and Arthur sued the bank for £118. They were not successful, because Mr. Arthur had not taken reasonable precautions to prevent forgery.

The customer had drawn carelessly a cheque for £2, which before being presented to the bank for payment was fraudulently and easily altered to £120. The customer was held to have acted in such a way as to justify the bank in believing that a certain state of facts existed, namely, that the cheque was genuinely for £120, and he was, therefore, barred from stating afterwards that the cheque was really only for £2.

2. Personal Bar by Notice

A person is normally entitled to assume that what he is told by another party is true, but he will not be entitled to do so if he has "notice," *i.e.* knows, that what he has been told is in fact not true.

3. Rei Interventus

"Rei interventus" may be translated as "subsequent actings."

This form of personal bar prevents a party from freeing himself from a contract merely on the ground that some formality has not been observed. For the principle to operate there must have been some important subsequent actings, based on the contract and producing some alteration of circumstances, loss, or inconvenience if the contract were to be held not to be binding; *e.g.* A and B may enter into a contract, which is not in the proper legal form, that A is to lease business premises to B; B, not realising the defect in the contract, may incur expense by repairing and decorating the premises to A's knowledge and with A's permission; A would not later be entitled to withdraw from the contract merely because it was "informal" (not in the proper legal form); he would be "barred from resiling" (prevented from drawing back). See also p. 264, below.

4. Homologation

This is similar to rei interventus, but refers to the actings of the party who attempts later to withdraw from the contract, not to the actings of the party who wishes it to be enforced.

It occurs when a person, knowing that he would be entitled to challenge something, refrains from doing so, and therefore leads the other party to believe that he has given up the grounds of challenge which were open to him; e.g. if a lease is not in the proper form, and the tenant, knowing that, nevertheless pays the rent, the lease is considered to have been homologated by the tenant. See also p. 264, below.

In some situations the term "ratification" is used rather than "homologation"; e.g. in the law of agency, if an agent has acted outwith the authority conferred on him by his principal but the principal nevertheless chooses to accept the agent's action as binding on him (the principal), then the principal's acceptance is referred to as "ratification."

5. Adoption

Adoption is similar to homologation, but applies where an agreement is void, whereas homologation applies where an agreement is voidable. If an agreement is void, it is a complete nullity; if it is voidable, it is valid until it is challenged and set aside.

The distinction between adoption and homologation, therefore, corresponds to the distinction between void and voidable.

Adoption would be the form of personal bar to operate where a person whose signature had been forged chose, in full knowledge of the forgery, to accept the signature as binding on him.

6. Acquiescence

This occurs when a person sees that his rights are being invaded, and yet takes no action to safeguard them, thus leading others to believe that he has no objection to the invasion; he is then barred from objecting at some later date.

Examples of acquiescence are failure to object to the existence of a "nuisance" on neighbouring property and failure to object to interference with a servitude (such as a right of way) over a neighbour's property.

7. Mora and Taciturnity

"Mora" means "delay," and "taciturnity" means "silence."

Although there is no general rule which requires a person to state his objections to another party's conduct immediately, there are various time-limits laid down by statute for different situations; these

time-limits are referred to as "prescriptive periods," and lapse of
the appropriate prescriptive period will cut off a person's right to
object. By the Prescription and Limitation (Scotland) Act 1973
certain rights are extinguished by a prescriptive period of five years
and other rights by a prescriptive period of twenty years.

The effect of the form of personal bar known as "mora and taciturnity" is to bar a claim where the prescriptive period has not run
its full length. This form is closely linked to acquiescence: a delay
of much less than the appropriate prescriptive period may bar the
exercise of a right where one party's failure to object has led the
other party to infer that the invasion of the right has been acquiesced
in. If the facts are not strong enough to amount to acquiescence,
mora and taciturnity may have the effect of placing such a heavy
onus (burden) of proof on the party who has delayed that he will
be unable to satisfy the court that he is entitled to the right which he
claims.

8. Waiver

Waiver is the giving up of a claim or objection which could otherwise be made; *e.g.* an arbiter, appointed to settle a dispute between
two parties, must as a general rule have no interest in the subject-
matter of the dispute, but, if he has some interest which is known
to the parties and not objected to, then the party who would otherwise have been entitled to object to the arbiter's award is considered
to have "waived" his objection.

9. Holding Out

This type of personal bar applies in partnership and in agency;
thus, if a person has represented himself, or knowingly allowed others
to represent him, as a partner in a particular firm, he may be held
liable for the debts of the firm as if he were in fact a partner; by the
principle of holding out, he is barred from saying that he is not a
partner.

LIABILITY "IN SOLIDUM" AND LIABILITY "PRO RATA"

Where there are co-obligants, *i.e.* where more than one person
is under an obligation, the liability of each obligant to the creditor
in the obligation (*i.e.* to the person who has the personal right) may
be either in solidum ("for the whole debt") or pro rata ("proportionate").

If in a contract the words used are "jointly and severally," or
similar words, the liability of each obligant is in solidum, but if the
contract uses the word "jointly" by itself, or some similar expression
then the liability is only pro rata.

Where there is no express provision, the general presumption is that liability of co-obligants is pro rata, but there are several important exceptions; *e.g.* all the parties to a bill of exchange are liable in solidum for the amount of the bill, and each partner in a firm is liable in solidum for the debts of the firm; joint wrongdoers are also liable in solidum to the person wronged.

Where there is joint and several liability, and one of the co-obligants has paid more than his pro rata share, he has a right of relief against the others; *e.g.* if one of two partners has paid to a creditor of the firm a debt of £500 due by the firm, he is normally entitled to recover £250 from the other partner.

CLASSIFICATION OF OBLIGATIONS

The fundamental classification of obligations in Scots law is into:
1. obligations deliberately undertaken; and
2. obligations imposed by law.

1. Obligations Deliberately Undertaken

Obligations in this group arise ex voluntate vel ex conventione (literally, "out of will or out of agreement"), *i.e.* they are either voluntarily undertaken by one party to another or are created by mutual agreement. The group is, therefore, subdivided into voluntary or unilateral obligations on the one hand and conventional or bilateral or mutual obligations on the other hand, and the former subdivision consists of unilateral gratuitous promises (dealt with in this chapter, below) while the latter subdivision consists of contracts (dealt with in Chapter 9, below).

2. Obligations Imposed by Law

Obligations in this group arise ex lege (literally, "out of law") *i.e.* they are imposed by law, independently of the intentions of the parties. The obligations may arise either because the parties find themselves in a position similar to that which they would have been in had they made a contract, or because one party has inflicted some legal wrong on another party; the former result from quasi-contract (dealt with in Chapter 12, below) and the latter from delict (dealt with in Chapter 13, below).

UNILATERAL GRATUITOUS PROMISES

A person may voluntarily undertake to pay a sum of money to another person or to do something for the benefit of another person, and, if he does so in definite terms, he is under an obligation to fulfil his undertaking. The undertaking may, for instance, be to make a donation, to give a reward, to leave a legacy, or to keep an offer open for a stated period. No acceptance of the promise by the promisee (the one to whom it is made) is necessary in order to make the undertaking binding, and there is no need for any return or "consideration" (a technical term of English law) to pass from the promisee to the promisor. The promise must have been communicated to the promisee in some way before he claims performance, and if he so desires he may reject the promise, in which case the promisor's obligation "falls" (*i.e.* is at an end). A promise may be enforced against the promisor's representatives after the promisor's death.

A unilateral gratuitous promise cannot be revoked by the promisor, but if the existence of the promise is disputed and the promisee brings an action in court to enforce the promise, the only evidence which can be used is either the writing of the promisor or an admission by him on oath that he made the promise. A case which illustrates this restriction on proof is *Smith* v. *Oliver*, 1911 S.C. 103:

This was an action brought by trustees for a church against the executor of a deceased lady who had been a member of the congregation. They were suing for payment of the cost of additions to the church which they alleged the deceased had urged them to make, and for which she had, they said, undertaken to pay by her will, an undertaking which she had not fulfilled.

The court held that this unilateral gratuitous promise could not be enforced because there was no written evidence to prove it and the alternative of reference to oath was, because of the party's death, no longer available.

Further Reading

Gloag and Henderson, *Introduction to the Law of Scotland*
T. B. Smith, *A Short Commentary on the Law of Scotland*
David M. Walker, *Principles of Scottish Private Law*
David M. Walker, *The law of Contracts and related obligations in Scotland* (Butterworths)
Enid A. Marshall, *Scottish Cases on Contract* (W. Green & Son Ltd.)

CHAPTER 9

CONTRACT

A CONTRACT may be defined as "an agreement which creates, or is intended to create, a legal obligation between the parties to it" (Jenks, *Digest of English Civil Law*, Book II, Title 1). This definition was quoted with approval by *Gloag on Contract*, which has been the most authoritative Scottish work on the subject (second ed. (1929), p. 8).

Points to note about this definition are:

1. "between . . . parties": there must always be at least two parties;

2. "agreement": there must be agreement, or, as it is commonly put, there must be "consensus in idem" (literally, "agreement with regard to the same thing"); and

3. "legal obligation": a merely personal or social agreement

(*e.g.* to play a game or to have a meal together) does not create a legal obligation; therefore, it is not a contract; a legal obligation is one which the courts will regard as enforceable; some "patrimonial" interest (*i.e.* some material gain or material loss) must be involved if the obligation is to be a legal obligation, and the terms of the agreement must also not be too vague.

While a contract is always "bilateral" or "mutual" in the sense that two or more persons are parties to it, it does not necessarily give rise to more than one obligation: one party only may be bound to do something or to pay a certain sum, and the other party will have a purely passive role, being neither required to do anything nor liable to pay any money; such a contract is referred to as a "gratuitous contract."

Usually, however, both or all the parties to a contract come under obligations; *e.g.* if by a contract A undertakes to perform some work for B, then normally B will be under an obligation to pay for the work. The normal type of contract is, when contrasted with the gratuitous contract, referred to as an "onerous contract."

The law of contract is mainly concerned with onerous contracts, but it is convenient to note at the outset the distinctive law relating to gratuitous contracts.

GRATUITOUS CONTRACTS

A gratuitous contract is binding in Scots law. English law, with its doctrine of "consideration," differs from Scots law on this point. According to Scots law, a person who has accepted an offer which amounts to a gift made to himself by another person is just as much entitled to enforce the contract as he would have been if he had himself made or agreed to make a full return in money or money's worth to the other party.

An illustration is *Morton's Trustees* v. *Aged Christian Friend Society of Scotland* (1899) 2 F. 82:

M. wrote to a charitable society offering "to become personally responsible for the pensions of fifty life pensioners of £6 each" on certain conditions. His offer was accepted, and the conditions were complied with. Pensioners were appointed, and M. duly paid the amount of their pensions annually to the society until his death.

M.'s representatives were held by the court to be bound to continue to pay to the society the sums necessary for the pensions of pensioners appointed before M.'s death.

A gratuitous contract, unlike an onerous contract, requires, if its existence is disputed, to be proved by writing of the party who is liable under it or by an admission of that party on oath. The method of proving an onerous contract is not restricted to writing or oath:

such a contract may, as a general rule, be proved prout de jure ("by any competent evidence"), *e.g.* by the oral evidence of witnesses.

It is often difficult to distinguish between a gratuitous contract (which, being a contract, is bilateral) and a unilateral gratuitous promise (see p. 248, above). Both require either writing or oath for their proof, but they differ in that, whereas a unilateral gratuitous promise can be enforced only by the promisee, a gratuitous contract can be enforced by either party because the donee, by accepting the offer, has become a party to a binding contract.

FORMATION OF A CONTRACT

A contract is usually regarded as consisting of an offer by one party and an acceptance by the other.

The offer, or the acceptance, or both, may be in words (either spoken or written words), or may be inferred from the actings of the parties. An instance of a contract being inferred from actings of the parties is seen in self-service shops: the customer's selection of the goods, followed by presentation of them at the cash-desk, is an offer; the cashier's action amounts to an acceptance.

The main rules as to offer and acceptance in relation to the formation of a contract are considered below under these headings:
1. offer;
2. acceptance;
3. recall of offer; and
4. recall of acceptance.

1. Offer

There must first be an offer: there can be no acceptance if an offer has never been made.

It is sometimes difficult to distinguish between an offer on the one hand and an expression of willingness to negotiate on the other hand.

Distinction between Offer and Expression of Willingness to Negotiate

This distinction is important, because, if an offer is accepted, there will be a contract, whereas if there is merely a willingness to negotiate, there can be no acceptance, because no offer has yet been made.

If A makes an offer to B, and B says, "I accept," there will be a contract; but if A says to B, "I am willing to negotiate with you," and B says, "I accept," that does not make a contract, because there has been no offer in the first place.

A person who indicates that he is willing to receive and to consider offers and that he intends to contract does not necessarily reach the stage of making an offer; he is free to change his mind.

The following are considered to be merely expressions of willingness to negotiate, not offers which are capable of being accepted: advertisements of goods for sale, catalogues, display of goods in a shop window or in a self-service shop, exposing of goods for sale by auction, requests for tenders for work to be done, and in some situations quotations of prices.

The question of whether there is in any particular case an offer or merely an expression of willingness to negotiate depends on the circumstances of the case; the words "offer" and "accept" are not always necessary, nor does their use always conclusively indicate that an "offer" and an "acceptance" in the legal sense of these terms have been made.

The difficulties which may arise in the distinguishing of an offer from an expression of willingness to negotiate may be seen in the three following cases:

. *Philp & Co.* v. *Knoblauch*, 1907 S.C. 994: In this case there were circumstances in which a quotation of a specific quantity of goods at a specific price was held to be an offer and not merely an expression of willingness to negotiate.

K., a merchant in Leith, wrote to P. & Co., oil-millers at Lower Largo: "I am offering to-day Plate (*a trade name*) linseed . . . and have pleasure in quoting you 100 tons at 41s. 3d., usual Plate terms. I shall be glad to hear if you are buyers, and await your esteemed reply."

The following day, P. & Co. telegraphed: "Accept hundred . . . Plate 41s. 3d.," and confirmed this by letter.

This was followed by a telegram from K. to P. & Co.: "Sorry 41s. 3d. now useless; sellers ask to-day 42s. 6d." This telegram also was confirmed by letter.

K. claimed that his first letter had been a "quotation" and not an "offer" in the legal sense, and refused to deliver the linseed, on the ground that there was no contract.

P. & Co. brought an action of damages for breach of contract.

The court held that K.'s first letter *was* an offer which had been duly accepted, and that, therefore, there was a contract.

If K.'s first letter had been merely a quotation, there would have been no contract, and P. & Co.'s communications would have been the offer which required acceptance if a contract was to be formed.

Harvey v. *Facey* [1893] A.C. 552, a case which came before the Judicial Committee of the Privy Council on appeal from the Supreme Court of Jamaica: In this case a statement by the seller of an estate of the lowest price which he would accept for it was held to be not an offer but merely an indication that he was willing to consider an offer of that amount.

H. sent a telegram which read: "Will you sell us Bumper Hall Pen? Telegraph lowest cash price."

F. telegraphed in reply: "Lowest price for Bumper Hall Pen £900."

H. then telegraphed: "We agree to buy Bumper Hall Pen for £900 asked by you. Please send us your title-deed in order that we may get early possession."

H. received no reply to that telegram, and in these circumstances there was held to be no contract; the final telegram was not the acceptance of an offer to sell, for none had been made; it was itself an offer to buy, which required acceptance from F. if the contract was to be complete.

The argument was put forward that F.'s telegram should have been read as saying "Yes" to the first question in H.'s first telegram, but that argument was rejected: F.'s telegram gave a precise answer to a precise question, namely the price, and an answer to the first question could not be implied; the mere statement of the lowest price at which the seller would be prepared to sell did not amount to an offer to sell at that price to the person who had made the inquiry.

Pharmaceutical Society of Great Britain v. *Boots Cash Chemists (Southern) Ltd.* [1952] 2 Q.B. 795: This concerned a self-service shop.

The case arose out of a provision of the Pharmacy and Poisons Act 1933, which required the sale of a listed poison to be supervised by a registered pharmacist. The vital question was when the "sale" took place, and the answer depended on whether the display of the goods on the shelves was an "offer" in the legal sense or merely an invitation to negotiate; if it was an offer, then the contract would have been complete when a customer put an article in one of the baskets provided, and the sale would therefore have been unlawful under the Act; if, however, the display of the goods was merely an invitation to negotiate, the customer would be making an offer which would be accepted only at the cash-desk, where a registered pharmacist might intervene, and so the sale would comply with the provision of the Act.

The court held that the sale took place at the cash-desk: the display of the goods on the shelves, therefore, amounted to no more than an invitation to negotiate.

2. Acceptance

If acceptance is to be effective it must meet the offer: there must be consensus in idem, and if there are terms in an "acceptance" which were not in the offer, no contract is formed; the purported acceptance is in fact a new offer, which must itself be accepted before there will be a contract.

This does not mean that an acceptance must repeat all the conditions contained in an offer. Normally, if a person gives a general acceptance to an offer which contains conditions, he will be considered to have agreed to all the conditions. There are, however, some exceptions to this, notably under the Unfair Contract Terms Act 1977 (see p. 312, below).

Express Acceptance not Always Necessary

An acceptance is said to be "express" when it is in the form of spoken or written words.

In some situations an express acceptance is not necessary for the completion of a contract:

1. The doing of an act by a member of the public sometimes amounts to an acceptance; *e.g.* if a reward is offered for lost property, the finding and returning of the lost property is sufficient acceptance, and an advertiser may make a general offer to the public in such a way that it may be accepted by the performance of some act by a member of the public; the best-known example of this type of general offer is the English case of *Carlill* v. *Carbolic Smoke Ball Company* [1893] 1 Q.B. 256:

The defendants, proprietors of a medical preparation called "The Carbolic Smoke Ball," issued an advertisement in which they offered to pay £100 to any person who contracted influenza after having used one of their smoke balls in a specified manner and for a specified period.

The plaintiff on the faith of the advertisement bought one of the balls at a chemist's, and used it according to instructions, but nevertheless contracted influenza.

She then claimed £100, and she was held entitled to it, although the company had not known of her acceptance of the offer made in the advertisement; she had accepted the offer in the way indicated in the advertisement, namely, by buying and using the smoke ball.

"Performance of the conditions is the acceptance of the offer," stated Lindley L.J. (Lord Justice Lindley) at p. 262.

The Scottish case of *Hunter* v. *General Accident Fire and Life Assurance Corporation Ltd.*, 1909 S.C.(H.L.) 30; 1909 S.C. 344, was concerned with a similar type of offer; in that case the offer was contained in a coupon for insurance in a Letts' diary.

2. An order for goods does not require an express acceptance: the mere act of supplying the goods is sufficient acceptance.

3. There may be an express or implied agreement between parties that an offer is to be regarded as accepted if it is not refused within a specified time; failure to refuse an offer may then amount to acceptance. This applies only if the parties have expressly so agreed

or have in the past dealt with one another in such a way that their agreement to this method of contracting can be inferred: a person is not entitled to force a contract on another by stating that he will regard his offer as accepted if it is not refused.

If, for instance, A writes to B that he assumes B accepts if he (A) does not hear to the contrary within a certain time, B would not be regarded as having accepted A's offer even although he made no reply, unless there was either some prior express agreement or some previous course of dealing between A and B to that effect.

Similarly, if goods are sent without having been expressly ordered and without there having been any previous course of dealing from which an order could be inferred, they may be rejected.

Time of Acceptance

Questions may arise as to the time within which acceptance must be made.

If an offerer states that his offer is to remain open for, say, three days, he must keep his promise: he cannot revoke the offer within that time, and if acceptance is made within the three days, a binding contract is formed.

If the offer does not state the time within which acceptance must be made, the offer, unless it is recalled, remains open for a reasonable time, and if acceptance is made within a reasonable time, a binding contract is again formed.

What is a reasonable time depends on the whole circumstances of the case; the question might, for instance, be decided by a custom of a particular trade. Business offers to buy or sell goods the price of which changes rapidly are generally regarded as being open for acceptance only by return of post.

An "acceptance" which is not "timeous" (*i.e.* which is too late) amounts to a new offer which in turn requires to be accepted if there is to be a contract.

In the following three cases, offers were held not to have been timeously accepted:

1. *Wylie and Lochhead* v. *M'Elroy and Sons* (1873) 1 R. 41: An offer to execute iron work for a new building had not been accepted for five weeks, during which time there was a considerable rise in the price of iron.

2. *Glasgow etc. Steam Shipping Co.* v. *Watson* (1873) 1 R. 189: An offer made on August 5 to supply a shipping company with coal for one year at 7s. a ton was held to be no longer open for acceptance on October 13, by which date the price had risen by 2s. a ton.

3. *Hall-Maxwell* v. *Gill* (1901) 9 S.L.T. 222 (O H.): An offer made on August 28 to sell Calderwood estate for £36,500, and in-

cluding the request, "Please let me know on receipt of this letter," was held to be no longer open for acceptance on October 12.

On the other hand, in *Murray* v. *Rennie & Angus* (1897) 24 R. 965, an offer of June 10 to execute the mason work required for the erection of a house was held to have been timeously accepted on June 21.

Postal Cases

The question of the time from which an acceptance is to operate is especially important in connection with contracts made by letter or telegram.

The general rule is that the contract is completed at the time when the acceptance is dispatched. The basis for this rule is that the offerer, by posting or telegraphing his offer, has made the Post Office his agent, intends (unless he states otherwise) that the acceptor will use the same means of communication, and impliedly agrees to be bound by an acceptance duly delivered to his agent, the Post Office.

It follows from this rule that if the offer states that acceptance must be made within a certain time, the contract is binding provided the acceptance is posted within the required time, even although it is not delivered until later to the offerer:

Jacobsen, Sons & Co. v. *Underwood & Son Ltd.* (1894) 21 R. 654: On March 2, 1893, U. offered to buy straw from J. The offer stated, "This for reply by Monday, 6th inst.".

On the 6th J. wrote to U. accepting the offer. The letter of acceptance was addressed to the offerer, Leith, the name and number of the street being omitted. It was posted in Edinburgh on the evening of the 6th, but owing to the insufficiency of the address did not reach its destination until the noon delivery of the 7th, instead of the morning delivery.

U. intimated that the contract was off as he had not received the acceptance on the 6th, but the court held that the offer had been accepted in time.

It is uncertain in Scotland what the legal position is if the acceptance, though posted, never arrives. In England, this situation came before the court in *Household Fire Insurance Co. Ltd.* v. *Grant* (1879) 4 Ex.D. 216, and the decision was that the contract was binding even although the acceptance never reached the offerer at all.

An offerer may find himself in an unsatisfactory position if he has stated that his offer is open for acceptance within a specified time, because he cannot be sure that an acceptance has not been delayed in the post. It is, therefore, safer for the offerer to state that acceptance must reach him before a certain date; the contract will then not be binding on him unless he actually receives the acceptance within the stated time.

3. Recall of Offer

The main rules as to recall or withdrawal of an offer are:

1. If the offerer undertakes to keep the offer open for a definite period, that promise is binding on him: he cannot recall the offer within that time.

2. If the offerer states that acceptance must be made within a specified time, and acceptance is not made within that time, the offer is automatically recalled.

3. If the offerer does not state a time within which acceptance must be made, the offer remains open, not indefinitely, but only for a reasonable time, and if not accepted within a reasonable time it is automatically recalled.

4. Where there is no promise to keep an offer open for a specified time, the offerer can recall his offer at any time before it has been accepted. As long as the parties are still at the stage of negotiation, and a contract has not yet been formed, either party has locus poenitentiae (literally, "room for repentance"), *i.e.* the right to "resile" or draw back. An offer cannot be withdrawn after it has been accepted:

Thomson v. *James* (1855) 18 D. 1: J., by letter dated November 21, 1853, offered to buy the lands of Renniston for £6,400 from T.

At first T. was not satisfied with this offer, but finally on December 1, 1853 he posted a letter of acceptance. On the same day, however, J. posted a letter withdrawing his offer. Both letters were delivered on December 2.

The court held that there was a binding contract of sale which J. was bound to fulfil, and that the withdrawal of the offer was too late, because it did not arrive until after the acceptance had been posted.

5. An offer is also automatically recalled by the death of either party or by the insanity or bankruptcy of the offerer.

4. Recall of Acceptance

An acceptance completes the contract: there can usually be no question of recalling or withdrawing the acceptance.

The question of recall of acceptance can arise only where the acceptance has been dispatched through the Post Office; *e.g.* the acceptance may have been sent by letter, and before it has reached the offerer, the acceptor, having changed his mind, may send off another communication, perhaps a telegram, which arrives before or at the same time as the acceptance.

If the second communication arrives after the first one, it is of no effect: the acceptance is binding.

If, however, the recall reaches the offerer before or at the same time as the acceptance, there is no binding contract. This is an exception to the general rule that in postal cases dispatch of an acceptance concludes the contract. The authority for this exception is:

Countess of Dunmore v. *Alexander* (1830) 9 S. 190: Lady Agnew had a servant Betty Alexander who wished to leave her service. The Countess of Dunmore, who was looking for a new servant, heard of this, and wrote to Lady Agnew stating that the wages which she gave were £12 12s. per annum and requesting information as to Betty's character.

Lady Agnew in answer stated that she could recommend Betty, who would gratefully accept the proposed wages. That amounted to an offer made by Betty to the Countess.

This offer was accepted by a letter posted by the Countess on November 5, but the following day the Countess posted another letter revoking the acceptance. Owing to a delay in the delivery of the first letter, both letters reached Betty at the same moment.

The court held that no contract had been formed.

FORMALITIES REQUIRED FOR CONTRACTS

As a general rule, the law of Scotland does not require any special formality in the making of contracts: a contract may be entered into orally or in writing, or may be inferred from the actions of the parties, and if there is a dispute as to whether a contract has been formed any evidence, written or "parole" (given orally by witnesses), may be brought before the court to resolve the dispute.

There are, however, two major exceptions to that general rule:

1. There are certain contracts which cannot be entered into except by writing; these are referred to as "obligationes literis" ("contracts requiring writing").

2. There are certain other contracts which may be entered into without writing but which cannot be proved except by the "writ" (writing) or oath of the person who has an interest to deny that they exist.

1.   Obligationes Literis

These are contracts which either by common law or by statute require writing for their constitution.

They include:

(a) contracts dealing with heritable property, such as land and buildings, *e.g.* offers and acceptances for sale or purchase of a house:

a lease of heritable property for not more than a year is an exception —it may be entered into orally;

(b)   contracts of service (*i.e.* employment) for a period of more than a year and contracts of apprenticeship;

(c)   formal submissions to arbitration and the decrees-arbitral which bring them to an end;

(d)   contracts which the parties agree should be constituted in writing;

(e)   possibly, contracts of insurance; and

(f)   various classes of contracts which, by different statutory provisions, require to be in writing, *e.g.* "cautionary[1] obligations" (guarantees) by the Mercantile Law Amendment (Scotland) Act 1856, bills of exchange (including cheques) by the Bills of Exchange Act 1882, and the memorandum and articles of a company by the Companies Act 1948.

Where a statutory provision applies, the form which the written contract must take depends on that statutory provision; *e.g.* under the Companies Act 1948 a company's memorandum and articles require to be signed before one (but not necessarily before more than one) witness.

Where no statutory provision has been made, the rule of the common law requires that the writing be "probative."

A probative writing is one which in court is presumed to be genuine. Documents which are not probative require in court to be proved genuine by the person who brings them forward as evidence.

The following are either probative writings or deemed equivalent to such writings:

(a)   attested writings;

(b)   holograph writings; and

(c)   writings in re mercatoria ("on a commercial matter").

(a)   *Attested Writings*

"Attested" means "witnessed" (from the Latin "testis," a witness), and an attested writing is one which is signed by two witnesses as well as by the party or parties to the contract.

This is the most formal of the three types of writing; it is used, for instance, in the title-deeds of heritable property, and is, in general, the form of writing adopted for "deeds" (formal legal documents) of all kinds.

The procedure for the signing of deeds is referred to as "authentication" or "execution," and in outline is normally as follows:

(i)   After the terms of the agreement have been settled by

[1] Pronounced as if there were no "u" ("kay-shun-ary").

negotiations between the parties, the deed is typed, and ruled in pencil for signature.

(ii) The parties who are granting the deed and two witnesses sign the deed. The witnesses are not concerned with the contents of the deed: they are witnesses to the execution of it only. They need not actually see the granter sign the deed: it is sufficient if they hear him acknowledge his signature.

(iii) A "testing" or "attestation" clause is then typed into the deed in a space deliberately left for this purpose at the end of the deed and above the signatures. This clause traditionally always starts with the words "IN WITNESS WHEREOF," and gives details of the signing of the document, such as the place, date, and names and addresses of witnesses; if there have been alterations in the deed, these are declared in this clause.

A testing clause is not necessary, provided the "designations" of witnesses are given after their signatures. By a "designation" is meant sufficient information to identify the witness, *i.e.* usually his occupation and address.

Notarial execution

A special procedure, known as "notarial execution" is provided for the authentication of deeds where the granter of the deed is blind or unable to write. The procedure is laid down in the Conveyancing (Scotland) Act 1924.

The document is read over to the granter by a notary public or other solicitor, or by a justice of the peace, or, in the case of wills only, by a minister, and then signed by the reader on behalf of the granter. Two witnesses must be present throughout, and must also sign. A special docquet relating to the execution of the document, is added at the end.

(b) *Holograph Writings*

The word "holograph" is derived from Greek, and means "written wholly in handwriting." A holograph document is one which is written entirely, or at least in all its essential parts, in the handwriting of the person who signs it.

Holograph writings are not probative until they are proved or admitted to be holograph, but, once that has been done, they are equivalent to attested writings.

A writing which is not actually holograph may be "adopted as holograph": the person who is signing the document writes the words "adopted as holograph" or words with the same meaning immediately before his signature, thereby giving a holograph character to a document which is typed, printed, or written by another person's hand.

Writings which are holograph or adopted as holograph are regularly used in the formation of contracts for sale and purchase of heritable property.

A document cannot be holograph of more than one party, but the same document may be holograph of one party and adopted as holograph by another; similarly, the document may be adopted as holograph by two or more parties.

(c) *Writings in Re Mercatoria*

Documents embodying ordinary commercial contracts are privileged in that they are treated as probative although they are neither attested nor holograph: they require only an ordinary signature, and their genuineness, if challenged, can be proved by parole evidence.

This privilege is based on the desirability of simplicity and speed in business transactions and also on the international character of trading relations.

Writings in re mercatoria include bills of exchange, orders for goods, contracts of agency, offers and acceptances to buy, sell, or transport merchandise, and in general all documents required in the ordinary course of trade.

A guarantee is a writing in re mercatoria if it is granted in the course of dealing between merchants (*e.g.* a guarantee granted by H. to suppliers of animal feedstuffs in order to secure future supplies to a company of grain merchants in which H. was the individual principally interested: *B.O.C.M. Silcock Ltd.* v. *Hunter*, 1976 S.L.T. 217), but not in other circumstances (*e.g.* if granted to a bank in connection with a loan made by the bank to one of its customers). Similarly, arbitration may, or may not, be a res mercatoria ("commercial matter") according to circumstances.

2.   Contracts Requiring Proof by Writ or Oath

Contracts in this category do not require writing as a solemnity for their formation, but if they are disputed they are enforceable only if they can be proved by the writing or oath of the party who would be interested in denying them. The writing is necessary, not for the constitution of the contract, but only in modum probationis ("by way of proof"), *i.e.* as evidence.

This category of contracts is to be distinguished from obligationes literis (which require writing for their formation) on the one hand, and from the great mass of ordinary contracts (which may be both constituted and proved prout de jure, *i.e.* by any competent evidence) on the other hand.

Contracts requiring writ or oath for proof are:

(a) gratuitous obligations, whether unilateral or bilateral;

(b) loans over £8·33 (£100 Scots);

(c) trust, *i.e.* the situation where a person holds property apparently absolutely and for his own benefit but really in trust for others (the beneficiaries in the trust);

(d) express obligations of relief, *e.g.* an agreement by a director of a company to relieve his co-directors of their liability for a bank overdraft; and

(e) innominate and unusual contracts; "innominate" means literally "without a name," and is used of contracts which do not fall into one or other of the well-recognised categories such as sale, hire or loan; to be classed as an "innominate and unusual contract" a contract must be of such a peculiar nature that the parties could be expected to have put it in writing; there is an example of such a contract in:

Garden v. *Earl of Aberdeen* (1893) 20 R. 896: A tenant alleged that, a year before the end of a nineteen-year lease of a farm, the landlord had agreed that, if the tenant would remain in the farm until the end of the lease and pay the rent, he, the landlord, would repay to the tenant all his loss for the nineteen years of the lease, however large the sum might be.

The court held that this was an innominate and unusual contract which could be proved only by the landlord's writ or oath.

Writing which is required merely to prove a contract does not need to be probative: the authority for this is *Paterson* v. *Paterson* (1897) 25 R. 144, in which the court held that a loan of £450 made to John Paterson by his mother could be proved by an acknowledgment which was not probative in form.

Contracts Defective in Form

Contracts which require probative writing for their constitution are defective in form if they have been entered into in writing which is "improbative" (*i.e.* lacking in the formalities of a probative writing).

The general rule is that either party to a contract which is defective in form may "resile" (*i.e.* withdraw): there is locus poenitentiae (literally, "room for repentance"), *i.e.* the contract is not binding.

For instance, a contract for the sale of heritable property requires for its constitution a probative offer, followed by a probative acceptance, and if either the offer or the acceptance is improbative, neither the seller nor the purchaser is, according to the general rule, bound by the contract.

Goldston v. *Young* (1868) 7 M. 188, is a striking example: Y. wrote out an offer, addressed to himself, for the purchase of his shop, and G. signed the offer. Y. wrote out and signed an acceptance, but later wished to resile from the contract.

The court held that he was entitled to do so because the contract was defective in form, G.'s offer being neither attested nor holograph.

In some situations, however, the doctrine of personal bar prevents a party from exercising his right to resile from a contract which is defective in form: locus poenitentiae may be barred either by rei interventus or by homologation (see pp. 245 and 246, above).

A case which illustrates this point, and also the distinction between rei interventus and homologation is *Mitchell* v. *Stornoway Trustees*, 1936 S.C.(H.L.) 56:

The case concerned a contract for the feuing of a triangular piece of ground by the Stornoway Trustees to M.

The contract, being one dealing with heritable property, required for its constitution probative writings on both sides. It did not have this form, and so there was locus poenitentiae as long as no action had been taken on the contract.

M., however, presented an application to the dean of guild court for the necessary authorisation to erect buildings on the ground. There were some difficulties as to the building plans, and the trustees gave assistance to M. in order that his plans might be approved by the dean of guild court.

The trustees later tried to resile from the contract claiming that it was not in proper form.

M. contended that there had been (a) rei interventus, and (b) homologation: the rei interventus, he said, was the action which he, the party loyal to the contract, had been taking, such as the lodging of the application with the dean of guild court for building permission; the homologation, he said, was the assistance given by the trustees when the matter was before that court; they had, M. alleged, consented to the contract's being binding on them in spite of its improbative form.

The House of Lords held that there had been homologation.

Rei interventus consists of actings of the party who wishes a contract to go on (M., in this case), whereas homologation consists of actings of the party who wishes to resile (the trustees, in this case).

Three out of the five Law Lords were also prepared to hold, if necessary, that there had been rei interventus as well as homologation.

If a contract which ought to have been constituted by probative writing has been entered into orally (*i.e.* without even an improbative writing), then, according to the generally accepted view, the doctrine of personal bar will not operate unless the existence of the oral contract can be proved by the writ or oath of the party who wishes to resile from the contract.

VALIDITY OF CONTRACTS

Even although a contract is in the proper form, it may have other defects which will affect its validity: the parties may not have full capacity to make the contract (*e.g.* a party may be too young); full consent may be lacking because of some error in the mind of one or both of the parties (*e.g.* one party may have been misled by a fraudulent statement made by the other party); or the contract may be one forbidden by law.

These defects make a contract void, or voidable, or unenforceable, according to circumstances.

Void

If a contract (or rather an apparent contract) is void, it has no legal effect at all: it is a mere nullity. Neither party can enforce it, and even a third party who knows nothing of the nullity cannot acquire any rights through it; *e.g.* if there is a void "contract" for the sale of goods by A to B, and B, having obtained the goods, re-sells them to C, C, the third party, has no right to the goods, even although he may know nothing about the invalidity of the "contract" between A and B.

Voidable

A voidable contract is one which may be "reduced" or "avoided" (legal terms meaning "set aside"), but which is valid and has full legal effect until that is done; if, therefore, there is a voidable contract for, say, the sale of goods by A to B, and B resells the goods to C before A exercises his right to set the voidable contract aside, C obtains a valid title to the goods, provided he knows nothing of the invalidity of the first contract.

Unenforceable

An unenforceable contract is one which cannot be enforced by a court action. It is not necessarily either void or voidable: it is simply of such a nature that a court will not order it to be carried out.

A contract may be unenforceable because of a rule of common law (*e.g.* contracts which lack the formalities required for their constitution or for their proof), or because of a statutory provision (*e.g.* under the Registration of Business Names Act 1916 contracts entered into by persons who have not duly registered their business names).

If, however, an unenforceable contract is performed or money is paid under it, the court will not interfere to cancel the contract or to order repayment of the money.

Capacity to Contract

Certain persons and bodies do not have full capacity to contract ("contractual capacity"), and contracts entered into by them may as a result be void or voidable.

There are limitations on the contractual capacity of:

1. pupils;
2. minors;
3. insane persons;
4. intoxicated persons;
5. enemy aliens; and
6. corporate bodies.

1. *Pupils*

For legal purposes, a pupil is a boy under fourteen or a girl under twelve.

Pupils have no power to contract: a contract which purports to be made by a pupil is as a rule void and therefore unenforceable, with the possible exception that a contract may be enforceable for the pupil's benefit (but not against him).

There is a provision of the Sale of Goods Act 1979 that if necessaries (such as food and clothing) are sold and delivered to a pupil, he must pay a reasonable price for them; that price is not necessarily the same as the contract price.

There is also a rule of the common law that if money has been lent to a pupil and spent for his benefit (*e.g.* in the repair of his house), he is liable to the extent of the benefit received.

Neither of these rules, however, is properly part of the law of contract.

Contracts are made on behalf of pupils by their "tutors" (guardians).

By the Guardianship Act 1973 either the pupil's father or the pupil's mother may act as his tutor, and, where the parents disagree, either of them may apply to the court for a settlement of the difference. Appointments of tutors can also be made by either parent's will or by the court.

Contracts made on behalf of a pupil by his tutor may in certain circumstances be set aside up to the end of a period of four years after the pupil attains the age of majority, which, since January 1, 1970, has been eighteen (Age of Majority (Scotland) Act 1969); the pupil must have suffered "enorm lesion" (*i.e.* some considerable loss) and the contract must have been one which was not proper and reasonable at the time when it was made.

2. *Minors*

A minor is a young person who is over the upper age-limits of pupillarity (fourteen or twelve, according to sex) and has not yet attained majority (eighteen).

Minors have a limited capacity to contract: their contracts may be void, or voidable, or fully binding.

The guardian of a minor is called a "curator."

By the Guardianship Act 1973 either the minor's father or the minor's mother may act as his curator, and, where the parents disagree, either of them may apply to the court for a settlement of the difference. Curators may also be nominated by either parent's will, and a minor who does not otherwise have a curator may petition the court for the appointment of one, if he so desires.

The rules relating to a minor's contracts depend partly on whether or not the minor has a curator. Unlike the tutor, the curator has no power to make contracts himself on behalf of the minor: contractual capacity lies in the minor, and the function of the curator is merely to consent to a contract.

There are three possible situations:

(a) A minor who has a curator contracts without his curator's consent

Any contract purporting to be made by a minor without his curator's consent is as a rule void, with the probable exception that contracts of service and contracts in the ordinary course of a trade carried on by the minor are fully binding and with the possible exception that contracts beneficial to the minor are enforceable by him. The provision of the Sale of Goods Act 1979 as to necessaries and the rule of the common law as to loans, mentioned under "1. Pupils," above, also apply to minors.

(b) A minor who has a curator contracts with his curator's consent

The general rule is that contracts made by a minor with his curator's consent are voidable, since they may be set aside by the minor himself up to the end of the period of four years after majority on the ground of enorm lesion. This four-year period is known as the quadriennium utile ("useful four-year period").

In order to prove enorm lesion it is not sufficient for the minor to prove that the contract has turned out badly for him: he must also show that the contract was not a proper and reasonable one at the time when it was made. If, for instance, the minor made a donation of his property or otherwise voluntarily surrendered his rights without receiving any return, it would be presumed that there was enorm lesion, and the minor would be entitled to reduce the contract.

(c) The minor does not have a curator

If both the minor's parents are dead, the minor does not necessarily have a curator at all.

Contracts made by a minor in such a position are governed by the same rules as contracts in (b) above.

It is, however, easier to prove that there has been enorm lesion if the minor has been acting without the guidance of any curator, and so contracts in this category are more likely to be set aside at a later date. This tends to make other parties reluctant to enter into contracts with a minor who does not have a curator.

Exclusion of the plea of minority and enorm lesion

In certain circumstances it is not possible for the minor's contracts to be set aside on the ground of enorm lesion; the contracts are fully binding. These circumstances are:

(i) where the minor has held himself out to be of full age and the person with whom he was contracting believed on reasonable grounds that he was in fact of full age;

(ii) where the minor has entered a trade or business and the contract was made by him in the ordinary course of that trade or business; and

(iii) where the minor, after attaining majority, has ratified the contract in full knowledge of his right to reduce it.

3. *Insane Persons*

An insane person has no power to contract: his "contracts" are void.

If, however, necessaries are sold and delivered to an insane person, he must pay a reasonable price for them (Sale of Goods Act 1979, s. 3).

Application can be made to the court for the appointment of a curator bonis ("guardian for his goods or property"), whose function is to manage the insane person's affairs.

A contract of a continuing nature, *e.g.* a contract of partnership, does not necessarily become void if a contracting party who was sane when he entered into the contract later becomes insane; thus, partnership is not automatically dissolved if a partner becomes insane, but the partner's insanity may be made the ground of an application to court for the purpose of having the partnership dissolved by an order of the court (Partnership Act 1890, s. 35).

4. *Intoxicated Persons*

Drunkenness is not a ground on which a contract can be made either void or voidable unless the drunkenness has reached such a stage that the person no longer knows what he is doing and is, therefore, incapable of giving the consent which is essential for a contract. If the drunkenness has reached that stage, then the contract is voidable, but can be set aside only if the intoxicated person repudiates it as soon as he recovers his senses and realises what he has done.

Taylor v. *Provan* (1864) 2 M. 1226: P., in the morning when sober, had offered to buy 31 cattle from T. at £13 10s., £13 15s., and £14 a head, but T. refused to sell at less than £15. P. returned at night, when partially drunk, but quite rational, and offered £15 a head.

He later attempted to set aside the sale on the ground of intoxication, but the court held that the contract was binding because the degree of T.'s intoxication was not sufficient to make him incapable of giving true consent to the contract.

5. *Enemy Aliens*

Aliens, other than enemy aliens, are not subject to any general incapacity to contract.

An enemy alien is a person of any nationality, who, in time of war, voluntarily resides or carries on business in an enemy country.

A contract entered into with an enemy alien is illegal, and a criminal offence.

Contracts already in existence at the declaration of war become void on that event if they involve intercourse with enemy aliens, but at the end of the war the rights of the former enemy aliens revive, with the result, for instance, that they may sue for the recovery of sums due to them under the pre-war contracts.

6. *Corporate Bodies*

Not all corporate bodies have the same degree of personality (see p. 133, above). They consequently differ from one another as to their contractual capacity.

The general principle is that the contractual capacity of a corporate body depends on its constitution, *i.e.* the document containing the state's authority for the creation of the body.

A body owing its corporate status to a royal charter has power to enter into any contract unless the charter expressly forbids it to do so. The activities of such a body, however, are sometimes open to challenge on the ground that it has acted in breach of trust.

In contrast, a corporate body created by statute cannot enter into any contracts except those expressly or impliedly authorised by the statute concerned. By the ultra vires ("beyond the powers") doctrine any purported contracts outside the statutory powers of the body are void, and cannot be made valid even by the unanimous consent of all members of the body.

When applied to those corporate bodies which are in the form of companies registered under the Companies Acts, this doctrine means that a registered company has no power to enter into contracts which are not necessary for or incidental to the attainment by the company of its objects as stated in its memorandum of association. The practical result is that registered companies usually state their objects in very wide terms. Nevertheless, persons contracting with registered companies have sometimes suffered hardship as a result of the ultra vires doctrine. The memorandum is a public document which anyone may consult at the office of the registrar of companies, and by the "doctrine of constructive notice" every person dealing with a registered company was considered by the law to "have notice of" (*i.e.* know of) any limitations on the company's contractual powers set out in the memorandum, although he would seldom in fact have consulted that document. The ultra vires doctrine as applied to registered companies was restricted by the European Communities Act 1972. Section 9 of that Act provides that in favour of a person dealing with a company in good faith any transaction decided on by the directors is now deemed to be one which is within the company's contractual capacity.

Contracts of corporate bodies are made by persons acting as agents for the bodies; these agents may have the title of "directors," "managers," "officers," etc., and their powers to contract on behalf of the particular body which they represent are not necessarily as wide as the contractual powers of the body itself; for instance, a director of a registered company may not have power to enter into all types of contracts which the company itself might, according to its stated objects, have power to enter into, and so a contract may be ultra vires of a director and yet intra vires ("within the powers") of the company; such contracts, unlike contracts which are ultra vires of the company itself, can be "ratified" and so made valid by the members of the company. Section 9 of the European Communities Act 1972 also gives protection here. It provides that in favour of a person dealing with a company in good faith the power of the directors is now deemed to be free of any limitation under the memorandum or articles of association.

Error

One or both of the parties to a contract may have entered into it under error, and this may affect the validity of the contract.

The law on this subject is controversial, and only the main traditional aspects of error are dealt with here.

A distinction must first be made between errors in law and errors in fact.

An error in law exists where a party is mistaken about his legal rights or about the legal effects of his words or conduct. The general rule is that error in law does not affect the validity of a contract. This is in accordance with the principle expressed in the maxim "ignorantia juris neminem excusat" ("ignorance of the law excuses no one").

There are some possible exceptions to this general rule; *e.g.* in gratuitous obligations the court may allow reduction on the ground that the granter was mistaken as to the legal consequences of his undertaking.

An error in fact exists where a party is mistaken about some matter of fact connected with the contract, *e.g.* the subject-matter or the price. It is, in general, this type of error, and not error in law, which affects the validity of contracts. Its effect varies according to circumstances.

Error in fact may be considered under five headings:

1. error which has not been induced by the other party;
2. error which has been induced by the innocent misrepresentation of the other party;
3. error which has been induced by the fraud of the other party;
4. error which has been induced by concealment or failure to disclose; and
5. error which has been induced by negligent misrepresentation.

1. *Error not Induced by the Other Party*

(a) **Error of expression**

There may be some error in the recording or expressing of the terms of the contract. Instances of this type of error are:

(i) a clerical error in a contractual document signed by both parties;

(ii) faulty transmission of a message in a telegram; or

(iii) a slip made by the offerer in the stating of the terms of his offer.

(i) *Clerical error in signed contractual document*

This refers to the situation where the parties have reached agreement, but the document embodying the terms of their agreement contains a clerical error and so is not a correct statement of what was agreed on by the parties.

In such circumstances the court does not allow one party to take advantage of the incorrect provision: the document may be reduced by the court in order that an accurate record of the contract may be substituted. Reduction is granted even where the interests of "third parties" (persons other than the parties to the contract) are involved, unless either:

1. the document is a "negotiable instrument" (see p. 318, below), such as a cheque, and the third party is a "holder for value" of it (*i.e.* has made some return for the transfer of the document to him); or

2. the document is one of the title-deeds of heritable property, and has been "recorded in the Register of Sasines" (*i.e.* registered in the land register kept at Register House, Edinburgh).

There is an illustration of a clerical error in *Krupp* v. *John Menzies Ltd.*, 1907 S.C. 903:

Mrs. K. was employed by M. as manageress of the Station Hotel, Mallaig. Her remuneration according to her written contract with M. was to be one-fifth of the net annual profit.

The clerk who had written out the contract had been given as a "style" another contract in which the remuneration was stated as one-tenth of the net annual profit, and he had been told to insert one-half of that in Mrs. K.'s contract. He had made the arithmetical mistake of calculating a half of a tenth as a fifth instead of a twentieth.

The error was not discovered by either party until immediately before the date of the action.

Mrs. K. claimed a fifth, and M. refused to pay.

The court allowed M. to show by parole evidence what the real contract was; the document did not record what had in fact been the agreement reached, and its terms were therefore not binding.

(ii) *Faulty transmission of message in telegram*

If an offer sent by telegram is misread by the telegraph operator, so that the message delivered is materially different from the original offer, there will be no contract created by an acceptance of the terms of the telegram, because there is no real consensus ("agreement") between the parties.

An illustration is *Verdin Brothers* v. *Robertson* (1871) 10 M. 35:

R. despatched a telegram from Peterhead to V. in Liverpool as follows: "Send on immediately fifteen twenty tons salt invoice in my name."

The telegram delivered at Liverpool read: "Send on rail immediately fifteen twenty tons salt Morice in morning name."

V. sent salt and invoices to "Morice, Peterhead."

Later V. brought an action for the price against R., but R. was held not liable because the offer had been wrongly transmitted: there had been no contract, because of the error of expression in the offer.

(iii) *Misstatement of terms by offerer*

The offerer may make some slip in the stating of the terms of his offer; *e.g.* he may, through a miscalculation or otherwise, quote a price which is lower than that which he means to quote. This misstated offer may then be accepted by the other party before the offerer notices his mistake.

There are conflicting authorities as to whether there is in such circumstances a binding contract. A distinction may require to be drawn between cases where the acceptor realises that the offerer is making a mistake and cases where the acceptor accepts in good faith, not aware that the offer is misstated. In the former type of case the contract is probably reducible. In the latter type the contract is possibly reducible, at least if the acceptor might reasonably be expected to have discovered the mistake.

(b) Error of intention

There may have been some erroneous belief in the mind of one or both of the parties when the contract was entered into, *i.e.* the error may be unilateral or bilateral.

(i) *Unilateral error*

The general rule is that error of one party only does not affect the validity of a contract. If, for instance, a person agrees to pay more for property than it is worth or to sell property for less than its true value, he will be required to stand by his price, and, in general, a person cannot reduce a contract merely on the ground that he would not have entered into it had he been aware of certain circumstances.

There is an example of the application of this general rule in the case of *Stewart* v. *Kennedy* (1890) 17 R.(H.L.) 1, and (1890) 17 R.(H.L.) 25:

S. offered to sell a property to K.; acceptance was to be "subject to the ratification of the court."

S. thought that the inclusion of these words meant that the court's approval of the bargain as fair and reasonable would be required.

The House of Lords at the earlier stage of the case held that this was a misunderstanding on S.'s part, and at the later stage of the case held that S.'s error was not a ground on which the contract could be reduced.

The general rule does not apply if the unilateral error is so fundamental that the party in error cannot be regarded as ever having agreed to the contract at all. The contract in that case is void.

(ii) *Bilateral error*

Bilateral error may be either **common** error or mutual error:

1. *Common error*

There is common error where both parties have made the same mistake about some fact which is "material to" (important for) the contract. The contract is then void.

For instance, "where there is a contract for the sale of specific goods, and the goods without the knowledge of the seller have perished at the time when the contract is made, the contract is void" (Sale of Goods Act 1979, s. 6).

If, however, the common error is not as to some fact but as to a matter of opinion (*e.g.* as to the value of an article being sold), the contract is valid; *e.g.* in the case of *Dawson* v. *Muir* (1851) 13 D. 843, the court held that where certain vats sunk in the ground had been sold to D. for £2 and were later found to contain white lead valued at £300, D.'s right to the lead was not open to challenge on the ground that both parties had been mistaken as to the real value of the subject-matter of the sale.

2. *Mutual error*

"Mutual error" is often used to denote common error, but since "mutual" means "experienced or undertaken by each towards the other," the term "mutual error" ought to be reserved for the situation where the parties have misunderstood one another. In this situation the court looks at the written contract or at the negotiations to ascertain which party's understanding was the reasonable and correct one, and the contract is valid unless the court holds that the misunderstanding was so fundamental that the parties had never in fact reached agreement.

In this connection a distinction is drawn between error concomitans ("collateral error" or "accompanying error") and error in substantialibus ("error in the substantials"), which is sometimes referred to as "essential error."

(a) *Error concomitans.* This is error as to matters which are merely collateral to the contract and not part of its essence. It does not impair the validity of the contract.

The case of *Cloup and anr.* v. *Alexander* (1831) 9 S. 448, gives an example of this type of error:

The managers of a French company of comedians hired the Caledonian Theatre, Edinburgh, "for their performances."

They later discovered that it was illegal for them to present their particular kind of performances in that theatre, and they hired the Theatre Royal instead.

The proprietor of the Caledonian Theatre brought an action against the comedians for the rent, and he was held entitled to it.

The fact that the comedians were in error as to the nature of performances which were permissible in the Caledonian Theatre did not allow them to treat the contract as either void or voidable.

(b) *Error in substantialibus.* This is error as to the fundamentals or essence of the contract. It makes the contract void, since the consensus in idem required for the making of a contract is lacking.

There are five generally recognised types of error as to the substantials, namely:

    (i)   error as to the identity of the parties;

   (ii)   error as to the subject-matter of the contract;

  (iii)   error as to the nature of the contract;

  (iv)   error as to the price; and

   (v)   error as to quality, quantity or extent.

(i) *Error as to identity.* If A believes that he is contracting with B, and in reality he is contracting with C, the contract is void if, but only if, personal identity is material to the particular contract, *i.e.* if A would not have entered into the contract at all if he had realised that he was negotiating with C instead of with B.

Error as to identity where identity is material may be illustrated by the three following cases:

1. *Cundy* v. *Lindsay* (1878) 3 App.Cas. 459: Blenkiron & Son, a well-known firm of good credit, carried on business at 123 Wood Street, Cheapside. At 37 Wood Street, a person called "Alfred Blenkarn" occupied a room on the top floor of a house which had windows looking into Wood Street but the entrance to which and the proper address of which was 5 Little Love Lane.

Blenkarn, using the address "37 Wood Street," at which he pretended to have a warehouse, wrote to L. & Co., linen manufacturers in Belfast, ordering a considerable quantity of goods. The signature of the letter looked very like "Blenkiron & Co.," and L. & Co., knowing of the respectable firm in Wood Street, sent the goods ordered addressed to "Messrs. Blenkiron & Co." at 37 Wood Street, Cheapside, where they were taken in at once by Alfred Blenkarn.

L. & Co. received no payment for the goods, which were disposed of by Blenkarn for his own profit. Amongst the sales which Blenkarn transacted was one of 250 dozen handkerchiefs to C.

After Blenkarn had been prosecuted for fraud and sentenced, L. & Co. brought an action against C., who had known nothing of the fraud.

The action was successful, because the sale of the goods to Blenkarn had been void. Blenkarn never had any title to the goods;

therefore he could not pass on any title to them to a purchaser from him.

It would have been different if Blenkarn had made a voidable contract, because the right of C., an innocent third party, could not then have been challenged.

As it was, there had never been any contract between L. & Co. and Blenkarn: the identity of the purchaser was material, since L. & Co. would not have supplied the goods unless they had believed that they were contracting with a firm whose credit was good; the contract with Blenkarn was void because of error as to identity.

2. *Morrisson* v. *Robertson*, 1908 S.C. 332; This is the best-known Scottish case on the same point.

M., a dairyman in Kirkcaldy, had in the past had dealings with Wilson, a dairyman at Bonnyrigg.

One day Telford, a man of no fixed residence, approached M., and said that he was the son of Wilson of Bonnyrigg and that he wished to buy two cows from M.

M. was completely deceived, and gave the cows on credit to Telford, who then sold them to R. and vanished.

M. brought an action against R. for redelivery of the cows, and his action was successful because of the error as to identity in M.'s sale to Telford. Since that contract had been void, not even an innocent third party, R., could acquire any rights through it.

Lord M'Laren stated, at p. 336:

" The case of the pursuer is that there was here no contract of sale. If Telford, the man who committed the fraud, had by false representations as to his own character and credit obtained the cows from the pursuer on credit, then I think that would have been the case of a sale which, although liable to reduction, would stand good until reduced. But then that was not at all the nature of the case. The pursuer never sold his cows to Telford. He believed that he was selling the cows to a man Wilson at Bonnyrigg, whom he knew to be a person of reasonably good credit, and to whom he was content to give credit for the payment of the price. This belief that he was selling the cows to Wilson was induced by the fraudulent statement of Telford that he was Wilson's son. It is perfectly plain that in such circumstances there was no contract between Telford and the pursuer, because Telford did not propose to buy the cows for himself, and because the pursuer would not have sold them on credit to a man of whom he had no knowledge. Neither was there any sale of the cows by the pursuer to Mr. Wilson, Bonnyrigg. Wilson knew nothing about them, and never authorised the purchase; the whole story was an invention. There being no sale either to Wilson or to Telford, and there being no other party concerned in the business in hand, it follows that there was no contract of sale at all, and there being no contract of sale the pursuer remained the undivested owner of his cows, although he had parted with their custody to Telford in consequence of these false representations.

". . . it follows that as Telford had no right to the cows, he could not give a good title to the defender even under a contract for an onerous consideration. He had no better title to sell the cows to any third person than he would have had if he had gone into the pursuer's byre and stolen the cows."

3.   *Said* v. *Butt* [1920] 3 K.B. 497: The plaintiff, S., a Russian, wished to attend the first performance of a new play, "The Whirligig," at the Palace Theatre, London, but knew that if he applied personally for a ticket he would be refused one because of his former relations with the theatre.

He got a friend to buy him a ticket, but when he presented his ticket at the theatre he was refused admission.

In his action against B., the managing director of the theatre, the court held that B. was entitled to refuse admission to the ticket-holder because he would not have sold the ticket at all if he had known that S. was the purchaser of it. The identity of S. was a material element in the formation of the contract.

(ii)   *Error as to subject-matter.* In this case the parties do not have the same subject-matter in mind when they make their contract.

An example is *Raffles* v. *Wichelhaus and anr.* (1864) 2 H. & C. 906:

Two ships of the name "Peerless" were both sailing with cotton on board from Bombay.

The defendant bought from the plaintiff cotton which was to "arrive ex 'Peerless.' " He was thinking of the ship which sailed from Bombay in October.

The plaintiff, however, was not ready to deliver any cotton which arrived by that ship, but only cotton which arrived by the other "Peerless," which had sailed from Bombay in December.

The court held that, since there had been no consensus in idem there was no binding contract.

(iii)   *Error as to contract.* This occurs when a party signs a document which he does not really intend to sign at all: he may think that he is signing as a witness merely, or he may not intend to sign that particular type of document.

An example is the English case of *Foster* v. *Mackinnon* (1869) L.R. 4 C.P. 704, in which an old man of feeble sight had been induced to indorse a bill of exchange for £3,000 by being told that the document was only a guarantee.

(iv) *Error as to price.* If error as to price is to make a contract void, both parties must have thought that the price had been fixed and must have had different prices in mind; it is not enough merely that the price has not been fixed: if the price has not been fixed and the contract has not been carried out, the parties would usually be held not to have passed beyond the stage of negotiation, while if the contract has been carried out, the court has power under the Sale of Goods Act 1979 to fix a "reasonable" price.

There is an example of error as to price making a contract void in *Wilson* v. *Marquis of Breadalbane* (1859) 21 D. 957:

There had been a misunderstanding about the price of eighty bullocks being sold by W. to B. W. thought that the price was to depend on the quality of the cattle, whereas B. thought that the price had been fixed at £13 a head.

The sale was carried into effect, and in an action by W. against B. for the price, B. was held liable to pay the market price, which was proved to have been £15 a head.

(v) *Error as to quality, quantity or extent.* Error as to the quality, quantity or extent of the thing contracted for makes a contract void if, but only if, the particular quality, quantity or extent is material to the contract. For this to occur the thing supplied must be of a different kind from the thing contracted for. This type of error as to the substantials may, therefore, be regarded as an instance of error as to subject-matter (see (ii), above) instead of as a distinct fifth type.

The following illustration is given by the Scottish Law Commission in Memorandum No. 37 (*Constitution and Proof of Voluntary Obligations: Abortive Constitution*), at p. 20:

"Where, for example, of two parties negotiating the sale (or hire) of a piece of machinery one believed that the equipment in question would maintain 100 horse-power, and the other that it would maintain 150 horse-power, the first question to be asked would be: is it possible for the court in the light of the words and actings of the parties (including any intention known by one of them to be in the mind of the other) to say that an agreement in particular terms (including the horse-power of the machine) was arrived at? If so, the court will recognise that agreement even though one of the parties claims that his intention or understanding or belief was otherwise. . . . Where, however, the court concluded that the negotiations ultimately resulted in a situation in which one party undertook to buy a machine of 150 horse-power and the other undertook to sell a machine of 100 horse-power, the result would be irresolvable misunderstanding or dissensus ("disagreement")—failure of offer and acceptance to meet—and, consequently, no contract."

2. *Error Induced by Innocent Misrepresentation*

It may be that the error in the mind of a contracting party has been "induced" (caused or produced) by misrepresentation (misleading statements or misleading conduct) of the other party. If the party making the misrepresentation honestly believed in the truth of what he was saying or doing, the misrepresentation is described as "innocent misrepresentation," as distinct from fraud or fraudulent misrepresentation.

Innocent misrepresentation may make a contract void or voidable: if the misrepresentation induces error as to the substantials of the contract in the mind of the other party, then the contract is void, but if the misrepresentation does not induce such error in the other party's mind, then the contract is merely voidable.

For the reduction of a contract on the ground of innocent misrepresentation the following conditions must be fulfilled:

(a) The misrepresentation must have been material and must not have related only to some unimportant aspect of the contract. The maxim "de minimis non curat lex" ("the law does not take notice of trivialities") applies here.

(b) The misrepresentation must have been relied on by the party misled, and must actually have been the factor or one of the factors which led him to enter into the contract.

(c) The party seeking the reduction must be able to give restitutio in integrum ("restoration to the original position"), *i.e.* he must be able to restore the other party to the position in which he was before the contract was carried out. This would not be possible, for instance, where building or engineering work has been done under the contract.

Innocent misrepresentation does not give the party misled any right to claim damages; this is because an innocent misrepresentation, unlike a fraudulent misrepresentation, is not a civil wrong.

The best-known Scottish case on innocent misrepresentation is *Boyd & Forrest* v. *Glasgow and South-Western Ry. Co.*, 1915 S.C. (H.L.) 20:

Contractors had undertaken to build a railway, and in estimating for its construction had relied on information regarding rocks which was supplied to them by the railway company.

When constructing the line the contractors discovered that there was much more rock than they had been led to believe, but they completed the work.

The additional rock made the work much more costly: the contract price was about £243,000, and the work cost about £379,000.

On inquiry they found out that the notes made by the borers had been altered by Melville, the company's engineer, before they were given to the contractors. It was, however, established that Melville had altered the notes because he honestly believed that they were wrong. Therefore no claim could be made on the ground of fraud.

The contractors brought an action to have the contract reduced on the ground that there had been innocent misrepresentation, but they were held not entitled to have the contract reduced because restitutio in integrum was by that time impossible; the railway had been constructed.

3. *Error Induced by Fraud*

Fraud (also referred to as "fraudulent misrepresentation"), like innocent misrepresentation, may induce error in the mind of the other contracting party, and the contract may, as a result, be either void or voidable. If the error is as to the substantials of the contract, then the contract is void; otherwise, it is merely voidable.

In addition to the right to have the contract reduced because of the misrepresentation, the victim of the fraud is entitled to damages since fraud is regarded as a "delict" (a civil wrong). The remedy of damages is as a general rule available even if the party deceived does not seek to have the contract reduced or cannot have it reduced because he is unable to give restitutio in integrum. A contract to take shares in a company is an exception to the general rule: the shareholder is not entitled to damages for the company's fraud unless he can and does reduce the contract.

A misrepresentation will not be regarded as fraudulent unless it has been made without any belief in its truth. There is fraud not only where a person makes a false statement knowing that it is false, but also where he makes a reckless statement, which is in fact false, without caring whether it is true or false. Mere carelessness does not amount to fraud, for a person who is careless may nevertheless honestly believe that his statement or other representation is true.

The leading English case on the nature of fraud is *Derry* v. *Peek* (1889) 14 App.Cas. 337:

A special Act of Parliament incorporating a tramway company provided that carriages might be moved by animal power, and, with the consent of the Board of Trade, by steam power.

The directors of the company issued a prospectus inviting

members of the public to take shares in the company and containing a statement that by the special Act of Parliament the company had the right to use steam power instead of horses, *i.e.* no mention was made of the consent of the Board of Trade.

P. took shares on the faith of this statement.

The Board of Trade afterwards refused consent to the use of steam power and the company was wound up.

P. brought an action against the directors claiming damages for fraudulent misrepresentation by them.

It was proved that the directors believed the misstatement to be true.

The House of Lords held that actual fraud had to be proved and that a false statement made in the honest belief that it was true was not fraudulent.

The directors were, therefore, not liable for fraud because the statement as to steam power had been made by them in the honest belief that it was true.

In that case Lord Herschell said, at p. 374:

"There must be proof of fraud, and nothing short of that will suffice . . . Fraud is proved where it is shewn that a false representation has been made (1) knowingly, or (2) without belief in its truth, or (3) recklessly, careless whether it be true or false . . . The third is but an instance of the second, for one who makes a statement under such circumstances can have no real belief in the truth of what he states. To prevent a false statement being fraudulent, there must, I think, always be an honest belief in its truth."

So far as the law on prospectuses of companies is concerned a statutory right of compensation was introduced by the Directors' Liability Act 1890 passed as a result of the decision in *Derry* v. *Peek*, but the explanation of the nature of fraud given in the case remains valid and has been much quoted.

The best-known Scottish case on the nature of fraud is the earlier stage of *Boyd & Forrest* v. *Glasgow and South-Western Ry. Co.*, 1912 S.C.(H.L.) 93: Melville, the company's engineer, was held not to have acted fraudulently in changing the notes made by the borers.

In that case Lord Atkinson said, at p. 99:

"It may well be that the data upon which Mr. Melville proceeded to form a judgment, were to some degree insufficient . . . but if he honestly thought they were sufficient, and, after full consideration, honestly came to the conclusion that the borer was mistaken in his description of the substances he had found, and that the description which he (Melville) inserted in the document was the true description, and further, inserted that description with the object of giving what was, in his opinion, true information, deliberate lying is, in my view, not only out of the case, but every element which renders recklessness in statement equivalent to lying, is absent from it as well."

The explanation of fraud given in *Derry* v. *Peek* was referred to with approval in the Scottish case.

4. *Error Induced by Concealment or Failure to Disclose*

The error in the mind of one of the parties may be due to the other party's concealment of, or failure to disclose, "material" facts (facts which, if known to the first party, would have caused him not to enter into the contract).

Fraudulent concealment has the same effect as fraudulent misrepresentation; there is an example of fraudulent concealment in *Gibson* v. *National Cash Register Co. Ltd.*, 1925 S.C. 500:

G., a Montrose butcher, brought an action for damages for fraudulent concealment on the ground that he had wished to purchase two new cash registers and the company had supplied him with two secondhand machines reconditioned so as to look new.

G. was successful in his claim for damages.

Where, however, there is no fraud, the general rule is that concealment or failure to disclose material facts does not affect the validity of the contract; the parties are said to be "at arm's length," which means that each party must look after his own interest by finding out for himself all the material facts: he is not entitled to rely on the other party's informing him of them (although, if questions are asked and answered, answers must be honest).

Examples of the general rule are:

(a) When A makes a contract with B, A does not need to inform B that he, A, has doubts about whether he will be able to pay for or to perform the contract.

(b) *Royal Bank of Scotland* v. *Greenshields*, 1914 S.C. 259: Hutchison had an overdraft of £300 on his bank account and also owed the bank an additional sum of £1,100. G., at Hutchison's request, agreed with the bank to act as Hutchison's guarantor in respect of his overdraft. He knew of the overdraft but not of the additional debt of £1,100. The bank did not inform G. of the additional debt, and G. would not have consented to act as guarantor if he had known about it.

The court held that G.'s guarantee was valid in spite of the bank's failure to disclose a material fact (the extent of Hutchison's indebtedness to the bank).

(c) *Gillespie* v. *Russel* (1856) 18 D. 677: In this action G. sought to reduce a lease of minerals to R. on the ground that, at the time when the lease was granted, R. knew, and was also aware that G. did not know, that a specially valuable seam of coal was included in the minerals let.

The court held that, since there had been no fraud, the lease was valid in spite of R.'s concealment of a material fact.

In that case Lord Curriehill stated the general rule, at p. 686, as follows:

"Concealment by a contracting party is not held in law to be fraudulent, if he is not under an obligation to disclose what he conceals to the other contracting party. The understood object of parties in entering into bargains in business matters is to make gain, and neither is bound to inform the other of the grounds upon which he makes his prospective estimate of gain, or of the extent of the profit he expects to realise; and in the ordinary case he is not guilty of fraud, although he conceal the grounds of his own calculations and expectations from the other contracting party, and although he in consequence obtain a better bargain than he might have got if the other contracting party had possessed the same degree of sagacity or knowledge."

Contracts uberrimae fidei ("of the utmost good faith") and contracts in which the parties stand in a "fiduciary" relationship (*i.e.* a relationship of trust) to each other are exceptions to the general rule.

(a) Contracts uberrimae fidei

To this category belong contracts of insurance, contracts guaranteeing the honesty of employees, contracts to form a partnership, and contracts to take from a company shares which it is offering to the public by a prospectus.

In these contracts there is a duty on the parties to disclose all the material facts known; failure by one party to disclose a material fact gives the other party the right to reduce the contract; *e.g.* when a person proposes to take out a life policy with an insurance company he is bound to declare (even without being asked to do so) any facts, such as his state of health or habits of life, which would influence the company's decision of whether or not to issue the policy; otherwise the company would not be bound to honour the policy.

(b) Contracts involving fiduciary relationships

This category includes contracts between parent and child, principal and agent, trustee and beneficiary, and between partners. Where the parties to a contract stand in any of these fiduciary relationships to each other, the contract will be open to reduction unless material facts have been disclosed.

Contracts between a solicitor and his client are treated with special strictness: the solicitor must not only disclose material facts but also be able to prove that the contract is one which he would have advised the client to make if he himself had had no personal interest in the contract.

The validity of contracts involving fiduciary relationships may also be challenged on the ground of undue influence (see p. 286, below).

5. *Error Induced by Negligent Misrepresentation*

Where a person, A, is under a duty to take care not to make a false statement to another person, B, and a contract is entered into by B, in reliance on a false statement negligently made by A, then B has a claim for damages against A for loss suffered as a result. The claim is based on A's failure in his duty to take reasonable care for the accuracy of his statements, and there is no need for B to prove either that the statement was fraudulent or that there was a fiduciary relationship between the parties. Damages are due because the "negligence" (in the sense of failure in a legal duty of care) is a delict.

Two contrasting House of Lords cases may be given in illustration:

Robinson v. *National Bank of Scotland Ltd.*, 1916 S.C.(H.L.) 154: R., who had, along with two other parties, guaranteed a loan, was compelled, because of the bankruptcy of the other parties, to pay the whole of the loan himself. He alleged that he had been induced to guarantee the loan by representations as to the financial standing of these other parties contained in a letter from their bank, the National Bank of Scotland Ltd., to another bank which had made inquiries on R.'s behalf.

R. brought an action against the National Bank of Scotland Ltd. to recover the amount of his loss.

The action was unsuccessful because neither were the representations fraudulent nor was there any relationship between R. and that bank which imposed on the bank a special duty to make sure that the information given was accurate.

Hedley Byrne & Co. Ltd. v. *Heller & Partners Ltd.* [1964] A.C. 465: This was an English case. Advertising agents, H.B. & Co. Ltd., had, on behalf of one of their clients, Easipower Ltd., placed orders for advertising time on television programmes and for advertising space in certain newspapers, and in that connection made inquiries through their own bank as to the credit-worthiness of Easipower Ltd.

In the course of these inquiries, H. & Partners Ltd., the bankers of Easipower Ltd., stated to H.B. & Co. Ltd. that Easipower Ltd. was in their opinion "trustworthy, in the way of business, to the extent of £100,000 per annum, advertising contract." This statement was made in a letter from H. & Partners Ltd. to H.B. & Co. Ltd.'s bank, and the letter was headed "Confidential" and "For your private use and without responsibility on the part of this bank." The substance of the letter was communicated to H.B. & Co. Ltd. by their bank.

Easipower Ltd. went into liquidation, and H.B. & Co. Ltd. suffered a loss of £17,000.

H.B. & Co. Ltd. sued H. & Partners Ltd. for damages on the ground of negligent misrepresentation.

The House of Lords held that in the circumstances of the case H. & Partners Ltd. did owe a duty to take reasonable care in the answering of inquiries made by other banks on behalf of customers who could be expected to rely on the answers given.

H. & Partners Ltd. were, however, held not liable, because they had expressly provided that their statement was made "without responsibility."

These two cases show that there may be circumstances in which a party to a contract may be entitled to damages for a negligent, though innocent, misrepresentation on which he has relied in the making of the contract.

As regards the validity of the contract, however, the effect of negligent misrepresentation does not differ from the effect of any other innocent misrepresentation.

Summary of Effect of Error on Validity of Contracts

The effect of the various types of error on the validity of contracts is summarised in the following table:

error in law—contract normally valid

error in fact

1. error not induced by the other party
    (a) error of expression—contract as expressed may not be binding
    (b) error of intention
        (i) unilateral error—contract normally valid
        (ii) bilateral error
            1. common error—contract void
            2. mutual error
                (a) error concomitans—contract valid
                (b) error in substantialibus—contract void
2. error induced by innocent misrepresentation
    (a) error concomitans—contract voidable (no damages)
    (b) error in substantialibus—contract void (no damages)
3. error induced by fraud
    (a) error concomitans—contract voidable (damages for fraud)

   (b) error in substantialibus—contract void (damages for
       fraud)
4. error induced by concealment or failure to disclose
   general rule—contract valid (except for fraudulent concealment)
   exceptions—(a) contracts uberrimae fidei
              (b) contracts involving fiduciary relationships
5. error induced by negligent misrepresentation
   (a) error concomitans—contract voidable (damages for negli-
       gence)
   (b) error in substantialibus—contract void (damages for
       negligence)

Facility and Circumvention

Facility is weakness of mind due, for instance, to old age or ill-health.
A person who is merely facile is not insane and so does have capacity
to contract.

Circumvention involves the motive to mislead, but does not
amount to actual fraud.

Facility and circumvention affect the validity of a contract only
when they are both present: if one party takes advantage of the
other party's facility so as to make a contract which causes loss to
that other party, then the contract is voidable.

Undue Influence

There is undue influence when a person abuses a position of influence or trust to make a contract which is a bad bargain for the
other party.

Examples are contracts by which a parent acquires a benefit
from a child, a clergyman from a parishioner, a doctor from a
patient, or a solicitor from a client.

In considering whether or not there has been undue influence
the court attaches importance to the fact that the party influenced
has or has not had adequate independent advice.

Undue influence makes a contract voidable.

Force and Fear

A contract induced by force or by threats sufficient to overcome the
bravery of a reasonable person is void.

Earl of Orkney v. *Vinfra* (1606) M. 16,481: The Earl summoned
Vinfra to his castle, presented him with a contract already signed
by the Earl by which Vinfra was to pay the Earl 2,000 merks,
and commanded him to sign it, "which the said Andrew Vinfra
refused, wherewith the said Earl was so offended, that with terrible

countenance and words, and laying his hand upon his whinger (*dirk*), he threatened with execrable oaths to bereave this Vinfra of his life, and stick him presently through the head with his whinger, if he subscribed not."

Vinfra signed, but later refused to pay. The Earl brought this action against him for 2,000 merks.

The Earl maintained that there was a valid contract because he had *done* nothing to Vinfra; he had only used boisterous words which could not be sufficient to induce "fear."

However, the court found Vinfra's defence of "fear" "very relevant," and the contract was declared void.

Extortion

The general rule is that no matter how extortionate a contract may be, it is not void or voidable merely because it is extortionate: a person who undertakes to pay an excessively high price for goods or who makes some other bad bargain has no remedy merely on the ground of extortion.

Certain moneylending transactions have been exceptions to this general rule. The Moneylenders Acts 1900 and 1927 made it necessary for a moneylender to obtain a licence, and they imposed other restrictions on moneylending transactions. These Acts are repealed by the Consumer Credit Act 1974 which contains provisions of more general application relating to " extortionate credit bargains." A credit bargain is extortionate under that Act if it requires the debtor or a relative of his to make payments which are grossly exorbitant, or otherwise grossly contravenes ordinary principles of fair dealing. Factors to be taken into account include interest rates, the debtor's age, experience, business capacity and state of health, the degree of risk accepted by the creditor and the relationship between the parties. The court has power to reopen the credit agreement " so as to do justice between the parties."

Pacta Illicita

Pacta illicita ("illegal agreements") are contracts which are prohibited by law. They may have been declared illegal by statute, or they may be illegal at common law.

The general rule is that pacta illicita have no legal effect: the court will not enforce them, or award damages for breach of them, or assist either of the parties in any other way. Two legal maxims expressing the general rule are "ex turpi causa non oritur actio" ("out of an immoral situation an action does not arise"), *i.e.* no action can be brought in court as a result of a legally objectionable agreement, and "in turpi causa melior est conditio possidentis" ("in

an immoral situation the position of the possessor is the better one"),
i.e. the court will not interfere to alter the status quo ("existing
position").

There are, however, exceptions to the general rule:

1.   In the case of agreements illegal by statute, the exact effect
of the illegality depends on the statutory wording and on the interpretation given to that wording by the court; the result sometimes
is that the court will enforce an agreement which is illegal by statute
or will in some other way assist one or other of the parties. (See also
under the heading " (a) Illegality by Statute," below.)

2.   Where the parties are not in pari delicto ("equally at fault")
the court may intervene to assist the party who is less blameworthy.
The principle applicable is that of restitution, a branch of quasi-
contract. Instances occur in the law of bankruptcy: a secret payment
made by the bankrupt to an individual creditor is a pactum illicitum
("an illegal agreement"), but, since the creditor was probably
exerting pressure on the bankrupt, the parties are considered not to
be in pari delicto, and while the court will not assist the creditor by
enforcing the agreement it will assist the bankrupt (who will be
represented by his trustee in bankruptcy) by ordering the creditor to
restore what the bankrupt has paid.

(a)   *Illegality by Statute*

(i)   A statute may declare a particular type of agreement void. The
court will then neither enforce such an agreement nor award damages
for breach of it.

However, the court may give effect to rights which are incidental
to the agreement declared void, in order to prevent one party from
gaining an unfair advantage over the other. The principle operating
is that of recompense, a branch of quasi-contract. An example of
such a situation is the case of *Cuthbertson* v. *Lowes* (1870) 8 M. 1073:

C. sold potatoes to L. at £24 per Scots acre. L. received the
potatoes but did not pay the full price, and when C. brought an
action for the balance, L. put forward as his defence that the contract
was void by the Weights and Measures Acts, since it used a local
measure instead of an imperial one.

The court held that, although the contract could not be enforced,
C. was entitled to receive the market price of the potatoes which he
had supplied; otherwise L. would have gained an unfair advantage
over C.

The court will not intervene in this way to give effect to incidental
rights if the agreement has been declared "unlawful" by statute or is
objectionable at common law: there must be no "turpis causa"
("turpitude," "immorality"). The doctrine of recompense was

therefore held not to operate in *Jamieson* v. *Watt's Trustee*, 1950 S.C. 265:

Defence Regulations declared certain construction work unlawful if done without a licence. W. instructed J. to execute work on a cottage, and J. obtained a licence for expenditure of £40. J. undertook additional work, and rendered an account for £114.

J. was held not entitled to payment for work not covered by the licence.

(ii) A statute may, without declaring the contract void, impose a penalty on parties who enter into it. The general presumption is that imposition of a penalty implies that the contract is void.

However, in exceptional cases the court may decide that the intention of Parliament in imposing the penalty was merely to provide for the collection of revenue (*e.g.* a statute imposing a penalty for failure to stamp a particular type of contract), not to make the contract itself void or even unenforceable. Further, if the statute has been passed in order to protect a certain class of persons, a member of that class can sue on the contract.

(iii) A statute may, without either declaring the contract void or imposing a penalty, provide that the contract is to be unenforceable; *e.g.* the Trade Union and Labour Relations Act 1974 provides that a "collective agreement" is conclusively presumed not to have been intended by the parties to be a legally enforceable contract unless it is in writing and contains a provision, however expressed, that the parties intend it to be legally enforceable; a "collective agreement" is an agreement made by a trade union and an employer or an employer's association and concerned with terms and conditions of employment.

(b) *Illegality at Common Law*

A contract is illegal at common law if its purpose is:

(i) criminal, *e.g.* a contract to commit a murder; or

(ii) fraudulent, *e.g.* a contract between two parties to defraud a third party; or

(iii) immoral, *e.g.* a contract for the furtherance of sexual immorality; or

(iv) contrary to public policy; this fourth category requires fuller treatment.

Agreements contrary to public policy

The following agreements are void as being contrary to public policy:

1. agreements which conflict with national foreign policy, *e.g.* a contract with an enemy alien;

2. agreements which interfere with the administration of the

law, *e.g.* a contract to bribe a judge or to evade the revenue laws by smuggling or other means;

3. agreements which restrict individual liberty, especially the liberty to work or to trade.

Contracts in restraint of trade

Contracts which restrict the liberty to work or to trade are referred to as "contracts in restraint of trade" or "restrictive covenants." They may be divided into four main categories:

(a) contracts between employer and employee;

(b) contracts between seller and purchaser of a business;

(c) joint agreements among manufacturers or traders; and

(d) "solus" agreements.

The general rule is that contracts in restraint of trade are void unless the restriction can be shown to be reasonable both for the parties to the contract and for the public. That general rule was stated by Lord Macnaghten in *Nordenfelt* v. *Maxim Nordenfelt Guns and Ammunition Co. Ltd.* [1894] A.C. 535, at p. 565, as follows:

"All interference with individual liberty of action in trading, and all restraints of trade of themselves, if there is nothing more, are contrary to public policy, and therefore void. That is the general rule. But there are exceptions: restraints of trade . . . may be justified by the special circumstances of a particular case. It is a sufficient justification, and indeed it is the only justification, if the restriction is reasonable—reasonable, that is, in reference to the interests of the parties concerned and reasonable in reference to the interests of the public, so framed and so guarded as to afford adequate protection to the party in whose favour it is imposed, while at the same time it is in no way injurious to the public."

The courts are especially vigilant where the parties are not negotiating as equals. One party may, for instance, produce a "standard form" contract and be strong enough to adopt a "take-it-or-leave-it" attitude towards the other party; it will then be for the party with the superior bargaining power to justify the restrictions in the contract. The decision in the English case of *A. Schroeder Music Publishing Co. Ltd.* v. *Macaulay* [1974] 1 W.L.R. 1308 illustrates this:

M., an unknown song-writer, aged twenty-one, had entered into an agreement with music publishers in their "standard form," whereby M. was to give them his exclusive services as a song-writer for five years; the full copyright for the whole world in all M.'s compositions for that time was to belong to the publishers; M.'s remuneration was to be by royalties, and if his royalties exceeded

£5,000 the agreement was to be automatically extended for a further
five years; the publishers, on the other hand, were to be entitled to
terminate the agreement at any time by one month's notice.

The House of Lords, after considering all the terms of the
agreement, held that it was for the publishers to justify such a one-
sided agreement and that since they had failed to do so the agreement
was contrary to public policy and void.

Lord Diplock stated (at p. 1315):

"In refusing to enforce provisions of a contract whereby
one party agrees for the benefit of the other party to exploit or to
refrain from exploiting his own earning power, the public
policy which the court is implementing is not some 19th-century
economic theory about the benefit to the general public of
freedom of trade, but the protection of those whose bargaining
power is weak against being forced by those whose bargaining
power is stronger to enter into bargains that are unconscionable."

(a) Contracts between employer and employee

An employee or apprentice may on entering employment or
apprenticeship agree to some restriction being placed on his future
employment or trade. The question of whether the restriction is
valid or not will not usually arise until the end of the employment
or apprenticeship, when the employee or former apprentice wishes
to regard the restriction as not binding on him. The employer may
then bring an action to have the employee or apprentice "interdicted" (forbidden by the court) from acting in breach of the
restriction.

The main factors considered by the court in deciding whether
the restriction is enforceable or not are:

(i) *Extent of restriction in area and time.* The restriction must
not be wider than is reasonably necessary for the protection of the
interests of employer or master. The court will consider the nature
of the business, the area from which customers come, the position
held by the employee or apprentice, and the length of time for which
he would probably be able to harm the interests protected under the
agreement.

The case of *Stewart* v. *Stewart* (1899) 1 F. 1158 gives an illustration of a restriction held enforceable:

A, a photographer in Elgin, and B, his brother, who had once
been his assistant, entered into an agreement by which B, in return
for a loan, bound himself not to start in business as a photographer
or to enter into the employment of any photographer, in Elgin or
within twenty miles of Elgin.

The court held that the area of twenty miles was no more than was reasonably necessary for A's protection.

In contrast, the restriction considered in the English case of *Mason* v. *Provident Clothing and Supply Co. Ltd.* [1913] A.C. 724 was held to be void:

M., a canvasser for a clothing company with branches all over England, agreed not to assist in a similar business for three years within twenty-five miles of London.

The court held that the restraint was wider than was reasonably necessary for the company's protection: M. had been only a local canvasser working on a fortnight's notice, and the area of the restraint was excessive in view of the dense population of the London area.

(ii) *Interests which employer may protect.* The employer may protect his trade secrets and prevent his customers from being enticed away from him, but he is not allowed to protect himself from competition of his former employee or apprentice or to prevent the employee or apprentice from using personal skill and knowledge.

The nature of the work, therefore, undertaken by the employee or apprentice affects the enforceability of a restrictive covenant, for the covenant is not normally enforceable unless the employee or apprentice has had access to trade secrets of the business or has come into contact with its customers.

The following two cases illustrate the interests which may be protected:

Bluebell Apparel Ltd. v. *Dickinson*, 1980 S.L.T. 157: D., a young man holding a degree in mechanical engineering and business studies, was appointed in January 1977 as a management trainee by B. Ltd., a subsidiary of an American company which had a world-wide business in the manufacture of "Wrangler" jeans. D. agreed that he would not make any unauthorised disclosure of any of the trade secrets of B. Ltd. or of other companies in the group, and also that he would not for two years after the end of his employment perform any services for any business competitor.

D. was trained at B. Ltd.'s main Scottish factory at Falkirk, and by July 1977 was about to be offered a post as manager of one of B. Ltd.'s Scottish factories. At the end of August, however, D. left B. Ltd.'s employment and took up employment with Levi Strauss & Co., one of B. Ltd.'s most important competitors in the world's jeans market.

The court held that as D. was in possession of trade secrets which would be of value to a business competitor, B. Ltd. was entitled to an order interdicting D. from continuing in employment with Levi Strauss & Co.

Fitch v. *Dewes* [1921] 2 A.C. 158: F. had been junior clerk, articled clerk, then managing clerk to a solicitor at Tamworth, and had agreed that he would not be engaged in the office, profession or business of a solicitor within seven miles of the Town Hall of Tamworth.

After the termination of his employment, F. intentionally committed a breach of the restrictive covenant to test its validity.

The court held that the restriction did not exceed what was reasonably required for the employer's protection and that it was not against the public interest.

F.'s position as managing clerk had enabled him to become intimate with clients: of the interviews with clients taken by F. and his employer from 1910 to 1913, F. had taken in 1910 25 per cent., in 1911 33 per cent., in 1912 48 per cent., and in 1913 52 per cent. F. was not entitled to use the intimacies and the knowledge which he had thus acquired, in order to undermine the business and the connection of his employer.

(iii) *Severability*. A contract may contain several restrictions some of which, if they appeared alone, would be enforceable, and the question may arise of whether these enforceable restrictions become void through their being linked with unreasonably wide, and therefore unenforceable, restrictions.

The rule is that the court will enforce the reasonable restrictions only if they can be "severed" (separated) from the unreasonable ones; the court regards the unenforceable restrictions as having been scored out (hence the phrase "the blue pencil rule" applied to such cases).

This rule as to severability does not allow the court to substitute for some unreasonable restriction a lesser restriction which it would have held to be reasonable. The court will not carve out of the void covenant the maximum which the employer might legally have required. This point may be illustrated by the English case *Empire Meat Co. Ltd.* v. *Patrick* [1939] 2 All E.R. 85, C.A.:

P., manager of a Cambridge butcher's business, worked in the shop and interviewed the customers who numbered about 350 and who came mostly from within a mile of the shop. P. had agreed not to engage in a butcher's business on his own or for others within five miles from the shop.

Shortly after leaving that employment P. opened a butcher's shop a few doors away. Many customers followed him and the first business which under his management had made a profit of about £6 per week began to make a loss of about £3 per week.

The court held that the area of the restraint was unnecessarily wide and that the covenant was therefore unenforceable; if the area of the restraint had been one mile instead of five miles, the covenant might have been enforceable, but the fact that too wide an area had been chosen meant that the employer could not restrain P. from obtaining employment even within the immediate vicinity.

There is an example of severable restrictions in *Mulvein* v. *Murray*, 1908 S.C. 528:

Mulvein employed Murray as a retail traveller in his boot business, and Murray agreed that for twelve months from the end of his employment he would not sell to or canvass Mulvein's customers and would not sell or travel in any of the towns or districts traded in by Mulvein.

After Murray had left Mulvein's employment, Mulvein brought this action to have Murray interdicted from acting in breach of the restrictions.

The court held that the first part of the agreement (the obligation not to sell to or canvass Mulvein's customers) was reasonable and valid but that the second part (the obligation not to sell or travel in any of the towns or districts traded in by Mulvein) was unreasonable and invalid, and further held that since the two parts could be separated the first part was enforceable.

The reasons for the invalidity of the second part were explained by Lord Ardwall, at p. 534, as follows:

"With regard to the agreement in question, I am of opinion that the first part of it in which the defender 'bound himself not to sell to or to canvass any of the said George Mulvein's customers' is a valid provision, and is separable from what follows. But the contract also binds the defender not 'to travel in any of the towns or districts traded in by the said George Mulvein for a period of twelve months from the date of the termination of this engagement.' The limitation in time which is applicable to both clauses I have quoted, is quite reasonable, but I am of opinion that the latter clause I have quoted imposes an unreasonable restraint upon the defender. It is too wide and too vague. For all that appears the pursuer may have traded in every district in Scotland and England too, and I may add that the word 'district' is in itself a very vague term, as it is not a known geographical division of either town or country. In short, this provision leaves the defender entirely in the dark as to what towns or districts he is precluded from selling or travelling in, and so far as its terms are concerned it might embrace the whole country, should it turn out that Mulvein had traded in each district thereof, whatever that may mean. It appears that according to his own evidence his business extends to 'Ayrshire,

Renfrewshire, Lanarkshire, Dumbartonshire, Stirlingshire, and Linlithgowshire,' and he adds after this enumeration, 'I have a traveller who goes to Bo'ness in Linlithgow.' So apparently the pursuer seems to think if a traveller of his visits one town in a county the restriction will apply to the whole of the county; but be this as it may, I am of opinion that an agreement of this sort in restraint of trade should at least be definite and distinct, and in such terms as that the person who is coming under the restraint should know what he is binding himself to refrain from doing. . . .

"But further, I am of opinion that the second clause I have quoted is invalid, inasmuch as it is a restraint against selling or travelling for any purpose in any of the towns or districts mentioned. Now I think it was wholly unnecessary for the protection of the pursuer that the defender should be prohibited from selling or travelling for any purpose whatever in these towns or districts, and was unreasonable in respect that the defender had a right to engage in any sort of business for himself, provided he did not interfere with the pursuer's class of business in such towns or districts."

(b) *Contracts between seller and purchaser of a business*

On the sale of a business the seller may bind himself not to set up a similar business within a certain area or for a specified time.

The courts regard these contracts with more favour than contracts between employer and employee or apprentice: the seller has probably received payment for goodwill, and it is considered only right that he should be bound to give the purchaser the advantage of the goodwill; further, seller and purchaser are looked upon as parties able to bargain on a footing of equality, whereas in contracts of employment or apprenticeship the employee or apprentice is looked upon as being more in need of the protection of the law than the other party to the contract.

Contracts in this category are subject to the same principles as those in category (a), above, except that the purchaser is quite entitled to protect himself from competition from the seller.

The English case of *Nordenfelt* v. *Maxim Nordenfelt Guns and Ammunition Co. Ltd.* [1894] A.C. 535, gives an example of an unusually wide restriction which was held to be valid: the seller of a cannon-manufacturing business had agreed that he would not engage in the manufacture of cannon anywhere in the world for twenty-five years after the sale; because of the nature of the business and the limited number of customers (namely, the governments of countries) the restriction was considered to be neither wider than necessary for the protection of the purchaser nor harmful to the public.

In contrast, the circumstances in *Dumbarton Steamboat Co. Ltd. v. MacFarlane* (1899) 1 F. 993, were more usual, and the restriction was held unenforceable:

M. and another had been in business as carriers between Dumbarton, Glasgow, Greenock and other places in the same area. They sold their business to a company and bound themselves not to carry on any separate business of a similar kind in the United Kingdom for ten years. The company carried on business only in the Glasgow and Dumbarton district.

In this action the company was seeking an interdict to prevent M. from carrying on business as a carrier between Glasgow and Dumbarton.

The court held that in view of the area of the company's business a restriction extending to the whole of the United Kingdom was unreasonably wide, and further the court refused to reform the restriction so as to confine it to what would have been a reasonable area.

(c) *Joint agreements among manufacturers or traders*

Into this category come agreements by which manufacturers and traders attempt to regulate output, selling price or other aspects of their trade relations. Such agreements are now governed mainly by statute.

The Restrictive Trade Practices Act 1956 introduced compulsory registration of many types of restrictive trade agreements. Registered agreements are brought before the Restrictive Practices Court, and if they are considered by that court to be contrary to the public interest, they are prohibited. The onus of proving that a restrictive agreement is not contrary to the public interest lies on the party who wishes to maintain it.

The Resale Prices Act 1964 made special additional provision for agreements by which minimum prices were fixed for the resale of goods, *e.g.* an agreement between a manufacturer and a retailer by which the retailer agreed that he would not sell the manufacturer's product for less than a certain price. The effect of the Act of 1964 was to abolish this scheme of "resale price maintenance," except that exemptions were allowed where the Restrictive Practices Court was satisfied that for some particular class of goods the abolition of resale price maintenance would be decidedly harmful to the public interest.

The Fair Trading Act 1973 created the office of Director General of Fair Trading, one of whose functions is to protect consumers against unfair trading practices. In this he is assisted by the Consumer Protection Advisory Committee. Greater power was conferred on the Restrictive Practices Court, and the Act of 1956 was extended to cover restrictive agreements relating to services.

The statutory provisions on this topic were consolidated by three Acts of 1976—the Restrictive Practices Court Act, the Restrictive Trade Practices Act, and the Resale Prices Act.

(d) *"Solus" agreements*

The term "solus agreement" is used of an agreement between a manufacturer, importer or other supplier on the one hand and a distributor, retailer or other dealer on the other hand, by which the person in the latter category binds himself, in return for favourable trading terms, to sell only the products supplied to him by the person in the first category. "Solus" is the Latin for "alone."

Two solus agreements were considered by the House of Lords in *Esso Petroleum Co. Ltd.* v. *Harper's Garage (Stourport) Ltd.* [1968] A.C. 269:

E.P. Co. Ltd., suppliers of motor fuels to dealers, entered into two agreements with a garage company.

One of the agreements related to the Mustow Green Garage, near Kidderminster. It provided that the garage company was for a period of between four and five years to buy from E.P. Co. Ltd. all the motor fuels which were to be on sale at that garage; in return, E.P. Co. Ltd. were to allow to the garage company a rebate of 1¼d. a gallon on all fuels supplied.

The other agreement, which related to the Corner Garage at Stourport-on-Severn, contained the same provisions except that the period was twenty-one years.

In 1961, when cheaper "cut-price" petrol came on the market, the garage company began to sell it instead of E.P. Co. Ltd.'s petrol, and E.P. Co. Ltd. sought from the court "injunctions" (the English law term corresponding to "interdicts" in Scots law) restraining the garage company from dealing in brands of petrol other than their own.

The House of Lords held that a period of five years was not in the circumstances longer than was reasonably necessary for the protection of the legitimate interests of E.P. Co. Ltd. in the maintenance of a stable system of distribution, but that a restriction of twenty-one years' duration was unreasonable and therefore unenforceable.

Sponsiones Ludicrae

The term "sponsiones ludicrae" ("sportive promises") is used of undertakings which are considered unworthy to occupy the time of the courts. Competitions and betting and gaming transactions come into this category. The court will, for instance, not allow proof of the result of a competition or enforce payment of a bet.

However, sponsiones ludicrae, although unenforceable, are not necessarily illegal or void, and so the court may protect rights which have arisen from these undertakings; *e.g.* if the result of a contest of skill or prowess (as distinct from a pure gamble or wager) is not disputed, the court will allow the winner to sue the stakeholder for the prize, and where a bet has been placed through an agent, the court will allow the agent to sue his principal for expenditure incurred on the principal's behalf.

The most important sponsiones ludicrae are now regulated by statute—betting by the Betting, Gaming and Lotteries Act 1963, gaming by the Gaming Act 1968, and lotteries, prize competitions and amusements with prizes by the Lotteries and Amusements Act 1976. There have also been some later amending Acts.

The Betting, Gaming and Lotteries Act 1963 (so far as unrepealed) provides that betting is legal only if it is conducted in certain places, principally licensed betting offices; the use of unlicensed private premises or of public places for betting is a criminal offence under the Act. Betting in contravention of the Act would, therefore, come under the heading of "pacta illicita."

The Gaming Act 1968, which repealed the provisions on gaming in the Act of 1963, allows commercial gaming to take place only under strict control, so that the number of establishments can be limited and their management supervised.

The Lotteries and Amusements Act 1976, which consolidated provisions from the Act of 1963 and later legislation, declares all lotteries, with certain exceptions, to be unlawful. The exceptions include small lotteries at fetes, dances and similar entertainments, private lotteries confined to, for instance, work-mates, lotteries promoted by charitable, athletic, cultural and similar societies, and local authority lotteries. All these permissible lotteries are made subject to specified conditions. Prize competitions connected with any trade or business are unlawful unless success depends to a substantial degree on the exercise of skill. The Act also sets out the restrictions which are imposed on the provision of amusements with prizes.

Reduction of Voidable Contracts

The fact that a contract is voidable does not necessarily mean that it may be "reduced" (set aside by the court). Reduction is "barred" (*i.e.* is not allowed) if:

    1.   restitutio in integrum ("restoration to the original position") is impossible; or

2. real rights of third parties are involved; or
3. there has been homologation; or
4. there has been undue delay.

1. *Restitutio in Integrum Impossible*

The party seeking to reduce the contract must be able to restore the other party to the position in which he was before the contract was entered into, *e.g.* by handing back an article which has been sold and delivered to him. If he cannot do so, he is not entitled to have the contract set aside. Therefore, if, for example, he has resold or consumed an article delivered to him under the voidable contract, or if work has been done under the contract in circumstances such as those of *Boyd & Forrest* v. *Glasgow and South-Western Ry. Co.*, 1915 S.C.(H.L.) 20 (see p. 279, above), he cannot offer restitutio in integrum and cannot reduce the contract.

For the purposes of restitutio in integrum it does not matter that the thing being restored may have diminished in value in the meantime; *e.g.* shares sold may have greatly depreciated in value but provided they can be returned by purchaser to seller there will be restitutio in integrum.

However, the rule that there must be restitutio in integrum is not applied too literally. In particular, it is not applied where its effect would be to allow a person to retain a benefit which he has derived from his own fraud.

2. *Real Rights of Third Parties*

"Real" is used here in its technical sense (see p. 242, above). If a third party (a person who is not one of the two parties to the contract) has acquired a real, as distinct from a personal, right as a result of the voidable contract, the contract can no longer be set aside. For example, if A and B enter into a contract for the sale of goods by A to B, and that contract is for some reason voidable, but the goods are then resold by B to C, a third party who buys the goods in good faith without knowing about the defect in the first contract, then C acquires a real right, a jus in re ("right in the thing"), and this prevents the contract between A and B from being reduced.

The situation is different if the third party acquires only a personal, as distinct from a real, right: the contract then remains voidable and can be set aside; the maxim applicable is "assignatus utitur jure auctoris" ("an assignee enjoys only the right which his cedent had"), which means that the third party can acquire no greater right than the right which belonged to the party to the voidable contract. For example, X may have taken out a life insurance policy, which he later transfers to Y as security for a loan made to him by Y; the claim which Y has against the insurance company is no better than the claim which X himself would have had, and so, if the policy could have been set aside by the insurance company in a question with X (*e.g.* because X had made some important misstatements about his health), it remains voidable in a question between the company and Y, since Y has acquired only a jus in personam ("right against a person"), a right which can be claimed only from one person, namely the insurance company.

3. *Homologation*

Where the party entitled to reduce a voidable contract gives up the grounds of challenge which he knows to be open to him, the contract becomes binding by homologation, one aspect of the doctrine of personal bar (see p. 243, above, and the case of *Mitchell* v. *Stornoway Trustees*, 1936 S.C.(H.L.) 56, p. 264, above).

4. *Undue Delay*

Reduction is not allowed if the party seeking it has delayed too long. The length of time necessary to make a voidable contract binding varies with circumstances; *e.g.* reduction of a minor's contracts on the ground of lesion is not allowed beyond the period of four years after the minor has attained majority, and under the Sale of Goods Act 1979 the right to reject goods which are not in accordance with the contract must be exercised within a reasonable time; in commercial transactions in general, the party seeking to reduce the contract, even on the ground of fraud, must act with reasonable speed.

INTERPRETATION OF CONTRACTS

When a dispute arises between parties to a contract as to the meaning of the contract, it will be for the court to "construe" (interpret) the terms used in the contract. The object of "construction" (interpretation) of a contract is to ascertain the intention of the parties. The court considers the words used by the parties and decides on the sense in which these words would appear to a reasonable man to have been used: the court does not go beyond the words used by the parties and probe the actual intention of the parties as distinct from their expressed intention.

The rules which are followed by the courts in the interpretation of contracts include the following:

1. Ordinary and Technical Words

Ordinary words are taken to be used in their ordinary sense and technical terms in their technical sense, unless the context indicates otherwise.

2. Effectiveness of Contract

Where more than one interpretation is possible, the court prefers an interpretation which gives effect to the contract to an interpretation which would result in the contract's being of no effect. If, however, the language used is too vague, the contract cannot be enforced at all.

3. Ejusdem Generis Rule

The ejusdem generis ("of the same kind") rule applies where there is a list of items, all of the same kind, followed by general words such as "and other things": the general words are interpreted as being limited to items of the same kind as those specifically mentioned; e.g. in the phrase "house, office, room, or other place," the words "other place" would be interpreted as being limited to other places of the same kind as house, office and room, and so would probably be considered not to cover places out of doors, such as a race-course (see p. 115, above).

There are two important limitations on the ejusdem generis rule:

(a) The rule is only a presumption, and it will not apply if the general words were clearly intended to be absolutely general; e.g. in Glasgow Corporation v. Glasgow Tramway and Omnibus Co. Ltd. (1898) 25 R. (H.L.) 77 the phrase "all expenses whatever" was interpreted as being completely general and as not being limited to expenses of the same class as the expenses of "borrowing" and "management" specifically mentioned in the contract.

(b) The items specifically mentioned must, if the rule is to be applied, all be of one genus ("kind"); if they are not all of the same class or category and do not have common characteristics, the general words will be interpreted as being absolutely general; e.g. in The Admiralty v. Burns, 1910 S.C. 531, the ejusdem generis rule was held not to apply to a clause in a lease which gave the landlord power to take off part of the land "for the purpose of planting, feuing, or letting on building leases, or for making, or altering, or widening roads, or for making railroads or canals, or for any other purpose"; the result was that the landlord was entitled to take off part of the land for the purpose of erecting buildings for a naval base.

4. Construction Contra Proferentem

If there is an ambiguity in a contract, the ambiguous phrase is construed contra proferentem ("against the person putting it forward"). This rule applies especially to those contracts the details of which are fixed by one party only and which are presented to the other party on a printed form which that other party has merely to sign. For instance, an ambiguous phrase in an insurance policy is given the meaning which is less favourable to the party putting forward the contract, namely, the insurance company. See also p. 307, below.

5. Expressio Unius est Exclusio Alterius

The rule "expressio unius est exclusio alterius" ("expression of one is exclusion of the other") means that express mention of one item, coupled with no mention being made of another similar or associated item, has the effect of excluding that other item; the presumption is that the parties would have expressly mentioned that other item if they had intended their contract to apply to it also.

6. Extrinsic Evidence

Extrinsic evidence is evidence from some source outside the contract itself. If the parties have put their contract into writing, extrinsic evidence includes not only parole evidence (*i.e.* oral evidence given by witnesses) but also correspondence and other previous writings which passed between the parties during their negotiations.

The general rule is that where there is a formal written contract, extrinsic evidence cannot be brought forward to contradict or modify the terms of that document; the court will confine itself to interpreting the words used in the document.

This general rule and the reason for it were explained by Lord Gifford in *Buttery & Co.* v. *Inglis* (1877) 5 R. 58, at p. 69, in a passage subsequently approved by the House of Lords (*Inglis* v. *Buttery & Co.* (1878) 5 R.(H.L.) 87):

> "Now, I think it is quite fixed, and no more wholesome or salutary rule relative to written contracts can be devised, that where parties agree to embody and do actually embody their contract in a formal written deed, then in determining what the contract really was and really meant a Court must look to the formal deed and to that deed alone. This is only carrying out the will of the parties. The only meaning of adjusting a formal contract is that the formal contract shall supersede all loose and preliminary negotiations, that there shall be no room for misunderstandings which may often arise and which do constantly arise in the course of long and it may be desultory conversations, or of correspondence or negotiations in the course of which the parties are often widely at issue as to what they will insist in and what they will concede. The very purpose of a formal contract is to put an end to the disputes which would inevitably arise if the matter were left upon verbal negotiations or upon mixed communings, partly consisting of letters and partly of conversations. The written contract is that which is to be

appealed to by both parties, however different it may be from their previous demands or stipulations, whether contained in letters or in verbal conversation."

The exceptions to the general rule that extrinsic evidence is not admitted in the interpretation of a written contract include the following:

(a) *Latent Ambiguity*

An ambiguity is "latent" where doubt about the meaning of words used in the contract arises only from a knowledge of the surrounding circumstances; *e.g.* X may have contracted to sell his red car to Y, and it may later be discovered that X has two red cars.

Where there is a latent ambiguity in a written contract extrinsic evidence is admitted to resolve the doubt.

A latent ambiguity is to be distinguished from a "patent" ambiguity, *i.e.* one which is obvious from the contract itself. There is said to be a rule that extrinsic evidence is not allowed where the ambiguity is patent, but that rule has not always been applied in decided cases.

(b) *Surrounding Circumstances*

Extrinsic evidence is admissible to show what the circumstances surrounding the parties were when the contract was made, *e.g.* to show the state of knowledge of the parties at that time.

(c) *Writ or Oath of Defender*

If the defender admits by writ or oath that the written contract does not contain the agreement which was in fact reached between him and the other party to the contract, extrinsic evidence is allowed in order to prove what the agreement really was. The defender is no longer taking his stand on the written contract.

(d) *Usage of Trade*

Extrinsic evidence is admitted to prove a usage of trade in order either:

(i) to interpret a technical term or an expression alleged to be used in some special sense in the trade; or

(ii) to introduce into the contract a term which is so usual in the trade that it must be considered to have been implied.

The usage must be reasonably fair and generally recognised in the trade.

A usage which conflicts with the express terms of the contract will not be given effect to by the court. This point is illustrated by the cases of *Tancred, Arrol & Co.* v. *Steel Co. of Scotland Ltd.* (1890) 17 R.(H.L.) 31; (1887) 15 R. 215, and *Duthie & Co. Ltd.* v. *Merson &*

Gerry, 1947 S.C. 43, cases in which attempts were made to prove usages for purposes (i) and (ii) above, respectively.

Tancred, Arrol & Co. v. *Steel Co. of Scotland Ltd.:* Tancred, Arrol & Co., contractors for the building of the Forth railway bridge, agreed to take from the Steel Co. of Scotland Ltd. "the whole of the steel required" for the bridge. The contract also stated that the estimated quantity of steel was "30,000 tons more or less."

There was an attempt in the case to prove that by a custom of the steel trade in Glasgow a contract for the supply of steel, in which the quantity to be supplied was described as the whole steel required, and which also contained a clause giving the estimated quantity, was regarded as a contract only for the estimated quantity, *i.e.* in this case 30,000 tons.

The House of Lords, however, affirming the judgment of the Court of Session, held that a custom could not be used to contradict the plain and unambiguous language of the contract.

The contractors were, therefore, bound to take the whole of the steel required for the bridge from the Steel Co. of Scotland Ltd. and were not free to go to another supplier for any excess over the 30,000 tons.

In the Court of Session Lord President Inglis stated (at p. 222): "It is impossible to admit evidence of custom to contradict the plain words of the contract."

Duthie & Co. Ltd. v. *Merson & Gerry:* Fish salesmen, who had been in the habit of allowing discount to buyers, intimated that the discount was to cease. The buyers, however, continued to deduct discount when making payments to the salesmen, and finally the salesmen brought an action for the sums deducted.

The buyers claimed that there was a custom of trade with regard to the discount and that the salesmen were not entitled to terminate it without the consent of the buyers.

The court, however, held that a custom of trade could not add an implied term to a contract in which the contrary was expressed; in this case the buyers had bought under an express condition that there was to be no more discount.

CONDITIONS IN CONTRACTS

Performance of a contract may be subject to a condition. In this connection the following classifications are made:

1. pure, future, and contingent obligations; and
2. potestative, casual, and mixed conditions.

1. Pure, Future, and Contingent Obligations

(a) *Pure Obligations*

An obligation is said to be "pure" when fulfilment of it is due at once: no conditions at all are attached to it.

An example is a debt payable immediately.

(b) *Future Obligations*

An obligation is "future" if it is to come into existence and become enforceable only on the occurrence of an event which is certain to happen, though the time at which it will do so is uncertain.

An example is a debt payable on the death of a named individual.

(c) *Contingent Obligations*

"Contingent" means "conditional." A contingent obligation is one which is subject to either a suspensive or a resolutive condition.

There is a suspensive condition when the obligation is to arise on the occurrence of an event which may or may not happen, *e.g.* payment of a sum of money when a person reaches a certain age.

There is a resolutive condition when an obligation requires to be fulfilled immediately but will cease to require to be fulfilled on the occurrence of some event which may or may not happen: *e.g.* a person may become tenant of property on the resolutive condition that the lease is to terminate if he becomes bankrupt.

The distinction between suspensive and resolutive conditions corresponds generally to a distinction made in English law between "conditions precedent" and "conditions subsequent."

2. Potestative, Casual, and Mixed Conditions

A condition is potestative when it can be fulfilled by an act which one or other of the parties has power to do (*e.g.* "if you go ski-ing").

A condition is casual when its fulfilment depends on chance or on the act of a third party (*e.g.* "if you break your leg").

A mixed condition is one which contains both potestative and casual elements (*e.g.* "if you go ski-ing and break your leg").

EXEMPTION CLAUSES IN CONTRACTS

The basic rule of the common law is that the parties to a contract are free to agree on whatever terms they see fit. They therefore appear at first sight to have the benefit of complete freedom of contract. It has, however, long been recognised that this apparent freedom, far from being a benefit, may cause considerable hardship and is in fact the very opposite of true freedom of contract. The reason for this often is that the parties are not of equal bargaining strength, *e.g.* one party may be an individual passenger or an individual employee and the other party is quite likely to be a large organisation. In theory, the terms of the contract are agreed on by both parties, but when such a situation is viewed on the practical level, the second party is seen as having the power virtually to *impose* his own terms on the first party. Of course, the first party could refuse to accept the "imposed" terms. Both parties would then lose the bargain, but it is obvious that the loss would generally fall much more heavily on the first party. In the interests of justice, the weaker party in negotiations is protected to some extent by rules of the common law and to an increasing extent by statutory provisions. The effect of such protection is to modify substantially the basic rule of the common law that parties are free to agree on their own terms in a contract.

Protection under the Common Law

Some important rules worked out by the courts for the protection of the weaker party to a contract are indicated in the following paragraphs:

(a) *"Ticket" Cases*

Attempts have often been made by carriers and others to incorporate conditions into their contracts by the issue of tickets, the aim usually being to exclude or limit liability for breach of contract or for negligence.

Whether these attempts were successful or not depended:

(i) on the nature of the ticket: the ticket had to be an integral part of the contract, not merely a voucher or receipt, if it was to have the effect desired by the person issuing it of imposing conditions on the other party; *e.g.* a ticket issued by a carrier of goods or of passengers was considered to be a contractual document, whereas a ticket issued by a beach attendant to persons who had chosen to sit on deck-chairs provided on a beach was held to be merely a receipt and not part of the contract for the hire of the chairs (*Chapelton* v. *Barry Urban District Council* [1940] 1 K.B. 532);

(ii) on the adequacy of the notice given of the conditions: if the ticket was signed by the party to whom it was issued, then (provided there was no fraud or misrepresentation) that party was bound by conditions contained in the document whether he had read them or not; usually, however, the ticket would not be signed, and in that case the following rules applied:

1. If the person receiving the ticket actually read the conditions, he was bound by them.

2. If he knew of their existence, but did not read them, he was bound by them provided they were reasonable and of a type to be expected on such a ticket.

3. If he did not know of their existence, he was bound by them only if he had been given adequate notice of them; *e.g.*, if the conditions were on the back of the ticket and there was no reference to them on the front of the ticket, that was not adequate notice.

(b) *Construction Contra Proferentem*

An ambiguous condition in a contract is interpreted contra proferentem ("against the person putting it forward"). This rule of construction can protect the weaker party where, for instance, the other party presents him with a "standard form" contract contained in a printed document, saying, in effect, "These are the conditions on which we contract; take them, or leave them."

In *North of Scotland Hydro-Electric Board* v. *D. & R. Taylor*, 1956 S.C. 1, the contra proferentem rule was applied to the interpretation of an indemnity clause in a contract made between a contractor, T., and the Board:

The indemnity clause provided that T. was to indemnify the Board against (*i.e.* free the Board from liability for) "all claims from third parties arising from the operations under the contract."

In the course of the work, one of T.'s employees was injured by an electric shock, and obtained damages from the Board on the ground that the accident had been due solely to the Board's negligence.

The Board then brought an action against T., claiming that T. was bound to indemnify the Board.

The court held that, as the indemnity clause might have been intended to cover only claims by third parties involving *no* negligence on the Board's part, it was not to be extended to claims arising out of the Board's negligence.

Lord Justice-Clerk Thomson said, at p. 7:

"The law has . . . in certain circumstances set a limit to the scope of such a clause of indemnity. A party is to be indemnified against a claim for which he would be legally responsible in virtue of his own negligence only if it is clear that the other party consented to the situation."

Lord Mackintosh explained the application of the contra proferentem rule, at p. 12, in these words:

"I am of the opinion that at the best for the Board the indemnity clause must be regarded as being one of ambiguous import. If that be so, then I am of opinion that, looking to the nature of the clause . . . and the purpose it is intended to serve, the clause is one which will fall to be construed contra proferentem, *i.e.* in this case, against the Board, at any rate in a question as to whether the scope of the clause is wide enough to cover third party

claims arising out of the Board's own negligence. . . . I think
that . . . this indemnity clause must be read as not extending to
cover the negligence of the pursuers or their servants, because
its terms do not clearly include such negligence and it has not
been established that the clause can have no other content. I
think therefore that . . . the clause would in view of its nature
fall to be construed . . . as not being intended to indemnify the
pursuers against the consequences of their own negligence."

The Court of Session's decision in this case was approved by the
House of Lords in the recent case *Smith* v. *U.M.B. Chrysler (Scotland)
Ltd. and South Wales Switchgear Co. Ltd.*, 1978 S.C.(H.L.) 1, in
which a similar indemnity clause was held not to extend to liabilities
arising from the negligence of the "proferens" ("the party putting
the clause forward") or his servants.

(c) *Penalty Clauses*

A contract may contain a provision that, in the event of a breach of
the contract, the party in breach will become liable to pay to the
other party a stipulated sum of money. This sum may be referred to
in the contract as "liquidate damages" or as "penalty." Whichever
term is used, a court will give effect to the provision only if the sum
is in reality liquidate damages, *i.e.* a genuine attempt to pre-estimate
the loss which the breach will probably cause. If the sum fixed is
truly an attempt by one party to impose on the other party a penalty
out of proportion to the probable loss, the court will not enforce the
provision. (See also p. 330, below.)

(d) *Doctrine of Fundamental Breach*

The doctrine of fundamental breach may have the effect of preventing a party from escaping liability by relying on an exemption
clause where his breach of contract amounts to a fundamental
breach, such as a total failure to perform the contract.

The phrase "fundamental breach" has been used to denote either:
  (i) breach of a fundamental term of the contract; or
  (ii) fundamental breach of the contract.
This distinction is a fine one.

(i) **Breach of a fundamental term of the contract**

Where there is breach of a fundamental term of the contract the
breach is "material": it is said to "go to the root of the contract."
There is a well-established rule of the common law that if one party
has been guilty of a material breach he is regarded as having
"repudiated" the contract, and this repudiation justifies the *other*

party in "rescinding" (cancelling) the contract; the result of rescission is that no further performance of the contract can be demanded.

The parties may themselves have settled which terms in their contract are fundamental. If they have not done so, and a breach occurs, it will be for the court to decide whether the breach is material or not. (See p. 324, below).

(ii) Fundamental breach of the contract

Here the court looks not at one or more of the individual terms of the contract, but at the contract as a whole and asks whether the breach which has occurred has made performance of the contract something quite different from what the parties contemplated. For instance, if a person made a contract to purchase peas and the seller supplied beans instead, that would not be breach of a *term* of the contract: it would be a total non-performance of the contract contemplated.

An exemption clause may not be wide enough to enable the party who is in breach to escape liability for a fundamental breach of the contract as distinct from a breach of one or more of the terms of the contract. A Scottish illustration is *Pollock & Co.* v. *Macrae*, 1922 S.C.(H.L.) 192:

A firm of engineers contracted to build and install a set of motor engines for M., a Stornoway fishcurer. The contract contained the following clause: "All goods are supplied on the condition that we shall not be liable for any direct or consequential damages arising from defective material or workmanship."

The court held that this clause, although it would have protected the engineers where parts of engines were defective, was of no avail where there had been a complete breach of contract owing to a series of defects which made the engines practically unserviceable: the article truly contracted for had not been supplied at all.

It is of course usual for an exemption clause to be in wide terms, and the question which has been controversial in recent years is whether the party in breach is entitled, by relying on a wide exemption clause in the contract, to escape from liability for a fundamental breach of the contract.

On the one hand, there were a number of decisions of the (English) Court of Appeal which seemed to establish a "rule of law" that if the breach was so fundamental as to bring the contract to an end, then the exemption clause in the contract would also be at an end, and the innocent party would therefore be entitled to claim full damages as if there had been no exemption clause at all. It can be understood that the application of this supposed "rule of law" gave some protection against harsh exemption clauses.

The best-known of these English decisions was *Harbutt's Plasticine Ltd.* v. *Wayne Tank and Pump Co. Ltd.* [1970] 1 Q.B. 447:

W. Ltd. had been installing in a mill where plasticine was manufactured equipment for storing and dispensing a hot molten wax used in the manufacturing process. W. Ltd. used a plastic pipeline of a type which was wholly unsuitable for the purpose because it was liable to distort at a high temperature.

When the installation had been completed, the heating system for the pipes was switched on at night so that the wax would be in the molten state required for the test of the equipment on the following day.

During the night there was a distortion in the pipes, the highly inflammable wax escaped and ignited, and as a result the mill was completely destroyed.

W. Ltd. resisted payment of damages of £172,966 on the ground that a clause in the contract limited their liability for accidents and damage to the contract price (£2,330).

The court held that the breach of contract had been so fundamental as to bring the contract automatically to an end, and that W. Ltd. could not in that situation rely on the limitation clause.

On the other hand, there was the view that there was no such rule of law, but that in each case the duty of the courts was to interpret the words used in the contract: if the exemption clause was wide enough in its terms, it would, according to this view, protect the guilty party from liability even for fundamental breach.

Two decisions of the House of Lords have established that this second view is the correct one.

The first of these decisions was *Suisse Atlantique Société d' Armement Maritime S.A.* v. *N.V. Rotterdamsche Kolen Centrale* [1967] 1 A.C. 361. The case arose out of a charterparty (a contract for the hire of a ship by its owners to charterers). The charterparty contained, as is usual, a demurrage clause (*i.e.* a clause setting out the calculation of agreed damages to be paid by the charterers to the owners for delay in loading and unloading). The owners claimed that, on account of excessive delay, the charterers had in this case been in fundamental breach of the charterparty and that therefore they, the owners, were entitled to damages greater in amount than the demurrage specified.

The House of Lords held that the damages which could be obtained were limited to the demurrage payments.

The speeches included statements to the effect that the question whether an exemption clause applied where there had been a fundamental breach of contract depended on the true interpretation of the contract. These statements, however, were not well understood (as can be seen from the later decisions of the Court of Appeal in *Harbutt's Plasticine* case and other cases) and a second decision of the House of Lords was required to clarify the statements.

This second decision was *Photo Production Ltd.* v. *Securicor Transport Ltd.* [1980] 2 W.L.R. 283:

P. Ltd. and S. Ltd., contemplating the risks of fire and theft, entered into a contract by which for a small weekly charge S. Ltd. was to provide a patrol service for P. Ltd.'s factory; the service consisted of four visits each night, two visits on Saturday afternoons and four day visits on Sundays. The contract was on S. Ltd.'s printed form incorporating a number of standard conditions.

On one of the visits a patrolman deliberately started a fire by throwing a match on to some cartons. The fire got out of control and a large part of the factory was burnt down. P. Ltd. claimed damages of over £600,000.

S. Ltd. sought to avoid liability by relying on one of the standard conditions which was a strongly worded exemption clause.

The House of Lords, reversing the decision of the Court of Appeal, held that the clause clearly covered acts such as that of the patrolman and that S. Ltd. was therefore not liable.

The case may be regarded as establishing beyond doubt that the question whether an exemption clause is applicable where there has been a fundamental breach is always a matter of interpretation of the contract. *Harbutt's Plasticine* case and other decisions of the Court of Appeal in the same line were overruled. The "rule of law" applied by the Court of Appeal to give protection against harsh exemption clauses has yielded to the principle of freedom of contract. The result is that the doctrine of fundamental breach now gives much less assistance than it was formerly thought, at least in England, to give. However, the need has also diminished because of the Unfair Contract Terms Act 1977. See especially the provisions of section 17 (p. 314, below), applicable to exemption clauses in consumer contracts and standard form contracts. (The contract in the *Photo Production* case was entered into before the passing of the Act of 1977.)

Finally, it is interesting to note the Scottish case *Alexander Stephen (Forth) Ltd.* v. *J. J. Riley (U.K.) Ltd.*, 1976 S.L.T. 269 (O.H.):

The case concerned a contract with ship repairers for the conversion of a dredger belonging to R. Ltd. The contract provided that, apart from liability for defective workmanship and for damage directly caused by negligence, the repairers were not to be liable even if circumstances arose in which R. Ltd. would be entitled to terminate the contract because of fundamental breach on the part of the repairers.

R. Ltd., on account of delay in the completion of the work, removed the ship and had the work completed at Rotterdam. R. Ltd. then claimed damages from the repairers for the additional cost involved by that move.

Lord Kincraig held that the wording of the exemption clause enabled the repairers to escape liability for the additional cost. He said (at p. 274) that the law of Scotland "allows parties to contract as they may deem fit, and to contract in such a way as to limit their liability, even in cases of so-called fundamental breach, or to put it in phraseology more familiar to Scots lawyers in cases where there has been a material breach of contract by one of the parties which entitles the other to rescind the contract."

The Lord Ordinary's interpretation of the *Suisse Atlantique* case is the interpretation which has since been confirmed as the correct one by the *Photo Production* case.

Protection under Statute

A number of statutory provisions have from time to time been introduced to meet special types of cases: these have had the effect of preventing employers and various categories of carriers by land, sea and air from excluding or restricting their liability beyond various specified limits. There was, however, no comprehensive legislation on the subject until the Unfair Contract Terms Act 1977 came into operation on February 1, 1978.

The Unfair Contract Terms Act 1977 is based on the recommendations in the Law Commissions' *Second Report on Exemption Clauses* (Law Com. No. 69, Scot. Law Com. No. 39, 1974–75 H.C.P. 605).

The Commissions' *First Report on Exemption Clauses in Contracts* (Law Com. No. 24, Scot. Law Com. No. 12, 1968–69 H.C.P. 403) recommended changes in the law relating to implied terms (as to title, conformity with description and sample, and quality and fitness) in contracts for the sale of goods. The Supply of Goods (Implied Terms) Act 1973 was passed to give effect to these recommendations.

The *Second Report* of the Law Commissions was of wider scope; in particular, it included consideration of exclusion of liability for negligence both in contracts of sale of goods and in contracts for the supply of services. There is, however, this limitation: the study and recommendations made by the Law Commissions, and the provisions of the Unfair Contract Terms Act 1977, relate only to things done, or left undone, in the course of a business. The Law Commissions considered that exemption clauses were not widely used, and did not give rise to serious concern, in contracts made "over the garden wall" as it were, *i.e.* where both parties were acting in a purely private capacity. The Act of 1977, therefore, does not apply where, for instance, two neighbours agree that one should repair the other's lawn-mower, car or television set: they may make such arrangements as they please about who is to bear the risk that the work may be done carelessly or unskilfully. (This does not mean that private transactions are completely uncontrolled: *e.g.* the Road Traffic Act 1972 provides that exclusion or restriction of liability for the death of or injury to a passenger is void even if the user of the vehicle is not acting in the course of a business.)

The Unfair Contract Terms Act has three Parts: Part I amends the law for England, Wales and Northern Ireland, Part II amends the law for Scotland, and Part III consists of provisions applicable to the whole of the United Kingdom. The differences between the provisions in Parts I and II are for the most part differences of expression rather than of substance. The matters dealt with in Part III of the Act include international supply contracts and choice-of-law clauses, and are beyond the scope of this introductory work. The following paragraphs are intended to provide a brief and simplified outline of the contents of Part II of the Act only.

Part II of the Act consists of sections 15 to 25. The most comprehensive provisions are in sections 16 to 18. The remaining provisions relate to specific types of transaction.

(a) *Sections 16 to 18*

These sections apply, by section 15, to contracts which:

    (i) relate to the transfer of goods (with or without work having been done on them); or

    (ii) are contracts of service or apprenticeship; or

    (iii) relate to services of whatever kind (including carriage, deposit and pledge, care and custody, mandate, agency, loan, and services connected with the use of land); or

    (iv) relate to the liability of an occupier of land; or

    (v) relate to permission to use land.

The sections do *not* apply to contracts which:

    (i) transfer the ownership of land; or

    (ii) are contracts of insurance; or

    (iii) relate to the formation, constitution or dissolution of bodies such as companies, partnerships and unincorporated associations.

There are some partial exceptions to the list of contracts to which the sections apply. The contracts affected are contracts:

    (i) of marine salvage or towage;

    (ii) for the charter of a ship or hovercraft; and

    (iii) for the carriage of goods by ship or hovercraft.

Sections 16 to 18 apply to these contracts to a limited extent only.

Section 16

This section deals with liability for breach of duty. It provides that a term excluding or restricting liability for breach of duty in the course of any business is:

(i) void if it relates to death or personal injury; and

(ii) of no effect in any other case *unless* it is proved to have been, at the time when the contract was made, fair and reasonable.

The phrase "breach of duty" is defined in the Act as covering the following three types of breach (whether they were caused by intentional conduct or by mere carelessness):

(i) breach of any obligation, arising from the express or implied terms of a contract, to take reasonable care or exercise reasonable skill in the performance of the contract;

(ii) breach of any common law duty to take reasonable care or exercise reasonable skill;

(iii) breach of the duty of reasonable care imposed by the Occupiers' Liability (Scotland) Act 1960 (see p. 425, below).

The liability with which section 16 is concerned may therefore be contractual (*i.e.* may arise out of contract) (as with the first type of breach), or it may be delictual (*i.e.* may arise out of a delict, a civil wrong) (as with the second and third types of breach). The section does not, however, affect either the "strict" liability which arises in certain circumstances in the common law of delict (see p. 426, below), or any statutory liability arising in the law of delict other than the statutory liability of an occupier under the Act of 1960.

The term "business" includes a profession and the activities of any government department or local or public authority.

The onus of proving that a term was fair and reasonable is always on the party who seeks to rely on the term.

Section 17

This section imposes a "reasonableness" test on exemption clauses in consumer contracts and standard form contracts. The effect is to make the doctrine of fundamental breach as applied to exemption clauses unnecessary: the test is now, not whether the exemption clause still operates in spite of a fundamental breach of the contract, but only whether the clause was, at the time of the making of the contract, a fair and reasonable one.

Section 17 has two provisions:

First, it provides that a term in a consumer contract or in a standard form contract cannot exclude or restrict liability to the consumer or customer for breach of the contract, *unless* the term was, at the time of the making of the contract, fair and reasonable.

This provision could, for instance, apply where a carrier's contract stated that he would not be liable unless advised of a claim within X days, or where a builder's contract provided that he would not be liable for more than £Y if he failed to complete the work within the contract period.

The second provision in section 17 is more far-reaching in that it extends to terms which might not be expressed as, or easily identified as, exemption clauses. It is aimed at protecting the rights which the consumer or customer might reasonably expect to enjoy under his contract.

The provision is that a term in a consumer contract or in a standard form contract cannot enable the other party to the contract to give no performance at all or to give a performance substantially different from that which the consumer or customer reasonably expected, *unless* the term was, at the time of the making of the contract, fair and reasonable.

The provision could, for instance, apply where a travel agent's contract stated that he had the right to substitute a different ship and a different route for those specified in the customer's cruise contract.

Both parts of section 17 affect only consumer contracts and standard form contracts.

"Consumer contract" is defined in the Act. An essential part of the definition is that one party to the contract deals, and the other party to the contract ("the consumer") does not deal, in the course of a business. The onus of proving that a contract is not a consumer contract lies on the non-consumer.

The Act does not define "standard form contract": it is left for the court to decide whether or not in any particular case the contract is a standard form contract. In such a contract *both* parties may be dealing in the course of a business: the contract will be on the standard terms of one of the parties, and the purpose of section 17 is to protect the weaker of the two commercial parties ("the customer")

Practical difficulties are likely to arise where the standard terms put forward by one party are adjusted by negotiation between the parties: how much adjustment will be necessary in order to take the contract outwith the description of a standard form contract for the purposes of section 17?

Section 18

This section relates to indemnity clauses in consumer contracts, *i.e.* to clauses which provide that the consumer is to free another person (whether a party to the contract or not) from liability which that other person may incur as a result of breach of duty or breach of contract. Any such indemnity clause is of no effect, *unless* the incorporation of it was fair and reasonable at the time when the contract was made.

(b) *Other Sections in Part II*

The specific contracts covered by the remaining sections in Part II are:

(i) guarantees of consumer goods, where the guarantee is not given by a party to the contract (*e.g.* a manufacturer's guarantee of an article sold by a retailer): by section 19, the manufacturer (or other party) can no longer exclude or restrict his liability if, through his breach of duty, loss or damage has been caused as a result of the goods proving defective when used or possessed by the consumer;

(ii) sale and hire-purchase contracts: the controls introduced by the Supply of Goods (Implied Terms) Act 1973 are for convenience briefly restated in section 20: the implied terms as to title can in no case be excluded or restricted, and the implied terms as to conformity with description or sample, or as to quality or fitness for a particular purpose, cannot, in a consumer contract, be excluded or restricted at all as against the consumer, and in any other case cannot be excluded or restricted *unless* the exclusion or restriction was fair and reasonable;

(iii) other contracts for the supply of goods (*e.g.* contracts of hire or loan, but not contracts for the charter of a ship or hovercraft unless they are consumer contracts): by section 21, any implied term as to title cannot be excluded or restricted *unless* the exclusion or restriction was fair and reasonable, and any implied term as to conformity with description or sample, or as to quality or fitness for a particular purpose cannot, in a consumer contract, be excluded or restricted at all as against the consumer, and in any other case cannot be excluded or restricted *unless* the exclusion or restriction was fair and reasonable; these provisions are an extension of the provisions in (ii) above, except that here exclusion or restriction of an implied term as to title is not necessarily void in every case.

A schedule to the Act sets out "guidelines" for the application of the reasonableness test in sections 20 and 21; *e.g.* matters to be considered include the bargaining strength of the two parties relative to each other, and whether the customer received an inducement to agree to the term or had the opportunity of making a similar contract with someone else without having to accept a similar term. (These "guidelines" were derived from the Supply of Goods (Implied Terms) Act 1973, and they have not been expressly made applicable to the reasonableness test in sections 16 to 18.)

ASSIGNATION OF CONTRACTS

"Assignation" is the term used of the transfer of a right under a contract from one of the contracting parties to a third party. The party who grants the assignation is called the "cedent," and the third party to whom the right is transferred is called the "assignee."

The two main questions which arise in relation to assignation are:

1. Which contracts are assignable? and
2. What is the effect of assignation?

1. Assignability

A distinction is drawn between executed contracts and executorial or executory contracts.

An executed contract is one which can be completed merely by the payment of a sum of money or by the handing over of an article. Such a contract is assignable unless there is express provision to the contrary.

An executorial or executory contract is one which contains an obligation to do or not to do something. The assignability of an executorial contract depends on whether or not the contract involves delectus personae ("choice of person").

There is delectus personae where one party has entered into the contract in reliance on the personal qualities or skill of the other party.

The following contracts involve delectus personae, and, therefore, cannot be assigned:

(a) a contract for the exercise of some artistic, literary or professional skill, *e.g.* for the painting of a portrait;

(b) a contract of employment: an employee cannot be transferred without his consent to the service of another employer; and

(c) a contract of partnership: one partner in a firm cannot assign his right in the firm to an outsider so as to make the outsider a partner in the firm.

2. Effect of Assignation

The general rule on the effect of an assignation is that the assignee can exercise the right which his cedent had. The maxim expressing this rule is "assignatus utitur jure auctoris" ("the assignee enjoys the right of his cedent").

The negative aspect of this general rule is that the assignee acquires no higher right than his cedent had. If, therefore, the contract was voidable (*e.g.* on the ground of fraud) before the assignation, it remains voidable in the hands of the assignee; this would apply, for instance, to an insurance policy which was voidable because of a material misstatement made by the insured in the proposal form and which was subsequently assigned by the insured to a third party. Similarly, if the cedent had, before the assignation, committed a material breach of the contract with the result that he would not have been able to enforce the contract against the other party, then the assignee is also unable to enforce the contract.

An important exception to the general rule is the principle of negotiability, which applies to a limited class of documents known as "negotiable instruments."

Negotiable Instruments

A negotiable instrument has three essential characteristics:

    (a) It contains a personal obligation to pay money.

    (b) It can be transferred by simple delivery, *i.e.* by the handing over of it, after it has been "indorsed" (signed on the back) in some cases, by the holder of it to the assignee; no intimation of the assignation need be made to the party who is to pay the money, as is required to complete the assignation of other personal obligations to pay money.

    (c) It confers on a bona fide holder for value a valid title to the obligation which it contains, in spite of any defect in the title of the transferor; an assignee is a "bona fide holder for value" if he has, without suspecting that the transferor's title is defective, himself handed over goods or made some other return for the document which is being transferred to him. In this respect a negotiable instrument resembles money, for any person who obtains money in good faith and for value is entitled to retain it even although it may have been lost by or stolen from its original owner.

A document becomes a negotiable instrument only through either mercantile custom recognised by the courts or Act of Parliament: parties cannot merely by agreement give to a document the character of "negotiability."

Examples are bank notes, bills of exchange (including cheques), promissory notes (written promises to pay a certain amount), dividend warrants (by which payment of dividends on a company's shares is made), and share warrants to bearer (which differ from share certificates in that they state that the bearer of the document, not a named party, is entitled to the shares mentioned).

The following are not negotiable instruments: Post Office money orders and postal orders, deposit receipts, "I.O.U.s" (which are merely acknowledgments that there is some outstanding debt), and bills of lading. A bill of lading is a receipt for goods shipped. It gives evidence of the terms of the contract of carriage, and is a "document of title" (*i.e.* it entitles the holder of it to take delivery of the goods from the ship), but it does not have characteristic (c), since the transferee of it does not obtain any better title than the transferor had.

TITLE TO SUE

As a general rule only the parties to the contract have the "title to sue" on it (*i.e.* have the right to bring a court action to enforce it): a third party, although he may receive some incidental benefit from performance of the contract has no title to sue on it. This absence of any title to sue is referred to as "jus tertii" (literally "right of a third party"), which is a succinct way of expressing the principle that a third party is excluded from making a claim under a contract to which he was not a party.

According to the general rule, therefore, if a third party, C, found that he would obtain some benefit for himself if a contract between A and B were to be performed, and if he attempted to enforce the contract in an action against A or B, he would be met by the defence "jus tertii," meaning that he had no title to sue.

There are, however, the following important exceptions to the general rule:

1. Agency

If one person is acting as agent for another in the making of a contract, then that other, called "the principal," may have a title to sue on the contract, although he is not personally one of the con-tracting parties.

2. Assignation

The rights under certain contracts can be assigned (see p. 317, above), and the assignee then has the right to sue to enforce the contract.

3. Transmission on Death or Bankruptcy

When one of the parties to the contract dies, the right to sue "trans-mits" to his executor (*i.e.* passes to his legal representative), unless there is an element of delectus personae (see p. 317, above), in which case the contract is terminated by the death.

Similarly, when one of the parties to the contract becomes bank-rupt, the right to sue may transmit to the trustee who is appointed to administer the bankrupt's estate. The trustee usually has the right to "elect" (choose) whether to adopt the bankrupt's contracts or not, and his choice would depend mainly on the likelihood of benefit to the estate; in some cases, however, the presence of delectus personae prevents the trustee from adopting the contract.

Bankruptcy, unlike death, may amount to or lead to breach of contract which will make the estate liable in damages to the other

contracting party; *e.g.* in a contract of employment bankruptcy of
the employer amounts to a breach of the contract, and if a trustee
elects not to adopt a contract entered into by the bankrupt this leads
to a breach of the contract.

4. Jus Quaesitum Tertio

Where a jus quaesitum tertio ("right accruing to a third party") has
been created by a contract, then a third party has a title to sue to
enforce the contract.

For a jus quaesitum tertio to arise the following conditions must
be satisfied:

(a) the contract must name or refer to the third party or the
class to which the third party belongs; and

(b) the contracting parties must be shown to have intended to
benefit the third party.

There may be an express provision in the contract to the effect
that the third party is to have a title to sue; *e.g.* money lodged with a
bank on deposit receipt may be made payable to a third party instead
of to the party who has lodged it: the third party then has the right to
sue the bank for payment.

If there is no express provision in the contract, the intention of the
contracting parties to confer a title to sue on the third party has to be
inferred from the contract.

Such an intention may be inferred where the only party having
any substantial interest in the fulfilment of the contract is the third
party; *e.g.* a promise made by A to B that he, A, will pay a sum of
money to C may give rise to a jus quaesitum tertio in favour of C.

The case of *Morton's Trustees* v. *Aged Christian Friend Society of
Scotland* (1899) 2 F. 82, illustrates this point:

M. wrote to a provisional committee which was promoting a
charitable society, offering on certain conditions to pay a subscription of £1,000 to the society if it was formed. The committee accepted
M.'s offer.

The society was formed, and the conditions were complied with.

The court held that a jus quaesitum tertio had been created in
favour of the society, although it had not been in existence when
M.'s offer was made. The society was therefore entitled to sue for
the subscription.

In most cases, however, at least one of the contracting parties
has an interest to enforce the contract, and it is then less easy to
infer an intention to create a jus quaesitum tertio; thus, if A and B
make a contract which A and a third party, C, both have an interest
to see performed, A will have a title to sue on the contract, but only
in special circumstances will C be entitled to sue on it; C's interest is

regarded as merely an incidental result of a contract to which he is not a party.

Co-feuars

One situation in which a question of jus quaesitum tertio may arise is that of co-feuars, who are persons owning different, but usually adjacent, pieces of land feued to them by the same superior. For instance, a superior, X, may divide an area of land into five feus, and make five separate feu-contracts with A, B, C, D, and E, each of whom undertakes to erect a building on his feu. These feu-contracts often contain building restrictions, e.g. that the feuar is to build a house and not a factory, or that the building is to be a certain height or a certain distance from the street. It is clear that if any of the co-feuars, say, B, commits a breach of his feu-contract by perhaps erecting a factory instead of the house required by the contract, the superior, X, can sue B in respect of that breach, for X and B are the two parties to the feu-contract.

It may be, however, that X takes no action; he may not live in the locality himself, and may be little affected by B's breach of the building restriction. The question may then arise of whether one of B's co-feuars, say, C, can enforce the restriction against B. C is a third party as far as the feu-contract between X and B is concerned, and he can enforce the restriction only if he can show that that feu-contract conferred a jus quaesitum tertio on him.

The mere fact that the same restrictions are imposed on all the co-feuars in a particular area is not enough in itself to give one feuar a title to sue another feuar; there must be in addition either a reference to a common building plan for the locality or a provision in each feu-contract that the same restrictions are to be imposed on all the other feuars.

BREACH OF CONTRACT

A breach of contract occurs where one party fails to "implement" (fulfil) his part of the contract and the other party becomes entitled to damages as compensation for the loss suffered by him as a result of the first party's failure. It is to be noted that failure to implement a contract is not considered as a breach of contract if the circumstances are such that no claim for damages can arise; e.g. where, by a change in circumstances between the date of the contract and the date at which it requires to be implemented, performance of the contract becomes impossible, there is failure to perform the contract, but not a breach of contract, since no claim for damages arises.

Although a breach of contract always gives to the party who is not in breach the right to claim damages, there are also, in certain circumstances, other remedies for breach of contract.

The remedies for breach of contract may be considered under four headings:

1. specific implement;
2. rescission;
3. damages; and
4. defensive measures.

A breach of contract may take place either before the date when performance is due or at the date of performance. The former type of breach is referred to as "anticipatory" breach. Although in point of time anticipatory breach is prior to ordinary breach (*i.e.* breach at the due date of performance), its significance will be more easily understood once the remedies for ordinary breach are known. Treatment of it is, therefore, reserved until later (see p. 333, below).

1. Specific Implement

When one party to a contract fails to fulfil his obligations, the other generally has the remedy of specific implement, by which he can apply to court for an order directing the party who is in breach to perform the contract, *i.e.* to give specific implement or fulfilment of it.

The court order takes the form of a decree ad factum praestandum ("for the performance of an act") if the order is positive, and of an interdict if it is negative.

A decree ad factum praestandum would be appropriate, for instance, if the order of the court was that a building be erected in accordance with the contract.

A situation where interdict would be the appropriate remedy would be where a restrictive covenant between the seller and the purchaser of a business had been broken: if the seller, in breach of the contract, set up business again in competition with the purchaser, the purchaser could apply to court for an interdict ordering the seller to refrain from doing so.

A person who wilfully fails to comply with the court order is liable to imprisonment for contempt of court.

In certain circumstances the remedy of specific implement is not open. These circumstances are:

(a) where the obligation is to pay money; the remedy of the creditor in that case is to enforce payment by diligence, *i.e.* by taking the debtor's property with the authority of the court, selling the property and using the proceeds to pay the debt; a contract with a company to take up and pay for debentures in the company is an exception, since, by the Companies Act 1948, s. 92, such a contract, although it involves payment of a sum of money to the company, can be enforced by an order for specific implement; another exception is that in some cases there may be an order to consign the money in court, *i.e.* to entrust it to the court;

(b) where the contract involves an intimate relationship as a result of which forced compliance would be worse than no compliance at all, *e.g.* contracts of employment and of partnership; however, under the Employment Protection (Consolidation) Act 1978 an industrial tribunal has power to make an order for reinstatement or re-engagement of an employee who has been unfairly dismissed;

(c) where compliance with the decree would be impossible or unlawful, *e.g.* if a person has undertaken to carry out work on land to which he has no right of access;

(d) where the court could not enforce the decree, *e.g.* where the defender is a foreigner who could not be imprisoned, or where the act is one which could be performed only by a corporate body, such as a company, and performance could not be enforced except by imprisonment of all the individual members of the body; this does not apply to acts which are to be performed by officials of a corporate body: these can be enforced by specific implement;

(e) where there is no pretium affectionis ("reason for preference"), *i.e.* where the article contracted for is not a specific one with its own characteristics, but is merely one of a class; *e.g.*, in the case of a sale of some commodity which can be obtained in the open market, the purchaser cannot insist on the seller's supplying him with the commodity: his remedy is to procure the commodity from another source and then sue the seller for any loss; or

(f) where in the opinion of the court it would be clearly "inequitable" (unjust or unfair) to grant specific implement, *e.g.* where it would cause special hardship to the defender; it is, however, the general rule that the pursuer has the remedy of specific implement as of right, and only in exceptional circumstances would the court exercise its discretion in refusing the remedy.

2. Rescission

The remedy of rescission is the right of the party who is loyal to the contract to "rescind" (cancel) the contract. It arises when the party who is in breach has "repudiated" the contract, *i.e.* has been guilty of some material breach of it. If the breach is only a minor one, there is no right of rescission.

The question, therefore, to be examined in connection with the remedy of rescission is what amounts to a *material* breach of contract.

If the parties in their contract state that a particular provision is material, then breach of that provision by one party will justify rescission of the contract by the other party, however trivial the provision may in fact be.

If the parties do not state which provisions in the contract are material, then it will be for the court to decide which are material and which are not.

Where there is complete failure on the part of one party to perform the contract, the court will hold that to be a material breach, and the other party will be justified in rescinding the contract, treating it as repudiated by the party guilty of the breach.

Where, however, the breach is only a partial one, it may or may not be material. The question of materiality of a partial breach may arise where:

(a) there are several stipulations in the contract;

(b) there is defective performance of the contract; or

(c) one party fails to perform his part of the contract at the agreed time.

(a) *Several Stipulations in the Contract*

A contract may contain several stipulations and one party may fail to comply with one of these stipulations. The other party will be entitled to rescind the contract if the stipulation in question goes to the root of the contract but not if it is merely incidental or trivial.

Two contrasting cases which illustrate this aspect of materiality of breach are *Graham & Co.* v. *United Turkey Red Co. Ltd.*, 1922 S.C. 533, and *Wade* v. *Waldon*, 1909 S.C. 571.

Graham & Co. v. *United Turkey Red Co. Ltd.*: G. had agreed to sell cotton goods for the United Turkey Red Co. Ltd. and for no-one else. He broke the second stipulation by selling for another party. His breach was held to be sufficiently material to justify rescission.

Wade v. *Waldon*: Waldon, owner of the Palace Theatre, Glasgow, had engaged Wade, whose stage name was "George Robey," to perform at his theatre. One of the stipulations in their contract was that Wade was to give fourteen days' notice before the engagement, together with "bill matter." Wade failed to do this, and Waldon claimed to be entitled to rescind the contract. The court held that he was not entitled to do so, because the breach of this one stipulation was not material.

(b) *Defective Performance*

Where one party's performance of his part of the contract is defective in a material respect, the other party is justified in rescinding the contract.

For instance, if a contract provides for goods or work to be of a certain quality, failure in quality is usually material, but a remediable defect in a piece of machinery sold would probably not be material.

The Sale of Goods Act 1979 provides that if the seller delivers to the buyer a smaller quantity of goods than was ordered, or a larger quantity than was ordered, or delivers goods ordered mixed with goods of a different description, then the buyer is justified in rescinding the contract.

(c) *Time of Performance*

Where one party fails to perform his part of the contract in time, the other party is entitled to rescind the contract, provided time is of the essence of the contract, *e.g.* a contract concerned with goods the market price of which fluctuates from day to day. If time is not of the essence of the contract, failure to perform the contract by a stated date does not give rise to a right of rescission, provided performance takes place within a reasonable time.

3. Damages

This is the most general remedy for breach of contract.

The object of an award of damages is to place the party who is not in breach in the same position as he would have been in had the contract been duly performed, so far as money can do so.

Damages are intended as compensation for the party who is loyal to the contract, but even if that party has not in fact suffered any financial loss through the breach of contract he may still claim damages for the trouble and inconvenience which necessarily result from the breach.

Where actual loss has resulted from the breach the damages which are awarded are referred to as "substantial" or "compensatory" damages, as opposed to "nominal" damages, the small sum awarded where there has been no actual loss.

Measure of Damages

A provision of the Sale of Goods Act 1979 may be given as a straightforward example of how damages are measured: where the seller wrongfully fails to deliver the goods to the buyer, the measure of the damages which the buyer can claim for non-delivery is "the estimated loss directly and naturally resulting, in the ordinary course of events, from the seller's breach of contract," and where there is an available market for the goods the measure of damages is "prima facie (*i.e.* 'at first appearance' or 'until the contrary is proved') to be ascertained by the difference between the contract price and the market or current price of the goods at the time or times when they ought to have been delivered, or (if no time was fixed) at the time of the refusal to deliver" (s. 51).

However, the party suing for damages may not be able to recover his full loss: his claim may be limited because either:

(a) he has not "minimised" (lessened) his loss; or

(b) the loss is too remote a result of the breach.

(a) Minimising the loss

The party claiming damages must have taken all reasonable steps to minimise his loss; *e.g.* an employee who has been wrongfully dismissed and is suing his former employer for damages for the wrongful dismissal must have tried to obtain other employment, and if, in a sale of goods where the seller is in breach because he has failed to deliver the goods, the buyer has waited for some time before supplying himself from another source and finds that there has meantime been a steep rise in the price of the goods on the market, he cannot claim for the rise which has taken place since the seller's breach of contract.

The principle of minimisation of loss is illustrated in *Ireland & Son* v. *Merryton Coal Co.* (1894) 21 R. 989:

A coal company contracted to supply a firm of coal merchants with 3,000 tons of coal at 7s. per ton, to be delivered "over the next four months" in "average" or "about equal" monthly quantities.

At the end of the period of four months the sellers had delivered only about half of the 3,000 tons, and the buyers brought an action of damages against them in which the buyers calculated the damages on the basis of the market price ruling at the end of the four months.

The court held that under the contract the sellers were bound to deliver no more than about 750 tons of coal during each month, and that the amount of damages was to be calculated on the basis of the market price ruling at the end of each month for the quantity short-delivered during that month.

The party claiming damages is not required to resort to extra-ordinary measures in order to mitigate his loss: he need do no more than what is reasonable in the circumstances. This point was given effect to in *Gunter & Co.* v. *Lauritzen* (1894) 1 S.L.T. 435 (O.H.); 31 S.L.R. 359:

A purchaser bought a cargo of Danish hay and straw with express notice to the seller that the goods were bought for resale. The goods were admittedly not in conformity with the contract, and were rejected by the purchaser on their arrival.

The purchaser brought an action of damages in which he claimed the loss of the profit which he would have made on the resale.

The goods had not been obtainable in the open market, but might have been purchased in three separate lots from private sellers in different parts of the country.

The purchaser was held entitled to recover from the seller the loss of the profit which he would have made on a resale; he was not bound to take other than ordinary measures to replace the goods.

(b) Remoteness of damage

The party claiming damages is not entitled to damages for a loss which is a remote and unforeseeable result of the breach of contract.

This principle is usually associated with the English case of *Hadley* v. *Baxendale* (1854) 9 Ex. 341, but the principle was recognised in Scots law before that case was decided.

The "rule in *Hadley* v. *Baxendale*" as expressed by Alderson B. in delivering the judgment of the Court of Exchequer is as follows (at p. 354):

"Where two parties have made a contract which one of them has broken, the damages which the other party ought to receive in respect of such breach of contract should be such as may fairly and reasonably be considered either arising naturally, i.e., according to the usual course of things, from such breach of contract itself, or such as may reasonably be supposed to have been in the contemplation of both parties, at the time they made the contract, as the probable result of the breach of it."

The facts of *Hadley* v. *Baxendale* were as follows:

The plaintiffs were owners of a Gloucester flour mill which had been brought to a standstill by a broken crank shaft. The shaft had to be sent to the makers at Greenwich as a pattern for a new one, and was handed to a carrier, who promised to deliver it at Greenwich in two days.

The only information given to the carrier was that the article was the broken shaft of a mill and that the plaintiffs were the millers of that mill.

Owing to the carrier's neglect, the shaft was unduly delayed in transit, and as a result the mill remained idle for a longer time than it would have done had there been no breach of the contract of carriage.

The plaintiffs claimed from the carrier damages for the loss of profit caused by the delay.

The court held that the plaintiffs were not entitled to such damages since *neither* (i) would the loss have flowed "naturally" from the breach of the contract in ordinary circumstances *nor* (ii) had the carrier been made aware of the special circumstances as a result of which loss of profit could have been contemplated by him as being "the probable result of the breach" of the contract by him; as regards (i), it was not a normal occurrence that the mill would remain idle: the plaintiffs might, for instance, have had a spare shaft; and as regards (ii), the special circumstances had not been disclosed to the carrier.

The rule in *Hadley* v. *Baxendale* has two branches: the first deals with the normal damage which occurs "according to the usual course of things," and the second with abnormal damage which results from exceptional circumstances. The defender in an action for damages is assumed to have had both types of damage in contemplation, but, in the case of abnormal damage, he must have been made aware of the exceptional circumstances.

A distinction, based on the two branches of the rule, is usually made between general or ordinary damages, on the one hand, and special or consequential damages, on the other hand. The defender is normally liable only for loss which occurs "according to the usual course of things." and the pursuer is then said to be entitled to general or ordinary damages. Where, however, there are exceptional circumstances of which the defender was aware at the time of the contract, so that he ought to have foreseen that some abnormal loss would probably result from a breach on his part, then the defender is liable for that abnormal loss and the pursuer is said to be entitled to special or consequential damages.

The test of "foreseeability" covers both general and special damages.

The following three cases illustrate the principle of remoteness of damage.

(i)   *Hobbs* v. *London and South Western Ry. Co.* (1875) L.R. 10 Q.B. 111, an English case, which is an example of a claim for damages being limited to loss arising "according to the usual course of things";

(ii)   *"Den of Ogil" Co. Ltd.* v. *Caledonian Ry. Co.* (1902) 5 F. 99, a Scottish parallel to *Hadley* v. *Baxendale*, giving an example of a case in which special circumstances were not disclosed sufficiently fully to the defender; and

(iii)   *Macdonald & Co.* v. *Highland Ry. Co.* (1873) 11 M. 614, an example of a claim which was successful because special circumstances had been sufficiently fully disclosed to the defender.

(i)   *Hobbs* v. *London and South Western Ry. Co.*: The plaintiff with his wife and two children took tickets on the railway from Wimbledon to Hampton Court to travel by the midnight train.

The train went along the wrong line to a different station where they were compelled to alight. It was too late at night for them to get a conveyance home or accommodation at an inn, and in fact they arrived home at 3 a.m. after walking five miles in the rain.

Mrs. Hobbs caught cold, and as a result was unable to assist her husband in his business for some time.

An action of damages was brought, and the court held that £8 could be awarded for the inconvenience of walking home, but that no damages could be awarded for the wife's illness and its consequences, as these were too remote results of the railway company's breach of contract.

(ii) *"Den of Ogil" Co. Ltd.* v. *Caledonian Ry. Co.*: Owners of a steamship of 4,000 tons, which had broken one of her pistons and was lying at Plymouth, got another one cast at Port Glasgow and sent it by rail from Port Glasgow to Plymouth.

There was a delay of between three and four days in delivery, and the shipowners sued the railway company for damages, including outlays and loss of profit caused by the detention of the ship, amounting to £300.

The railway company had been told that the new part was in a "big hurry," but had not been made aware that such a large ship, with a cargo and crew on it, was being kept waiting.

The court held that the railway company was not liable for the loss of profit, and was liable for only part (estimated at £50) of the outlays, caused by the detention of the ship, since the notice of the special circumstances had not been specific enough to make it liable for more.

(iii) *Macdonald & Co.* v. *Highland Ry. Co.*: Confectionery for the celebration of the coming of age of Lord Macdonald was being sent by the Highland Railway from Inverness to Dingwall and Strome Ferry and then to Skye.

The confectionery was marked "perishable," and it was the custom of the railway company to forward perishable goods in preference to others.

However, the truck in which the confectionery was placed was not marked "perishable," and at Dingwall was taken off the train to lighten it, while goods not of a perishable nature were forwarded.

As a result, the confectionery did not reach Strome Ferry until too late for the steamer of that day. It arrived at its destination too late for the celebration, and was also much spoiled by the delay.

In an action brought against the railway company for damages the company was held liable.

Conventional or Liquidate Damages

Parties to a contract may agree at the time when they make the contract that in the event of breach by one party the other party will be entitled to a certain sum as damages. That sum is called "conventional damages" or "liquidate damages." If a breach occurs, then the party not in breach has a claim for the sum fixed, and for that sum only, whether his actual loss is greater or less than the estimate. In a contract for work to be done, for example, a clause is often included providing for payment of a certain sum for each day (or week or month) during which the work remains uncompleted after a specified date.

Liquidate damages must be distinguished from a penalty. While the former are valid, the latter is not. The court will not give effect to a "penalty" clause in a contract if the clause is really an attempt by the parties to impose a punishment for breach instead of to fix the sum to be paid by way of compensation for probable loss. To qualify as liquidate damages the amount fixed must be a genuine pre-estimate of the loss, and not merely in the nature of a threat.

The distinction between liquidate damages and penalty was considered by the House of Lords in the Scottish case of *Lord Elphinstone* v. *Monkland Iron and Coal Co. Ltd.* (1886) 13 R.(H.L.) 98:

A mineral lease contained a stipulation that the tenants should within a certain time level and soil over deposits of slag which by the lease they were authorised to make, and that if they failed to do so they were to be liable to pay to the landlord "at the rate of £100 per imperial acre for all ground not so restored, together with legal interest thereon from and after the date when the operations should have been completed until paid."

In a later part of the lease this payment was referred to as a "penalty."

The sum was held to be liquidate damages and not penalty.

The case brings out two important points about the distinction:

(i) The mere fact that the parties have in their contract called the sum to be paid in the event of a breach "liquidate damages" or "penalty" is not conclusive: the court may decide that what the parties have called "liquidate damages" is in fact a penalty and therefore unenforceable, or that what the parties have called a "penalty" is in fact liquidate damages and therefore enforceable.

(ii) A single lump sum is more likely to be held to be a penalty than is a sum which is proportionate to the degree of failure in performance of the contract. Lord Watson explained this second point as follows (at p. 106):

"When a single lump sum is made payable by way of compensation, on the occurrence of one or more or all of several events, some of which may occasion serious and others but trifling damage, the presumption is that the parties intended the sum to be penal, and subject to modification. The payments stipulated in article 12 are not of that character; they are made proportionate to the extent to which the respondent company may fail to implement their obligations, and they are to bear interest from the date of the failure."

A later case which illustrates these two points is *Cameron-Head* v. *Cameron & Co.*, 1919 S.C. 627:

Timber merchants entered into a contract with a landed proprietor by which they bought the standing timber in the vicinity of the mansion-house.

The contract contained the condition that the wood was to be cleared away by April 1, 1918, "under a penalty of 10s. a day until such is done."

By April 1919 the wood had still not been completely cleared away, and the proprietor brought an action against the timber merchants for payment of one year's "penalty" at the rate stated in the contract.

The court held that, although the sum of 10s. was described in the contract as a "penalty," yet, as it appeared to be a reasonable pre-estimate and not a mere random or extortionate figure, it was to be regarded as liquidate damages and not as a penalty.

The case of *Dingwall* v. *Burnett*, 1912 S.C. 1097, on the other hand, gives an illustration of circumstances in which a single lump sum was held to be a penalty:

An agreement for the lease of a hotel contained mutual obligations, some important and others not, with a provision for the payment of £50 for breach of any of them.

The tenant later refused to carry out his part of the agreement at all, and the landlord claimed damages for breach of the contract to the amount of over £300.

The tenant maintained that he could be made liable for only £50.

The court held that the £50 stipulated in the agreement was not liquidate damages but a penalty and that the landlord's claim for damages was therefore not limited to £50, since that provision was unenforceable.

In some situations it is impossible at the time when the contract is entered into to make any substantially accurate pre-estimate at all of the loss which would be likely to result from a breach. The court will then allow as liquidate damages any sum fixed by the parties, provided it is reasonable in the circumstances. The case of *Clydebank Engineering and Shipbuilding Co. Ltd.* v. *Castaneda* (1904) 7 F.(H.L.) 77, gives an example of such a situation:

By two contracts made in 1896 the Spanish government had contracted with a Clyde shipbuilding company for the building of four torpedo boats at the price of £67,180 under one contract and

£65,650 under the other, for each vessel, delivery to be within periods varying from 6½ to 7¾ months from the date of the contracts.

The contracts provided that "the penalty for late delivery shall be at the rate of £500 per week for each vessel."

At the date of the contracts the Spanish government was trying to suppress an insurrection in Cuba and feared armed intervention by the United States.

All the vessels were delivered many months after the stipulated dates of delivery and were too late to be of service.

The Spanish government brought an action against the shipbuilders for £500 for each week of late delivery of each vessel—a total of £75,500.

The defenders pleaded that the sum of £500 stipulated for in the contract was a penalty and not liquidate damages.

The House of Lords, however, affirming the judgment of the Court of Session ((1903) 5 F. 1016), held that, since it was impossible to make any substantially accurate pre-estimate of the loss which might result to a government through the lack of torpedo boats, the sum was to be regarded as liquidate damages and not as penalty. The Spanish government was therefore entitled to the full amount claimed.

4. Defensive Measures

These are:

    (a)   retention; and

    (b)   lien.

Retention is the right to refuse to pay a debt which is due, whereas lien is the right to refuse to deliver a particular thing. (Sometimes, however, the term "retention" is used to include lien.)

These remedies are used mainly where rescission would confer no advantage (*e.g.* where the contract has already been partly performed), or where the breach is not sufficiently material to justify rescission. They are based on the principle of mutuality.

(a) *Retention*

Retention is an exception to a general rule.

The general rule is that a debtor has no right to refuse to pay his debt merely on the ground that he has himself some claim against his creditor, unless "compensation" (see p. 338, below) can be pleaded. For compensation to operate, both debts must be "liquid" (*i.e.* actually due and of ascertained amount).

An example of the general rule is as follows: a seller, A, supplies goods to B, and B pays for them; the goods prove to be of defective quality, with the result that B has a claim for damages against A; meantime, however, B has bought more goods from A, and payment is due but has not yet been made; B is not entitled to refuse to pay for the second lot of goods merely on the ground that he has an illiquid claim for damages for the defective quality of the first lot.

Retention is permissible in the following three situations:

(i)   where compensation can be pleaded (see p. 338, below);

(ii) where both claims arise under the same contract; *e.g.* if in a sale of goods the seller fails to deliver the goods within the specified time, the purchaser, who has a claim for damages, has a right to retain the price until his claim for damages is settled; similarly, if a carrier of goods is liable for damages for injury done to the goods during their carriage, the carrier's demand for the cost of the carriage can be resisted by the party who has engaged him;

(iii) where the creditor is bankrupt; it would be a special hardship if the debtor had himself to pay the full amount of what he owed to the bankrupt creditor and then received only part-payment of the debt which the bankrupt owed to him; accordingly, if the creditor is bankrupt, the law allows the debtor who has an illiquid claim against him to refuse payment until the amount of his illiquid claim is ascertained, and then to compensate the one debt with the other even although the two debts arise out of different contracts.

(b) *Lien*

The right of lien is available to a person who is in possession of an article on which he has been employed to do work; he can refuse to return the article to its owner until payment for the work done on it is made.

Lien is a "right in security" (see p. 485, below).

Anticipatory Breach of Contract

Anticipatory breach of contract takes place where before the time for performance has arrived one party indicates conclusively by his words or actions that he will not perform his part of the contract. Parties to a contract are entitled not only to performance when it is due but also to the expectation that there will be performance when it is due, and so an anticipatory breach by one party may be treated by the other as a repudiation of the contract as at the time when it occurs. The party who is not in breach may therefore at once rescind the contract and claim damages instead of waiting for the actual breach to occur as at the date when actual performance is due.

To explain the effect of anticipatory breach one may take as an instance a contract between A and B, which has been entered into in January and which is to be performed in July. In March B intimates that he will not carry out the contract. A then has a choice of remedy:

(a) He may rescind the contract in March and claim damages; if, after March, B changes his mind and offers to perform the contract after all, his offer comes too late.

(b) He may wait until July and then either claim specific implement (if appropriate) or rescind the contract and claim damages; in adopting this course A is keeping the contract alive; it follows that if B changes his mind and performs the contract in July after all, A will be bound to accept that performance and will have no claim for breach of contract, and also that if between March and July performance becomes impossible or illegal (*e.g.* owing to outbreak of war), A will have no claim for breach of contract when, in July, B fails to perform the contract.

Whichever course A chooses, the damages are calculated with reference to the date when performance is due. Where the time for performance has not yet arrived, this may involve a difficult forecast.

For an anticipatory breach to occur the refusal to perform must be definite: it is not enough that one party has merely indicated that he doubts whether he will be able to perform the contract; nor will there be anticipatory breach where A, having contracted to sell a particular article to B, sells that article to C in the interval between the making of the contract and the date on which the article is due to be delivered to B, because A might, before that date, buy back the article from C; it would be different if A had contracted to deliver the article to B on demand instead of at some fixed future date.

EXTINCTION OF CONTRACTUAL OBLIGATIONS

The obligations contained in a contract may be brought to an end by:

1. discharge;
2. novation;
3. delegation;
4. confusion;
5. compensation;
6. prescription;
7. impossibility, illegality and frustration; and
8. breach of the contract.

1. Discharge

The term "discharge" is sometimes used to cover all modes of termination of contracts, but here it is used in the more restricted sense of termination by acceptilation, performance or payment.

(a) *Acceptilation*

This is the technical term used where a creditor discharges his debtor without payment or performance being made. Acceptilation may result from agreement between the two parties to a contract or from a voluntary unilateral surrender of his rights by the creditor.

(b) *Performance*

When both parties have fully performed their obligations the contract is at an end. Performance which is only partial or is defective in some other way is a breach of contract.

If one party is ready duly to perform his part of the contract but is prevented from doing so by the other party, then that other party is in breach of contract.

The term "performance" may be used of fulfilment of any contractual obligation, or it may be restricted to obligations ad factum praestandum ("for the performance of an act"), *e.g.* for the execution of work or the delivery of goods, and not extend to obligations which are discharged by payment of a sum of money.

(c) *Payment*

It is the duty of the debtor to tender payment to the creditor at the proper place and in the proper manner, and if he does so the debt is extinguished.

Legal tender

Where there is no provision to the contrary in the contract the creditor is entitled to refuse to accept payment in any form other than "legal tender."

By the Coinage Act 1971 the coins which are legal tender are:

(i)   gold coins, for payments of any amount;

(ii)   cupro-nickel or silver coins of more than 10p, for payments up to £10;

(iii) cupro-nickel or silver coins of 10p or less, for payments up to £5;

(iv)   bronze coins, for payments up to 20p; and

(v)   other coins, as specified in any proclamation made under the Act by the Queen with the advice of the Privy Council.

By the Currency and Bank Notes Act 1954 Bank of England notes for less than £5 are legal tender in Scotland. Notes of the Scottish banks are not legal tender anywhere.

A cheque is not legal tender, but, if the creditor objects to payment by cheque he must return the cheque at once; otherwise he will be held to have accepted it in payment.

Where a cheque is accepted, the payment is considered to be conditional, *i.e.* the debt is immediately extinguished, but will revive if the cheque is dishonoured; this is an example of a resolutive condition (see p. 305, above).

Ascription of payments

This is also referred to as "appropriation of payments."

The question of ascription or appropriation of payments arises where a debtor owes more than one debt to the same creditor and makes a payment which is not sufficient to meet all the debts.

If the debtor on making the payment ascribes it to a particular debt, the creditor if he keeps the payment must ascribe it in accordance with the debtor's instructions.

If the debtor gives no instructions, the creditor is free to ascribe the payment to any debt he pleases; e.g. the creditor may have security over some property of the debtor for one debt and no security for another debt, and he would be quite entitled to ascribe the payment to the debt for which he holds no security.

Where there is a continuous account, such as a current account at a bank, a rule known as "the rule in *Clayton's case*" (*Devaynes* v. *Noble* (*Clayton's Case*) (1816) 1 Mer. 529, 572) applies: the rule is that payments on the credit side extinguish payments on the debit side in order of date. The rule is important where there is a "cautioner"[2] (guarantor) who has agreed to guarantee an overdraft for a fixed period: if after the expiry of the agreed period of the guarantee the account is allowed to continue without any settlement, then any later payments made by the customer into the account go towards the cancellation of the debit balance for which the cautioner was liable, with the result that the cautioner may be freed from liability although the overdraft may, owing to subsequent withdrawals made by the customer, not have been reduced at all.

The rule in *Clayton's case* has, however, only a limited application: it probably does not apply except to parties who stand in the relationship of banker and customer and to parties in substantially the same relationship: it does not apply to a trademan's account or to two separate accounts kept at a bank.

Proof of payment

The general rule as to proof of payment is that a debt arising from a written contract requires for proof of its payment either the writ or the oath of the creditor, whereas a debt arising from an oral contract may be proved to have been paid by parole evidence except where the debt exceeds £100 Scots (£8·33), in which case proof is again limited to the creditor's writ or oath. The creditor's "writ" usually takes the form of a receipt, and by the Cheques Act 1957 a cheque which appears to have been paid by the drawer's bank is evidence of the receipt by the payee of the sum payable by the cheque.

There are several exceptions to the general rule as to proof of

[2] Pronounced as if there were no " u " (kay-shun-er).

payment; *e.g.* payment for goods sold over the counter for cash may be proved by parole evidence, even although the price exceeds £100 Scots, whereas if delivery of goods is postponed or the sale is on credit, proof is restricted to the seller's writ or oath, even although the contract is an oral one.

In certain situations the alleged debtor derives assistance in the proof of payment from "presumptions of payment." These presumptions include the following:

(i) Where a guest has left a hotel, it is presumed, until the hotel-keeper proves the contrary, that the guest's bill has been paid.

(ii) Where a debtor produces receipts for three consecutive instalments of any termly payment, such as feu-duty, rent, wages or interest, it is presumed that all prior instalments have been paid. This presumption is referred to as "the apocha trium annorum" (literally, "receipt of three years"), but the payments need not be yearly payments.

(iii) Where a "document of debt" (*i.e.* a document which is an admission of a debt) is found in the hands of the debtor, even although it has no receipt or other discharge on it, the debt is presumed to have been paid. The maxim applicable is "chirographum apud debitorem repertum praesumitur solutum" ("a document found in the possession of the debtor is presumed to have been paid").

2. Novation

Novation takes place when a new obligation by the same debtor is substituted for the prior obligation in such a way that all liability on the prior obligation is extinguished; *e.g.* the debtor may sign a new document of debt which is to take the place of an earlier document, as where he accepts a new bill of exchange and the earlier bill is torn up.

However, it is often difficult to prove that where a new obligation has been undertaken the prior obligation is extinguished; if the original document of debt is not torn up or given up or cancelled, the presumption is that the new obligation gives the creditor additional rights and does not extinguish the right which he enjoys under the prior obligation.

The term "novation" is also used in a wider sense to cover the case where the new obligation is undertaken by a different person.

3. Delegation

Delegation is the substitution of a new debtor for the existing debtor, and is a form of "novation" in the wider sense of that term.

The consent of the creditor is necessary for delegation: the debtor is not entitled, without the creditor's consent, to substitute for himself another person who may have no means.

4. Confusion

Confusion, also referred to by its original Latin name "confusio" ("combination"), takes place where the same person becomes both debtor and creditor. A person cannot be his own debtor or his own creditor, and the obligation is therefore extinguished confusione ("by combination").

Confusion may arise where a creditor assigns to his debtor his right to receive the debt, and it may arise through succession if a debtor becomes the heir of his creditor on the creditor's death.

For confusion to operate, the person must be debtor and creditor in the same capacity; if, for instance, X owes a debt to Y and later becomes Y's executor or trustee, he is debtor in his individual capacity, and creditor in his capacity as executor or trustee, and the debt is not extinguished confusione.

5. Compensation

Compensation is the right of a person who finds himself both the debtor and the creditor of another person to set off the one debt against the other with the result that there is total or partial extinction of the debt which he is due to pay. For instance, if A owes B £50 and B owes A £20, and B brings an action against A for £50, A may be able to plead compensation to the extent of the £20 which B owes to him, with the result that A would be required to pay only £30.

Where the effect of compensation is to extinguish part only of a debt and not the whole of it, the debt is said to be extinguished "pro tanto" ("to such an extent").

The law on compensation is based on a Scots Act, the Compensation Act 1592.

For compensation to operate, the following conditions must be fulfilled:

(a) Compensation must be pleaded in an action; it does not ipso facto ("of itself") extinguish a debt.

(b) Both debts must be "liquid" (*i.e.* actually due and of ascertained amount), unless the debts arise out of the same contract or one of the parties is bankrupt; compensation will, therefore, not normally operate if the debt sued for is payable immediately and the debt due by the pursuer to the defender is future (*i.e.* due only on some future date) or contingent (*i.e.* dependent on some condition).

(c) There must be concursus debiti et crediti ("concurrence of debt and credit"), *i.e.* the parties must be debtor and creditor in the same capacity as well as at the same time; if, for instance, A sues B for a debt due by B personally, B cannot plead compensation of a debt due to him, B, as a trustee or executor by A: he is not debtor and creditor in the same capacity; he is debtor in his individual capacity and creditor in his representative capacity.

6. Prescription

Prescription deals with the effect of lapse of time on rights and obligations. Different types of prescription apply to different circumstances and the effect is not always to extinguish a right or obligation; *e.g.* one type of prescription, called "positive" or "acquisitive" prescription, enables the possessor of land who has an apparently valid, but actually defective, title to the land to acquire a valid title to it on the lapse of ten years (see p. 452, below).

Important changes in the law relating to prescription were made by the Prescription and Limitation (Scotland) Act 1973 which gave effect to recommendations of the Scottish Law Commission. The Act repealed, as from July 25, 1976, a variety of early statutes on the subject, and replaced them with a modernised scheme, applicable comprehensively to all rights and obligations.

By the Act of 1973, there are now two negative prescriptions:

    (a)   the five-year prescription; and

    (b)   the twenty-year prescription.

The Act also provides that certain rights and obligations are:

    (c)   imprescriptible rights and obligations.

Both of the prescriptions actually extinguish rights and obligations: they do not merely (as was the case with some of the former short negative prescriptions) alter the onus ("burden") of proof or limit the method of proof to the writ or oath of the debtor.

"Contracting-out" is not allowed: any provision in any agreement purporting to exclude these prescriptions is null.

The Act, however, does not exempt any deed from challenge at at any time on the ground that it is ex facie ("apparently" or "obviously") invalid or was forged.

(a) *Five-year Prescription*

This, which is now the only short negative prescription, is of wider application than the various former short negative prescriptions. It applies in general to obligations:

    (i)   to pay a periodical sum of money (*e.g.* interest, an instalment of an annuity, feu-duty, ground annual and rent);

    (ii)   arising from quasi-contract, including restitution, repetition, recompense and negotiorum gestio;

    (iii)   to make reparation;

    (iv)   under a bill of exchange or a promissory note;

    (v)   of accounting, other than accounting for trust funds; and

(vi) arising from, or because of any breach of, a contract or promise not already covered by (i) to (v) above.

The prescription, therefore, extends in general to all three branches of the law of obligations—contract, quasi-contract and delict. There are, however, some exceptions: the prescription does not apply to any obligations:

1. to obey a decree of court, an arbitration award or an order of a tribunal or similar body;

2. arising from the issue of a bank note;

3. constituted or evidenced by a probative writ (but cautionary obligations and obligations to pay periodical sums of money (see (i), above) are excepted from this);

4. under a continuing contract of partnership or agency;

5. relating to land (but periodical payments within (i) above are excepted from this);

6. to satisfy any legal or prior rights in the law of succession;

7. to make reparation for personal injuries or death (these are dealt with by other provisions of the Act); or

8. specified as an imprescriptible obligation.

If an obligation to which the five-year prescription applies has subsisted for a continuous period of five years—

(i) without any "relevant claim" having been made, and

(ii) without the subsistence of the obligation having been "relevantly acknowledged,"

then as from the expiry of the five years the obligation is extinguished. In relation to bills of exchange and promissory notes only condition (i) need be satisfied.

A "relevant claim" may take the form of a claim for implement made by the creditor in court or in an arbitration, the lodging of a claim in the debtor's sequestration or liquidation or the execution of any diligence directed at enforcing the obligation.

The subsistence of an obligation is regarded as having been "relevantly acknowledged" if, and only if, one of the following conditions is satisfied:

1. there has been such performance by the debtor or on his behalf towards implement of the obligation as clearly indicates that the obligation still subsists; or

2. there has been made by the debtor or on his behalf to the creditor or the creditor's agent an unequivocal written admission clearly acknowledging that the obligation still subsists.

In the calculation of the prescriptive period of five years the following periods are excluded:

(i) any period during which by the fraud of the debtor or by error induced by him the creditor was led to refrain from making a relevant claim (this does not, however, cover any time occurring after the creditor could with reasonable diligence have discovered the fraud or error); and

(ii) any period during which the creditor was under legal disability, *i.e.* was under age or of unsound mind.

(b) *Twenty-year Prescription*

The long negative prescription applies to an obligation of any kind (including an obligation to which the five-year prescription applies), other than an imprescriptible obligation.

The conditions for its operation correspond to those applicable to the five-year prescription: there must for a continuous period of twenty years have been no "relevant claim," and, with the exception of bills of exchange and promissory notes, the subsistence of the obligation must not have been "relevantly acknowledged" during that time.

No deduction is made in the case of this prescription on account of the debtor's fraud or the creditor's error or disability.

The twenty-year prescription also applies to rights relating to heritable and moveable property, *i.e.* to rights which are correlative to duties as distinct from rights which are correlative to obligations (see p. 243, above). The Act provides that if a right relating to property, other than an imprescriptible right, has subsisted for a continuous period of twenty years unexercised or unenforced, and without any "relevant claim" having been made, then as from the expiry of the twenty years the right is extinguished.

(c) *Imprescriptible Rights and Obligations*

These are rights and obligations which are not extinguished by any lapse of time, even though they are not exercised or enforced.

The following are imprescriptible rights and obligations:

(i) any real right of ownership in land;

(ii) the right in land of the lessee under a recorded lease;

(iii) any right exercisable as a res merae facultatis ("a matter of mere power"), *i.e.* a right of such a kind that non-exercise of it, even for the whole of the prescriptive period, does not result in its being extinguished (*e.g.* the right to the ordinary uses of property such as the opening of a door, and the right of a superior to feu-duty: the mere fact that the door has not been opened or that no feu-duty has been paid for even twenty years does not prevent the right from being exercised in future);

(iv) any right to recover property extra commercium ("outside commerce"), *i.e.* property belonging to the public or to the Crown in trust for the public, such as highways and navigable waters;

(v)   certain obligations of a trustee, namely a trustee's obligation to produce accounts showing how he has dealt with the trust property, to make reparation for fraudulent breach of trust and to hand over trust property, or make good its value, to the beneficiaries;

(vi) any obligation of a third party to hand over trust property in his possession, unless he received the property in good faith;

(vii) any right to recover stolen property from the thief or from a person who knew of the theft; and

(viii) the right to challenge a deed on the ground that it is invalid ex facie ("on its face") or was forged.

7.   Impossibility, Illegality and Frustration

It may be impossible or illegal to perform a contract. The impossibility or illegality may either:

(a)   have existed at the date when the contract was made; or

(b)   be "supervening" impossibility or "supervening" illegality, *i.e.* have arisen between the time of the making of the contract and the date of its performance.

The term "frustration" (or "frustration of the adventure") is used in two senses: in its wider sense it covers supervening impossibility, supervening illegality, and also other supervening circumstances which, although they do not make performance of the contract either impossible or illegal, make it quite different from what the parties contemplated; in its narrower sense the term "frustration" denotes only these other supervening circumstances, and supervening impossibility and supervening illegality are then treated as distinct from frustration.

(a)   *Impossibility or Illegality Existing at Date of Contract*

If it is either impossible or illegal for the parties to perform the contract both at the time when it is made and at any future time, then the contract is void from the beginning, and no rights or obligations arise out of it.

Impossibility occurs when the parties are under some material error about the facts of their "contract"; *e.g.* by the Sale of Goods Act 1979 where there is a contract for the sale of specific goods, and the goods without the knowledge of the seller have perished at the time when the contract is made, the contract is void. Illegality occurs when the parties "contract" to do something which is void by statute or at common law.

In situations coming under this heading there is no question of extinction of contractual obligations, since the "contracts", being void, have never had any legal existence at all.

(b) *Frustration*

The term "frustration" is here used in its wider sense as including supervening impossibility and supervening illegality.

Frustration is sometimes described as an exception to the general rule that a party who fails to perform his part of a contract is liable for breach of contract even where his failure is not due to any fault on his part. This general rule would apply, for instance, if a party found that he did not have enough money to perform the contract when performance became due.

Frustration exists where, without fault on the part of either party, certain sets of circumstances arise which prevent the contract from being performed by one or both of the parties either at all or in any manner similar to that contemplated by the parties. The contract is at an end, and no damages can be claimed for failure to perform it.

The circumstances giving rise to frustration may be:

   (i) supervening impossibility;

   (ii) supervening illegality; or

   (iii) other supervening circumstances which fundamentally alter the nature of the contract.

(i) Supervening impossibility

A contract may be terminated by supervening impossibility where performance of the contract depends on the existence of a certain state of facts which has ceased to exist by the time when performance is due. The impossibility may result from:

   1. rei interitus ("destruction of the subject-matter");

   2. "constructive total destruction"; or

   3. change in the condition of one of the parties.

1. *Rei interitus*

This, the most obvious example of supervening impossibility, occurs where specific property essential to the contract is accidentally destroyed, as where a music hall hired for a concert on a particular day has been burned down (*Taylor* v. *Caldwell* (1863) 3 B. & S. 826, an English case), or where specific goods which are the subject-matter of an agreement to sell perish without any fault on the part of seller or buyer before the ownership of the goods passes to the buyer (Sale of Goods Act 1979, s. 7).

2. *Constructive total destruction*

Actual total destruction is not always necessary for supervening impossibility: where the subject-matter is so changed that, although it is still in existence, it is no longer available for the purposes of the contract, there is said to be "constructive total destruction," and this has the same legal effect as actual total destruction.

Examples of constructive total destruction are a house becoming uninhabitable during a lease because of subsidence caused by mining operations (*Allan* v. *Robertson's Trustees* (1891) 18 R. 932), a mansion-house which has been let being requisitioned by military authorities on the outbreak of war (*Mackeson* v. *Boyd*, 1942 S.C. 56), and a right of salmon fishing being made incapable of being exercised when the area came to be used as a danger zone for aerial gunnery and bombing practice (*Tay Salmon Fisheries Co. Ltd.* v. *Speedie*, 1929 S.C. 593).

3. *Change in condition of one of the parties*

Performance may become impossible because of some change in the condition of one of the parties: the effect of a party's death, bankruptcy, insanity or serious illness may be to terminate the contract. Thus, a contract involving delectus personae ("choice of person"), such as a contract of employment or of partnership, is dissolved by the death of the person who was specially chosen because of his personal qualities; the bankruptcy of a partner dissolves a partnership unless there is agreement to the contrary (Partnership Act 1890, s. 33); insanity dissolves a contract which is of such a nature that it can be performed only by a sane person; and there is an instance of illness dissolving a contract in the English case of *Robinson* v. *Davison* (1871) L.R. 6 Ex. 269, which concerned the inability of a pianist to perform her contract because of illness.

(ii) **Supervening illegality**

If a change in the law makes performance of a contract illegal, the contract is dissolved. For instance, by the Partnership Act 1890 a partnership is dissolved by the happening of any event which makes it unlawful for the business of the firm to be carried on or for the members of the firm to carry it on in partnership.

Supervening illegality often results from the outbreak of war, *e.g. James B. Fraser & Co. Ltd.* v. *Denny, Mott & Dickson Ltd.*, 1944 S.C.(H.L.) 35:

In 1929 two companies, F. and D., entered into a contract for the supply of imported red and white pine wood by D. to F. In 1939, as a result of the outbreak of war, restrictions were, by emergency legislation, imposed on transactions in that type of timber. One effect of the legislation was to make it unlawful for D. to supply F. in accordance with the terms of the contract.

The contract was held to have been terminated by this supervening emergency legislation.

If, however, a change in the law merely makes performance of a contract more expensive or more difficult, the contract is not dissolved; *e.g.* a contract for the supply of certain goods would not be dissolved merely because later legislation imposed a new tax or duty on the goods with the result that the contract became unprofitable.

(iii) Other supervening circumstances fundamentally altering nature of contract

Between the time of the making of the contract and the time for its performance, events may occur which, although they do not make performance of the contract either impossible or illegal, make it quite different from that which the parties contemplated. To cases in this category the term "frustration" in its narrower sense is applied. The principle operating in these cases is an extension of the principle which operates where there is supervening impossibility or supervening illegality.

There are examples in a series of English cases, known as "the Coronation cases," which arose out of contracts to hire rooms on the route of Edward VII's coronation procession, which was postponed owing to the King's illness.

Similarly, the English case of *Jackson* v. *Union Marine Insurance Co. Ltd.* (1874) L.R. 10 C.P. 125, shows how unforeseen delay, even although neither party may be liable for it, may bring a contract to an end where performance of the contract after the delay would in a business sense be quite a different thing from the performance originally intended:

J. contracted to send his ship with all possible speed, unless prevented by perils of the sea, from Liverpool to Newport, and there load for San Francisco a cargo of iron rails which were required for the construction of a railway.

The ship sailed from Liverpool on January 2, 1872, went aground upon the rocks of Carnarvon Bay the following day, was refloated on February 18, and was repaired by the end of August, but meantime, in February, the charterers had thrown up the contract and chartered another ship to take the rails to San Francisco.

In spite of the fact that the delay had been caused by perils of the sea, for which according to the contract the shipowner was not to be responsible, the court held that the shipowner could not enforce the contract after such a long delay.

Theoretical basis of doctrine of frustration

There are several different views as to the theoretical basis of the doctrine of "frustration" in its wider sense, *e.g.*:

(a) There is the "implied term" theory, according to which there is an implied term in every contract that performance is to be given only if it remains possible, legal and fundamentally the same as the parties contemplated; that theory was criticised in *James B. Fraser & Co. Ltd.* v. *Denny, Mott & Dickson Ltd.*, 1944 S.C.(H.L.) 35, (see p. 344, above), on the ground that it did not explain *why* such a term should be implied.

(b) There is the "material change" theory, according to which, since contract is based on consent, a party is not bound to perform something which turns out to be radically different from what he consented to perform.

(c) The theory favoured in *James B. Fraser & Co. Ltd.* v. *Denny, Mott & Dickson Ltd.* was that the doctrine is a device by which the rules as to contracts expressed in absolute terms are reconciled by the courts with what justice demands; the doctrine enables the court to intervene to supply a just and reasonable solution in a situation which the parties did not anticipate.

Money paid before frustration occurs

When payment has been made in advance for a contract which is not performed because of "frustration" in the wider sense, it can be recovered in accordance with the doctrine of restitution, a branch of quasi-contract (see p. 405, below). The action which may be brought is an action for "repetition" (repayment) referred to as the "condictio causa data causa non secuta" ("action applicable when consideration has been given and consideration has not followed").

An instance of such an action is the case of *Cantiere San Rocco* v. *Clyde Shipbuilding and Engineering Co. Ltd.*, 1923 S.C.(H.L.) 105:

A Scottish company agreed to supply engines to an Austrian firm and payment was to be by instalments.

The first instalment had been paid but no engines had been built on the outbreak of the 1914–18 war which made performance of the contract impossible.

At the end of the war the buyers were held entitled to recover the instalment which they had paid, on the ground that the consideration for it had failed.

8. Breach of the Contract

Breach of the contract does not of itself bring a contract to an end, but if it is sufficiently material the party who is not in breach may treat the breach as a repudiation of the contract and himself rescind the contract. On rescission, see p. 323, above.

(A breach which is not sufficiently material to justify rescission and which therefore does not lead to the termination of the contract may still give rise to a claim of damages for the loss caused by the breach.)

Irritancies

A breach of contract may entitle the party who is not in breach to put an end to the contract if the contract includes an "irritancy" (a right to terminate the contract in certain circumstances).

There are two types of irritancies:

(a) Legal irritancies

These are irritancies imposed by law and not requiring to be expressly provided for. The only legal irritancies are for non-payment of feu-duty and for non-payment of rent. Legal irritancies can be "purged" at any time before decree is granted, *i.e.* they become unenforceable if the feuar or tenant pays the arrears at any time before the court finally declares that he has lost his right.

(b) Conventional irritancies

These are irritancies provided for by agreement between the parties; *e.g.* a contract may contain a clause that if A commits a particular breach of the contract B is to have the right to treat the contract as at an end. Conventional irritancies cannot normally be purged. However, the court would not enforce a conventional irritancy which was intended to be really a penalty, rather than a pre-estimate of the loss likely to arise from the breach.

There is an instance of a conventional irritancy in *Dorchester Studios (Glasgow) Ltd.* v. *Stone*, 1975 S.C.(H.L.) 56:

A sub-lease included a clause of irritancy according to which the sub-lease would come to an end if the sub-tenants allowed any part of their rent to remain unpaid for twenty-one days.

The rent due at Martinmas (November 11) 1972 was, by an oversight, not paid by the sub-tenants until December 13, 1972.

The principal tenants were held entitled to irritate (*i.e.* terminate) the lease, since the irritancy, being a conventional one, had not been purged by payment tendered on December 13.

Further Reading

Gloag and Henderson, *Introduction to the Law of Scotland*

J. A. Lillie, *The Mercantile Law of Scotland*

T. B. Smith, *A Short Commentary on the Law of Scotland*

David M. Walker, *Principles of Scottish Private Law*

David M. Walker, *The law of Contracts and related obligations in Scotland* (Butterworths)

David M. Walker, *The Law of Prescription and Limitation of Actions in Scotland* (W. Green & Son Ltd.)

Enid A. Marshall, *Scottish Cases on Contract* (W. Green & Son Ltd.)

EMPLOYMENT

THE law of employment is traditionally referred to in Scotland as "the law of master and servant." For legal purposes the more modern terms "employer" and "employee" have exactly the same meaning as "master" and "servant" respectively.

Employment is basically a contractual relationship by which the employee gives his services to the employer for a certain period in return for remuneration. The law of employment is, therefore, basically a branch of the law of contract.

However, there is much more to the relationship between employer and employee than the express terms in a contract between these two parties, and some writers take the view that in the twentieth century the employee has a "status," *i.e.* a position fixed by law, rather than a contractual relationship governed by a bargain made between him as an individual and his employer. It is certainly true that most employees at the present day are in reality not free to negotiate individually about the terms and conditions of their contracts of employment. There are two principal reasons for this:

1. A great mass of legislation has been passed in the nineteenth and twentieth centuries to regulate health, safety, welfare, wages, unemployment, industrial injury and redundancy, and for many other social and economic purposes; normally these statutory

provisions cannot be varied by a contract between an individual employer and an individual employee.

2. The rise of trade unions has resulted in widespread "collective bargaining," according to which terms and conditions of employment are settled for all the members of a category of employees by negotiations entered into by the trade union which represents them; there is little scope for an individually negotiated contract of employment.

These modern aspects of the relationship between employer and employee have added so much to the content of the law of master and servant that what was originally a branch of the law of contract has emerged in the twentieth century as a subject in its own right under the title of "industrial law" or "labour law," the former term being the one more generally adopted in Britain and the latter having American associations.

This chapter, however, is confined to the basic contractual relationship between employer and employee and the common law consequences of that relationship. While the existence of the main statutory provisions is indicated where necessary in the following sections, for the substance of these provisions reference must be made to works devoted to industrial law as a subject in its own right.

GENERAL NATURE OF RELATIONSHIP BETWEEN EMPLOYER AND EMPLOYEE

In some situations it is not easy and it may be important to distinguish employment, the relationship which arises from a contract of service, from other apparently similar relationships. In particular, an employee must be distinguished from:

1. an independent contractor;
2. an agent;
3. a partner;
4. a company director; and
5. a tenant.

1. Employee and Independent Contractor

Whereas an employee is under a contract of service, an independent contractor is under a contract for services. The distinction corresponds to that in Roman law between locatio operarum ("hiring of services") by which an employer engaged an employee, and locatio operis faciendi ("the letting out of work to be done") by which an employer engaged an independent contractor. The distinction is easy to recognise but difficult to define precisely.

As an illustration the case may be taken of a person, X, who wishes to build a house for himself: either he may himself engage

all the workmen required for the operation and give them the
necessary instructions, or he may take the more usual course of
placing the work in the hands of a builder who will have the responsibility of providing the necessary workmen; in the first situation the
workmen will be the employees of X, and X will have the right to
direct them not only as to what is to be done but also as to how it is
to be done, whereas in the second situation the relationship between
X and the builder will be that of employer and independent
contractor, and X will have no right to give detailed instructions as
to how the work is to be done.

There are three main reasons for the importance of the distinction
between employee and independent contractor:

(1) *Vicarious liability*

As a general rule an employer is liable "vicariously" (*i.e.* in the
place of the employee) for wrongs done by an employee within the
scope of the employment, but not liable for wrongs done by an
independent contractor. A traditional illustration is the contrast
between the coachman or chauffeur and the cabman:

> "My chauffeur is my servant; and if by negligent driving he
> runs over someone in the street, I am responsible. But the
> cabman whom I engage for a particular journey is not my
> servant; he is not under my orders; he has made a contract
> with me, not that he will obey my directions, but that he will
> drive me to a certain place: if an accident happens by his
> negligence, he is responsible and not I" (Salmond's *Law of Torts*,
> 15th ed., p. 610).

(2) *Duty to provide for safety*

An employer is under a common law duty to take reasonable
care for the personal safety of his individual employees, but is under
no such common law duty in relation to independent contractors
whom he employs.

(3) *Statutes*

For the purposes of very many modern statutes it is necessary to
distinguish an employee from an independent contractor; *e.g.* the
Employment Protection (Consolidation) Act 1978 applies to
employees only, and the Social Security Act 1975 provides for
different contributions and different benefits for "employed earners"
from those applicable to "self-employed earners" such as independent contractors. In deciding whether a person is an employee for
the purposes of a statutory provision the court must consider any
definition of that term included in the Act itself.

Guidance on the question of whether a person is an employee

or an independent contractor may be derived from the following factors:

(a) *Remuneration*

If the remuneration takes the form of salary or wages, the person is more likely to be an employee, whereas if it takes the form of a lump sum or of commission, he is more likely to be an independent contractor.

(b) *Number of employers*

An employee usually works for only one employer at a time, whereas an independent contractor often works for several employers at the same time.

(c) *Hours of work*

An employee normally has his hours of work fixed by his employer, whereas an independent contractor works at his own discretion.

(d) *Internal rules*

An employee is generally subject to a greater degree than an independent contractor to internal rules of the organisation for which he works.

None of these factors, however, gives a conclusive answer, and in many cases the courts have attempted to lay down a more general test which might be equally valid in differing circumstances. Of the various general tests which have been suggested the most notable are:

(a) the "control" test; and
(b) the "integration" (or "organisation") test.

(a) **The "control" test**

This is the traditional test. The relationship of employer and employee is considered to exist only where one person has the right to control the work done by, and the method of working of, another person.

This test is prominent in the two following Scottish cases:

(i) *Stephen* v. *Thurso Police Commissioners* (1876) 3 R. 535: This was a claim by Stephen for £500 as damages for severe injuries suffered when he stumbled in the dark over a heap of rubbish in a Thurso street. The commissioners were, Stephen said, in breach of a duty imposed on them by the Police and Improvement (Scotland) Act 1850 either to remove rubbish before dark or to fence and light it.

The commissioners put forward the defence that they had contracted with Swanson, a carter, for the removal by him of all rubbish from the streets and that, if there was negligence on the part of any one, it was Swanson who was liable, not the commissioners, *i.e.* they were claiming that Swanson was an independent contractor and that they could not, therefore, be made liable for Swanson's negligence.

The court held that, since the commissioners retained control over the execution of Swanson's work, he was their employee and they were liable for his negligence.

The narrowness and the importance of the distinction in some cases between employee and independent contractor are emphasised by Lord Gifford, at p. 541:

"The delicacy and difficulty of the case arises from the necessity of distinguishing between the negligence of a servant employed by a master, and the negligence of a tradesman employed by a person to do some work on his property, or the negligence of the workmen of such a tradesman. A master is liable for damage occasioned by the act or by the negligence of his servant acting in his employment. . . . On the other hand, a person who employs an independent tradesman or contractor to build or to repair or to take down his house, or to execute some specific work, is not liable for the fault or negligence of such tradesman or contractor, or of the workmen whom they may employ . . .

"But there are many cases where it is exceedingly difficult to tell whether the party directly guilty of the fault or negligence is the servant of a master who will be responsible in the damage caused or merely the independent employee of an employer who will not be answerable for the employee's or contractor's fault and not liable in damages occasioned thereby. The present case is one in which there is great difficulty in determining whether the persons who were directly negligent, that is, the persons who were to blame for leaving the heap on the public street unlighted and unfenced, were in point of law to be held the servants of the commissioners, or were merely the workmen of an independent contractor, for whose negligence the commissioners are not answerable."

(ii) *Scottish Insurance Commissioners* v. *Church of Scotland*, 1914 S.C. 16: This case concerned the interpretation of the phrase "employment in the United Kingdom under any contract of service," as used in the National Insurance Act 1911.

The court held that assistant ministers were not employed persons within the meaning of the Act because they were not subject to the control and direction of a master under a contract of service.

Lord Kinnear, after referring to the "order and control" which an employer had over the work done by the employee, stated, at p. 23:

> "In a contract by which one undertakes to produce a given result, but so that in the actual execution of the work he is not under the direction of the person for whom it is done, but may use his own discretion in things which are not specifically fixed by the contract itself, the relation of master and servant does not exist. The employer, in cases of that kind, is not liable for the acts and defaults of the person employed, just because, although he may take benefit from the work and pay for it, he is not in the position of an employer of a servant, entitled to interfere in the direction and control of his work."

It must be noted that the "control" test does not mean that the employer actually controls the work done by his employee; the *right* to control, even although not usually exercised, is all that is required.

Further, the control is often exercised, not by the employer personally, but by him through some other employee who is the superior of the person actually doing the work; in any undertaking other than a very small-scale one the employer necessarily delegates his right of control. Hence the "control" test is sometimes given the title of "the direction-or-delegation test." It is only in this form that the "control" test can be applied to most employment situations in modern industrial life.

There are, however, some employees for whom the "control" test, even in its developed form of the "direction-or-delegation" test, is not appropriate. Many persons who exercise professional skills or do work of a highly technical nature cannot properly be regarded as having their methods of working "controlled" by their employers, and yet they may undoubtedly be employees. Difficulties have arisen especially in connection with hospital boards, which could be sued for the negligence of qualified medical staff appointed by them, although they had no right themselves to control the treatment of patients. Not only may an employer have insufficient skill or knowledge to control some of his employees: he may even be prohibited by statute from doing so; *e.g.* by the Mines and Quarries Act 1954 the owner of a mine is not entitled to appoint himself as the manager of it unless he has certain qualifications.

Other tests have been suggested in order to overcome the objections to the "control" test, which is still, however, the most generally accepted test.

(b) **The "integration" (or "organisation") test**

According to this test a person is an employee if he is an integral part of the organisation for which he works, and not merely accessory to that organisation.

An explanation of the test was given by Denning L.J. in *Stevenson, Jordan and Harrison Ltd.* v. *Macdonald and Evans* [1952] 1 T.L.R. 101, at p. 111:

> "It is almost impossible to give a precise definition of the distinction (*between a contract of service and a contract for services*). It is often easy to recognise a contract of service when you see it, but difficult to say wherein the difference lies. A ship's master, a chauffeur, and a reporter on the staff of a newspaper are all employed under a contract of service; but a ship's pilot, a taxi-man, and a newspaper contributor are employed under a contract for services. One feature which seems to run through the instances is that, under a contract of service, a man is employed as part of the business, and his work is done as an integral part of the business; whereas, under a contract for services, his work, although done for the business, is not integrated into it but is only accessory to it."

That case concerned the copyright of a textbook on business management written by an accountant who had been employed by a company engaged in business management. Part of the book had been composed by the accountant for the purpose of a particular assignment given him by the company; another part consisted of public lectures prepared and delivered by him during his employment. The question which the court had to decide was whether the copyright belonged to the company (as it would do if the accountant's authorship was part of his service) or to the accountant himself (on the ground that his authorship was independent of his contract of service).

The court held that there was here a mixed contract, partly of service and partly for services: the copyright of the section dealing with the particular assignment belonged to the company, whereas the copyright of the section consisting of the public lectures belonged to the accountant himself. The court further held that, since the two sections could be separated, the company was entitled to restrain the publishers from publishing the first section.

The "integration" test is, however, open to the objection that it is too wide, since persons other than employees can be regarded as integrated into an organisation, *e.g.* partners in a firm and directors in a company.

The conclusion is that no one test is valid in all situations where it is necessary to distinguish the employee from the independent contractor.

2. Employee and Agent

An agent is a person who has express or implied authority to act on behalf of another person called "the principal." Agency involves two contracts:

(a) a contract of agency between the principal and the agent; and

(b) a contract made by the agent on behalf of his principal with a third party.

Once the agent has made the contract with the third party, he drops out of the transaction, and the law recognises a contractual relationship as existing between the principal and the third party. For example, A, the owner of a house, may instruct B, an estate agent, to sell his house for a certain sum; the function of B is to bring A into a contractual relationship with a purchaser, C; the law will then recognise a contract for the sale of the house as existing between A as seller and C as purchaser.

An employee as such is not an agent, but some employees are agents: *e.g.* the worker at a factory bench has normally no authority to make contracts with third parties on behalf of his employer, and is therefore normally not an agent, but the purchasing officer of a company will have authority to buy goods from third parties as agent for the company.

(Similarly, an independent contractor may or may not be an agent for the person employing him; *e.g.* an estate agent instructed to sell a house is normally both an independent contractor and an agent, whereas an independent contractor instructed to build a bridge is normally not an agent.)

3. Employee and Partner

By the Partnership Act 1890 partnership is the relationship which exists between persons who carry on a business in common with a view of profit and without being either registered as a company or incorporated in some other way.

The distinction between an employee and a partner may cause difficulty in the following situations:

(a) A person working in a business may own business property jointly with others.

For example, in *Sharpe* v. *Carswell*, 1910 S.C. 391, the facts were that S. had owned ten sixty-fourth shares of the sailing schooner "Dolphin" and had been employed as master at a fixed remuneration.

S. died as a result of injuries sustained on board and his widow claimed compensation under the Workmen's Compensation Act 1906, on the ground that S. had been a "workman."

The court held that the fact that S. held shares did not make him a partner in the trading of the vessel: he was a "workman," and so his widow was entitled to compensation under the Act.

The Partnership Act 1890 provides that part-ownership does not of itself create a partnership.

(b) A person working in a business may share gross returns of the business.

For example, in *Clark* v. *Jamieson*, 1909 S.C. 132, the question arose of whether C., a member of the crew of a small cargo boat who was remunerated by a share of the gross earnings of the vessel, was a workman for the purposes of the Workmen's Compensation Act 1906 so that his mother and sister might claim compensation on his death.

The court held that C. was a workman, not a partner.

The Partnership Act 1890 provides that sharing of gross returns does not of itself create a partnership.

(c) A person working in a business may receive a share of net profits (which are the returns of the business after deduction of the expenses of the conduct of the business).

The Partnership Act 1890 provides that receipt by a person of a share of the net profits of a business is prima facie evidence that he is a partner in the business; this means that he is presumed to be a partner until evidence is brought forward to "rebut" (contradict) the presumption; receipt of a share of the net profits is not conclusive evidence that a partnership exists, and there is an express provision in the Act that a contract for the remuneration of a servant of a person engaged in a business by a share of the profits of the business does not of itself make the servant a partner in the business.

4. Employee and Company Director

A director of a company is not as such an employee of the company; he is an "officer" of it.

However, a director may hold a salaried employment in addition to his directorship, and he would then be an employee of the company, but his rights and duties as a director would remain distinct from his rights and duties as an employee.

5. Employee and Tenant

Where a person lives in a house owned by his employer, it may be difficult to decide whether he occupies the house as employee or as tenant. The former type of occupancy is not tenancy but merely "service occupancy," and the person living in the house does not have the rights and duties of a tenant.

The test generally accepted is that if the occupancy of the house is necessary for the performance of the contract of service then it is a service occupancy, and that otherwise it is a tenancy.

The distinction is often important on the termination of employment: in the case of service occupancy the employee must remove from the house immediately, whereas in the case of a tenancy he will have the rights of a tenant as regards notice to quit and other matters.

FORMATION OF THE CONTRACT OF EMPLOYMENT

A contract of service for a period of more than a year requires probative writing, or the equivalent of probative writing, for its formation. If the writing is only informal (*i.e.* is not attested, holograph, or adopted as holograph), a contract of service for a period of more than a year may become binding for its full duration by the operation of the principle of rei interventus (see p. 245, above). The rei interventus usually takes the form of the employee's entering upon the employment and being paid wages by the employer for the work done. Where there is no writing at all, rei interventus may make an oral contract binding for a period applicable by custom or usage to the particular employment but in no case for a period longer than a year.

A contract of service for a period of less than a year may be constituted orally and may be proved by parole evidence. If there is in fact writing in such a case, parole evidence may still be brought forward to show that the contract included additional terms which are not set out in the writing. Where terms and conditions of employment are contained in notices exhibited at the place of employment or are issued in some other form by the employer, they are imported into an oral contract of employment, provided the employee has been made aware of them. It is for the party who is basing his claim on the contract of employment to prove its terms.

A contract of service may be created by implication where without any written or oral agreement two parties act in the capacities of employer and employee respectively, the former paying remuneration in return for services rendered by the latter. There is a presumption that remuneration is payable for services which are rendered by one party and accepted by the other, except where the first party resides with and is a child or other close relative of the second party. The presumption may be rebutted by proof that it is a professional or trade custom to render the services in question gratuitously. Implied contracts of service often arise where there is a change in the legal status of an employer, *e.g.* where an individual or a partnership is converted into a limited company and so becomes a different legal person, or where a company goes into liquidation and its business is continued by the liquidator.

The formation of a contract of service is now affected by a number of statutes. Several of these modify the rule of the common law that an employer is free to choose whomsoever he wishes as his employee: in engaging an employee, an employer must now have regard to:

1. the Sex Discrimination Act 1975;
2. the Race Relations Act 1976;
3. the Rehabilitation of Offenders Act 1974; and
4. the Disabled Persons (Employment) Act 1944.

In addition, while a contract of service may still be *formed* without writing, the employer will require to comply with statutory provisions as to:

5. particulars of the terms of employment.

1.   Sex Discrimination Act 1975

By this Act it is unlawful to discriminate, directly or indirectly, in employment matters on the grounds of sex or marital status. There are specified exceptions to the principle of the Act (*e.g.* employment in a private household or in a business employing not more than five persons).

An employee or disappointed applicant has the right to apply to an industrial tribunal if he has suffered unlawful discrimination, and may be awarded compensation.

The Act established the Equal Opportunities Commission to promote the principle of the Act. The Commission can issue notices to employers requiring them to discontinue certain acts which contravene the legislation, and it can also bring proceedings against offending employers before courts of law and industrial tribunals.

2.   Race Relations Act 1976

This Act repeals and extends earlier legislation on racial discrimination. By the Act it is unlawful for an employer to discriminate against an employee or applicant on racial grounds (*i.e.* grounds of colour, race, nationality or ethnic or national origins). There are specified exceptions, but these are more limited than the exceptions in the Sex Discrimination Act (*e.g.* an exception is made for employment in a private household, but there is no exception for small businesses).

Other provisions of the Act are parallel to those of the Sex Discrimination Act: the individual has a right to apply to an industrial tribunal, and the Act established the Commission for Racial Equality.

3.   Rehabilitation of Offenders Act 1974

The purpose of this Act is to draw a veil over "spent convictions" of persons who have been convicted of criminal offences in the past.

The conviction becomes "spent" when a specified period has elapsed without any further conviction. The period varies according to the sentence (*e.g.* if the sentence was imprisonment for not more than six months, the rehabilitation period is seven years). The Act does not apply to sentences of more than thirty months' imprisonment.

A spent conviction, or failure to disclose a spent conviction, is declared by the Act to be not a proper ground for excluding a person from any employment, or for prejudicing him in any way in any employment.

4. Disabled Persons (Employment) Act 1944

The aim of this Act is to assist handicapped persons to obtain employment. The Act established a register of disabled persons, and provides that every employer of twenty or more persons must include a quota of registered disabled persons. The quota fixed by the Disabled Persons (Standard Percentage) Order 1946 is three per cent.

It is an offence for an employer to employ a person other than a registered disabled person if by so doing his quota becomes less than the statutory quota. An employer may, however, apply for a permit exempting him from complying with the Act in respect of a particular person or persons.

5. Particulars of the Terms of Employment

By provisions now contained in the Employment Protection (Consolidation) Act 1978 an employer must, within thirteen weeks after the beginning of an employee's period of employment, supply the employee with written particulars of the terms of employment. Some categories of employees are excluded (*e.g.* merchant seamen and civil servants).

An employee has a right to apply to an industrial tribunal for a declaration of particulars which ought to have been supplied to him. A dispute over particulars which have been supplied may be referred to a tribunal by either the employer or the employee.

DUTIES OF EMPLOYEE TO EMPLOYER

The duties of an employee to his employer still depend mainly on the common law.

The contract of employment may specify what the employee's duties are to be, but if there is no express provision to the contrary in that contract, certain general duties of the employee to his employer are implied by the common law. The main ones are:
1. personal service;
2. obedience;
3. loyalty;
4. reasonable care.

The most important statutory addition to an employee's duties is that contained in the Health and Safety at Work etc. Act 1974. By that Act it is the duty of every employee while at work to take reasonable care for the health and safety of himself and of other persons who may be affected by his conduct; he must co-operate with his employer and other persons in securing compliance with their duties under the Act, and he must not intentionally or recklessly interfere with or misuse anything provided under the Act for health, safety or welfare.

1. Personal Service

The relationship between employer and employee is a personal one, and the employee is not entitled, without his employer's consent, to delegate performance of his duties to another person.

2. Obedience

The employee must obey all lawful orders given to him by his employer.

Whether a particular order is lawful or not is sometimes a difficult question. An employee would be quite justified in disobeying an order to do something criminal or to do something illegal or immoral. The law would not protect an employee who chose to obey orders of that kind: if prosecuted for a crime the employee could not put forward as a defence that he committed the crime on his employer's orders, and if the employee were guilty of some civil wrong done to a third party on his employer's orders, the third party would be entitled to sue the employee for damages.

An employee would also be justified in disobeying an order which would expose him to a risk which was not reasonably within the contemplation of the parties when the contract of employment was made.

An employer cannot lawfully, except in an emergency, order an employee to do work of a different kind from that for which he was engaged.

Whether an employer can lawfully order an employee to change from one place of employment to another depends on circumstances, including especially the position held by the employee and the nature of the employer's business. If the service is personal, such as that of a domestic servant, a private secretary, or a chauffeur, the employee must accompany the employer wherever he goes within the United Kingdom. If the contract is for work to be done at a place of employment rather than for personal service, the general rule apparently is that the employer is not entitled to remove the employee to another place of employment which would be inconvenient for the employee, but circumstances might indicate that the parties intended otherwise; *e.g.* the general rule would probably apply to an employee doing routine work at his employer's premises, but not to an employee occupying a high position in a business carried on by his employer at several different premises throughout the country; the employer may be entitled to direct the employee to work at a particular place outside the United Kingdom, if work abroad was contemplated at the time when the contract was entered into, but he cannot lawfully transfer the employee to a country in which the employee's life would be endangered by risks which he had not agreed to undertake.

3. Loyalty

An employee must not allow any personal interest to conflict with loyal service to his employer. He must act with good faith towards his employer, and put his employer's interests before any conflicting interest of his own. This general duty takes different forms according to circumstances.

If the employee handles money belonging to his employer, or transacts with his employer's goods, he must account to his employer for money received and profits made, and is not entitled to retain additional benefits secretly conferred on him by third parties with whom he deals in the course of his employment. In some cases, however, the employer may consent, expressly or impliedly, to his employee's retaining benefits conferred by third parties, *e.g.* in occupations where tips are customary.

The duty of loyalty also requires the employee to refrain from doing, even in his spare time, anything which would harm his employer's interests; he must not, for instance, secretly work for a rival of his employer, or divulge trade secrets or other confidential information obtained in the course of his employment. It is advisable for the employer to safeguard his own position by having appropriate provisions about such matters included in the contract of employment, rather than to rely on this general, but rather vague, duty of loyalty implied by the common law.

It is to be noted that the employee's duty of loyalty emerges only after the relationship of employer and employee has been established: the contract of employment is not one of the contracts uberrimae fidei ("of the utmost good faith") (see p. 283, above), which require full disclosure of material facts at the time when they are entered into; a person seeking employment is therefore not bound to disclose past misconduct to a prospective employer.

Whether the employee's duty of loyalty makes it necessary for him to disclose to his employer misconduct or fault on the part of his fellow-employees depends on the position held by the employee and the other circumstances of the case.

Duty of loyalty and employee's inventions

The employer's common law duty of loyalty has been considered by the courts in the past in connection with inventions made by an employee.

Questions arose as to whether the employer or the employee was the "true and first inventor" for the purposes of the Patents Act 1949, whether the employee had undertaken in his contract of service to assign his right to apply for a patent to his employer, and whether, if the employee was entitled to take out the patent, he was bound to hold it in trust for his employer, giving the employer the benefit of it.

The English case of *British Syphon Co. Ltd.* v. *Homewood* [1956] 1 W.L.R. 1190, [1956] 2 All E.R. 897, illustrates how the court could decide at common law that it was inconsistent with the employee's duty of loyalty for the employee to take the benefit of a patent for himself:

The company manufactured syphons for soda water, and H. was employed as chief technician in charge of design and development.

The company had been given the benefit of H.'s invention of a plastic top which he had been requested to devise.

Later, without any request being made to him by the company, H. invented a soda-water dispenser, and applied for a patent for it.

The court held that it was not consistent with good faith as between employer and employee that H. should be entitled to invent something relating to the company's business and withhold it from the company; the nature of H.'s employment made it his duty to give to the company the best possible advice on design and development.

Substantial modernisation of the legislation on patents was made by the Patents Act 1977. One of the important features of this Act is the inclusion of statutory provisions relating to employees' inventions. The provisions do not apply to pre-1978 inventions.

In future, therefore, the common law on this topic will be gradually replaced by the provisions of the Act of 1977, which in outline are:

(a) *Ownership*

An invention made by an employee belongs to his employer only if either:

(i) it was made in the course of the normal duties of the employee or in the course of duties specifically assigned to him, *and* the circumstances in either case were such that an invention might reasonably be expected to result from the duties; or

(ii) the invention was made in the course of the employees' duties *and*, because of the nature of his duties and responsibilities, he had a special obligation to further the interests of the employer's undertaking.

In all other circumstances, the invention belongs to the employee.

(b) *Compensation*

Where an employer owns an invention which was made by his employee and the employer has obtained a patent for it, then the employee may claim an award of compensation from the employer if the patent has been of "outstanding benefit" to the employer. For the purposes of this test the size and nature of the employer's undertaking are amongst the matters to be considered.

Where the invention belonged initially to the employee, and the employee by contract assigned his rights in the invention to his employer, the employee is still entitled to an award of compensation in so far as the benefit derived by him from the contract is inadequate in relation to the benefit derived by the employer from the patent.

The award of compensation under these provisions is intended to secure for the employee a fair share of the benefit which the employer has derived, or may reasonably be expected to derive, from the patent.

(c) *Contracts relating to inventions*

Any term in a contract entered into by an employee with, or at the request of, his employer is unenforceable against the employee in so far as it diminishes the employee's rights in inventions or patents. This provision, however, is not to be taken as derogating from any duty of confidentiality owed by the employee to his employer.

4. Reasonable Care

An employee must exercise reasonable care in his work. This is a standard which varies according to the facts of the case, such as the nature of the employment and the qualifications and experience which the employee professes to have.

If as a result of an employee's failure to take reasonable care a third party is injured and successfully claims damages from the employer, then the employer is entitled to be "indemnified" by the negligent employee, *i.e.* to recover from the negligent employee what he himself has had to pay to the third party. In practice, however, the employer is insured against such claims made by third parties, and neither he nor the insurance company would enforce this right of indemnity against the employee.

DUTIES OF EMPLOYER TO EMPLOYEE

Modern statute law has greatly extended the duties of employers to employees.

Many of an employer's duties are now of purely statutory origin, *e.g.* the employer's duty not to discriminate against an employee on grounds of sex or marital status under the Sex Discrimination Act 1975 or on racial grounds under the Race Relations Act 1976, and the employer's duty to allow time off work to an employee who is a trade union official or who wishes to take part in trade union activity or who has public duties to perform (*e.g.* as a member of a local authority) under the Employment Protection (Consolidation) Act 1978.

Where an employer fails to fulfil a statutory duty, the course normally open to the employee is to apply to an industrial tribunal for an appropriate remedy, which will often be payment of compensation. An industrial tribunal normally consists of three members—a chairman who is legally qualified and two lay members, one from a trade union panel and one from an an employers' panel. On a question of law, an appeal may be made against the decision of the industrial tribunal to the Employment Appeal Tribunal ("EAT"), with the possibility of a further appeal to the Court of Session. The Employment Appeal Tribunal consists of judges (one at least of whom must be a Court of Session judge) and of persons appointed for their special knowledge or experience of industrial relations (either as representatives of employers or as representatives of workers). It may sit at any place in Britain, and either as a single tribunal or in two or more divisions. Normally proceedings are taken before a judge and either two or four appointed members (with equal representation as between employers and workers).

Reference must be made to works on industrial law for any adequate treatment of the employer's many statutory duties to his employee. The main statute on individual employment law is now the Employment Protection (Consolidation) Act 1978 which consolidated provisions formerly contained in the Redundancy Payments Act 1965, the Contracts of Employment Act 1972, the Trade Union and Labour Relations Act 1974, the Employment Protection Act 1975 and statutes which had amended these Acts. The Act of 1978 has itself been amended by the Employment Act 1980.

It should further be borne in mind that to view the contract of employment as now giving rise to duties of an individual employer to an individual employee is to over-simplify the situation: the employer, in practice and by law, owes many duties to and through trade unions, and "collective bargaining", and codes of practice have a vital importance which finds no recognition in the principles of the common law.

In the following paragraphs, the employer's common law duties are considered under the headings:

1. remuneration;
2. providing work;
3. testimonials and references;
4. indemnity; and
5. providing for the employee's safety.

1. Remuneration

The employer must pay the agreed remuneration. If no express provision has been made about remuneration before the employee enters on his employment, the employer will be bound to pay remuneration on the ground that there is an implied undertaking to pay for the employee's services.

Where there is no provision as to how the remuneration is to be calculated, the employee is entitled to receive the remuneration which is customary in the particular locality for the type of work in question. If there is no custom applicable, the employee is apparently entitled to be paid on a "quantum meruit" ("as much as he deserved") basis.

Of the statutory provisions applicable to remuneration the most important are:

(a) Truck Acts of 1831, 1896 and 1940

These made contracts to pay workmen their wages otherwise than in current coin of the realm "illegal, null and void" and prohibited deductions from workmen's wages for fines, bad or negligent work, or use of the employer's materials, unless certain conditions were fulfilled.

Although the evil of paying wages in goods ("truck") or of requiring the employee to spend his wages at a specified place or in a specified manner is not part of the twentieth century industrial scene, the Truck Acts of 1831 and 1896 are still in force and must be taken account of by an employer who wishes to make deductions (other than those authorised by statute for such purposes as income tax and social security) from the wages of employees engaged in manual labour; deductions for meals supplied at the employer's premises, for instance, are permissible only on conditions laid down by the Act of 1831, and it was to confirm that point that the Truck Act 1940 was passed as a result of the case of *Pratt* v. *Cook, Son & Co. (St. Paul's) Ltd.* [1940] A.C. 437, in which a packer who had been employed by wholesale drapers for over fifteen years, successfully claimed from his employers the illegal deductions of 10s. weekly which they had been making for dinners and teas served on the premises.

The Truck Acts were, however, modified by the Payment of Wages Act 1960, which provides that the employer may, at the written request of an employee, pay wages into a bank account in the employee's name or by postal order, money order or cheque.

(b) Wages Councils Act 1979

Wages councils are the successors of the trade boards introduced in 1909 to deal with "sweated" industries in which workers' remuneration was notoriously low.

The establishment and operation of wages councils are now governed by the Wages Councils Act 1979 which consolidated the legislation on the subject previously contained mainly in the Wages Councils Act 1959 (itself a consolidating Act) and the Employment Protection Act 1975.

An order establishing a wages council may be made by the Secretary of State for Employment either on his own initiative or on the recommendation of the Advisory, Conciliation and Arbitration Service ("ACAS"). An application for the establishment of a wages council may be made jointly by the employers' side and the workers' side of an industry to the Secretary of State who may refer the application to ACAS. The Secretary of State may also abolish a wages council or vary its field.

A wages council has power to make orders fixing remuneration, requiring holidays to be allowed and fixing any other terms and conditions for the workers in the particular industry or trade.

A wages council may be converted into a "statutory joint industrial council" by an order made by the Secretary of State after consultation with representative organisations of employers and workers. The object of this provision is to ease the transition from a wages council to voluntary collective bargaining: a statutory joint industrial council is the "half-way house," differing from a wages council in that it is composed solely of representatives from the employers' and the workers' sides without any independent members.

The occupations for which wages councils exist are those which are typically low-paid, substantially staffed by women, and difficult for trade unions to organise (*e.g.* dressmaking, hairdressing and retailing).

The number of wages councils was reduced in 1979 from forty-one to thirty-four by an amalgamation of nine councils for the retail trade into two new councils. Further amalgamations are under consideration. No new wages council has been established since 1956.

(c) Equal Pay Act 1970, as amended

This Act, which took effect as from December 29, 1975, provides for equal pay as between the sexes for "like work" or work which is "rated as equivalent." The Act was amended by the Sex Discrimination Act 1975, and is set out in full in its amended form in a schedule to that Act.

(d) Employment Protection (Consolidation) Act 1978, as amended

This Act consolidated most of the legislation on individual employment passed since 1963. Amongst the provisions affecting remuneration are:

(i) the requirement that the employer must, within thirteen weeks after the beginning of an employee's period of employment, supply the employee with written particulars of the terms of employment, including specific information relating to remuneration; and

(ii) the rights of an employee to an "itemised pay statement," showing gross remuneration, deductions, and net remuneration to a "guarantee payment" for "workless" days, to remuneration where he is suspended from work on medical grounds, to remuneration for time off for carrying out certain trade union duties if he is a trade union official, and to maternity pay.

Some amendments were made by the Employment Act 1980 (*e.g.* the addition of a new right to paid time off for ante-natal care).

2. Providing Work

An employer is not always under a duty to provide work for his employee.

The duty to provide work exists where the employee's remuneration depends on the actual performance of work, *e.g.* where the employee is a piece-worker or is paid wholly or partly by commission.

In other circumstances, however, the general rule is that the employer is not bound to provide work, and so the employee has at common law no legal right to complain if he is kept idle or if his employer dismisses him instantly with a payment of wages in lieu of notice.

There are exceptions to this general rule in the case of those employees whose careers depend on publicity; *e.g.* an actor who is not provided with work in accordance with his contract of employment may lose an opportunity of enhancing his reputation, and may sue his employer for damages for loss of publicity even although the employer is willing to pay the agreed remuneration.

3. Testimonials and References

An employer is at common law not under any duty to provide an employee with a testimonial or a reference, or to answer inquiries from interested parties as to the employee's character. The employee has, therefore, no remedy against his employer or former employer, however great the loss resulting to the employee from the lack of a testimonial or reference.

If, however, the employer chooses to give a reference or testimonial, he may become liable to pay damages to:

(a) the employee; or

(b) the third party, such as another employer, to whom the testimonial or reference is addressed.

(a) Liability to employee

The employer may become liable to the employee for defamation of the employee's character: if the employer makes a statement, either written or oral, which is false and imputes to the employee a bad character or incapacity in his trade, profession or occupation, the employee is entitled to damages.

The liability arises whether the statement is made to the employee himself (as in a testimonial) or to a third party (*e.g.* a prospective employer who "takes up" a reference). On this point the law of England differs from that of Scotland: under English law no damages can be claimed unless the statement has been communicated to a third party.

An employer who is sued for defamation of an employee's character may put forward the defence of veritas ("truth") or the defence of qualified privilege.

Veritas

To succeed in this defence the employer must prove that the statement was substantially true. It may not be necessary for him to prove the truth of *every* part of the statement, since the Defamation Act 1952 provides that where a statement contains two or more distinct charges against the pursuer, a defence of veritas will not necessarily fail just because the truth of every charge is not proved, *provided* the words not proved to be true do not materially injure the pursuer's reputation when one considers the truth of the other words; *e.g.* an employer might have made a statement that an employee was "dishonest and incompetent," and the employer might have been able to prove that the employee was incompetent but not that he was dishonest; in that case the defence of veritas would probably fail because the charge not proved to be true (dishonesty) would materially injure the reputation even of an incompetent employee; if, on the other hand, the employer had been able to prove that the employee was dishonest but not that he was incompetent, then he might very well be successful in his defence of veritas because the charge not proved to be true (incompetence) would in many situations not materially injure the reputation of an employee who had been proved to be dishonest.

Qualified privilege

This is a much more probable defence for the employer. To be successful in this defence the employer need prove only that he made the statement honestly (*i.e.* that he *believed* it to be true), and that he made it on a "privileged occasion." An occasion is "privileged" where the person making the statement is doing so because of some legal or moral duty; *e.g.* the occasion would be privileged if an employer were making a statement about his employee to a prospective employer or to an employment agency through which the employee had been engaged, since these parties would have a legitimate interest in knowing about the employee's character; on the other hand, the occasion would not be privileged if the employer communicated his statement about the employee to outsiders who had no legitimate interest in the matter; this accounts for the words "to those whom it may concern" which often appear at the beginning of a testimonial.

The employee can counter the defence of qualified privilege by proving "malice," *i.e.* by proving that the employer was not acting in good faith but out of spite.

(b) Liability to third parties

Third parties, such as another employer, may suffer loss as a result of a false statement included in a testimonial or reference.

If the statement is fraudulent, *i.e.* was made by the employer in the knowledge that it was false or in reckless disregard of whether it was true or false, the third party will be entitled to damages for fraud.

If the statement was made negligently but without deliberate dishonesty, the employer will be liable for loss incurred by a third party to whom he owed a duty of care; he would owe this duty to a prospective employer of his own employee. Mere carelessness in the making of statements which cause loss to third parties does not make the employer liable for the loss; for negligence to exist there must first be a duty of care.

4. Indemnity

An employer must indemnify his employee for all losses, liabilities and expenses properly incurred by the employee within the scope of his employment.

This duty does not exist where the employee knew that what he was doing was unlawful.

5. Providing for the Employee's Safety

An employer is at common law under a personal duty to take reasonable care for the safety of his individual employees. Points to note about this statement are:

(a) *"Personal duty"*

The employer may, of course, in practice delegate his duty to a manager, foreman, safety officer, or other person, but the duty remains "personal" in the sense that the employer will be liable to an employee injured as a result of the negligence of the person to whom the employer has delegated his duty. The employer cannot put forward the defence that he selected the manager or other person with the greatest care.

The employer is personally responsible even where he is compelled by statute to delegate his duty to a technically qualified person. This was established by the case of *English* v. *Wilsons and Clyde Coal Co. Ltd.*, 1937 S.C.(H.L.) 46:

An action was brought by an employee against his employer for injuries suffered as a result of the employer's failure to instal a safe system of working in a mine. Provision of the system of working was part of the technical management of the mine, and by the Coal Mines Act 1911 a mine owner was prohibited from interfering in the technical management of the mine unless he was himself qualified to be manager of a mine.

The employer put forward the defence that he had delegated his duty to provide a safe system to a competent manager.

The House of Lords, however, held that this duty, although compulsorily delegated to a subordinate, remained the personal duty of the employer in that he was liable for injury caused to the employee through the absence of a safe system.

(b) *"Reasonable care"*

The employer's liability is not absolute: he is required to take the care which a reasonable and prudent person in his position would take, but he does not guarantee that his employees will suffer no injury.

The degree of care which will be held to be reasonable varies according to circumstances. The greater the likelihood of danger to the employee, the greater is the care required to be taken by the employer.

An English case which illustrates this aspect of the employer's duty is *Latimer* v. *A.E.C. Ltd.* [1953] A.C. 643:

During an unusually heavy rainstorm the floors of a factory were flooded and an oily cooling mixture, normally in a channel on the floor, rose and mixed with the flood-water, leaving the floor slippery afterwards. Sawdust was spread on the floor, but there was not enough of it to treat all areas.

A workman slipped and injured his ankle.

The House of Lords held that his employer had done all that a reasonable employer could have been expected to do in the circumstances, and was therefore not liable in damages.

(c) *"Individual employees"*

The employer's duty is owed to his employees as individuals, and not merely collectively. Greater care must be taken by him of employees who because of youth, inexperience, or any physical disability such as defective vision, or for any other reason are specially vulnerable.

The best-known case on this point is the English case *Paris* v. *Stepney Borough Council* [1951] A.C. 367:

A workman employed as a garage-hand had had only one good eye, and he lost this when a metal chip flew off his work. His employers had not provided goggles, and the workman claimed damages.

The House of Lords held that, although it was not the custom for goggles to be provided for the type of work in question, the employers were negligent in failing to provide goggles for this particular employee.

The employer's duty to provide for his employee's safety is often described as being a threefold one (*e.g.* by Lord Wright in *English* v. *Wilsons and Clyde Coal Co. Ltd.*, 1937 S.C.(H.L.) 46, at p. 60):

   (i) to select competent fellow-employees;

   (ii) to provide and maintain suitable materials; and

   (iii) to institute and operate a safe system of work.

(i) Competent staff

The employer must exercise reasonable care in the selection of fellow-employees, and must give proper instruction to inexperienced workers, especially where there is dangerous machinery.

If an employee is injured by a fellow-employee as a result of the latter's incompetence, lack of experience, or lack of instruction, he can sue his employer for damages on the common law ground that the employer has been negligent in his selection or instruction of staff.

Where a particular employee is known by the employer to be a source of danger to other employees, the employer may incur liability if he fails either to reform that employee or to dismiss him. An illustration is the English case of *Hudson* v. *Ridge Manufacturing Co. Ltd.* [1957] Q.B. 348:

For four years an employee had made a nuisance of himself to fellow-employees including H., and had been warned by his employer about the danger of his conduct.

In this action H. was claiming damages for injuries received when he was tripped up by this fellow-employee as a practical joke.

The employer was held liable, since by allowing this potentially dangerous conduct to continue for such a long time he had failed to take reasonable care for the safety of his other employees including H.

(ii) Suitable materials

The employer must exercise reasonable care in the provision and maintenance of plant, tools and equipment.

He need not provide the latest improvements, unless it would be reasonable in the circumstances for him to do so.

Where there is dangerous machinery, the employer must do what is reasonable to minimise the danger. Amongst the matters which the court would consider in deciding whether he had acted reasonably would be the likelihood of injury and the cost of a safety device.

Inspection should be made at reasonable intervals, and defects should be put right without unreasonable delay.

At common law the employer was not liable for injury caused by defective tools obtained from reputable sources unless he had some means of discovering the defect; this point was established by the House of Lords' decision in the English case of *Davie* v. *New Merton Board Mills Ltd.* [1959] A.C. 604:

A maintenance fitter was knocking out a metal key by means of a drift (a tapered bar of metal) and hammer when a particle of metal flew off the drift and entered his eye.

The drift, although apparently in good condition, was of excessive hardness, and had been negligently manufactured. Its makers were, however, reputable, and the tool had been purchased by the fitter's employer from a reputable firm of suppliers. The employer's system of maintenance and inspection was not at fault; the employer had no means of discovering the latent defect in the tool.

In those circumstances the fitter was held not entitled to damages from his employer.

The law on this point was altered by the Employer's Liability (Defective Equipment) Act 1969, which provides that where an employee is injured in the course of his employment because of a

defect in equipment provided by his employer and the defect is due
wholly or partly to the fault of a third party, his employer is to be
liable. An employee in Davie's position would, therefore, under this
Act now have a right to damages from his employer.

(iii) Safe system

The phrase "safe system" is sometimes used in a sense wide
enough to cover all aspects of the employer's duty to provide for
the employee's safety, including those of competent staff and suitable
materials.

It does, in any case, cover numerous miscellaneous aspects of the
employer's duty, including the provision of:

1. safe premises, with adequate ventilation and lighting, and of
a reasonable temperature;

2. proper lay-out for the performance of the work; and

3. adequate warnings, notices, and instructions.

"System" does not necessarily refer to a permanent system: it may
apply to a single special operation as well as to a series of repeated
and usual operations. If the operation is a routine one, the employer
need not lay down the system in such great detail as he would be
required to do if the operation were complicated or unusual.

Illustrations of the employer's duty to provide a safe system are:

(a) *Work in danger areas*

If employees are working in a danger area, *e.g.* surfacemen on
a railway line, lookouts or some other adequate warning system
must be provided.

(b) *Welsh* v. *Moir* (1885) 12 R. 590

A crane was improperly used to tear up rails and sleepers of a
disused railway line. The pivot on which the crane rested broke and
the jib of the crane fell suddenly killing one of the workmen.

His widow was held entitled to damages.

(c) *General Cleaning Contractors Ltd.* v. *Christmas* [1953] A.C. 180

This was an English case which went to the House of Lords.

A window-cleaner was standing on a sill to clean a window, and a
defective sash caused the window to come down on his finger. As
a result he fell and was injured.

Although the usual practice had been followed, the employer
was held to have failed in the duty to devise a reasonably safe
system of work for an obvious danger, since instructions were not
given that windows should be tested before being cleaned nor was
any apparatus, such as wedges, supplied to prevent windows from
becoming closed.

Trade practice

In considering whether a system of work is reasonably safe the court gives great weight to recognised practice in a trade. It is comparatively easy for an employee to prove negligence on the part of his employer where the latter has failed to take some very ordinary precaution. On the other hand, the employee may in some cases, as in *General Cleaning Contractors Ltd.* v. *Christmas*, be able to show that, even where the usual trade practice has been followed, the system is not reasonably safe; in such cases, however, the onus of proof on the employee is a heavy one.

In this connection a passage is often quoted from the judgment of Lord Dunedin in *Morton* v. *William Dixon Ltd.*, 1909 S.C. 807, at p. 809, an action of damages brought by a miner who alleged that he had been injured by a fall of coal:

"Where the negligence of the employer consists of what I may call a fault of omission, I think it is absolutely necessary that the proof of that fault of omission should be one of two kinds, either—to shew that the thing which he did not do was a thing which was commonly done by other persons in like circumstances, or—to shew that it was a thing which was so obviously wanted that it would be folly in anyone to neglect to provide it."

Defences to actions for breach of employer's duty to provide for employee's safety

(a) *Denial of the existence of negligence*

The employer may be able to prove that he did all that was reasonable in the circumstances, and that he was therefore not negligent.

(b) *Volenti non fit injuria*

The defence of "volenti non fit injuria" (literally, "to a person who is willing a wrongful act is not done") means that the person injured had voluntarily "waived" (surrendered) his right to the duty of care which would otherwise have been owed to him by the other party; the injury suffered is then not an "injuria" ("a legally wrongful act"), but "damnum absque injuria" ("loss or suffering without legal wrong").

In the law of employment the defence of "volenti non fit injuria" has the effect of preventing an employee from recovering damages from his employer for injury resulting from risks necessarily incidental to dangerous work which the employee has voluntarily undertaken to do. It might, for instance, be put forward by an employer sued by an employee who was a lion-tamer, a steeplejack, worked in an explosives factory, or was paid "danger-money."

However, the defence is of only limited application. In particular, it does not apply where the employee merely knows of some risk, but has not actually consented to his employer's doing nothing about it; this point is often expressed by the statement that the defence is "volenti non fit injuria," not "scienti non fit injuria" (literally, "to a person who knows, a wrongful act is not done").

The application of the defence is expressly limited by a provision in the Unfair Contract Terms Act 1977: a term in a contract of employment is void if it purports to exclude or restrict the employer's liability for breach of duty which results in the employee's death or personal injury, and the fact that the employee "agreed to, or was aware of" the term is not of itself sufficient evidence that he "knowingly and voluntarily assumed any risk."

(c) Contributory negligence

This third defence is much more likely to be available to the employer than the defence of "volenti non fit injuria."

For the defence of contributory negligence to be successful the employer must show that the employee has contributed to his injury by his own carelessness, *i.e.* that the employee has not taken reasonable care for his own safety; *e.g.* he may have disobeyed orders given by the employer for safety, disregarded obvious dangers, or failed to use protective equipment supplied.

An important change in the law relating to contributory negligence was made by the Law Reform (Contributory Negligence) Act 1945. Before that Act an employee could recover no damages if he had even in the slightest degree contributed to the causing of the accident; in other words, contributory negligence was a complete defence for the employer.

The Act provided that contributory negligence was no longer to be a complete defence, but was to have the effect of reducing the damages which could be claimed by the injured person according to the extent of his responsibility for the injury.

[(d) Former defence of common employment

The defence of common employment was not originally part of the common law of Scotland, but was introduced from English law by decisions of the House of Lords in Scottish cases about the middle of the nineteenth century.

The effect of the defence of common employment was that an injured employee could not recover damages from his employer if the injury had been caused by a fellow-employee (a person in "common employment" with himself under the same employer). The underlying theory of the defence was that the employee by accepting employment had voluntarily undertaken the risk of being injured by the negligence of fellow-employees.

The doctrine of common employment was much criticised. It was modified by the Employers' Liability Act 1880 and by workmen's compensation legislation, and was finally abolished, both in Scotland and in England, by the Law Reform (Personal Injuries) Act 1948.]

Statutory extensions of employer's duty to provide for employee's safety

The legislation which now gives an employee better protection than he enjoyed at common law forms a major part of industrial law. It falls into three main categories:

(a) Statutory safety provisions

In the nineteenth and twentieth centuries there has arisen a great mass of legislation making specific provision for the safety of employees in certain occupations. The earliest statutes in this category were those applying to factories, and later statutes applying to other situations have mostly followed the same general pattern. Examples are the Factories Act 1961, the Mines and Quarries Act 1954, the Offices, Shops and Railway Premises Act 1963, and the Agriculture (Safety, Health and Welfare Provisions) Act 1956.

Detailed provisions on the safety measures applicable to particular machinery or work are generally not included in the Acts themselves, but are dealt with in subordinate legislation, such as "regulations" and "rules," made under authority of the Acts.

If an employer fails to observe a statutory duty designed to protect his employees from injury (e.g. section 14 of the Factories Act 1961, which requires the occupier of a factory to fence dangerous parts of machinery), then he is liable not only to penalties in the criminal courts but also to claims for damages made in the civil courts by an injured employee. In many cases it will be easier for an employee to show that his employer has failed to implement a statutory duty, often expressed in absolute terms, than to prove that the employer has failed to satisfy the vaguer, though wider, common law standard of "reasonable" care. An injured employee, therefore, often bases his claim alternatively on statutory and common law grounds.

A major advance on earlier statutory safety provisions was made by the Health and Safety at Work etc. Act 1974, which was passed to give effect to the main recommendations of the *Report of the Committee on Safety and Health at Work* ("the Robens Report") published in 1972 (Cmnd. 5034). The Act creates a more unified, integrated system aimed at making the state's contribution to health and safety at work more effective. The existing statutory provisions contained in the several Acts mentioned above and in the associated subordinate legislation are being progressively replaced by regulations and codes of practice under the Act of 1974. The duty of an employer to his employees is stated in general terms in the Act as being "to ensure, so far as is reasonably practicable, the health, safety and welfare at work of all his employees." Breach of this duty however, is not a ground for proceedings in a civil court.

(b) *Statutory benefit for industrial injuries*

Since the National Insurance (Industrial Injuries) Act 1946 employees have been entitled to claim industrial injury benefits from a state fund. This state scheme of insurance against "industrial injury" (a phrase which covers injury in employment generally and is not restricted to injury in manual occupations) was developed out of the workmen's compensation legislation which originated in 1897 and which gave injured workmen the right to claim compensation from employers even where there had been no negligence on the part of the employers.

Recommendations for some extensions of the present industrial injuries scheme have been made by the Royal Commission on Civil Liability and Compensation for Personal Injury 1973–78 ("the Pearson Commission") (Cmnd. 7054).

The statutory provisions on benefit for industrial injuries now form Chapter IV of the Social Security Act 1975.

Where an employed earner suffers personal injury caused by accident arising out of and in the course of his employment as an employed earner, the benefits are:

(i) injury benefit payable to the earner for up to 156 days if he is, as a result of the injury, incapable of work;

(ii) disablement benefit payable to the earner, after the lapse of the 156 days, if he suffers, as a result of the accident, from loss of physical or mental faculty; the benefit may be a lump sum (referred to as "a disablement gratuity") or a pension; and

(iii) industrial death benefit payable, if the earner dies as a result of the injury, to other persons such as his widow and dependent relatives.

Corresponding benefits are payable under Chapter V of the Act of 1975 where the earner suffers from a prescribed disease or prescribed personal injury not caused by accident but due to the nature of his employment.

The fact that an employee is entitled to a benefit from the state fund does not prevent him from claiming damages from his employer, but the Law Reform (Personal Injuries) Act 1948 provides that in the assessment of damages for loss of earnings or profits, there must be taken into account one half of the benefits which have been paid or probably will become payable to the claimant in the five years from the time of the injury; this statutory provision has the effect of reducing the damages which the employer has to pay by approximately the same proportion as the employer's share of the contribution made to the state fund.

(c) *Legislation applying to common law actions*

In spite of the improvements referred to in (a) and (b) above, an employee may still find that his only remedy, or only substantial remedy, is to sue his employer for damages for negligence on the ground that the employer has failed in his common law duty to take reasonable care for the employee's safety. Several statutes have been passed for the purpose of giving the employee a better chance of success in an action based on common law.

Amongst these statutes are the Employer's Liability (Defective Equipment) Act 1969 (see p. 372, above), the Law Reform (Personal Injuries) Act 1948 (see p. 376, above), and the Employers' Liability (Compulsory Insurance) Act 1969. This last Act requires employers to insure against their liability to pay damages to employees for injuries sustained in employment. It was passed to remedy the situation where an employee, although he had a good ground for claiming damages and might have had substantial damages awarded to him by the court, failed to have his claim satisfied because his employer was neither insured against the liability nor financially able himself to meet the claim.

VICARIOUS LIABILITY OF EMPLOYER

An employer may become liable "vicariously" (*i.e.* in the place of another, namely, the employee in this case) for injury or loss suffered by a third party as a result of a wrongful or negligent act of an employee. For this vicarious liability to arise the act must have been done within the scope of the employment.

The third party who has suffered from the wrong or negligence has a claim for damages against the employee, whether the employee was acting within the scope of the employment or not, but usually the third party prefers to claim damages from the employer since the employer is usually better able financially to make actual payment of a substantial sum than his employee would be. The third party, therefore, usually attempts to prove that the wrongful or negligent act was done within the scope of the employment.

In very many cases it is difficult to decide whether the employee was acting within the scope of the employment or not; the employee may, for instance, be disobeying his employer's instructions as to the method of working or may, when on a journey, deviate from the expected route.

An act which the employee was authorised to do is still within the scope of the employment although it is done in an unauthorised way, and an employer may be made vicariously liable even for acts which he expressly prohibited. If, on the other hand, the employee is acting purely for his own purposes, even although he may be doing so within working hours, he will not be considered to be acting within the scope of the employment and his employer will therefore not be liable vicariously for any wrongful or negligent act of the employee which injuries a third party. (See also p. 435, below.)

TERMINATION OF THE CONTRACT OF EMPLOYMENT BY NOTICE

The contract of employment may be brought to an end by due notice being given by either party.

The general rule of the common law is that if the period of notice is neither specified in the contract nor fixed by custom, it must be reasonable; an important factor to be considered in the decision of whether the period of notice is reasonable or not is the nature of the employment; the mere fact that remuneration is paid at, say, monthly intervals does not necessarily mean that a month's notice would be reasonable in the circumstances.

Important changes in the law relating to dismissal with due notice have been made by recent statutes. These changes relate to:

1. minimum period of notice;
2. redundancy payments; and
3. unfair dismissal.

1. Minimum Period of Notice

Minimum periods of notice were first provided for by the Contracts of Employment Act 1963. Extensions were made by further legislation, and the provisions were consolidated in the Contracts of Employment Act 1972. The Act of 1972 was itself amended by the Employment Protection Act 1975, and there was a further consolidation in the Employment Protection (Consolidation) Act 1978.

It is always open to the parties to specify a longer period of notice in their contract, and longer notice than the statutory minimum is also required where custom or the common law standard of reasonableness makes it necessary.

The provisions at present in force apply to persons who have been continuously employed for four weeks or more for at least sixteen hours a week. There are detailed statutory provisions on the calculation of the employee's period of employment and on the question of whether or not its continuity has been broken; *e.g.* a week in which the employee is incapable of work because of sickness or injury counts as a period of employment, and transfer of a business from one employer to another does not break the continuity of the employee's period of employment in the business.

The minimum notice required by the Act to be given by employer to employee is:

(a)   one week's notice if the period of continuous employment is less than two years;

(b)   one week's notice for each year of continuous employment if the period of continuous employment is two years or more but less than twelve years; and

(c)   twelve weeks' notice if the period of continuous employment . is twelve years or more.

The minimum notice required by the Act to be given by employee to employer is one week's notice.

The Act further provides that an employer must supply to an employee written particulars of the terms of employment not later than thirteen weeks after the beginning of the period of employment. One of the particulars required to be included is the length of notice which the employee is bound to give and entitled to receive for the termination of the contract. As a result of this provision doubts as to the length of notice required arise less often than they did before 1963.

2.   Redundancy Payments

Before the Redundancy Payments Act 1965, an employee was not entitled to any special payment if he became redundant: his employer was bound only to give the appropriate notice of termination of the contract or to pay wages in lieu of notice.

The provisions for redundancy payments introduced by the Act of 1965 were amended by subsequent legislation including the Employment Protection Act 1975, and are now to be found in the Employment Protection (Consolidation) Act 1978.

The basic principle is that where an employee who has been continuously employed for two years is dismissed by reason of redundancy (or in certain circumstances is "laid-off" or kept on "short-time"), he is entitled to receive from his employer a redundancy payment based on his length of service. Certain categories of employees are excluded, *e.g.* men over the age of 65, women over the age of 60, and civil servants.

"Dismissal" has been given a statutory definition: it includes, for instance, the situation where an employee is employed for a fixed term and the term expires without renewal of his contract. The burden of proving "dismissal" lies on the employee.

There is also a statutory definition of "redundancy." The dismissal must be attributable wholly or mainly to:

(a) the fact that the employer has ceased, or intends to cease, to carry on his business either at all or at the employee's place of employment; or

(b) the fact that the need for work of a particular kind to be carried out, either at all or at the employee's place of employment, has ceased or diminished or is expected to cease or diminish. The burden of proving that the reason for the dismissal has not been "redundancy" lies on the employer, *i.e.* the employee (provided he has proved that he has been "dismissed") is presumed, until the contrary is proved by his employer, to have been dismissed because of redundancy.

The legislation on redundancy is extensive and includes important provisions as to offers of alternative employment, as to the employer's right to claim a rebate out of the Redundancy Fund, as to the employer's duty to consult representatives of a recognised trade union, and as to the right of an employee to make a direct claim on the Redundancy Fund in the event of his employer's insolvency.

3. Unfair Dismissal

The Industrial Relations Act 1971 conferred on most employees the right not to be unfairly dismissed. That Act was repealed by the Trade Union and Labour Relations Act 1974, but the provisions as to unfair dismissal were re-enacted, with some changes, in the Act of 1974. Further amendments were made by the Employment Protection Act 1975, and the provisions are now contained in the Employment Protection (Consolidation) Act 1978, as amended by the Employment Act 1980.

"Unfair dismissal" must be distinguished from "wrongful dismissal." "Unfair dismissal" has a special statutory meaning, whereas "wrongful dismissal" is the phrase used in the common law for the situation where an employer dismisses his employee without giving proper notice and without having good grounds for "summary" dismissal (see p. 384, below).

In the statutory provisions relating to unfair dismissal, the basic principle is that an employee who has been continuously employed for twenty-six weeks has the right not to be unfairly dismissed by his employer. Certain categories of employees are excluded, *e.g.* employees who have reached the normal retiring age, and employees who ordinarily work outside Great Britain. The right does extend to civil servants in spite of the rule that they may be dismissed at the will of the Crown.

"Dismissal" has the same statutory definition as in the redundancy provisions, and it is for the employee to prove that he has been "dismissed."

The burden of proof then shifts to the employer, and in most cases it will be for him to show:

    (a) what the principal reason for the dismissal was; and

    (b) that the reason was one of five specified statutory reasons.

A reason is one of the five acceptable reasons if it:

    (i)   related to the capability or qualifications of the employee for performing his work; or

    (ii) related to the employee's conduct; or

    (iii) was that the employee was redundant; or

    (iv) was that the employee could not continue to work in the position which he held without contravention of a statutory duty or statutory restriction (*e.g.* if the employee was disqualified from driving); or

    (v) was some other substantial reason of a kind such as to justify the dismissal of an employee holding the position which that employee held.

Once the employer has fulfilled the requirements (a) and (b) above, the question of whether the dismissal was fair or unfair depends on whether the employer acted reasonably or unreasonably in treating the reason as a sufficient reason for dismissing the employee, and that question must be decided "in accordance with equity and the substantial merits of the case"; amongst the circumstances to be considered are the size and administrative resources of the employer's undertaking.

There are further special rules for particular situations, *e.g.* for dismissal relating to trade union membership; where there is a "closed shop," the dismissal of an employee who falls out of membership or refuses to join the union is "fair" unless the employee genuinely objects on grounds of conscience or other deeply-held personal conviction to being a member of any trade union whatsoever or of a particular trade union; the effect of amendments made by the Employment Act 1980 is to enlarge the occasions on which dismissal in a "closed shop" situation is "unfair"; this is in accordance with the general policy of the Act to tilt the balance between individual interests and collective interests in favour of the former.

An employee who has been successful in his claim may obtain from the industrial tribunal an order for reinstatement or an order for re-engagement or an award of compensation. Important changes were made in this area by the Employment Protection Act 1975 with a view to strengthening these remedies: in particular, the remedies of reinstatement and re-engagement were given more prominence, and awards of compensation were made to consist of a basic award and a compensatory award. The provisions are now in the Employment Protection (Consolidation) Act 1978 as amended by the Act of 1980.

TERMINATION OF THE CONTRACT OF EMPLOYMENT WITHOUT NOTICE

In certain circumstances the contract of employment may be brought to an end without notice being given by either party.

1. Death or Bankruptcy

Since employment is a personal relationship, it is automatically terminated by the death of either employer or employee.

If the employer becomes bankrupt, this is considered to be a breach of the contract on his part, and the employee is entitled to leave, claiming as damages for breach of contract the wages which he would have earned during the appropriate period of notice.

2. Crown Service

Civil servants, although in practice they enjoy a high degree of security of employment, can legally be dismissed by the Crown at any time without notice. They are, however, protected by the statutory "unfair dismissal" provisions (see p. 381, above).

3. Wages in Lieu of Notice

If an employer dismisses an employee without giving the proper notice, he will be liable for damages for breach of contract, the amount being based on the remuneration which the employee would have earned during the appropriate period of notice.

At common law an employee normally had no ground for complaint if his employer chose to dismiss him instantly at the same time paying him wages in lieu of notice. This did not apply to those employees, such as actors, for whom the employer was bound to provide work in order that they might enhance their reputations.

While the employee may still choose to accept a payment in lieu of notice, the statutory provisions as to redundancy and unfair dismissal give him, in certain circumstances, the right to additional payments.

An employee has no legal right to terminate his employment instantly by making a payment to his employer of the remuneration which he would have earned during the period of notice; he cannot

be compelled to continue in employment, but if he leaves in breach
of his contract he is liable to pay damages to his employer.

4. Summary Dismissal

The employer is sometimes entitled to dismiss an employee "summarily," *i.e.* instantly without either notice or wages in lieu of notice
and without becoming liable to make a redundancy payment
or to pay compensation for unfair dismissal. The employer has this
right where the conduct of the employee or other circumstances make
a continuance of the proper relationship of employer to employee
impossible.

Summary dismissal is justified at common law on the following
grounds:

(a) Disobedience to orders

The order must be a lawful order, and usually the disobedience
would require to be habitual.

(b) Incompetence or neglect

In accepting employment the employee may expressly or by
implication have professed a particular skill or capacity, and if he
fails to show a reasonable standard of competence his employer is
justified in dismissing him summarily.

Neglect (including carelessness in the performance of work and
absence without leave) rarely justifies summary dismissal unless it is
habitual or would have especially serious consequences (*e.g.* a
signalman's failure to put a signal at "danger").

(c) Misconduct

The misconduct need not be during working hours, provided it
is sufficiently serious and affects the employee's capacity to perform
his part of the contract of employment. The type of misconduct
which justifies summary dismissal varies according to the nature of
the employment; *e.g.* dishonesty, insolence, drunkenness, or immorality would often, but not always, justify it.

(d) Illness

The illness of an employee may be such as to "frustrate" his
contract of employment (see p. 342, above). If so, the employer is
entitled to dismiss the employee summarily, and is not liable to pay
wages or damages, since the contract is at an end.

Factors to be considered would be the nature of the employment,
the likely duration of the illness, and the need for, and availability of,
a substitute.

If an employer dismisses an employee summarily in circumstances in which he is not entitled to do so, he is liable to pay damages to the employee for the wrongful dismissal.

The common law on summary dismissal as justified by the circumstances mentioned in (a) to (d) above has not been abolished by the recent statutes, but in practice most claims in respect of dismissal are now brought before industrial tribunals under the statutory "unfair dismissal" provisions; an employee would be unlikely now to resort to court proceedings unless either:

(i) he belonged to one of the categories excluded from the statutory provisions; or

(ii) his claim exceeded the statutory maximum (*i.e.* since February 1, 1980, £3,600 as basic award plus £6,250 as compensatory award).

Further Reading

Isaac P. Miller, *Industrial Law in Scotland* (The Scottish Universities Law Institute Series) (W. Green & Son Ltd.)

Gloag and Henderson, *Introduction to the Law of Scotland*

David M. Walker, *Principles of Scottish Private Law*

Smith and Wood, *Industrial Law* (Butterworths)

G. Barrie Marsh, *Employer and Employee* (Shaw & Sons Ltd.)

William Leslie, *Industrial Tribunal Practice in Scotland* (W. Green & Son Ltd.)

AGENCY

AGENCY is the relationship which exists where one person, the principal, authorises, or is deemed to authorise, another person, the agent, to act on his behalf in a transaction with a third party. The agent's function is to bring his principal into legal relations with the third party, and in return for doing so he receives a commission or some other form of remuneration.

A person who is an agent does not necessarily use the term "agent" of himself in his transactions with the third party; *e.g.* in partnerships a partner is an agent of the firm, in companies a director is an agent of his company, and in the law of domestic relations a wife is the agent of her husband in the ordering of goods for the household.

Mandate is a relationship similar to agency except that no payment is made for the services rendered. In mandate the terms "mandant" and "mandatary" correspond to the terms "principal" and "agent" respectively in agency.

CONSTITUTION OF AGENCY

Agency may be constituted in any of the following four ways:

1. express appointment;
2. implied appointment;
3. holding out;

4. ratification; and
5. necessity.

Both principal and agent must have the contractual capacity to perform their different parts. A principal cannot extend his own capacity to contract merely by appointing as agent a person who as an individual has greater contractual capacity than himself; *e.g.* if the principal is a minor, contracts made with third parties by an agent who is of full age are no more binding on the principal than they would have been if he had not acted through an agent.

1. Express Appointment

An agent may be appointed expressly, either orally or by writing. If there is writing, the writing may be informal, *e.g.* "letters of mandate," or formal, *e.g.* a "power of attorney" which is often used where a person going abroad wishes to entrust the management of his affairs in this country to another person.

The agent's authority is in this case "express" and "actual" authority.

2. Implied Appointment

Circumstances may indicate that a person has been impliedly appointed as agent; the creation of agency is then inferred by the law from the circumstances; *e.g.* a partner dealing with partnership affairs is treated by the law as agent of the firm, and an employer who engages an employee as a shop manager or in some other capacity involving transactions with third parties is treated by the law as the principal in an implied contract of agency between himself and his employee.

Here the agent's authority is "implied" authority. Implied authority includes "usual" authority because the agent is regarded as having authority to do the kinds of things which a person in his particular line of business usually has authority to do.

Implied authority is, no less than express authority, "actual" authority: the difference is that it has not been expressly conferred, either orally or in writing.

3. Holding out

This mode of constituting agency differs from the first two modes in that the agent has no actual authority at all conferred on him, either expressly or by implication: he only *appears* to have authority.

The principle of personal bar by holding out (see p. 247, above) applies here. The effect of the principle is that if A has acted in such a way as to make it appear that B had power to contract on his behalf and C has been induced by A's conduct to make a contract with B as agent for A, A is liable as principal on the ground that he held himself out as principal. For instance, if A, the owner of goods, allows B, a person whose ordinary business includes the selling of that class of goods, to have possession of the goods, and B sells the goods to C who believes that B had the proper authority to sell them, A will be bound by the sale on the ground that the law infers the creation of agency between A and B in these circumstances.

The agent is said to have "ostensible" or "apparent" authority.

The distinction between implied authority and ostensible authority is a fine one. Both types of authority often involve a consideration of what the agent's "usual" authority is in the circumstances.

Ostensible authority can arise where the principal has withdrawn an agent's actual authority without giving proper notice to third parties of the withdrawal. It may also arise where the principal has made some private arrangement with his agent, limiting the agent's usual authority and has not notified third parties of these special limitations. Two illustrations of ostensible authority are:

(a) The Partnership Act 1890 provides that "where a person deals with a firm after a change in its constitution he is entitled to treat all apparent members of the old firm as still being members of the firm until he has notice of the change." A third party who has had dealings with the firm and has known X to be a partner is entitled to continue dealing with X as if he were still a partner until he (the third party) has been personally notified that X has retired, *i.e.* X has ostensible authority to enter into contracts which will be binding on the firm; on account of his retirement X no longer has any actual authority (whether express or implied) to enter into such contracts.

(b) *International Sponge Importers Ltd.* v. *Watt & Sons*, 1911 S.C.(H.L.) 57: Cohen, a commercial traveller for a sponge importing company, was in the habit of selling to saddlers parcels of sponges which he was allowed to carry with him and hand over to purchasers. He had no actual authority to receive payment except by crossed cheques in favour of the company.

Occasionally W. & Sons paid for sponges by cheques in favour of Cohen, and the company knew of this but did not object. On one occasion W. & Sons paid £120 in cash to Cohen.

W. & Sons were held to have been justified in believing that Cohen did have authority to receive payment in these ways, and so when Cohen was found to have been embezzling the money W. & Sons were not liable to pay a second time to the company.

Cohen was regarded as having had the necessary ostensible authority to receive payment on behalf of his company.

4. Ratification

When an act has been done on behalf of a person, A, without his authority by another person, B, who purports to act as A's agent, A may by ratifying the act make it as valid as if it had been originally done with his authority. This applies whether B was an agent exceeding the powers which A had conferred on him or was a person with no authority at all to act for A. Ratification may be express or implied.

The right to create agency by ratification is subject to the following conditions:

(a) The agent must have purported to act as agent for an identifiable principal who later ratifies the agent's action. The agent must not have been contracting in his own name with the mere expectation that his act would be ratified, nor must he have been acting for a person other than the principal who ratifies his act.

(b) The act must be one which the principal would have been legally capable of authorising; *e.g.* if the directors of a company enter into a contract which is void because it is ultra vires ("beyond the powers") of the company itself, the contract cannot be ratified by the company.

It follows that the principal must have been in existence at the time when the act being ratified was done and not merely at the time of ratification. This point is important in connection with "pre-incorporation" contracts of companies, which are contracts entered into by promoters or other persons acting on behalf of proposed companies; until a company receives its certificate of incorporation from the registrar of companies it is legally not in existence, and any contracts made by persons purporting to act as its agents before that time cannot be ratified by the company.

(c) If the validity of an act depends on its being done within a certain time, ratification must take place before the time elapses.

5. Necessity

The term "agency of necessity" is used of situations where a person must, in an emergency, take some action on behalf of another person who has not in fact given him any authority to do so; *e.g.* a carrier of perishable goods may find himself in a position in which he must dispose of the goods by selling them or otherwise, even although he has no authority from their owner to do so, and masters of ships who are unable to communicate with the owners of the ship or cargo have in case of emergency power to "hypothecate" (*i.e.* grant security over) the ship or cargo in order to raise money to enable the voyage to continue (the documents by which such security is created being referred to as "bonds of bottomry" if the security is over the ship itself and "bonds of respondentia" if the security is over the cargo) (see p. 480, below).

Agency of necessity applies in only a limited number of situations, and with improvement in communications has become increasingly rare since it cannot arise except where communication is impossible.

Agency of necessity is a form of negotiorum gestio ("management of affairs") (see p. 410, below).

CLASSES OF AGENTS

There are many different kinds of agents, and the authority which an agent has depends mainly on the category to which he belongs. A general distinction is drawn between general agents and special agents, and there are within these two classes groups of persons who, by professional and trade usage, have distinctive rights and duties depending on their particular calling and function.

General and Special Agents

A general agent is one who has authority to act for his principal in all the principal's affairs or in all his affairs of a particular kind, *e.g.* the master of a ship or a solicitor. A special agent is one who has authority to act for his principal in some particular transaction only.

Third parties dealing with a general agent are entitled to assume that he has general powers or at least the powers which an agent of the particular class to which he belongs usually has by the custom of his trade or profession. On the other hand, third parties dealing with a special agent must satisfy themselves as to the exact extent of the agent's powers, for if the special agent goes beyond what he has been instructed to do the third party cannot hold the principal liable.

A general agent has implied or "ostensible" (apparent) authority to act according to the trade or professional usage applicable, and provided he does not overstep his ostensible authority his actions are binding on his principal even although the principal may have given the agent no authority for the particular action or indeed may have expressly forbidden it. A special agent, on the other hand, has no ostensible authority, and so if he oversteps his actual authority his actions are not binding on his principal.

Mercantile Agents

Mercantile agents may be factors or brokers. Both are employed to buy and sell goods, and have ostensible authority to act in accordance with the custom of the particular market on which they deal.

A factor differs from a broker in that a factor has possession of his principal's goods, whereas a broker has not, and in that a factor has authority to sell in his own name, whereas a broker has not. Auctioneers are a special class of factors. Examples of brokers are stockbrokers, shipbrokers ("middlemen" between shipowners and persons who wish to have goods shipped and between buyers and sellers of ships), and insurance brokers (who have an intermediate position between insurance companies and persons wishing to take out insurance).

A mercantile agent may be a del credere agent, *i.e.* he may by agreement with his principal and in return for an extra commission undertake to indemnify his principal if the third party fails to pay what is due under the contract. Del credere agency is an exception to the normal rule that a principal cannot hold his agent liable for the third party's failure to fulfil the contract.

Property Agents

Into this category come house agents and estate agents (whose function is to offer houses and other heritable property for sale on behalf of the owners), and house factors and estate factors (who are employed to manage, on behalf of the owners, houses and other heritable property occupied by tenants).

Estate agency work is controlled by the Estate Agents Act 1979. Under this Act the Director General of Fair Trading has power to prohibit unfit persons from continuing to do such work, particulars of all orders, including warning orders, issued by the Director being entered on a register open to public inspection. The Act also includes accounting and insurance provisions designed to protect clients' money.

Solicitors

Solicitors were formerly called "law agents." They act in legal affairs as agents for their clients.

The extent of a solicitor's ostensible authority varies according to the nature of the work which he is employed to do; *e.g.* a solicitor instructed to purchase heritable property has ostensible authority to take the usual steps to verify that his client will obtain a good title to the property, and a solicitor instructed to bring an action in court has ostensible authority to take any ordinary step in procedure but not to appeal to a higher court.

Bankers

Where the customer of a bank has a current account, the banker is the agent of the customer for the purpose of paying sums of money

out of the account according to the instructions given on the customer's cheques.   The banker also acts as agent in collecting the
proceeds of cheques paid into the customer's current account.

Masters of Ships

These may act as agents for the owners of the ship, for the
charterers of the ship (the persons who have by a contract known
as a "charterparty" obtained the right to have goods carried on the
ship), and also for the owners of the cargo. Amongst the normal
functions of shipmasters as agents is the signing of bills of lading
for goods on board the ship. The authority of shipmasters in
emergencies to grant bonds of bottomry and respondentia has been
mentioned above (pp. 389–390).

Partners

Although a firm (*i.e.* a partnership, as distinct from a registered
company) is a legal person, it does not have the ability to enter into
contracts except through agents.

By the Partnership Act 1890 every partner is an agent of the firm
for the purpose of the business of the partnership, and the acts of
every partner who does any act for carrying on in the usual way
business of the kind carried on by the firm bind the firm unless:

(a) the partner has in fact no authority to act for the firm in the
particular matter; *and*

(b) the person with whom he is dealing either knows that he has
no authority, or does not know or believe him to be a partner.

The question whether a particular contract falls within the scope
of acts "for carrying on in the usual way business of the kind carried
on by the firm" depends largely on the nature of the firm's
business.

An act which is outside the scope of the firm's business will be
binding on the firm if the partner was specially authorised to do it or
if the firm later ratifies what he has done.

Directors

Limited and other registered companies, being artificial and not
natural legal persons, also necessarily engage natural persons to
enter into contracts on their behalf. These natural persons may be
directors, managers or other senior officials. They derive their
authority from the company's memorandum and articles of association and the resolutions of the board of directors. In large companies
there will be wide-spread delegation enabling numerous persons
other than the directors themselves to enter into contracts on the
company's behalf.

The authority of a company's agents is limited by the ultra vires
("beyond the powers") doctrine and by any limitations placed on it

by the memorandum and articles of association, but there is some protection for third parties under the European Communities Act 1972 (see p. 270, above).

In so far as the authority of any agent of the company depends on the internal procedures of the company and is not discoverable by consulting public documents such as the memorandum and articles, third parties are entitled to assume that the necessary procedure has been regularly followed; *e.g.* if the authority to borrow more than a stated amount could be conferred on a director only by the passing of an ordinary resolution of the company, the lender would be entitled to assume that such a resolution had been properly passed. This rule concerning the company's "indoor management" is referred to as the "rule in *Turquand's Case*" (*Royal British Bank* v. *Turquand* (1856) 6 E. & B. 327). The rule is, however, subject to exceptions; *e.g.* it does not protect a third party who "is put on his inquiry" (*i.e.* ought, in the circumstances, to have suspected some irregularity).

DUTIES OF AGENT TO PRINCIPAL

The agent is in a fiduciary relationship (a position of trust) towards his principal, and must therefore always act in a way which justifies the principal's confidence in him. He is engaged to look after his principal's interests, and must not seek additional profit for himself out of his position beyond the commission or other remuneration allowed to him by the principal. This fiduciary relationship underlies all the specific duties considered below.

The fact that agency is of a fiduciary nature does not mean, however, that the agent is restricted from acting as agent for other principals or from conducting business on his own account. There is no *implied* condition in a contract of agency that the agent must not sell the products of another party who is in competition with his principal: *Lothian* v. *Jenolite Ltd.*, 1969 S.C. 111. There may, of course, be an *express* condition to that effect, as in *Graham & Co.* v. *United Turkey Red Co. Ltd.*, 1922 S.C. 533 (p. 324, above).

1. Carrying out Instructions

The agent must carry out the principal's instructions. These may be express, or implied either by usage of trade or by the previous course of dealing between the parties. If there are no instructions at all on some matter the agent must act as he thinks best for the interests of the principal.

The standard of care which the agent must exercise is that which is expected of a reasonably competent and careful member of the profession or other class to which the agent belongs.

If an agent fails to carry out instructions or fails to show the required standard of care, he becomes liable in damages to the principal.

2. Acting in Person

Since agency is a personal relationship, the general rule is that an agent must act in person and is not entitled to delegate. The maxim in which this general rule is expressed is "delegatus non potest delegare" ("a person to whom something has been delegated cannot delegate it to another"). The general rule applies where the agent has been selected because of his personal skill.

In very many situations, however, agents have implied power to delegate. This implied power may arise from the nature of the work or from usage of trade.

A solicitor is an example of an agent who has no implied power to delegate, whereas an architect has been held entitled to delegate to a surveyor (*Black* v. *Cornelius* (1879) 6 R. 581).

3. Keeping Accounts

The agent must keep the money and property of his principal separate from his own and from that of other persons, must keep accounts of his dealings in the course of the agency, and hand over to his principal in accordance with the contract of agency money and property received in the course of the agency.

4. Giving the Principal Full Benefit

The agent must give his principal the full benefit of the contracts made with third parties. He is not entitled without the principal's consent to make a profit out of his position as agent beyond the remuneration agreed on in the contract of agency. Any additional benefit received by the agent without his principal's consent is classed as a "secret commission," and the agent is not entitled to retain it, however fair the transaction may have been and even although the principal may have suffered no loss. For instance, if the agent receives discount when he is paying accounts for his principal, he must give the principal the benefit of that discount; an agent who has been engaged to sell goods for his principal must not without his principal's consent buy them himself, and if he did so the principal could take the goods back from the agent or sue the agent for profit made by the agent on a resale; similarly, an agent who has been engaged to buy goods for his principal from third parties must not without his principal's consent sell his own goods to the principal, and if he did so the principal would be entitled to refuse the goods or alternatively to claim the profit made by the agent on the transaction.

Consequences of receipt of secret commission

Receipt by an agent of a secret commission may have both civil and criminal consequences.

(a) Civil consequences

(i) The principal may dismiss the agent from his service.

(ii) The principal may recover the amount of the commission from the agent.

(iii) Since the giving of a secret commission is a civil wrong the principal may recover damages from the person who gave the commission.

(iv) The agent forfeits all claim to his agreed commission, and if the principal has already paid it the principal may recover it. This applies, however, only to the particular transaction in question, not to other transactions in which the agent acted properly.

(v) The principal when he discovers that his agent has been bribed may refuse to perform the contract made on his behalf with the third party, and if the contract is a sale to him and he has made a deposit he may recover the deposit.

(vi) The agent is not allowed to sue the third party for the secret commission, since the agreement for the payment of it is a pactum illicitum ("illegal agreement").

(b) Criminal consequences

The Prevention of Corruption Act 1906 provides that it is a criminal offence for an agent corruptly to accept or agree to accept or attempt to obtain any gift or consideration as an inducement or reward for doing or not doing anything in connection with his principal's business. Further, any person who corruptly gives or offers any gift or consideration to an agent is guilty of an offence under the same Act.

Increased penalties were provided for by the Prevention of Corruption Act 1916 in the case where the matter in question is a government contract or a contract with a "public body" (*e.g.* a gas board set up under the Gas Act 1948: *Reg.* v. *Manners* [1977] 2 W.L.R. 178 (H.L.) (E.)).

RIGHTS OF AGENT AGAINST PRINCIPAL

An agent has the following rights against his principal:

1. Remuneration

The rate of the agent's remuneration may be expressly stated in the contract of agency, but if it is not it will depend on usage of trade. Where there is neither any express provision nor any usage of trade applicable, the agent is entitled to be paid on a quantum meruit ("to the extent which he deserved") basis.

There is a general rule that an agent is not entitled to remuneration unless he has brought the transaction for which he was engaged to completion, but this rule does not apply where there is an express provision to the contrary in the contract of agency or where usage of trade confers on the agent the right to remuneration in spite of his failure to complete the transaction; *e.g.* the contract may provide that the agent is to be entitled to commission on his finding a prospective purchaser of his principal's property, and by custom in certain trades commission becomes due on the mere introduction of buyer to seller.

2. Reimbursement of Expenses

The principal must reimburse the agent for all expenses properly incurred by the agent in the course of the agency. The agent is entitled to deduct these from money received by him on behalf of his principal.

3. Relief

The principal must relieve the agent of all liabilities necessarily incurred in the performance of the agency. For instance, if the principal refuses to carry out his part of a contract entered into by the agent on his behalf and as a result the agent becomes liable in damages to the third party, the principal is bound to relieve the agent of that liability.

If, however, the agent incurs liability through doing something which is not part of his duty as agent, the principal is not bound to relieve him of that liability; such a situation occurred in *Tomlinson v. Liquidators of Scottish Amalgamated Silks Ltd.*, 1935 S.C.(H.L.) 1:

T., a company director, had been tried for fraud in relation to acts done by him as a director. He was acquitted and lodged a claim in the liquidation of his company for expenses of £11,500 incurred by him in his successful defence.

The House of Lords held that he was not entitled to be relieved of this liability by the company because the incurring of these expenses had not been part of his duty as a director.

4. Lien

An agent has a lien over property of the principal which comes into his hands in the course of the agency. This right enables the agent to retain his principal's property until the principal has paid the appropriate remuneration, has reimbursed the agent for expenses and has relieved the agent of liabilities incurred to third parties.

The lien is referred to as a "possessory" lien because it is lost when the property passes out of the agent's possession.

An agent's lien is usually a general lien, *i.e.* he has a right to retain the property until some general balance arising out of the whole course of the agency has been met. A general lien is distinguished from a special lien which is a right to retain property until payment of a debt arising out of the contract under which possession of the property was obtained. Carriers and repairers of goods have special liens. Most agents, *e.g.* factors, stockbrokers, solicitors and bankers, have general liens.

RIGHTS AND LIABILITIES OF THIRD PARTIES

The essential purpose of agency is to create a legal relationship between the principal and the third party. The general rule, therefore, is that the third party will have rights against, and may be liable to be sued by, the principal, but will neither have rights against, nor be liable to be sued by, the agent, since the agent is regarded as having dropped out of the transaction once he has established the relationship between his principal and the third party.

In some situations, however, the general rule does not apply, and the third party may have rights against, and be liable to be sued by, the agent. The law applicable to these situations depends on whether the agent was:

1. acting within his authority; or
2. exceeding his authority.

1. Agent Acting within his Authority

The third party's rights and liabilities in this case vary according to the way in which the agent has contracted with him. There are three possibilities:

(a) The agent may have contracted expressly as agent for a named principal.

(b) The agent may have contracted expressly as agent without naming his principal.

(c) The agent may have contracted "ostensibly as principal," *i.e.* as if he were himself the contracting party.

(a) As agent for named principal

Where the agent discloses to the third party at the time of the making of the contract the name of the principal for whom he is acting, the rights and liabilities arising out of the contract exist as between the third party and the principal, and the agent normally cannot either sue or be sued by the third party on the contract.

In the following exceptional cases the agent may incur personal liability to the third party:

(i)   where he expressly undertakes personal liability;

(ii)   where, by the custom of his particular trade, he is personally liable; and

(iii)   where the named principal has no legal existence, *e.g.* is an unincorporated body, such as a club or a congregation, which cannot be sued, or is a proposed company not yet registered.

(b)   As agent for unnamed principal

The law applicable to this situation is rather uncertain.

On the one hand the view may be taken that the third party, knowing that the person with whom he is dealing is only an agent, is relying on the credit of the principal, and this view suggests that the same rules would apply to this situation as to (a), above, with the addition that the agent would also incur personal liability to the third party:

(iv)   where he refuses to name his principal on being asked to do so by the third party after the making of the contract.

However, the court would probably be more ready to infer in this situation that the agent had undertaken personal liability or was made personally liable by usage of trade (see (i) and (ii) under (a)) than it would be where the principal had been actually named when the contract was made.

On the other hand the view may be taken that the third party, since he does not know the identity of the principal, must have been relying on the credit of the agent, and according to this view the rules to be applied would be the same as those applying to the situation where the agent contracts ostensibly as principal (see (c), below).

In many cases custom of trade will make it clear whether the agent is personally liable to the third party or not, but so far as other cases are concerned no definite rule as to the agent's liability appears to have been established other than the very general one that the agent is in this situation more likely to be held personally liable than where he named his principal, but less likely to be held personally liable than where he contracted ostensibly as principal.

It is, however, a well-recognised rule that if the third party discovers at a later date the identity of the principal for whom the agent was acting and "elects" (chooses) to exercise against the principal the rights which arise out of the contract, he cannot afterwards hold the agent also personally liable. An illustration of this rule is *Ferrier v. Dods and ors.* (1865) 3 M. 561:

D., an auctioneer, sold a mare guaranteed to be a good worker to F. The name of the seller was not disclosed, and F. paid the price to D.

Later F. learned that the seller was Bathgate.

The mare proved unsound and F. returned it to Bathgate.

F. then brought an action to recover the price against both the auctioneer and the seller.

The court held that by returning the mare to Bathgate F. had elected to sue the principal and could no longer sue the agent.

The rule as to the third party's right of election was explained thus by Lord Justice-Clerk Inglis at p. 564:

"Dods sold the mare to him (*the pursuer*) as agent, and did not disclose his principal. He was known to be an agent; an auctioneer is presumably an agent. Soon after the sale he did disclose his principal. This was the position which the pursuer then occupied. He was entitled to go against either Dods as seller, because the principal had not been originally disclosed, or against the true owner, now disclosed. But he was not entitled to go against both. What the law gave him was an election or option. He was entitled to have his choice of action against the ostensible or the real seller. But here he proposes to go against both. Not only so, but he proposes to go against the agent, though, in my opinion, he has already elected to go against the true owner. This I gather from . . . the return of the mare to Bathgate. . . . It was to the owner he returned her. He was not entitled to get back the money unless he returned the mare, nor from any one, except the person to whom he returned her."

(c) Ostensibly as principal

In this situation the agent is contracting in his own name, and the third party does not know that he is in fact an agent. The parties to the contract are the agent and the third party and it is they who have in the first instance the right to sue on it.

The principal may, however, after the contract has been made, either disclose himself or be disclosed by his agent, and rights of action will then arise between him and the third party:

(i) The principal will be entitled to sue the third party on the contract, but the third party can put forward as a defence to the principal's action any defence which he might have put forward if the action had been brought by the agent (*e.g.* the third party may plead compensation of a debt which is due to him by the agent).

(ii) The third party will have the right to choose between suing the principal and suing the agent.

The right of election referred to in (ii) does not entitle the third party to sue both the agent and the principal at the same time (see *Ferrier* v. *Dods and ors.*, above), or to sue first one, and, if he fails to obtain full redress from that party, then to sue the other: the liability of the agent and the principal to the third party is alternative liability, not "joint and several" liability, and election, once made, is final.

However, the third party is entitled to have full knowledge of the facts when he exercises his option. Therefore, if some time elapses between the date of the contract and the time when the third party discovers the principal, the third party will not be considered to have made his election during that interval. Election may be express or implied; *e.g.* in *Ferrier* v. *Dods and ors.* election to hold the principal liable was inferred by the court from the return of the mare to Bathgate. What amounts to election varies with the circumstances. The mere fact that the third party has commenced proceedings against the agent does not prevent him from electing to sue the principal, but if the third party has reached the stage of obtaining a "decree" (a court order made at the conclusion of proceedings) against either agent or principal, his right of election is at an end and the party whom he has not sued is freed from liability to him.

2. Agent Exceeding his Authority

Where the agent has exceeded both his actual and ostensible authority, the third party will have no right to sue any principal on the contract, but will have the following rights against the agent:

(a) Where the agent was professing to contract on behalf of a non-existent principal (such as a company not yet incorporated), the third party is entitled to treat the agent as the contracting party, and, if necessary, sue him to perform the contract.

(b) Where the principal did in fact exist but had not expressly, impliedly or ostensibly conferred the necessary authority on the agent, the contract becomes binding on the principal if he ratifies his agent's unauthorised action, and the third party can then sue the principal. If, however, the principal does not ratify the contract, the third party's remedy is an action of damages for fraud against an agent who has been fraudulent or an action of damages for "breach of warranty of authority" against an agent who has innocently misrepresented the extent of his authority.

The action of damages for "breach of warranty of authority" is based on the principle that an agent impliedly "warrants" (guarantees) to the third party that he does have the necessary authority to enter into a contract which will be binding on his principal.

The damages which can be claimed in such an action are measured by the loss suffered by the third party as a result of his not having a binding contract with the principal.

An instance of a successful action of this type is *Anderson* v. *Croall & Sons Ltd.* (1903) 6 F. 153:

At Musselburgh races a mare, "Ethel May," which the owner did not mean to sell, was by an innocent mistake on the part of C. & Sons Ltd., the auctioneers, "sold" to Mrs A. for thirty-five guineas. The owner refused to part with the mare at that time, but seven months later it fetched seventy guineas when sold by auction at York.

Mrs A. sued C. & Sons Ltd., and was held entitled not only to the return of the purchase price which she had paid but also to twenty-five guineas for loss of her "bargain" and for any trouble and outlay to which she had been put as a result. She would, the court estimated, have been about twenty-five guineas richer if the auctioneers had had the owner's authority to sell.

In contrast, the case of *Irving* v. *Burns*, 1915 S.C. 260, shows that if the third party has suffered no loss through his not having a binding contract with the principal he will obtain no damages for the agent's breach of warranty of authority:

A contract had been made between I., a plumber, and B., a chartered accountant who was secretary of the Langside Picture House Ltd.

In accordance with that contract plumber-work was carried out at the company's premises, but the contract was not binding on the company because B. had been acting without authority in making it.

An action for damages for breach of warranty of authority was raised by I. against B., but since the company was insolvent and had no assets the court held that the plumber had suffered no loss from the fact that the contract was not binding on the company and so he was not entitled to damages from the company's unauthorised agent.

TERMINATION OF AGENCY

Agency comes to an end when the agent ceases to have authority to create a contractual relationship between his principal and the third party. Cessation of the agent's authority may result from:

1. completion of the transaction or expiry of time;
2. mutual agreement;
3. revocation by the principal;
4. renunciation by the agent;
5. frustration.

1. Completion of Transaction or Expiry of Time

Agency terminates on the completion of the transaction or expiry of the time for which the authority was granted.

2. Mutual Agreement

Principal and agent may agree that the agency is to be at an end.

In some situations, however, this does not take effect until third parties are properly notified, because, though the agent's actual authority is at an end, he may have ostensible authority; *e.g.* under the Partnership Act 1890 a retiring partner's authority is not terminated effectively unless notice of the retirement is given in the Edinburgh Gazette and to individual customers of the firm.

3. Revocation by Principal

The principal may revoke the agent's authority. Unless it is a "procuratory in rem suam" ("authority solely for agent's own benefit").

Here again, the principal must give proper notice to third parties if he wishes to avoid the possibility that third parties will hold him liable on the ground of the agent's ostensible authority.

Moreover, the principal may be liable in damages to the agent if the revocation amounts to a breach of a "term of their contract."

4. Renunciation by Agent

The agent may renounce his agency.

The renunciation will in some situations be a breach of the contract of agency between principal and agent, making the agent liable in damages to the principal.

5. Frustration

On frustration generally see p. 342, above. An agency will, for instance, terminate where there is rei interitus ("destruction of the subject-matter"), such as would occur if property which the agent was employed to sell was accidentally destroyed.

Special mention may be made here of:
   (a)   death;
   (b)   bankruptcy;
   (c)   insanity; and
   (d)   discontinuance of the principal's business.

(a) **Death**

The death of either principal or agent terminates the agency.

It is, however, said to be the rule that if an agent continues to act bona fide ("honestly") believing that the deceased principal is still alive, the transactions will be binding on the principal's estate. This is supported by the House of Lords decision in the Scottish case *Campbell* v. *Anderson* (1829) 3 W. & S. 384, which concerned transactions by a factor of an estate whose owner had died on a visit to the West Indies. The authority of the case may, however, have diminished somewhat owing to the passage of time and the improvement in communications; in addition, the case appears to be contrary to the generally accepted rule that death is a public fact of which no notice need be given.

(b) Bankruptcy

The bankruptcy of the principal terminates the agency (*M'Kenzie* v. *Campbell* (1894) 21 R. 904, a case in which a law-agent's authority to act in the defence of a person arrested on charges of forgery was held to have terminated when the accused, in custody and awaiting his trial, was found to be bankrupt).

The bankruptcy of the agent also terminates the agency. Because of the delectus personae ("choice of person") involved in the contract of agency between principal and agent, the trustee in bankruptcy is not entitled to adopt the agency. A new agreement to which the principal, the agent and the trustee would be parties could enable the bankrupt agent to continue his work as agent.

Bankruptcy, like death, is regarded as a public fact of which no notice need be given.

(c) Insanity

Permanent insanity of the principal, if known to the third party, terminates the agency. According to the views expressed in *Pollok* v. *Paterson*, 10 December 1811, F.C., a principal's permanent insanity does not of itself terminate an agency and a third party who is in good faith (*i.e.* is unaware of the insanity) is entitled to regard the agent as still having authority until notification of the insanity has been given.

Temporary insanity of the principal does not terminate the agency; thus in *Wink* v. *Mortimer* (1849) 11 D. 995 an agent who had continued to act as agent during a period when the principal was confined to a lunatic asylum was held entitled, on the principal's recovery, to claim remuneration for having so acted.

Insanity of the agent terminates the agency.

(d) Discontinuance of principal's business

If the principal discontinues the business in which the agent is engaged, the agency is terminated and the agent is not entitled to damages for breach of contract unless he can show that it was an express or implied term of the agency that the principal should continue the business for a specified period.

Patmore & Co. v. *B. Cannon & Co. Ltd.* (1892) 19 R. 1004: P. & Co. were Scottish agents for the sale of leather goods, dip and glue manufactured by an English company, C. Ltd. The agreement between P. & Co. and C. Ltd. stated that the agency was to continue for five years from October 1891.

In January 1892 C. Ltd. intimated its intention to give up its leather trade.

P. & Co. were held not entitled to damages for breach of contract, because C. Ltd. had not in the agreement bound itself to carry on its business or any part of it, for five years or for any other period.

Further Reading

Gloag and Henderson, *Introduction to the Law of Scotland*

J. A. Lillie, *The Mercantile Law of Scotland*

David M. Walker, *Principles of Scottish Private Law*

J. J. Gow, *The Mercantile and Industrial Law of Scotland* (W. Green & Son Ltd.)

David M. Walker, *The law of Contracts and related obligations in Scotland* (Butterworths)

Enid A. Marshall, *Scottish Cases on Agency* (W. Green & Son Ltd.)

QUASI-CONTRACT

CERTAIN obligations implied by law arise from quasi-contract, and are referred to as "quasi-contractual obligations."

A quasi-contractual obligation resembles a contractual obligation in being an obligation to pay something or to perform some act, but differs from a contractual obligation in that it arises, not from the consent of the parties, but ex lege ("out of law"), *i.e.* by operation of law. In that respect it resembles a "delictual" obligation, *i.e.* the obligation which the law imposes on a wrongdoer to make "reparation" (compensation) for the wrong which he has done.

The underlying idea in quasi-contract is that the parties, although they have made no contract with each other, are in much the same position "as if" (the meaning of the Latin word "quasi") they had made a contract. The law, therefore, in the interests of "equity" (fairness or justice), imposes on the parties obligations similar to the obligations which they would have been under if they had actually made a contract.

The main branches of quasi-contract are:
1. restitution;
2. recompense;
3. negotiorum gestio ("management of affairs");
4. salvage; and
5. general average.

1. *RESTITUTION*

A person comes under an obligation of restitution when he is in possession of goods belonging to another person without being entitled to retain them. He may have found the goods, or stolen them, or had them delivered to him by mistake, or purchased them from a thief, or he may be a person who has had a limited right to possess the goods and who continues in possession of them after his right has come to an end.

A person in such a position is bound to restore the goods to the person entitled to possession of them, and if he has consumed them he is bound to pay their value.

In the case of stolen goods the obligation of restitution exists even when the person possessing the goods does not realise that they have been stolen. The goods are said to be affected by a "vitium reale" ("inherent defect"), which prevents even a "bona fide purchaser" (one who has paid for the goods "in good faith," *i.e.* without being aware that the seller had no right to the goods) from retaining them when their true owner claims them.

If a bona fide purchaser of stolen goods has resold them before his title to them is challenged, he is freed from the obligation of restitution, but where he has made a profit on the resale he will, by the principle of recompense (see p. 407, below), be bound to hand over his profit to the owner if the goods themselves cannot be recovered.

The obligation of restitution may arise where a contract between the parties proves, for some reason, to be ineffective; *e.g.* it may be unenforceable because it was not entered into in the proper form, it may have been reduced because it was voidable, performance of it may have been frustrated by supervening impossibility (see p. 343, above), or it may have been justifiably rescinded by one party because of a material breach of it by the other party (see p. 323, above). The party who has received property in accordance with the terms of the contract must restore it, or, if he has consumed the property, pay its value.

There is, however, usually no obligation of restitution if the reason for the ineffectiveness of the contract is that it is a pactum illicitum ("illegal agreement"): the general rule is summarised in the maxim "in turpi causa melior est conditio possidentis" ("in an immoral situation the position of the possessor is the better one"); the effect of the rule is that the court will not interfere to alter the status quo ("existing position") by ordering restitution. There are exceptions to the general rule where the parties are not in pari delicto ("equally at fault"): the party who is less blameworthy may then have a claim for restitution.

Repetition

This is a special aspect of restitution. It applies to situations where money may be recovered either because it was not due at all or because the "consideration" for it has not followed, *i.e.* where the other party to the contract has not made the agreed return for the sum paid. The remedies available in these situations are often referred to by the Roman law terms, "condictio indebiti" ("action for what was not due") referring to the recovery of money which was not due, and "condictio causa data causa non secuta" ("action applicable when consideration has been given and consideration has not followed") referring to the recovery of money for which the agreed return has not been made.

The condictio indebiti is appropriate where a payment was made under an error in fact (*e.g.* where a debtor forgot that he had already paid his debt) or because of a misinterpretation of a document affecting the parties only (*e.g.* a private commercial contract). The condictio is not applicable where the payment was made under an error as to a general principle of law or because of a misinterpretation of an Act of Parliament (as in *Taylor* v. *Wilson's Trustees*, 1975 S.C. 146, where a liquidator, having misinterpreted the Finance Acts, had paid out to shareholders money which he ought to have retained to meet the company's tax liability to the Inland Revenue); the reason is expressed in the maxim "ignorantia juris neminem excusat" ("ignorance of the law excuses no one").

There is an example of the condictio causa data causa non secuta in *Cantiere San Rocco* v. *Clyde Shipbuilding and Engineering Co. Ltd.*, 1923 S.C.(H.L.) 105 (see p. 346, above).

2. *RECOMPENSE*

The institutional writer Bell defined the principle of recompense as follows (*Principles of the Law of Scotland*, § 538):

> "Where one has gained by the lawful act of another, done without any intention of donation, he is bound to recompense or indemnify that other to the extent of the gain."

That definition indicates the general nature of recompense, but has been criticised as being too wide. For instance, Lord President Dunedin in *Edinburgh and District Tramways Co. Ltd.* v. *Courtenay*, 1909 S.C. 99, at p. 105, gave the following illustration in support of that criticism:

> "One man heats his house, and his neighbour gets a great deal of benefit. It is absurd to suppose that the person who has heated his house can go to his neighbour and say—'Give me so much for my coal bill, because you have been warmed by what I have done, and I did not intend to give you a present of it.' "

Lord Dunedin concluded that it was impossible to frame a completely satisfactory definition of recompense: the doctrine was an equitable one, and each case had to be judged of according to its own circumstances. However, he referred with approval to the Latin

maxim "nemo debet locupletari ex aliena jactura ("no-one ought to
be enriched as a result of another person's loss").

According to that maxim there are two essential elements in
recompense:

(a) loss ("jactura") suffered by one party; and

(b) gain conferred on another party as a result of that loss.

A third essential element was brought out in *Varney (Scotland)
Ltd.* v. *Burgh of Lanark*, 1976 S.L.T. 46:

(c) absence of any other legal remedy.

(a) Loss Suffered by One Party

This element was not given sufficient weight in Bell's definition.
The need for the person claiming recompense to have lost something
is illustrated by the case of *Edinburgh and District Tramways Co. Ltd.*
v. *Courtenay*, 1909 S.C. 99:

A tramway company let to C., an advertising contractor, the right
to advertise on the company's tram-cars, and by the contract C. was
to supply the fittings necessary for the advertisements.

New tram-cars, however, constructed for the company already
had the necessary fittings which were required by the company for
other purposes. This resulted in a saving for C., and the company
claimed a sum, additional to the agreed rent, by way of recompense
for the use by C. of the fittings.

The claim failed because the company had suffered no loss; C.'s
benefit was merely incidental to expenditure incurred by the company
for other purposes.

(b) Gain Conferred on Another Party as a Result of that Loss

The person against whom a claim for recompense is made must
have gained as a result of the other's loss. He must be lucratus
("enriched").

Accordingly, a claim for recompense is measured not by the
amount of the pursuer's expenditure but by the amount of the
defender's gain. The defender is liable only quantum lucratus ("so
far as enriched").

(c) Absence of Any Other Legal Remedy

The facts in *Varney (Scotland) Ltd.* v. *Burgh of Lanark* were that
building contractors had built a number of houses in Lanark for sale
to the public, and that, as the Burgh of Lanark was unwilling to
construct the necessary sewers for the housing development, the
contractors themselves constructed the sewers and then claimed
reimbursement of the cost of construction from the burgh.

The court held that the contractors were not entitled to succeed in this claim based on recompense since they had had another legal remedy available to them, namely a petition for specific implement based on the Burgh Police (Scotland) Act 1892 under which the local authority was bound to construct the sewers; recompense was available only as a last resort.

Examples of Recompense

(i) If a person spends money on property in the mistaken, but honest, belief that the property belongs to him, he can be compelled to give up the property to the owner, but he has a claim on the principle of recompense for his expenditure on it in so far as the expenditure has proved beneficial to the owner.

(ii) If a person has done work under a contract, but has departed so radically from the terms of the contract that he cannot claim the contract price, he may have a claim against the other party on the ground of recompense. An illustration is the case of *Ramsay & Son* v. *Brand* (1898) 25 R. 1212:

R. agreed to do mason-work on a cottage for B. for £79 10s., but departed from the plan without B.'s consent. B. refused to pay,

The court held that although R. could not claim the contract price, he was entitled to recompense if and in so far as B. had been lucratus by the work done.

(iii) If a contract which the courts do not recognise as being enforceable has been performed, a claim of recompense may be open; the contract may, for instance, be unenforceable because the proper evidence to prove it is lacking or it may have been declared void by statute. An illustration is the case of *Cuthbertson* v. *Lowes* (1870) 8 M. 1073, concerning the sale of potatoes under a contract which was void by the Weights and Measures Acts (see p. 288, above).

Distinction between Recompense and Implied Contract

The principle of recompense properly applies only where there is no contract or where a claim based on an existing contract cannot be made.

An implied contract, on the other hand, exists where there is assumed by law to be a contract, although the parties have not expressly agreed on its terms.

There is an example of implied contract in the provision of the Sale of Goods Act 1979 that where necessaries have been sold and delivered to a person who because of non-age, mental incapacity or drunkenness is unable to contract he must pay a reasonable price for them.

A claim based on implied contract is also possible where work has been done under a contract which does not contain any express provision about the price, or where extra work has been subsequently agreed on by the parties.

The importance of the distinction between recompense and implied contract lies in the fact that a person claiming recompense is entitled only to the amount by which the other party is lucratus, whereas a person basing his claim on implied contract is entitled to payment quantum meruit ("to the extent which he deserved"), which will in normal cases be the market price of his goods or services; in the case of implied contract it does not matter that the recipient has received no benefit.

It is, therefore, usually to the advantage of a party to base his claim on implied contract rather than on recompense, but this course is not open to him where there is in existence a binding contract expressly providing for his rights; *e.g.* in the circumstances of *Ramsay & Son* v. *Brand* (1898) 25 R. 1212 (see p. 409, above), R. could claim neither the contract price (because he had not complied with the contract) nor quantum meruit payment (because the contract expressly provided for the work to be done and for the price to be paid for it); similarly in *Boyd & Forrest* v. *Glasgow and South-Western Ry. Co.*, 1915 S.C.(H.L.) 20 (see p. 279, above), the contractors were held not entitled to payment on a quantum meruit basis for the extra cost because the contract (which could not, in the circumstances, be set aside) expressly provided for the price to be paid for the work.

3. *NEGOTIORUM GESTIO*

This occurs when a person, referred to as a "negotiorum gestor" ("manager of affairs"), intervenes, without authority, in the affairs of another person who is permanently or temporarily unable to attend to them himself; the circumstances must be such that it is reasonable to assume that actual authority would have been given to the negotiorum gestor if it had been possible for him to apply for it.

There may be negotiorum gestio where it becomes necessary for a person to act on behalf of an insane person, a person who is abroad or in prison, or a person who is for some other reason unable to take or authorise the necessary action himself. There is no negotiorum gestio if actual authority has been conferred on the person who takes the action.

A negotiorum gestor is entitled to be repaid all the expenditure which he has properly incurred, even although it may not have proved beneficial. His claim is therefore wider than a claim based on recompense.

On the other hand, he must account for his "intromissions" (transactions with the property of the other person) and must exercise the degree of care which is reasonable in the circumstances.

The principle of negotiorum gestio operates in agency of necessity (see p. 389, above).

4. *SALVAGE*

Salvage is the reward given to persons who voluntarily save or contribute to the saving of a ship or cargo or of the lives of persons endangered at sea. At common law salvage applied only to ships and their cargoes; by statute it was extended to the saving of life at sea (Merchant Shipping Act 1894) and to the saving of cargo or life from an aircraft on or over the sea (Civil Aviation Act 1949).

The term "salvage" is also used of the services rendered as well as of the reward for the services. The person rendering the services is referred to as a "salvor."

The persons entitled to salvage are the owners, masters and crew of the ships which have come to the rescue. The assistance must have been given voluntarily; therefore, the master and crew of the ship salved are not entitled to salvage, because they are under a duty to do all in their power to save ship and cargo; passengers on the salved ship become entitled to salvage if they voluntarily remain on the ship to assist in rescue operations, but are not entitled to it otherwise.

The persons liable to pay salvage are those who have an interest in the property which has been saved—usually the owners of the ship and of the cargo and the persons entitled to the freight (the charge for the carriage of the cargo).

No salvage is due for rescue operations which prove unsuccessful, unless there is a salvage agreement containing an express provision to the contrary.

The amount of salvage is, unless agreed on by the parties, fixed by the court. Amongst the factors taken into account by the court are the value of the property saved, the degree of peril of the ship, the risks run by the salvors, and the cost in labour and time to the salvors. The general policy given effect to by the court is that salvage should be a generous amount in order that persons may be encouraged to undertake similar rescue work.

5. *GENERAL AVERAGE*

"Average" is a term of shipping law meaning loss or injury to a ship or cargo during a voyage. Average may be particular or general.

Most ordinary losses and injuries come under the head of particular average, *e.g.* loss of a cargo through its being washed overboard or injury to a ship when it strikes a rock. A particular average loss is borne solely by the party whose property is involved (or by his insurer in his place).

A general average loss, on the other hand, occurs where any extraordinary sacrifice or expenditure is intentionally and reasonably made or incurred for the common safety or to preserve the ship or other property from peril. The sacrifice or expenditure is referred to as a "general average act."

A general average act may result in loss to any of the three main interests at stake during a voyage, namely, the ship, the cargo, and the freight; *e.g.* there is a general average loss to the ship if part of it is deliberately and reasonably sacrificed or used in an abnormal way for the common safety, and there is general average loss to the cargo and the freight if the cargo is jettisoned to save the ship from sinking.

A general average loss must be borne by all the parties whose interests were at stake. Therefore, a party whose property has been saved by the general average act is under a quasi-contractual obligation to make a general average contribution, in proportion to his interest, to the other parties whose property has been deliberately sacrificed.

Further Reading

Gloag and Henderson, *Introduction to the Law of Scotland*
T. B. Smith, *A Short Commentary on the Law of Scotland*
David M. Walker, *Principles of Scottish Private Law*
David M. Walker, *The law of Contracts and related obligations in Scotland* (Butterworths)

DELICT

A "DELICT" is a legal wrong, *i.e.* harmful conduct by a person which causes loss or injury to another person and subjects the person responsible for the loss or injury to legal liability to "make reparation for" (*i.e.* to make good) the loss or injury caused. The liability is referred to as "delictual liability."

The harmful conduct may be an act or an omission, and it may be deliberate and intentional or merely negligent and unintentional.

The conduct may or may not be a criminal offence, and it may or may not be morally, as well as legally, wrong. The law of delict or reparation is concerned only with civil liability for the conduct, *i.e.* liability which can be enforced in the civil courts by the person who has suffered against the person who is responsible.

The reparation required to be made always takes the form of damages, *i.e.* of payment of a sum of money by the wrongdoer or his executor to the person who has suffered or his executor. Where personal injuries have resulted in the victim's death, the wrongdoer is liable to pay damages also to certain relatives of the deceased in accordance with the Damages (Scotland) Act 1976.

Where a delict is threatened or is likely to be repeated or continued, the remedy of interdict may be granted. An interdict is an order given by the court to the wrongdoer to refrain from harmful conduct. It is the appropriate remedy for delicts such as trespass and nuisance.

The leading principle in the law of delict is that the loss or injury must have been caused by culpa ("fault") before reparation in the form of damages can be claimed. The term "culpa" is here used to cover both dolus ("intentional wrongdoing") and negligence. In some contexts the term is given a more restricted meaning, namely negligence.

There are some situations where delictual liability arises without culpa. These come under the heading "strict liability." They are always treated as part of the law of delict, although the leading principle referred to above does not apply to them. An obvious instance is statutory liability: a statute may provide that liability for some act or omission is to arise even where there has been no culpa.

There are also other situations, not regarded as part of the law of delict, where compensation may be obtained without the need to prove culpa. The prominent instance is the state industrial injuries scheme (see p. 377, above): it has a "no fault" basis of compensation for persons who suffer personal injury caused by accident arising out of and in the course of their employment.

The Royal Commission on Civil Liability and Compensation for Personal Injury 1973–1978 ("the Pearson Commission") considered some possible extensions of "no fault" compensation. The Commission's *Report* (Cmnd. 7054) includes recommendations for extension of the industrial injuries scheme, a new scheme for motor vehicle accidents modelled on the industrial injuries scheme and financed by a levy on petrol, and a new benefit for severely handicapped children (financed by the state); also recommended are further developments of strict liability, including a new system of products liability (by which producers would be strictly liable for death or personal injury caused by defective products) and a new system for the benefit of vaccine-damaged children.

GENERAL NATURE OF DELICT

The general nature of delict is summed up in the maxim "damnum injuria datum" ("loss caused by a legal wrong"). The three essential elements are:

1. damnum, *i.e.* loss or injury suffered by the party who has been wronged;
2. injuria, *i.e.* conduct which amounts to a legal wrong; and
3. a causative link between 1 and 2, *i.e.* the loss or injury must have been caused ("datum") by the legal wrong.

1. Damnum

This may take the form of "patrimonial" (financial) loss or of physical injury and suffering.

In the case of some delicts there may be damnum in the shape of an affront or hurt feelings, even although no substantial loss or injury has been caused. In such cases the damages are considered to be a solatium ("comfort") for wounded feelings. An insult, for instance, may give rise to a claim for damages.

The phrase "injuria sine damno" ("a legal wrong without loss") is used to describe the situation where no harm has resulted from wrongful conduct, e.g. where careless driving has *almost* caused injury.

2. Injuria

For a delict to exist there must have been some act or omission which was wrongful, *i.e.* which was a breach of a legal duty. For instance, a trader, A, may find that he is suffering loss as a result of competition from another trader, B, who has recently established a business in a locality where A formerly had a monopoly; competition is not a legal wrong (an "injuria"); therefore there is no delict and A has no right to damages from B, although he suffers loss as a result of B's conduct. In such cases there is said to be "damnum absque injuria" ("loss without legal wrong").

The duty may be imposed by statute or by common law, and in some cases there may be both a statutory and a common law duty; e.g. there have been many cases in which factory workers have claimed damages from their employer, the factory occupier, both under the Factories Act 1961 and on the ground of negligence at common law.

The question of whether or not there is in a particular situation a duty, breach of which amounts to a delict, is a question of law, and must be decided by reference to statutory provisions or "precedents" (earlier cases) which are in point. This question of law must be distinguished from the questions of fact which arise in actions based on delicts, e.g. the question of whether in fact the defender was in breach of the duty which the law imposed on him.

This distinction may be illustrated by the best-known of all cases on this branch of law, *Donoghue* v. *Stevenson*, 1932 S.C.(H.L.) 31:

Mrs D. alleged that one evening in August 1928 in Francis Minchella's cafe in Paisley a friend had ordered for her ice cream and ginger beer suitable to be used with the ice cream as an iced drink, that the beer was supplied in an opaque sealed bottle, that Minchella poured some of the beer from the bottle into a tumbler containing the ice cream, that Mrs D. drank some of the contents of the tumbler, that her friend then lifted the bottle and was pouring out the remainder into the tumbler when a decomposed snail floated out of the bottle, and that as a result Mrs. D. suffered shock and illness. These points were questions of fact.

Mrs. D. brought an action of damages against the manufacturer of the beer. For the success of this claim the court had to be satisfied not only of the probable truth of Mrs. D.'s story but also that she was in law entitled to sue the manufacturer. The question of law was whether the manufacturer owed to probable consumers, such as Mrs. D., a duty to guard against harmful foreign bodies being present in the opaque sealed bottles intended to reach the consumer without having their contents inspected by any other person. It was this question of law which caused the case to be taken on appeal to the House of Lords, and which made the case a famous and important one.

Mrs. D. was successful in her appeal to the House of Lords, since the House, reversing the judgment of the Court of Session, held that the manufacturer did owe a duty to the consumer in circumstances such as these, and that therefore Mrs. D., *if* she could prove the facts of her case to the satisfaction of the court, was entitled to damages from the manufacturer for failure in that duty.

It is from this case that the standard formulation of "duty" at common law was developed: the case is regarded as authority for the principle that A has a legal duty to take precautions against his harming B, if A should reasonably have foreseen that failure on his part to take precautions would probably result in harm to B.

(Like many other cases involving important questions of law this case was, once the question of law had been authoritatively decided, settled out of court by agreement between the parties. Whether or not Mrs. D. could have proved the facts of her case cannot be discovered from the law reports.)

The breach of duty which is essential for delict may be a deliberate and intentional act or omission, *e.g.* interference with personal security or with a person's reputation or property; assault, slander and trespass are instances of delicts which may be in this category.

Alternatively, the breach of duty may be unintentional. It will then normally require to amount to what the law regards as "negligence" (see p. 419, below). There are, however, some situations where, even although there has been no negligence, the law holds that there has been a breach of duty giving rise to delictual liability; in these situations there is said to be "strict liability" (see p. 426, below).

3. Causation

For delictual liability to arise the "damnum" must have been caused by the "injuria"; the person suing for reparation must be able to show that the breach of duty was the effective cause of the loss or injury which he suffered. There is an illustration of this theory of causation in *M'Williams* v. *Sir William Arrol & Co. Ltd. and Lithgows Ltd.*, 1962 S.C.(H.L.) 70:

A steel erector had been killed when he fell seventy feet from a steel lattice tower being erected at a shipyard in Port Glasgow. His widow brought an action of damages against his employers on the ground that they had failed in their duty to provide a safety belt.

Evidence was heard in court, and while it was proved that the employers had been in breach of that duty it was also proved that if a safety belt had been provided the deceased would not have worn it.

The employers were held not liable, since the widow had failed to establish a causal connection between the breach of duty and the accident.

Lord Reid stated (at pp. 82 and 83):

"If I prove that my breach of duty in no way caused or contributed to the accident I cannot be liable in damages. And if the accident would have happened in just the same way whether or not I fulfilled my duty, it is obvious that my failure to fulfil my duty cannot have caused or contributed to it. . . .

"A pursuer must prove his case. He must prove that the fault of the defender caused or contributed to the damage which he has suffered."

Difficult questions may arise where there are several factors leading up to the act or omission which is the immediate cause of the injury. The factors which are material causes must be separated from those which are not, the harm done must not be too remote a result of the breach of duty, and there must be no break in the "chain of causation."

A new factor which disturbs the sequence of events is referred to as a "novus actus interveniens" ("new intervening factor"). It breaks the chain of causation, and so the person guilty of the original breach of duty is not liable for injury occurring after that point. The novus actus ("new factor") may be some action of the injured party himself or a deliberate intervention by a third party.

In deciding whether the chain of causation has been broken the court applies the test of "reasonable foreseeability." This means that the person guilty of the original breach of duty will be liable if a reasonable man in his position would have foreseen that the breach of duty was likely to result in injury to the party who has in fact suffered. The test of reasonable foreseeability may be illustrated as follows:

(a) If the wrongdoer has created a situation which was likely to lead to the injured party's taking emergency action, then the chain of causation is not broken and the wrongdoer will be held liable for the injury, although the immediate cause of it was the emergency action taken by the injured party himself.

(b)   If the foreseeable result of the wrongdoer's action is intervention by a third party which causes injury to the party claiming damages, the chain of causation is not broken; *e.g.* if X throws a lighted squib into a crowded market place where it is passed quickly on from A to B and from B to C before it explodes and injures C, X will be liable to C because the action which A and B took for their own safety was foreseeable.

(c)   *Macdonald* v. *David Macbrayne Ltd.*, 1915 S.C. 716: A steamship company negligently delivered to M., a shopkeeper in Fort William, along with two barrels of paraffin a third barrel containing naphtha which ought to have been delivered to someone else. The three barrels were placed in M.'s store by one of M.'s assistants, and M. was not made aware that more than two barrels had been delivered.

Some three weeks later, one of M.'s assistants, desiring to obtain paraffin, went to the store with a lighted candle and tapped the barrel of naphtha. There was an explosion, and the store was set on fire and destroyed.

M. brought an action of damages against the steamship company for the loss which he had suffered as a result of the destruction of the store and its contents, and for this loss the company was held liable, because, as was stated by Lord Guthrie (at p. 725): "There is sufficient sequence of causation to warrant us in holding that what took place was a natural consequence of the defenders' initial fault."

However, M. also claimed damages of £200 for personal injuries which he had received in falling from an adjoining roof on to which he had climbed with a hose to help to extinguish the fire. The court held that these injuries were too remote a result of the company's negligence to give M. a valid claim for damages. Of M.'s action Lord Justice-Clerk Macdonald stated (at p. 722): "I cannot say that that was a natural consequence of what took place. It was his own act."

(d)   *McKew* v. *Holland & Hannen & Cubitts (Scotland) Ltd.*, 1970 S.C.(H.L.) 20: M., a steel fixer, had sustained injuries to his left leg as a result of an accident caused by the negligence of his employer.

Three weeks later M. had another accident: he was about to go down a flight of stairs leading from a house which he had been visiting when he felt a sudden weakness in his left leg, jumped down several steps to the next landing, and as a result sustained severe injuries to his right leg.

M. brought an action claiming damages from his employer in

respect of both accidents. He was awarded damages for the injuries to his left leg, but the court held that the injuries to his right leg had been caused by a deliberate and voluntary action (M.'s jump on to the landing) which broke the chain of causation.

Lord Wheatley stated (at 1969 S.C. p. 27):

"The test of reasonable foreseeability is not always an easy one to apply. It has been observed time and again that it is not to be judged by the test of hindsight on the one hand or inspired crystal gazing on the other. It is what the reasonable man might reasonably anticipate would happen if placed in the given set of circumstances. Circumstances can vary infinitely, and there is no set standard or norm for qualification as the reasonable man. That, too, will be determined by the circumstances of the particular case. . . . Each case must be considered on its own facts. In the present case . . . the pursuer was undoubtedly suffering from a weakness in his left leg consequent upon his initial injuries, and it was this weakness which triggered off the chain of events which resulted in the injury to his right ankle. . . . The issue narrows to this: it being reasonably foreseeable that the pursuer might have this episodic weakness in his leg, and that he might be descending stairs without a support, was it reasonably foreseeable that the pursuer would find himself in danger of falling through that weakness and would act as he did in the circumstances which prevailed, or was his action such as no reasonable man would have anticipated or done in the circumstances? Was there in fact a nova causa interveniens[1]? The decision to jump was a conscious and voluntary one. . . . To make a conscious decision to jump in that situation . . . was something which, in my opinion, no reasonable person would have done in the circumstances, and which no reasonable person would have regarded as being a reasonably foreseeable course of action. It was in fact a nova causa interveniens which broke the chain of causation."

NEGLIGENCE

Very many actions of damages for delict are based on negligence, the pursuer alleging that he has suffered injury as a result of the defender's negligence. In this legal context "negligence" does not simply mean "carelessness"; negligence exists when a person allows harm to occur in circumstances in which he ought to have taken precautions to prevent its occurrence. The commonest categories

[1] Literally "new cause intervening."

of negligence are those concerned with road accidents and employment accidents.

The nature of the negligence which will be the ground of a successful action of damages may be examined under the following headings:

1. duty of care;
2. standard of care; and
3. proof of negligence.

1. Duty of Care

For negligence to exist there must first have been a duty of care on the defender to prevent the loss or injury which has been suffered by the pursuer. "Negligence" in its technical legal sense implies a duty owed and neglected. The distinction between negligence and carelessness was expressed thus by Lord Macmillan in *Donoghue* v. *Stevenson*, 1932 S.C.(H.L.) 31, at p. 70 (see p. 415, above):

"The law takes no cognisance of carelessness in the abstract. It concerns itself with carelessness only where there is a duty to take care and where failure in that duty has caused damage. In such circumstances carelessness assumes the legal quality of negligence, and entails the consequences in law of negligence. What then are the circumstances which give rise to this duty to take care? . . . The categories of negligence are never closed. The cardinal principle of liability is that the party complained of should owe to the party complaining a duty to take care, and that the party complaining should be able to prove that he has suffered damage in consequence of a breach of that duty."

In that case the decision was that the manufacturer of a product which was intended to reach its ultimate consumer in the form in which it left the factory, without intermediate inspection, owed a duty of care to that consumer.

The duty of care is owed, not to all the world, but to persons to whom the defender (if he were a reasonable man) would anticipate that injury would probably result from carelessness on his part. It is, therefore, quite possible for two or more persons to be injured as a result of the same act or omission of the defender and for only one or more, but not all, of them to have a valid claim for damages, since they may not all be within the ambit or range of the duty which is owed.

The persons to whom a duty of care is owed may be regarded as the defender's "neighbours" in the legal sense of that word, as was explained by Lord Atkin in *Donoghue* v. *Stevenson* (at p. 44):

"But acts or omissions which any moral code would censure cannot, in a practical world, be treated so as to give a right to every person injured by them to demand relief. In this way rules of law arise which limit the range of complainants and the extent of their remedy. The rule that you are to love your neighbour becomes in law, you must not injure your neighbour; and the lawyer's question, Who is my neighbour? receives a restricted reply. You must take reasonable care to avoid acts or omissions which you can reasonably foresee would be likely to injure your neighbour. Who, then, in law is my neighbour? The answer seems to be—persons who are so closely and directly affected by my act that I ought reasonably to have them in contemplation as being so affected."

A case which illustrates the range of the duty is *Bourhill* v. *Young*, 1942 S.C.(H.L.) 78:

Y., riding a motor cycle carelessly in Colinton Road, Edinburgh, collided with a car and was fatally injured. About fifty feet away was a stationary tram-car which Y. had overtaken on its near side shortly before the collision.

Mrs. B. was a fishwife who had alighted from the tram-car, and who, at the moment of the collision, was getting her creel on to her back from the off side of the driver's platform. She was out of sight of the collision, but she alleged, and succeeded in proving, that, although she had no reasonable fear of immediate physical injury to herself from the collision, she sustained nervous shock as a result of the noise of it.

Her action of damages against Y.'s executor, however, was unsuccessful because Y. could not reasonably have foreseen that nervous shock to a person in Mrs. B.'s position would be the probable result of his careless driving; the occupants of the car were, but Mrs. B. was not, within the range of the duty owed by Y.

Lord Macmillan stated (at p. 88):

"The late John Young was clearly negligent in a question with the occupants of the motor-car with which his cycle collided. He was driving at an excessive speed in a public thoroughfare and he ought to have foreseen that he might consequently collide with any vehicle which he might meet in his course, for such an occurrence may reasonably and probably be expected to ensue from driving at a high speed in a street. But can it be said that he ought further to have foreseen that his excessive speed, involving the possibility of collision with another vehicle, might cause injury by shock to the appellant? The appellant was not within his line of vision, for she was on the other side of a tramway-car which was standing between him and her when he passed, and it was not until he had proceeded some distance beyond her that he collided with the motor-car. The appellant did not see the accident, and she expressly admits that her 'terror did not involve any element of reasonable fear of immediate bodily injury to herself.' She was not so placed that there was any reasonable likelihood of her being affected by the cyclist's careless driving. In these circumstances I am of opinion . . . that the late John Young was under no duty to the appellant to foresee that his negligence in driving at an excessive speed and consequently colliding with a motor-car might result in injury to her; for such a result could not reasonably and probably be anticipated. He was, therefore, not guilty of negligence in a question with the appellant."

By way of general description of the duty of care which is essential for "negligence" in the legal sense, the same judge stated (at p. 88):

"The duty to take care is the duty to avoid doing or omitting to do anything the doing or omitting to do which may have as its reasonable and probable consequence injury to others, and the duty is owed to those to whom injury may reasonably and probably be anticipated if the duty is not observed."

2. Standard of Care

The standard of care required is that expected of the hypothetical or notional "reasonable man," a man of ordinary care and prudence who is neither over-cautious nor over-confident.

The degree of care varies according to circumstances: the greater the risk involved, the greater the degree of care required to satisfy the reasonable standard; special precautions may be necessary, for instance, where an obviously dangerous task is being performed or where the persons within a danger area are specially susceptible to injury (*e.g.* children and disabled persons). A professional man must exercise the degree of care which is expected of a reasonably careful member of that profession.

In deciding whether the defender has attained the necessary standard of care the courts take an objective, as opposed to a subjective, view of the situation, *i.e.* they are not concerned with whether or not the defender was doing what *he* thought was reasonable to prevent injury, but only with whether or not the defender acted as carefully as *a reasonable man* would have acted in his circumstances.

3. Proof of Negligence

The onus (burden) of proof of negligence lies initially on the pursuer, *i.e.* it is for the pursuer to prove that the defender has been negligent. During the course of the case, however, the evidence may have the effect of shifting the onus of proof on to the defender, with the result that it will be for the defender to prove that he has not been negligent, if he is to escape liability for delict.

As regards the standard of proof, negligence need not be established by conclusive evidence or even beyond reasonable doubt; it need be established only on "the balance of probabilities," *i.e.* the court will hold that there has been negligence if the pursuer has shown that there *probably* was negligence and the defender has been unable to prove the contrary.

Res ipsa loquitur

In some cases the pursuer is assisted in his proof of negligence by the application of the rule expressed in the maxim "res ipsa loquitur" ("the thing itself speaks"), which means that an occurrence sometimes tells its own story.

The maxim applies where a thing is shown to have been under the management of the defender, and the accident is such as in the ordinary course of events would not have happened if those who had the management of it had exercised proper care. There is then considered to be reasonable evidence of negligence unless the defender is able to explain how the accident might have occurred without negligence on his part. If the defender provides such an explanation, the pursuer is left where he began, *i.e.* he must prove that there has been negligence. The maxim applies to occurrences such as a bag of flour falling out of a warehouse on to a passer-by.

The maxim does not apply if the pursuer can reasonably be expected to know the exact cause of the accident; the pursuer must then state the cause and prove negligence.

Further, the maxim does not apply where the thing causing the accident is under human control at the time, *e.g.* is a vehicle under the control of a driver. In such cases once the pursuer has proved the circumstances of the accident (*e.g.* that the vehicle suddenly swerved for no apparent reason), it is for the defender to prove that he was in fact not negligent. This contrasts with the situations to which the maxim res ipsa loquitur applies, because in those situations the onus of proof shifts back to the pursuer provided the defender offers some reasonable explanation of how the accident *might* have occurred without fault on his part.

The case of *Devine* v. *Colvilles Ltd.*, 1969 S.C. (H.L.) 67, gives an illustration of circumstances in which the maxim applies:

D., an employee of Colvilles Ltd. at their Ravenscraig steel works, was injured when he jumped from a platform about fifteen feet above the ground. His action was due to a violent explosion which had occurred a short distance from the place where he was working.

D., alleging that the explosion had been caused by the negligence of his employers, claimed damages from them for his injuries.

His employers were able to show how the explosion might have been caused, but they did not establish that it could have been caused *without fault on their part.*

The maxim res ipsa loquitur was applied, which meant that the employers had to show that the explosion was "just as consistent with their having exercised due diligence as with their having been negligent" (*per*[2] Lord Donovan, at p. 102). If they had been able to prove that point, then "the scales which had been tipped in the pursuer's favour by the doctrine of res ipsa loquitur" would have been once more in the balance, and D. would have had to begin again and prove negligence in the usual way. The employers, however, did not prove that the accident was equally consistent with no negligence on their part (*e.g.* they failed to show that inspections were properly carried out), and so, as Lord Donovan expressed it: "The scales remained at the end of the day tilted by the doctrine of res ipsa loquitur in the pursuer's favour."

D. was accordingly awarded damages of £1,350.

The circumstances in which the maxim is applicable and the effect of its application were fully explained in the opinions of Lord Justice-Clerk Grant and Lords Wheatley and Milligan in the Court of Session, and the House of Lords approved of these opinions.

The maxim, said Lord Wheatley (at p. 83), applied only if the pursuer proved two points:

"(a) that the 'thing' causing the accident was under the management of the defender or his servants, and (b) that the accident was such as in the ordinary course of things would not happen if those who had the management had used proper care."

In this case both these points were held to have been proved: the plant in which the explosion had occurred had been under the management of Colvilles Ltd., and "plant which is properly operated and maintained does not normally explode" (*per* the Lord Justice-Clerk at p. 80).

The effect of application of the maxim was to create a presumption that the defenders had been negligent: the explosion was "prima facie" evidence of negligence, *i.e.* it was evidence of negligence until the contrary was shown to be the case.

This presumption could, however, have been rebutted if the defenders had explained how the explosion could have happened without negligence on their part. They had failed to give that explanation, and so the res ("thing") had, as the Lord Justice-Clerk said (at p. 83), "the last word as well as the first."

[2] Meaning "in the words of."

OCCUPIERS' LIABILITY

Liability for negligence in connection with the occupation of premises is now governed by the Occupiers' Liability (Scotland) Act 1960.

Before that Act the liability of an occupier depended on whether the person injured was an "invitee" (a person who had been invited), a "licensee" (a person who was there by leave or licence, express or implied), or a "trespasser" (a person whose presence was not known to the occupier, or if known was objected to by him).

This division into three rigid categories was not originally part of the common law of Scotland, but had been introduced to Scots law from the common law of England by the decision of the House of Lords in the Scottish case *Dumbreck* v. *Robert Addie & Sons (Collieries) Ltd.*, 1929 S.C.(H.L.) 51:

A machine used by a colliery company in a field beside their colliery was started without warning, and D., a child of four, was caught and killed in the mechanism.

The field was separated from the public road by a hedge in which there were many gaps, and adults and children often trespassed in the field. Warnings had constantly been given by the company against trespassing.

D. was held to have been a trespasser, and since the only duty of the occupier to a trespasser was not maliciously to injure him (as by the setting of a trap), the colliery company was not liable for D.'s death.

If the company had taken no steps to try to prevent trespassing, D. would have been classed as a licensee, and the company would have owed to him a higher duty of care.

The effect of the Occupiers' Liability (Scotland) Act 1960 was to remove the rigid categories rule and to restore the former common law of Scotland.

The main provisions of the Act are:

1.   The care which an occupier is required to show to a person entering his premises is such care as in all the circumstances of the case is reasonable to see that that person will not suffer injury or damage because of some danger due to the state of the premises. The occupier may modify this obligation by agreement between himself and the person entering his premises, but the circumstances in which he may now do so are restricted by the Unfair Contract Terms Act 1977 (see p. 314, above): if a term in a contract to which that Act applies is an attempt by the occupier to exclude or restrict his liability under the Act of 1960 for death or personal injury, it is void.

2.   The same duty of care is owed by a person who has control

of fixed or moveable structures, including vessels, vehicles and aircraft; *i.e.* the person in control of such a structure has the same duty to those entering it as the occupier has to those who enter his premises.

3. The occupier's duty of care extends to property which is on his premises, including property of persons who have not themselves entered the premises. Freedom to modify this statutory duty by agreement is limited in circumstances where the Unfair Contract Terms Act 1977 applies: in those circumstances, an occupier attempting to exclude or restrict his liability would require to be able to prove that the agreement had been fair and reasonable.

4. The liability of a landlord towards persons who are or whose property is on premises let to a tenant is the same as that of the occupier under 1 above in so far as dangers arising from faulty maintenance or repair are concerned. This provision of the Act applies only to tenancies in which the landlord is by contract or by Act of Parliament responsible for maintenance or repair.

A case which illustrates the application of the Act is *McGlone* v. *British Railways Board*, 1966 S.C.(H.L.) 1:

McG., a boy of twelve, was seriously injured when he climbed up an electric transformer on ground occupied by British Railways Board at Cambuslang. The transformer was fenced and carried notices of danger. McG. had passed through barbed wire before being injured.

The House of Lords held that an occupier in such circumstances discharged his duty to show "reasonable" care if he erected an obstacle which children had to take some trouble to overcome before they reached the danger. British Railways Board had erected such an obstacle in this case, and there was therefore no liability on the Board for McG.'s injuries.

STRICT LIABILITY

The general principle of Scots law is that there is no liability for delict unless there is culpa ("fault"). Liability which arises in the absence of fault is referred to as "strict liability." The categories of strict liability are important exceptions to the general principle mentioned, and may be considered under the following headings:

1. statutory liability;
2. edictal liability;
3. liability for animals;
4. liability for nuisance;
5. liability for non-natural use of property;
6. liability for unintentional slander; and
7. vicarious liability.

1. Statutory Liability

Liability for harm done is often based on breach of a duty imposed by statute. Failure to exercise the standard of care prescribed by the statute is described as "statutory negligence." The standard of care varies according to the words used in the statute, and is often considerably higher than the "reasonable" standard of the common law; e.g. the Factories Act 1961 imposes on factory occupiers the duty to have dangerous parts of machinery "securely fenced," and an occupier who fails to satisfy that standard cannot put forward the defence that he did all that was reasonably practicable to make the dangerous part safe.

Some statutory provisions impose an absolute duty, with the result that a person who is in breach of the duty incurs liability, however great his efforts to fulfil the duty may have been. In such cases the statutory liability is strict liability.

There is an illustration of strict statutory liability in *Millar* v. *Galashiels Gas Co. Ltd.*, 1949 S.C.(H.L.) 31:

A workman was killed through the failure of the brake mechanism of a hoist in his employers' factory.

The Factories Act 1937 provided that every hoist had to be "properly maintained," and "maintained" was defined by that statute as meaning "maintained in an efficient state, in efficient working order, and in good repair."

The employers had taken every practicable step to ensure that the mechanism worked properly and that the hoist was safe; the failure was unexplained and could not have been anticipated.

The House of Lords, however, affirming the judgment of the Court of Session, held that the duty imposed by the statute was absolute, and that the fact that the brake mechanism had failed was enough to establish that the employers were in breach of their statutory duty.

2. Edictal Liability

This refers to the praetorian edict of Roman law, known as the edict "nautae, caupones, stabularii" ("sailors, innkeepers and stable-keepers"), which required a higher standard of care to be shown by these categories of persons in respect of their customers' property.

This edict, as incorporated into the common law of Scotland, made "common carriers" of goods by land, innkeepers and stable-keepers liable for loss of or damage to property unless they could prove that the loss or damage had been caused by circumstances such as negligence of the owner, act of the Queen's enemies or damnum fatale ("predestined loss"). A "common carrier" is one who undertakes for a charge to carry the goods of any member of the public who chooses to employ him; he is contrasted with the private carrier, who makes no general offer to carry the goods of anyone choosing to employ him and who enters into individual contracts with customers. A damnum fatale, also called "an act of God," is some accident which has resulted directly and solely from natural causes without human intervention and which could not have been prevented by any amount of foresight and care (*e.g.* an earthquake or a purely accidental fire).

The effect of the common law was to place these categories of persons in the position of insurers of the property, since they were liable for loss or injury even although no negligence on their part had been proved.

The common law has been altered by several statutes, the most important of which are the Carriers Act 1830 and the Hotel Proprietors Act 1956.

Before 1830 a common carrier might limit or exclude his edictal liability by a public notice or advertisement. The Carriers Act 1830 removed this possibility, but left it open to the carrier to make special contracts with individual customers. The Act further provided that in the case of certain classes of goods the carrier was not to be liable if the package exceeded £10 in value, unless the sender had declared the nature and value of the goods when handing them over to the carrier. The specified classes of goods include precious stones, jewellery, watches, bank notes, china, lace and other articles which have the common characteristic of being more valuable than their bulk would suggest. The carrier is entitled to make an increased charge provided he has a notice of the increased rates conspicuously affixed at the place where the goods are received. The Act, however, does not protect the carrier from liability for loss or injury arising from felonious acts (*e.g.* theft) by his employees.

The Mercantile Law Amendment (Scotland) Act 1856 made the common carrier of goods by land liable for loss caused by accidental fire, which had been considered a damnum fatale at common law.

Under the Hotel Proprietors Act 1956 the edictal liability of an innkeeper is now limited to proprietors of hotels where sleeping accommodation has been engaged and the loss or damage occurs between the midnight before and the midnight after the period during which the guest was entitled to use the accommodation. Further, the Act provides that there is no edictal liability for loss of or damage to any vehicle or property left in a vehicle, or any horse or other animal or its harness or other equipment. These provisions apply only to the edictal, *i.e.* the strict, liability of the hotel proprietor; they do not prevent liability from arising out of the proprietor's negligence or out of a special contract entered into between him and the guest.

The Act of 1956 also enables the hotel proprietor to limit his liability by putting up a statutory notice at the reception desk.

The validity of terms in any special contract made with a carrier or hotel proprietor usually now depends on whether or not the standards imposed by the Unfair Contract Terms Act 1977 have been satisfied (see p. 314, above). The general effect of the provisions of that Act is that there can be no exclusion or restriction of liability for death or personal injury, and that any other exclusion or restriction will be effective only if it was, at the time when the contract was made, fair and reasonable.

3. Liability for Animals

A person who is in charge of animals must take reasonable care to prevent them from injuring other persons or the property of other persons, and if he fails in this duty he will be liable for negligence according to the general principle of delictual liability.

In certain circumstances, however, liability for animals can arise quite apart from negligence. This strict liability exists where the person in charge of an animal knows (or is presumed to know) of its "dangerous propensities," *i.e.* knows (or is presumed to know) that if he does not confine it or control it, it is likely to do damage to the persons or property of other people.

In this connection a distinction is drawn between animals mansuetae naturae ("of a gentle disposition") and animals ferae naturae ("of a wild disposition"). The former category includes domestic and farm animals such as dogs, cats, fowls, horses, cattle (including bulls), sheep and sows. The latter category includes lions, elephants, bears, boars, monkeys and zebras. The distinction is a distinction of law, and is not affected by the fact that a particular animal, normally of a wild disposition, has been tamed or domesticated: for legal purposes it remains an animal ferae naturae.

The importance of the distinction is that the person in charge of an animal ferae naturae is presumed by law to know of its dangerous propensities, whereas the person in charge of an animal mansuetae naturae must be proved to have known that the animal had dangerous propensities (*e.g.* from its behaviour in the past). For instance, a person injured by a bull, an animal mansuetae naturae, must, if he is to recover damages, prove that the person in charge of it was negligent or knew that the bull was a dangerous one, but a person injured by a pet monkey, an animal ferae naturae, could recover damages without proving either negligence or knowledge of its savage tendencies on the part of the person in charge of it.

Statutes make special provision for liability for injury done to farm animals by dogs: by the Dogs Act 1906 the owner of a dog is liable for injury done to "cattle" (defined as including horses, mules, asses, sheep, goats and swine) even although he has neither been negligent nor known of any dangerous propensity in the dog; by the Dogs (Amendment) Act 1928 that absolute liability was extended to cover injury done by dogs to poultry.

By the Dangerous Wild Animals Act 1976 a person who keeps any "dangerous wild animal" (*i.e.* an animal of one of the kinds listed in the Schedule to the Act) is required to obtain a licence for doing so from the local authority (the islands or district council).

4. Liability for Nuisance

"Nuisance" in the legal sense is an infringement of a neighbour's right of comfortable enjoyment of his heritable property. The maxim applicable is "sic utere tuo ut alienum non laedas" ("use your own property in such a way that you do not harm another's property"). What amounts to a nuisance depends on the locality of the property and on other circumstances. The nuisance may take the form, for instance, of excessive noise or of harmful fumes. It must be of a continuing nature and must not be merely trivial. The remedy often sought for nuisance is interdict (see p. 413, above).

The liability of the person who is responsible for the nuisance is strict liability, since he cannot, if sued by his neighbour for damages, put forward the defence that he took all reasonable care to prevent the nuisance.

What would be a nuisance at common law is sometimes authorised by an Act of Parliament, and the words used in the Act may be such that all right to complain of the nuisance is cut off. If, however, the Act merely authorises something to be done and nuisance would not necessarily result from the doing of the thing authorised, then liability for nuisance would still exist.

On nuisance, see also p. 462, below.

5. Liability for Non-natural Use of Property

Non-natural use of property occurs where a person brings on to his land and keeps there some object or erection which is not part of the natural scene and which is a potential source of danger to his neighbours. The person who does so is liable for damage caused to neighbouring property if he allows the dangerous agency to escape from his own land. His liability is "strict" in the sense that he cannot defend himself by showing that he exercised all reasonable care. He may, however, in certain circumstances have the defence of "damnum fatale" ("act of God") (see p. 428, above).

The typical instance of non-natural use of property is the collection of water in a reservoir or dam.

This branch of strict liability is usually associated with the English case of *Rylands and anr.* v. *Fletcher* (1868) L.R. 3 H.L. 330; (1866) L.R. 1 Ex. 265:

F. was the lessee of certain coal mines known as the "Red House Colliery."

R. had in 1860 employed competent persons to construct a reservoir to store water for use about a mill.

Water from the reservoir overflowed into F.'s mines.

F. was held entitled to recover damages from R. for the injury caused.

In the House of Lords the Lord Chancellor (Lord Cairns), after explaining what he meant by the term "non-natural use," quoted with approval that part of Mr. Justice Blackburn's judgment in the Court of Exchequer Chamber which expressed the rule now known as "the rule in *Rylands* v. *Fletcher*" ((1868) L.R. 3 H.L. at p. 339; (1866) L.R. 1 Ex. at p. 279):

> "The person who, for his own purposes, brings on his land and collects and keeps there anything likely to do mischief if it escapes, must keep it in at his peril; and if he does not do so, is prima facie answerable for all the damage which is the natural consequence of its escape."

It was considered just and reasonable that a person who brought on to his property something which was not naturally there and which was harmless so long as it was confined to his own property but which he knew would be mischievous if it got on to his neighbour's should be required to make good the damage which resulted from his failure to confine that thing to his own property, since, but for his act in bringing the thing on to his property, his neighbour would have suffered no harm.

It is, however, doubtful whether the rule in *Rylands* v. *Fletcher* is properly regarded as part of the law of Scotland. Two Scottish cases which involved similar questions to that in the English case were *Kerr* v. *Earl of Orkney* (1857) 20 D. 298, and *Caledonian Ry. Co.* v. *Greenock Corporation*, 1917 S.C.(H.L.) 56.

Kerr v. *Earl of Orkney*: K. had built a grain mill, and the Earl had constructed a large dam covering many acres above the mill.

At a time of extraordinary, but not unprecedented, flooding the water broke out from the dam and swept away all K.'s property including the mill.

The Earl was held liable to K.

Caledonian Ry. Co. v. *Greenock Corporation*: Greenock Corporation had altered the channel of a burn in order to form a paddling pool in a public park.

After a rainfall of an intensity unknown to Greenock (though not unprecedented in Scotland), the pool caused flooding which damaged the railway.

The Corporation was held liable; the extraordinarily heavy rainfall was not a damnum fatale ("act of God").

These and other Scottish cases probably do not justify the acceptance in Scotland of such an extreme form of strict liability as that expressed in the rule in *Rylands* v. *Fletcher*. The Scottish cases can probably all be brought within the general principle of the Scots law of delict that there must be culpa ("fault") before liability will arise; they may be treated as giving instances of circumstances which "raise an almost irrebuttable presumption" of negligence; this means that it is presumed until the contrary is proved (and such proof will be almost impossible) that a person who constructs a dam or uses his land for some other similarly "non-natural" purpose has been negligent if in fact the obviously foreseeable damage to neighbouring property results from an escape of the water or other danger from his own land.

It is questionable whether this type of strict liability extends to personal injuries: it may be confined to damage done to property. Further, it may be restricted to forces such as water which get out of control on the defender's lands, and which escape from those lands with resulting damage to the pursuer's property. It does not apply to harm done *within* the defender's lands.

6. Liability for Unintentional Slander

In an action of damages for slander, the pursuer does not need to prove that the defender intended his statement to be "defamatory of" the pursuer, *i.e.* intended it to harm the honour or reputation of the pursuer. A claim for damages may be successful provided the words used might reasonably have been read as referring to the pursuer and were in fact read as referring to him. The defender need not even have known of the existence of the pursuer.

An example of unintentional slander occurred in the case of *Wragg* v. *D. C. Thomson & Co. Ltd.*, 1909, 2 S.L.T. 315 and 409:

This was an action for slander brought by W., a music-hall comedian whose stage name was "George Reeves," against the proprietors of the "Weekly News," a newspaper circulating generally throughout Scotland.

At a time when W. was performing at the Palace Theatre,

Glasgow, a paragraph had been published in that newspaper under the headings "GEORGE REEVES SHOOTS WIFE TWICE. THEN ENDS HIS OWN LIFE." The incident described had occurred in New York, but the paragraph did not mention that fact or give any other express indication of where the incident had occurred or who the George Reeves was who featured in it. The publishers claimed that they were not even aware of W.'s existence.

The court, considering the semi-public position held by W., who was known to the public as "George Reeves," and the fact that that name was not a common one, held that the paragraph might reasonably have been read as referring to W., and that the publishers might be made liable even although they had not actually intended to refer to the pursuer and even although they had not been aware of his existence.

It may be that liability for unintentional slander is less strict in Scotland than in England: *Wragg's* case, for instance, did involve an element of negligence in that the publishers failed to take the reasonable precaution of identifying the particular George Reeves who had been involved in the incident.

Common law liability for unintentional slander has been modified by the Defamation Act 1952, which allows a person who has innocently published a defamatory statement to put forward in certain circumstances the defence that he made an "offer of amends," *i.e.* offered to publish a suitable correction and apology and to take reasonable steps to notify the falseness of the statement to persons known to have received it. The publisher must in his offer specify the facts which indicate that the publication of the statement was "innocent," *i.e.* not intended to be defamatory. Even if the party who alleges that he has been defamed refuses the publisher's offer, the publisher is still entitled to use the offer as a defence, but the defence is not available where the publisher himself has not been the originator of the statement, unless he proves that the originator was writing without malice.

7. Vicarious Liability

The general rule is that a person is liable for his own delicts, and not for those of another person. The maxim which expresses this general rule is "culpa tenet suos auctores" ("blame attaches to its own authors"). It is, therefore, no defence for a person who committed a wrongful act to say that he was obeying the instructions of another party.

Important exceptions to this general rule are the situations where there may be "vicarious liability," *i.e.* liability incurred by one person for wrongful acts done by another.

Vicarious liability arises from a contractual relationship between the parties. This relationship may be:

(a) partnership;
(b) agency; or
(c) employment.

The general theory underlying vicarious liability is that the person under whose direction and for whose benefit a thing has been done ought to be responsible for harm caused to others through the performance of that action. This theory is, however, only a general one, and does not apply to every situation where vicarious liability may arise; *e.g.* an employer may be liable for a wrong done by his employee even where he has expressly forbidden the employee's action and has himself derived no benefit from it.

Vicarious liability is a principle which has very important practical consequences, since it enables an injured party to sue the person who is behind the actual wrongdoer and who is more likely to be financially able to pay substantial damages or to be adequately insured against such claims (in which case the injured party is entitled to the benefit of the insurance). Therefore, although the injured party may always sue the actual wrongdoer, he will usually be more interested in establishing that another person (*e.g.* the wrongdoer's employer) is vicariously liable.

The principle of vicarious liability is not intended to benefit the actual wrongdoer. The general rule "culpa tenet suos auctores" overrides the principle of vicarious liability in the sense that not only may the injured party choose to sue the actual wrongdoer instead of his employer or other superior, but the superior who has been made vicariously liable to the injured party has a right to recover from the actual wrongdoer what has been paid to the injured party.

Two maxims used in connection with vicarious liability are:

"respondeat superior" ("let the superior answer"); and

" qui facit per alium facit per se" ("he who does something through the agency of another person does it himself").

(a) Vicarious liability in partnership

By the Partnership Act 1890 a firm is liable for any wrongful act or omission of any partner acting in the ordinary course of the business of the firm or with the authority of his co-partners; this is vicarious liability because the firm is a legal person distinct from the partners of whom it is composed. The same Act provides that every partner is liable for everything for which the firm becomes vicariously liable in that way, and this is itself another instance of vicarious liability.

(b) Vicarious liability in agency

A principal is liable for the wrongs done by his agent in carrying out the transaction entrusted to him, and also for wrongs done by the agent within the scope of his authority even although the agent was not at the time carrying out a transaction for which he had the actual authority of his principal.

(c) Vicarious liability in employment

In this connection it is vital to distinguish between the relationship which exists between employer and employee (or between "master and servant," to use the older terminology) and the relationship which exists between employer and independent contractor, for while an employer is vicariously liable for the wrongs of his employee committed within the scope of the employment, it is only exceptionally that he can be made liable for the wrongs of his independent contractor. On the distinction between an employee and an independent contractor, see p. 349, above. (See also p. 378, above.)

(i) *Wrongs committed by employee*

For vicarious liability to arise the employee must have been acting within the scope of his employment. The employer may not have obtained any benefit from his employee's action, and, provided the wrong has been committed within the scope of the employment, the employer incurs liability to an injured third party although he may have expressly forbidden his employee to act in the particular way which has resulted in the injury.

On the other hand, the employer is not responsible for acts of his employee which are not within the scope of the employment. An injured third party will then be restricted to claiming damages from the employee who actually committed the wrong.

In many situations it is difficult to decide whether the wrong was committed within the scope of the employment or not. The general rule applied is that if an employee does what he is authorised to do but does it in an unauthorised way, his action is within the scope of the employment, whereas if he does something which is altogether unauthorised, his action is not within the scope of the employment. For instance, if an employee wrongfully smokes when working with highly inflammable materials such as petrol and as a result a third party's property is damaged by fire, his employer may be made vicariously liable to the third party, but if a driver goes off on an independent expedition (as distinct from a merely incidental deviation from a prescribed route) and as a result a third party sustains injury, the employer will not incur vicarious liability.

(ii) *Wrongs committed by independent contractor*

The general rule, to which there are important exceptions, is that a person who engages an independent contractor to perform a piece of work for him is not liable for wrongs committed in the course of the work by the independent contractor or by the employees of that contractor. An injured third party will be entitled to recover damages from the actual wrongdoer or, if the actual wrongdoer is an employee of the contractor and was acting within the scope of his employment, from the contractor himself, but he will not as a general rule be entitled to sue the person who has engaged the contractor.

The general rule may be illustrated by the case of *M'Lean* v. *Russell, Macnee & Co.* (1850) 12 D. 887:

R., M. & Co., proprietors of a house in Princes Street, Edinburgh, contracted with builders for the execution of alterations upon it. The builders entered into a sub-contract with Tait to do the plasterwork.

Tait deposited a heap of lime on the street without taking the necessary precautions of fencing it or keeping lamps burning at it during darkness to guard against accidents.

M'L., a coach-hirer, drove his cab and horse into this heap of lime, was thrown off his seat and killed instantly.

M'L.'s widow brought an action for £600 damages against the proprietors of the house, the builders and the plasterer.

The jury found her entitled to £50 damages and left it to the court[3] to decide on which party the liability lay.

The court held that liability rested solely on the plasterer.

The contrast between liability for an employee's wrongs and absence of liability for an independent contractor's wrongs is brought out in the opinions of Lords Mackenzie and Fullerton in that case.

Lord Mackenzie stated (at p. 892):

"The general rule of law is culpa tenet suos auctores. Men are answerable for themselves, not for others. No doubt that rule, if carried to its full extent, would exempt the master from responsibility for his servants; but we do not carry it so far. Every master is liable for what is done by his servants in his employment. . . . There is no reason to extend the master's liability for servants to contractors. . . . There was nothing culpable here in the conduct of any one but Tait. . . . On the whole, I am not inclined to carry the doctrine of liability any further than to servants."

[3] Meaning in this context the judge or judges.

Lord Fullerton stated (at p. 892):

"The question comes to be, whether the proprietor of a house bona fide employing a tradesman to execute repairs upon it, is to be held liable for every thing done by the contractors—whether he is bound to watch every thing they do? I cannot carry the law so far as that. . . .

"As regards a servant, the employer is in a much more unfavourable position than as regards a contractor. The master is bound to watch over the doings of the servants, and their acts are his. This is very different from his position with regard to a person duly qualified, who has been employed as a contractor."

The exceptions to the general rule that the employer of an independent contractor is not liable for wrongs committed by the contractor are instances not of vicarious liability, but of personal liability. The main ones are as follows:

1. where the employer retains control over the method by which the work is done and actually directs the contractor's operations;

2. where the employer has been negligent in that he has selected an incompetent contractor;

3. where the employer has engaged a contractor to do unlawful work or to do lawful work in an unlawful manner;

4. where the work is inherently dangerous so that negligence in the performance of it would naturally result in damage or injury, *e.g.* excavation of streets, and building operations which expose neighbouring property to a risk of damage; and

5. where personal liability is imposed by statute on the employer.

LIABILITY OF THE CROWN

Before 1947 the main principle of the common law relating to liability of the Crown for delicts committed by officials in the course of their employment was "The king can do no wrong," a theory which had its origins in the feudal system and had been introduced to Scots law from the common law of England. The result of this principle was that a person injured by a delict of an official was restricted to claiming damages from the actual wrongdoer.

This principle became increasingly unsatisfactory with the increase in governmental intervention in the life of the community and was abolished by the Crown Proceedings Act 1947, which provided that the Crown was to be liable for delicts committed by its servants or agents wherever the servants or agents would have been themselves liable before the date of the Act. The effect of the Act is to make the Crown liable vicariously for wrongs committed by its agents and servants, liable in the exceptional circumstances indicated above (p. 437) for wrongs committed by independent contractors engaged by it, and liable as an employer for injury sustained by its own servants in the course of their employment. The Crown also incurs the same statutory liability as an individual would incur provided the Act in question "binds the Crown"; *e.g.* the Occupiers' Liability (Scotland) Act 1960 binds the Crown and so the Crown may incur liability for injury caused by dangerous premises.

The Act of 1947, however, provided for certain immunities formerly enjoyed by the Crown to be continued, *e.g.* in connection with the acts of judges and other judicial persons, with injuries suffered by members of the armed forces in the course of their service and with powers and authorities of a prerogative nature (*e.g.* for the defence of the realm).

LIMITATION OF DELICTUAL LIABILITY

A person who has committed a delict is not necessarily liable for all the damage which has resulted. His liability may be limited:
    1. by statute;
    2. by contract;
    3. by allocation of responsibility where he is not the only party at fault; or
    4. by the principle of "remoteness of damage."

1. Limitation of Liability by Statute

An Act of Parliament may provide that the wrongdoer is not to be liable beyond a certain amount for his delict; *e.g.* the Railway Fires Acts of 1905 and 1923 made the railway authority liable for damage to agricultural land caused by sparks from engines, but provided that the amount was not to exceed £200 in each case.

Further, some statutes provide that persons in certain positions can be sued only subject to special qualifications; *e.g.* judges in a district court are protected by a provision now incorporated in the Criminal Procedure (Scotland) Act 1975 (see p. 442, below).

2. Limitation of Liability by Contract

At common law a person could by a term in a contract which he was making with another party limit, or even exclude, liability for damage which might be sustained by the second party in the course of the contract. Such "exemption clauses" were not looked on with favour by the courts, and were read contra proferentem ("against the person putting them forward"), *i.e.* were interpreted, if there was any ambiguity, in favour of the party who sustained the damage. The courts, however, were bound to give effect to such clauses if the exclusion or restriction of liability had been clearly expressed.

The common law was considered to be unsatisfactory, and the Law Commissions made recommendations for important cha nges (*Second Report on Exemption Clauses*, Law Com. No. 69, Scot. Law Com. No. 39, 1974–75 H.C.P. 605). These recommendations were substantially adopted in the Unfair Contract Terms Act 1977, which came into force on February 1, 1978. There is now a whole range of contracts in which exemption clauses are:

(a)   void, if they purport to exclude or restrict liability *for death or personal injury;* and

(b)   of no effect *in any other case*, unless it was *fair and reasonable* to incorporate them.

See p. 313, above.

3. Allocation of Responsibility

Where two or more persons have contributed to a delict, they are liable "jointly and severally," *i.e.* they are all liable jointly and each one is also liable individually to the injured party for the full amount of the damage. The injured party may, therefore, choose to sue only one of the joint wrongdoers, and to leave it to that wrongdoer to recover from the other or others an appropriate proportion of what he has had to pay. This is to the benefit of the injured party, since one or more of the joint wrongdoers may be financially unable to pay substantial damages or may be unidentified or beyond the court's jurisdiction.

The Law Reform (Miscellaneous Provisions) (Scotland) Act 1940 provides that where a court finds two or more defenders jointly and severally at fault, it must allocate responsibility by stating the percentage of fault applicable to each defender. This does not deprive the pursuer of his right to claim the full damage from any one of the wrongdoers whom he has sued. If the fault cannot be apportioned accurately, liability is allocated equally.

A wrongdoer may also be relieved of liability for some of the damage caused, if he is successful in a defence of contributory negligence (see p. 445, below); responsibility is then allocated between the wrongdoer and the injured party.

4. Remoteness of Damage

The phrase "remoteness of damage" is used in two distinct senses in the law of delict:

(a)   The phrase is used in connection with causation: the damage for which reparation is being claimed must not be too remote from the breach of duty which caused it.

The test of reasonable foreseeability applies here: the wrongdoer will not be liable if he could not reasonably have foreseen that his breach of duty would result in injury to the party who has in fact suffered.

"Remoteness of damage" in this sense has been dealt with under "Causation" (see p. 416, above, and especially the case of *Macdonald* v. *David Macbrayne Ltd.*, 1915 S.C. 716, on p. 418, above).

(b) The phrase is more properly used in connection with the extent of liability: the wrongdoer is liable only for the damage which has arisen naturally and directly out of his breach of duty. His liability for *some* of the damage has been either admitted or proved and the question of remoteness of damage is concerned solely with the extent of his liability.

The test of reasonable foreseeability does not apply here: the wrongdoer must "take his victim as he finds him," *i.e.* the wrongdoer's liability depends on the actual damage sustained as the natural and direct result of his breach of duty, even although the damage is, perhaps because of the victim's poor state of health, greater than could reasonably have been foreseen. The point may be illustrated by the case of *McKillen* v. *Barclay Curle & Co. Ltd.*, 1967 S.L.T. 41:

McK., a plumber's mate, fractured a rib when he slipped and fell while descending some staging steps on a ship under construction. He sued his employer for damages on the ground that the accident had been caused by the employer's negligence, and he was awarded the sum of £600 by the Lord Ordinary.

The employer in an appeal to the Inner House did not dispute the finding of negligence, but maintained that the award of £600 was excessive. The Lord Ordinary had in assessing damages taken account not only of the fractured rib but also of tuberculosis from which McK. had formerly suffered and which had, McK. alleged, been reactivated by the accident.

The employer argued that the reactivation of McK.'s tuberculosis was not a foreseeable result of the accident, but the court held that the doctrine of reasonable foreseeability did not apply to the measure of damage once liability had been established, since the negligent party had to take his victim as he found him.

The employer's appeal was, however, successful on the separate ground that McK. had not given legally satisfactory proof that the fracture of his rib did cause the reactivation of the tuberculosis. He was held entitled to only £218 damages.

Lord President Clyde stated (at p. 42):

"In my opinion it has never been the law of Scotland that a man guilty of negligence towards another is only liable for the damage in respect of physical injuries which a reasonable man would foresee as likely to follow from it. On the contrary it has always been the law of Scotland as I understand it that once a man is negligent and injures another by his negligence he is liable for all the damage to the injured man which naturally and directly arises out of the negligence. He must take his victim as he finds him, and if his victim has a weak heart and dies as a result of the injury the negligent man is liable in damages for his death, even although a normal man might only in the same circumstances have sustained a relatively trivial injury. . . . The doctrine of reasonable foreseeability with all its subtle ramifications may be applied in determining questions of liability. It has no relevance once liability is established and the measure of damage is being determined. Indeed any other conclusion than this would have startling results. The measure of damages would depend not upon the actual injuries naturally and directly following from the negligence, but upon the injuries reasonably to be anticipated to follow. These might be very much less or might even be larger than the unfortunate victim in fact sustained. That was never our law."

SUBROGATION

The principle of subrogation applies where a party who has sustained damage as a result of another party's delict and who is insured against such damage chooses to make a claim against his insurance company rather than to sue the wrongdoer. The insurance company is then "subrogated to" the injured party's right to recover damages from the wrongdoer, i.e. is entitled to stand "in the shoes of" the injured party and recover from the wrongdoer the amount which the injured party himself might have recovered from him.

Subrogation is one of the consequences of the principle of indemnity, which operates generally in the law of insurance and prevents an insured person from making a profit out of his loss.

DEFENCES TO ACTIONS FOR DELICT

The party who is sued in an action of reparation for delict may obviously defend himself by showing that some factor which is essential for the emergence of delictual liability is lacking; e.g. he may be able to satisfy the court that in law he owed to the pursuer no duty of care, that he was not in fact negligent, or that liability was excluded by a fair and reasonable " exemption clause."

In addition to these defences, which apply generally in the field of delict, there are certain other defences one or more of which may, according to the circumstances, be available to the defender and which may sometimes wholly and sometimes partially relieve him of liability. They include the following:

1. immunity or privilege;
2. statutory authority;
3. damnum fatale ("act of God");
4. self-defence or necessity;
5. volenti non fit injuria (literally, "to a person who is willing a wrongful act is not done");
6. contributory negligence; and
7. extinction of the claim through personal bar or lapse of time.

1. Immunity or Privilege

The underlying reason for these defences is public policy.

The Queen in her personal capacity is immune from actions based on delict. This immunity no longer extends to all acts done by Crown servants (see p. 437, above).

Judges of the higher courts and probably also of the sheriff court enjoy absolute immunity for anything done by them in their judicial capacity. Judges of the inferior courts could probably be made liable at common law for acts outside their jurisdiction or for acts done with malice. The Lord Advocate and procurators-fiscal acting on his instructions enjoy absolute immunity in connection with criminal proceedings on indictment. In summary criminal proceedings there is no absolute immunity but by a provision now included in the consolidating Criminal Procedure (Scotland) Act 1975 judges in district courts, and clerks of court and prosecutors in summary criminal proceedings, can be made liable to pay damages only if certain conditions are fulfilled; in particular, the person claiming damages must have been imprisoned as a result of the proceedings and must be able to prove that the defender acted with malice.

Immunities and privileges enjoyed by foreign sovereigns, ambassadors, consuls, Commonwealth representatives, foreign states and international organisations and also by the families and staff of such persons are now mainly defined by statutes based on international conventions. Prominent amongst these statutes are the Diplomatic Privileges Act 1964 and the Consular Relations Act 1968 which grade immunities and privileges according to whether the defender is of diplomatic rank or a consular officer, a member of the administrative or technical staff, or a member of the service staff. The general effect of the State Immunity Act 1978 is to restrict the immunity of a foreign state to activities of the state in its sovereign capacity while making it subject to the jursidiction of the courts in connection with its commercial activities. Immunities and privileges may be "waived" (surrendered) in any particular case by the person entitled to them.

In an action of defamation the defender may be able to claim absolute or qualified privilege for the statement which he has made. The effect of absolute privilege is that no liability can ever arise for the defamation: it makes no difference that the defender may have been acting with malice. Examples of statements enjoying absolute privilege are statements made in Parliament, statements made by advocates and witnesses in court and fair reports of proceedings in Parliament or in court.

The effect of qualified privilege is to exclude liability provided the pursuer fails to prove that the defender was acting with malice. The defence of qualified privilege is available where the defamatory statement has been made on a "privileged occasion"; *i.e.* the defender must have been discharging some legal or moral duty in making the statement. An example of a privileged occasion is when an employer makes a statement about the capacity of his employee to someone (*e.g.* a prospective employer) who has an interest to receive it (see p. 369, above). The Defamation Act 1952 conferred qualified privilege on several types of statements which had not been privileged at common law, *e.g.* fair and accurate newspaper reports of public proceedings at international organisations and conferences and of proceedings at public meetings, meetings of local authorities, company meetings and tribunals.

2. Statutory Authority

An Act of Parliament may authorise a person to do something which would otherwise be wrongful and would give rise to delictual liability. The statutory authority may be so expressed that the act in question may be performed whether or not it causes damage to the interests of other persons. It is, however, more usual for statutory authority to be subject to the condition that the person authorised takes all reasonable precautions to safeguard the interests of other persons; in that case the person authorised would incur liability for negligence in the performance of the act authorised.

3. Damnum Fatale

A damnum fatale or "act of God" as it is sometimes called is some extraordinary happening produced by natural causes and such that it could not have been provided against by human foresight and prudence. No liability is incurred for damage caused by a damnum fatale. An earthquake would probably be a damnum fatale but extraordinarily heavy rain would be unlikely to be considered a damnum fatale (see the case of *Caledonian Ry. Co.* v. *Greenock*

Corporation, 1917 S.C.(H.L.) 56 (p. 432, above) and also the section on Edictal Liability (p. 427, above)).

4. Self-defence or Necessity

The defender in an action for reparation may justify conduct which would otherwise have been wrongful if he proves that he was acting in self-defence, in defence of other persons whom he had a duty to protect, or out of necessity.

These defences are not usually available except in cases of emergency, and the harm inflicted on the pursuer or on the pursuer's property must not exceed what is reasonable in the circumstances; *e.g.* a person is entitled to use reasonable force in warding off a personal assault or in protecting a member of his family from assault, but if he uses excessive force he will be liable in damages; similarly, trespass on and damage to another person's property give rise to no liability if they were necessary, for instance, in order to escape from imminent danger.

Where the defender is unable to establish self-defence or necessity as a complete defence, he may still be able to use either of these defences "in mitigation of damages," *i.e.* to reduce the amount for which he is liable; *e.g.* if the pursuer's assault provoked the defender to make an excessive counter-assault, the defender may put forward the provocation in mitigation of damages.

Similar to the right to protect one's person is the right to use reasonable force to retain or recover one's property; *e.g.* a thief may be unable to recover damages for injury inflicted by the owner of the property in an attempt to recover it, and a reasonable amount of force may be used to evict squatters on land, passengers who refuse to pay a fare and persons who cause disturbance at a meeting. However, the law does not regard with favour a resort to self-help where the right to property is in dispute; normally the proper course is for the party claiming the property to enlist the aid of the courts in order to retain it or recover it and if he resorts to self-help in circumstances which do not justify it he will be liable in damages for resulting loss or injury sustained by the other party.

5. Volenti Non Fit Injuria

The effect of this defence is to bar the pursuer from recovering damages for an injury the risk of which he had voluntarily undertaken to run. The literal translation of the maxim is "a wrongful act ('injuria') is not done to one who is willing"; there is deemed to have been no injuria, and so the situation is an instance of damnum absque injuria ("loss without a legal wrong"), for which no damages can be claimed (see p. 415, above).

The defence is available where an injury results from:

(a) surgical or medical treatment which the pursuer has consented to undergo;

(b) participation in a lawful sport or game played according to the rules;

(c) watching a contest or display, provided the participants are not recklessly disregarding the spectators' safety;

(d) dangerous work which an employee has voluntarily undertaken to do (see p. 374, above); or

(e) continued occupation of dangerous premises by a tenant who does not notify his landlord of the defects or who does not abandon the lease after allowing the landlord a reasonable time to remedy the defects.

On the other hand, the defence is not available in rescue cases, since a person who deliberately exposes himself to risk of injury in order to save life or property is considered to be acting in the discharge of a social or moral duty and not completely voluntarily. Further, the defence is of only limited application in the law of employment (see p. 375, above).

6. Contributory Negligence

In the phrase "contributory negligence" the word "negligence" means "carelessness"; it does not here have the technical meaning of failure in a duty to take care (see p. 420, above).

Contributory negligence is carelessness on the part of the pursuer which has contributed to the injury which he has sustained. In putting forward this defence, the defender is alleging that the injury was caused either wholly or partially by the pursuer's failure to take reasonable care for his own safety.

At common law contributory negligence was a complete defence. This meant that if the defender could prove that the pursuer's carelessness had been a joint cause of the injury along with the defender's negligence, no damages could be claimed however much the defender might have been at fault.

The law was altered by the Law Reform (Contributory Negligence) Act 1945, which provided that in future where a person suffered damage as the result partly of his own fault and partly of the fault of another person, a claim for damages would not necessarily fail just because of the pursuer's carelessness but the amount of damages which could be recovered would be reduced according to the pursuer's share in the responsibility for the damage. Where pursuer and defender have jointly caused the damage, therefore, the responsibility is apportioned on a percentage basis between them, and the pursuer is entitled to recover only the appropriate percentage of the damage which he has sustained.

If the defender has placed the pursuer in a position of danger, and the pursuer suffers injury through adopting what turns out to be the wrong course of action, the defender cannot put forward the defence of contributory negligence. This is referred to as "the agony rule."

7. Extinction of Claim through Personal Bar or Lapse of Time

A claim of damages for delict may be extinguished by:

(a) personal bar;
(b) prescription; or
(c) statutory limitation.

(a) Personal bar

The injured party may have acted in such a way that he is barred from asserting his right to damages; *e.g.* he may have acquiesced in the wrong ("acquiescence"), delayed too long before making objections ("mora and taciturnity") or waived his claim ("waiver"). On these forms of personal bar see pp. 246 and 247, above).

(b) Prescription

A change was made by provisions of the Prescription and Limitation (Scotland) Act 1973 which came into force on July 25, 1976.

By that Act the five-year prescription extinguishes obligations to make reparation with the exception of obligations to make reparation for personal injuries or death; these latter are extinguished only by the twenty-year prescription.

The date from which either of these prescriptions runs is the date when the loss, injury or damage occurred, except that where the injured party was not aware (and could not with reasonable diligence have been aware) that the loss, injury or damage had occurred, the prescription runs from the date when he first became (or could with reasonable diligence have become) aware of the occurrence.

As to the conditions for the operation of these two prescriptions see pp. 339 and 341, above.

(c) Statutory limitation

Statutes sometimes provide that claims connected with types of action must be made within certain limited periods. These statutory limitations do not extinguish a claim: their effect is merely to make the claim unenforceable by legal action.

The limitation most generally applicable is that contained in the

Prescription and Limitation (Scotland) Act 1973, which consolidated rules introduced by three earlier Acts. These provisions of the Act of 1973 came into force when the Act was passed (July 25, 1973).

By the Act of 1973 an action of damages for personal injuries or death must be commenced within three years from the date when the injuries were sustained or the death occurred. An extension of the three-year period is allowed:

(i) where the person entitled to bring the action is under legal disability (because he is under the age of majority or is of unsound mind) *and* is not in the custody of a parent, step-parent or grand-parent; the action may then be brought within three years from the date when the disability ended; and

(ii) where material facts of a decisive character were not known to the pursuer until a date later than the date when the injuries were sustained or the death occurred; the action may then be brought within three years from the date when these facts became known to the pursuer.

A provision of the Law Reform (Miscellaneous Provisions) (Scotland) Act 1980 adds a further relaxation: the court may allow an action to be brought after the expiry of the three-year period if it seems equitable to the court to do so.

Further Reading

David M. Walker, *The Law of Delict in Scotland* (The Scottish Universities Law Institute Series) (W. Green & Son Ltd.)

David M. Walker, *Principles of Scottish Private Law*

Gloag and Henderson, *Introduction to the Law of Scotland*

T. B. Smith, *A Short Commentary on the Law of Scotland*

Royal Commission on Civil Liability and Compensation for Personal Injury 1973–1978 (Chairman: Lord Pearson), *Report* (1978: Cmnd. 7054) (H.M.S.O.)

PROPERTY

THE word "property" may denote the right which an owner of things has, or it may denote the things themselves. "Property" in the first of these senses has the same meaning as "ownership." On the other hand, when "classification of property" is referred to, the word "property" is being used in the second sense.

GENERAL NATURE OF PROPERTY OR OWNERSHIP

The institutional writer Erskine defined "property" as "the right of using and disposing of a subject as our own, except in so far as we are restrained by law or paction" [*i.e. agreement*] (*An Institute of the Law of Scotland*, II, 1, 1).

Property is the largest right which a person can have in a thing, but it is seldom a completely unrestricted right; *e.g.* the owner of a house has the right of property or ownership in the house, but his right is restricted in several respects: the common law requires him to have proper regard for his neighbours; statutes, such as the Town and Country Planning Acts, regulate the use which he makes of the house and may even deprive him of it altogether; and by agreement with another person the owner may be barred from exercising full rights (*e.g.* if he had let the house, he would be barred from occupying it himself). It is because of these restrictions that words such as "except in so far as we are restrained by law or paction" must be included in the definition of "property."

Jura in Re Propria and Jura in Re Aliena

A distinction is made between jura in re propria ("rights in a thing belonging to oneself") and jura in re aliena ("rights in a thing belonging to another person").

The former are the rights which an owner may exercise over his own property, *i.e.* using it, enjoying the fruits of it, and consuming, selling or otherwise disposing of it, in all cases in so far as his ownership is not limited by operation of law or by the rights of other persons.

Jura in re aliena exist where some of the mass of rights which together make up full or absolute ownership are separated from the mass and come to belong to persons other than the owners of the property. They are not rights *of* property, but rights *in* property, and their effect is to limit to a greater or lesser extent the owner's rights over his own property.

Examples of jura in re aliena are:

1. the right of a tenant in property which has been let; the landlord remains the owner;

2. a right in security, *i.e.* a right which enables a creditor to use some particular part of his debtor's property to meet a debt which has not been paid in full by the debtor;

3. servitudes, such as a person's right of way over his neighbour's property; and

4. the right of beneficiaries in property held in trust for them; the trust property belongs to the trustees.

GENERAL NATURE OF POSSESSION

A person whose ownership of property is unrestricted is entitled to exclusive possession of the property and so may prevent all other persons from interfering with it; *e.g.* an owner of land may "interdict" trespassers, *i.e.* obtain an order from the court forbidding those who have been trespassing on his land from doing so in future.

There are, however, many situations where the owner does not have the right to exclusive possession, and sometimes he is not entitled to any possession at all.

The exact nature of possession has been the subject of much controversy among jurists, and is one of the principal topics of jurisprudence.

The institutional writer Stair defined "possession" as "the holding or detaining of any thing by ourselves, or others for our use" (*The Institutions of the Law of Scotland*, II, 1, 17). There must, he stated, be "an act of the body" (detention and holding) and "an act of the mind" (the intention to make use of the thing).

The material element, the detention, varies according to the nature of the thing possessed: obviously, the same kind of act is not appropriate for all classes of property.

The mental element, referred to as the "animus possidendi" ("intention to possess"), is the intention of the person to detain the thing for his own interest.

If there is no animus possidendi, there may be custody, but there can be no possession. For instance, an employee in charge of his employer's property is not legally the possessor of it: he has merely the custody of it. On the other hand, a thief is regarded as having possession of stolen goods because he satisfies both the material and the mental requirement.

Possession may be either natural or civil. Natural possession is actual physical possession of the property; e.g. a person is in natural possession of land if he cultivates it, in natural possession of a house if he occupies it, and in natural possession of goods if he keeps them in his hands or amongst his belongings.

Civil possession is possession through some other person who represents the possessor; e.g. a person may have civil possession through his employees or agents, a landlord has civil possession through his tenant, and trustees who own a house have civil possession through a liferenter who is in natural possession of it.

Possession is said to be "exclusive," by which is meant that two or more persons cannot each have the full possession of the same property at the same time. There may, however, be concurrent possession by two or more persons who have different rights of possession which do not conflict; e.g. both landlord and tenant have possession of property, each for his own interest.

IMPORTANCE OF POSSESSION

There are many situations where the possessor of property is not the owner of it. Possession without ownership is a rather precarious right, since the possessor may find himself evicted by the owner or by someone else to whom the owner has transferred the title to the property.

However, there is some legal basis for the layman's saying that "possession is nine-tenths of the law":

1. So far as goods are concerned, there is a presumption that the possessor is the owner. This presumption may be "rebutted" (displaced or contradicted) by proof, but unless and until there is proof that the possession is not legally justified the possessor is entitled to continue in possession. Thus, even a thief has his possession protected by the law to the extent that the owner must show not only that he lost possession but also that the goods were stolen from him.

This presumption of ownership, however, is sometimes not strong, *e.g.* where the possessor is a carrier or the goods are the kind of goods which are commonly rented or made the subject of a hire-purchase contract.

2. So far as heritable property is concerned, possession has three important practical effects:

(a) If it has lasted for at least seven years, it makes available to the possessor certain "possessory remedies."

(b) If it is "bona fide possession" ("possession in good faith"), it gives the possessor certain advantages connected with his use of the property.

(c) It may in certain circumstances ripen into ownership after the lapse of ten years through the operation of the positive prescription.

(a) Possessory Remedies

The possession must for seven years have been open, peaceful and exercised as a matter of right, and the possessor must have some title to the property, but not necessarily a registered title; *e.g.* a lease is enough.

The possessory remedies are "interdict," used to defend possession which is threatened, and an "action of removing," available for the recovery of lost possession.

(b) Bona Fide Possession

A "bona fide possessor" is one who honestly, but mistakenly, believes himself to be the owner, and has probable grounds for his belief. A bona fide possessor becomes a "mala fide possessor" ("a possessor in bad faith") if the true owner produces clear evidence of his own right to the property.

The bona fide possessor enjoys the three following advantages:

(i) Fruits

He is entitled to retain the fruits of the property which were severed by him during his period of possession. The term "fruits" includes not only natural fruits of the soil but also "industrial fruits" (such as crops on which labour must be expended) and "civil fruits" (such as rents).

(ii) Improvements

He is entitled to recover from the true owner expenditure on improvements in so far as the expenditure benefits the true owner. The principle operating here is that of recompense, a branch of quasi-contract (see p. 407, above).

(iii) Violent profits

He is not liable for "violent profits," as a possessor in bad faith would be. By "violent profits" are meant all the profits which the rightful owner could have made if he had been in possession and also all damage caused to the property by the wrongful possessor.

(c) Positive Prescription

If the possessor has a title which is ex facie (apparently) valid and which has been duly recorded in the Register of Sasines (the register of heritable property kept at Register House, Edinburgh), then he may become the owner of the property after he has possessed it as if he were the owner for ten years. This positive or acquisitive prescription was introduced by the Prescription Act 1617, and the period was originally forty years. The Conveyancing (Scotland) Act 1924 reduced the period to twenty years except for servitudes, rights of way and other public rights, and the Conveyancing and Feudal Reform (Scotland) Act 1970 substituted ten years for the twenty years in the Act of 1924.

Since July 25, 1976, positive prescription has been governed by the Prescription and Limitation (Scotland) Act 1973. By that Act the prescription operates where:

(i) the land has been possessed for a continuous period of ten years openly, peaceably and without any "judicial interruption" (*i.e.* proceedings by a rival claimant in court or in an arbitration); and

(ii) the possession was founded on a recorded deed sufficient to confer a title to the land.

The title is then exempt from challenge except on the ground that the deed is ex facie (" apparently " or " obviously ") invalid or was forged. For the following the prescriptive period is twenty years:

(i) the foreshore and salmon fishings when claimed by the Crown as regalia (see p. 467, below);

(ii) the interest of the lessee under a lease;

(iii) allodial land (see p. 471, below);

(iv) positive servitudes; and

(v) public rights of way.

In (ii), (iii), (iv) and (v) there is no need to have a recorded deed.

CLASSIFICATION OF PROPERTY

Property may be classified in various ways:

1. Corporeal Property and Incorporeal Property

Corporeal property consists of things which can be seen or touched, *e.g.* buildings, clothing, and cash. Incorporeal property consists of rights, *e.g.* the right to a debt which is due, a claim for damages, goodwill of a business, shares in a company, and patent rights. All jura in re aliena (see p. 449, above) are incorporeal.

2. Fungibles and Non-fungibles

Fungibles are things which can be weighed or measured and can be replaced by equal quantities of the same quality, *e.g.* money and grain. Non-fungibles are things which have an individual value and which cannot be replaced by other things of the same kind, *e.g.* a picture or a horse.

3. Heritable Property and Moveable Property

This is the most important classification of property.

Heritable property consists of land and its "pertinents" (things going with it, including buildings on it). All other property is moveable.

Both heritable and moveable property may be either corporeal or incorporeal; *e.g.* while land itself and buildings are corporeal, rights connected with land and buildings, such as leases and servitudes (see p. 462, below), are incorporeal, and while items such as furniture, jewellery, and cash are corporeal moveable property, rights such as shares in a company, patent rights and copyright are incorporeal moveable property.

The distinction between heritable and moveable was formerly vital to the law of intestate succession, since before the Succession (Scotland) Act 1964 different rules of succession applied to the two kinds of property. As a general rule the distinction does not now require to be made for that purpose, but it is still important for several other purposes, *e.g.* in the calculation of the legal rights of a surviving spouse or children in a deceased person's estate (these rights being due only out of moveables), and in connection with diligence (the formal legal process by which a successful pursuer may attach the defender's property in order to satisfy his claim and which takes different forms according to whether the property is heritable or moveable).

Difficult questions can arise in the case of property which may be either heritable or moveable; *e.g.* the goodwill of a business is heritable if it is closely associated with the business premises, but moveable if it depends on an individual trader's skill and reputation.

Difficulties also arise where there is the possibility that property has been converted from one type to the other; *e.g.* stones, minerals, trees and crops are heritable as long as they are partes soli ("parts of the ground"), but once they are separated from the land they become moveable, and in the law of succession a deceased person may be held to have converted heritable property into moveable property or vice versa by the terms of his will. Especially notable in this connection are "fittings and fixtures," moveable property which has been brought into connection with heritable property;

on this subject there is a mass of decisions which embody what is known as "the law of fixtures."

Law of fixtures

"Fixture" means anything annexed to heritable property, *i.e.* fastened to or connected with it (not merely set beside it). It may be annexed either directly to the soil or to some other property, such as a building, which has itself become annexed to the soil.

There are two general rules applicable to fixtures.

The first of these rules is expressed in the maxim "inaedificatum solo, solo cedit" ("a thing built on the ground goes with the ground"). which means that a moveable which has become a fixture belongs to the owner of the heritage.

The second rule is that no person other than the absolute owner of the heritage is entitled to remove a fixture. There are, however, several exceptions to this second rule.

Two main problems, corresponding to these two rules, arise in connection with fixtures:
(a) whether the thing in question is a fixture; and
(b) whether a limited owner has the right to remove a fixture.

(a) *Nature of fixtures*

In deciding whether the thing in question is a fixture the court considers:
(i) the purpose of the annexation; and
(ii) the degree of the annexation.

(i) *Purpose of annexation.* If the motive was to improve the heritage, the thing is likely to be a fixture, whereas if the motive was to secure fuller enjoyment of the thing itself, the thing is likely to be still a moveable.

(ii) *Degree of annexation.* As a general rule there must be some physical attachment between the thing and the heritage, and if the attachment is permanent or such that the thing cannot be removed without injury either to itself or to the property to which it has been attached, the thing is likely to be a fixture. However, attachment does not necessarily make a moveable into a fixture; *e.g.* things only slightly attached to heritage, such as carpets nailed to floors, pictures hanging on walls, and tents placed on ground, are not fixtures.

Prima facie ("until the contrary is proved") a thing which is unattached is not a fixture, but there are some items which, though unattached, are considered fixtures; *e.g.* heavy machinery, held in position merely by its own weight, and articles specially adapted or designed for a particular heritage may be proved to be fixtures; in addition, items which are accessory to heritable property, such as the key of a house, the bell of a factory and tools designed for use with particular fixed machinery only, are treated as fixtures and are referred to as "constructive fixtures."

(b) *Right to remove fixtures*

The answer to the question of whether a thing which has become a fixture may later be removed from the heritage varies according to the relationship of the parties between whom the question arises. The rival claimants may be, or stand in the position of:

   (i)   heir and executor;
  (ii)   seller and purchaser;
 (iii)   heritable creditor and general creditors;
 (iv)   liferenter and fiar; or
  (v)   tenant and landlord.

(i) *Heir and executor.* Before the Succession (Scotland) Act 1964 heritable property passed to the heir and moveable property to the executor. Where a conflict arose as to the right of the executor to remove a fixture from the heritage, the courts tended to favour the heir, thus allowing him to take the heritage with the fixture attached as it had been during the deceased's ownership.

Under the Act of 1964 the executor now administers both heritable and moveable property, but the question of removal of fixtures can still arise between parties in the position of heir and executor; *e.g.* a division of the estate into heritage and moveables is still required for calculation of legal rights of a surviving spouse or children, and if a bequest of heritage in a will does not clearly indicate the extent of the bequest, it may be necessary to decide whether the legatee is entitled to a particular fixture or whether on the other hand it may be removed and treated as part of the residue of the estate.

(ii) *Seller and purchaser.* When heritage has been sold the contract of sale may and ought to make it quite clear exactly what is included in the sale. If a dispute arises, the courts tend to favour the purchaser, and the rule applied seems to be the same as that applied as between heir and executor except that in this case greater weight may be given to the element of the intention of the parties.

(iii) *Heritable creditor and general creditors.* A creditor who holds security over heritable property of his bankrupt debtor may have his claim to a fixture challenged on behalf of creditors who hold no security by the trustee in bankruptcy. The rule is the same as that applicable as between seller and purchaser.

(iv) *Liferenter and fiar.* When a liferent (a right to use property for some limited period which is often, but not always, the liferenter's lifetime) comes to an end, a dispute may arise between the liferenter or the liferenter's representatives on the one hand and the "fiar" (the person entitled to the property on the termination of the liferent) on the other hand as to the ownership of fixtures attached to the property by the liferenter during the liferent.

It is to the general advantage of the community that a liferenter should not be discouraged from enhancing property of which he has only a liferent, and he would be discouraged from doing so if the rule of law was that any fixtures attached by him could not be removed by him or his representatives at the end of the liferent. The law, therefore, allows a greater right of removal than in cases (i) to (iii), above.

A liferenter is regarded as being in this respect in a similar position to that of a tenant, entitled to remove trade and ornamental fixtures. A liferenter's claim may, however, be less strong than that of a tenant.

(v) *Tenant and landlord.* The same element of public policy operates here as in (iv), above.

A tenant is entitled to remove a "trade fixture" (a fixture attached by him for the purposes of his trade) and an "ornamental fixture" (a fixture which he has attached for ornament or for the better enjoyment of the fixture itself), provided these fixtures can be removed without substantial injury to the heritage and without being themselves destroyed or losing their essential character.

In agricultural subjects to which the Agricultural Holdings (Scotland) Act 1949 applies the tenant has a statutory right to remove any engine, machinery, fencing or other fixture affixed by him, and buildings erected by him, up to six months after the expiry of the lease.

Modification by agreement of the right to remove fixtures

The rules given above as to the right to remove fixtures may be modified by agreement between the parties. The tenant, for instance, may, when he affixes some article to the heritage, arrange with his landlord that he, the tenant, is to be entitled to remove the article at the end of the lease, although according to the law of fixtures it might not be removable.

Any such agreement is binding on the parties to it but not on other persons who do not know of it; *e.g.* if equipment supplied on hire-purchase under the condition that it is not to become the property of the owner of the heritage until all instalments have been paid has become a fixture, a heritable creditor who has lent money to the owner of the heritage without knowing about that condition is entitled to enforce his security over the heritage with the equipment attached.

LANDOWNERSHIP

Scope of Landownership

The owner of land is entitled to use it as he pleases except in so far as he is restricted by:

1. statute;
2. common law; or
3. agreement.

1. Restrictions imposed by statute ·

In modern times the owner of land has been increasingly restricted by statute in the use which he may make of his land. Obvious examples of statutes imposing restrictions on him are Town and Country Planning Acts, Rent Acts, and Acts which authorise compulsory purchase for specified purposes.

2. Restrictions imposed by common law

Of special importance under this heading are the restrictions arising from what is known as the "law of neighbourhood."

The maxim which embodies the law of neighbourhood is "sic utere tuo ut alienum non laedas" ("use your own property in such a way that you do not harm another's property"). A person is not entitled to use his own property in such a way as to cause unlawful discomfort to his neighbour or unlawful damage to his neighbour's property; *e.g.* the common law requires the owner of a mine not to conduct mining operations in such a way as to cause subsidence of his neighbour's land; other examples are given below under "Natural Rights of Property" (p. 459, below).

If the interference with the neighbour's property is unlawful it amounts to the delict known as "nuisance" (see p. 462, below), and entitles the neighbour to an "interdict" (a court order forbidding continuance of the nuisance) and to damages for the loss or inconvenience which he has suffered.

If, on the other hand, some act lawfully done by A on his own property interferes with B's enjoyment of his (B's) property, B is not normally entitled to restrain A's action, whatever A's motive may be; the law presumes that A is acting for his own benefit, and not purely to disturb B. However, if B can show that A was acting purely "in aemulationem vicini" ("to spite his neighbour"), *i.e.* for the sole purpose of causing loss or inconvenience to B, A's action is illegal and can be restrained by B. An example might be interception of underground water by A on his own land solely to prevent the water from benefiting B's land.

3. Restrictions imposed by agreement

The agreement may be that of the owner himself or of previous owners; *e.g.* an owner may expressly agree with his neighbour not to use his property for a specified purpose, or a feu charter may contain conditions which "run with the land" and these will be binding on all subsequent owners of the land, although they have been expressly agreed to only by the first owner. Servitudes (see p. 462, below) are an important class of restrictions imposed by agreement.

The Conveyancing and Feudal Reform (Scotland) Act 1970 enabled owners to have some restrictions varied or removed on application to the Lands Tribunal for Scotland.

Apart from the restrictions mentioned in 1, 2 and 3, above, the owner of land has a right to exclusive possession of it "a caelo usque ad centrum" ("from the sky to the centre of the earth"), *i.e.* he alone is entitled to possess the property without any vertical limit: he has a right not only to the surface but also to everything above and below the surface. For instance, he can insist on the removal of a cornice on his neighbour's house if the cornice projects beyond the boundary, and may cut off overhanging branches of his neighbour's trees, and he has a common law right (modified to a considerable extent, however, by statute and by contract) to all minerals and other substances so far as they are in a strict vertical line between his surface land and the centre of the earth.

Unlawful interference with the owner's right of exclusive possession amounts to trespass, for which he may obtain damages (if the trespasser has injured the property) and an interdict (ordering the trespass to be discontinued).

Interdict is, however, an equitable remedy which the court has a discretion to grant or to refuse: it is not granted automatically wherever there has been some unlawful encroachment on land; it is refused, for instance, if the trespass is unlikely to be repeated, or is too insignificant to occupy the attention of the court. There is a picturesque illustration of the latter type of trespass in the case of *Winans* v. *Macrae* (1885) 12 R. 1051, in which an interdict was refused on the ground that de minimis non curat lex ("the law does not concern itself about trifles"):

W., the tenant of the estate of Kintail in Ross-shire, brought an action against M., a cottar, whose cottage was close to a road passing through the estate, to have M. interdicted from grazing any lamb or other bestial on any part of his 200,000-acre deer forest.

The ground of the application for interdict was that a pet lamb kept by the cottar often strayed off the road on to the forest which was not fenced.

Lord Young stated (at p. 1063):

"Interdicts are granted by this and other Courts of law where appreciable wrong to a man, whether in his property or in his other rights, is threatened. Here there was no appreciable wrong. This lamb, saved and brought up (*by the cottar and his family*), when a few weeks old followed the cottar and his wife and children, and even the dogs along the road, scampered on the grass occasionally, and I daresay took a blade of grass, but did no appreciable wrong whatever, and I decline, by any interdict, to protect unenclosed lands against trespass of that kind. To talk about the lamb growing into flocks of sheep and herds of cattle is really to talk in a way which makes no impression on my mind whatever. If a man wants to protect his lands from being invaded in this way—against children toddling on to the grass at the roadside, or a lamb going on to it, or a cat, or a kitten—I say, if he wants to exclude that he must do so by other means—by fencing the lands, for example—but not by applying to Her Majesty's Judges for interdict."

(A layman's account of this case can be read in *Scot Easy* by Wilfred Taylor (published by Max Reinhardt), in the chapter entitled "The Pet Lamb.")

Natural Rights of Property

Ownership of land carries with it certain rights, referred to as "natural rights," which are considered necessary for the comfortable enjoyment of the property. The owner may choose by contract to give up some part of his natural rights, but on the termination of the contract they would regain their full original force.

Natural rights are distinguished from servitudes (see p. 462, below) in that natural rights arise ex lege ("by operation of law"), whereas servitudes arise from agreement or prescription. Natural rights may be considered under three headings:

1. right of support for land;
2. rights in water; and
3. rights protected by the law of nuisance.

1. Right of support for land

Land usually requires to be supported both from below and by surrounding land, and if the necessary support is taken away subsidence occurs.

Questions as to the right of support usually arise in connection with mining, and in many cases are governed by statute or by contract. What follows here is confined to the principles of the common law which apply only where there is no statutory or contractual provision to the contrary.

A distinction must be made between (a) land in its natural state, and (b) land carrying buildings, for it may be that a neighbouring owner will be bound to give sufficient support for land in its natural state, but will not be bound to give the additional support which is necessary for land carrying heavy buildings.

(a) *Land in its natural state*

The owner of land has a right to the support which is necessary to maintain his land in its natural state; *e.g.* if A transfers the surface of his land to B, but reserves the minerals for himself, B is entitled to have the surface supported unless there is some provision to the contrary; any subsidence caused by A's working of the minerals would be a legal wrong for which B could claim damages, and later subsidences would be new wrongs giving rise to further claims, even although A had discontinued mining operations.

Similarly, damages may be claimed for subsidence resulting from a neighbour's mining or quarrying too close to the edge of his own land: an adjacent owner must stop his operations at such a distance from the boundary as will leave sufficient support for the neighbouring land.

(b) *Land carrying buildings*

There is no natural right of support for land carrying buildings, but a right of support may be acquired by express grant or implied grant. For instance, if ownership of minerals is separated from ownership of the surface after buildings have been erected, the mineral owner must give sufficient support for the existing buildings, and similarly if at the time of the separation of the ownership of minerals from that of the surface the parties contemplate that buildings will be erected, then support must be given for the contemplated buildings; in both these situations there would be an implied grant of a right of support. On the other hand, there would be no implied grant of a right of support for all buildings, however heavy, which were not contemplated by the parties but which might afterwards be erected on the surface; in that case an express grant would be necessary.

2. Rights in water

Water which is not in a definite channel must be distinguished from streams and lochs.

(a) *Water not in a definite channel*

Surface or underground water not in a definite channel may be appropriated by the owner of the land. A neighbour has no right to object to such an appropriation. For example, if A appropriated underground water on his own land by sinking a well and as a result the well of his neighbour, B, dried up, B would have no right to object.

Usually, however, the owner of land wishes not to appropriate this type of water but to rid himself of it by drainage or other means. If the water drains naturally on to lower ground, the owner of the lower ground cannot object to it, but the owner of the higher ground is not entitled to increase the volume of water beyond the volume which would naturally run that way (*e.g.* by pumping operations). Agricultural drainage is an exception: it is regarded as a necessary operation, and an adjacent owner is bound to submit to alteration in the natural flow of water on to his land if the alteration results from agricultural drainage on his neighbour's land.

There are also statutory provisions dealing with flood prevention and with agricultural drainage.

(b) *Streams*

Water in the form of a stream with a defined course is not, however small the stream may be and whether it is on the surface or below it, under the sole control of the owner of the land where it happens to be. All the "riparian proprietors" (owners of land on the banks of the stream) from the source of the stream to its mouth have a "common interest" in it and are entitled to object if their rights in the water are interfered with by other riparian proprietors.

The alveus ("bed") of a stream (other than a tidal river), *i.e.* the actual ground over which the water flows, belongs to the owner of the land on either side of it or, if the stream is a boundary between the lands of two proprietors, to each of them up to the medium filum ("middle line"), an imaginary line drawn down the middle of the stream. The right of ownership of the alveus, however, must be exercised in such a way as not to interfere with the common interest in the water itself.

A riparian proprietor is entitled to take water from the stream for the "primary" uses, namely, drink for man and beast and ordinary domestic purposes such as cooking and washing, even although the result is to exhaust the stream, but he is not entitled to draw off water for other purposes, such as irrigation and manufacturing operations, unless this can be done without infringing the rights of other riparian proprietors. Both quantity and quality of the water are taken into account.

A lower proprietor would normally have no right to object to an upper proprietor's diverting the stream provided the water was returned to the stream before the stream reached the lower proprietor's land. A proprietor on the opposite bank would, however, be entitled to object to such a diversion because it would diminish the quantity of water flowing past his property.

As regards pollution, the common law has been altered by

statute. Under the Control of Pollution Act 1974, which replaces most of the provisions of the Rivers (Prevention of Pollution) (Scotland) Acts of 1951 and 1965, it is an offence to cause any poisonous, harmful or polluting matter to enter a stream.

(c) *Lochs*

Sea-lochs are for legal purposes extensions of the sea, and cannot be acquired by the owner of adjoining land.

Inland lochs fall into two classes:

(i) Some are entirely surrounded by the lands of one proprietor. That proprietor then owns the whole loch—both the solum ("ground") of it and the water in it. It is under his sole control except that if a stream runs out of it he must have due regard for the rights of riparian proprietors.

(ii) Other lochs have the lands of several proprietors adjoining them. It is then presumed that each proprietor owns the solum opposite his own land as far as the middle of the loch, but that all proprietors have a joint right to the water and may sail and fish on the loch. However, provisions in the title-deeds and evidence of possession may rebut this presumption.

3. Rights protected by the law of nuisance

"Nuisance" in its legal sense consists of disturbance of an adjacent owner's right to the comfortable enjoyment of his property, *e.g.* noise and fumes.

In deciding what amounts to a nuisance one must take into account the character of the locality; *e.g.* what is a nuisance in a residential area is not necessarily a nuisance in an industrial area.

A person alleged to be causing a nuisance cannot defend himself by saying that another person, even the complainer himself, is contributing to the nuisance, or that the public derives benefit from the operation which causes the nuisance, or that he is himself merely making a normal use of his own property.

A nuisance which has existed for the period of the negative prescription (twenty years) can no longer be objected to, but any increase in the extent of the nuisance after that time could still be challenged. Objection to a nuisance may also be barred if the complainer has consented to the nuisance or if the nuisance has been authorised by statute.

Servitudes

A servitude may be defined as "a burden on land or houses, imposed by agreement—express or implied—in favour of the owners of other heritable property, whereby the owner of the burdened property and his heirs and successors must either submit to something being done by the owner of the other property or himself refrain from doing something on his own property."

The word "tenement" is used for property in this connection, although the property may not be a "tenement" in the ordinary sense and may consist of land with no buildings on it at all. The burdened property is referred to as the "servient tenement" and the other property as the "dominant tenement." Servitudes may be divided into:

1. positive servitudes and negative servitudes; or
2. urban servitudes and rural servitudes.

1.   Positive servitudes and negative servitudes

A positive servitude is one which entitles the owner of the dominant tenement to exercise a right over the servient tenement, the right being one which can be actively exercised, *e.g.* a right of way entitling the owner of the dominant tenement to walk over the servient tenement.

A negative servitude consists of a restraint imposed on the actions of the owner of the servient tenement, as where the owner of the servient tenement is restrained from building in such a way as to cut off light from the dominant tenement. A negative servitude cannot be actively possessed.

The distinction between positive and negative servitudes is indicated in the definition given above, a positive servitude being one in which the owner of the servient tenement must "submit to something being done by the owner of the other property," and a negative servitude being one in which he must "himself refrain from doing something on his own property."

2.   Urban servitudes and rural servitudes

Urban servitudes are those which relate to buildings (whether situated in the town or in the country), whereas rural servitudes relate to land.

(a) *Urban servitudes*

The established urban servitudes are:

  (i)   support;
  (ii) stillicide; and
  (iii) light or prospect.

  (i) *Support.* This includes the servitudes tigni immittendi ("of letting in a beam"), by which the owner of the dominant tenement has the right to insert into the wall of the servient tenement a beam or other structural part of the dominant tenement and to keep it there, and oneris ferendi ("of bearing the burden"), by which the owner of the dominant tenement has the right to have his building supported by the servient tenement.

(ii) *Stillicide*. The servitude of stillicide or eavesdrop entitles the owner of the dominant tenement to have the rainwater from his own building fall directly on to the servient tenement.

(iii) *Light or prospect*. Under this heading come the servitudes non aedificandi ("of not building"), by which the owner of the servient tenement must not build on his own land, altius non tollendi ("of not raising higher"), by which he must not raise his buildings beyond a certain height, and non officiendi luminibus ("of not harming the light"), by which he must not build in such a way as to cut off the dominant tenement's light or view.

Servitudes of light or prospect are the only recognised negative servitudes.

(b) *Rural servitudes*

Rural servitudes include:

   (i) way;
  (ii) aquaehaustus ("drawing of water");
 (iii) aqueduct;
 (iv) pasturage; and
  (v) fuel, feal and divot.

(i) *Way*. This may be a footpath, a horse-road or a carriage-road, which last might be used for motor cars.

The owner of the servient tenement is not required to keep the road in repair, and he is free to erect gates on the path or road provided this does not interfere with the exercise of the servitude.

A servitude of way must be distinguished from a public right of way. The former is for the use of the owner of the dominant tenement only, and no-one else would be entitled to bring an action in court to have it established. A public right of way, on the other hand, is a right of the public to use a particular route between one public place and another public place; it can be claimed by any member of the public.

(ii) *Aquaehaustus*. This is the right to take water from or to water cattle at a well, stream or pond on the servient tenement.

(iii) *Aqueduct*. This is the right to convey water by pipes or canals through the servient tenement. The duty of maintenance lies on the dominant owner, and he is entitled to reasonable access to the servient tenement for this purpose.

(iv) *Pasturage*. This is the right to pasture cattle and sheep on the servient tenement.

(v) *Fuel, feal and divot*. This is the right to take from the servient tenement peat for fuel and turf for fencing and roofing.

Characteristics of servitudes

1. Servitudes go with ownership of heritable property; they are "real rights" in the technical sense, as opposed to personal privileges which an owner of land may choose to grant to the person who is his neighbour for the time being. A classification is sometimes made of servitudes into "praedial" servitudes (servitudes relating to land) and personal servitudes, but the only possible example of a personal servitude is liferent (see p. 504, below), and the view now generally accepted is that liferent is a distinct interest in property and should not be classified as a servitude; accordingly all proper servitudes are praedial.

2. A servitude is for the benefit of the owner of the dominant tenement as such. It cannot be separated from ownership of that tenement: only the owner of that tenement can claim it, and he cannot transfer the benefit of the servitude to anyone else, unless he also transfers ownership of the tenement itself to that person.

3. A servitude does not require the owner of the servient tenement to do anything active: his role is to submit to something active done by the owner of the dominant tenement or to refrain from doing something himself; *e.g.* in the servitude of way, the owner of the servient tenement is not bound to repair the road. A servitude is said to consist "in patiendo" ("of suffering or allowing") and not "in faciendo" ("of doing").

4. A servitude must be exercised civiliter ("courteously"), *i.e.* in the way which is least burdensome for the owner of the servient tenement. The servient owner's right to use his own property as he pleases is not restricted beyond what is necessary to satisfy the servitude; *e.g.* in the case of the servitude of pasturage, the servient owner is entitled to the surplus pasturage.

Constitution of servitudes

Servitudes do not necessarily appear in the title-deeds of a property. They may be created by:
1. express grant;
2. implied grant or implied reservation; or
3. prescription.

1. *Express grant*

Both positive and negative servitudes may be created in this way, and this is the only way in which a negative servitude can be created.

The grant is made by the owner of the servient tenement, and, since it relates to heritable property, must be contained in a probative document, which may be, but is not necessarily, one of the registered title-deeds of the property.

2. *Implied grant or implied reservation*

A positive servitude may be created by implication where the servitude is necessary for the use of the property. This can occur when the owner of heritage separates it into two or more parts and transfers one or more of these parts to another person. For instance, A, the owner of an estate, may transfer part of the estate to B and retain the rest for himself; if the only means of access to B's property is over the part of the estate retained by A, then a servitude of way in favour of B and his successors in the property will have been created by implied grant, and if the only means of access to the part retained by A is over B's property, then a servitude of way in favour of A and his successors in the property will have been created by implied reservation. The courts, however, do not readily hold that a servitude has been created by implied reservation: they take the view that the person transferring his property ought to have provided expressly at the time of the transfer for any servitude which he wished to enjoy over the property transferred.

3. *Prescription*

By the Prescription and Limitation (Scotland) Act 1973, a positive servitude may be created by prescription, *i.e.* by being possessed for a continuous period of twenty years "openly, peaceably and without judicial interruption." There would be a "judicial interruption" if the possession were challenged in court proceedings or in an arbitration. The actings of the dominant owner in the exercise of the servitude claimed must have been such that they indicated beyond doubt to the servient owner that a right was being asserted: it is not enough if the dominant owner has been relying on some mere permission or privilege granted to him by the servient owner or has secretly taken some liberty which would have been objected to, if known about, by the servient owner.

Extinction of servitudes

Servitudes may be extinguished in the following ways:

1. By a change in circumstances: Examples are permanent destruction of the dominant or the servient tenement and acquisition of land by compulsory purchase under some statutory provision.

2. Confusione ("by combination"): This occurs when both tenements pass into the ownership of the same person; the servitude does not automatically revive if they later come to belong to different persons again.

3. By renunciation: A servitude is extinguished if it is expressly renounced by the dominant owner in a probative document.

4. By prescription: A servitude may be lost by the operation of the negative prescription of twenty years. Under the Prescription

and Limitation (Scotland) Act 1973 a positive servitude, if unexercised and unclaimed (in court proceedings or in an arbitration) for a
continuous period of twenty years, is extinguished as from the
expiry of the twenty years. For the extinction of a negative servitude
the servient owner would require to have done something inconsistent with the servitude (*e.g.* built higher than the servitude altius non
tollendi allowed him) and his action would require to have remained
unchallenged by the dominant owner for the next twenty years.

5. By personal bar: The conduct of the dominant owner may
have been such as to indicate that he intended to give up the servitude, and he will then be barred from insisting on it. The form of
personal bar usually applicable in this connection is acquiescence.

6. By discharge ordered by the Lands Tribunal for Scotland: This
may be obtained under the Conveyancing and Feudal Reform
(Scotland) Act 1970 where the servient owner satisfies the Tribunal
that the servitude is unreasonable, inappropriate or unduly burdensome.

Regalia

"Regalia" is the term used of the rights of the Crown (the King or
Queen for the time being) in heritable property.

Regalia are divided into regalia majora (literally, "the greater
royal rights") and regalia minora (literally, "the lesser royal rights"),
the former being rights which the Crown holds in trust for the public
and which cannot be alienated by the Crown, and the latter being
rights which the Crown may exercise or alienate as it pleases.

Examples of regalia majora are:

1. *The sea.* The sea within the limits of territorial waters (*i.e.*
in general, up to three miles out from the shore) belongs to the
Crown in trust for the public rights of navigation and fishing.

2. *The foreshore.* The foreshore consists of the land lying between the high and low water-marks of ordinary spring tides. It is
held by the Crown in trust for the public rights of navigation and
fishing, and possibly also recreation.

3. *Tidal rivers.* These are subject to the same rules as territorial
waters: the solum ("ground" or "bed") belongs to the Crown in
trust for the public rights of navigation and fishing. A public right
of navigation also exists in non-tidal rivers, but in such rivers the
solum belongs not to the Crown but to the riparian proprietors (see
p. 461, above).

Examples of regalia minora are:

1. *Precious metals.* Mines of gold and silver and mines of lead
of a specified fineness belong to the Crown, but the Crown must,
when required, make a grant of these minerals to the owner of the
land in which they are found in return for payment of a "royalty"

(a payment proportionate to the amount of minerals). Coal belongs to the National Coal Board, and other minerals belong to the owner of the land in which they are found.

2. *Salmon fishings.* Salmon fishing is a separate heritable right which does not necessarily belong to the owner of the land on which that fishing is available. It is a right belonging in the first instance to the Crown and which the Crown may grant to the person of its choice, who is not always the owner of the land. Where the owner of the salmon fishing is not the owner of the surrounding land he has a right of access to the fishings over that land and other incidental rights such as to moor boats and dry nets, but he must have due regard for the interests of the landowner.

Salmon fishing is extensively regulated by statute.

3. *The foreshore.* The foreshore, as well as being one of the regalia majora, is one of the regalia minora since the Crown's right to the foreshore can be alienated except in so far as is necessary for the safeguarding of the public rights in the foreshore. Where the Crown has granted the foreshore to the owner of the adjacent land or to some other person, that person is entitled to take sea-weed and other materials and in general make what use of the foreshore he wishes but he must not obstruct the public in the exercise of their rights.

Principles of Land Tenure

The main principles of the present system of land tenure in Scotland are outlined below under the headings of:

1. feudal tenure; and
2. Register of Sasines.

From April 6, 1981, there is to be a gradual introduction of:

3. registration of title.

The major reforms now being undertaken in the system of land tenure are based on the work of three committees:

(a) the Reid Committee, under the chairmanship of Lord Reid, which recommended in its report in 1963 (*Registration of Title to Land in Scotland*, Cmnd. 2032) that two further committees be appointed, one to consider amendment of the statutes on conveyancing and another to work out the details of a scheme of registration of title;

(b) the Halliday Committee, under the chairmanship of Professor J. M. Halliday, which issued its report in 1966 (*Report of Committee on Conveyancing Legislation and Practice*, Cmnd. 3118); and

(c) the Henry Committee, under the chairmanship of Professor G. L. F. Henry, which issued its report in 1969 (*Report on the*

Scheme for the Introduction and Operation of Registration of Title to Land in Scotland, Cmnd. 4137).

The Halliday Committee's recommendations led to the following legislation:

(i) the Conveyancing and Feudal Reform (Scotland) Act 1970, which introduced a new form of heritable security ("the standard security"), made other amendments of the law relating to heritable securities, conferred power on the Lands Tribunal for Scotland to vary or discharge "land obligations" (*e.g.* conditions imposed by a feu charter), reduced the period of positive prescription (see p. 452, above), and included several other conveyancing reforms;

(ii) the Redemption of Standard Securities (Scotland) Act 1971, a short Act amending the Act of 1970 on a single point which was proving unsatisfactory in practice; and

(iii) the Land Tenure Reform (Scotland) Act 1974, which prohibited the creation of new feu-duties and enabled owners to redeem existing feu-duties,

The major recommendations of the Henry Committee were given statutory force by the Land Registration (Scotland) Act 1979.

1. Feudal tenure

Land tenure (*i.e.* the way in which land is held by its owner) is still basically feudal. The theory of the feudal system was that all the land in the country belonged to the king, and that the right of every landowner to his land was derived directly or indirectly from a grant made by the king. Powerful nobles held their land "immediately" under the king, *i.e.* by a direct grant from the king to them or to their predecessors, and lesser subjects held their land "mediately" under the king, *i.e.* by a grant made to them or to their predecessors by a superior intermediate between them and the king.

The granting of ownership under the feudal system of land tenure is referred to as "feuing," and the land granted is referred to as a "feu." The person who feus the land is called the "superior" and the person to whom it is feued is called the "vassal" or the "feuar."

There is no limit to the number of times a piece of land may be subfeued, and there may be many intermediate superiors between the Crown and the vassal who is in actual occupation of the land as owner. The land system may, therefore, be pictured as being in the form of a pyramid, with the monarch at the top and an increasing number of vassals and sub-vassals below him, the base of the pyramid representing the vassals who actually possess the land.

The process of subinfeudation is to be distinguished from outright sale of land. The former is the creation of a new feudal estate, and a new vassal-and-superior relationship: the person who was formerly the vassal in actual occupation of the land becomes a superior but does not disappear from the feudal chain since he continues to hold the land of his own superior. In an outright sale, on the other hand, the vassal substitutes another vassal for himself in the feudal chain and himself ceases to form part of that chain.

Subinfeudation often involves subdivision of a piece of land, *e.g.* where new feus are created on a building estate, but does not necessarily do so: an owner may choose to subfeu the whole of his land to one other person and himself remain in the feudal chain as the new and additional superior, the link between his own superior and the new vassal. In earlier times, when a superior had the right to object to the substitution of a new vassal on an outright sale of the land, the process of subinfeudation was sometimes used as a device to achieve the same purposes as sale since the superior had no right to object as long as the vassal of his choice remained immediately below him in the feudal chain.

In earlier times the return made by the vassal to the superior for the grant of the land was military service as and when required. This type of tenure, known as "ward holding," was abolished just after the Jacobite rebellion of 1745.

The normal tenure is now feu holding, in which the vassal pays a certain periodic sum, known as "feu-duty," to the superior and may also be bound to observe certain conditions, *e.g.* as to the type of building which may be erected on the feu.

In feudal tenure both superiors and vassals are regarded as having rights of ownership in the land. In making a feudal grant the Crown or any other superior retains a radical right to the land, referred to as the "superiority" or "dominium directum" ("direct ownership"). The right which the vassal receives is referred to as the "dominium utile" ("useful ownership"). Where the vassal subfeus, he will, in relation to the sub-vassal, have the dominium directum, and the sub-vassal will have the dominium utile. The same division of ownership takes place at each stage of subinfeudation.

The dominium directum is the higher right in the feudal sense, but the dominium utile is the more valuable right. The dominium directum entitles the superior to exact feu-duty and enforce the other conditions on which the feu has been granted but gives him no right to use the land. The dominium utile, on the other hand, entitles the vassal to use the land as his own provided he pays the feu-duty and observes the other conditions of the feu.

Proposed reforms of land tenure include the abolition of feudal tenure, with the existing owners of the dominium utile becoming absolute owners of the land. While feu-duty would disappear, there would still be the possibility under the proposed new system of creating conditions running with the land similar to the conditions which are under the feudal system of land tenure often included in the feu-charter or other document which creates the new feudal estate. The Lands Tribunal for Scotland would be given power to annul or modify unreasonable conditions. These proposals were outlined in a White Paper published in 1969—*Land Tenure in Scotland —A Plan for Reform* (Cmnd. 4099).

The first step was taken by the provision in the Conveyancing and Feudal Reform (Scotland) Act 1970 that an owner may apply to the Lands Tribunal for Scotland for variation or discharge of unreasonable, inappropriate or unduly burdensome conditions in existing feus.

The Land Tenure Reform (Scotland) Act 1974 marks the second stage. This prohibits the creation of new feu-duties, confers on an owner the right to redeem his feu-duty at any term of Whitsunday (May 15) or Martinmas (November 11) on giving to his superior the statutory "notice of redemption" and paying the appropriate "redemption money," and provides for compulsory redemption of feu-duty when land is sold (the redemption money being paid to the superior by the seller). The "redemption money" is the sum of money which if invested in $2\frac{1}{2}\%$ Consolidated Stock would produce an annual sum equal to the feu-duty. For the calculation of this sum the price taken is the middle market price at the last close of business before the date occurring one month before the date of redemption. For instance, if the feu-duty was £7 per annum and the owner redeemed it at Martinmas 1974, the calculation would have been:

> Middle market price of $2\frac{1}{2}\%$ Consolidated Stock at close of business on October 10: $15\frac{3}{4}$
> Divide this by $2\frac{1}{2}$ (or multiply it by 4 and divide by 10).
> The result is the figure $6 \cdot 3$, referred to as the "multiplier" or the "redemption factor."

The redemption money is then £7 $\times$ $6 \cdot 3$, *i.e.* £44·10.

It is to be noted that the Act of 1974 does not abolish feudal tenure or prohibit the creation of new feus. A superior still has the right to impose and enforce feuing conditions in new and existing feus respectively.

Allodial land

By far the greater part of the land in Scotland is held on feudal tenure, but there is a small portion of it which is held "allodially," *i.e.* absolutely and under no superior. Allodial land includes:

(a) The paramount superiority of the Crown: There is no

further superior beyond the Crown; therefore, the Crown's dominium directum is itself allodial.

(b) The "property" of the Crown in the sense of the full ownership of the land: This refers to land in respect of which there has been no division of ownership into dominium directum and dominium utile because the Crown has retained full ownership for itself.

(c) Certain property belonging to the Church of Scotland: This includes churches, churchyards, manses and glebes.

(d) Land acquired by compulsory purchase: This was provided for by the Lands Clauses Consolidation (Scotland) Act 1845.

(e) Udal land in Orkney and Shetland: Some of the land in Orkney and Shetland is held on a tenure known as "udal tenure" introduced to those parts by the Vikings, who considered themselves as not being vassals of any king or lord. In recent times, however, there has been a tendency for udal land to be brought gradually within the feudal system.

2. Register of Sasines

The Register of Sasines is the register of heritable property in Scotland. It is kept at Register House, Edinburgh, and is open to public inspection. It now takes the form of photographic copies of the title-deeds of properties throughout Scotland. Registration in this register is referred to as "registration for publication," because it enables any member of the public to find out who has the title to a particular property and what burdens (such as heritable securities) there are over the property. The register was originally set up by the Registration Act 1617.

It is through the system of registration of deeds in the Register of Sasines that "personal" rights in heritable property are converted into "real" rights. The terms "personal" and "real" are used here in their technical senses; for the distinction between a personal right, a "jus in personam," and a real right, a "jus in re," see p. 242, above. If A enters into a contract with B by which B is to purchase A's land, B has a right as against A to have that contract implemented and he can sue A for damages if A fails to implement it; that is a personal right. The contract of itself does not, however, give B a real right to the land: B can claim the land from A, but cannot assert his right to it against all and sundry. B obtains a real right to the land only when the "conveyance" (the formal legal document transferring the land) is "recorded," i.e. registered in the Register of Sasines. The distinction between B's personal right and his real right is of particular importance where A has contracted to sell the land to another party, C, also. A conflict may then arise as to whether B or C is entitled to the land. The party who is the first to register his title in the Register of Sasines is (unless he has been guilty of fraud) entitled to the land, even although the contract under which he obtained it and the conveyance itself may have been the later in date.

Registration has a similar effect on heritable securities. Where a loan has been made to A by B, and A, as well as undertaking to repay the loan, has granted to B a "bond" or other security over his (A's) land so that B may, if A defaults in payment, recover the amount of the loan by selling the land, B's "right in security" becomes a real right only when the appropriate document constituting the security is registered in the Register of Sasines. Once the burden appears on that register, it "runs with" the land, affecting the ownership of anyone into whose hands the land may come. Should A, for instance, sell his land to C, B would still have the right to enforce his security against the land on A's default in payment of the loan. C would be deemed to have been aware of the entry on the register which gave B his real right over the land, and to have bought the land with the burden attaching to it. B would require to discharge his right (which be would normally do only on repayment of the loan) before C could obtain a "clear" title to the land.

The Register of Sasines derives its name from the fact that it was originally composed of "instruments of sasine," formal legal documents which were regarded as being evidence of the ceremony known as "sasine" (compare the modern English word "seizing").

The basic rule of the common law was that the only means of transferring property, whether heritable or moveable, was delivery. In accordance with that rule, heritable property was in early times transferred from one person to another by "symbolical delivery," the nearest possible approach to actual delivery which was impossible because of the nature of the property. The symbols varied with the property; *e.g.* for land and houses they were earth and stone, for salmon fishings a net and coble, and for a right of ferry an oar and some water. Originally the symbols were actually handed over on the land in the presence of witnesses—the ceremony of sasine. By this ceremony the new owner became "infeft" (legally entitled to the land), and the maxim applicable was "nulla sasina, nulla terra" ("no sasine, no land"), *i.e.* the transferee, although he might have a contractual right against some other specific person, had no real right to the land: "infeftment" depended on sasine.

By 1617, when the Register of Sasines was set up, it had become the usual practice for the ceremony of sasine to be narrated in a "notarial instrument" (a formal legal document drawn up by a notary) known as an "instrument of sasine," and it was these instruments of sasine which by the Registration Act 1617 had to be registered in order that the public might be made aware of the change in the ownership of the land.

In course of time it came to be realised that the appearance of the instrument of sasine on the Register of Sasines was of greater legal importance than the ceremony itself, and finally the Infeftment Act 1845 provided that the ceremony was no longer to be essential and that infeftment might be achieved by the mere recording of an instrument of sasine in the Register of Sasines. After that date the instrument of sasine was usually of a fictitious nature in that it narrated a ceremony which had never in fact taken place.

Subsequent legislation on conveyancing made instruments of sasine unnecessary by allowing deeds of conveyance, such as feu-charters and dispositions (by which transfers of land are made by superior to vassal or seller to purchaser, respectively) to be themselves recorded, and so the Register of Sasines is now largely composed of conveyances. A feuar or purchaser now becomes infeft by recording the feu-charter or the disposition granted to him by the superior or the seller respectively, and similarly a creditor who holds a heritable security obtains a real right which will run with the land by recording his security document.

The present system of registration in the Register of Sasines is a system of registration of *title deeds* and must be distinguished from a system of registration of *title* according to which the state guarantees the validity of a recorded title.

When the system of registration of title (see 3, below) is fully in operation, the Register of Sasines will be closed.

3. Registration of title

A system of registration of title is being introduced by phases starting from April 6, 1981. The main statutory provisions for this are in the Land Registration (Scotland) Act 1979, which authorises the Secretary of State for Scotland to make rules prescribing the various details of procedure.

The Act is to be brought into operation area by area, the first area being Renfrew in part of which a pilot scheme has already been operating. The introduction is expected to extend over nine years according to the following plan:

Year 1: Renfrew;
Year 2: Barony and Regality of Glasgow;
Year 3: Lanark and Dumbarton;
Year 4: Midlothian;
Year 5: remainder of Central Belt;
Year 6: Angus, Kincardine and Aberdeen;
Year 7: Ayr, Dumfries and Galloway;

Year 8:   Southern Rural Areas; and
Year 9:   Northern Rural Areas.

The Act establishes the "Land Register of Scotland," which is to be under the management and control of the Keeper of the Registers of Scotland. The register is based on the Ordnance Survey map. For each property as it comes to be registered the Keeper makes up a title sheet, entering on the title sheet a description of the land including a description based on the Ordnance map. The title sheet will also state the name and designation of the person entitled to the property and heritable securities affecting the property. Appropriate changes will be made on the title sheet as occasion demands, *e.g.* when the property is sold to another person or where a heritable security is discharged. If an owner sells part only of his property the Keeper will make up a new title sheet for the part sold.

On completion of a registration the Keeper issues to the owner a copy of the title sheet, this copy being known as a "land certificate." Where the registration is that of a heritable security over the property, the Keeper issues to the creditor a certificate known as a "charge certificate." Both types of certificate include a statement of the indemnity provided by the Keeper under the terms of the Act. The indemnity is to the general effect that if a person suffers loss as a result of:

 (a) a rectification of the register made by the Keeper;

 (b) the refusal or omission of the Keeper to make a rectification;

 (c) the loss or destruction of any document while lodged with the Keeper; or

 (d) an error or omission in any land or charge certificate or in any written information given by the Keeper,

that person is entitled to be indemnified by the Keeper for the loss suffered. There are numerous exceptions to the right to an indemnity; *e.g.* no indemnity is due to a person who has by his fraudulent or careless act or omission himself caused the loss.

A person who is aggrieved by a refusal of the Keeper to rectify the register may appeal to the Lands Tribunal for Scotland, and there is a further right of appeal to the Court of Session. The Keeper will be bound to comply with an order for rectification made by the Lands Tribunal or by the court.

Although an area may have become an operational area, this does not mean that every transaction must thereafter be registered under the new system. As a general rule the first registration will require to be made only when there is a transfer for valuable consideration (as in the ordinary sale and purchase transaction or on the creation of a new standard security). Other transactions (*e.g.*

gratuitous transfers and the assignation of existing standard securities over a property) *may* be brought under the new system, but the applicant is entitled to elect to have his title continued as a recording in the Register of Sasines.

The Act also permits voluntary registration outwith an operational area if this is acceptable to the Keeper. For instance, the Keeper might exercise his discretion to accept such registration if the transaction related to a building development in an area which would soon be an operational area.

As the new system spreads through the different areas, by compulsory and voluntary registration, the need for recording in the Register of Sasines will gradually diminish. The transitional period will be of considerable duration, but the Act includes a provision enabling the Secretary of State for Scotland by statutory instrument to require remaining interests in unregistered land in any specified area to be registered, with the result that the Register of Sasines for that area would then be closed.

JOINT PROPERTY, COMMON PROPERTY AND COMMON INTEREST

Where the same property, whether heritable or moveable, is owned by two or more persons their ownership may be either joint or common, while questions of "common interest" can arise as between the owners of different, but neighbouring or otherwise associated, properties.

Joint Property

Where two or more persons hold property jointly, they have no separate rights in the property. They are said to have the property vested in them "pro indiviso" ("indivisibly").

A joint owner cannot dispose of his right to another person either inter vivos ("during his lifetime") or mortis causa ("on his death"); if he surrenders or loses his right or when he dies, the right "accresces to" (*i.e.* is added to the ownership of) the other joint owners.

Examples of joint ownership are the rights of trustees in trust property, of partners in partnership property, and of members of a club in club property.

Common Property

In this case each owner has a title to his own share, and he may dispose of that share as he pleases. On his death his share passes according to the terms of his will or, if he fails to dispose of it by will, then according to the rules of intestate succession.

Each co-owner is entitled to take part in the management of the property. He may veto extraordinary use of the property and alteration in the condition of it except that he cannot stop necessary operations for rebuilding or repair. The maxim generally applicable to the management of common property is "in re communi melior est conditio prohibentis" ("in common property the position of the one who forbids something is the better position").

Any one co-owner can insist on division of the common property, or, if that is impracticable or unreasonable, on a sale followed by division of the proceeds.

Examples of common property occur in flatted houses (see "Law of the Tenement," below), and in most of the situations where property is owned by two or more persons who do not stand in any special legal relationship (such as trust or partnership) to one another. Before the Succession (Scotland) Act 1964 if heritable property passed to female heirs, as daughters, sisters, etc., of the deceased, these heirs, referred to as "heirs-portioners," were also common proprietors.

Common Interest

Common interest exists where two or more owners, each of whom has an individual right of ownership in his own property, have their rights of ownership restricted by the rule of law that they must have proper regard for the interests of the other or others.

Common interest is distinct from common property, since common interest involves several different properties, whereas in the case of common property there is only one property involved. Questions of common interest cannot be solved by division or sale of the properties, but only by agreement between the owners or, where there is no agreement, by rules of law.

Riparian proprietors have a common interest in the water of a stream (see p. 461, above), and owners of houses in a street have a common interest in the space above the street for the purpose of entry of light to their premises (e.g. if two opposite houses came to belong to one person, he would not be entitled to bridge over the street if this would deprive other owners in the street of light). Most examples of common interest, however, occur in flatted properties (see "Law of the Tenement," below).

Law of the Tenement

Where different storeys or parts of a single building belong to different persons, and there is no express provision in the title-deeds to regulate the rights and obligations of these different owners amongst themselves, then a body of rules, referred to as "the law of the tenement," applies. The general principle underlying the law of the tenement is that the rights of ownership of each proprietor are modified by the common interest of all the proprietors in the building as a whole.

Examples of the rules embodying the law of the tenement are:

1. The solum ("ground") on which the building is erected and any garden or area in front of or behind the building belong to the owner of the ground floor, but the owners of the other floors have a common interest to prevent injury to their own flats, such as injury resulting from the erection in the garden of a building which excludes light from their flats.

2. The external walls of the building belong to the owner of each storey or part in so far as they enclose his own flat, but the other owners have a common interest which entitles them to object to operations which would endanger the security of their flats.

3. The owners of lower storeys must uphold them as support for upper storeys. The roof belongs to the owner of the highest storey in so far as it is above his property, but the common interest of the other proprietors requires him to maintain it, at his own cost unless there is provision to the contrary, as an effective cover for the building as a whole.

4. Gables, and floors and ceilings give examples of common property, since, where they separate flats which are in different ownership, they are regarded as being divided in ownership along an imaginary middle line. Of more practical importance, however, is the common interest of all proprietors to see that gables, and floors and ceilings are so treated by their owners as not to injure the stability of the building.

5. Entrances, passages and stairs are the common property of all to whose premises they give access.

RIGHTS IN SECURITY OVER PROPERTY

A "right in security" means some additional right which a creditor has for the recovery of the debt due to him should the debtor himself fail to make full payment.

A right in security may be a personal right or a real right. Where it is a personal right it is known as a "cautionary [1] obligation," and gives the creditor the right to claim from a third party the outstanding balance of the debt. The third party, referred to as a "cautioner" [2] (the term corresponding to "guarantor" in English law), has guaranteed the debt, i.e. has undertaken that if the principal debtor fails to make paymen the, the cautioner, will do so in his place.

[1] Pronounced as if there were no "u" ("kay-shun-ary").
[2] Pronounced as if there were no "u" ("kay-shun-er").

Where a right in security is a real right, it gives the creditor a nexus ("bond") over some property, heritable or moveable, with the result that he can resort to that property for satisfaction of the debt in so far as it has not been paid. It is with these real rights in security that the rest of this section is concerned.

The ultimate test of any real right in security comes in the bankruptcy of the debtor, for the creditor holding a real right in security will then be entitled to take the property over which his right extends out of the bankrupt estate and use it to pay the debt which is due to him. If the proceeds of the property are not sufficient to meet the debt in full, the creditor will be entitled to rank along with the ordinary creditors on the remainder of the bankrupt's estate for the balance not satisfied out of the secured property, but on that balance the creditor is likely to receive only a "dividend" of so much in the £, which will be the same proportion as the ordinary creditors receive on the whole amount of their debts. If the secured property is more than sufficient to satisfy the debt, the creditor must restore the excess to the bankrupt estate so that the other creditors may have the benefit of it.

The general principle of Scots law as to rights in security over property is that there must be some form of delivery of the property to the security holder: mere agreement is not enough to give the creditor the real right which alone will give him an advantage over the other creditors should his debtor become bankrupt. This general principle is expressed in the maxim "traditionibus, non nudis pactis, dominia rerum transferuntur" ("by delivery, not by mere agreements, are real rights in property transferred"). Delivery takes different forms, varying with the nature of the property and the type of transaction.

The most important exceptions to this general principle are:
1. floating charges; and
2. hypothecs.

1. Floating Charges

Floating charges are rights in security which can be granted only by companies and industrial and provident societies. They are so called because they do not attach to any particular property of the company or society but "float over" all its property for the time being, until some event occurs (*e.g.* the winding up of the company or society) which causes the charge to "crystallise"; until that occurrence the company or society is free to dispose of any of the property in the usual way.

Floating charges were not valid by the common law of Scotland, but were introduced from the common law of England by the

Companies (Floating Charges) (Scotland) Act 1961 because Scottish companies were thought to be at a disadvantage, compared with their English counterparts, in not being able to grant this type of security to their creditors. The Act of 1961 applied only to companies, but its provisions were extended to industrial and provident societies by the Industrial and Provident Societies Act 1967. The statutory provisions now applicable are contained in the Companies (Floating Charges and Receivers) (Scotland) Act 1972.

A floating charge is created by an "instrument or bond or other written acknowledgment of debt or obligation" but there is no longer any prescribed statutory form. The charge may cover all the company's or society's property, heritable and moveable, or specified items only.

The validity of floating charges depends on their being registered in accordance with statutory provisions the aim of which is to enable any member of the public to ascertain what floating charges have been granted over the property of a company or society with which he may wish to deal.

2. Hypothecs

Hypothecs are those common law rights in security for the existence of which the creditor does not require to have possession of the property. Hypothecs are either:

(a) "conventional," *i.e.* created expressly by contract; or

(b) "legal," *i.e.* implied by law.

(a) Conventional hypothecs

The only conventional hypothecs recognised by Scots law are bonds of bottomry and bonds of respondentia. These are rights in security granted by the master of a ship in an emergency when he finds it necessary to raise money in order to continue the voyage. If the security is over the ship itself, the security document is a bond of bottomry, and if the security is over the cargo, the document is a bond of respondentia. The purpose of both types of bond is to enable the ship and cargo to be brought safely to their destination, and if that end is not achieved the lender has no right in security.

Before granting such bonds the master must communicate with the owner of ship or cargo as the case may be, if that is possible. If communication is impossible, the master may act as agent of necessity (see p. 389, above).

Where several bonds have been granted by the master at different stages of the same voyage, the latest bond has priority over the earlier ones, since it was presumably the last loan which enabled the voyage to be completed.

Such bonds have been made practically obsolete by improvement in communications.

(b) Legal hypothecs

The recognised legal hypothecs are those of the landlord, the superior, and the solicitor, and certain maritime hypothecs or maritime "liens."

(i) *Landlord's hypothec for rent*

A landlord has a hypothec over certain moveables of the tenant, called the "invecta et illata" ("things brought in and carried in"), moveables brought into the premises by the tenant, including articles obtained by the tenant on hire-purchase.

The hypothec does not apply to the tenant's clothes or money, or to goods belonging to other persons which the tenant is to repair.

By the Hypothec Abolition (Scotland) Act 1880 it was abolished in the case of agricultural property over two acres in extent.

The hypothec gives the landlord security for one year's rent, not for prior arrears, and he loses the right if he does not enforce it within three months of the last term of payment.

The sheriff court process by which the hypothec is enforced is known as "landlord's sequestration for rent."

(ii) *Superior's hypothec for feu-duty*

A superior has a hypothec over invecta et illata, which is similar to, but has priority over, a landlord's hypothec.

(iii) *Solicitor's hypothec for costs of action*

A solicitor has in certain cases a hypothec for the costs which he has incurred in bringing a court action on behalf of a client.

At common law if the client has been found entitled to recover expenses from the other party to the action, then the solicitor has a hypothec over these expenses.

The common law gave the solicitor no security over any property recovered in the action, but by the Solicitors (Scotland) Act 1980 the court may declare in any action that the solicitor is to have security over property recovered on behalf of his client.

(iv) *Maritime hypothecs or maritime "liens"*

These securities are properly hypothecs because there is no possession, but they are usually referred to as "liens."

They give to certain creditors rights in security over a ship which is not in the creditors' possession.

The main examples are those of seamen for wages, of the master of the ship for his wages and disbursements, of a salvor for the amount due to him as salvage (see p. 411, above), and of the owner of another-vessel for damages as a result of a collision.

Scots law on this topic does not differ from English law (*Currie* v. *McKnight* (1898) 24 R.(H.L.) 1; (1895) 22 R. 607).

Securities Requiring Delivery

The rights in security dealt with under this heading are those which conform to the general principle that some form of delivery is essential for the creation of a real right. The property over which the security exists may be either:

1. heritable; or
2. moveable.

1. Heritable securities

No actual delivery is possible in the creation of security over heritable property: the equivalent was originally symbolical delivery, and is now registration of the security document in the Register of Sasines.

An important change in the law of heritable securities was made by the Conveyancing and Feudal Reform (Scotland) Act 1970, which introduced a new form of heritable security, known as a "standard security."

The outline of the form of standard security given as "Form A" in a schedule to the Act is as follows:

> "I, A.B., hereby undertake to pay to C.D., the sum of £ . . . with interest from . . . (the date of the loan) at . . . per centum per annum on . . . (a certain date) in each year commencing on . . . (the first date when interest is to be payable); For which I grant a standard security in favour of the said C.D. over ALL and WHOLE . . . (a description of the property is given here): The standard conditions specified in Schedule 3 to the Conveyancing and Feudal Reform (Scotland) Act 1970, and any lawful variations thereof operative for the time being, shall apply: And I grant warrandice: And I consent to registration for execution.
> (To be attested)"

Another form ("Form B") is provided for use where the personal obligation (contained in the first part of Form A) has been created by some other document. Form B is concerned only with the constitution of the real right which is to be C.D.'s security for the amount due to him under the other document.

The standard conditions of Schedule 3 referred to in both Forms include:

(a) an obligation on the debtor to maintain the property in good repair;

(b)   an obligation on the debtor not to alter buildings except with the creditor's consent;

(c)   an obligation on the debtor to comply with the requirements of the law in connection with the property, *e.g.* to pay rates;

(d)   an obligation on the debtor to insure the property;

(e)   the conditions on which the creditor, having "called-up" the security, is entitled to treat the debtor as being "in default" and exercise certain rights such as selling the property, entering into possession, having repairs done, etc.;

(f)   the procedure to be followed when the debtor wishes to exercise his "right of redemption," *i.e.* to free the property from the security by payment of the whole amount due; and

(g)   a provision that the expenses connected with the security are payable by the debtor.

The phrases "I grant warrandice" and "I consent to registration for execution" are part of the technical language of conveyancing; they relate to the "warrandice" (guarantee) which the debtor is giving that the security being granted is a valid one, and to a specially speedy procedure for enforcing payment which may be available to the creditor if the document is registered "for execution."

Heritable securities cannot now be created by any means other than a standard security.

Before the Act of 1970 the main forms of heritable securities were:

(a)   the bond and disposition in security, a deed in which the debtor first undertook to repay a certain sum of money with interest to the creditor and then transferred the heritable property to the creditor in security of that personal obligation; and

(b)   the ex facie ("apparently" or "seemingly") absolute disposition, qualified by a back bond or a back letter, the creditor obtaining a title which on the face of the disposition was an absolute one (such as he would have obtained if the debtor had made an outright sale) but which was really only in security of some indebtedness, as explained in the separate document known as the "back bond" or "back letter."

2.   Securities over moveable property

Rights in security over moveable property may be either:

(a)   constituted by express contract; or

(b)   implied by law ("liens").

(a)   *Securities constituted by express contract*

The method of creation of the security depends on whether the property is (i) corporeal, or (ii) incorporeal (for the distinction see p. 452, above).

(i) *Corporeal moveable property*

The ordinary method of creating security over corporeal moveables is the contract of pledge. The articles are handed over to the creditor who retains them as security for the debt and must return them when the debt is paid. The person who grants the security is called the "pledger" and the person to whom it is granted is called the "pledgee."

Pawn is a special form of pledge, the pledgee being a "pawnbroker" (a person who lends money on the security of goods which are left with him "in pawn" until repayment is made in accordance with the contract). The transactions of pawnbrokers are regulated by the Consumer Credit Act 1974 which repeals the Pawnbrokers Acts of 1872 and 1960 and the Moneylenders Act 1927.

Although pledge requires delivery of the property to the pledgee (with the result that a mere agreement to pledge will not confer a right superior to that of the general creditors of the debtor), delivery does not always involve physical transfer of the moveables. Delivery may be:

1. actual;
2. symbolical; or
3. constructive.

1. *Actual delivery.* This occurs where the moveables are physically transferred from the pledger to the pledgee, and it can also occur where moveables are in a confined space and complete command of that space is given to the pledgee, *e.g.* where the moveables are separately enclosed by a locked fence and the key is handed over to the pledgee.

2. *Symbolical delivery.* The main instance of this form of delivery is the bill of lading, which is regarded as a symbol of the goods shipped. If the bill of lading is transferred, that amounts to symbolical delivery of the goods themselves.

Intimation to the master of the ship is not necessary.

3. *Constructive delivery.* This applies where goods are in a store, and the pledger addresses a delivery order to the storekeeper, directing him to deliver the goods to the pledgee instead of to himself. On receiving intimation of this delivery order, the storekeeper holds the goods on behalf of the pledgee.

Intimation to the storekeeper is essential for the creation of a real right in the goods. This is the point of contrast between symbolical and constructive delivery.

The storekeeper must be an independent third party, not, for instance, an employee of the pledger, and the goods must be ascertained, *i.e.* distinguishable from other goods kept by the pledger in that particular store.

(ii) *Incorporeal moveable property*

A right in security is created over incorporeal moveable property, such as a debt to a person, by a written assignation followed by intimation of it to the debtor. Here intimation has the same legal effect as has delivery in the case of corporeal moveables. It gives the person who is due to pay the debt notice that he must make payment to the assignee of the creditor instead of to the creditor himself. An assignation which has not been intimated to the debtor does not give the assignee a real right.

Incorporeal moveable property which is often used as security includes insurance policies and stocks and shares.

In the case of a life insurance policy, the amount of the policy is a debt due to the policy-holder by the insurance company and can be used by the policy-holder as security for a loan which he may wish to obtain. If the policy-holder merely hands over the policy to the lender, no real right in security will have been created: for such a right there must be a written assignation of the policy to the lender and then intimation of that assignation to the insurance company.

Similarly, in the case of shares in a company, mere deposit of the share certificate with the lender gives him no real right in security. The only way in which the lender can obtain a fully binding right in security over shares is to have the borrower transfer the shares to him and then register himself as owner of the shares with the company concerned; the lender would undertake to retransfer the shares to the borrower on repayment of the loan. In practice, partly to avoid expense, the lender is often satisfied if the borrower hands over to him the share certificate together with a transfer duly signed; the lender is then in a position to complete his security at any time he pleases by sending in these documents to the company, and he normally would not actually take this step unless the borrower failed to make due repayment. However, where this practice is adopted the lender, until he registers the transfer, has no real right and therefore runs the risk of losing his "security" if, for instance, another creditor of the shareholder "arrests" the shares (*i.e.* attaches them for satisfaction of his debt), or if the shareholder fraudulently transfers them to another party who knows nothing of the earlier security transaction.

(b) *Liens*

A lien is a right implied by law to retain moveable property belonging to another person until some debt or other obligation has been satisfied. It is founded on possession and is said to be "possessory." Liens are divided into:

(i) special liens; and

(ii) general liens.

(i) *Special liens*

A special lien is one which entitles the holder of the article to retain it until satisfaction of some obligation arising out of the contract through which he obtained possession of the article; *e.g.* a carrier has a lien over every parcel which he carries for the price of the carriage of that particular parcel only, not of other parcels no longer in his possession, and a person who has been placed in possession of an article in order that he may repair it or do other work on it is entitled to retain the article until he is paid for the work which he does under that particular contract.

(ii) *General liens*

A general lien is one which entitles the holder of the article to retain it until some general balance arising out of a course of dealing or out of a series of transactions has been met.

General liens are recognised by usage in certain professions and trades, and include those of the factor, the banker, the solicitor and the innkeeper.

1. *Lien of factor.* A factor has a general lien over all goods, documents and money belonging to his principal which have come into his possession in the course of the agency.

The lien covers the factor's remuneration, any liabilities incurred by him on behalf of his principal and advances made by him to his principal.

2. *Lien of banker.* A banker has a general lien over negotiable instruments, such as bills of exchange (including cheques) and promissory notes, belonging to his customer, provided they have come into his possession in the course of banking transactions and have not been deposited with him merely for safe-keeping.

The banker can avail himself of this lien to secure any balance due to him by his customer.

3. *Lien of solicitor.* A solicitor has a general lien over documents, including title-deeds and share certificates, entrusted to him by his client. He has, however, no right to dispose of the documents, and he must produce them if they are required for a court action.

If the client becomes bankrupt, the trustee in bankruptcy can insist on the solicitor's surrendering all documents to him, but the solicitor would then be entitled to rank as a preferred creditor on the bankrupt's estate.

The lien covers professional fees and also payments made in the ordinary course of business on behalf of the client to other persons such as counsel. It does not extend to advances made by the solicitor to the client himself.

4. *Lien of innkeeper.* The innkeeper's lien is over the guest's luggage. It does not extend to the person of the guest: the innkeeper is not entitled to detain the guest or to exercise a lien over the clothes which the guest is wearing.

The lien enables the innkeeper to retain the luggage until his bill has been paid.

By the Innkeepers Act 1878 the innkeeper is entitled on certain conditions to sell goods left at his inn if a bill for board and lodging has been outstanding for six weeks.

Table of Rights in Security over Property

The following table may assist the understanding of the arrangement of the law as to rights in security over property:

general principle—delivery essential
    (traditionibus, non nudis pactis, dominia rerum transferuntur)

exceptions to general principle
  (securities without possession)
    1. floating charges
    2. hypothecs
      (a) conventional hypothecs
        (bonds of bottomry
        bonds of respondentia)
      (b) legal hypothecs
        (i) landlord's hypothec for rent
        (ii) superior's hypothec for feu-duty
        (iii) solicitor's hypothec for costs of action
        (iv) maritime hypothecs or maritime "liens"

instances of general principle
  (securities requiring delivery)
    1. heritable securities
    2. securities over moveable property
      (a) securities constituted by express contract
        (i) over corporeal moveable property
        (pledge)
        (ii) over incorporeal moveable property
        (assignation followed by intimation)

    (b) securities implied by law (liens)
       (i) special liens
          (carrier, repairer, etc.)
      (ii) general liens
         1. lien of factor
         2. lien of banker
         3. lien of solicitor
         4. lien of innkeeper

Further Reading

Gloag and Henderson, *Introduction to the Law of Scotland*
T. B. Smith, *A Short Commentary on the Law of Scotland*
David M. Walker, *Principles of Scottish Private Law*
J. A. Lillie, *The Mercantile Law of Scotland*
John M. Halliday, *The Conveyancing and Feudal Reform (Scotland) Act 1970* (W. Green & Son Ltd.)
John M. Halliday, *The Land Tenure Reform (Scotland) Act 1974* (W. Green & Son Ltd.)
John M. Halliday, *The Land Registration (Scotland) Act 1979* (W. Green & Son Ltd.)

CHAPTER 15

TRUSTS AND LIFERENT AND FEE

TRUSTS

THE essence of a trust is that property "vests in," *i.e.* comes into the ownership of, a person, usually called a "trustee," who is under an obligation to administer the property not for his own benefit but for the benefit of some other person, usually called the "beneficiary."

The trustee is the legal owner of the property, but not the beneficial owner of it. The beneficial interest, referred to as the "jus crediti" ("right to the benefit of the trust"), belongs to the beneficiary. While the trustee's function is merely to administer the property in accordance with the terms of the trust, the beneficiary is entitled to use and dispose of the benefits which he receives from the trust; they are said to be his own "beneficial property."

It is quite usual for there to be more than one trustee and more than one beneficiary in a trust, and it is possible for one or more of the trustees to be amongst the beneficiaries, but a sole trustee cannot be the sole beneficiary.

The person who formerly owned the trust property and through whom it has come to be vested in the trustee is called the "truster." He may himself be one of the trustees or beneficiaries, or even the sole trustee or sole beneficiary.

The law relating to trusts is partly common law and partly statute law. The main Acts now applying to trusts are the Trusts (Scotland) Acts of 1921 and 1961.

The administration of trusts is supervised by the Court of Session in the exercise of its nobile officium ("equitable power") (see p. 106, above).

Classification of Trusts

Trusts may be classified in various ways. The two principal classifications are:

1. inter vivos (literally, "among the living") trusts and mortis causa (literally, "for the sake of death") trusts; and

2. private trusts and public trusts.

1. Inter vivos trusts and mortis causa trusts

An inter vivos trust is one which has been set up while the truster is still alive, and a mortis causa trust is one which operates only on the truster's death.

There are the following points of distinction between inter vivos trusts and mortis causa trusts:

(a) An inter vivos trust may arise not only out of a donation made by the truster, but also out of a contract between him and another party and by operation of law; *e.g.* an inter vivos trust may be set up by a "marriage contract" (a contract entered into by parties in contemplation of a marriage), or may be held to exist where one party, A, who stands in a "fiduciary" position (a position of trust) towards B, acquires some property or other benefit for which he is liable to account to B as if he, A, were in fact holding the benefit as a trustee for B; the latter type of trust, arising by operation of law without any express intention on the truster's part to create it, is called a "constructive" trust; instances of constructive trusts occur where an agent acquires in the course of his agency some additional benefit which he must hand over to his principal and where a partner acquires in the course of the partnership business some personal profit for which he must account to the firm.

A mortis causa trust operates as a donation made by the truster at the time of his death to the beneficiaries in the trust.

(b) An inter vivos trust does not require writing for its constitution, although its existence can be *proved* only by the writ or oath of the trustee; the writ required for proof need not be probative.

A mortis causa trust requires probative writing for its constitution. The writing is a "testamentary document" (a will) usually in the form known as a "trust disposition and settlement."

(c) An inter vivos trust may or may not, according to its purposes, be revocable by the truster: if it has been set up voluntarily by the truster merely for the purpose of administering his estate for his own benefit or if all the beneficiaries other than the truster himself are to take no benefit until after the truster's death, then the trust is revocable; if, however, immediate benefits are conferred on parties other than the truster or if the terms of the trust-deed make it clear that the truster intended the trust to be irrevocable, then it is irrevocable.

A mortis causa trust, since it comes into operation only on the truster's death, can never be revoked. The trust disposition and settlement or other testamentary document by which the trust is set up may be revoked by the truster during his lifetime, but the effect of that revocation is to prevent the trust from ever being set up at all, not to discontinue the operation of an existing trust.

(d) In an inter vivos trust, if the purposes of the trust fail or do not exhaust the trust-estate, the trustees hold the property not disposed of or not required, on behalf of the truster. The truster is said to have a "reversionary interest" or a "radical right" in the trust-estate, and in so far as the trust funds transferred by him to his trustees are not used for the trust purposes, they still belong to him and can be disposed of by him as he wishes. The trustees hold these unused funds by way of a "resulting" trust in which the truster himself is the beneficiary.

In a mortis causa trust, property not used for the trust purposes belongs to those who would have been entitled to succeed to it had the truster died intestate.

2. Private trusts and public trusts

A private trust is one in which the beneficiaries are private individuals, whereas a public trust is one set up for the benefit of the public or a substantial portion of the public, the beneficiaries being identifiable religious, educational, charitable or other public organisations or causes.

There are the following points of distinction between private trusts and public trusts:

(a) A private trust can be enforced only by the individuals who are named or otherwise identified as the beneficiaries under the trust or who have some other interest in the proper administration of the trust (*e.g.* the executor).

A public trust can be enforced by popularis actio ("popular action"), *i.e.* by an action on behalf of the public.

(b) In a private trust, if the trust purposes fail (*e.g.* where beneficiaries die before the truster himself), no further effect can be given to the trust and the trust-estate will fall to be treated as if the trust had not been set up, *i.e.* it will in an inter vivos trust revert to the truster and in a mortis causa trust pass to the "residuary legatee" (the person to whom the residue has been bequeathed) or, where there is no residuary legatee or the trust itself relates to the residue, be divided as on intestacy.

The purposes of a private trust once it has come into operation may to a certain extent be varied. At common law the powers of variation were very limited: *e.g.* the beneficiaries might compel the trustees to divide up the trust-estate before the date contemplated by the truster if, but only if, all the beneficiaries were legally capable of giving their consent; an " alimentary liferent " (a benefit intended to provide aliment during the beneficiary's lifetime) could not, once accepted, be renounced even by a beneficiary of full legal capacity.

The common law was altered to a certain degree by the Trusts

(Scotland) Act 1921 and more radically by the Trusts (Scotland) Act 1961. Under the latter Act the Inner House of the Court of Session may grant approval for variation of trust purposes on behalf of beneficiaries who are under the age of majority or suffer from some other legal disability or who are not yet born, provided the interests of the beneficiaries concerned are adequately protected (*e.g.* by insurance), and it may authorise revocation of an alimentary liferent, provided the arrangement is reasonable in view of the beneficiary's income from all sources and of other factors and provided either the alimentary beneficiary or the court acting in his interest approves of the arrangement.

To public trusts, on the other hand, the cy près ("approximation") principle applies. This principle means that if the intention of the truster cannot be given effect to in the exact way directed by him, the court does not allow the trust to fail but directs that the trust-estate is to be applied instead in a way which is as close as possible to that directed by the truster. The trustees petition the Inner House of the Court of Session which in the exercise of its nobile officium ("equitable power") settles a cy près scheme on the lines proposed by the trustees with any amendments which the court considers just.

The cy près principle, however, does not operate in a public trust in which the truster has expressed a clear intention to benefit a particular institution only; in that case if it is no longer practicable to confer the benefit on that institution, the trust fails to that extent. The reason is that the principle is based on the assumption that the truster had a "general charitable intention," *i.e.* that he intended the trust-estate to be applied for the benefit of public purposes *such as* those which he specified rather than to revert to himself (in an inter vivos trust) or to be treated as intestate estate (in a mortis causa trust).

(c) Both in private and in public trusts the beneficiaries must be indicated with reasonable certainty; the trustees must not be allowed complete discretion in the choice of beneficiaries, and if the truster does not give sufficiently definite directions, the trust fails on the ground of uncertainty.

It is not essential for the beneficiary to be actually named: descriptive terms (*e.g.* "the children of X") may be adequate. Difficulties, however, often arise, especially in public trusts, in the decision of whether or not the trust purposes have been sufficiently definitely indicated by the truster; *e.g.* the truster, instead of naming a particular institution, may have specified educational or religious purposes in a limited locality. A trust does not fail merely because the truster has left to his trustees the selection of the precise objects to be benefited, provided he has adequately defined the class of objects or the purposes.

There have been many decisions of the court on this subject, each based on the interpretation of particular wording used by the truster. In private trusts there is no scope for any general rules of interpretation, but in public trusts the following general rules have been established:

(i) Where the truster has described the trust purposes as "public purposes," or as "educational purposes," or as "religious purposes," without giving any further specification, the wording is considered to be too vague and the trust fails from uncertainty.

(ii) The term "charitable" is sufficiently definite by itself, and so if the truster has used this term either by itself or along with one of the same meaning (*e.g.* "philanthropic," "benevolent" or "beneficent"), the trust can be given effect to.

(iii) Where the term "charitable" is linked alternatively to another expression which would by itself be too vague (*e.g.* where the trustees are directed to apply the estate for "public or charitable purposes" or for "educational, religious or charitable purposes"), the trust fails from uncertainty because the trustees are free to choose an alternative which would be too vague (*e.g.* "public," or "educational," or "religious").

(iv) Where the term "charitable" is linked cumulatively to another expression which would by itself be too vague (*e.g.* "public and charitable purposes" or "educational, religious and charitable purposes"), the wording is held not to be too vague, because the trustees are being directed to select from the class of charities (a class sufficiently definite in itself) objects which also fit the other expression (*e.g.* purposes which are not only charitable but are also public, or purposes which are not only charitable but are also educational and religious).

For the purposes of rules (iii) and (iv) the use of the words "or" and "and" respectively is not conclusive: the court may hold in interpreting the truster's language that he used the word "or" in a cumulative sense or the word "and" in an alternative sense; *e.g.* in the case of *M'Conochie's Trustees* v. *M'Conochie*, 1909 S.C. 1046, a direction to a trustee to divide trust-estate "amongst such educational, charitable, and religious purposes within the city of Aberdeen as he shall select" was interpreted by the court as a bequest to any one or more of the three purposes as the trustee should select, *i.e.* the word "and" was held to enlarge the group from which selection might be made; the bequest was therefore void from uncertainty. Normally, however, the words "or" and "and" are interpreted in their ordinary senses.

(d) Although the same general principles apply to the administration of both private and public trusts, the court would probably be more lenient towards honest mistakes of management made by trustees in a public trust than to such mistakes in a private trust. In cases of doubt, however, the trustees ought to seek guidance from the court.

Trustees

The legal position of trustees, particularly as regards their powers, is now mainly regulated by the Trusts (Scotland) Acts of 1921 and 1961, but in some respects, particularly as regards their fundamental duties, is still governed by the common law.

For statutory purposes the term " trustee " is defined as including a trustee ex officio ("as a result of office"), who is a person occupying a position of trust by virtue of his holding of some office, an executor-nominate (a person appointed by a will to divide up the deceased's estate), an executor-dative (a person appointed by the court for the same purpose), a tutor (a parent or guardian of a pupil), a curator (a person in charge of the property of a minor or of some other person not of full capacity) and a judicial factor (an officer of court appointed to manage and administer property where this is necessary for the protection of the property or to resolve deadlock in the administration of it). So far as the common law is concerned, however, the persons included in this extended statutory definition of " trustee " are not fully trustees, since the property held on trust does not vest in these persons as it does in the case of "trustees" proper.

Acceptance of office

A person cannot be compelled to accept the office of trustee.

No special form is required for acceptance: there should preferably be writing, but acceptance may be oral or inferred from actings.

Where a person nominated as trustee wishes to decline the office, his declinature may similarly be written, oral, or inferred from circumstances such as prolonged delay in acceptance of office.

Assumption of new trustees

Where there are no trustees left to continue the administration of the trust and the truster has not provided for this situation (e.g. by conferring on some person such as the holder of an office the right to nominate new trustees), new trustees may be appointed by the truster himself (in an inter vivos trust) or by the Court of Session either in the exercise of its nobile officium or under powers conferred on it by the Trusts (Scotland) Act 1921.[1] There is also a power in the court to appoint a judicial factor on a trust-estate to administer the estate under the supervision of the Accountant of Court.

Although the court does not allow a trust to fail merely because

[1] The Law Reform (Miscellaneous Provisions) (Scotland) Act 1980 conferred these same statutory powers on the sheriff court.

there are no accepting or no acting trustees, it is usual for difficulties which would arise through declinature, death, absence, insanity or other legal disability to be avoided by express provisions in the trust-deed, *e.g.* nomination of several trustees rather than of only one. In addition, the Act of 1921 provides that existing trustees have, unless the contrary is expressed, power to assume new trustees.

The trust-estate vests in new trustees jointly with existing trustees, and, except in so far as the trust-deed provides otherwise, new trustees have the same powers and duties as trustees originally nominated by the truster, including the power to assume further new trustees.

Resignation of trustees

By the Trusts (Scotland) Act 1921 every trust includes, unless the contrary is expressed in the trust-deed, a power to any trustee to resign his office except that:

1. A sole trustee is not entitled to resign unless either he has assumed new trustees and they have accepted office or the court has appointed new trustees or a judicial factor; and

2. A trustee who has accepted a legacy given to him on condition of his becoming a trustee or who receives remuneration for his services as trustee is, unless there is provision to the contrary in the trust-deed, not entitled to resign; he may, however, apply to the court for authority to resign; the court may, if it grants such authority, impose the condition that a legacy accepted by the trustee be repaid.

Resignation has the effect of divesting the resigning trustee of his joint ownership of the trust-estate which is thereafter vested in the remaining trustee or trustees.

Removal of trustees

At common law the court has power to remove a trustee, but does not readily exercise the power unless the trustee has been acting dishonestly or has shown himself unfit for the office. Such circumstances as mere negligence on the part of the trustee or mere disagreement between trustees normally do not justify the exercise of this common law power of removal. The court may, however, appoint a judicial factor to administer the trust-estate in place of the trustees where there are not grounds to justify removal (*e.g.* in a case of deadlock in the administration); the factor's appointment is a temporary measure and may be recalled at any time by the court; the trustees whom he had superseded would then resume their powers and duties.

By the Trusts (Scotland) Act 1921 the court has power to remove a trustee who:

1. is insane; or

2. is incapable of acting because of physical or mental disability; or

3. has been absent continuously from the United Kingdom for at least six months; or

4. has disappeared for at least six months.

Application to court for the removal is made by a co-trustee, beneficiary or anyone interested in the trust-estate. If the ground of the application is insanity or incapacity, the court must remove the trustee, but if the ground is absence from the United Kingdom or disappearance, the court has a discretion and is not bound to remove the trustee. If the trustee removed was a sole trustee, the court has power to appoint a new trustee or new trustees to take his place.

Powers of trustees

The truster may have expressly conferred certain powers on the trustees by the trust-deed; otherwise, the trustees must look to the common law or to statutory provisions for their powers; in exceptional circumstances the court may in the exercise of the nobile officium grant further powers to trustees, *e.g.* where the trust is unworkable.

The common law powers include the power to do, without the court's authority, acts of ordinary administration.

Statutory powers are set out in the Trusts (Scotland) Act 1921 as amended by the Trusts (Scotland) Act 1961. Examples from the list of powers which may be exercised, provided they are not at variance with the terms or purposes of the trust, are:

1. to sell the trust-estate or part of it, whether heritable or moveable;

2. to grant feus and leases of heritable property;

3. to borrow money on the security of heritable or moveable property;

4. to purchase heritable property, but only for the limited purpose of providing residential accommodation reasonably required for a beneficiary (a power added by the Act of 1961);

5. to appoint factors and solicitors and pay suitable remuneration to them; and

6. to grant all deeds necessary for carrying their powers into effect.

The Act of 1921 further provides that if trustees desire to exercise one of the powers in the statutory list but that power is at variance with the terms or purposes of the trust, the trustees may apply to the court for authority to exercise the power. The court before granting such authority must be satisfied that exercise of the power would be expedient for the execution of the trust.

A statutory power which always requires the authority of the court (unless the power has been expressly conferred on the trustees by the trust-deed) is the power to make advances of part of the capital of a fund to the beneficiary for whom it is destined but who is not yet entitled to receive it. This statutory power can be authorised only where:

1. the beneficiary is not of full age;
2. the advance is necessary for the maintenance or education of the beneficiary;
3. the advance is not expressly prohibited by the trust-deed; and
4. the beneficiary's right to the capital of the fund does not depend on the fulfilment of any condition other than the condition that he must survive until a certain future time.

In circumstances not covered by the statutory provision (*e.g.* where the beneficiary has already attained the age of majority) power to make advances of capital can be obtained only by resort to the nobile officium.

Where there are two or more trustees, their powers belong to them as a body. Acts of a majority are binding on the minority, but this does not entitle trustees who are in a majority to administer the estate without consulting their co-trustees who form the minority. All must be given the opportunity to attend meetings and to participate in other ways in the administration of the trust.

The trust-deed may provide for a certain number (*e.g.* two or three) out of a greater number of trustees to be a "quorum," *i.e.* the minimum number required for meetings and for acts of administration. By the Act of 1921 there is implied in every trust, unless the contrary is expressed, a provision that a majority of the accepting and surviving trustees shall be a quorum.

Duties of trustees

The function of a trustee is to administer the trust-estate in accordance with the instructions given by the truster. If the truster has ordered the trustee to do something, then the trustee must carry out the order so far as that is possible and lawful. Similarly, the trustee must refrain from doing what the truster has expressly forbidden him to do. In very many situations, however, the trustee will have a discretion and must decide for himself whether or not, considering the best interests of the trust-estate, he should exercise a power which has been conferred on him. A trustee who is faced with some practical difficulty in the administration of the estate may by the Administration of Justice (Scotland) Act 1933 apply to the court for directions.

In administering the trust-estate a trustee has the following general duties in addition to any specific instructions given to him by the truster:

1. a duty to ingather and distribute the estate;
2. a duty to exercise due care;
3. a duty not to delegate;
4. a duty not to be auctor in rem suam ("one who acts for his own personal benefit");
5. a duty to keep accounts; and
6. a duty in a continuing trust to keep the funds properly invested.

1. Duty to ingather and distribute estate

In a mortis causa trust the trustee's initial duties are the same as those of an executor: he must "ingather" the trust-estate (*i.e.* bring it under his control), enforce payment of debts due to the deceased, pay debts due by the deceased, selling as much of the trust-estate as is necessary for that purpose, and then distribute the estate among the beneficiaries in accordance with the deceased's expressed wishes. Whereas, however, the distribution made by an executor is a once-for-all payment of the capital of the estate, the distribution required of the trustee usually entails his holding the capital for a substantial time (*e.g.* until a beneficiary attains the age of majority, or until the death of a liferenter (see p. 504, below)) and meantime paying out only the income of the estate to that or to another beneficiary.

2. Duty to exercise due care

A trustee must in administering the trust exercise the care which a reasonably prudent man would exercise in the management of his own private affairs. This is an objective (as opposed to a subjective) standard of care: the law of trusts does not concern itself with the care which the trustee does in fact exhibit in the management of his own affairs, but only with the question of whether or not he has as trustee attained the standard of the reasonably prudent man.

A trustee who does not exercise due care is guilty of negligence and may be made liable for loss resulting from his negligence.

3. Duty not to delegate

A trustee must not delegate his administration of the trust to his co-trustees or to advisers and other agents. He may, and in certain circumstances must, obtain the advice of experts and employ agents, but he must never surrender his judgment: however skilled the adviser and however technical the subject-matter may be, the trustee must always apply his own mind to the decisive steps, scrutinising the advice given to him and exercising reasonable supervision over any agent employed.

The maxim applicable is "delegatus non potest delegare" ("a person to whom something has been delegated cannot delegate it to another").

4. Duty not to be auctor in rem suam

It is of the essence of the trust relationship that the trustee must act not for his own personal benefit but solely for the benefit of the beneficiaries in the trust; there must not be even the possibility of a conflict arising between the trustee's interest as an individual and his duty as a trustee. This principle has three main aspects:

(a) The trustee must act gratuitously. Even if the trustee is a professional person (e.g. a solicitor) performing work of a professional nature, he is not entitled to make any charge unless the truster has authorised him to do so or all the beneficaries consent.

(b) The trustee must make no personal profit out of the trust. Any commission or other advantage obtained by him from his position as trustee must be communicated to the trust-estate and held on a "constructive" (see p. 490, above) trust on behalf of the beneficiaries, unless the truster has authorised the trustee to retain the commission or other advantage as his own private property or all the beneficiaries consent.

(c) The trustee must not transact as an individual with the trust-estate; e.g. he must not purchase for himself property which is being sold by the trust. Any such transaction is voidable and can be set aside by the beneficiaries, however fair the terms of the transaction may have been (e.g. where the trustee has been the highest bidder at a public auction of trust property). Transactions authorised by the truster or sanctioned by the beneficiaries in full knowledge of their legal rights are not open to challenge. Further, a trustee is free to transact with a beneficiary concerning that beneficiary's share of the trust-estate, but such a transaction would be regarded with suspicion because of the fiduciary position of the trustee and would be upheld by the court only if the trustee could show that he acted fairly and honestly, giving the beneficiary full information and full value.

5. Duty to keep accounts

The trustee must keep proper accounts showing not only all the capital and income of the estate expressly committed to his charge but also all property which is contructively part of the trust-estate, such as property which he has acquired while acting as auctor in rem suam.

6. Duty to keep funds properly invested

In a continuing trust the trustee must keep the trust funds invested in authorised and appropriate investments. This may involve the sale by the trustee of some investments made by the truster and reinvestment of the proceeds: the mere fact that the truster has approved of the investment when the property was his own does not mean that it is an authorised or appropriate one for the trustee to hold.

The trustee must not retain an unreasonably large amount of uninvested cash nor must he delay unreasonably in reinvesting the proceeds of a sale; otherwise, he may be made liable for the income lost by the trust-estate as a result.

The trust-deed may specify how the funds are to be invested, conferring on the trustee wider or narrower powers than would be implied by law.

At common law the trustee was restricted to fixed-interest securities of the Government and of public and local authorities in the United Kingdom and to heritable securities. Common law powers have been extended by statute, especially by the Trustee Investments Act 1961.

By that Act a trustee may divide the trust funds into two equal parts; one part he must invest in investments referred to as " narrower-range investments "; the other part he may invest in investments known as " wider-range investments." " Narrower-range investments " are subdivided into those not requiring advice (*e.g.* British savings bonds, national savings certificates and deposits in trustee savings banks) and those requiring advice (*e.g.* fixed-interest securities of the Government, of nationalised undertakings and of local authorities, debentures of (*i.e.* loans made to) companies registered in the United Kingdom, building society deposits and heritable securities). " Wider-range investments " always require advice; they include ordinary stocks and shares, shares in building societies and units of unit trust schemes. The advice required for the purpose of these provisions is that of a person who is reasonably believed by the trustee to be qualified to give it by his ability and experience of financial affairs.

The trustee must not only confine himself to investments authorised by the trust-deed or by statute: he must also exercise due care in selecting out of authorised investments those which are appropriate in the circumstances and for the purposes of the trust; *e.g.* he must avoid investments which, although falling within the class of authorised investments, are at the time attended with undue risk and he must have due regard for the need to spread the trust funds over different sectors of investments.

Liabilities of trustees

In their administration of the trust trustees may incur liability:

1. to creditors; and
2. to beneficiaries.

1. *Liability to creditors*

So far as debts incurred by the truster himself are concerned, trustees are not liable beyond the value of the trust-estate.

On the other hand, they are personally liable for debts contracted by themselves in the course of their administration, unless the particular creditor concerned has agreed that only the trust-estate is to be liable; the mere fact that trustees are registered as holding a company's shares "as trustees" does not limit the liability of the trustees for any amount unpaid on the shares to the value of the trust-estate: they must, if required, pay the deficiency out of their private resources.

Trustees are, however, entitled to recover from the trust-estate any liability properly incurred. Further, it is possible for there to be an agreement between trustees and beneficiaries by which the trustees undertake transactions involving greater liability than the amount of the trust-estate on the understanding that the beneficiaries are to indemnify the trustees against personal loss; such an agreement does not, however, prevent creditors from holding the trustees personally liable to them.

Liability of trustees to creditors is joint and several (see p. 247, above).

2. *Liability to beneficiaries*

Failure in any of the duties imposed on trustees by the trust-deed or by law makes them liable to the beneficiaries for breach of trust.

If the breach of trust has resulted in loss to the trust-estate, the trustees are liable to pay as damages the amount of the loss; *e.g.* if the trustees have delayed unreasonably in paying beneficiaries, they are liable to pay interest from the date on which payment ought to have been made, and, if they have failed to invest the trust funds properly, they are liable for the difference between the interest which would otherwise have been earned and that actually earned.

Even if the breach of trust has not resulted in loss to the trust-estate, the trustees are liable to hand over to the beneficiaries the profit which accrues to the trustees from their breach of trust; *e.g.* if the trustees have used the trust funds for their private purposes, they are liable to the beneficiaries not only for the capital of the funds but also for either the profit made by the use of the funds or interest at a rate fixed by the court, whichever the beneficiaries may choose.

Where a trustee has in breach of trust disposed of trust property with the result that the beneficiary cannot actually recover the property from him, the beneficiary has the right to "follow" the property. This right enables the beneficiary to claim from the trustee the property into which the trust property has been converted (*e.g.* other property purchased with the proceeds of an unauthorised sale). The right to follow trust property also extends to persons whose rights to the property are derived from the trustee unless these persons acquired the property for value (*e.g.* by paying a full price for it) and in good faith, not knowing of the breach of trust.

Liability of trustees to beneficiaries for breach of trust is joint and several.

Trustees are protected to a certain extent from liability for breach of trust by:

(a)   clauses in the trust-deed; and

(b)   statutory provisions.

(a)   *Protective clauses in trust-deed.* It is usual for a trust-deed to contain a clause providing that the trustees are not to be liable for omissions, errors or neglect of management, or singuli in solidum ("jointly and severally") but that each is to be liable for his own actual "intromissions" (dealings) only.

Such clauses, however, are given a restrictive interpretation by the courts, and so do not protect trustees from liability for gross negligence or for conduct which is inconsistent with the good faith which is essential to the trust relationship.

(b)   *Statutory protection.* The Trusts (Scotland) Act 1921 gives trustees the following protection:

(i)   All trusts, unless the contrary is expressed, are held to include a provision that each trustee is to be liable only for his own acts and intromissions and is not to be liable for the acts and intromissions of co-trustees or for his own or their omissions. This provision does little more than declare the common law. It does not protect a trustee who acquiesces in breaches of trust committed by co-trustees, nor does it relieve a trustee of liability for omission to perform a trustee's essential duties.

(ii)   If a breach of trust has been committed by a trustee at the instigation or request or with the written consent of a beneficiary, the court may, if it thinks fit, order that the beneficiary's interest in the trust-estate or part of that interest be used to indemnify the trustee.

(iii)   If it appears to the court that a trustee has acted honestly and reasonably and ought fairly to be excused for his breach of trust, the court may relieve him wholly or partly from personal liability for it.

(iv) A trustee is not liable for breach of trust merely because he continues to hold an investment which has ceased to be an authorised investment.

Restrictions on Trust Purposes

The "trust purposes" are the intentions expressed by the truster as to how the trust funds are to be applied. A trust will fail if the trust purposes are contrary to the common law or to statute.

1. Common law restrictions on trust purposes

The trust purposes must be declared in sufficiently definite terms: disposal of the trust funds must not be left completely to the discretion of the trustees.

The trust purposes must not be illegal, immoral or contrary to public policy. The last of these three categories includes purposes which confer no benefit on any person, such as the trust purpose with which the well-known case of *M'Caig* v. *University of Glasgow*, 1907 S.C. 231, was concerned:

John Stuart M'Caig of Oban died unmarried in 1902 leaving a holograph will with a codicil, in which he nominated the Court of Session and alternatively the University of Glasgow as his trustees.

His will stated that the purpose of the trust was that his heritable property be not sold but let to tenants and the income be used to erect monuments and statues of himself and his brothers and sisters "on the Tower or circular Building called the Stuart M'Caig Tower situated on the Battray Hill above Oban," and also that "artistic Towers be built on the hillock at the end of Airds Park in the Parish of Muckairn" and in other prominent places. The statues were to be made by Scottish sculptors, and M'Caig expressed his wish as being to encourage young and rising artists by the offer of prizes for the best plans for the proposed statues.

The codicil was aimed at removal of any possibility of vagueness. It stated:

> "I particularly want the Trustees to erect on the top of the Wall of the Tower I built in Oban Statues in large Figures of all my five Brothers and of myself namely . . . and of my father . . . and of my mother . . . and of my sisters . . . these statues will cost not less than One thousand pounds Sterling."

M'Caig left heritable estate in and near Oban with a yearly rental of between £2,000 and £3,000 and moveable estate of about £10,000. The Court of Session did not accept the office of trustees but the University of Glasgow did.

M'Caig's sister brought an action against the university maintaining that the trust purposes were void and of no effect and that she was therefore entitled to succeed to her brother's estate as if he had died intestate.

The court held that the trust purposes mentioned were of no effect because no beneficial interest was conferred on any person or class of persons. M'Caig's sister was therefore entitled to assert her right of succession.

2.   Statutory restrictions on trust purposes

It is lawful at common law to create a trust "in perpetuity" (to continue for ever), but certain limitations on that right have been introduced by statute. The most important of these limitations relate to accumulation of income and creation of liferents; see pp. 533 and 534, below.

LIFERENT AND FEE

Liferent was regarded by the institutional writers as a servitude, the only personal servitude known to Scots law, but the view now generally accepted is that liferent is not a servitude but a distinct interest in property.

Liferent may be defined as a right to possess, use and enjoy property during one's life without destroying or encroaching upon the substance or corpus (literally, "body") of the property. It is a right to receive the fruits, profits and income yielded by property as contrasted with the right to the capital or property itself, and it can be exercised only salva rei substantia ("provided the substance of the property remains intact").

The person entitled to the liferent is called the "liferenter," and the person entitled to the property which is burdened with the liferent is called the "fiar." The interest of the fiar in the property is referred to as the "fee."

Although a liferent, as its name implies, necessarily comes to an end with the liferenter's death, it may also be brought to an end by some earlier event, e.g. the marriage of the liferenter.

A liferent must be distinguished from an annuity. Whereas the liferenter has no right to any part of the capital, the annuitant is entitled to a certain sum for every year (or for some other period of time), even although the income may be insufficient to meet the payment and encroachment upon capital is necessary. A further point of contrast is that an annuity, unlike a liferent, is not necessarily limited to the lifetime of a human being but may be granted for a longer period of time or even in perpetuity.

A liferent must also be distinguished from a right of occupancy, which is a more limited right. For instance, a person may provide in his will that his widow is to have "the use of" his house. Such words would give the widow a right of occupancy but would not make her a liferenter. The rights and liabilities of a mere occupant differ from those of a liferenter; *e.g.* an occupant, unlike a liferenter, is not entitled to let the property and, on the other hand, is not liable for burdens, such as feu-duty, which fall on a liferenter.

Classification of Liferents

Liferents may be classified in the following ways:
1. legal liferents and conventional liferents;
2. liferents by constitution and liferents by reservation; and
3. proper liferents and beneficiary liferents.

1. Legal liferents and conventional liferents

By a "legal liferent" is meant a liferent created by operation of law, whereas a conventional liferent is one arising out of some expressed intention of the parties concerned (*e.g.* out of provisions in a person's will).

Terce and courtesy, the liferents of the widow and widower respectively in a deceased person's heritable property (see p. 514, below), were legal liferents. They were abolished by the Succession (Scotland) Act 1964, and all liferents are now conventional liferents.

2. Liferents by constitution and liferents by reservation

A liferent by constitution, also called a "simple liferent," is created when the owner of property, A, grants to another person, B, a liferent of the property; A may retain the fee for himself or he may grant the fee to a third party, C. For instance, in a testamentary trust the truster may direct his trustees to allow one beneficiary the liferent of property and to hold the fee on behalf of another beneficiary.

A liferent by reservation is created when the owner of property reserves a liferent of his property for himself in transferring the fee to another person.

3. Proper liferents and beneficiary liferents

Proper liferents are created by a direct grant which results in the emergence of two distinct rights of ownership in the property, namely, the liferent and the fee, the one limiting the other.

Beneficiary or "improper" liferents are created through the medium of a trust: the property is vested in the trustees and the liferenter does not have a direct right to it but only a jus crediti (see p. 489, above) against the trustees. It is for the trustees in their administration of the trust to hold a proper balance between the interests of the fiar and those of the liferenter.

Beneficiary liferents are now much more common than proper liferents.

Rights of Liferenter

Since it is of the essence of liferent that the right is to be enjoyed only salva rei substantia (without destruction of the substance), a true liferent cannot be created over fungibles, such as wine, which necessarily perish by being used. A liferent may, however, be created over property, such as furniture, which, although it wears out in time, continues fit for use for the duration of an ordinary life. Formerly heritable property was the most common subject of liferent, but in modern times the most familiar type of liferent is that created by a testamentary deed over the whole of the deceased's heritable and moveable estate.

The revenue or income to which the liferenter is entitled takes different forms according to the nature of the property liferented; *e.g.* if the property is heritage, the liferenter's right, if he does not himself occupy the heritage, normally takes the form of rents paid by the tenants of it, and if the property is shares in a company, the liferenter's right is normally in the form of dividends paid by the company on the shares.

In general, any payment made to the trust-estate falls to the liferenter, provided it can properly be regarded as part of the profit as distinguished from part of the corpus (or substance) of the estate. Difficulties, however, arise in practice in the decision of whether certain payments made to the trust-estate should go as capital to the fiar or as income to the liferenter. Especially noteworthy are the difficulties which can occur in connection with:

1. timber;
2. minerals; and
3. shares in companies.

1. Rights in timber

The liferenter is entitled to ordinary windfalls, to copse-wood cut from time to time as it reaches maturity and to wood necessarily cut for estate purposes such as the repair of fences.

The fiar, on the other hand, is entitled to growing trees and to trees blown down in an extraordinary storm; he may cut wood, provided he does not interfere with the liferenter's enjoyment of the estate (*e.g.* by depriving the estate of shelter or amenity).

2. Rights in minerals

Minerals are part of the substance of the soil, and so strictly the returns, whether in the form of rents or "royalties" (payments proportionate to the quantity of minerals extracted), received by the trust-estate from a tenant of mineral workings on the estate could not be claimed by the liferenter. It is, however, settled law that where trustees are directed to pay the income of an estate to a beneficiary in a mortis causa (testamentary) trust, rents and royalties from mines which have been either worked or let during the truster's lifetime fall to the liferenter as income. On the other hand, returns from mines not let until after a truster's death belong to the fiar as capital unless the truster has indicated a contrary intention (*e.g.* by directing the trustees to have the minerals worked).

3. Rights arising from the holding of shares

The liferenter is entitled to dividends on shares and also prima facie ("at first appearance" or "until the contrary is proved") to cash payments made by the company out of accumulated profits.

Special difficulties arise in connection with bonus shares. The ruling factor is the intention of the company; *e.g.* if a company which has power to increase its capital does so by capitalising accumulated profits and then issues the new capital as bonus shares to shareholders, the bonus shares fall to the fiar because the distribution is intended by the company to be one of capital, but if a company declares a cash bonus and at the same time offers, as an alternative to cash, additional shares of an amount equal to the bonus, it may be that the company's real intention is to distribute cash and if so the liferenter is entitled to the cash bonus or to the additional shares accepted as its equivalent.

When shares forming part of the trust-estate are sold by the trustees, part of the price received usually represents a portion of the dividend which is expected to be paid on the shares on the next date for payment of dividends; the liferenter is entitled to receive as income the appropriate part of the proceeds of sale.

Similarly, apportionment of dividends on a time-basis may require to be made at the beginning and end of a liferent in order that the liferenter (or his representatives if he is dead) may receive that portion of the dividends paid to the trust-estate which is applicable to the period of the liferent. This is because by the Apportionment Act 1870 dividends are to be considered as accruing from day to day and must be apportioned in respect of time accordingly. Such apportionment, however, is awkward in practice and is usually avoided by an express provision to that effect in the trust-deed.

Liabilities of Liferenter

A liferenter must bear the annual and other periodical burdens on the property, such as feu-duty, local rates, and interest on heritable securities over the property.

He must have proper regard for the interests of the fiar, but is not liable for ordinary wear and tear or for accidental destruction of the property liferented.

He must pay for ordinary repairs, but the cost of extraordinary repairs and of rebuilding falls on the fiar.

Alimentary Liferents

A beneficiary liferent may be declared in the trust-deed to be "alimentary," *i.e.* for the personal maintenance of the liferenter. The effect of such a declaration is that the liferent cannot be assigned by the liferenter and cannot be attached by the liferenter's creditors.

For the creation of an alimentary liferent the following conditions must be fulfilled:

1. There must be a continuing trust: a "proper" liferent cannot be alimentary.

2. The truster who creates it must normally be a person other than the alimentary beneficiary: the law does not generally allow a person to make an alimentary provision for himself and so put his property beyond the reach of his creditors. There is one exception to this rule: a woman may by an "ante-nuptial marriage contract" (*i.e.* a contract entered into in contemplation of marriage) make an alimentary provision in her own favour out of her own property; the provision remains alimentary only for the duration of the marriage.

3. The liferent must be reasonable in amount; in so far as a liferent declared "alimentary" exceeds what is required for maintenance of the beneficiary it may be attached by the beneficiary's creditors.

At common law an alimentary liferent could not be terminated even where all the parties were of full legal capacity and consented to its termination. The Trusts (Scotland) Act 1961, however, gave to the court power to vary or revoke alimentary provisions, provided certain conditions are fulfilled (see p. 492, above).

Assignation of Liferents

A proper liferent cannot be assigned, but the liferenter may assign the income arising from the liferent; the assignee will have only a personal right against the liferenter and the "real" right will remain with the liferenter.

A beneficiary liferent, other than an alimentary one, may be assigned by the liferenter to another person. The assignation must be intimated to the trustees who must then pay the income to the assignee instead of to the original liferenter.

Assignations of liferents are subject to the rule "assignatus utitur jure auctoris" ("the assignee enjoys the right of his cedent") which applies to assignations in general (see p. 317, above). A liferent which has been assigned will, therefore, come to an end on the happening of the event (often the death of the original liferenter) which would have brought it to an end had there been no assignation.

Termination of Liferents

A liferent may be terminated:

1. by the death of the liferenter or by the happening of the earlier event which has been fixed for the end of the liferent;

2. unless the liferent is alimentary, by discharge of the liferent by the liferenter; or

3. unless the liferent is alimentary, by consolidation of the liferent with the fee, *i.e.* if the liferent and the fee come to be vested in the same person.

Further Reading

W. A. Wilson and A. G. M. Duncan, *Trusts, Trustees and Executors* (The Scottish Universities Law Institute Series) (W. Green & Son Ltd.).

Gloag and Henderson, *Introduction to the Law of Scotland*

David M. Walker, *Principles of Scottish Private Law*

T. B. Smith *A Short Commentary on the Law of Scotland*

SUCCESSION

A PERSON who succeeds to a deceased's estate is referred to as a "universal successor," as distinct from a "singular successor," who is a person acquiring an object or a right inter vivos ("between living persons"), *e.g.* by purchase or by gift.

The law of succession falls into three main parts:

1. prior and legal rights, some of which are not strictly rights of succession at all;

2. the law of intestate succession, which applies where the deceased has not indicated how he wishes his estate to be disposed of; and

3. the law of testate succession, which applies where the deceased has left a will or other "testamentary" document, such as a "trust disposition and settlement," indicating how he wishes his estate to be disposed of.

Where there is partial intestacy, *i.e.* where the deceased has left a testamentary document which does not dispose of the whole of his estate, the division of the estate is governed partly by the law of intestate succession and partly by the law of testate succession.

Three conditions must be fulfilled before the rules in any of the three main parts of the law of succession can operate:

(a) There must have been a death.

(b) The person succeeding to the deceased's estate must have survived the deceased.

(c) The debts of the deceased must have been paid in full.

(a) Death

In this connection difficulties can arise where a person has disappeared and it is not known whether he is still alive or not.

The rule of the common law was that a person was presumed to continue in life for a reasonable time: no precise period was established, and the court would be more easily persuaded in some cases than in others that the explanation for a person's disappearance was his death.

However, difficulties have usually been resolved by resort to statutory provisions. The Act now applicable is the Presumption of Death (Scotland) Act 1977, which repealed earlier statutory provisions and re-enacted them in an improved form.

The Act provides that where a missing person is thought to have died or has not been known to be alive for at least seven years, any person having an interest may raise an "action of declarator" of the death of the person. In such an action the court, if satisfied "on a balance of probabilities," declares that the missing person died at a particular time or at the end of seven years after the date on which he was last known to be alive. The court has also power to decide any question concerning any interest in property which arises as a result of the death.

The decree in an action of declarator may be varied or recalled by a subsequent order of the court. The need for such a "variation order" would arise if, for example, the missing person reappeared or if his death was later discovered to have occurred at a time other than that stated in the decree (with the result that the succession to his estate would be different). The variation order does not itself affect any property rights which have been acquired under the original decree, but the court makes a further order concerning these rights if, in the court's view, it is fair and reasonable in all the circumstances to do so. A further order of this kind does not affect any income which has arisen between the date of the original decree and the date of the variation order. It is also a condition of such a further order being made that the variation order has been applied for within five years after the date of the original decree. Where any property right has been acquired by a third party in good faith and for value, the third party's title cannot be challenged. The general aim of the provisions is, on the one hand, to give adequate protection to the interests of the missing person while, on the other hand, enabling other parties, such as his relatives, to be reasonably free from insecurity in transacting with his estate.

(b) Survivorship

Difficulties may arise in this connection where several persons die in a "common calamity," e.g. in a road accident.

Rights of succession "vest in" (i.e. pass to, or come to belong to) the survivor, however short may be the interval between the two deaths; if, for instance, A and B have made wills in favour of each other and die as the result of the same accident, then, provided A is proved to have survived B even by only a few moments, B's estate will have passed to A and the two estates will be distributed to those who are entitled to succeed to A's estate.

At common law, there was no presumption that of persons dying in a common calamity the younger survived the elder: rights of succession could arise only if survival was established.

The common law on this point was altered by the Succession (Scotland) Act 1964, which provides that where two persons have died in circumstances which suggest that they died simultaneously or which make it uncertain which of the two survived the other, then as a general rule the younger person is presumed to have survived the elder.

To this general rule there are two exceptions:

(i) If the two persons were husband and wife, the presumption does not apply. The effect is that the estates of husband and wife would each be distributed as if there were no widow or widower, and in practice this will usually result in the wife's estate passing to members of her own family and the husband's estate to members of his.

(ii) If the elder has left a will in favour of the younger containing a provision that, in the event of the younger failing to survive, a certain third party is to have the right to succeed, and if also the younger person dies intestate, then the elder is, for the purposes of that provision only, presumed to have survived the younger. The effect is to prevent a legacy from passing to the relatives of the younger person, perhaps against the wishes of the elder person.

(c) *Debts*

No prior or legal rights or rights of succession arise unless the deceased's debts can be paid in full. The executor (the person who distributes the deceased's estate) cannot be compelled to pay away any part of the estate until the expiry of six months after the death, because all creditors who make valid claims within that time are entitled to be treated pari passu ("equally").

1. *PRIOR AND LEGAL RIGHTS*
(a) **Prior Rights**

Prior rights, as distinct from legal rights, are statutory claims which arise only where there is total or partial intestacy. They therefore form part of intestate succession, and differ from legal rights in that they can be defeated by provisions in the deceased's will.

Where, however, prior rights do emerge, they rank in priority not only to rights of succession but also to legal rights.

Only a surviving spouse (widow or widower) has prior rights, and if the intestacy is merely partial the surviving spouse is entitled to prior rights only out of the intestate part of the estate.

The scope of prior rights was greatly extended by the Succession (Scotland) Act 1964. Under that Act a surviving spouse has three prior rights:

(i) a right in the dwelling-house;

(ii) a right to furniture and plenishings; and

(iii) a right to a financial provision.

To take account of inflation the Succession (Scotland) Act 1973 increased the amounts of these rights and conferred on the Secretary of State power to fix by order larger amounts from time to time.

(i) Dwelling-house

The surviving spouse is entitled to the deceased's interest in the dwelling-house in which the surviving spouse was ordinarily resident up to a value of £50,000.[1] The deceased may have been the owner or merely the tenant of the house, except that the right does not arise if the tenancy is one to which the Rent (Scotland) Acts 1971 to 1975 apply.

If the deceased's interest exceeds £50,000, the surviving spouse is entitled to a sum of £50,000 only. There are two other situations where the surviving spouse's claim is not to the actual interest of the deceased but merely to a sum of money:

1. where the house forms part only of the subjects comprised in one tenancy; and

2. where the house forms the whole or part of subjects used by the deceased for carrying on a trade, profession or occupation and it is likely that the value of the estate as a whole would be substantially diminished if the house were to be disposed of separately from the assets of the trade, profession or occupation.

If there are two or more houses in which the surviving spouse was ordinarily resident, then that spouse is entitled to choose within six months of the death which one to take.

(ii) Furniture and plenishings

The surviving spouse is entitled to the furniture and plenishings of a dwelling-house in which he or she was ordinarily resident up to a value of £10,000.[1] This right exists even although the dwelling-house itself may not be part of the intestate estate.

The term "furniture and plenishings" does not include articles or animals used for business purposes, or money or securities for money (such as share certificates).

Here again, if there are two or more houses involved, the surviving

[1] As from August 1, 1981 (Prior Rights of Surviving Spouse (Scotland) Order 1981).

spouse has a right of election (*i.e.* a choice) which must be exercised within six months of the death. This right of election does not depend on which house may have been chosen under right (i) above.

(iii) Financial provision

This right arises only after rights (i) and (ii) above have been satisfied.

If the deceased is survived by issue (children, grandchildren, and any more remote direct descendants) the right is[1] to £15,000, otherwise it is to £25,000. In both cases interest is due on the sum from the date of death until payment. Under the Act of 1964 the rate of interest was four per cent; a different rate may now be fixed by statutory instrument (Law Reform (Miscellaneous Provisions) (Scotland) Act 1980).[2]

Where the intestacy is partial only, and the surviving spouse is entitled to a legacy under the deceased's will (other than a legacy of the dwelling-house or of its furniture and plenishings), then the surviving spouse is entitled only to the sum necessary to bring the legacy up to £15,000 or £25,000, as the case may be.

(b) Legal Rights

Legal rights are mainly common law rights, and are in favour of a surviving spouse and issue. They apply to both intestate and testate succession.

Legal rights are not strictly rights of succession because they must be given effect to (if claimed) before division of the estate is made according to the rules of intestate succession or according to the deceased's will. They are postponed to debts due to creditors of the deceased and also to the prior statutory rights which may arise on intestacy, but they cannot be defeated by any provision in the deceased's will.

Considerable changes in legal rights were made by the Succession (Scotland) Act 1964.

For the purpose of calculating legal rights it is still necessary to divide the estate into heritage and moveables.

(i) Legal rights in heritage

There were formerly two legal rights in heritage:

1. *Terce*

This was the right of the widow to a liferent of one-third of the deceased's heritable property.

2. *Courtesy*

This was the right of the widower to a liferent of the whole of

[2] Rate increased to seven per cent as from August 1, 1981 (Interest on Prior Rights (Scotland) Order 1981).

the deceased's heritable property. It was a condition of this right that a child, who had been heard to cry, had been born to the couple and that the child would have been (if he had survived) the heir of the deceased; therefore, if the deceased had had by a former marriage a child who succeeded to her heritage, her surviving husband had no right of courtesy.

Both terce and courtesy were abolished by the Succession (Scotland) Act 1964.

Children have never had any legal rights in heritable estate, a fact which enables a parent to defeat or restrict claims by children on his estate by converting his assets during his lifetime into heritage.

(ii) Legal rights in moveables

These are:
1. jus relictae ("right of the widow");
2. jus relicti ("right of the widower"); and
3. legitim, *i.e.* the right of issue.

For the purpose of ascertaining these rights, the deceased's moveable estate is divided into two or into three parts according to circumstances: if the deceased is survived both by a spouse and by issue the estate is divided into three parts, namely, jus relictae or jus relicti as the case may be, legitim, and "dead's part" (which is the term used of that part of the estate which is free from legal rights and is distributed according to the rules of testate or intestate succession); if the deceased is survived by either a spouse or issue, but not by both, the estate is divided into two parts, namely, jus relictae, jus relicti, or legitim as the case may be, and dead's part.

1. *Jus relictae*

This is the common law right of the widow to one-third (if there are surviving issue) or one-half (if there are no surviving issue) of her deceased husband's moveable estate.

2. *Jus relicti*

This is the corresponding right of the widower to one-third or one-half of his deceased wife's moveable estate.

It was introduced by the Married Women's Property (Scotland) Act 1881.

3. *Legitim*

Legitim or "bairn's part" is the right belonging to surviving children, or to the issue of children who have already died, to either one-third or one-half of the deceased parent's or other ancestor's moveable estate, according to whether there is or is not a surviving spouse.

At common law only surviving children of the deceased were entitled to legitim: grandchildren and remoter issue had no claim. The Succession (Scotland) Act 1964, however, introduced the principle of representation in connection with legitim. The effect of this principle is that if the deceased has had a child who has predeceased (*i.e.* has died before) him but left issue (grandchildren or remoter issue of the deceased), the issue have the same right to legitim as the child himself would have had if he had survived the deceased.

If all those claiming legitim are related in the same degree to the deceased (*e.g.* if they are all children or all grandchildren), the division amongst them is equal, and is referred to as "division per capita" ("according to individuals"). If, however, the claimants on the legitim fund are not all related in the same degree to the deceased (*e.g.* if there are both children and grandchildren, the latter representing children who have already died), the division amongst them is based on the class of claimants which is nearest to the deceased, and is referred to as "division per stirpes" ("according to branches of the family tree").

The distinction between division per capita and division per stirpes may be made clearer by two examples:

(a)

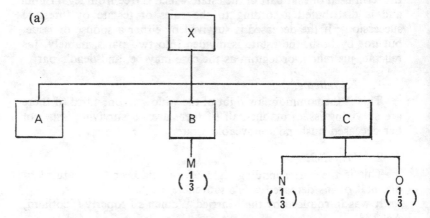

X, the deceased, had three children, A, B, and C, all of whom predeceased him; A never had any children, B had one child, M, and C had two children, N and O; M, N, and O all survived X, The legitim fund would be divided per capita, M, N, and O taking one-third each.

(b)

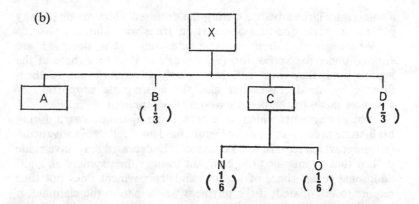

X, the deceased, had four children, A, B, C, and D, of whom A and C had predeceased him; A never had any children, but C had two children, N and O, both of whom survived X. The claimants on the legitim fund would therefore be B, D, N, and O, and, being in different degrees of relationship to X, they would have the fund divided amongst them per stirpes, B and D taking one-third each and N and O one-sixth each as representing their parent C, who failed to survive X.

Since the Succession (Scotland) Act 1964, adopted children have been treated for the purposes of legitim as children of the adopter.

By the Law Reform (Miscellaneous Provisions) (Scotland) Act 1968 illegitimate children have a claim to legitim equal to the claim of legitimate children. Illegitimate issue of a child (whether the child was himself legitimate or not) have no claim.

Step-children have no claim to legitim.

Collation inter liberos. The purpose of the doctrine of collation inter liberos (" among children ") is to maintain equality among the claimants on the legitim fund.

The doctrine means that a claimant who has received advances of his share of the fund during the deceased's lifetime must "collate" these advances, *i.e.* bring them in to increase the total legitim fund. In the distribution of that fund these advances will then be set against the claimant's share, with the result that he will receive on the parent's death that much less than the other claimants who have had no advances made to them.

Collation inter liberos applies only to claims on the legitim fund: it has no effect on jus relictae or jus relicti, or on rights of "succession" in the strict sense, and if a child (or some remoter descendant) chooses to make no claim on the fund either because he has received a sufficiently large advance during the deceased's lifetime or for any other reason, no question of collation arises with him.

Where grandchildren or remoter issue of the deceased are entitled under the Succession (Scotland) Act 1964 to a share of the legitim fund, they must collate not only advances made to them directly by the deceased but also the appropriate proportion of advances made to the person whom they represent.

Not all payments which have been made by the deceased during his lifetime to claimants on the legitim fund are "collatable advances" (advances which require to be collated): the deceased may have made it clear that he intended the claimant to have the payment as a gift additional to his share of legitim, and the payment does not then require to be collated; if the payment was a loan to the claimant, it is not a collatable advance but a debt due to the estate as a whole; remuneration for services rendered by the claimant does not require to be collated, nor do sums paid under the natural duties of main- tenance and education of the claimant.

Examples of collatable advances given by the institutional writer Bell in his *Principles* (§ 1588) are advances made to set up a child in trade, or for a settlement in the world, or for a marriage portion.

Discharge of legal rights during deceased's lifetime

Legal rights of the surviving spouse and of children or other issue may be discharged during the lifetime of the deceased by those prospectively entitled to them.

Jus relictae and jus relicti may be discharged by an agreement between the spouses before or during the marriage, *e.g.* by a provision in an "ante-nuptial marriage contract" (a contract made before and in contemplation of marriage) or by a provision in a "post-nuptial marriage contract" (a contract made during the marriage).

Before 1964 intending spouses might also, by an ante-nuptial marriage contract, discharge in advance the right of any child of the marriage to claim legitim; normally such a contract would provide some alternative benefit for any children to be born, but the alter- native benefit might be much less valuable than legitim. By the Succession (Scotland) Act 1964, however, a claim for legitim cannot now be discharged without the consent of the child or other descen- dant concerned.

Where there has been a discharge of legal rights during the deceased's lifetime by one or more of the claimants, the effect is that the grantor of the discharge is treated as dead; thus, if jus relictae has been discharged during the husband's lifetime, the estate will be divided equally between legitim and dead's part, unless there are no surviving issue, in which case the whole of the estate will be dead's part; similarly, if all claims to legitim have been discharged during the parent's lifetime, there will be no legitim fund on the parent's death; if, however, one or more, but not all, of those entitled to legitim have discharged their claims during the ancestor's lifetime, those who have not discharged their claims have the right to the whole of the legitim fund.

Satisfaction of legal rights by testamentary provisions

Spouses and children cannot be deprived of legal rights by any provision in the deceased's will or other testamentary document. They may, however, be required to "elect" (*i.e.* choose) between a testamentary provision, such as a legacy, in their favour and their legal rights. The principle applicable is referred to as "approbate and reprobate"; this means that a person cannot both accept and reject the same document.

Therefore, if a legacy is stated in the will to be in satisfaction of legal rights, the legatee is not entitled both to take the legacy and to upset other provisions in the will by claiming legal rights.

Before 1964 a legatee was entitled both to his legacy and to his legal rights unless there was an express or implied term in the will that the legacy was in satisfaction of legal rights. The Succession (Scotland) Act 1964, however, provides that in wills made after 1964, if there is a provision in favour of the testator's spouse or issue, a declaration that the provision is made in full and final satisfaction of legal rights is implied unless there is an express provision to the contrary.

Where a person entitled to claim legal rights has, by accepting a testamentary provision, forfeited his legal rights, the portion of the estate consequently not required to be paid to him as legal rights is added to dead's part, and does not increase the amount which may be claimed by other persons entitled to legal rights out of the estate. This is in contrast to the effect of a discharge of legal rights during the deceased's lifetime; *e.g.* if X is survived by six children, five of whom elect not to claim legitim, the sixth child is entitled only to one-sixth of the legitim fund, whereas if five of X's six children have during X's lifetime discharged legitim, the sixth child is entitled on X's death to the whole of the legitim fund.

2. *INTESTATE SUCCESSION*

If the deceased has left no will or has failed in his will to dispose of his whole estate, the division of the estate, after payment of debts, prior rights and legal rights, is, wholly or in part, governed by the rules of intestate succession.

Before 1964 there were important differences between the

rules applying to heritage and those applying to moveables; especially notable features of heritable succession were the principles of primogeniture (according to which the eldest child, with his issue representing him, was preferred to any younger child) and of preference for males (according to which females were excluded from succession unless no males, or their issue, survived in the same class).

By the Succession (Scotland) Act 1964 the distinctive rules of heritable succession were, with some minor exceptions (*e.g.* for titles and coats of arms), abolished, and the rules which had before that Act applied to moveables only were for the most part made to apply to the whole estate.

The general principles underlying the order of succession which is set out in that Act are:

(a) The succession opens first to descendants (children and remoter issue), then (if there are no descendants) to collaterals (brothers and sisters and their issue), and thirdly, if necessary, to ancestors and their issue. Parents and spouses are exceptions to this general scheme.

(b) Representation is applied throughout the succession: a person who would have succeeded if he had survived the deceased is represented by his issue, who are entitled to take what would otherwise have been his share of the deceased's estate. "Issue" means "lawful issue however remote": illegitimate issue have no right to represent their deceased parents.

(c) Where there are two or more persons with rights of succession, the division between or amongst them is per capita if the persons are all related in the same degree to the deceased, and per stirpes in other cases (see p. 516, above).

(d) Collaterals of the whole blood exclude collaterals of the half-blood; the latter are entitled to succeed only if there are no collaterals of the whole blood. No distinction is now made between collaterals of the half-blood "consanguinean" (half-brothers and half-sisters who have the same father) and collaterals of the half-blood "uterine" (half-brothers and half-sisters who have the same mother).

The order of succession is as follows:

(a) children, including adopted children and, by the Law Reform (Miscellaneous Provisions) (Scotland) Act 1968, illegitimate children; children who have predeceased the intestate are represented by their issue;

(b) parents, brothers, and sisters; if the intestate is survived *both* by one or both of his parents *and* by his own collaterals, one half of his estate falls to his parent or parents and the other half is divided amongst his collaterals, with nephews, nieces, and remoter issue

representing brothers and sisters of the intestate who have predeceased him; if the intestate is survived by one or both of his parents
but not by his own collaterals or their issue, his whole estate goes
to his parent or parents, and similarly if only collaterals or their
issue, but no parents, survive the intestate, the whole estate is divided
amongst the collaterals and the issue of any collaterals who have
predeceased the intestate;

(c) husband or wife; there is no right of representation here;
hence step-children have no rights of succession;

(d) uncles and aunts, without distinction between those on the
father's and those on the mother's side; cousins represent those
uncles and aunts who have predeceased the intestate;

(e) grandparent or grandparents, both paternal and maternal;

(f) collaterals of grandparents, with issue representing those
collaterals who have predeceased the intestate;

(g) remoter ancestors of the intestate, generation by generation;
collaterals of any ancestor have the right to succeed before the
succession opens to the next more remote degree of ancestors;

(h) the Crown as ultimus haeres ("ultimate heir"), where no
person, however remotely related, is entitled to succeed under (a) to
(g) above.

3. TESTATE SUCCESSION

A "will" may be defined as "a declaration of what a person wishes
to be done with his estate after his death."

A person who makes a will is said to "test," he is the "testator,"
and a will is often referred to as a "testament" or as a "testamentary
document." A will which sets up a trust is usually called a "trust
disposition and settlement."

A person who dies leaving a spouse or issue is not entitled to
dispose by will of his whole estate, but only of his heritage and of
that third or that half, as the case may be, of his moveables which is
not required for the satisfaction of legal rights. The statutory prior
rights of the surviving spouse, however, do not arise if, and in so far
as, the deceased has disposed of his estate by will.

Capacity to Test

For a will to be valid the testator must have had capacity to test.

A pupil has no testamentary capacity. A minor had at common
law capacity to test on his moveables only, but, by the Succession
(Scotland) Act 1964, a minor can now test on his heritable estate
also; his curator's consent is not required.

Where the testator's mental state is such that he cannot understand the nature and effect of what he is doing, his "will" is void
and of no effect: an insane person has no capacity to test except

during lucid intervals; if a person is not generally insane but suffers from delusions, his will can be set aside if it was affected by his delusions; a will made at a time when the testator was so affected by drink or drugs or otherwise as to be without the necessary understanding of his action is also open to reduction; other grounds of reduction are misrepresentation, force and fear, facility and circumvention (*i.e.* where the testator, although he has testamentary capacity, is so "facile" (weak in mind), owing, for instance, to old age or ill-health, that he is easily misled by a person who seeks to obtain some benefit under the will), and undue influence (*i.e.* where the person who benefits under the will stood in a position of trust towards, or exercised a dominating influence over, the testator); a solicitor who benefits under a will which he himself has drawn up has the onus (burden) of proving, if the will is challenged, that he did not exercise undue influence.

Form of Wills

A legacy of not more than £100 Scots (£8·33) may be made orally; it is termed a "nuncupative" or "verbal" legacy.

Otherwise, probative writing or its equivalent is required, *i.e.* the will must be attested, holograph, or adopted as holograph.

No particular words are essential, but it must be clear that the person executing the document had "testamentary intention," *i.e.* really intended the document to be a will. The document must not be merely a list of names and sums of money, or notes or instructions intended to be used as the basis for the drawing up of a will. There must be a final testamentary writing (however imperfectly it may be expressed): a draft will, even if probative in form, is not given effect to, since the testator is regarded as not having finally decided how he wishes his estate to be distributed.

A will may consist of several documents of different dates and in different forms; *e.g.* there may be a formal attested document and also some later holograph documents containing minor alterations. A later document which adds to, or in some other way alters, an existing will which is still intended by the testator to be the major testamentary document is called a "codicil."

Revocation of Wills

It is of the essence of a will that it may be revoked at any time by the testator. Revocation may be of the whole will or of part of it only, and may be effected by:

    (a)   intentional cancellation or destruction by the testator;

    (b)   express or implied provisions in a later testamentary writing; or

(c) operation of the conditio si testator sine liberis decesserit ("the condition that the testator will have died without children").

(a) Intentional cancellation or destruction

There must be animus revocandi ("intention to revoke") on the part of the testator.

A will is revoked if the testator intentionally tears it up or intentionally destroys it in some other way, and a particular provision is revoked if it is obliterated or scored out in such a way that it can no longer be deciphered. Any attempted revocation which does not result in complete destruction of the whole will or in complete obliteration of the particular provision is of no legal effect unless it is authenticated by the testator's signature or initials; thus a provision scored out but still legible would be given effect to unless the testator had signed or initialled the alteration.

Where there has been no animus revocandi, the will or the provision in question is not revoked: therefore a will which has been destroyed by accident, or when the testator was insane, or without the testator's authority, will still be given effect to if its terms can be proved by other evidence, such as surviving fragments or a draft or a copy; an action for proving the tenor of the will would require to be raised in the Court of Session (see p. 27, above).

(b) Provisions in later testamentary writings

A later will may expressly revoke a provision in an earlier will, or the whole of an earlier will, or all earlier wills.

Revocation is implied where a provision in a later will is inconsistent with a provision in an earlier will, but so far as possible all existing testamentary writings which have not been expressly revoked are read together and all are given effect to. Revocation will be implied to the extent necessary to avoid inconsistency, but no further.

If a will revoking an earlier will is itself invalid, the earlier will remains effective.

Where a first will is revoked by a second will which in turn is revoked by a third will, the first will revives and if it is extant will be given effect to so far as it is consistent with the third will.

(c) Conditio si testator sine liberis decesserit

A will which makes no provision for children of the testator who are not yet born is presumed to be revoked by the subsequent birth of a child to him. The presumption is based on the supposition that the testator would not have wished a will which made no provision for the later-born child to be given effect to.

Such a presumption is obviously appropriate where a testator who was childless when the will was made has died so soon after the birth of the child that he has had no reasonable opportunity of making a new will, but the presumption is also applied where a considerable period of time has elapsed between the birth of the child and the death of the testator.

The presumption may, however, be rebutted (contradicted and excluded) by circumstances which show that the testator intended that his will should stand in spite of the subsequent birth of the child; e.g. the presumption may be rebutted if the testator has made an inter vivos (literally, " between living persons ") provision for the child.

Only the later-born child, and not any other party, can invoke this conditio for the purpose of having the will reduced.

If the presumption is not rebutted, the effect is that the whole will is revoked, but that earlier wills revoked by it are not revived.

(A will is not revoked by the subsequent marriage of the testator.)

Mutual Wills

A mutual will is a testamentary document in which two or more persons give directions for the disposal of their estates after their deaths.

Sometimes mutual wills are partly contractual in nature, and this can give rise to problems, especially to the problem of whether they can be altered or revoked by one of the parties either before or after the death of the other or others; e.g. a mutual will containing a gift to the survivor of two parties and on the death of the survivor to a third party would usually be held to be contractual and so would not be revocable.

There is a presumption that a mutual will is merely two wills within one document and is therefore revocable.

If the parties are spouses the court is more easily persuaded that the provisions in the mutual will in favour of the surviving spouse and the children are contractual, and so irrevocable, than it is in the case of provisions in favour of other parties.

Interpretation of Wills

In interpreting a will the aim of the court is to give effect to the intention of the testator. That intention must, as a general rule, be ascertained only from the language of the will itself and not from any outside sources: extrinsic (outside) evidence is in general inadmissible; it is, for instance, incompetent to bring forward evidence to show what the testator himself believed the effect of his will to be.

Extrinsic evidence is, however, admitted in some exceptional circumstances:

(a) to help the court to decide whether there was the necessary testamentary intention (see p. 521, above);

(b) where an unusual text or a foreign language has been used in the will, to decipher the text or to translate the language;

(c) to show the circumstances known to the testator at the time when he made the will, such as the state of his family and of his property;

(d) to resolve ambiguities and uncertainties as to the persons whom the testator intended to benefit and as to the property which he intended to dispose of; the maxim applicable in this connection is falsa demonstratio non nocet dummodo constet de persona (or de re) ("a false description is not fatal provided there is certainty as to the person (or as to the thing)"); *e.g. Wedderspoon* v. *Thomson's Trustees* (1824) 3 S. 396: T. had bequeathed a legacy of £500 to "Janet Keiller or Williamson, confectioner in Dundee"; the legacy was successfully claimed by Agnes Keiller who had been married to Wedderspoon and who was a confectioner in Dundee; the court held that "Williamson" was merely a clerical error for "Wedderspoon"; another instance of admission of extrinsic evidence in connection with the same will is *Keiller* v. *Thomson's Trustees* (1826) 4 S. 724: T. had left a legacy of £200 to "William Keiller, confectioner in Dundee," and there was no such person; the legacy was claimed both by William Keiller, confectioner in Montrose, and by James Keiller, confectioner in Dundee; after considering extrinsic evidence, including evidence of intimacy between T. and James Keiller, the court decided that T. had intended to benefit that person; if, however, after all competent evidence has been considered, the identity of the legatee or of the subject-matter bequeathed still remains ambiguous or uncertain, the legacy is of no effect.

Where there is doubt as to the meaning of a testamentary provision, the court will, if possible, interpret the provision in such a way as to avoid total or partial intestacy.

If two provisions in a will cannot be reconciled with one another, then it is presumed that the later provision is the one to be given effect to, on the ground that it is a later expression of the testator's intention.

Legacies

In a will the deceased disposes of his estate or part of it by means of legacies or bequests, and a person receiving a legacy or bequest is referred to as a "legatee."

The subject bequeathed may be a particular article, or a sum of money. It may also be some claim which the testator had against a third party, or it may take the form of a cancellation of a debt due by the legatee himself to the testator.

Types of legacies

General legacies

A general legacy is one in which the subject given has no individual character distinguishing it from other subjects of the same kind, *e.g.* a sum of money or a quantity of goods answering to some generic (general) description.

Special legacies

A general legacy is contrasted with a special or specific legacy, which is a bequest of some definite object, such as a particular house, a particular investment held by the testator, or a debt due to the testator by a particular person.

Demonstrative legacies

Special legacies include demonstrative legacies, which are legacies in which the testator indicates the source from which the legacy is to come, *e.g.* "such of my furniture as the legatee may choose up to the value of £1,000," or "one-half of the debt due to me by X."

Ademption of special legacies

It may be that the subject of a special legacy ceases, before the testator's death, to be part of his estate, because he transfers the thing to another person or because the thing is destroyed or in some other way taken from him (*e.g.* by compulsory purchase). This is referred to as "ademption," and the legacy is said to have been "adeemed" (taken away). The legatee has then no claim.

Doubts may arise in some cases as to whether there has been ademption or not, *e.g.* where the legacy is a holding of shares in a company, and the company's capital structure is altered in some way. The general test applied is whether the asset which forms part of the deceased's estate is substantially the same thing as the asset mentioned in the will; *e.g.* if the legacy is of a particular block of shares in a company, and the company has, between the date of the will and the testator's death, subdivided the shares or converted them into stock, the legacy would probably be held not to have been adeemed.

Bequests of residue

The residue of a deceased person's estate is that part of it which is left over after debts have been paid, legal rights have been satisfied, and the claims of legatees to their general and special legacies have been met.

It is advisable for a person who wishes to dispose of his whole estate by will always to include a bequest of residue; otherwise any bequest which fails (*e.g.* because the legatee dies before the testator) will pass to the persons who would have been entitled to the deceased's estate had he died intestate.

The person to whom the residue is bequeathed is termed "the residuary legatee." He is in many cases the person who receives the major benefit under the will. There may be more than one residuary legatee, the will specifying how the residue is to be divided among them.

Cumulative and substitutional legacies

If a deceased person's testamentary writings provide two or more legacies for the same legatee, there may be doubt as to whether these legacies are cumulative (*i.e.* are all due) or are substitutional (*i.e.* replace one another, so that only the legacy which is latest in date is effective).

In deciding whether legacies are cumulative or substitutional the court attempts to ascertain the intention of the testator, but if the testator's intention cannot be ascertained the court applies the following presumptions:

(a) If the legacies are contained in the same document *and* are of the same amount they are presumed to be substitutional; the testator is considered to be merely repeating himself or to have forgotten his earlier mention of the legacy.

(b) In other cases (*i.e.* where the legacies are contained in different documents or are of different amounts) they are presumed to be cumulative; this is in accordance with the principle that all extant unrevoked testamentary writings of the deceased must be read together and, so far as they are consistent with each other, given effect to.

Legatum rei alienae

This means "a legacy of a thing belonging to another person."

If a testator has bequeathed something in fact belonging to another person, he is presumed to have believed that the thing was his, and because of this error on the testator's part the legacy fails.

If, however, it can be proved that the testator knew that the thing did not belong to him, then the legacy is interpreted as an instruction to the executor to purchase the thing from its owner and hand it over to the legatee, or, if it cannot be purchased, to pay its value to the legatee.

Abatement of legacies

Abatement or cutting down of legacies is necessary where the testator's estate is not sufficient for the satisfaction of all the bequests which he has made. If the testator has not himself indicated the order in which the bequests are to abate or be cut down, the rules applied are:

(a) Bequests of residue abate first: residuary legatees are not entitled to anything unless all other legatees are paid in full.

(b) General legacies abate next, the abatement being pari passu ("equal" or "proportionate"), *i.e.* all the legatees will receive the same proportion of the bequests made to them.

(c) Special legatees are entitled to their legacies in full even although the result may be that nothing is left for the general legatees.

The mere numbering of legacies in the will is not considered to indicate the order of priority intended by the testator.

Legatees

A legatee must be capable of being identified; otherwise the legacy fails from uncertainty. A testator is not allowed to delegate to other persons his power to make a will; therefore, if he sets up a trust, he must not give to the trustees complete discretion as to who the beneficiaries are to be; it is, however, permissible for a testator to confer on his trustees power to choose beneficiaries from some definite class.

Legatees are often not named in a will, but are referred to by some descriptive term, such as "issue," "children," "heirs," "next-of-kin," "servants," etc. Difficult questions of interpretation can arise in respect of some of these descriptive terms, and, while the more commonly used terms have acquired recognised meanings, the court will always consider the context in which a term is used and may hold that the testator used the term in a sense different from its generally recognised one. If, however, the descriptive term used is a vague one with no recognised definite meaning (*e.g.* "dependants"), the bequest will fail from uncertainty.

Competing claims to legacies are especially liable to emerge where two or more persons are named or described as being entitled to the legacies. Difficulties arise in connection with:

(a) division per capita and division per stirpes;

(b) accretion; and

(c) destinations-over.

(a) *Division per capita and division per stirpes*

For the distinction between these two types of division, see p. 516, above.

If the legacy is to a number of named individuals without any indication of how it is to be divided among them, then the testator is considered to have intended an equal division.

If, however, the legatees are described by some group term, *e.g.*

" my brother's and sister's children," then there may be doubt as to whether the testator intended division per capita or division per stirpes; *e.g.* in a bequest to "my brother's and sister's children," if the number of children in the two families was not equal, the question would arise of whether each nephew and niece was intended to have the same share (division per capita) or whether the brother's children were together to take one-half and the sister's children the other half (division per stirpes).

A properly composed will ought to leave no room for doubt, but in the absence of indication to the contrary the testator is presumed to have intended division per capita.

(b) *Accretion*

Accretion occurs where one or more of several legatees dies before the testator and his share of the legacy "accresces to" (*i.e.* is added to the share(s) of) the other or others.

If the legacy is joint, there will be accretion, but if it is several, there will be no accretion.

Normally, unless the testator has indicated otherwise, a legacy will be held to be joint; *e.g.* if the legacy is simply "to A and B," and A dies before the testator, B will be entitled to the whole of the legacy.

Where there are "words of severance," however, the legacy will in general be held to be several. Words of severance indicate that the testator was thinking of separate shares being taken by the different legatees. Examples of such words are, "equally," "equally among them," "in equal shares," and "share and share alike." Thus, if the legacy is "to A and B equally between them," and A dies before the testator, B will be entitled only to one-half of the legacy, and the other half will fall into the residue of the estate and pass to the residuary legatee, or, if there is no residuary legatee, will be dealt with according to the rules of intestate succession.

The testator, however, may by other words which he has used in his will indicate that he intended that words of severance should not exclude accretion; the court will give effect to his intention.

Moreover, the presumption that words of severance indicate that accretion was not intended does not apply to bequests to a class; *e.g.* in a bequest to "my nephews equally among them." the share of any nephew who died before the testator would accresce to the surviving nephews.

(c) *Destinations-over*

A destination-over in a bequest is a provision such as "to A, whom failing, to B." A is referred to as "the institute"; B may be either a "conditional institute" or a "substitute."

The primary effect of a destination-over is that if A fails to survive the testator, then B is entitled to the legacy; provided B survives the testator, the legacy will not fall into residue or (if there is no bequest of residue) lapse into intestacy. For the purpose of this primary effect it does not matter whether B is a conditional institute or a substitute.

A destination-over may have an additional effect if B is a substitute, and not merely a conditional institute.

Where B is merely a conditional institute, he has no right to the legacy if A, by surviving the testator, becomes entitled to it; once A takes the legacy, the destination-over to B is said to "fly off."

Where B is a substitute, however, he will have the right to the legacy not only in the event of A's not surviving the testator, but also if A takes the legacy but later dies before B without having "defeated" (*i.e.* cancelled) the substitution; A is quite free to use and dispose of the subject of the legacy during his lifetime and to bequeath it by his own will to whomsoever he wishes, but if he dies intestate, and the subject forms part of his estate, then B is entitled to the subject in accordance with the destination-over.

In deciding whether a destination-over is merely a conditional institution or is a substitution the court gives effect to the testator's intention as declared in his will, but where the testator's intention is not clear the court presumes that, if the bequest is one of moveables, the destination-over is merely a conditional institution, whereas if the bequest is one of heritage, the destination-over is a substitution.

Vesting of legacies

A legacy is said to "vest" in the legatee when it becomes his property. Once the legacy has vested in the legatee he has the right to dispose of it either inter vivos ("between living persons"), *i.e.* by a transfer of it during his lifetime, or mortis causa ("in contemplation of death"), *i.e.* by a testamentary provision; if the legatee dies without providing for the succession to a legacy which has vested in him, the legacy will form part of the legatee's intestate estate.

A vested interest is contrasted with a mere spes successionis ("hope or expectation of succession"); *e.g.* since there can be no vesting of a legacy until the testator has died, a legatee has during the testator's lifetime a mere spes successionis.

A legatee in whom a legacy has vested does not necessarily have a right to immediate possession of the subject; *e.g.* where a trust has been set up by the testator and the trustees have been directed to hold the subject of the legacy for A in liferent and to make it over to B only on A's death, B acquires a vested interest in the legacy at the testator's death, but is not entitled to possession of the subject until A has died.

The date of vesting is decided in accordance with the testator's intention as declared in the will. If the testator's intention is not clear, there is a presumption in favour of early vesting. Since the earliest possible vesting date is the death of the testator, the court will, where this is possible, interpret the will in such a way as to give the legatee a vested interest " a morte testatoris " (" from the death of the testator ").

A legacy which is unconditional, vests in the legatee on the testator's death, as does also a legacy which is to be payable at a fixed future time or on the occurrence of an event which is bound to happen (e.g. the death of a liferenter).

Where, however, a condition is attached to a bequest and it is uncertain whether the condition will ever be fulfilled, vesting is in some cases postponed. In this connection a distinction is drawn between suspensive conditions and resolutive conditions.

A suspensive condition postpones vesting until the condition has been fulfilled; e.g. if a testator provides a legacy for X in the event of X's attaining majority, the legacy does not vest in X as long as he is a minor, and if X fails to attain majority the legacy will never have been part of X's property; it would be different if the testator made an absolute bequest to X with a condition attached to it that payment was not to be made until X reached majority: such a bequest would vest in X at the testator's death.

A resolutive condition does not postpone vesting, but makes the vesting liable to be defeated. This is termed "vesting subject to defeasance." It operates in only a limited number of situations.

An example of vesting subject to defeasance is: A testator directs his trustees to hold a fund for A in liferent and for A's issue in fee, and failing issue of A, then for B in fee; the testator is survived by both A and B, but A has at that time no issue; B then takes a vested right in the fund, but his right is subject to defeasance, i.e. is liable to be defeated, if A later has issue.

In some cases vesting is subject to partial defeasance; this occurs in legacies to a class if the time of payment of the legacies is postponed; e.g. if the testator makes a bequest to A in liferent and to A's children in fee, the legacy vests in those children of A who are alive at the testator's death subject to partial defeasance so far as is necessary to allow children born to A before the date of payment arrives to share in the legacy.

The conditio si institutus sine liberis decesserit in legacies

In some cases there is read into a bequest a condition that if the legatee dies without acquiring a vested interest but leaving issue, the issue, although not mentioned in the will, have a right to the legacy in preference to the conditional institute, or the residuary legatee, or the heirs on intestacy, as the case may be. This condition is referred to as "the conditio si institutus sine liberis decesserit" (" the condition that the institute will have died without children").

It applies only to the following types of bequests:

(a)   bequests to the testator's own descendants (children, grand-children, etc.); and

(b)   bequests to the testator's nephews and nieces provided the testator has placed himself " in loco parentis " (" in place of a parent ") to them, *i.e.* has treated them in his will in a way in which a parent would be expected to treat them.

The conditio is based on the presumption that if the testator had foreseen that the legatee was to predecease him leaving issue, he would have expressly provided that the issue were to take their parent's share.

If the language used in the will indicates that the testator intended the conditio not to apply, then his intention is given effect to; *e.g.* the conditio does not apply if there is evidence of delectus personae ("choice of person"), *i.e.* where the testator has made the bequests out of personal favour to the descendants or nephews and nieces concerned, and not merely because of their relationship to him, and it does not apply if in other legacies the testator has made express provision for the issue of legatees who predecease him.

Objectionable conditions and directions in legacies

In some cases conditions attached to legacies and directions given by a testator are considered legally objectionable and are not given effect to. The most noteworthy of these restrictions on a testator's power to dispose of his estate as he wishes relate to:

(a)   void conditions;

(b)   repugnancy;

(c)   accumulation of income; and

(d)   creation of liferents.

(a)   *Void conditions*

A condition attached to a legacy is void if it is uncertain, im-possible, illegal, immoral, or contrary to public policy; an example of a condition contrary to public policy is one which prohibits the legatee from ever marrying, or a wife from living with her husband.

A void condition is held pro non scripto ("as not having been written"), and the legacy is given effect to as if it had been unconditional.

(b) *Repugnancy*

There is repugnancy where conditions attached to a legacy are inconsistent with it. The principal examples of repugnancy are:

(i) where in a trust disposition and settlement a testator confers a vested, unconditional, and "indefeasible" (*i.e.* not subject to defeasance) right of "fee" (*i.e.* full ownership, as distinct from limited ownership such as liferent) on a beneficiary and then directs his trustees to hold the capital and pay only the income to the beneficiary; in such a situation the beneficiary is entitled to be paid the capital; and

(ii) where the testator directs that an annuity be purchased for a beneficiary (*e.g.* by payment of a lump sum to an insurance company in return for an annual payment by the company to the beneficiary for the rest of his life), and the beneficiary could immediately sell the annuity and so receive a lump sum; in that case the beneficiary is entitled to payment of the lump sum which would have been the purchase price of the annuity; alimentary liferents are an exception to this rule (see p. 508, above).

(c) *Accumulation of income*

The Accumulations Act 1800, often referred to as "the Thellusson Act," imposed restrictions on the accumulation of income for prolonged periods. The restrictions are now in the Trusts (Scotland) Act 1961, as amended by the Law Reform (Miscellaneous Provisions) (Scotland) Act 1966.

So far as mortis causa (testamentary, as opposed to inter vivos) trusts are concerned, the leading restriction is that income must not be accumulated for more than twenty-one years from the testator's death. Income directed to be accumulated contrary to the statutory provisions goes to the person or persons who would have been entitled to it had accumulation not been directed.

The operation of these provisions may be illustrated by the case of *Elder's Trustees* v. *Treasurer of Free Church of Scotland* (1892) 20 R. 2:

A testator, E., directed his trustees, after providing for an annuity to be paid to his widow, to hold the whole residue of his estate until the death of his widow and on her death to set aside £10,000 as an endowment of a chair in a Free Church college, to apply another sum of £10,000 in erecting and endowing a Free church, and to provide such further sum as they thought proper for a manse for that church. The trustees were further directed to pay any remaining estate to such four schemes of the Free Church of Scotland as they might select.

The income of the estate was more than sufficient to pay the widow's annuity, and the surplus was accumulated by the trustees in accordance with E.'s direction to hold the residue of the estate. The widow, however, survived E. by more than twenty-one years, and further accumulation of surplus income was void under the Thellusson Act.

Claims to the surplus income were lodged by (i) E.'s next-of-kin, who claimed it as intestate estate, and (ii) the Free Church of Scotland, which maintained that the surplus income fell to be paid to such four schemes of the Free Church as the existing trustees shonld select.

The court held that the four schemes could not be selected until the widow's death, that until that event had occurred there was no residuary legatee, and that therefore E.'s next-of-kin were entitled to the surplus income as intestate estate.

(d) *Creation of liferents*

The Law Reform (Miscellaneous Provisions) (Scotland) Act 1968 provides that if a liferent is created in favour of a person who was not yet born at the date of the testator's death, then that person is, once he has reached the age of majority, entitled to absolute ownership of the property, and if the property has been vested by the testator in trustees, then the trustees must transfer the property to the beneficiary.

These provisions replace provisions of earlier Acts, notably the Entail Amendment Act 1848 for heritable property, and the Entail Amendment (Scotland) Act 1868 and the Trusts (Scotland) Act 1921 for moveable property.

Donations Mortis Causa

A donation mortis causa ("for the sake of death," or "in contemplation of death") is a gift made by one person, A, to another person B, on the condition that, although the property is immediately transferred to B, B is not to obtain an absolute right to it until A's death.

The gift must have been made in contemplation of death, but the testator need not have been in immediate fear of death.

Donations mortis causa resemble legacies in that:

(a) they do not take effect unless the donee survives the donor;

(b) they can be revoked by the donor during his lifetime;

(c) they can be taken to pay the donor's debts if this is necessary; and

(d) they are postponed to the legal rights of the donor's spouse and issue.

On the other hand, they differ from legacies in that:

(a) they do not require writing for their constitution, whereas legacies over £8·33 do; the person claiming the gift, however, must prove that there was animus donandi ("the intention to make a gift"), and this may be a difficult task since there is a presumption against donation; and

(b) the property is transferred to the donee during the donor's lifetime.

EXECUTORS

The term "executor" denotes the person who "ingathers" the deceased's estate, pays the debts, and then distributes the balance among those entitled to it by way of legal rights and according to the rules of testate and intestate succession.

Appointment of Executors

An executor may have been appointed by the deceased's will; such an executor is called an "executor-nominate." If there is no executor-nominate, the court may appoint an executor, called an "executor-dative."

Executors-nominate include not only persons expressly nominated as executors in the will but also testamentary trustees and those legatees to whom the whole or the residue of the estate has been bequeathed.

For the appointment of an executor-dative an application in the form of a petition must be made to the sheriff court of the sheriffdom in which the deceased was domiciled.

The persons entitled to the office are those who have rights in the estate. In outline the order of priority is:

1. the surviving spouse if that spouse has prior rights which exhaust the estate;
2. the deceased's next-of-kin;
3. other persons in the order in which they are entitled to succeed on intestacy (see p. 520, above);
4. creditors of the deceased;
5. legatees; and
6. the procurator-fiscal or a judicial factor.

Where there are two or more applicants within the same category, all are entitled to the office jointly.

Confirmation of Executors

Neither executors-nominate nor executors-dative have any authority to "intromit" (transact) with the estate, until they have obtained "confirmation," which is a decree of the sheriff court authorising the executor to "uplift, receive, administer and dispose of" the estate.

A person who acts as executor without having applied for and obtained confirmation is referred to as a "vitious intromitter." He may be held liable for the whole of the deceased's debts, even although he had no fraudulent intention.

In applying for confirmation an executor must present a full inventory of the heritable and moveable estate. Capital transfer tax (formerly estate duty) is payable if the estate exceeds £50,000.

An executor-dative, but not an executor-nominate, is required to "find caution to make the estate forthcoming" (*i.e.* provide a guarantee that he will hand over the estate) to the parties entitled to it. Caution is usually supplied by an insurance company in return for payment of a premium by the executor to the company.

If the confirmation is in favour of an executor-nominate, it is called a "testament-testamentar"; if it is in favour of an executor-dative, it is called a "testament-dative."

Confirmation must as a general rule be to the whole estate known to exist. The only exception is that a creditor may, where there has been no confirmation of an executor, himself apply for the office and be confirmed as "executor-creditor" to so much of the estate as is required to meet his debt.

For small estates a simple mode of obtaining confirmation is available to an executor on application to the sheriff clerk, who undertakes the work of filling up the inventory. The upper limit for a "small" estate is at present £10,000, a figure which may be altered by statutory instrument (Confirmation to Small Estates (Scotland) Act 1979).

There are scattered through many statutes, some originating in the nineteenth century, various provisions which permit small sums to be paid without any confirmation being exhibited at all. The provisions apply to payments such as those from certain pension funds, building society funds and trade union funds; they do not apply to sums, however small, payable by private individuals. By the Administration of Estates (Small Payments) Act 1965 a uniform limit of £500 was made applicable to all the varied statutory provisions and power was conferred on the Treasury to substitute a higher limit for £500 by statutory instrument.

Eik[2] to confirmation

If an executor discovers that he has omitted or undervalued part of the estate, he must lodge an amending inventory, and the court

[2] Pronounced as "eke."

will grant an "eik to the confirmation" (an additional confirmation, "ekeing out" the earlier one).

Confirmation ad omissa

A creditor or any other interested party has the right, where the executor has not obtained an eik, to apply himself for "confirmation ad omissa vel male appretiata" ("confirmation in respect of property omitted or undervalued").

Confirmation ad non executa

This applies where a confirmation has become inoperative because of the death or incapacity of all the executors in whose favour it was granted. In those circumstances creditors and other interested parties are entitled to be granted "confirmation ad non executa" ("confirmation in respect of property not administered"), which authorises them to complete the administration of the estate.

Effect of confirmation

The effect of confirmation is to vest the deceased's estate, as set out in the inventory, in the executor for the purposes of administration.

Before confirmation, an executor cannot enforce payment of a debt due to the estate, nor grant a valid discharge of it: therefore a debtor of the deceased is not bound to pay his debt to anyone other than the executor who has confirmed to it, and if he chooses to pay to some other person he may find himself liable to pay twice.

Duties of Executors

So far as creditors of the deceased are concerned, the executor is eadem persona cum defuncto ("the same person as the deceased"): he is liable to the creditors to the same extent as the deceased himself was liable; an executor's liability is limited to the amount of the estate which he is administering.

If the estate is not sufficient to meet the claims of all the deceased's creditors in full, the executor must give preference to certain privileged debts, including the expenses of confirmation, deathbed and funeral expenses, widow's and family's mournings, aliment for the widow and family, and wages of farm and domestic servants.

Where all preferential claims have been paid in full but the remaining estate is not sufficient to meet all the claims of ordinary creditors in full, all claims made within six months after the death are entitled to rank pari passu ("equally"). Therefore, it is not safe for an executor, unless he is convinced that the estate is solvent (*i.e.* is sufficient to meet all debts in full), to pay any ordinary creditor until six months have expired from the date of death. Even after the expiry of that period the executor is still bound to pay, so far as he has funds in hand, any valid claim subsequently lodged by a creditor, and if the executor, even after the expiry of that period, knowing that there are outstanding debts, chooses to distribute the whole estate to the beneficiaries, he can be made personally liable for a debt which has not been paid.

When all claims of creditors have been met, it is then the executor's duty to distribute the estate to the persons entitled to it in accordance with the rules relating to prior and legal rights, and testate or intestate succession.

Further Reading

Michael C. Meston, *The Succession (Scotland) Act 1964* (W. Green & Son Ltd.)

James G. Currie, *The Confirmation of Executors in Scotland*, 7th edition by A. E. McRae (W. Green & Son Ltd.)

Gloag and Henderson, *Introduction to the Law of Scotland*

David M. Walker, *Principles of Scottish Private Law*

T. B. Smith, *A Short Commentary on the Law of Scotland*

CHAPTER 17

HUSBAND AND WIFE

THE institutional writer Erskine described marriage as a contract (*An Institute of the Law of Scotland*, I, 6, 2).

This is true in that marriage is based on consent of the parties, but there are several important respects in which marriage differs from ordinary commercial contracts: there are distinctive rules as to capacity and as to formality applicable to the constitution of marriage, and (what is most important) marriage creates a new status for the parties and affects the status of their children.

It is because of the creation of a new status that the effects of marriage and the ways in which it may be brought to an end are in general regulated not by the will of the parties but by rules of law.

Marriage, therefore, if it is, as Erskine held it to be, truly a contract, is a contract of a very special nature.

ENGAGEMENT

A marriage is often preceded by an engagement, which, unlike marriage itself, is an ordinary contract:

1. It is subject to the ordinary rules of capacity to contract, not the rules of capacity to marry; therefore, parties who are still too young to marry may validly enter into an engagement.

2. It requires no special formalities.

3. It does not change the status of the parties; the result is that the parties are quite free to agree to rescind (*i.e.* cancel) the contract at any time by "breaking off" their engagement.

Breach of the contract of engagement by one party entitles the other party to bring an action for damages for "breach of promise." The damages awarded consist of a sum representing solatium ("comfort") for hurt to feelings, and a sum to compensate the party not in breach for loss of financial advantages which that party would have obtained as a result of the marriage and also for any expenses incurred on account of the promised marriage.

The Law Reform (Miscellaneous Provisions) Act 1970, which abolished breach of promise actions in England, does not apply to Scotland.

When an engagement is brought to an end by agreement or by breach of promise, gifts made by the parties to one another in contemplation of marriage may be recoverable, but outright gifts are not recoverable.

Marriage gifts made by third parties should, as Stair stated (*The Institutions of the Law of Scotland*, I, 7, 7), be returned if the marriage does not take place.

CONSTITUTION OF MARRIAGE

For the ceremony of marriage itself to be valid:

1. there must be no legal impediments to the marriage, such as exist where one of the parties is already married to someone else, or is too closely related to the other party, or lacks the legal capacity to marry; and

2. certain formalities must be observed.

In 1967 a committee was appointed under the chairmanship of Lord Kilbrandon "to inquire into the requirements (both fundamental and formal) for the constitution of marriage in Scotland." Most of the changes recommended in that committee's Report—*The Marriage Law of Scotland* (1969: Cmnd. 4011)—were enacted by the Marriage (Scotland) Act 1977, which came into force on January 1, 1978. The Act repealed a considerable amount of earlier legislation, starting from the Marriage Act 1567, and is now the sole source of almost all the law relating to the constitution of marriage.

1. Impediments to Marriage

By the Marriage (Scotland) Act 1977, there is a legal impediment to a marriage if:

(a) the parties are related to one another in one of the degrees of relationship listed in Schedule 1 to the Act; the list is divided into three parts:

(i) relationships by consanguinity (blood relationships), whether of the full blood or of the half blood, and even where traced through a person of illegitimate birth; a marriage solemnised in Scotland or at a time when either party is domiciled in Scotland is void if one party is the parent, child, brother, sister, uncle, aunt, grandparent or great grandparent of the other;

(ii) relationships by affinity (relationships by marriage), even where traced through a person of illegitimate birth; *e.g.*, a man is prohibited from marrying the daughter of his former wife, and a woman from marrying the former husband of her mother;

(iii) relationships by adoption; the only relationship under this heading is that of parent and child;

(b) either party is already married;

(c) either party is under the age of sixteen;

(d) either party is incapable of understanding the nature of a marriage ceremony or of consenting to marriage;

(e) both parties are of the same sex; or

(f) in the case where either party is not domiciled in Scotland, there is some other ground on which a marriage in Scotland between the parties would be void ab initio ("from the beginning") under the law of the party's domicile.

2. Formalities of Marriage

Marriages are classed as regular or irregular according to the way in which they are constituted.

(a) Regular marriage

The Marriage (Scotland) Act 1977 made important changes, including the repeal of the provisions concerning proclamation of banns and sheriff's licence.

There are two forms of regular marriage:

(i) religious marriages; and

(ii) civil marriages.

Certain preliminaries are common to the two forms. These preliminaries are as follows:

1. *Notice of intention to marry.* Each of the parties must submit to the registrar for the registration district in which the marriage is to be celebrated a notice in a prescribed form of intention to marry (referred to as a "marriage notice"). This notice must be accompanied by the prescribed fee, the person's birth certificate, and in appropriate circumstances by other documents, namely, a copy of the decree of divorce, the death certificate of the former spouse, and, if a party is not domiciled in any part of the United Kingdom and has been resident in the United Kingdom for less than two years, a certificate, issued by the state in which he is domiciled, that he is not known to be incapable of marrying under the law of that state.

An alternative to compliance with these provisions is available if a party to the intended marriage resides in another part of the United Kingdom: it is normally sufficient for him to submit to the district registrar a valid certificate for marriage (referred to an "approved certificate") issued in that other part.

2. *Publicity.* On receiving a marriage notice or an approved certificate, the district registrar must immediately enter particulars in his "marriage notice book." Any person claiming that he may have

reason to object to the intended marriage is entitled to inspect the entry in the marriage notice book without charge.

The district registrar must also enter the names of the parties and the proposed date of their marriage (but not further information) in a list displayed in a conspicuous place at the registration office until the date has elapsed.

3. *Objections.* Any person may at any time before the solemnisation of the marriage submit a written objection to the district registrar. If the objection is on the ground that one of the parties is incapable of understanding the nature of a marriage ceremony or of consenting to marriage, the objection must be supported by a medical certificate.

If the objection relates to no more than a misdescription or inaccuracy in the marriage notice or approved certificate, the district registrar must notify the parties and make such inquiries as he thinks fit, and must then, subject to the approval of the Registrar General of Births, Deaths and Marriages for Scotland, make any necessary correction.

In the case of any other objection, the district registrar must notify the Registrar General, and the marriage cannot then take place until the Registrar General is satisfied that there is no legal impediment to the marriage.

4. *The Marriage Schedule.* If the district registrar is satisfied that there is no legal impediment to the marriage (or has been so informed by the Registrar General), he prepares a Marriage Schedule in a prescribed form. The Marriage Schedule serves two purposes: it authorises the marriage to take place, and it is a means of recording the particulars of the ceremony. It is signed immediately after the marriage by the two parties, by two witnesses and by the person who solemnised the marriage.

Normally, a Marriage Schedule cannot be issued, nor can a marriage take place, until fourteen days have elapsed since the date of the marriage notice, but this requirement may be modified in any particular case if the parties make a written request to the district registrar, stating the reason for the request, and the Registrar General authorises a specified earlier date for the issue of the Marriage Schedule or for the solemnisation of the marriage.

If the marriage is to be a religious one, the Marriage Schedule is issued by the district registrar to the parties, but if the marriage is to be a civil one, the Marriage Schedule is retained by the district registrar.

After these preliminaries, the procedure depends on whether the marriage is a religious one or a civil one.

(i) *Religious marriages*

The term "religious marriage" is used in the Act of 1977 to denote a marriage solemnised by an "approved celebrant." There are four categories of "approved celebrants," namely:

1. ministers of the Church of Scotland;

2. other ministers, clergymen, pastors, or priests of religious bodies prescribed by regulations made by the Secretary of State for Scotland; the prescribed religious bodies include the Roman Catholic Church, churches of the Anglican communion, the Congregational Union, the Baptist Union, the United Free Church, the Free Church, the Methodist Church, the Salvation Army, the Hebrew Congregation and the Religious Society of Friends;

3. persons nominated by other religious bodies, provided the Registrar General accepts the nomination; before doing so the Registrar General must be satisfied that the marriage ceremony used by the body is in an appropriate form, *i.e.*, that it includes a declaration by the parties, in the presence of each other, the celebrant and two witnesses, that they accept each other as husband and wife, and also a declaration by the celebrant that the parties are then husband and wife; the nomination must not be for more than three years but is renewable; if the Registrar General rejects the nomination, the nominating body may appeal to the Secretary of State, whose decision is final except that if the reason for the rejection is that the nominating body is not a religious body at all, the nominating body has the further right of appeal to the Court of Session; and

4. persons who have been granted by the Registrar General a temporary written authorisation to solemnise either a specified marriage or marriages during a specified period.

A religious marriage cannot take place unless the parties produce the appropriate Marriage Schedule to the approved celebrant before the ceremony and unless both parties to the marriage are present at the ceremony. Two witnesses professing to be at least sixteen years of age must also be present at the ceremony. The date and place of the ceremony must be as specified in the Marriage Schedule; otherwise, a new Marriage Schedule, or an authorised alteration in the existing Marriage Schedule, will be required. The place for the ceremony need not be a church or any other specific type of building.

Immediately after the ceremony, the Marriage Schedule is signed by the parties contracting the marriage, by both witnesses and by the approved celebrant. It must then, within the next three days, be delivered or posted to the district registrar, who enters the particulars from it in his register of marriages.

An amendment of the Marriage (Scotland) Act 1977 made by the Law Reform (Miscellaneous Provisions) (Scotland) Act 1980 protects the validity of a marriage once the particulars have been entered on the register. The only ground of challenge open is that both parties were not present at the ceremony.

(ii) *Civil marriages*

A civil marriage is one solemnised by an "authorised registrar." The authority is derived from appointment by the Registrar General, whose duty it is to appoint a sufficient number of district registrars, and in addition, if he thinks it necessary, assistant registrars, for the purpose of solemnising marriages.

Normally, the marriage can take place only in the registration office of the authorised registrar. However, at the request of one of the parties to the marriage, the authorised registrar may solemnise the marriage at a different place if he is satisfied that one of the parties is unable to attend at the office because of serious illness or serious bodily injury and that there is good reason why the marriage cannot be delayed until the party is able to attend. If the authorised registrar is not satisfied as to these points, he must consult the Registrar General, who has a discretion either to grant or to refuse the party's request.

A marriage must not be solemnised by an authorised registrar unless he has available to him at the time of the ceremony the appropriate Marriage Schedule, and the prescribed fee for the marriage has been paid. Both parties to the marriage must be present, and also two witnesses professing to be at least sixteen years of age.

Immediately after the ceremony, the Marriage Schedule is signed by the parties contracting the marriage, by both witnesses and by the authorised registrar. Then as soon as possible the particulars from the Marriage Schedule are entered in the register of marriages kept at the registration office.

The validity of civil marriages also is protected by the provision of the Law Reform (Miscellaneous Provisions) (Scotland) Act 1980 referred to above.

(b) Irregular marriage

Formerly there were three modes of irregular marriage:
  (i) cohabitation with habit and repute;
  (ii) declaration de praesenti ("there and then"); and
  (iii) promise subsequente copula ("with intercourse following upon it").

Modes (ii) and (iii) were abolished by the Marriage (Scotland) Act 1939 as from July 1, 1940.

The Marriage (Scotland) Act 1977 has only one provision under this heading: it provides that where a decree of declarator has been granted by the Court of Session establishing that, on a specified date, a marriage was constituted by one of the irregular modes, particulars must be intimated to the Registrar General for registration.

(i) *Marriage by cohabitation with habit and repute*

This is now the only valid form of irregular marriage.

Marriage is constituted by this mode where a man and a woman constantly ("habit") live together ("cohabitation") "at bed and board" with the result that they are generally believed ("repute") to be husband and wife. No particular period of cohabitation is required, but usually the period would require to be considerable.

The parties must have intended to be married, and they must have been free to marry (*e.g.* they must both have been of single status). However, it is not essential that they should, right from the start of their cohabitation, have either intended or been free to marry.

(ii) *Marriage by declaration de praesenti*

Marriage could formerly be constituted by a declaration by the parties that they took each other as husband and wife. The declaration might be written or oral, and witnesses were not essential; the parties need not have ever lived together. However, in disputed cases the court had to be satisfied that the parties had in their declaration genuinely consented to marriage there and then, and this consent was obviously difficult to prove without evidence such as writing, witnesses and subsequent living together.

The Gretna Green and other "runaway" Scottish marriages were usually marriages by declaration de praesenti.

The scope of this form of irregular marriage was greatly restricted by the Marriage (Scotland) Act 1856, which required at least one of the parties to have had twenty-one days' residence in Scotland before the marriage.

(iii) *Marriage by promise subsequente copula*

For marriage to be constituted in this way there had to be both a promise of marriage and intercourse in reliance on that promise.

In disputed cases the promise could not be proved by "parole" evidence (*i.e.* the oral evidence of witnesses): it could be proved only by the writing of the party who was claiming that there had been no marriage, or, perhaps, by a "reference to the oath" of that party (*i.e.* by an admission made on oath by that party). The intercourse could be proved prout de jure ("by any competent evidence"), *i.e.* there was no restriction on the mode of proving it.

The parties must have consented to marriage and the intercourse must have been permitted on the faith of the promise, but, provided the promise and the intercourse were proved, it was then presumed both that the parties had consented to marriage and that the intercourse had been on the faith of the promise. These two presumptions might be "rebutted" (contradicted) by other evidence.

The marriage dated from the time of the intercourse, not from the time of the promise.

EFFECTS OF MARRIAGE

Marriage gives rise to certain rights and duties as between the spouses, and also affects their property and their obligations to third parties in some respects.

1. Duty of Adherence

Spouses are under a duty to adhere to each other. The court would not compel a spouse to fulfil this duty, but failure in the duty would give the other spouse grounds for a divorce.

The husband has the right of fixing the place of residence and the duty to provide it, and it is the duty of the wife to accompany her husband unless she has adequate legal justification for not doing so. Non-adherence is justified where there are grounds for judicial separation (*i.e.* separation approved by the court) or for divorce, but only exceptionally is it justified in other circumstances.

Spouses may enter into an agreement for voluntary separation, but a contract of that kind will not be enforced by the court and can be revoked by either party at any time. However, if the contract provides for aliment and payments have fallen into arrear, the court will "grant decree for" the arrears, *i.e.* will order the arrears to be paid.

2. Duty to Aliment

The husband is under a common law duty to aliment his wife provided she is willing to adhere. By the Divorce (Scotland) Act 1976 a wife voluntarily living apart, even if she has no reasonable cause for non-cohabitation, is entitled to aliment unless the husband is willing to cohabit.

In normal circumstances the husband fulfils the duty to aliment by maintaining or offering to maintain his wife in the home of his choice. In other circumstances he must provide her with the necessary food, clothing and accommodation. Where an action is brought in court for aliment the amount of aliment awarded depends on the circumstances of the parties and may be altered on a change in these circumstances.

By the Married Women's Property (Scotland) Act 1920 a wife has a statutory duty to aliment her husband, but only if:

(a) she has separate financial resources which are more than reasonably sufficient for her own maintenance; and

(b) her husband is unable to maintain himself.

Reform of the law on aliment has been recommended by the Scottish Law Commission (Scot. Law Com. No. 67, Nov. 4, 1981).

3. Wife's Praepositura

When spouses are living together it is presumed that the wife is praeposita negotiis domesticis ("placed in charge of domestic affairs"), and this position of the wife is referred to as her "praepositura" ("command" or "supervision"), *i.e.* her presumed authority.

The presumption is based on the fact that the ordering of household necessities is usually entrusted to the wife.

The effect of the praepositura is to make the wife an agent of her husband, with the result that he is liable to pay for the necessities supplied.

The praepositura covers items such as food, clothing and furniture, but it does not extend to goods or services which are not normal household necessaries; for these extras the husband will be liable only if he has given his wife express authority to purchase them. The definition of "necessaries" varies according to the husband's position in life and to his style of living.

Where the praepositura applies the supplier of the goods or services is considered to have been relying on the husband's credit.

Therefore, the praepositura does not apply if the supplier is shown to have been relying only on the credit of the wife herself.

A housekeeping allowance was regarded by the common law as the husband's money entrusted to the wife to enable her to pay the debts for which the husband himself could be made liable. It followed that any savings made by the wife out of the housekeeping allowance belonged to the husband. The common aw was altered by the Married Women's Property Act 1964: mo :ey and property derived from a housekeeping allowance now belong equally to husband and wife unless they make an express agreement to the contrary.

The wife's praepositura may be brought to an end by the husband either formally or informally.

(a) Formal termination of the praepositura

The husband presents a petition to the Outer House of the Court of Session, and obtains from the court, as a matter of course, "Letters of Inhibition," which is a formal document "inhibiting" (forbidding) the wife from disposing of her husband's goods or contracting debts on his behalf, and inhibiting members of the public from transacting with her as agent of her husband unless she has special authority from him for the transaction. This document must then be registered in the "Register of Inhibitions and Adjudications," which is kept in Edinburgh and is open to public inspection.

The effect of inhibition is to free the husband from liability for items which would otherwise come under the praepositura, except that if he fails to provide what is necessary for the maintenance of his wife and his family he can still be made liable to a person who has supplied the necessaries. The effect of inhibition does not depend on whether the supplier was actually aware of the inhibition or not.

(b) **Informal termination of the praepositura**

The husband may notify a particular supplier that he will not accept liability for transactions entered into by his wife. In addition he may insert in a newspaper or publish in some other way a statement that he will not be responsible for debts contracted by his wife.

These informal methods of terminating the praepositura, however, do not affect the rights of suppliers who were unaware of the husband's advertisement.

4. Donations between Spouses

At common law donations made by one spouse to the other could be revoked by the donor. They were made irrevocable by the Married Women's Property (Scotland) Act 1920, except that if the donor becomes bankrupt and has his estate "sequestrated" (distributed among his creditors) within a year and a day afterwards, his creditors have the right to revoke the gift in order that their debts may be more fully paid.

5. Policies of Assurance

By the Married Women's Policies of Assurance (Scotland) Act 1880 a policy of assurance taken out by a married man on his own life for the benefit of his wife or children or both is considered to be a trust for her or them. It cannot later be revoked or controlled by him, nor does it form part of his estate on his death. If the man becomes bankrupt, his creditors have no right to the proceeds of the policy except that if the policy was taken out in order to defraud creditors or if the bankruptcy occurs within two years of the date of the policy creditors are entitled to the amount paid as premiums under the policy.

By the Married Women's Policies of Assurance (Scotland) (Amendment) Act 1980 the provisions of the Act of 1880 were made applicable to a policy taken out by a married woman on her own life for the benefit of her husband or children or both.

The settlement of such policies may be altered by the court on divorce.

[6. Jus Mariti

The jus mariti ("right of the husband") was formerly a very important effect of marriage. It was abolished by the Married Women's Property (Scotland) Act 1881.

By the jus mariti the husband automatically acquired all his wife's moveable property except her "paraphernalia" (clothing, jewellery and their receptacles) and property from which the jus mariti had been expressly excluded (*e.g.* by a provision in an antenuptial marriage contract). The husband also became liable for all the moveable debts which had been incurred by his wife before the marriage.

A wife's moveable property is now her own separate estate, and a husband is not liable for debts incurred by his wife before the marriage.]

[7. Jus Administrationis

Another right which was formerly a very important effect of marriage was the jus administrationis ("right of management"). It was abolished by the Married Women's Property (Scotland) Act 1920.

Under the common law the husband was the curator of his wife, and obligations undertaken by the wife without her husband's consent were, as a general rule, void. The jus administrationis gave the husband the right of management over that part of the wife's property which he did not himself actually come to own, namely the wife's heritable property and any part of her moveable property which was not subject to the jus mariti.

A wife is no longer, unless she is a minor, under the curatory of her husband; she has the same capacity to deal with her property as if she were unmarried.]

TERMINATION OF RELATIONSHIP OF HUSBAND AND WIFE

The relationship of husband and wife comes to an end on "declarator of nullity of marriage" (*i.e.* a declaration by the court that the parties are not married) or on dissolution of the marriage by death or divorce. There is also the possibility of judicial separation, which leaves the marriage standing but frees the parties from the duty of adherence which is one of the effects of marriage.

1. Nullity of Marriage

A marriage may be void or voidable, and in either case a petition may be brought in court to obtain from the court a declarator of nullity of marriage.

A void marriage differs from a voidable marriage in the following respects:

(a) A void marriage is ab initio ("from the beginning") a nullity, whereas a voidable marriage is valid until it is set aside by the declarator.

(b) A void marriage may be challenged by any person who has an interest to do so, whereas a voidable marriage cannot be challenged except by one of the parties to it. It follows that a voidable marriage becomes unchallengeable on the death of one of the spouses.

(c) A void marriage cannot be ratified by the parties, whereas a voidable marriage may be.

(d) The effect of a declarator of nullity is in the case of a void marriage to provide an official record of the fact that the parties are not married and in the case of a voidable marriage to change the status of the parties from married to single with retrospective effect (*i.e.* with effect as from the date of the voidable marriage) except that the children of the marriage remain legitimate.

For the grounds on which a marriage may be declared void ab initio, see "Constitution of Marriage," p. 540, above. Examples are non-age, mental incapacity, an existing marriage and a forbidden degree of relationship.

The only ground on which a marriage is voidable is sexual impotence of either party. The impotence may be either physical, the party being physically incapable of sexual intercourse, or psychological, the party having an insuperable repugnance to sexual intercourse either generally or with the particular individual who is the other party to the marriage.

2. Dissolution of Marriage

Dissolution of marriage differs from nullity of marriage in that a marriage which is dissolved is considered to have been valid for all purposes while it lasted, whereas a marriage declared null is considered for most purposes never to have existed at all.

Marriage cannot be dissolved by mere agreement of the parties. Apart from death, the only way in which a marriage may be dissolved is by a decree of the court. The decree may be on the ground of the presumed death of one of the spouses or it may be a divorce.

(a) Dissolution on ground of presumed death

Where one spouse has become a "missing person" for the purposes of the Presumption of Death (Scotland) Act 1977, an action of declarator of his death may be raised in the Court of Session or the sheriff court, and one effect of a decree in such an action will be to dissolve the marriage. For an outline of the provisions of the Act, see p. 511, above. The Act expressly provides that if the decree in the action of declarator is later varied or recalled (*e.g.* on the reappearance of the missing person), that variation order will not revive the dissolved marriage.

(b) Divorce

An action for divorce can be brought only in the Court of Session.

By the Divorce (Scotland) Act 1976, which repealed earlier legislation on divorce and came into force on January 1, 1977, the only ground for divorce is "that the marriage has broken down irretrievably," Irretrievable breakdown must be established in one of the five ways set out below under these headings:

  (i) adultery;

  (ii) behaviour;

  (iii) desertion;

  (iv) two years' separation plus the defender's consent;

  (v) five years' separation.

With a view to the encouragement of reconciliations, the Act of 1976 provides that if at any time before granting decree the court believes that there is a reasonable prospect of a reconciliation between the parties, it must continue the action for an appropriate period to enable an attempt to be made to effect a reconciliation.

(i) *Adultery*

Irretrievable breakdown is established if the defender has committed adultery since the date of the marriage. One act of voluntary sexual intercourse between a married person and a person of the opposite sex other than his spouse is sufficient; there need not have been a course of adultery. Formerly, adultery had to be proved "beyond reasonable doubt," a high standard of proof applicable normally to criminal cases but not to civil ones. The Act of 1976 altered the standard of proof to proof "on balance of probability," the standard applicable to the other cases of irretrievable breakdown also.

Defences to an action based on adultery are:

1. condonation; and

2. lenocinium ("encouragement of adultery") or connivance.

1. *Condonation.* The court will refuse to grant a decree of divorce if the adultery has been condoned (*i.e.* forgiven) by the pursuer. As a general rule there would be condonation if the spouses in full knowledge of the previous adultery continued or resumed cohabitation (*i.e.* living together as man and wife), but, for the purpose of encouraging reconciliations, there is a statutory exception to this: adultery is not to be held to have been condoned merely because the

pursuer has continued or resumed cohabitation with the defender, provided the pursuer has not cohabited with the defender at any time after the expiry of three months from the continuance or resumption of the cohabitation; *e.g.* if the adultery causes a breakdown of the marriage on January 1, and cohabitation is resumed on February 1, the three-month period allowed by the Act for reconciliation begins to run on February 1 and, however short the actual duration of the cohabitation may be, will expire at the end of April, with the result that if there is a further resumption of cohabitation in May, that will count as condonation of the adultery.

2. *Lenocinium or connivance.* This defence means that the husband has created opportunities for or actively encouraged his wife's adultery; mere indifference about it does not amount to "connivance" in this legal context.

The following are *not* defences to an action based on adultery:

1. *Delay.* If the pursuer did not know of the adultery, lapse of time between the date of the adultery and the date of the court action is not a defence at all. If the pursuer knew of the adultery, delay in the bringing of proceedings is a defence only if it is combined with other circumstances which suggest that the adultery has been condoned or acquiesced in.

2. *Adultery of the pursuer.* The pursuer is still entitled to obtain a decree of divorce where he has himself been guilty of adultery. There may be cross-actions of divorce.

(ii) *Behaviour*

Irretrievable breakdown is established if since the date of the marriage the defender has at any time behaved in such a way that the pursuer cannot reasonably be expected to cohabit with the defender. The behaviour may have been either active or passive, and it may, or may not, have been due to mental abnormality. The phrase "at any time" indicates that the behaviour may have been an isolated act and is not necessarily a continuous course of conduct.

(iii) *Desertion*

Irretrievable breakdown is established if the defender has wilfully and without reasonable cause deserted the pursuer and if, during a continuous period of two years immediately after the desertion, the two following conditions are also fulfilled:

1. There has been no cohabitation between the parties.
2. The pursuer has not refused a genuine and reasonable offer by the defender to adhere.

In considering whether the two-year period has been "continuous," no account is taken of any periods of up to six months in all during which the parties have cohabited with one another, but any such periods of cohabitation are not counted as part of the two-year period. Thus, if the parties, after, say, one year of the desertion period has already run, resume cohabitation for, say, four months, that would not break the continuity of the period of desertion, but the two-year period would not be completed until two years and four months had elapsed since the initial act of desertion.

If, after the expiry of the two-year period, the pursuer has resumed cohabitation with the defender *and* has cohabited with the defender at any time after the end of three months from the resumption of cohabitation, then irretrievable breakdown will be held not to have been established.

A decree will not be granted if the defender had a reasonable cause for deserting; *e.g.* the defender would have a reasonable cause for deserting, and so a divorce would not be granted, if he knew of adultery by the pursuer or if the pursuer had behaved in the way described in paragraph (ii) above.

(iv) *Two years' separation plus the defender's consent*

Irretrievable breakdown is established if there has been no cohabitation between the parties at any time during a continuous period of two years immediately before the bringing of the action, and the defender consents to the granting of the decree of divorce.

As in (iii) above, in considering whether the two-year period has been "continuous," no account is taken of any periods of up to six months in all during which the parties have cohabited with one another, but any such periods of cohabitation are not counted as part of the two-year period.

Mere non-objection is not enough; the consent must be a positive consent, given in a manner prescribed by Act of Sederunt.

(v) *Five years' separation*

Irretrievable breakdown is established if there has been no cohabitation between the parties at any time during a continuous period of five years immediately before the bringing of the action.

There is the same provision as to the interpretation of "continuous" as in (iv) above.

In this fifth case (but not in any of the other four cases) the court has a discretion: it is not bound to grant a decree of divorce if that would, in the court's opinion, result in "grave financial hardship" to the defender. "Hardship" includes the loss of the chance of acquiring some benefit, such as the right to a pension.

Financial provision on divorce

In an action for divorce, either party may, at any time before the decree is granted, apply to the court for one or more of the following orders:

1.   an order for the payment by the other party of a periodical allowance;

2.   an order for the payment by the other party of a capital sum;

3.   an order varying a marriage settlement so far as it takes effect at the termination of the marriage.

If such an application is made, the court has a discretion as to the order which it makes: it takes account of the means of the parties to the marriage and all the circumstances of the case, including any arrangements made for financial provision for children of the marriage.

If an application for a periodical allowance has not been made or has been refused, and after the date of the decree of divorce there is a change in the circumstances of either party, an application may be made to court for a periodical allowance at that later stage.

Any order for payment of a periodical allowance may on a change in circumstances be varied or recalled by a subsequent order. Application may be made by either party.

On the death of the party who has been paying the periodical allowance, his executor is bound to continue payments, but may apply to the court for a variation or recall of the order.

On the remarriage or death of the party who has been receiving the periodical allowance, the order for payment of the allowance ceases to have effect (except as regards any arrears due at the date of the remarriage or death as the case may be).

The Scottish Law Commission has recommended changes in the law relating to financial provision on divorce (Scot. Law Com. No. 67, Nov. 4, 1981).

3.   Judicial Separation

A judicial separation is an order of the court freeing a spouse from the duty of adherence, and is to be distinguished from a voluntary separation which is a matter of private agreement between the parties, can be revoked, and is not enforced by the courts.

An action for separation (or for separation and aliment) may be brought either in the sheriff court or in the Court of Session.

Important changes in the law relating to judicial separation were made by the Divorce (Scotland) Act 1976. The only ground for judicial separation now is the same as that for divorce, namely, "irretrievable breakdown" established in one of the five modes described above under "Divorce."

Further Reading

Eric M. Clive and John G. Wilson, *The Law of Husband and Wife in Scotland* (The Scottish Universities Law Institute Series) (W. Green & Son Ltd.)

Gloag and Henderson, *Introduction to the Law of Scotland*

David M. Walker, *Principles of Scottish Private Law*

T. B. Smith, *A Short Commentary on the Law of Scotland*

Eric M. Clive, *The Divorce (Scotland) Act 1976* (W. Green & Son Ltd.)

CHAPTER 18

PARENT AND CHILD

MUCH of the common law of Scotland relating to the relations between parent and child has been derived from Roman law; *e.g.* the division of persons under the age of majority into pupils (boys from birth up to the age of fourteen and girls from birth up to the age of twelve) and minors (young persons over fourteen or twelve, according to sex, and not yet of full age) is based on Roman law.

The common law has, however, been altered in many respects by statute; *e.g.* the Age of Majority (Scotland) Act 1969 reduced the age of majority from twenty-one to eighteen. The most important statute on the subject in recent years is the Children Act 1975, which has made substantial amendments on the topics of adoption, custody, and care by local authorities. It is not, however, either a codifying or a consolidating Act. Some of its provisions have not yet been brought into force. The sections of the Act which relate to adoption of children are now incorporated in the consolidating Adoption (Scotland) Act 1978.

LEGITIMACY

A maxim applicable in connection with disputes about legitimacy is pater est quem nuptiae demonstrant ("the father is the person whom the marriage points out (as the father)"). Therefore, a child born to a married woman during the marriage is presumed to be legitimate; the presumption extends to the case where a child is born so soon after the dissolution of a marriage that it could have been conceived during the marriage; on the other hand, the presumption does not apply where the child is born so soon after the celebration of the marriage that it could not have been conceived during the marriage.

Another presumption which applies is that a man who marries a woman in the knowledge that she is pregnant is the father of her child provided there have been opportunities for pre-marital intercourse.

These presumptions in favour of legitimacy are very strong, but they can be "rebutted" (overcome).

The fact that the parties have registered their child as legitimate is not conclusive evidence that it is legitimate.

The presumptions in favour of legitimacy apply even where the husband and wife are voluntarily living apart, but not where they have been judicially separated (see p. 554, above).

Legitimation

A child born illegitimate may later be legitimated.

Before 1968 legitimation depended on the common law principle of legitimation per subsequens matrimonium ("legitimation by means of subsequent marriage") which was part of Roman and canon law.

According to this principle an illegitimate child was legitimated by the subsequent marriage of his parents, if, but only if, the parents were free to marry at the time when the child was conceived; the legitimation had retrospective effect: the child was deemed legitimate as from the date of his birth.

It followed from the condition attached to the operation of the principle that children born as a result of adultery could not be legitimated. This hardship for illegitimate children was removed by the Legitimation (Scotland) Act 1968, which provides that a child is legitimated by the subsequent marriage of his parents in spite of any impediments to their marriage which may have existed at the time of the child's conception or birth; the legitimation takes effect only from the date on which it occurs: it does not have retrospective effect.

ALIMENT[1]

Until a child is able to maintain himself by his own exertions, his father is under a natural obligation to "aliment" (support) the child.

This obligation is not brought to an end by the attainment by the child of any particular age: it may last for the whole of the child's life, if the child is, because of physical or mental incapacity or inability to obtain employment, unable throughout his life to support himself. The court is less ready to award aliment to a child who has completed his education and training than to one who has not.

The father is not bound to give more by way of aliment than what is sufficient to maintain the child from want, but the term "want" denotes a standard which varies according to the social and financial circumstances of the parties.

[1] Changes have been recommended (Scot. Law Com. No. 67, Nov. 4, 1981).

The father is entitled to discharge his obligation in the way which is least burdensome to himself; this will often be by maintenance of the child in the family home.

If the father does not, by maintaining the child in the family home, or by making an allowance to the child, or by some other provision, discharge his obligation to aliment the child, he can be made liable to tradesmen who supply the child with necessaries.

If the father is dead or is unable to give aliment, the child is entitled to aliment from other relatives in the following order:

1. his mother;
2. his paternal ascendants in their order—first his paternal grandfather, next his paternal grandmother, and then higher ascendants in the paternal line; and
3. his maternal ascendants in their order.

A person has no legal right to aliment from his brothers and sisters except in so far as they represent the father; e.g. if the father has left his whole estate to one of his children, that child comes under an obligation to aliment his brothers and sisters out of the estate; this obligation would not arise if the father's estate had been divided equally among his children.

A father is not bound to aliment his daughter-in-law.

The obligation to aliment is reciprocal: parents and other ascendants have a corresponding claim to be alimented by their children and other descendants in case of need.

If a person who is unable to support himself has both ascendants and descendants who are able to aliment him, the obligation to aliment him lies on his descendants.

Where a child's parents are divorced or judicially separated, and the mother has been granted custody, she is normally also awarded aliment, since the father remains primarily liable to aliment the child.

Aliment of Illegitimate Children

Where it cannot be established who is the father of an illegitimate child, the whole expense of alimenting the child falls on the mother.

Where a person admits that he is the father, or where he is proved to be the father, both parents are liable jointly and severally to aliment the child, and if the mother alone supports the child she has a right of relief against the father for his share, which is fixed according to circumstances and is not necessarily a half; if the mother deserts the child and the father supports it, he has a corresponding right of relief against the mother for her share.

If paternity is disputed, the mother may, in order to obtain a contribution towards the child's aliment, bring an action of "affiliation and aliment" against the alleged father. When such an action is brought by a married woman against a man who is not her husband, she must first rebut the presumption pater est quem nuptiae demonstrant.

If the mother is dead, an action of affiliation and aliment may be brought by the illegitimate child through his tutor.

EDUCATION

Parents are under a statutory obligation to have their children educated, usually by ensuring that the children attend a local-authority, or other, school until they attain the minimum school-leaving age.

That obligation and the other statutory provisions on education are consolidated in the Education (Scotland) Act 1980.

PATRIA POTESTAS

"Patria potestas" ("paternal power") denotes the authority which at common law a father might exercise over his child.

The extent of the patria potestas varied according to the age of the child and other circumstances.

The patria potestas was said to amount to "dominion" as long as the child was in pupillarity (Stair, *The Institutions of the Law of Scotland*, I, 5, 3): the father was entitled to govern the person of the child and to decide how the child was to be brought up.

When the child attained puberty (fixed for legal purposes as fourteen years of age for males and twelve years of age for females), the patria potestas became weaker, and was regarded not as a right of dominion or even as a privilege conferred mainly for the father's own benefit, but as a benefit for the guidance and comfort of the child: the wishes and feelings of the minor were entitled to some weight varying according to his age, intelligence, and other circumstances, and a father might lose his right to control his minor child if he either abandoned the right by leaving the child to his own guidance, or in any other way showed that he was unable or unwilling to discharge his parental duty towards the child.

The patria potestas came to an end when the child attained majority. It ended earlier if:

1. the father died;
2. the child was "forisfamiliated," *i.e.* had with the father's consent set out on an independent course of life (*e.g.* by leaving home, marrying, or taking up employment); or
3. the father forfeited his power by unnatural treatment of the child.

By the Guardianship Act 1973 a mother has now the same rights and authority as the common law allowed to the father; the rights and authority of mother and father are equal and may be exercised by either parent without the other. An agreement to give up such rights and authority is unenforceable, except that an agreement made between husband and wife which is to operate only during their separation can be given effect to unless in the court's opinion it would not be for the benefit of the child to do so. Where a father and mother disagree on any question affecting their child's welfare, either parent may apply to court for a settlement of the difference.

GUARDIANSHIP

Guardianship is either tutory (if the child is a pupil) or curatory (if the child is a minor).

Under the Guardianship Act 1973, a child's mother and father are his tutors or curators. Where the consent of the child's guardian is required for any purpose, normally the consent of either parent is sufficient. This does not apply to the consent required for adoption (see p. 565, below): the consent of both of the child's parents is required for that except where consent may be dispensed with on certain grounds such as persistent ill-treatment of the child.

For the guardian's role in relation to a child's capacity to contract, see pp. 266–268, above.

CUSTODY

Normally a child's guardian is also the child's custodier, but in some situations it is important to distinguish between guardianship and custody, *e.g.* where, because the parents are separated or divorced, a relative has custody, or where the child is in the care of a local authority and the authority has not assumed parental rights. The custodier has authority to take day-to-day decisions affecting the child's welfare (including education and medical treatment), but is not entitled to deal with the child's property or take legal proceedings on his behalf, change the child's name, nationality or domicile, or consent to the child's adoption. These are matters for the guardian to decide.

At common law, the father was, by his patria potestas, entitled to custody of his pupil child. The Inner House of the Court of Session could, in the exercise of its nobile officium (see p. 106, above), control the father's right of custody, but would do so only if the child's health or morals were in danger. The mother was entitled to custody after the father's death, unless the court conferred custody instead on a "factor loco tutoris" (an agent or officer "in place of the tutor").

The common law relating to custody has been substantially altered by statutes since the Conjugal Rights (Scotland) Amendment

Act 1861. The sheriff court and the Outer House of the Court of Session now have a statutory jurisdiction in questions of custody.

The main statutory provisions on custody are now in the Guardianship of Infants Acts 1886 and 1925, as amended by the Guardianship Act 1973, and in the Children Act 1975. [1a] They relate to children under the age of sixteen.

The leading principle given effect to in these Acts is that in deciding questions of custody the court must regard the welfare of the child as the first and paramount consideration, and must not consider whether from any other point of view the claim of the father to custody is superior to that of the mother or vice versa; hence it is quite usual for a divorced wife to be allowed the custody of young children although it was her adultery or desertion which caused the irretrievable breakdown of the marriage.

Questions of custody often arise in actions of divorce, nullity or separation. In such actions the court must not grant decree (*i.e.* must not make the order sought by the pursuer) unless and until it is satisfied *either* that arrangements which are satisfactory or are at least the best which can be devised in the circumstances have been made for the care and upbringing of all the children, *or* that it is impracticable for the parties appearing before the court to make such arrangements (Matrimonial Proceedings (Children) Act 1958). If the court holds that it is impracticable or undesirable for the child to be entrusted to either of the parties, it may make an order committing the child to the care of another person, such as a grandparent, or to the care of a local authority; it may also place the child under the supervision of a local authority (Matrimonial Proceedings (Children) Act 1958, as amended by Social Work (Scotland) Act 1968). These provisions extend to any child (whether legitimate, illegitimate or adopted) of one of the parties, who has been accepted as one of the family by the other party (Matrimonial Proceedings (Children) Act 1958).

Where proceedings for divorce, nullity or separations are unsuccessful, the court may nevertheless deal with questions of custody arising in connection with these proceedings (Matrimonial Proceedings (Children) Act 1958).

Even though no proceedings for divorce, nullity or separation are being brought, the court has jurisdiction to regulate custody on an application being made to it by either parent (Custody of Children (Scotland) Act 1939).

Most applications for custody are by a parent, but some are by other persons, such as a relative, step-parent or foster parent. The Children Act 1975 recognises the right of such non-parents to apply

[1a] These provisions of the Children Act 1975 are not yet in force.

for custody, but the applicant will require to show cause why the court (regarding the welfare of the child as the first and paramount consideration) should make an order awarding him custody.

The Act of 1975 requires an applicant for custody to give notice of his application to each known parent of the child, and provides for orders to be varied or discharged on an application being made to the court or by the court ex proprio motu ("on its own initiative"). There is also provision for the local authority to be notified of applications for custody made by relatives (other than parents), step-parents or foster parents. The local authority may make payments for or towards the maintenance of a child where the court has awarded custody to a non-parent. This provision enables foster parents who have been receiving a boarding-out allowance to have an equivalent sum paid to them after they have been awarded custody.

Restrictions are imposed by the Act of 1975 on the removal of a child from a foster parent or other applicant for custody if:

1.   the child has been in the care and possession of that person for at least three years; and

2.   the application for custody is pending in any court.

The Act of 1975 also provides that the court may in certain circumstances treat an application for adoption as if it were an application for custody (see p. 568, below).

As regards illegitimate children, the mother had at common law the primary right to custody. Under the Illegitimate Children (Scotland) Act 1930, however, the court now has power to make such order as it thinks fit concerning custody, taking into consideration the welfare of the child, and the conduct and wishes of both father and mother.

A person who fails to obey a court order relating to custody may be imprisoned for contempt of court.

ACCESS

A parent who does not have custody of a child is normally entitled to reasonable access to the child.

If the parties fail to agree about access, the court may make provision for access. In doing so the court has a discretion, and, although it will normally allow access, it may refuse it where the parent's circumstances, character or conduct make access undesirable in the child's interests.

ADOPTION

The common law of Scotland did not recognise arrangements for the adoption of a child as being binding or as having the effect of giving the child different parents from his natural parents: however solemn and formal the agreement was by which the natural parent handed over the child to an adoptive parent, the natural parent remained free to reclaim the child at any time; further, the adopted child acquired no legitim or rights of succession in the estate of an adoptive parent and lost none of these rights in the estate of a natural parent.

Legal force was first given to adoptions by the Adoption of Children (Scotland) Act 1930, and the statutory provisions were consolidated in the Adoption Act 1958. Substantial parts of the Act of 1958 were repealed by the Children Act 1975, which implemented recommendations of the Houghton-Stockdale Committee's Report (*Report of the Departmental Committee on the Adoption of Children* (1972: Cmnd. 5107)), and a further consolidation followed with the passing of the Adoption (Scotland) Act 1978.

Except where otherwise stated the statutory provisions on adoption noted below are now to be found in the Adoption (Scotland) Act 1978. Some of the provisions are not yet in force.

The "keynote" of the statutory provisions, now comprising section 6 of the Adoption (Scotland) Act 1978, is in these terms:

> "In reaching any decision relating to the adoption of a child, a court or adoption agency staff shall have regard to all the circumstances, first consideration being given to the need to safeguard and promote the welfare of the child throughout his childhood; and shall so far as practicable ascertain the wishes and feelings of the child regarding the decision and give due consideration to them, having regard to his age and understanding."

Adoption Agencies [2]

The adoption agency may be either a local authority or an approved adoption society.

1. Local authorities

Every regional or islands council is under a duty to establish and maintain within its area as part of its social services an adoption service to meet the needs of:

(a) children who have been or may be adopted;

(b) parents and guardians of such children; and

(c) persons who have adopted or may adopt a child.

The facilities of the service, such as temporary accommodation, assessment arrangements and counselling, must be provided in conjunction with the local authority's other social services and with approved adoption societies in the area, so that "help may be given in a co-ordinated manner without duplication, omission or avoidable delay."

[2] These provisions are not yet in force.

The service maintained by local authorities is collectively known as "the Scottish Adoption Service."

2. Approved adoption societies

A body wishing to act as an adoption society must obtain, and then renew every three years, an approval from the Secretary of State for Scotland. The matters which the Secretary of State takes into account in granting or refusing approval include the society's adoption programme, the number and qualifications of its staff, its financial resources, and the organisation and control of its operations. The Secretary of State must be satisfied that the society is likely to make an effective contribution to the Scottish Adoption Service. If the society is likely to operate extensively within the area of a particular local authority, the Secretary of State must ask that authority whether it supports the application, and take account of the authority's views.

Where the Secretary of State decides to refuse the application, he must give the applicant an opportunity to make representations to him before any final notification of refusal is issued.

Approval may also be withdrawn by the Secretary of State from a body which is not in his opinion making an effective contribution to the Scottish Adoption Service. An opportunity must be given to the body concerned to make representations to the Secretary of State before the withdrawal becomes final.

Adoption Orders

Adoption proceedings commence with a petition in the sheriff court or Court of Session, and the adoption is effected by a court order, which vests in the adopters the parental rights and duties relating to the child, and extinguishes parental rights and duties which were vested in persons other than the adopters.

All proceedings take place "in camera" ("in private") unless the court orders otherwise.

Persons who may adopt

Adoption may be by two persons provided they are a married couple. Otherwise, adoption must be by one person only.

1. *Adoption by married couple*

Where the application for an adoption order is by a married couple, each of the applicants must be over twenty-one years of age.

The effect of the order is that the child is treated in law as if he had been born as a legitimate child of the marriage, and as if he were not the child of any person other than the adopters. An exception is made in connection with the rules which forbid marriage between persons within certain degrees of relationship to one another (see p. 540, above): for the purposes of these rules, the child is considered to be still the child of his natural parents and not the child of his adoptive parents; *e.g.* there would be no impediment to a person's marrying his adoptive sister. There is, however, this additional rule: marriage is forbidden between a person and his adopted (or former adopted) child.

2. *Adoption by one person*

Where the application for an adoption order is by one person, that person must be over twenty-one, and either:

(a) he or she must not be married; or

(b) the court must be satisfied that his or her spouse cannot be found, or is permanently separated from the applicant, or is incapable owing to ill health of making an application for an adoption order.

The effect of the order is that the child is treated in law as if he had been born as a legitimate child of the adopter, and as if he were not the child of any person other than the adopter. The rules on impediments to marriage are again exceptional: for the purpose of these rules the child continues to be treated as the child of his natural parents except that he is not permitted to marry his adopter.

If the application for adoption is by the mother or the father of the child alone, the court must be satisfied that either:

(a) the other natural parent is dead or cannot be found; or

(b) there is some other reason justifying the exclusion of the other natural parent.

These strict requirements are laid down because the adoption order will have the serious effect of terminating the relationship of the non-applicant parent to his or her child.

Parental agreement

The agreement of each of the child's parents or guardians is normally required before an adoption order can be made. The father of an illegitimate child is not a "parent" for this purpose, but if he has been granted custody by an order under the Illegitimate Children (Scotland) Act 1930 he will be a "guardian."

There are two procedures by which the necessary agreement may be made evident:

1. *Agreement at the time of the specific adoption order*

The court must normally be satisfied that each parent or guardian freely, and with full understanding of what is involved, agrees unconditionally to the making of the adoption order. A mother cannot give a binding agreement until six weeks after the child's birth.

The parent's or guardian's agreement may be dispensed with if he or she:

  (a) cannot be found or is incapable of giving agreement; or
  (b) is withholding agreement unreasonably; or
  (c) has persistently failed without reasonable cause to discharge the parental duties to the child; or
  (d) has abandoned or neglected the child; or
  (e) has persistently ill-treated the child; or
  (f) has seriously ill-treated the child *and* rehabilitation of the child within the household of the parent or guardian is unlikely.

Ground (f) was added by the Children Act 1975 to cover the situation where there had been a single brutal attack.

2. *The freeing procedure*[2]

This alternative was introduced by the Children Act 1975. It enables an adoption agency to apply to court for a court order declaring that the child is free for adoption. The court must normally be satisfied that each parent or guardian freely, and with full understanding of what is involved, agrees *generally* and unconditionally to the making of an adoption order. A mother cannot give a binding agreement until six weeks after the child's birth.

The parent's or guardian's agreement may be dispensed with on any of the grounds listed under 1. above.

Before making a freeing order, the court must satisfy itself that each parent or guardian who can be found has been given an opportunity of making a declaration that he prefers not to be involved in future questions concerning the adoption of the child. Where the parent or guardian chooses to make such a declaration, the adoption agency is released from the duty of furnishing certain progress reports on the adoption to that person.

In the case of an illegitimate child whose father is not its guardian, the court must further satisfy itself that the person who claims to be the father either:

  (a) does not intend to apply for custody under the Illegitimate Children (Scotland) Act 1930; or
  (b) would be likely to be refused custody if he applied for it.

The effect of a freeing order is to vest the parental rights and duties in the adoption agency.

A freeing order is final except that the former parent or guardian may apply to court for a revocation of the order provided that:

  (a) twelve months have passed since the making of the freeing order; and

(b) no adoption order has yet been made; and

(c) the child does not have his home with a person with whom he has been placed for adoption.

The effect of a revocation is to vest the parental rights and duties again in the parent or guardian. If an application for a revocation is dismissed, the adoption agency is released from the duty of furnishing progress reports and the former parent or guardian is not entitled to make any further application for revocation except by leave of the court.

The freeing procedure is designed to eliminate some of the problems which can arise where parental agreement is withdrawn (as it may be under the other procedure) at a late stage in the proceedings.

The child and his interests

The person being adopted must be between nineteen weeks and eighteen years old, and must never have been married. He may, or may not, have been previously adopted by other adoptive parents.

There are several statutory provisions which have the general aim of protecting the child's interests in accordance with the principle quoted above from section 6 of the consolidating Act.

1. *Minor's consent*

If the child is a minor (*i.e.* over twelve years old if female, and over fourteen years old if male), his consent to the adoption order is required, unless the court is satisfied that the minor is incapable of giving his consent.

2. *Home with adopters before order made*

Before an adoption order can be made, the child must, at all times during the preceding thirteen weeks, have had his home with the adopters or one of them. Further, the court, must be satisfied that the adoption agency or the local authority has been given sufficient opportunities to see the child with the adopter (or, in the case of an adoption by a married couple, with both adopters together) in the home environment.

3. *Prohibition of arrangements by unauthorised persons*[2]

A person other than an adoption agency or a relative of the child must not make arrangements for a child's adoption or place the child for adoption. Both the person arranging the adoption and the person receiving the child would be committing offences and be liable to penalties. The prohibition would apply to professional persons such as doctors, ministers and solicitors just as much as to unapproved adoption societies.

The prohibition does not, however, mean that the court would not grant an adoption order in such circumstances. It could do so provided the child, at all times during the preceding twelve months, had had his home with the adopters or one of them.

4. Custody order in preference to adoption order[2]

Where a relative or step-parent applies for an adoption order, and the court thinks that the child's welfare would not be better safeguarded by an adoption order than by a custody order and that it would be appropriate to make a custody order, the court must treat the application as if it were an application for custody (Children Act 1975).

The underlying reason for this provision is that it might be damaging for a child to discover suddenly that his "parents" were in fact his grandparents and that his older "sister" was in fact his mother.

5. Protection of existing fostering arrangements

There are various restrictions on the removal of a child from foster parents while an application for his adoption is pending. A new restriction introduced by the Act of 1975 is that where the person with whom the child has had his home for five years applies for an adoption order, no one has the right, without leave of the court, to remove the child from the applicant's custody while the application for adoption is pending.

6. Appointment of curator ad litem

In an application for a freeing order or for an adoption order, a curator ad litem ("guardian in connection with the court proceedings") may be appointed. The function of such a guardian is to safeguard the interests of the child. He must be an independent party, not employed by the adoption agency.

7. Conditions in adoption order

An adoption order may contain such terms and conditions as the court thinks fit. An example could be a condition as to the religious upbringing of the child. (Since the Children Act 1975, an adoption agency must in placing a child for adoption have regard (so far as practicable) to any wishes of the child's parents and guardians as to religious upbringing, but parents and guardians are no longer entitled to make their agreement to the adoption conditional on the child's receiving any particular form of religious upbringing.)

8. Information and counselling

Adopted persons have access to their birth records at the age of seventeen, by making an application to the Registrar General of Births, Deaths and Marriages for Scotland.

Local authorities and approved adoption societies are under a duty to provide counselling for adopted persons who have been furnished with information by the Registrar General and who apply for counselling with regard to that information.

9. *Payment of allowance to adopters*[2]

The general rule is that payments to adopters are unlawful, but the Children Act 1975 introduced a limited exception to the rule by providing that an adoption agency may submit to the Secretary of State for Scotland a scheme for the payment by the agency of allowances to persons who have adopted or intend to adopt a child. The Secretary of State has full discretion to approve, alter or revoke a particular scheme. The purpose of this exception is to facilitate the adoption of children who would otherwise be difficult to place for adoption (*e.g.* because of a physical handicap), and also to encourage long-term foster parents to adopt their foster children in circumstances where the loss of the boarding-out allowance was proving an obstacle to adoption.

CARE

The care of children by a local authority is governed by provisions of the Social Work (Scotland) Act 1968, as amended by the Children Act 1975.

The leading principle is that in reaching any decision relating to the child, the local authority must give first consideration to the need to safeguard and promote the welfare of the child throughout his childhood, and must, so far as practicable, ascertain the child's wishes and feelings about the decision and give due consideration to them, having regard to the child's age and understanding.

A child taken into care may be placed in a residential establishment managed by the local authority or may be boarded out with foster parents.

In certain circumstances a local authority may pass a resolution assuming parental rights over the child or vesting parental rights in a voluntary organisation (which must be either an incorporated body or a trust for the purposes of the Trusts (Scotland) Act 1921). The circumstances are:

1. that the child's parents are dead and he has no guardian; or
2. that a parent or guardian is in some way unfit to have the care of the child; or
3. that throughout the three years before the passing of the resolution the child has been in the care of a local authority or voluntary organisation.

There are statutory provisions aimed at protecting the child's interests where such proceedings are being taken.

It is the duty of the local authority to review at least every six months the case of a child who is in care, and there are statutory restrictions, extended by the Act of 1975, on the removal of children who have been in care for that period of time.

———————

Further Reading
Gloag and Henderson, *Introduction to the Law of Scotland*
David M. Walker, *Principles of Scottish Private Law*
T. B. Smith, *A Short Commentary on the Law of Scotland*

INDEX

a caelo usque ad centrum, 458
a morte testatoris, 531
abatement of legacies, 527
acceptance, 254–258
  express, 255–256
  recall of, 258–259
  time of, 256–257
acceptilation, 334–335
access to child, 562
accresces to, 476, 529
accretion in legacies, 529
accumulation of income, 533–534
acquiescence, 246
action, 17
actions, law of, 131, 139, 141
actor sequitur forum rei, 22
Acts of Adjournal, 86, 88, 191
Acts of Parliament, *see* statutes
Acts of Sederunt, 86, 88, 191
ad factum praestandum, 49, 322, 335
ad non executa, confirmation, 537
ad omissa, confirmation, 537
ademption of special legacies, 526
adherence, duty of, 546
adjective law, 126, 128
Adjournal, Acts of, 86, 88, 191
adjudication, 49–50
administrative law, 8, 9, 129, 130–131,
  140, 183, 184
administrative tribunals, 18–19, 183–
  184, 200, 226–232
  appeals from, 231–232
  classification of, 229
  membership of, 230
  procedure at, 230–231
adopted as holograph, 261–262
adoption (form of personal bar), 244,
  246
  (of children), 132, 562–569
advocate, 43–45
advocate-depute, 47
affidavits, 27
agency, 135, 141, 319, 386–404
  classes of agents, 390–393
  constitution of, 386–390
  duties of agent, 393–395
  ostensible authority, 388
  rights of agent, 395–397
  termination of, 401–404
  third parties, 397–401
  vicarious liability in, 434–435
agony rule, 446
aliment, duty to, 132, 546–547, 557–559
alimentary liferents, 491–492, 508, 509

Alison, Archibald, 100
allodial land, 452, 471–472
altius non tollendi, servitude, 464
alveus, 461
amendment of statutes, 85
analytical jurisprudence, 123
Anglo-American school of legal
  thought, 3, 13, 108, 123
Anglo-Saxon law, 121
animals, liability for, 426, 429–430
animus donandi, 535
animus possidendi, 450
animus revocandi, 523
annuity, 504, 533
answers, 29, 70
anticipatory breach of contract, 322,
  333–334
apocha trium annorum, 337
application-to-Scotland section, 82
apprising, 49
Appropriation Act, 163–164
appropriation of payments, 336
aquaehaustus, 464
aqueduct, 464
arbitration, 64–76, 139, 260
  arbiters and oversmen, 67–69
  challenge of award, 72–75
  conduct of arbitration, 69–72
  judicial references, 75–76
arrestment to found jurisdiction, 41, 42
Articles of Union, 175–176
artificial persons, 132, 133–134, 141
ascription of payments, 336
Assembly, proposed Scottish, 197
assignation, 317–319, 485, 487
assignatus utitur jure auctoris, 13, 299,
  317, 508
assoilzie, 29
assurance, policies of, 548–549
attestation clause, 261
attested, 260–261
attorney, power of, 387
auctioneers, 391, 398–399, 400, 401
auctor in rem suam, 498, 499
audi alteram partem, 192
Auld Alliance, 2
Austin, John, 123
authoritative writings, 78, 99–102
average, general and particular, 405,
  411–412
avizandum, 28

back bond, 483
back letter, 483

571